Europe Today

National Politics, European Integration, and European Security

SECOND EDITION

EDITED BY RONALD TIERSKY

ROWMAN & LITTLEFIELD PUBLISHERS, INC.
Lanham • Boulder • New York • Toronto • Oxford

ROWMAN & LITTLEFIELD PUBLISHERS, INC.

Published in the United States of America
by Rowman & Littlefield Publishers, Inc.
A wholly owned subsidary of The Rowman & Littlefield Publishing Group, Inc.
4501 Forbes Boulevard, Suite 200, Lanham, MD 20706
www.rowmanlittlefield.com

P.O. Box 317, Oxford OX2 9RU, UK

British Library Cataloguing in Publication Information Available

Library of Congress Cataloging-in-Publication Data

Europe today. National politics, European integration, and European
security / edited by Ronald Tiersky—2nd ed.
    p. cm.— (Europe today)
  Includes bibliographical references and index.
  ISBN 0-7425-2804-9 (cloth : alk. paper)—ISBN 0-7425-2805-7 (pbk. :
alk. paper)
    1. Europe—Politics and government—1989– 2. Europe—History—1989–
I. Title: National politics, European integration, and European
security. II. Tiersky, Ronald, 1944– III. Europe today (Rowman and
Littlefield, Inc.)
JN12 .E867 2004
320.94—dc22

                                    2003024438

Printed in the United States of America

Europe Today

Europe Today
Series Editor: Ronald Tiersky

Contents

Preface to the Second Edition

A Note to Students

Introductory textbooks are notoriously difficult for professors to write. Success demands from authors not only a mastery of subject matter but an ability to explain things to beginning students without talking down to them. The job isn't easy.

For your part, you, the student, must be willing to read seriously and to engage the book in good faith. You must be willing to try to imagine what most of you have not yet seen, that is, Europe and its vividly different separate countries and societies. You need to arrive at the first page with a willingness to get interested—an intellectual availability that amounts to not much more than a simple curiosity about the world. I can assure you that knowledge of what is beyond your own hometown and country will repay you in ways you will begin to realize only when you have reached the other side of your college course. You will have discovered the empowerment of traveling with your mind. You will, we hope, soon go to Europe and realize after a day or two that you are not quite so much a stranger as your parents, who may know London, Paris, Berlin, or Rome only as tourists.

That, then, is the issue in this book: professors working hard to produce accessible yet not overly watered-down introductory writing, students making the effort of intellectual seriousness and availability. It's a matter of a close encounter of a different kind.

It has always been true that serious knowledge of international politics requires some basic familiarity with at least one or a few countries, in order to have a foundational knowledge stone upon which to pile smaller stones. As a wise European friend once put it to me, one must be a specialist before becoming a generalist. Thus you will find several country chapters in this book, but you will find the separate countries again in every European-gauge chapter. So be aware that your job is to hold the two ends of a rope. To know separate countries in isolation is no longer even plausible as Europe integrates and globalization affects both the national and European "domestic" levels. Yet, despite everything, the French are still the French (even though they worry a great deal about the loss of their distinctive national identity).

The world, the international order, the importance of national states and societies, all these, as we have known them for a long time, are transforming before our very eyes. For students just arriving on the scene, there is, naturally, the advantage of naïveté. For you, at eighteen or twenty-two years old, the new jumbling of the national and international in Europe must seem totally unremarkable. How fortunate you are not to arrive with the heavy baggage of the past! Yet how much you don't know of what you need to know—that is, the past!

A Note to Teachers

In what I've just said I've put teachers on the spot. I hope you will, at the end of your courses, say that our authors have kept the faith.

Not surprisingly, given my comments above, the order of presentation in this text has been reversed from what it was in our first edition, published only a few years ago. Thus this book is different from the first edition, not only because the analysis is new but because we have put the chapters on European integration and European security ahead of the country chapters. It seems to us—first of all to me, as editor of the book—that the "European" has now trumped the "national" in so many respects that it is only good pedagogy to begin with the European Union (EU) and Europe's international relations rather than with the country chapters. But let me add that, for myself and others, this is a bit of *bonjour tristesse*, because so much of our professional interest began emotionally, that is, by falling in love with France, or Italy, or Spain, or even, for those with less hedonistic self-indulgence, with Britain, or Scandinavia, or Poland. Nostalgia for the uniqueness, the particular pleasures of each European society, is not what it used to be. But while the allure of old beauties fades, the New Europe of our times has become, if more soberly than in the 1950s and 1960s, a kind of political cause. Some Europeanist academics and intellectuals have enrolled in it, seeing the movement of European integration widening and deepening and the new prospect of a real EU Constitution as the leading edge of world political development. Others, also passionate rather than really objective, have maintained a kind of permanent "Euroskepticism." The a priori positions regarding European integration seem to me to be a sublimation of the great European ideological struggles of the twentieth century, now the "last century."

So be it. Professors do not live by grants and fellowships alone. The relevant point for teachers is simply to be alert for the sublimated bias of even this volume's authors. Good teaching is, as always, also a matter of explaining to students where a book or a chapter finds its intellectual and emotional core. Teaching against, rather than with, the fundamentals of a text can be a powerful pedagogical strategy: it places into question the implicit authority of what it published in black and white on a page.

European political life, as indicated above, has been thrown into constant flux since the Great Revolution of 1989–1991. The rapidity of decisive events renders the business of conceptualizing, the bread and butter of academics, a more difficult job than ever.

Timeliness is not just a theoretical point. As revision of this textbook neared completion in early 2003, the crisis over Saddam Hussein's regime in Iraq was moving toward climax. War or no war? Disarmament or regime change? American empire or democratic imperialism? Impossible to know, let alone to forecast or to take account of what would happen, even regarding a Europe that is principally on the sidelines, although France itself, in the person of President Jacques Chirac and his foreign minister, Dominique de Villepin, has been at the center of UN Security Council debate.

What I can say in this too-early-or-too-late introduction is that the three pillars of the West—American-European relations, solidarity within NATO, and the European Union itself—have been thrown into disarray. It is not sure that Humpty-Dumpty can be put together again. However, our chapters can provide frameworks for understanding the past, on which teachers can structure an understanding of current events. While difficult, it is an invigorating teaching task. We ourselves welcome it, as will our colleagues in the United States and in other countries where this textbook has been adopted. Above all else, we continue to provide first-rate writing and an array of intellectual handles and hooks that facilitate teaching with conviction. And, because *Europe Today, Second Edition*, strives mightily, as in our first edition, to be teacher-friendly, we look forward to feedback from you all as to how it can be improved.

I'd like to close this preface by reiterating our thanks to Susan McEachern, senior editor at Rowman & Littlefield Publishers, who has done so much for the Europe Today series. It is a pleasure to acknowledge our professional friendship, now spanning more than a few years. Susan is, as I said in the first edition, a formidable force in publishing fine books on European subjects. She is, as well, knowledgeable to such an extent that I have always felt that we are colleagues in this together. We all wish her long life. She makes so much happen, and saves us from so many errors along the way.

*As of May 1, 2004, joining the EU will be Cyprus, the Czech Republic, Estonia, Hungary, Latvia, Lithuania, Malta, Poland, Slovakia, and Slovenia.

**Bulgaria, Croatia, Romania, and Turkey are actively seeking membership.

Timeline of Events Leading to the Current State of the European Union

May 1945   End of World War II in Europe.
June 1945   The United Nations is founded.
June 1947   Marshall Plan (European Recovery Program) is launched.
April 1948   Organization for European Economic Cooperation (OEEC) is established.
May 1949   Council of Europe is formed.
April 1951   Treaty of Paris signed, which establishes the European Coal and Steel Community (ECSC).
March 1957   Treaties of Rome are signed, which establish the European Atomic Energy Community (Euratom) and the European Economic Community (EEC). Members of EEC are France, Netherlands, Belgium, Luxembourg, Germany, and Italy.
February 1958   Benelux Economic Union is founded.
July 1958   Common Agricultural Policy is proposed.
December 1960   OEEC is reorganized into the Organization for Economic Cooperation and Development (OECD).
August 1961   Denmark, Ireland, and the UK apply for EEC membership. (De Gaulle vetoes UK application twice: in 1963 and 1967.)
April 1962   Norway applies for EEC membership.
April 1965   Merger Treaty signed, which consolidates the institutions created by the Treaty of Paris and Treaties of Rome.
July 1968   EEC customs union is finalized and the Common Agricultural Policy is enacted.
January 1972   EEC membership negotiations concluded with UK, Denmark, Ireland, and Norway.
September 1972 National referendum in Norway goes against its membership in EEC.
January 1973   UK, Denmark, and Ireland join the EEC.
January 1974   Creation of the European Social Fund.
January 1975   Creation of the European Regional Development Fund.
June 1975   Greece applies for EEC membership.

March 1977	Portugal applies for EEC membership.
July 1977	Spain applies for EEC membership.
March 1979	European Monetary System is established.
June 1979	First direct elections of the European Parliament.
January 1981	Greece joins EEC.
January 1986	Spain and Portugal join the EEC.
February 1986	Single European Act signed in Luxembourg removing most of the remaining physical, fiscal, and technical barriers to the formation of a European common market. EEC now referred to as simply EC.
June 1987	Turkey applies for EC membership.
July 1989	Austria applies for EC membership.
December 1989	Turkey's membership application is rejected.
July 1990	Malta and Cyprus apply for EC membership.
October 1990	German reunification brings the former East Germany into the EC.
1991	Sweden applies for EC membership.
1992	Finland applies for EU membership.
February 1992	Treaty on European Union (Maastricht Treaty) signed, which expands process of European integration and creates a timetable for European Monetary Union (EMU). The European Community (EC) is now referred to as the European Union (EU).
June 1992	Danish voters reject Maastricht Treaty.
May 1993	Danish voters approve Maastricht Treaty after certain compromises are inserted into treaty.
January 1995	Austria, Sweden, and Finland join the EU after respective national referendums favor membership. National referendum in Norway rejects EU membership.
October 1997	Treaty of Amsterdam signed, which aims, among other things, to equalize tax structures among members of the EU in preparation for upcoming monetary union.
January 1999	EMU goes into effect. The eleven EU member states participating are Austria, Belgium, Finland, France, Germany, Ireland, Italy, Luxembourg, the Netherlands, Portugal, and Spain.
May 1999	Treaty of Amsterdam enters into force.
September 1999	European Parliament approves new European Commission led by Romano Prodi.
December 1999	European Council meeting in Helsinki decides to open accession negotiations with Bulgaria, Latvia, Lithuania, Malta, Romania, and the Slovak Republic and to recognize Turkey as a candidate country.

June 2000	A new partnership agreement (2000–2020) between the EU and the ACP countries is signed in Cotonou, Benin.
December 2000	European Council agrees on Treaty of Nice (to be ratified by all member states). EU leaders formally proclaim the Charter of Fundamental Rights of the European Union.
January 2001	Greece joins the euro area.
February 2001	Regulation adopted establishing the Rapid Reaction Force.
Jan.–Feb. 2002	The euro becomes legal tender and permanently replaces national currencies in EMU countries.
December 2002	Copenhagen European Council declares that Cyprus, Czech Republic, Estonia, Hungary, Latvia, Lithuania, Malta, Poland, Slovak Republic, and Slovenia will become EU members by May 1, 2004.
February 2003	The Treaty of Nice enters into force.
April 2003	Treaty of Accession (2003) is signed in Athens.
May 2004	Cyprus, Czech Republic, Estonia, Hungary, Latvia, Lithuania, Malta, Poland, Slovak Republic, and Slovenia become EU member states.

Sources

Harrison, D. M. *The Organisation of Europe: Developing a Continental Market Order.* London: Routledge, 1995.

McCormick, John. *The European Union: Politics and Policies.* Boulder, Colo.: Westview Press, 1996.

"The European Union: A Guide for Americans," at www.eurunion.org/infores/eugu ide/.milestones.htm.

PART ONE

INSTITUTIONS AND ISSUES

CHAPTER 1

Europe

International Crisis and the Future of Integration

Ronald Tiersky

Europe was not, in 2003, what it was when the first edition of this book appeared only a few years earlier. History has accelerated, as it did when communism fell in 1989–1991. The writers of textbooks are always rushing to catch up, and this revision of *Europe Today* will be the first textbook, or one of the first, to take account the Iraq war, the imminent enlargement of the European Union (EU) in 2004, and the Convention on the Future of Europe's draft constitution outlining the EU's future—if this constitution is ratified by the member states.

Thus Europe today is coping with what the French call a *nouvelle donne*, a new shuffle of the cards, internally and in the international system.

Let us look at European integration first. The European Union is, in a world with few such successes, a stunning economic and political achievement. It is compacting Europe's historic, nationalist, sovereignty-obsessed nation-states into an intergovernmental, transnational, and supranational framework whose goals are stability, peace, democracy, and prosperity. Fifty years on, Euroskeptics—continuously arguing that integration could not go further or would even fall apart—have been proven consistently wrong. No successes are complete, and integrationist enthusiasts should avoid any idea of inevitability. On the other hand, neither disdain nor anguished hand-wringing should obscure the essential fact: European integration, as such things go, is one of the most impressive political and economic advances of the twentieth century. Why not say it?

In 1999 the EU successfully launched the single European currency, the euro. This new currency has to date replaced the patriotic currencies of twelve countries: the much-loved German mark, the much derided (but beautiful) Italian lira, and the beautiful (and once derided) French franc. The euro soon may rival the dollar as a world reserve currency and is already the money of choice for huge amounts of international commerce and saving.

Today, after imposing respect for the euro, the EU continues an ambitious agenda of "widening" and "deepening" the unification of the Old Continent. "Widening," in European Union jargon, means enlargement of the EU by admitting more members. More than a decade after the Cold War's end and the collapse of the Soviet Union, the long-awaited "eastern" enlargement of the EU, once again, a historic achievement—the end of divided Europe, "Yalta Europe"—was approved in spring 2003 and will begin in May 2004. Ten central and eastern European countries (former Soviet bloc countries plus the islands of Cyprus and Malta) will join up. The European Union will, in the space of just a few years, have almost doubled its size from fifteen to twenty-five countries. This enlargement will create a huge and imposing new Gulliver in world politics. The Union will henceforth span the whole continent, creating a "Europe whole and free," as the first President Bush aptly put it when the Berlin Wall fell in 1989. In effect, a full stop was put after the Cold War. Or, perhaps one should say, this was the end of four centuries of fratricidal European wars, beginning with the religious wars of the sixteenth century. No crystal ball predicted this.

The history of European integration is, in a way, hard to follow simply because of the continually changing names of the European Union's ancestor organizations. "European Union" is likely to be the last name for this strange international beast—unless, someday far in the future, a "United States of Europe" is created. This is not necessary. It would come to pass only if the Europeans concluded that they needed a United States of Europe to compete in geopolitical power terms with the United States of America and other world powers, such as a rising China.

Integration began with reconstruction organizations set up after World War II, especially important being the European Coal and Steel Community (ECSC), created in 1951–1952. The ECSC's purpose in the first instance was economic. But its founders had a political strategy hidden from view. This strategy was to prevent another European war—to "pacify the Rhine River"—by combining German and French coal and steel industries so that neither country (obviously, Germany) could prepare secretly for another round of revenge, as in the three bloody wars that engulfed the Continent after German unification in 1870–1871.

The official ancestor of the European Union was launched on January 1, 1958, as the European Economic Community (EEC). The EEC was a straightforward customs union with just six members: France, Germany, Italy, and the three Benelux countries (Belgium, the Netherlands, and Luxembourg). Several vital if small enlargements thereafter brought all the western European countries into the fold, most notably Britain, the last of Europe's "Big Four" to join. (The three others are, of course, France, Germany, and Italy.) Of the other countries, the Norwegians voted twice not to join, and the Swiss—home of fine chocolates, hordes of gold, and a penchant for self-satisfaction and international banking secrecy—couldn't be bothered with European integration.

Moving from six members to fifteen in four decades was, according to some, an intolerably slow business. Others, however, thought that, for such a momentous undertaking as the integration of old bloody Western Europe during a situation of Cold War when warm and fuzzy Soviet feelings couldn't be taken for granted, a gradual expansion was the only way to do it. There were many unknowns. Would the Russian Bear accept European integration, since it implicitly threatened the Soviet empire in Eastern Europe? Could powerful and historically expansionist Germany be finally contained in an embrace with France and a European strait jacket?

It worked. The western European entity, instead of being swallowed by the Soviet Bear, saw the Soviet Union collapse. Yalta Europe was gone; Europe's geopolitical map was transformed.

Today, in 2003–2004, a sweet revenge of history is occurring. All the formerly captive communist bloc countries (except the Balkan states, i.e., former Yugoslavia) are nestling into the European Union. Europe, despite all its doubts and dangers, will be "Europe."

Russia, the erstwhile master of a menacing Soviet Empire, is now a rump state plagued with disintegrative tendencies. Its once-vaunted military is devastated (as shown in its inability to win a war against the small Muslim republic of Chechnya). Russia's gross domestic product is, astonishingly, about the size of the Netherlands'. And its declining population is almost an object of pity. Average life spans have fallen at an unprecedented rate (now about fifty-seven years for men, early sixties for women), and Russia's population is ebbing away in absolute terms because of alcoholism, tuberculosis, and AIDS. The small eastern countries that had long been prisoners of the Soviet communist empire are liberated and are "returning to Europe." Russia sits often on the sidelines, chastened and in many ways with hat in hand.

The accompanying aspect of today's European Union transformation, along with "widening," is the so-called deepening of the European Union's institutions. "Deepening," in EU jargon, originally meant enriching integration by moving toward further economic and political union. Today it means, specifically, reconfiguring the EU's internal decision-making structure. The key element is to specify (finally) exactly who decides what.

Since the end of the Cold War, the European Union has faced a choice: whether to "widen" first or to "deepen" first. The remarkable fact, in Simon Serfaty's nice phrase, is that the EU is doing both at the same time, "deepening in order to widen, widening in order to deepen."

And finally, there is the so-called Convention on the Future of Europe that met in 2002–2003, chaired by former French president Valéry Giscard d'Estaing.

The job of the Convention was to write a draft constitution for the EU, a concise statement of basic principles. This draft proposal is being discussed by the member-state governments in 2003–2004, with formal ratification procedures necessary in each country

The EU has never had a real constitution. It has worked solely on the basis of treaties such as those made in 1957, 1987, 1991, and 2001 among the sovereign member states. On this reading, the heretofore European Union might have been called basically an international organization, since contracting parties could renounce treaties and opt out of them, at least in theory. But the draft constitution goes further. It also contains an EU-wide bill of rights, modeled on the American precedent. But the notion of "rights" is more expansive; it includes, for example, the right to large social protection and a complex, potentially litigious formula on equal rights for women and men. The bill of rights, according to integrationists, is another step toward making the European Union into a federation.

It cannot be said that debate on the constitution in 2002–2003 attracted the attention of Europe's citizens. Most people had no idea what the constitution might contain, and many—far too many—had not even noticed that a constitutional convention was under way.

The other great issue for Europe today has been, of course, the Iraq crisis, the invasion, and its aftermath. A major alteration in Europe's position in the international system has occurred. The key factor has been disagreements with the United States and destabilization of NATO. The core of "old Europe," to use Secretary of State Rumsfeld's notorious term—essentially France and Germany—opposed the Bush administration's unilateralism in going to war. The governments of old Europe are espousing a new international order: a multilateral world very different from a unipolar international security regime based on American hegemony. The idea of a multipolar world that would constrain American power was welcomed, not surprisingly, by the Russian and Chinese governments. They have reason enough to worry about American hegemony in the international system.

In March–April 2003 an American-British–led war overthrew Saddam Hussein's unlamented regime. The invasion was supported by most European governments, but was opposed by many people—in fact, not only by the governments named above, but by huge majorities of European public opinion. They demonstrated in the millions in Europe's cities great and small, arguing that the war was illegal according to international law and illegitimate in the eyes of the world. They pointed up the fact that war was launched without clear Security Council approval. Smaller but still strong majorities said they opposed a war against Saddam Hussein *even with* United Nations approval.

But even the severest opponents of the war, whether in Europe or in the United States, had to agree, in spite of themselves, that the destruction of Saddam's totalitarian tyranny was welcome. In its wake, many of the previously opposed governments—in particular, France and Germany—are, at this writing, committing themselves to "pragmatism" in dealing with the Bush administration's effort to reconstruct the economic, political, and cultural fabric of the ancient Mesopotamian civilization "between the two rivers," the Tigris and the Euphrates.

Without a doubt, the Bush administration believes that this Franco-German turnabout seeks to reinsure commercial and economic interests in a new Iraq. But even Secretary of State Colin Powell, considered a moderate, said in a television interview that France would be "punished" for its diplomatic behavior in the UN Security Council leading up to war. The Washington slogan at the end of hostilities was, "Forget Germany, forgive Russia, and punish France."

However the consequences of the Iraq war play out, an unexpected upheaval of the international system has been launched. George Bush came to office not planning to be overly involved in world affairs, but now he is remaking world affairs.

The epicenter of this upheaval is the Middle East. Destroying the Saddam Hussein regime has made possible other assertive American policies. In early June 2003, the Bush administration, building aggressively on the changed geopolitics of that region, began pushing Israelis and Palestinians into practical negotiations toward a final settlement of their decades-old conflict, on the basis of the "road map" for peace drawn up by an international diplomatic "quartet" made up of the United States, the UN, Russia, and the European Union. The Bush administration also directly warned Syria and Iran not to meddle in post-Saddam Iraqi politics and to end support for terrorist groups.

Altogether, much more than in the 1999 first edition of *Europe Today*, to understand Europe after Iraq requires sustained concentration on foreign policy and geopolitics. The Iraq crisis has thrown into question an already wobbly Atlantic Alliance and NATO. Can there be true transatlantic partnership after Iraq? What will Europe (and America) do if the Atlantic partnership begins to crumble? Will there be a serious effort to repair the break, or not? This is all the more a question mark given NATO's already halting search for a sense of mission after the end of the Cold War and the demise of the Soviet Union.

On the other hand, if Europeans cannot feel certain of their own security without America's background presence—for example, with respect to global terrorism—and if, in addition, differing national foreign policies mean that Washington can "cherry-pick" among European countries when it wants to construct ad hoc "coalitions of the willing," what will be the effect on European unity and integration as a whole? What happens to European integration's goal of a European Union foreign and security policy? Can the European Union go forward without integration of foreign and security policies?

The answers to these questions are not simple. On one hand, the response may be a simple no. European integration may have to continue toward a mutual EU foreign policy, or else the current EU will begin to unravel back toward a single market, perhaps even giving up the euro, the single currency. On the other hand, the answer may be yes. An integrated Europe would not necessarily require a lockstep common foreign policy. Integration need not lead to a super-state. The European Union could very well remain a kind of confederacy combined with certain aspects of federalism and of national sovereignty. In short, as an Italian political proverb has it, the European Union could well be a "giraffe," meaning an animal that by all appearances should not exist, but does. (*Eppure si muove. . . .*)

Or, finally, the shock of such profound disagreements among European Union governments' foreign policy may have a paradoxical effect. It may lead EU governments to push harder for a common foreign and security policy precisely because their different worldviews and strategies have now been so publicly exposed to the world.

In addition to conflict about the Iraq war, Europeans generally agreed that, in other respects, the Bush administration's aggressive policies damaged European interests and moral concerns, from antitrust legislation, to trade in agriculture and steel tariffs (the "banana and steel wars"), to the World Trade Organization's admission of Russia, to genetically modified food, to the Kyoto treaty dealing with global climate change, nonproliferation issues, and the purview of the new International Criminal Court (ICC).

The solidity of transatlantic relations seems destabilized. Europe's anchor in world politics is shaking. Is "the West" breaking apart? Some Europeans, it is true, are not distraught by the disagreements with America. They think, having said it loudly over several years, that Europe and America have been drifting apart anyway. What is more, this parting of the ways is natural after the disappearance of a Soviet threat to Europe. Not to worry, or at least not to be surprised. Gerhard Schröder, upon taking office as the first German chancellor born after World War II, asserted in his speeches that, so to speak, the Germans had repented long enough for the Nazi period, that German governments would henceforth pursue their national interests just as would any normal country. German self-assertion is now an accomplished fact. Likewise, Europe as a whole may increasingly follow its own "national," continental interest in the future.

At this writing—as our authors in this book admirably demonstrate—whether the "Atlantic Community," what has long been called "the West," will survive differences not only of strategy but of political culture and moral worldview remains to be seen.

European *national* or *domestic* politics, for their part, continue to be focused on problems and conflicts similar to those of 1999. These are (1) national-level effects, both positive and negative, of European integration and globalization; (2) related dilemmas of economic stagnation, job guarantees and unemployment, and immigration problems; and (3) a looming demographic crisis, the so-called birth dearth.

Low birthrates and more retired people have led to bitter protests by government civil servants and private sector employees alike, hoping to stave off government strategies to cut social security and pension benefits and health-care coverage that are no longer sustainable because increasingly fewer workers are obliged to support an increasingly large retirement generation.

Another consequence of withering demography will be sharply increased numbers of legal immigrants into the European Union area. These will come, necessarily, largely from North African and other Muslim countries. While the U.S. population will, on current trends, tend to be stable, largely because of continuous and widely accepted immigration, massive new immigration into European societies will undoubtedly be a divisive phenomenon, even in societies in which one child or none is now a pattern. A rise in the potential for demagogic, populist political parties in connection with new immigration is already foreseeable, perhaps a radicalization of European politics as a whole.

Power and Weakness: Are Europeans from Venus?

The American intellectual Robert Kagan, in an essay published in *Policy Review* in spring 2002, shocked European intellectuals and political elites with a brutal assessment of contemporary Europe's new political and "strategic" culture. Europe's outlook toward world problems and crises, he wrote, has separated from American perceptions of the international order. The new core values animating European policies do not bode well for the Atlantic Alliance or for a larger mutual support in international security affairs. Americans are taking care of the world, Europeans are enjoying it.[1]

Kagan's analysis of European/American differences provoked a violent response from many Europeans fed up with what they perceived as American arrogance, of which Kagan himself seemed to them to be a perfect example. On the other hand, Kagan was enthusiastically taken up by a whole crowd of American government officials and policy intellectuals who had long believed that European pretensions to being taken seriously as international geopolitical actors were at bottom a game of smoke and mirrors. American elder statesman Henry Kissinger welcomed Kagan's essay as "one of those seminal treatises without which any discussion of European-American relations would be incomplete and which will shape that discussion for years to come." It was noteworthy that a leading French strategic specialist, François Heisbourg, agreed, commenting, without necessarily agreeing with Kagan, that "No academic piece in this realm has generated quite as much heat and interest since Samuel Huntington's 'Clash of Civilizations' article in 1993 or Francis Fukuyama's 'End of History' in 1989." Just a year later, as diplomatic negotiations over Iraq became acrimonious, the Kagan argument was no longer merely an academic exercise. European and American differences had become a practical matter of war and peace.

One must quote Robert Kagan's opening lines in full to convey the biting edge of his polemic:

> It is time to stop pretending that Europeans and Americans share a common view of the world, or even that they occupy the same world. On the all-important question of power—the efficacy of power, the morality of power, the desirability of power—American and European perspectives are diverging. Europe is turning away from power, or to put it a little differently, it is moving beyond power into a self-contained world of laws and rules and transnational negotiation and cooperation. It is entering a post-historical paradise of peace and relative prosperity, the realization of Immanuel Kant's "perpetual peace." Meanwhile, the United States remains mired in history, exercising power in an anarchic Hobbesian world where international laws and rules are unreliable, and where true security and the defense and promotion of a liberal order still depend on the possession and use of military might. That is why on major strategic and international questions today, Americans are from Mars and Europeans are from Venus.[2]

Kagan's last, epigrammatic phrase—"Americans are from Mars and Europeans are from Venus"—quickly became a cause célèbre, provoking loud applause from most Americans (and some Europeans, mainly privately), along with much European resentment.

According to Kagan, Europeans and Americans agree on precious little in the post-post–Cold War era. The problem is long-term, not transitory. "When it comes to setting national priorities, determining threats, defining challenges, and fashioning and implementing foreign and defense policies, the United States and Europe have parted ways."[3]

Europeans would like to believe that, after centuries of war, they look at international relations with wisdom, nuance, and experienced diplomacy. Europeans today are little given to the use of hard or coercive power in their relations with the rest of the world. Theirs is a strategy of influence, not of brutality. Their tactics emphasize subtlety and indirection, as opposed to American forthrightness and assertiveness. In the end, Europeans have become more tolerant, even of failure, than are Americans.

Increasingly, Europeans prefer process and mutual accommodation rather than the American penchant for confrontation and clear solutions, including, where necessary, bullying or even military force. Europeans hope that the international order is coming more and more under the sway of international law and institutions, including more responsiveness by national governments to the court of world public opinion. Europeans want a peaceful world, not only for

Europe, but because the preference against using military force to serve national interests *requires* peace. Otherwise Europe would need much more military power than it has mustered since World War II, not to say more than it is willing to pay for.

International peace, or at least peace for Europe, allows Europe's governments to concentrate on prosperity, first of all on the huge welfare state benefits that are (unfortunately) unlikely to be sustainable very far into the future. Overall, Europeans as a whole have, Kagan says, become more or less allergic to military action. Commercial and economic ties are, they believe, the surest way to build an international community. The American belief that its hegemony is not only possible but necessary to provide security in the new era seems to Europeans not only hubris, but a recipe for destabilization of the international order, including Europe and not excluding the United States itself. Concludes Kagan, Europeans thus "often emphasize process over result, believing that ultimately process can become substance."[4]

Europeans are even willing to tolerate terrorist attacks, insofar as they cannot be stopped. They believe the world is too fraught with causes for terrorism, justified or not. They point to their own past (Algerian or Middle Eastern terrorism in France, or homegrown Red Brigade or Red Faction terrorism in Italy and Germany) to demonstrate that, however tragic for victims, it is, in the end, better to live with such violence than try to stamp it out. For, as far as one can estimate, terrorism in western countries (and elsewhere) will not go away.

Europeans therefore did not see 9/11 as a watershed in international affairs. Despite all their compassion and solidarity, despite their realization that Americans suddenly were conscious of a catastrophic vulnerability, Europeans did not see the World Trade Center attacks as opening a new era in world history. September 11 to them was basically another terrorist attack, albeit on a larger scale than terrorism at home.

The American reaction to 9/11 was, of course, very different; Americans saw in the attack the beginning, not merely of a new American vulnerability, but of a new era of dangers for the United States and the world. The Bush administration quickly proclaimed that the struggle against global catastrophic terrorism was a "war," one that would last a long time. It would be fought, unlike earlier wars, not between countries and armies but between, on one hand, traditional states and, on the other, stateless networks of terrorists capable not only of catastrophic attacks but, in the future, of attacks using weapons of mass destruction.

Europe and America had ended the twentieth century with radically opposed "strategic cultures." The question became, Were Europe and the United States to live in radically different worlds as well?

The Europeans, Kagan alleged, are able to live in a sort of "post-historical" paradise of perpetual peace. They have an antiwar, pro-commerce-and-trade view of the world and of their responsibilities in it, but only because the United

States provides them with the international security that they are unable or unwilling to provide for themselves. Europeans, in short, continue, in the twenty-first century as during the Cold War, to be free riders on American power, expecting it to protect them from the dangers of world politics beyond the Old Continent.

If post-historical, post-industrial, postmodern European society is to survive, it must be protected. But Europeans are not willing to sign up for this task themselves, inasmuch as it would mean giving up the culture and the policies that make the pacifistic paradise possible. Thus the solution, according to a British writer, is for Europeans, hypocritically or not, "to get used to the idea of double standards." Within Europe, international relations may "operate on the basis of laws and open cooperative security." But outside, "we need to revert to the rougher methods of an earlier era—force, preemptive attack, deception, whatever is necessary. Among ourselves, we keep the law, but when we are operating in the jungle, we must also use the laws of the jungle. [Europeans must therefore provide themselves new arms] both physical and psychological."[5]

The trouble with Robert Cooper's prescription is that, while it might apply to future Europe as a whole, the necessity of double standards already applies to America. It is America that can deal peacefully enough with other *liberal* societies but is obliged, today as yesterday, in the larger world to play the policeman. The "reluctant sheriff," as Richard Haass put it several years ago, has now become a "preemptive sheriff." The unhappy paradox for the United States is that, having done the largest part to create Europe's pacified international relations, America cannot enter this world itself without, by the absence of its power, putting the global order at stake. (The debate over Iraq, of course, found many governments making the opposite argument: an aggressive, "democratic imperialist" America may turn out to be *itself* most responsible for destabilizing the international order.)

Robert Kagan himself recognizes that his Mars and Venus distillation of American-European differences is a caricature, although, in the nature of caricature, it is an exaggeration of an underlying reality. One writer even suggests that Kagan "is too kind to Europe," in the sense that "he elevates to a deliberate, coherent approach what is, in fact, a story of muddled seeking and national differences." Garton Ash continues,

> But a second, less obvious question is: Do Europeans and Americans wish this to be true? The answer seems to be yes. Quite a lot of American policymakers like the idea that they are from Mars—on the understanding that this makes them martial rather than Martian—while quite a lot of European policymakers like to think they are, indeed, programmatic Venutians.[6]

The Kagan polemic leads directly to the issue of a dangerous mutual disdain separating Europeans and Americans as peoples and societies rather than merely as governments and policies.

European Anti-Americanism, American Anti-Europeanism

As war against Iraq approached, and as it became clear that Security Council diplomacy was likely to fail, huge antiwar demonstrations appeared on the streets of Europe's largest cities. Not spared were capitals of European countries whose governments supported the Bush administration. Everywhere within European Union boundaries, strong public opinion majorities formed against the prospect of war.

Beyond this, on both sides of the Atlantic, a deeper incompatibility of European and American cultures seemed to be revealed, less amenable to change than simple attitudes. The "breakup of the West" hypothesis seemed to have a societal and cultural component, in addition to the geopolitical.

In Europe, more may be at stake than resentment over the Bush administration's evident brutality in dealings with European allies. Is there a new anti-Americanism in Europe? This is one of the crucial issues in the coming years.

In the 1979–1983 Euromissile crisis over introducing medium-range NATO missiles to counter a Soviet deployment of SS20 missiles, tens of thousands of Germans took to the streets on the motto that "the shorter range the missile, the deader the Germans." But at that time, the Helmut Kohl government withstood popular pressure and left-wing parliamentary opposition. He won support for the NATO deployment in parliament. But opposition to the American-British war in Iraq was something quite new in Germany, since it was the government itself, led by Chancellor Gerhard Schröder, which broke with the erstwhile American protector.

French anti-Americanism is quite another matter. The French left, dominated politically and above all culturally until the early 1970s by the massive French Communist Party, had for decades preached knee-jerk, anticapitalist anti-Americanism, almost as if the United States were even then a "Great Satan," as it is for Islamists today. This reflex anti-Americanism (against General Ridgway, "the plague" in 1953 during the Korean war, against the "Coca Cola-ization of France" later on) died away when the Machiavellian Socialist leader François Mitterrand became president of France in 1981. In power for fourteen long years, he undid the decades-old political domination of the Socialist party by the Communists, reversing their cultural dominance on the French left as well. But even conservative elements in French society, in spite of their admiration for many aspects of American achievement, have always contained anti-American feelings, some dating back to fascist inspirations of the 1930s.

In any case there has been a long-standing, wider European sympathy for "Gaullist" resistance to America's international dominance, the nationalist response of General Charles de Gaulle, France's heroic World War II leader and first president of the Fifth Republic (1958–1969), to Cold War constraints on French independence. De Gaulle wanted Europe's liberation from the United States as well as the USSR. Is this the larger meaning of transatlantic conflicts over Iraq?

Americans have long displayed a similarly self-contradictory attitude toward France and the French. French culture—cuisine, movies, fashion—was traditionally admired by Americans. But at the same time, tourists resented what they took to be French arrogance and an intolerable sense of cultural superiority. In the government and foreign-policy circles of Washington and New York, disdain for the French reached a peak. Belief was (and is) widespread that French foreign policy and diplomacy are cynical and hypocritical. French motives are believed to be not the enlightened façade that is presented in international diplomacy, but a reason of state mercantilism—a mixture of hidden, corrupt state support for France's commercial interests, combined with the desire of French elites to maintain the powerful state that is the source of their privileged positions in society.

The immediate and universal European solidarity with America after the terrorism of 9/11 surprised people on both sides of the Atlantic. The leading French daily, *Le Monde*, always skeptical of Washington, titled its front-page editorial, "*Nous sommes tous des americains*" ("We are all Americans"). However, Europeans became progressively less supportive of the American war in Afghanistan. A widely quoted survey of American and European opinion found that Americans endorsed President Bush's argument that the United States was waging a fight against "evil," the beginning battle in a global war against global terrorism. They accepted Bush's emotionally and religiously charged "axis of evil" labeling of Iraq, Iran, and North Korea. But Europeans in the four countries surveyed—Britain, France, Germany, and Italy—on the whole said that America was looking after its own national interests.[7] It was increasingly clear that Europeans did not understand the depth of American reactions to 9/11, a belief that a new, more dangerous era had dawned for America, fraught with permanent threats of mass destruction to the homeland. Europeans, with their history of frequent but less devastating terrorist attacks, thought that 9/11 was nothing qualitatively different from their own experience.

A Pew Center public opinion poll in twenty-one countries, released in June 2003, shows a sharp decline in mutual esteem across the Atlantic.[8] This trend has many Europeans and Americans committed to transatlantic friendship extremely concerned. Study groups, such as those at the Council on Foreign Relations in New York and at the Brookings Institution and the Center for Strategic and International Studies in Washington, not to mention European groups such as those at the French Institute of International Relations and the German Society for Foreign Affairs, are advising governments about what can be done.

Whereas in a summer 2002 poll 79 percent of Americans had a favorable view of France, in the 2003 poll this figure had plummeted to 29 percent. Those having an unfavorable view went up from 16 percent to 60 percent. In Germany, France, and Spain, favorable opinions of America dropped precipitously: in Germany from 78 percent in 2000 to 61 percent in 2002, to only 25 percent in 2003. In France the numbers were 63 percent in 2002 and 31 percent in 2003. In Spain, those having a favorable view of the United States dropped from 50 percent in 2000 to only 14 percent in 2003. Britain, not surprisingly, is the country most favorably viewed by Americans, and vice versa, with favorable American views in the 80 percent range. Italy is not far behind, with favorable percentages in the seventies. South Korea, Kuwait, and Nigeria were all more favorably viewed than France and Germany by American opinion!

The Iraq war has clearly had a deep effect on public opinion, increasing mutual disdain on both sides of the Atlantic. Congress's decision to rename French fries "freedom fries" and the Fox News Channel's nickname of "the axis of weasels" for France, Germany, and Russia, did express the angry mood of the moment. Nevertheless, to suppose the permanence of the new anti-Europeanism among Americans, and the new anti-Americanism among Europeans, is not yet justified. European governments, however, must now take care not to affront their public opinion.

European Unity, or Not?

In February 2003, in the last weeks of Security Council debate, an EU summit meeting tried to reconcile differences among the Europeans over how to deal with Iraq. This meant as much how to deal with Washington as how to disarm the Saddam Hussein regime, as became clearer as negotiations proceeded.

For several weeks, France's president Jacques Chirac and Germany's chancellor Gerhard Schröder had been refurbishing the Franco-German partnership, the "motor force" that traditionally commanded European Union policies. From this admittedly narrow point of view, the Iraq crisis arrived just in time.

In late 2002 Gerhard Schröder, about to lose reelection to his conservative opponent, the Bavarian Christian Democrat Edmond Stoiber, suddenly—and opportunistically—adopted an antiwar stance. This, in the circumstances, seemed not only anti-Bush but anti-American. In any case Schröder's late antiwar platform worked. He was narrowly reelected. On the other hand, the head of Germany's Christian Democracy, Angela Merkel, came to Washington to say that, had *they* won the election, a conservative government would have supported American policy. Schröder's success, and the arrival of Germany on January 1, 2003, as a nonpermanent Security Council member, hardened President Chirac's diplomacy. Huge antiwar demonstrations throughout Europe floated Chirac's boat, already rowing against Washington. Chirac, known as a past master of opportunism himself, suddenly became a kind of international hero, struggling to stop Washington's rush to war.

Remarkably, a few days later French and German control of European Union diplomacy was publicly challenged by other European governments. An unprecedented open letter, published in the *Wall Street Journal* and signed by the heads of eight EU member and candidate member states (Britain, Spain, Italy, Portugal, Denmark, and, among the candidate countries, Poland, Hungary, and the Czech Republic) endorsed the Bush administration's policy. This so-called Letter of the Eight observed that it was American and British military pressure alone on Iraq's borders that had forced Saddam to readmit weapons inspectors. Then a second letter appeared, signed by the so-called Vilnius Ten, composed mainly of EU candidate member countries, all recently admitted to NATO and due to join the EU as full members in 2004. The eighteen leaders of governments had not even apprised EU councils—that is, France and Germany—of their plans. Not informing the French was a sure recipe for diplomatic trouble.

Such bold behavior, especially daring for governments of candidate member states—they could, after all, suffer retaliation—provoked expressions of contempt from President Chirac—ironic, given the French president's criticisms of the Bush administration's "arrogant" attitudes.

Chirac, resembling an angry parent, scolded the candidate governments. In a press conference he said that the two letters were "dangerous" meddling in a delicate political situation that the French were handling, it was implied, quite well enough for all. Chirac thought to add that this was really "bad behavior" (they were *pas très bien élevé*). Our French specialist in this book, writing in his capacity as a journalist for the *Financial Times*, said, "Never before [had] Mr. Chirac used such undiplomatic language in public during almost eight years as French head of state."[9] The French president singled out Bulgaria and Romania, to join the EU in a second wave of the enlargement, whose leaders had strongly supported the Bush administration. The pro-Washington attitude of these two weak states was, for one thing, gratitude for America's role in the Cold War defeat of the Soviet Union, which led to their own national liberation. But it was also a matter of an implicit strategy, obviously worrisome to a French leader, to use American influence as a counterweight in the EU against domination by France and Germany.

"Particularly thoughtless," was Jacques Chirac's denunciation of this lèse-majesté. He then added, ominously, that Bulgaria and Romania "had done their best to reduce their chances of ratification of full European Union membership." Since ratification under EU rules must be unanimous, this implied that France might blackball the Bulgarian and Romanian candidacies. Robert Graham observed that Chirac's threat indicated that he believed the candidate countries were taking EU membership to be more or less synonymous with NATO membership. This amounted to putting Atlantic solidarity before France's pet project of fostering a common European foreign and security policy, in which France would have the leading voice.

Thus it remains to be seen whether foreign-policy harmony in the European Union, let alone a common European defense, is a viable, or even desirable, goal of EU development.

Conclusion

What can one conclude, as a general introduction to the chapters that follow? What is the outlook for Europe? What is the likely future of European/American relations?

One often prescient writer, Timothy Garten Ash, sees three broad tendencies on which the post-Iraq West could be built.

The first is the realist, hegemonic American idea that (1) American might makes it possible for the United States to organize the international system, and that (2) it is America's geopolitical and fundamentally moral responsibility to do so. No other state, or group of states, has either the political will or the necessary capability to do so.

As "the hyperpower of the free," America's first concern will be the war on terrorism and the struggle to limit, by force if necessary, proliferation of weapons of mass destruction. It is an ancient, if sad, truth that a durable, just peace may sometimes require making war. It may also mean the better task of fostering open societies. Iraq, for the Bush administration, means both.

American power, in any case, will be the center of the new world order. If other governments, especially the Europeans, will help the United States in this benevolent though sometimes brutal American hegemony, all the better. If America has to do the world's work alone, then so be it. The obstacle to success for America is that, while its military might is overwhelming, the United States must not only win wars, it must win the peace. And for this, America cannot go it alone. The Europeans can be absolutely vital to making and keeping the peace.

The second possibility, proposed by France, Russia, and others (including China), is a multilateral or multipolar world order, in which American hyperpower is balanced by another power center or centers.

The third idea is British prime minister Tony Blair's. It involves developing a new, larger version of "the West," to face the new threats of the twenty-first century, above all the intersection of global terrorism and weapons of mass destruction. On this view, America's strategic power, since it cannot be rivaled, should be partnered. "Partners are not servants," as Timothy Garten Ash rightly says.[10] Despite not speaking with one voice in the Iraq crisis, Europe ought now to do everything to keep U.S. administrations working through international institutions, in spite of their insufficiencies.

Altogether, the Iraq crisis has shaken the crucial institutions of international order. "Before a shot has been fired," wrote the *International Herald Tribune* on February 12, 2003,

> the political tensions ahead of a looming Iraq war are inflicting grievous wounds on the triad of institutions that embody aspirations for multilateral security cooperation among Western democracies: the European Union, NATO, and the UN Security Council. This combination of interlocking security arrangements, which has enabled the West to ride out trans-Atlantic tempests for decades, faces a simultaneous challenge from within that could spell change or even irrelevance for all parts of the system.[11]

The French government's Security Council diplomacy, which was either exemplary or disastrous according to one's point of view, prevented, by threatening a veto, a second Security Council resolution that the Bush administration could accept. In private, however, the French were less rigid: Their foreign minister and ambassador told the Americans just to "pass us by," that is, not to present a second resolution, and that is what happened.

The new transatlantic divide has a special meaning for the authors of this book. When history accelerates as it has in the past two years, the difficulty is great, for people whose education and worldview were formed in another age, to see with new eyes. On the other hand, *students* who use this book as an introduction to European politics and thus, to some extent, to world politics, have their own difficulty.

Naturally, students ought to immerse themselves in current events, to follow "what is going on," to be well-informed. But students should also be interested in the past; they should learn the history out of which current events arise.

In any case, no matter whether the readers of this book are political science majors or not, the world they will live in for a long time is being decided now. Their interest is to understand it and engage with it—not only in terms of the facts, but psychologically and emotionally as well.

Predictions of great changes and new worlds are, of course, easy enough to make. They are much more difficult to get right. Myopia is not only a weakness of the eye; it is a common mistake in looking at history. The myopic view can see clearly only what is near to the eye. Thus people—historians, political scientists, journalists—often confuse what is near, that is, current events, with what is far, that is, history in the large sense. People tend too often to believe that the changes before their eyes, so clear and sharp, amount to a total overthrow of a world system. Our authors try to avoid this mistake.

Nevertheless, broad changes in world politics since the collapse of communism, accelerated by 9/11 and international concern with proliferation of weapons of mass destruction, do support the hypothesis that some fundamental reordering of world political relationships is under way. While today's European-American differences should not be exaggerated, neither should the possibility of a progressive growing apart of Europe and America be underestimated.

Notes

1. Robert Kagan's article, "Power and Weakness," appeared in *Policy Review,* June/July 2002. The expanded version is *Of Paradise and Power: America and Europe in the New World Order* (New York: Alfred A. Knopf, 2003).

2. Kagan, *Of Paradise and Power,* 3.

3. Kagan, *Of Paradise and Power,* 3–4.

4. Kagan, *Of Paradise and Power,* 5.

5. Quoted in Kagan, *Of Paradise and Power,* 75. Robert Cooper is, significantly, an advisor to British prime minister Tony Blair, who has tried to lead his country back toward a more determined (his critics would say more reckless) view of Britain's responsibilities.

6. Timothy Garton Ash, "Anti-Europeanism in America," online at www.nybooks .com/articles/1059.

7. The survey, released April 17, 2002, was conducted by the Pew Research Center, in association with the Chicago Council on Foreign Relations and the International Herald Tribune.

8. "Views of a Changing World, June 2003," The Pew Center for the People & the Press (Washington, D.C.).

9. Robert Graham, "Chirac Vents Ire over Behaviour of EU Candidates," *Financial Times,* February 19, 2003.

10. For this, and the discussed ideas in general, see Garton Ash, "The War after War with Iraq," *New York Times,* sec. A, March 20, 2003.

11. Joseph Fitchett, *International Herald Tribune,* February 12, 2003.

CHAPTER 2

The European Union

From Community to Constitution

John Van Oudenaren

Introduction

Philosophers have dreamed about a united Europe for centuries, but it was not until World War II that a serious movement toward European integration began. Postwar leaders, many of them veterans of the anti-Nazi resistance, believed that if Europe were to achieve a durable peace and economic prosperity after the war, it needed to overcome the nationalism and economic autarky that characterized the 1930s and that had reached their epitome in Hitler's Germany and Mussolini's Italy. The question was how to begin the process of building a more united Europe, especially in the aftermath of a six-year conflict that had left deep hatreds and widespread economic destruction.

In the immediate postwar period, the western European countries took some initial steps toward integration. France and Britain concluded an alliance in the 1947 Treaty of Dunkirk. In March 1948, these two powers and the three Benelux countries—Belgium, the Netherlands, and Luxembourg—concluded the Brussels treaty, establishing the organization that later became the **Western European Union (WEU).** The five signatories pledged to come to each other's defense in the event of external attack; hold regular consultations among their foreign ministers; and cooperate in the economic, social, and cultural spheres.

The United States also played an important role in encouraging the Europeans to work together. By early 1947, the Truman administration had concluded that the Soviet Union was not prepared to cooperate with the western powers in establishing a stable European order. In eastern Europe, communist regimes were consolidating their grip on power. In western Europe, people were still suffering the aftereffects of war, including shortages of food and fuel, unemployment, and hopelessness about the future.

In a speech at Harvard University in June 1947, U.S. Secretary of State George C. Marshall proposed a program of aid designed to pull Europe to its feet. The United States offered to provide Europe with money and goods, but only if the Europeans themselves came up with a plan for using aid effectively, and only if the plan were designed as a joint effort rather than a hodgepodge of national requests. After a series of preliminary meetings, in April 1948, sixteen European states founded the **Organization for European Economic Cooperation (OEEC)**. Based in Paris, this organization helped to administer Marshall aid and provided a forum in which the member states negotiated arrangements to lower intra-European trade and currency barriers. The European Recovery Program, as the **Marshall Plan** formally was known, thus provided a powerful external stimulus to intra-European cooperation.

The conclusion of the Brussels Pact and the founding of the OEEC were important first steps on the road to integration, but they fell short of meeting the aspirations of those in Europe who wanted a complete break with the past and whose objective was nothing less than the establishment of a United States of Europe. Known as federalists, they believed that integration should not be a matter just for governments, but that it should be based directly on the will of the people. In 1947, the federalists launched a campaign to convene a European Assembly, whose members would not be chosen by or under the control of the national governments, that would undertake the task of constituting a new organization to unite the peoples of Europe. The federalists succeeded in convincing the five Brussels Pact signatories to convene a ten-power conference in London in early 1949 to discuss their ideas.

The conference quickly revealed a split, however, between Britain and the Scandinavian countries, who wanted integration to proceed on the basis of agreements among states, and those on the Continent who favored more radical forms of integration. The London conference led to the creation of the **Council of Europe**, a Strasbourg-based organization that works to harmonize laws and promote human rights in Europe. Although useful in its own way, the Council of Europe never became a truly federal institution for Europe. The elected governments in key countries had proven unwilling to cede sovereign powers to a supranational body such as the federalists were proposing. Integration was endorsed, but largely on the basis of intergovernmental agreement. As will be seen, the tension between **supranationalism** and **intergovernmentalism** has been a permanent feature of the integration process that persists to the present day.

The other major development of the late 1940s was the creation of the North Atlantic Alliance. The United States had emerged from World War II committed to promoting economic and political stability in Europe, but it did not intend to conclude a military alliance with western European states, which went against the U.S. tradition of "no entangling alliances" and was opposed by powerful isolationist forces in Congress. However, the communist takeovers in eastern Europe and the onset of the Cold War led to a shift in attitudes. In April 1949 the United States, Canada, the five Brussels powers, and four other European states signed the North Atlantic Treaty, in which they pledged to come to each other's assistance in the event of external attack. The signing of the treaty was followed by the creation of the **North Atlantic Treaty Organization (NATO)** and the establishment of an integrated military command. Like the Marshall Plan, NATO was an important U.S. contribution to the postwar revival of Europe and to the fledgling process of building a united Europe. It allowed the European countries to concentrate on economic cooperation, leaving sensitive and contentious matters of defense to the transatlantic organization.

Establishing the Community
THE EUROPEAN COAL AND STEEL COMMUNITY

The accomplishments and disappointments of the late 1940s began the process that led, in the 1950s, to the creation of the three sister institutions known as the European Communities and that became the basis for today's European Union: the **European Coal and Steel Community (ECSC)**, the **European Economic Community (EEC)**, and **the European Atomic Energy Agency (Euratom)**. The first of these institutions, the ECSC, was the inspiration of Jean Monnet, a French businessman who had spent the war years in the United States and who had devoted much thought to the problem of bringing about a European Union.

Like the federalists, Monnet was convinced that integration had to be based on something more than intergovernmental agreement. Europe needed institutions and laws of its own—a pooling of sovereignty that could survive the vagaries of national politics. But Monnet also believed that the federalists had been naïve in thinking that a united Europe could be brought about through a constitutive assembly that directly challenged the powers of the nation-states. In his view it was essential to start the process of integration on a different basis. Geographically, the key to building a new Europe was reconciliation between France and Germany. He thus was willing to go ahead, if necessary, without the British and the Scandinavians. He also believed that it was more important to achieve practical results in a few important sectors than to make broad commitments to economic, political, cultural, and defense cooperation that were impossible to implement. While proposing to narrow the geographic and sectoral scope of the European integration process, he was convinced that integration had to be far-reaching and irreversible, with real powers transferred to a supranational body whose decisions would be binding on the countries forming the community.

Working behind the scenes, Monnet managed to convince the French and West German governments to embrace his ideas. On May 9, 1950, French Foreign Minister Robert Schuman formally proposed to the French cabinet Monnet's plan for France and Germany to combine their coal and steel industries under a joint authority. This authority was to be independent of the governments of the two countries and would guarantee each country full and equal access to a common pool of resources. The significance of this proposal was as much political as economic. With the production of coal and steel—the very sinews of modern military capability—subject to a joint authority, war among west European states would become unthinkable.

The Schuman Declaration, as the proposal became known, was enthusiastically welcomed by the West German chancellor, Konrad Adenauer. Belgium, Luxembourg, the Netherlands, and Italy also expressed interest in joining the new community. The Benelux countries already had established an economic union among themselves and were eager to cooperate on a new basis with their larger neighbors. For Italy, joining the ECSC reflected a decision by its postwar leaders to "scale the Alps"—to turn Italy's energies toward northern Europe and away from the disastrous African and Balkan ambitions of the former dictator, Benito Mussolini.

The treaty establishing the ECSC was negotiated in the months following Schuman's dramatic declaration and signed in Paris in April 1951. The ECSC became operational in July 1952. For the commodities covered—coal, coke, iron ore, steel, and scrap—the ECSC created a common market in which all tariff barriers and restrictions on trade among the six member countries were banned. To ensure the operation of this common market, the ECSC treaty provided for the establishment of four institutions, roughly corresponding to the executive, legislative, and judicial branches of government, with extensive legal and administrative powers in the coal and steel sectors.

The **High Authority** was established as a nine-member commission with executive powers to administer the workings of the common market. The members of the authority (two each from France, Germany and Italy; one each from Belgium, Luxembourg, and the Netherlands) were to be "completely independent in the performance of their duties." They were to decide what was best for the ECSC as a whole, rather than to represent the views of the member countries. The High Authority was empowered to issue decisions, recommendations, and opinions prohibiting subsidies and aids to industry that distorted trade, to block mergers and acquisitions and other types of agreements among firms, and under certain circumstances to control prices. It could impose fines to ensure compliance with its decisions. Monnet was named the first head of the High Authority, and for several years he lent his energies and reputation to building its powers.

The **Council of Ministers** was established as a counterweight to excessive power in the hands of the High Authority. It consisted of ministers from the national governments of the member states, with each state represented by one minister. For some policy actions, the Council of Ministers had to endorse the decisions of the High Authority. Some decisions were taken by unanimity, others by majority voting. Thus, even within the Council of Ministers, member states could not always exercise a veto over collective decision making. This was quite different from organizations such as NATO, where decisions were taken only by consensus and where a single state could always block adoption of a decision to which it was opposed.

The **Common Assembly** was designed to introduce an element of legislative participation in the work of the ECSC. Its members were not directly elected by the people but were chosen by the national legislatures. Its power, moreover, was to advise rather than to pass legislation. Still, the principle of parliamentary participation was established, and the powers of what later was to become the European Parliament were to expand greatly in subsequent decades.

The other institution of the ECSC was the **European Court of Justice (ECJ),** which was set up to settle conflicts between the member states of the Community, between member states and the institutions of the Community (e.g., the High Authority), or between the institutions of the Community itself. The Court of Justice thus was established as a nascent "supreme court" for the ECSC, whose judgments were enforceable on the territory of the member states.

These institutions were the first genuinely supranational bodies in Europe. They could exercise authority—in their limited areas of competence—over the national governments of the member states. Establishment of the ECSC thus entailed a transfer of sovereignty from the national level to the central institutions, which were to be located in Luxembourg.

The ECSC was an immediate success. Along with steps already under way in the OEEC, the elimination of barriers to trade in the coal and steel sectors contributed to the European economic renaissance of the early 1950s. Politically, the community began the process of reconciliation between France and West Germany. It also embodied the commitment of a group of states to begin practicing some of what the federalists were preaching.

At the same time, however, ECSC's scope of activity was by definition quite limited. It dealt with a single economic sector, and it lacked an external profile. It could not, for example, negotiate tariffs with foreign countries. It therefore was understandable that the ECSC members should try to build upon their success and look for ways to broaden the scope of integration. Initially, they turned to defense—a reasonable choice, given the perceived military threat from communism, but one that proved to be disastrous. In May 1952, the six ECSC countries signed a treaty establishing a European Defense Community (EDC) in which decisions over defense and a jointly commanded European army were to be made by supranational EDC institutions patterned on those of the ECSC. However, in August 1954, the French National Assembly rejected the EDC treaty, rendering the process of European integration a severe, albeit temporary, setback. Whereas national governments and parliaments were willing to surrender sovereignty in some key economic areas, the EDC experience

showed that defense was too sensitive—too close to core issues of national identity—to be treated the same way. The emphasis thus shifted back to economics.

THE EUROPEAN ECONOMIC COMMUNITY

Following the EDC setback, the foreign ministers of the six ECSC states met
in Messina, Italy, in June 1955 to consider ways to energize the integration
process. At the time, two potential courses of action were widely discussed in
Europe: a further stage of *sectoral* integration based on a proposed atomic energy community, and a plan for *market* integration through the elimination of
barriers to trade and the eventual creation of a common market. Those in Europe, including Monnet and many in France, who saw integration primarily as a
process of building up shared institutions and accomplishing common projects,
tended to stress the importance of the atomic energy community. Others, especially in West Germany, who saw European integration more as a process of
tearing down intra-European barriers, emphasized the common market. These
two approaches came to be known as "positive" and "negative" integration,
and both have played a role in the development of Europe.

At Messina, the ministers agreed to establish a committee charged to study
these options and to formulate concrete proposals. The Spaak Committee
(named for its chairman, Belgian Foreign Minister Paul-Henri Spaak) presented
its report to the May 1956 Venice meeting of foreign ministers. It struck a balance between the two approaches to integration and proposed that the ECSC
states create both a European Atomic Energy Agency (Euratom) and a European Economic Community (EEC). Following detailed and arduous negotiations, in Rome on March 25, 1957, the six signed two treaties creating these new
entities.

Like the European Coal and Steel Community, Euratom subsequently
came to play an important role in a single sector of the economy. It promoted
the development of nuclear power and established a common pool of radioac-
tive fuels for western Europe's growing stock of nuclear reactors. Of the two
institutions created in 1957, however, the EEC—or Common Market as it was
widely known—was by far the more important. The agreement establishing the
EEC became known as the Treaty of Rome and remains in many ways the core
constitutional document of today's European Union.

The basic objective of the EEC was simple in principle, albeit sweeping in
its implications: to create an internal market characterized by the free movement of goods, services, persons, and capital. Initially, the overwhelming emphasis was on eliminating obstacles to trade in goods. The Treaty of Rome provided for the phasing out, in stages, of all tariffs and quantitative restrictions on
trade among the member states. The creation of a common internal market also
necessitated the establishment of a common external tariff and a common com-

mercial policy. Since goods that entered one member state could travel freely to other EEC countries, it was desirable for these countries to adopt the same tariffs toward third countries, lest goods simply be diverted to ports in countries with the lowest tariff for a given import. The EEC thus was empowered to speak with one voice in international negotiations conducted within the framework of the **General Agreement on Tariffs and Trade**.

The Treaty of Rome used the basic institutional framework established for the ECSC. The High Authority for the EEC was called simply the **European Commission**, a less grandiose name that reflected the desire on the part of the founding member states to cut back somewhat the powers of the supranational authority. Nonetheless, the Commission was endowed with broad executive powers, including the sole right to initiate EEC legislation. The member states were responsible for selecting the commissioners, who were chosen for four-year terms (five-year since 1979). The Commission president, also provided for under the treaty and selected by the member states, quickly emerged as the most visible champion of and spokesperson for the Community.

A Council of Ministers was to be the main decision-making body of the EEC, in which representatives of the member states would vote on proposals put forward by the commission. Votes could be made on the basis of unanimity or by qualified majority—a weighted system that assigns votes in rough proportion to the population sizes of the member states and that requires a certain critical mass of votes to pass a measure. France, Italy, and West Germany each had four votes, Belgium and the Netherlands two, and Luxembourg one. Twelve of the seventeen votes were considered a qualified majority. In practice, qualified majority voting was disliked by some member-state political leaders, especially in France, as being too supranational, and it was little used until the 1980s. As in the ECSC, the chairmanship of the Council rotated, with each member state serving as Council president for a six-month period. In addition, the member states agreed that the three communities—the ECSC, Euratom, and the EEC—all could share the same Common Assembly and Court of Justice. The ECSC High Authority remained in Luxembourg, but the new European Commission was established in Brussels, which became the de facto capital of uniting Europe. The Common Assembly was situated in Strasbourg, France. The treaty also provided for the establishment of two other institutions, the Economic and Social Committee and the European Investment Bank, that were to play much lesser roles in Community decision making.

As in the case of the ECSC, the impetus for creating the EEC was as much political as economic. Operating under a concept that became known as "functionalism," promoters of European federalism believed that the gradual expansion of economic ties and of cooperation in various practical spheres such as atomic energy eventually would "spill over" into the political realm, as governments, parliaments, and national electorates yielded sovereignty and national prerogatives in small but politically manageable steps. This aspiration to go beyond mere economic cooperation was expressed in the very first sentence of the Treaty of Rome, in which the signatories declared their determination "to lay the foundations of an ever closer union among the peoples of Europe."[1]

Although the focus of the EEC was on the creation of a common market through the elimination of barriers, the Treaty of Rome also provided for the establishment of common policies in other areas. Agriculture was the most important, but others included transport, competition (antitrust), and policy toward colonies and former colonies in Africa and the Caribbean. Over time, the EEC was to assume a role in a growing range of policy areas, some, like telecommunications and industry, closely linked to the internal market, but others, such as the environment and education, much broader in scope.

Completion of the common market for goods took place between 1958 and 1968, a period of rapid economic growth and rising prosperity. Businesses became more efficient and productive as they were able to sell to a larger market and were forced to invest in new machinery and research to meet competition from firms in other countries. France and Italy, whose backward industries initially feared the full force of competition in a common market, especially benefited from the new circumstances. Italy became a major producer of cars, machinery, and home appliances for the whole of the EEC, while France saw a general strengthening of its competitive position and was able to assert European leadership in a number of high-technology sectors such as nuclear power and aerospace.

Notwithstanding these successes, there were many gaps in the integration process, and a number of unresolved economic and political problems would come back to haunt Europe in the more difficult economic climate of the 1970s. The elimination of barriers and the expansion of trade in the EEC were mainly confined to goods. Of the "four freedoms"—free movement of goods, services, persons, and capital—the last three existed mainly on paper. Transportation, telecommunications, banking, insurance, and other service businesses still were organized along national lines, with little competition across borders. Most European governments maintained controls on the cross-border flow of capital. And free movement of labor within the EEC was mainly limited to the large number of workers from southern Italy who went to work in the factories of northern Europe to meet the growing labor shortages of the 1960s.

The **Common Agricultural Policy (CAP)** was established in 1962 in accordance with the general goals laid down in the Treaty of Rome. Its design was based on the assumption that agricultural production had unique characteristics that required a set of rules for farmers different from those establishing a free-trade regime for industry. Because European farms were smaller and less efficient than those in certain other parts of the world, European agricultural products generally were more expensive than imports. To protect European farmers and ensure them a stable or rising standard of living, the CAP relied on tariffs and subsidies. Importers of food from non-EEC markets paid a variable levy (tariff) intended to raise the price of imported food to that of domestic production. The EEC also established the European Agricultural Guidance and Guarantee Fund to finance purchases of farm products on the European market in order to bolster domestic prices. This system worked in sustaining farmers' incomes and ensuring stability of supplies, but it also led to higher food prices for consumers, overproduction (the famous "wine lakes" and "butter mountains"), and disputes with trading partners who were being progressively squeezed out of the protected EEC market. Indeed, the first serious trade dispute between the United States and the EEC was the "chicken war" of 1963, which resulted from U.S. loss of access to the large West German poultry market as a result of CAP.

DE GAULLE AND THE "EMPTY CHAIR"

As the EEC developed in the 1960s and proved its economic value, it somewhat paradoxically faced a growing political challenge within its own ranks. The source of this challenge was French President Charles de Gaulle, a leader of the French resistance in World War II who had retired from an active role in politics in 1946. He returned to power in 1958 amid the crisis caused by France's colonial war in Algeria and pushed through a series of constitutional changes that created a strong presidency, a post he himself occupied for the next decade.

The French leader broke with his European partners on two major issues: the powers and responsibilities of the Community's institutions and the question of British membership in the Community. Although on the surface these were different and unrelated issues, de Gaulle's approach to both reflected his nationalism and his questioning of the path down which Europe was headed. De Gaulle believed that France needed to be strong and independent—to recover the national greatness that it had lost in World War II. He thus instituted economic and political reforms aimed at modernizing French industry and society and making France more competitive with Germany. These measures indirectly benefited the cause of integration by helping to create the rough balance of power between France and Germany that was the basis for the EEC's development. At the same time, however, de Gaulle was extremely wary of surrendering French sovereignty to the newly created supranational bodies in Brussels.

The issue of supranationalism came to a head in mid-1965 over the question of CAP financing. With the phasing in of the common market running ahead of schedule, in the spring of 1965, European Commission president Walter Hallstein proposed that the EEC acquire its "own resources" (i.e., revenue raised directly by the EEC, rather than contributed to the EEC budget by the member states) in July 1967, some three years ahead of schedule. Hallstein further proposed a new budgetary mechanism in which the Commission and the European Parliament would have enhanced powers, as those of the member states in the Council of Ministers would diminish through the introduction of qualified majority voting in place of unanimity for certain issues. De Gaulle saw these proposals as a grab for power by a nascent European superstate in Brussels and as an attack on French sovereignty. He responded by announcing the policy of the "empty chair." Throughout the second half of 1965 France boycotted all meetings of the Council of Ministers. The Commission and the other member states deplored this tactic, but for six months Community business all but ground to a halt.

The crisis was resolved in January 1966 with the adoption by the six of what became known, after the site of the meeting, as the Luxembourg Compromise. The "compromise" was little more than an agreement to disagree. The six pledged that when issues very important to one or more states were to be decided, the Council of Ministers would try to reach decisions by unanimity. France registered its view—not endorsed by others—that when important issues were at stake unanimity *had* to be reached to take a decision. While noting the disagreement on this constitutional point, the six concluded that there was no need to prolong the impasse in EEC decision making. Hallstein retreated from his proposals, France took its place in the Council of Ministers, and normal business resumed.

The effect of the 1965 crisis on the Community was profound. Although the other five members would not yield to de Gaulle's attempt to reinterpret the Treaty of Rome by imposing the unanimity requirement, they had no wish to provoke another crisis. They thus tended to make decisions by consensus—a practice that lasted until well into the 1980s. The powers of the European Commission were cut back, as it was widely blamed for provoking the crisis by reaching prematurely for more authority. These developments all tended to slow decision making in the EEC and helped to reverse the momentum toward a federal Europe that had built up in the late 1950s and early 1960s.

Britain had been active in the early postwar moves toward European integration, but it had declined to join the original six in forming the ECSC and the Common Market. The British economy at that time was still considerably larger than those of the continental European powers, and Britain retained strong links with its colonies, the Commonwealth, and the United States, with which it had a "special relationship" growing out of World War II. It thus was unwilling to surrender sovereignty to a fledgling enterprise based in Brussels. Instead, Britain took the lead in founding the **European Free Trade Association (EFTA),** a looser grouping of states whose other founding members were Austria, Denmark, Norway, Portugal, Sweden, and Switzerland. By the 1960s, however, the empire was dissolving, and Britain's ties with the Commonwealth and the United States were diminishing in importance. British economic growth was lagging behind that of continental Europe, where British industry saw new and growing markets. Britain increasingly was coming to see its economic and political future in Europe. Thus, in the summer of 1961, Britain, along with Denmark and Ireland, applied to become an EEC member.[2]

The British government received a rude shock when, at a news conference in January 1963, de Gaulle announced that he would veto Britain's application. This decision was rooted in de Gaulle's distrust of the "Anglo-Saxon powers" and his view that Britain in the EEC would be a stalking horse for the United States, whose influence in Europe he wanted to diminish. This view made the other Community countries, and especially the West Germans, uncomfortable, but it was not something they could change, given the requirement for unanimity in key Community decisions. The same three countries subsequently reapplied for membership in May 1967, but de Gaulle would not lift his opposition to British membership.

Despite these many problems, by the end of the 1960s European leaders could be satisfied with the progress of integration since the early 1950s. The Common Market largely was completed, and the economic results were positive. Franco-German reconciliation was a reality. Moreover, de Gaulle relinquished his post in April 1969 and his successor, Georges Pompidou, although adhering to the basic Gaullist line, was less suspicious of European integration than his predecessor. He announced, in July of the same year, that France no longer would oppose Britain's admission to the Community. The time thus seemed right for bold new initiatives. At the Hague summit in December 1969 the leaders of the six agreed to explore ways to strengthen the EEC's institutions, to establish an "economic and monetary union" by 1980, and to begin cooperation in the foreign policy sphere. As will be seen, however, many of these initiatives were soon put on hold or implemented very slowly, as the EEC entered a more difficult phase under worsening international circumstances.

DEVELOPMENTS IN THE 1970s

The 1970s saw a number of milestones in the process of European integration. Cooperation in the field of foreign policy, or **European Political Cooperation (EPC),** was launched in 1970. The member states agreed to "consult on all questions of foreign policy" and where possible to undertake "common actions" on international problems. However, EPC was to take place outside the federal structures and institutions of the Community. The European Commission and the European Court of Justice thus did not have competence or jurisdiction in foreign policy matters, making EPC a much weaker form of cooperation than that established in the economic sphere by the Treaty of Rome.

On January 1, 1973, the first enlargement of the EEC occurred, as Denmark, Ireland, and Britain became members. This was the first of four enlargements (see Table 2.1), each of which has required complex negotiations on such matters as payments into and from the Community budget, transition periods

Table 2.1   Membership and Enlargements of the EC/EU

Belgium, France, Germany, Italy, Luxembourg, the Netherlands	Founding Members, 1958
Britain, Denmark, Ireland	1973
Greece	1981
Portugal, Spain	1986
Austria, Finland, Sweden	1995
Cyprus, Czech Republic, Estonia, Hungary, Latvia, Lithuania, Malta, Poland, Slovakia, Slovenia	May 1, 2004
Bulgaria, Romania	Expected, 2007
Turkey	No date set

for phasing in Community rules, and the weight of each member state in the Community's institutions.

Despite these achievements, the optimistic expectations of the late 1950s and the 1960s were disappointed in the 1970s, as the integration process was slowed by unfavorable external economic and political conditions. Economic policymakers worldwide became preoccupied with the problems of the U.S. dollar and the breakdown of the Bretton Woods monetary system. In August 1971, U.S. President Richard M. Nixon announced the suspension of convertibility of dollars into gold. This was followed by devaluation of the dollar and a worldwide shift to floating exchange rates. EEC finance ministers and central bankers tried to maintain a "joint float" of their currencies against the dollar, but in the absence of a stable and predictable global monetary system, European plans to achieve economic and monetary union by 1980 were put on hold.[3]

The oil crisis of 1973–1974 delivered another external shock to the integration process. When war broke out in October 1973 between Israel and its Arab neighbors, the Arab countries cut off the export of oil. Importing countries scrambled to find supplies to keep their economies going. In Europe, divergent national responses to the embargo strained the new EPC. Even after the embargo ended, oil prices had shot up to four times their 1970 level. One result was the economic recession of 1974–1975, the most severe since the 1930s.

The responses of the EEC member states to the recession were damaging to the process of integration. Governments tended to look to national solutions to combat rising unemployment. The Treaty of Rome prohibited the reimposition of tariffs and import quotas, but governments increased many open and hidden subsidies to industry, and in some cases imposed new nontariff barriers to trade that undermined the single market. The European economies eventually recovered from the recession, but for the remainder of the decade the industrialized world in general was plagued by "stagflation," the devastating combination of low growth and high inflation.

Among the few positive developments of the 1970s were the strengthening of the Franco-German relationship under French president Valéry Giscard d'Estaing and German Chancellor Helmut Schmidt and the founding, at their urging, of the **European Council**. At the December 1974 Paris summit the leaders of the member states agreed to hold such meetings three times (later changed to twice) each year. These regular gatherings constituted the European Council as a new institution.

Unlike the Council of Ministers, which was assigned extensive legislative responsibilities under the Treaty of Rome, the European Council was to operate more informally. It was a forum in which leaders could get together behind closed doors for discussion and bargaining. It became the preferred means by which European leaders reached compromises on deadlocked issues and launched new initiatives relating to the future of the community. Actual policy was still implemented in and through the existing treaty-based institutions—the Commission, the Council of Ministers, and to some extent the European Parliament—but the European Council became the "motor" behind the integration process.

Along with Commission president Roy Jenkins, Giscard and Schmidt also were instrumental in the founding, in March 1979, of the **European Monetary System (EMS).** All three individuals were former finance ministers who had been involved in the global financial upheavals of the early 1970s. Under the old Bretton Woods system, the value of most currencies was fixed against the dollar, which in turn was set relative to gold. With the breakdown of this system, the value of currencies relative to each other was set by the markets, and wild swings over periods of weeks and months frequently occurred. EMS was designed to eliminate sharp changes in the value of the European currencies against each other. These changes were a deterrent to cross-border trade and investment, which thrive on stable and predictable prices, and tended to weaken the single market (since a change in the relative value of currencies easily could swamp the trade-promoting effects of tariff elimination).

The EMS was a system of fixed but adjustable currency rates built around a central unit of account, the **European Currency Unit (ECU).** The latter was an artificial currency whose value was set by a weighted basket of EEC member-country currencies. In the EMS, each national currency had a fixed rate against the ECU. The central rates in ECUs then were used to establish a grid of bilateral exchange rates. Authorities in each country were responsible for ensuring that this rate fluctuated by no more than 2.25 percent (6 percent in the case of Italy). The central rates were not intended to be set for all time, but they could only be changed with the consent of the other members of the EMS. The EMS thus provided a high degree of at least intra-European monetary stability in the 1980s and paved the way for a still more ambitious project, economic and monetary union (EMU), at the end of the decade.

Two other developments in the late 1970s were especially important for the EEC. The first direct elections to the European Parliament were held in June 1979, bringing to Strasbourg a popularly elected body of men and women who could claim to speak for "Europe" on behalf of the electorate. The Community also began accession negotiations with the three Mediterranean countries, Greece, Portugal, and Spain. These countries were much poorer than the EEC average, and all three were emerging from authoritarian rule and attempting to establish democratic systems. While many in Europe questioned whether the Community could afford to absorb these applicants, European leaders saw an overriding political imperative for Mediterranean enlargement. The EEC thus began accession negotiations in 1976–1979, although membership was only achieved for Greece in 1981 and Portugal and Spain in 1986.

The Single European Act
CRISIS IN THE EARLY 1980s

EMS, direct elections to the European Parliament, and the start of enlargement negotiations with the Mediterranean countries were all stirrings of a new dynamism in European integration that was to take hold in the mid-1980s. Throughout the early 1980s, however, the EEC remained bogged down by myriad economic and political problems. The 1979 revolution in Iran produced a second oil shock and another deep recession. Relations between the United States and the Soviet Union deteriorated over the December 1979 Soviet invasion of Afghanistan and the December 1981 imposition of martial law in Poland, and the EEC had difficulty in formulating a coherent response to the new international climate. The terms "Europessimism" and "Eurosclerosis" were coined to sum up a widespread sense that Europe's internal structures—businesses, the welfare state, the educational system—were resistant to change and unable to respond to increased competition from Japan, the United States, and the newly industrializing countries.

This was also a time of extensive leadership change in Europe. Already in 1979, in Britain the Labour government was replaced by Conservative prime minister Margaret Thatcher, a forceful leader known for her skepticism about European integration.[4] In France, the center-right coalition led by Giscard was replaced in 1981 by a Socialist-Communist alliance led by François Mitterrand, and in Germany the following year Social Democrat Helmut Schmidt was succeeded by a more conservative leader, Christian Democrat Helmut Kohl. At least for a while these new governments headed off in radically different directions. In Britain, for example, the free enterprise–oriented Thatcher was busy privatizing state-owned firms such as British Steel and British Airways, while in France Mitterrand was carrying out a program of nationalizing many industrial and financial firms that previously had been in private hands.

Within the Community, Thatcher presented a particular challenge in that she was committed to redressing an imbalance in Britain's budgetary contribution to the EEC. This imbalance resulted from the fact that Britain imported large amounts of food and industrial goods from outside the EEC on which it paid customs duties and agricultural levies to Brussels, while it received far less back from the CAP, owing to the small size of its farming sector relative to those in other EEC countries. By 1979, this imbalance was well over $1 billion per year and growing. For five years, Thatcher pressed her counterparts in the European Council for a rebate, all but crippling political decision making in the Community. After several partial compromises, the British budgetary question finally was resolved at the Fontainebleau summit in June 1984, where the heads of government agreed to cut Britain's contribution as well as to undertake a wider budgetary reform.

The Fontainebleau summit was a turning point in other respects as well. Responding to growing concerns in the European Parliament, the business community, and elsewhere about the seeming drift in the Community, the leaders agreed to a proposal by President Mitterrand to establish a committee to explore ways to improve the functioning of the Community and of EPC. This committee consisted of one high-level representative from each member state, and became known as the Dooge Committee, after its chairman, former Irish foreign minister James Dooge. One month after Fontainebleau, the EEC governments took another important step by agreeing that French Finance Minister Jacques Delors would become president of the European Commission when a new term began on January 1, 1985. Delors's leadership, and the willingness of European leaders, including Thatcher, to consider major changes in the working of the EEC helped revive it in the second half of the 1980s.

THE SINGLE-MARKET PROGRAM

Discussion about the internal market had intensified in the late 1970s and early 1980s, both among government officials and the leaders of large European corporations, who were increasingly concerned about Europe's lackluster economic performance. The Treaty of Rome stated that the EEC was *supposed* to become an internal market characterized by the free flow of goods, services, persons, and capital. As a practical matter, only a free market in goods had been established, and even this was riddled with exceptions and had been undermined to some extent in recent years by the erection of new nontariff barriers. Differing national standards and technical regulations hindered the import of products from other EC countries. Paperwork at the borders and disparate national policies on taxation, health and safety, company law, and subsidies to industry all tended to fragment the European market.

The situation with regard to services, capital, and persons was even worse. Service industries remained largely national, controls on capital were in place and in fact served as important instruments of national economic policy (central banks, for example, could lower interest rates and be confident that savers would not be able to take their money and invest it in a neighboring country where banks might be offering a higher rate of return), and the ability of Europeans to work or set up businesses in other EEC countries was strictly limited by rules on residency, working permits, and nationally oriented pension and insurance schemes.

Shortly after taking office, Delors announced that the European Commission would introduce a program to eliminate all barriers to the internal market by the end of 1992. This concrete program of action with a firm date for completion was to capture the imagination and win the support of business, government, and ordinary citizens and workers. Soon, "1992" became the slogan of the late 1980s and early 1990s.

Delors entrusted implementation of the 1992 program to Lord Cockfield, the British commissioner responsible for the internal market. Cockfield and his staff produced, in the first half of 1985, a detailed plan that was presented in the form of a white paper to the European Council. In an appendix to the report, the Commission listed approximately three hundred proposals that needed to be turned into Community law to complete the internal market. Each proposal was assigned a target date, so that the whole program would be implemented by December 31, 1992. The report identified three kinds of barriers to the operation of the internal market—physical, technical, and fiscal—all of which it proposed to dismantle. Physical barriers included customs posts and paperwork and inspections at borders. Technical barriers included a vast array of national standards and regulations that did not always have the intent of impeding commerce among EC member states, but that in practice had this effect. They included rules on the content and labeling of foods, chemicals, and pharmaceuticals; car safety standards; different procedures for public procurement (including those in important state-owned sectors such as water supply, the railroads, telecommunications, and electricity); different banking and insurance regulations; national rules on air, rail, road and water transport; different rules on copyright and trademark protection; and many other barriers to the free flow of goods, services, capital, and people. Fiscal barriers related both to types and levels of taxation, including value-added and excise taxes, which varied widely across Europe.

While the single-market program as a whole generated enthusiasm throughout the Community, Delors and his advisors realized from the beginning that many of its specific measures would be difficult to turn into law. Much Community legislation takes the form of directives, which lay out general guidelines as to "the result to be achieved" but leave it to the member states to enact appropriate national legislation. Governments were reluctant to pass directives that might adversely affect domestic interests or that could be controversial to implement at the national level. With each of several hundred proposed measures requiring unanimous approval by twelve governments, there was little chance that the ambitious single-market program could be implemented. Institutional reform, meaning change in the way the Community took decisions, thus was needed.

RELAUNCHING THE COMMUNITY

In his July 1985 speech to the European Parliament, Delors noted that a new treaty would be needed if the member states were to complete an ambitious single-market program. Dooge's Ad Hoc Committee on Institutional Reform presented its final report to the Brussels summit, in which it called for both a broadening of the EEC's objectives and areas of responsibility and for selected institutional reforms that would strengthen the Community and speed decision making. To achieve these objectives, it recommended convening an Intergovernmental Conference (IGC) among the member states that would draw up a new treaty of European Union. The report did not command universal support for all of its points. The British, Danish, and Greek members declined to endorse its central recommendation for an IGC, and other members dissented on lesser points. But the general thrust of the report was toward significant changes in the Treaty of Rome as a way of restarting the integration process and ensuring that the single-market program would be implemented.

The European Council took up the Dooge Report at its June 1985 session in Milan, the same meeting at which it endorsed the Commission's white paper on the internal market. Italy, a founding member and traditionally a strong proponent of European integration, occupied the Council presidency, and Prime Minister Bettino Craxi was determined to move the Community forward. Under the Treaty of Rome, the member states were empowered to call at any time, by simple majority vote, an IGC to negotiate treaty revisions. This provision never had been invoked, however, in part because there was limited interest in such revisions but also because, following the Luxembourg Compromise, governments invariably took major decisions by consensus, even when the treaties allowed for majority or qualified majority voting. After hours of discussion in which Prime Minister Thatcher argued against convening an IGC, Craxi forced a vote on whether to call an IGC. The result was seven-three, with Britain, Denmark, and Greece opposed.

Thatcher was furious at what she saw as an unprecedented disregard of the rule of consensus within the European Council and concerned that the more integration-minded states would use the IGC to push forward a strengthening of the EEC's supranational powers. But Britain also supported the single-market program, the substance of which by then was closely intertwined with the perceived need for procedural reform. Thus Britain as well as the other dissenters approached the IGC ready to play a constructive role, although determined to block the most ambitious reform proposals.

The IGC began during the Luxembourg presidency in September 1985, and over the next six months entailed seven meetings of the Community foreign ministers, numerous other meetings of two high-level working groups, written submissions on the part of national governments, and intense bargaining among the Community leaders at the December 1985 Luxembourg summit. The result was a new treaty, called the **Single European Act (SEA)**, that was formally signed in Luxembourg on February 17, 1986. The treaty came into effect on July 1, 1987, after all of the member states had ratified.

The SEA both broadened the Community's areas of responsibility and, as had long been suggested by proponents of institutional reform, made important changes in Community decision-making processes. New policy areas not mentioned in the Treaty of Rome but added to Community competence included environment, research and technology, and "economic and social cohesion" (meaning regional policy aimed at narrowing income disparities between different parts of the Community). The SEA also inserted a new article in the Treaty of Rome that specified completion of the internal market by the end of 1992.

Changes in decision-making procedures dealt with the Council of Ministers, the European Parliament, and the Court of Justice. The SEA specified that for certain policy areas the Council was empowered to take decisions by qualified majority vote. These areas included some social-policy matters, implementation of decisions relating to regional funds and Community research and development programs, and, most important, most measures "which have as their object the establishment and functioning of the internal market." This last amendment, expressed in a new article inserted in the Treaty of Rome, was the crucial change that Delors and others saw as essential to allowing the completion of the single-market program by the end-of-1992 deadline.

The SEA also increased the power of the European Parliament, partly at the urging of its members, who since 1979 could claim with some justification to be the only popularly elected "European" politicians. Whereas the Treaty of Rome required only that the parliament be consulted on a piece of legislation (proposed by the Commission) before its adoption or rejection by the Council of Ministers, the SEA introduced a cooperation procedure under which the parliament could demand from the Council of Ministers an explanation as to why its proposed amendments had not been adopted. The treaty also introduced an assent procedure under which the parliament was required to approve, by simple majority vote, certain key legislative actions, including the Community budget and association agreements with countries outside the EC. These changes expanded the power of the European Parliament and marked a further stage in its transition from a consultative to a genuinely legislative body. In the judicial sphere, the SEA made one important change, by providing for the establishment of a new Court of First Instance. In the decades since the establishment of the ECSC, the importance of the European Court of Justice had steadily increased, as the Court interpreted Community law and adjudicated legal disputes between the Community and its member states, among institutions of the Community, and between private firms and citizens and member state governments. One effect of the growing importance of the European Court of Justice, however, was a rising workload. To address this problem, the SEA empowered the Council to found a new Court of First Instance to hear many lesser cases.

Finally, the Single European Act introduced an important change in the foreign policy sphere by creating a legal basis for European Political Cooperation. Under the terms of the act, the signatories henceforth were bound by legal agreement, rather than just a political commitment, to consult and cooperate with each other in the foreign policy sphere. However, the EPC itself was not (unlike, for example, such new policy areas as environment or regional policy) incorporated into the Treaty of Rome. There thus was no such thing as a Community foreign policy but, rather, only an agreement among the member states that they would forge a common foreign policy. This meant that foreign policy would remain a matter for intergovernmental cooperation rather than supranational coordination. Community institutions such as the Commission would not have a role in EPC, and foreign policy decisions would not be subject to the jurisdiction of the European Court of Justice.

The SEA was an uneasy compromise between those in Europe who wanted progress toward political union and those, like the British and the Danes, who would have preferred not to convene an IGC at all. It introduced important reforms in the Community's founding treaty and demonstrated that the member states could use the mechanism of an intergovernmental conference to push the integration process forward. Above all, it elevated to the level of a legal principle the key goal—a single market by the end of 1992—that was to preoccupy the EEC in the late 1980s and become all but synonymous with the "relaunch" that Delors had sought to achieve. It also provided added means to achieve that goal through expanded use of qualified majority voting and created the basis for a stronger external profile on the eve of what was to become an extraordinary period of international change.

The late 1980s was a period of dynamism and growing optimism in Europe. Economic growth improved and the rate of unemployment fell, as millions of new jobs were created. Good economic performance was partly attributable to favorable trends worldwide, but the enthusiasm generated by the 1992 program also contributed to it. European and non-European firms alike increased their investments in the Community to prepare for the increased competition as well as expanded opportunities of the single market. The late 1980s also were marked by favorable international political trends. The reform-minded Mikhail Gorbachev took power in the Soviet Union in March 1985 and gradually steered the Soviet Union on a path of reform. Change in the east provided new vistas for the Community's foreign economic policy and for the member states through European Political Cooperation. Virtually no one in the EEC was prepared, however, for the dramatic events of 1989, which were to lead to new intergovernmental conferences and yet another treaty revision.

The Treaty on European Union

The Treaty on European Union, or the **Maastricht Treaty**, as it was commonly known after the Dutch city in which it was signed, was by far the most extensive revision of EEC treaties ever attempted. Many of the changes wrought by Maastricht had been under discussion for decades, and some likely would have come about under any circumstances. But there can be little doubt that the sweeping changes in central and eastern Europe—the fall of the Berlin Wall, the unification of Germany, and the collapse of Communism throughout the region—gave a powerful external push to reform.

Economic and Monetary Union (EMU) had been on the Community agenda since 1969, but was all but forgotten in the 1970s and only slowly revived as an issue in the 1980s. Despite Thatcher's distaste for the idea and the skepticism of others, including in the powerful central banking community, by 1988 talk of EMU again was becoming fashionable. The EMS had been operating for nearly a decade and had been quite successful in its original goal of insulating intra-European trade from turbulence in global currency markets and from the wild swings in the value of the dollar that marked the Reagan years. As the EMS evolved toward a de facto fixed-rate regime, a growing number of economists and political leaders argued that Europe should take the next logical step and move to full EMU.

The single-market program also strengthened the case for EMU. Proponents argued that there was an inconsistency between the creation of a single internal market and the maintenance of separate currencies, since changes in the value of these currencies affected the prices of goods and services traded in the internal market and thus constituted a barrier to trade. National currencies also imposed transactions costs on businesses and consumers. The idea that the 1992 program virtually required EMU later was captured in a European Commission report entitled *One Market, One Money*. A second factor strengthening the case for EMU was the elimination, under the single-market program, of all national controls on capital. Free movement of capital had been enshrined in the Treaty of Rome, but it never was put into effect, as national governments relied on controls to manipulate the value of their currencies. However, in 1988 the twelve agreed, as part of the single-market program, to remove all such controls by 1990. Economists warned that it would be very difficult to sustain the EMS—a system that retained different national currencies but that tightly regulated variations in the value of these currencies relative to each other—in circumstances in which investors had complete freedom to move money across borders to seek the highest rate of return.

Responding to the growing interest in EMU, at the June 1988 Hanover summit the European Council agreed to establish, under the chairmanship of Delors, a committee to propose concrete steps leading to economic and monetary union. Composed mainly of the central-bank heads from the member states, the Delors Committee developed a detailed three-stage plan for the establishment of EMU. It proposed that in stage three exchange rate parities be "irrevocably fixed" and full authority for determining economic and monetary policy be transferred to EC institutions. The report stressed that with the expected completion of the single market (including for capital), and the establishment of competition and regional policies, the Community already had accomplished much of the work toward EMU.

Although many in Europe still were skeptical of EMU and unwilling to endorse a single currency, at the June 1989 summit the European Council approved the Delors Committee's three-stage approach and declared that stage one of EMU should begin on July 1, 1990, with the closer coordination of member state economic policies and completion of plans to free the movement of capital. The European leaders further agreed that another IGC would be held to consider moving to stages two and three, which, unlike stage one, required extensive amendment of the EC treaty. Before these plans could be implemented, however, developments in central and eastern Europe radically changed the international context in which the Community approached its future development.

The EEC had evolved primarily as an economic institution, but it had been profoundly shaped by the political and ideological conflict on the Continent. Strengthening western Europe against Soviet pressures always had been an important motivation for supporters of the Community. The division of Germany had helped to further integration by making France and West Germany roughly equal in size and ensuring that the latter would look to its western neighbors for economic and political partnership. This was a major change from earlier periods, in which Germany had always had strong economic and political links with eastern Europe.

The unexpectedly rapid collapse of communism in 1989–1991 thus raised questions about the future of European integration. The opening of the Berlin Wall in November 1989 and the fall of the East German regime raised the question of German reunification. After elections in East Germany and a set of fast-moving two-plus-four negotiations involving the governments of the two German states and the Soviet Union, Britain, France, and the United Kingdom (the four victor powers of World War II), Germany was reunited in October 1990.

The five states of the former East Germany, with some sixteen million inhabitants, automatically became part of the EEC.

Although leaders such as Mitterrand had come around to accepting German reunification as inevitable, they were concerned that creation of a larger and more eastward-oriented Germany could damage the process of European integration. The Community was a child of the Cold War, and the latter's impending end inevitably raised questions about the former's future. Mitterrand was determined to push forward with plans to "deepen" the Community, and thereby to ensure that the new Germany would remain firmly anchored in the west. He was supported in this by the Germans themselves, especially Kohl.

EMU most likely would have gone ahead in any case, but developments in eastern and central Europe lent new urgency to this project. In December 1989, at the Strasbourg summit, the European Council agreed to convene an IGC on EMU by the end of 1990. The leaders also agreed to adopt a social charter—a Community-wide agreement on labor standards that the trade unions had pressed for as a concomitant to the single European market. Britain did not sign the social charter and it opposed the IGC, but on both issues it was unable to dissuade the other member states from moving forward.

Alongside these developments in the economic sphere, the changing international situation gave new momentum to the old project for European Political Union (EPU). In April 1990, Kohl and Mitterrand jointly called for new and concrete steps to realize the aspirations to EPU already expressed in the Single European Act. The Kohl-Mitterrand proposal set the agenda for an extraordinary session of the European Council in Dublin in April 1990, at which the twelve leaders reaffirmed their commitment to political union. Meeting in the same city two months later, the European Council agreed to convene an IGC on political union to begin at the same time as the IGC on EMU and to run in parallel with it. Both IGCs formally opened at the Rome summit in December 1990. Thus, after not holding a single such conference in the three decades after 1955, the Community was to have three IGCs in five years, two of which would run concurrently. This extraordinary situation reflected the extent to which, as Delors had phrased it, history was "accelerating," forcing the Community to respond.

NEGOTIATING THE MAASTRICHT TREATY

The IGCs were conducted as formal diplomatic conferences involving regular meetings at the ministerial and working levels. Their focus was on strengthening the decision-making process in areas in which the EC already had competence and on extending the range of issues subject to common policy making. If these were the general goals, there was little agreement among the twelve about how and how quickly they were to be accomplished. Italy and the Benelux countries were the strongest supporters of European integration and pressed for the most sweeping revisions. Britain and Denmark were leery of change and sought to block many of the most extensive reforms. France wanted a strong Europe, but tended to be skeptical of the transfer of supranational powers to Brussels. It thus favored expanded use of intergovernmental cooperation along the lines already established in EPC. Germany tended to align its positions with those of France, but on foreign policy and defense matters it was wary of endangering NATO and transatlantic cooperation by building up a European defense alternative. On EMU it wanted strong safeguards to ensure that the future European currency would be as stable as the German mark. The negotiations lasted a year and concluded at the December 1991 Maastricht European Council with agreement on what was officially called the Treaty on European Union (TEU). The TEU, or Maastricht Treaty, both extensively amended the Treaty of Rome and added new provisions on matters beyond the scope of the latter treaty. However, the text was agreed only after last-minute negotiations in which Britain and Denmark secured the right to "opt out" of certain of the treaty's provisions. Agreement to disagree was in some cases the most that could be achieved.

Still, the reforms achieved at Maastricht were substantial and went far beyond anything that had been achieved in the previous thirty-five years of the Community's existence. As the name indicated, the treaty brought into being a new entity called the European Union, which was defined in the treaty as "mark[ing] a new stage in the process of creating an ever-closer union among the peoples of Europe." The Union itself was set up as a complicated structure of three "pillars" dealing with different and partially overlapping policy areas using different decision-making processes. The first pillar would consist of the three existing communities—the EEC (renamed the European Community, or EC, to reflect its broadened and no longer strictly economic areas of responsibility), the ECSC, and Euratom—in which the member states have pooled sovereignty and transferred decision-making powers to the European Commission, the Council of Ministers, the European Parliament, and the European Court of Justice, with a powerful guiding role also assigned to the European Council.

The second pillar, **Common Foreign and Security Policy (CFSP),** replaced and was based upon EPC. Decisions made in the second pillar, unlike those made in the first, were to remain largely intergovernmental in character, with only a limited role for Community institutions. Such decisions would not be subject to the jurisdiction of the Court of Justice. The European Commission could suggest actions under CFSP, but it was not given the sole right of initiative in this area, as the member states also could initiate policy actions under CFSP. The Maastricht Treaty specified certain foreign policy goals that were to be pursued under CFSP, such as safeguarding the common values, fundamental interests, and independence of the European Union; strengthening its security; and promoting peace and respect for human rights. These objectives were to be pursued through "common positions" and "joint actions" by the member states, with decisions on these matters taken primarily by unanimity. CFSP also provided for the "eventual framing of a common defense policy" and assigned implementation of EU defense decisions to an existing body, the Western European Union, previously not linked to the structures of the European Community.

The third pillar consisted of cooperation in the fields of Justice and Home Affairs (JHA), including asylum policy, control of external borders and immigration from outside the EU, and combating drug addiction and international crime. The completion of the single European market and the abolition of controls on the movement of people and capital had made EU-level cooperation in these areas increasingly necessary. Proponents of cooperation often stressed that international crime syndicates had adjusted to the single market, while the police and judges still were very national in their outlook. At the same time, the member states with their very different legal traditions and approaches to such sensitive internal matters were reluctant to surrender sovereignty to Brussels in these areas. The twelve thus agreed to establish the third pillar on an intergovernmental basis, with decision-making procedures similar to those used in CFSP. The members were committed to collaborating with each other, and there were provisions in the treaty for strengthening this collaboration over time and for establishing new and centralized bodies such as the European Police Office (Europol).

The Maastricht Treaty established the principle of "subsidiarity," a concept that attempts to define which decisions are to be taken at which levels. Issues of primarily local importance are to be taken as close to the citizen as possible. Subsidiarity was introduced in part as a response to fears of excessive centralization of powers in Brussels. The treaty also established a European citizenship, to exist alongside and in addition to national citizenship, that brings with it certain rights, such as the right of an EU citizen to be represented by the consulate of another member state while overseas or to vote in local elections while resident in another member state.

Continuing the pattern established in the SEA, the Maastricht Treaty strengthened the European Parliament by adding a new procedure, called co-decision, under which the EP for the first time could block legislation introduced by the Commission and passed by the Council of Ministers. Co-decision was prescribed only for a limited number of policy areas, although one of these—internal market—was quite important. In another change that strengthened its power, the parliament was given a say in the appointment of the Commission and the Commission president, hitherto a matter of exclusive concern for the Council of Ministers. The treaty also established a new institution, the Committee of the Regions, to provide a means whereby regional entities in Europe—states and provinces—can give direct input to policy making in Brussels.

Perhaps the most significant achievement of the Maastricht Treaty was the establishment of EMU. Building upon the Delors Committee report and the experience of EMS, the treaty established a detailed timetable and institutional provisions for the phasing out of national currencies and the introduction of a European money, initially called the ECU and later renamed the **euro**. Stage two of EMU was to begin on January 1, 1994, and bring about increased economic coordination and preparations for the single currency. In stage two, the member states were to meet certain economic convergence criteria relating to inflation, national debt and deficits, currency stability in the EMS, and long-term interest rates designed to ensure that the economies entering the economic and monetary union would have broadly similar economic performance. The emphasis in the convergence criteria was on price stability and the continued fight against inflation.

The treaty stipulated that stage three would begin no later than January 1, 1999, and would entail the "irrevocable locking" of the value of the European currencies against each other and their eventual phasing out by July 2002. The treaty and associated protocols provided for the establishment of a European Central Bank and a European System of Central Banks that would be responsible for conducting monetary policy at the EU level. Britain and Denmark, both traditional skeptics of EMU, secured "opt-outs" from the main provisions of EMU, and were not required to surrender their national currencies in 1999–2002 if they chose not to do so.

Britain also achieved an opt-out from one other Maastricht innovation, the social protocol. Eleven of the member states were strongly committed to incorporating, in the EU's first pillar, extensive new provisions on worker health and safety, working conditions, social security, and related matters. Britain was opposed to this change, which it saw as an encroachment by Brussels on traditional member-state responsibilities. Although opposition of a single state normally is sufficient to block treaty revision on any matter, on this issue it was agreed that the eleven states would adopt an EC social policy in a separate protocol, which Britain would not be bound to observe. This, along with the British and Danish opt-outs from EMU, was the first time in the history of the Community that a member state was granted a major derogation from a treaty provision. Along with the other complexities of the Maastricht Treaty, notably the three-pillar structure and the vagueness surrounding the subsidiarity concept, these derogations reflected the degree to which Maastricht itself was a compromise among widely different perspectives on European integration. It permitted the more integration-minded states to move ahead in sensitive areas, while allowing the skeptics to preserve cherished national prerogatives. Not surprisingly, to the extent that they understood the treaty at all, the European voters were less than enthusiastic about Maastricht, as soon became apparent in the debate on ratification.

BEYOND MAASTRICHT: AMSTERDAM AND NICE

After nearly a decade of rapid change, it was perhaps inevitable that the pace
would slow and that a reaction to further integration would set in. With western
Europe racing toward union and the old order in eastern Europe rapidly disin-
tegrating, people needed time to digest the changes that had occurred. After a
short-lived economic boom, the costs of German reunification helped to pre-
cipitate another recession in Europe, bringing to an end the job growth of the
late 1980s. The war in the Persian Gulf and the outbreak of civil war in the
former Yugoslavia caused added uncertainty. The mood in Europe became in-
trospective, more focused on local and national concerns such as crime, immigration, and unemployment and more skeptical of the headlong rush to union.

The first highly visible sign that sentiments had changed occurred in June
1992, when voters in Denmark narrowly rejected the Maastricht Treaty in the
national referendum that was required under the Danish constitution. Since all
twelve signatories had to ratify the treaty for it to go into effect, the Community was thrown into crisis. By September 1992, the political crisis had spilled
over into the financial markets, threatening the integrity of the EMS, one of the
key building blocks of the planned EMU. In the same month the French electorate approved the Maastricht Treaty, but only by the narrow margin of 51 to
49 percent. In Germany, the treaty was challenged in the supreme court, where
opponents argued that it contravened the German constitution by transferring
powers of the German states to Brussels.

In the end the Maastricht Treaty was ratified. The European Council negotiated additional opt-outs for Denmark, and in May 1993 the Danish voters approved the treaty by a healthy margin in a second referendum. Legislatures in
the other countries approved the treaty, as did the German federal court. Thus
Maastricht went into effect on November 1, 1993, some ten months later than
originally planned. The European Union was born, even though many voters
were confused about the new name and uncertain what it meant for them.

The inadequacies of the Maastricht Treaty were well recognized by its cre-
ators even before the difficulties with ratification arose. In many areas, disagreements among the member states had led to vague compromises and statements
of intent that could be interpreted in different ways. For example, the article
that introduced defense into the EU structure stated: "The common foreign
and security policy shall include all questions related to the security of the
Union, including the eventual framing of a common defense policy, which
might in time lead to a common defense." But how were terms like "eventual"
and "might in time" to be interpreted and translated into action? Recognizing
that such vagueness could not be tolerated indefinitely, the twelve agreed in the
Maastricht Treaty to hold another conference in 1996 to review the workings
of the treaty and to introduce such amendments as were deemed necessary.

As 1996 approached, the impending IGC became ever more closely associated with enlargement. On January 1, 1995, the membership of the European Union expanded to fifteen, with the accession of Austria, Finland, and Sweden. These were neutral countries that previously had declined to join an organization of NATO member states (Ireland being the only non-NATO member of the Community), but that had revised their position with the end of the Cold War. Even more important for the EU was the prospect of membership for the former communist countries of central and eastern Europe. When the Maastricht Treaty was signed, it was still unclear whether these countries would become full members, or whether they would settle for a looser form of association based on free trade and cooperation in other spheres. Increasingly, however, the leaders of these countries pressed for full EU (and NATO) membership. In doing so, they were motivated by a strong desire to be fully integrated into the West, to buffer themselves against instability in the former Soviet Union and a possible resurgence of Russian power, and to have influence over the institutions shaping the development of Europe. After a period of debate about the wisdom of committing to absorb a relatively poor region with over one hundred million inhabitants, the EU leaders concluded that they had no choice. At the June 1993 Copenhagen summit, the European Council in principle agreed that these countries could become members, but only after a period of transition in which they prepared their economies and established working democracies.

The prospect of adding ten or more members lent new urgency to calls for the reform of EU institutions. At fifteen, the Union already was too large to function with essentially the same set of institutions that had been devised in the 1950s for a community of six. With twenty members, the European Commission had lost its collegial character. The European Parliament, with 626 members, was already larger than most national parliaments. Under the rotating system of presidencies, member states could expect to chair the European Council and the Council of Ministers only once every seven-and-a-half years.

The IGC convened in Turin in March 1996. In addition to streamlining decision making in advance of enlargement, its goals were to strengthen a CFSP that was widely seen as having been ineffectual in the face of the wars in the former Yugoslavia and to develop the EU's third pillar, which had made little progress in forging common EU policies on immigration, asylum, and combating cross-border crime. After more than a year of intense negotiations among the member states, the IGC concluded in June 1997 with the approval of a new treaty amending Maastricht and the other founding treaties. Called the Treaty of Amsterdam after the city in which it was signed, the agreement provided for some strengthening of the union's CFSP, for example, by creating the post of High Representative for CFSP and by developing "common strategies" toward third countries and regions as a new policy instrument. It also mandated closer cooperation in third-pillar matters such as immigration and asylum policies, in large part through a phased shift of these responsibilities from the third to the first pillars. As in past revisions, the powers of the European Parliament were expanded somewhat. In addition, Britain, under the newly elected prime minister, Tony Blair, joined the Social Protocol.

On balance, however, the changes in the Treaty of Amsterdam were modest compared to those agreed at Maastricht. Because enlargement was not imminent and because national governments were preoccupied with making the painful adjustments to be ready for EMU, the member states largely postponed to a future IGC extensive reforms of the EU's decision-making apparatus. Instead, they adopted a legally binding protocol to the treaty that stipulated that at least one year before the membership of the Union reached twenty, a new IGC would be convened to carry out a review of the institutions and to examine in particular three questions: the size and composition of the Commission, the weighting of votes in the Council of Ministers, and the possible extension of qualified majority voting in the Council. Dubbed by the press somewhat misleadingly the Amsterdam "leftovers," these seemingly technical questions related to the fundamental character of the Union and to such matters as the balance of power between small and large states and the relative mix of supranationalism and intergovernmentalism in the makeup of the EU.

The third and decisive stage of EMU began on January 1, 1999. The euro was introduced as scheduled, with eleven EU members (all but the United Kingdom, Denmark, Sweden, and Greece) adopting the common currency and forming their own grouping of economic and financial ministers to coordinate euro-related policy matters. The technical switchover to the euro over the long New Year's holiday went surprisingly well, without computer crashes or increased volatility on financial markets. Nonetheless, broader questions continued to hang over the future of the common currency. Governments committed to creating jobs and cutting rates of unemployment pressed the newly formed European Central Bank to adopt more expansionary monetary policies, raising anew old questions about the balance between political control and central bank independence. The member states also differed over the future of the EU budget, with Germany and the Netherlands insisting that their large net contributions be trimmed and Spain and the other Mediterranean countries holding out for continued large regional aid payments from Brussels.

The enlargement process also inched forward. In July 1997, the Commission issued a detailed plan called *Agenda 2000* for bringing an initial round of candidate countries into the Union early in the twenty-first century and for reforming the Union's own budgetary and agricultural policies to cope with enlargement. Based upon the recommendations in *Agenda 2000*, the European Council decided that accession negotiations with six leading candidate countries—the Czech Republic, Cyprus, Estonia, Hungary, Poland, and Slovenia— could begin in March 1998. At Helsinki in December 1999, the member states further declared that all of the central and east European candidate countries and Malta (although not yet Turkey) had made sufficient progress in bringing

sion and effectiveness of the Commission, the "big five" gave up their second commissioner. The treaty further stipulated that after membership reached twenty-seven, the EU would shift to a rotation system in which the number of Commissioners would be less than the number of member states. For the foreseeable future, however, each member could still have its "own" commissioner. The relative weighting of the big states was increased, but France (along with Italy and the United Kingdom) continued to have the same number of votes in the Council of Ministers as Germany. To give somewhat greater weight to population and to defuse German complaints of unfairness, a complex "triple majority" was put in place, under which a qualified majority vote had to have not only the required number of Council votes, but also be formed by countries representing at least 62 percent of the Union's population.

Although Nice technically cleared the way to enlargement by deciding the distribution of decision-making power in an enlarged Union, the treaty was hardly the simplification and streamlining of decision making that many European commentators thought was essential. Its provisions were more complicated than ever, leaving plenty of scope for determined minorities to block legislation. At the insistence of the member states, policy decisions in such key areas as taxation, social policy, cohesion policy, policy on asylum and immigration, and, above all, such constitutional issues as reform of the treaties remained subject to unanimity rather than qualified majority voting. Perhaps most tellingly, the treaty was long, complicated, and difficult for the average citizen to understand and support, a circumstance that was underscored dramatically in June 2001 when the traditionally pro-Europe Irish electorate voted down the treaty. Nice finally went into effect after the Irish voters approved the treaty in a second referendum in October 2002. By this time it was clear, however, that Nice would only be an interim arrangement—an updating of the existing treaties that would allow enlargement to proceed—that would be superseded by a new and more ambitious constitutional treaty.

At the same time that it wrestled with these internal questions, the EU was beginning to assert itself more on the international scene. Euro notes and coins came into circulation in January 2002, successfully completing the transition to EMU and giving the Union tangible proof of its cohesion and its ability to accomplish ambitious, long-term goals. After the debacle in the former Yugoslavia in the early 1990s, the Europeans moved to strengthen CFSP and to add to it a defense dimension that would cooperate with NATO but could act autonomously if necessary. At the December 1999 Helsinki summit the EU adopted a decision to establish a fifty-to-sixty-thousand-person military force that would be capable of taking on the full range of peacekeeping and peace enforcement tasks, either in cooperation with NATO and the United States or, if need be, acting alone. Member states were slow to approve the added defense spending that was needed to turn these plans into reality, but the EU clearly was intent on building a defense and defense industrial identity apart from NATO and the United States.

Enlargement and the Constitution

The perceived shortcomings of the Nice treaty led to renewed efforts at institutional reform and in particular to attempts to involve a wider circle of citizens and interest groups in the reform process. Even before the treaty had been concluded, political leaders such as German foreign minister Joschka Fischer, British prime minister Tony Blair, and French president Jacques Chirac had given speeches calling for more vigorous and imaginative debate about the envisioned endpoint of the integration process ("finality") and the need for radical reforms going beyond institutional tinkering. Among the ideas suggested in the debate were creating an elected post of EU president, scrapping the Commission altogether to create an executive of member state government representatives, and setting up an additional legislative chamber parallel to the European Parliament that would be composed of members of national legislatures.[5]

To thrash out these ideas, the European Council agreed, at the December 2001 Laeken summit, to launch a **European Convention** composed of representatives of member state governments, members of national parliaments, Commission representatives, and representatives of the European Parliament. Even though they were not yet members of the Union, the candidate countries were invited to participate. Chaired by former French president Valéry Giscard d'Estaing, the Convention was charged with drawing up proposals for a European Constitution. These proposals then could be presented to the member states for discussion at an IGC to be convened in late 2003 or early 2004. This approach reflected the emerging sense in Europe that, after more than fifty years of integration, the EU needed a basic set of rules that would not be subject to change at frequent IGCs and that could be understood by and serve as a rallying point for the European citizenry. Whether a written constitution could resolve all of the internal disagreements and uncertainties about power sharing and Europe's "finality" remained unclear. Nonetheless, the Convention began work in March 2002 with great enthusiasm, its members conscious that they were embarking on a constitution-building exercise that in some ways paralleled (although in others was very different from) the one that had taken place in the United States in the 1780s.

After sixteen months of intense work and deliberation, the Convention adopted a draft constitutional treaty and forwarded it to the European Council for further consideration by the member states. If adopted by an intergovernmental conference scheduled to convene in the fall of 2003, the treaty would effect the most sweeping and radical changes in the history of the European integration project (see Table 2.3). The 1957 Treaty of Rome and all subsequent

Table 2.3   Key Reforms Proposed in the 2003 Draft Constitutional Treaty

Institution/Issue Area	Situation as Established by the Maastricht, Amsterdam, and Nice Treaties	Projected Situation after Adoption and Ratification of the Constitutional Treaty
European Council	Mentioned in the treaties but not formally recognized as an EU "institution."	Recognized as one of the five institutions.
European Council President	No such post. Chairmanship held on a rotating basis (six months) by the presidency country.	Elected by QMV for two-and-a-half-year term, renewable once. Chairs European Council; represents the Union externally at summit level.
Council of Ministers	Some coordinating role for the General Affairs Council (foreign ministers). All Council formations chaired by the rotating 6-month presidency.	Number and composition of specialized Councils to be determined by the European Council. Different member states to chair different Council formations at the same time for one-year period. Concept of a single presidency country effectively abolished. Foreign Affairs Council to be chaired by the EU Foreign Minister.
European Commission	Will be enlarged to 25 members under the Treaty of Nice—one from each member state.	Nice system in effect until 2009. After 2009, Commission to be reduced to 15: President, Vice President, and 13 voting Commissioners chosen on a rotating basis from among member states.
European Parliament	732 total members.	736 total members. Legislative power extended to 35 new areas, including aspects of police cooperation, agricultural policy, and social policy.
European Court of Justice	Responsibilities divided between the Court and the Court of First Instance.	Sets up three-tier system: the European Court, the High Court (renamed Court of First Instance), and specialized judicial panels.

Table 2.3   (Continued)

Institution/Issue Area	Situation as Established by the Maastricht, Amsterdam, and Nice Treaties	Projected Situation after Adoption and Ratification of the Constitutional Treaty
EU Foreign Minister	No such post. External representation shared by the High Representative for CFSP, the External Affairs Commissioner, and the foreign minister of the rotating presidency country.	Merges the current functions of the High Representative and the External Affairs Commissioner ("double-hatted" to the Council and the Commission).
National parliaments	No appreciable role other than to oversee national ministers.	May vote to send reasoned opinions to the EU institutions on compliance of proposals with the subsidiarity principle.
Competences	Competences added on an ad hoc basis by successive treaty amendments.	Catalog of "exclusive competences," "shared competences," and "supporting actions."
Qualified majority voting	Countries assigned weights roughly according to population; qualified majority consists of 232 of 321 votes, representing a majority of the member states comprising at least 62% of the Union's population. Systematic underweighting of largest countries (corrected somewhat at Nice but still a factor).	Majority of the member states representing at least three-fifths of the Union's population.
Structure of the Union	Three-pillar structure consisting of the European Community, CFSP, and Justice and Home Affairs.	Three-pillar structure abolished to create a single European Union.
Legal personality	EU has no legal personality. International agreements concluded either by the EC or as "mixed" agreements of the EC and the member states.	EU has legal personality.

Table 2.3 (Continued)

Institution/Issue Area	Situation as Established by the Maastricht, Amsterdam, and Nice Treaties	Projected Situation after Adoption and Ratification of the Constitutional Treaty
Types of legislation	Directives (addressed to the member states; require national transposition); Regulations (directly applicable); Decisions (addressed to specific party).	European framework laws (replace directives); European laws (replace regulations); Non-legislative acts (European regulations and European decisions) that are binding.
Charter of Fundamental Rights of the Union	Proclaimed as a political declaration. Legal status unclear.	Integrated as Part II of the Constitution. Justiciable in the ECJ.
Legal status of the treaties	All treaties technically in effect, albeit extensively amended (some renumbering and simplification at Amsterdam).	All former treaties repealed from date of entry into force of the new constitutional treaty.
Ratification and entry into force	Strict unanimity.	European Council to discuss situation if four-fifths have ratified and "one or more" others have not. (No real way around unanimity.)
Enhanced cooperation	No national veto and must involve 8 member states (Nice threshold lowered from Amsterdam requirement of a "majority" of states participating).	To be open to all and authorized by decision of the Council of Ministers; no other thresholds.

amendments and additions (the Single European Act, Maastricht, Amsterdam, and Nice) would be repealed and replaced by the new agreement. The three-pillar structure will be abolished and replaced by a single European Union that will have legal personality and the ability to conclude binding agreements with other countries and international organizations.

The new constitutional treaty preserves the five key institutions but makes important changes in how they operate, including the establishment of a Council president who is to be elected by the member states for a two-and-a-half-year term and who will replace the rotating six-month presidency in chairing Council meetings, the establishment of the post of EU foreign minister empowered to shape EU foreign policy and represent the Union abroad, and new roles for the national parliaments in ensuring the proper application of the subsidiarity principle in EU legislation. The powers of the European Parliament are extended to new (although still not all) policy areas, and the complicated triple majority system enshrined in the Nice treaty is to be abolished. In place of the system of national weights, the new system (to be in effect from November 1, 2009, onward) will require that for legislation to be adopted it must be supported by a majority of the member states representing three-fifths of the total Union population.

The proposed constitutional treaty was a compromise among many competing interests. To many European federalists, its adoption marked a continuation of the trend away from federalism that began after Maastricht and toward a more intergovernmental approach. The enhanced powers for the member states in the proposed Council presidency, the new role of the national parliaments in monitoring EU decisions, and the reluctance of the Convention to confer sweeping new powers on the Commission all were indications of the intergovernmentalist drift. In this sense, the constitution-building exercise was an ironic and, for traditional federalists at least, disappointing experience. Whereas a constitution had long been seen by the latter as the capstone of a powerful and united Europe with strengthened central institutions (just as the U.S. constitutional convention had marked the shift from confederation to federation), in the political climate of the early 2000s the constitution was becoming a vehicle for enshrining in law the rights and identities of the individual member states and for limiting the powers of Brussels. Although Giscard hoped that the draft constitution would be approved quickly by the member states in the IGC, this did not happen. France and Germany were satisfied with the draft, but many of the small countries had reservations about the seeming diminution of their power in the new arrangements. Most important, Poland and Spain were very unhappy with the new voting system proposed for the Council, which would drastically diminish their relative weight from what had been set in the Treaty of Nice. These differences prevented the adoption of the constitution at the December 2003 European Council and ensured that difficult negotiations would continue into 2004.

As the EU of the fifteen struggled to sort out its internal constitutional situation, the long preaccession process for the candidate countries moved toward conclusion. At the December 2002 Copenhagen summit, final agreement was reached on admitting ten new member states on May 1, 2004. Two countries, Bulgaria and Romania, were making slower progress but were expected to be ready for membership by 2007. The leaders of the ten accession countries met in Athens on April 16, 2003, with their member state counterparts to sign the accession treaty.

Along with constitutional reform and enlargement, the other major EU preoccupation was with CFSP and carving out a more distinct role for the Union in global politics. While U.S. policymakers generally applauded both enlargement and the EU's efforts to streamline its decision-making procedures, tensions with the United States increased over a range of economic, political, and security issues. European politicians spoke openly about building a new European identity by distinguishing Europe from the United States over such issues as the death penalty and the role of the welfare state. Differences between the EU and the United States arose over policy toward the Middle East, the International Criminal Court, the Kyoto Protocol on global warming, and other issues. These strains were already evident in the late 1990s under the Clinton administration, but they became particularly acute after the arrival of the Bush administration in Washington in January 2001 and, even more so, after the September 11, 2001, terrorist attacks on the United States. The Iraq crisis of 2002–2003 caused further strains in U.S.-EU relations, but also badly split the EU itself, as France and Germany took the lead in opposing a war that was deeply unpopular with European public opinion, while leaders in other member states—especially Britain but also Spain, Italy, and the accession countries—were more supportive of the effort to oust Saddam Hussein. These fissures had begun to heal by mid-2003, but their effects are likely to be felt within the Union for many years.

Whatever the future holds, the EU can be proud of its historical accomplishments. In the second half of the twentieth century, Europe, beginning with the core six countries, managed to overcome the bloody conflicts that ravaged the Continent in the first half of that century. Although the early postwar proponents of a United States of Europe perhaps would have been disappointed with the failure to achieve full political union, there is little doubt that the two basic objectives—peace and prosperity—were accomplished. The great unknown is how the EU will respond to the triple challenges of enlargement, constitutional reform, and the more complex and turbulent international environment. With twenty-five and eventually more member states, a territorial expanse stretching from the Arctic Circle to the Mediterranean and from the Atlantic to the Black Sea, and a diverse population approaching five hundred million, the EU will need to fashion and implement policies to maintain its economic vitality, carry through on plans to become a more influential international force, and cope with such problems as international terrorism, environmental degradation, and the economic burdens of an aging population. The challenge is to complete the historic task of extending peace and prosperity to the remainder of the Continent while maintaining Europe's place in a twenty-first-century world in a way that will not only benefit Europeans themselves but will also help to make the EU an inspiration to other, less prosperous and more turbulent, parts of the world.

Notes

1. For the texts of the treaties, see European Commission, *European Union: Selected Instruments from the Treaties* (Luxembourg: Office for Official Publications of the European Communities, 1995). The treaties also can be found online at europa.eu.int.

2. For the UK's complex relationship to the EU, see Hugo Young, *This Blessed Plot: Britain and Europe from Churchill to Blair* (Woodstock, N.Y.: Overlook Press, 1999).

3. For the monetary turmoil of the 1970s, see Paul Volcker and Toyoo Gyohten, *Changing Fortunes: The World's Money and the Threat to American Leadership* (New York: Times Books, 1992).

4. For Thatcher's views on Europe, see her memoirs, *Downing Street Years* (New York: HarperCollins, 1993).

5. For a more detailed analysis of the issues, see Youri Devuyst, *The European Union at the Crossroads: An Introduction to the EU's Institutional Evolution* (Brussels: PIE-Peter Lang, 2002).

Suggestions for Further Reading

Dinan, Desmond. *Ever Closer Union: An Introduction to European Integration.* Boulder, Colo.: Lynne Rienner, 1999.

Gilbert, Mark F. *Surpassing Realism: The Politics of European Integration since 1945.* Lanham, Md.: Rowman & Littlefield, 2003.

Grant, Charles. *Delors: Inside the House that Jacques Built.* London: Nicholas Brealey, 1994.

Kenen, Peter B. *Economic and Monetary Union in Europe: Moving Beyond Maastricht.* New York: Cambridge University Press, 1995.

Monnet, Jean. *Memoirs.* Garden City, N.Y.: Doubleday, 1978.

Moravcsik, Andrew. *The Choice for Europe: Social Purpose and State Power from Messina to Maastricht.* Ithaca, N.Y.: Cornell University Press, 1998.

Nugent, Neill. *The Government and Politics of the European Union.* 4th ed. Durham, N.C.: Duke University Press, 1999.

Tsoukalis, Loukas. *The New European Economy Revisited.* New York: Oxford University Press, 1997.

Van Oudenaren, John. *Uniting Europe: European Integration and the Post–Cold War World.* Lanham, Md.: Rowman & Littlefield, 2000.

CHAPTER 3

European Monetary Union and the Problem of Macroeconomic Governance

Erik Jones

The debate about economic and monetary union (EMU) in Europe has changed tack. Before EMU started in January 1999, the focus was on macroeconomic convergence.[1] Policymakers in the European Union (EU) argued over which policies they should follow in order to create a single currency, called the euro. Opinions differed both as to the merits of having a multinational currency and as to methods through which a European monetary union should be brought about. Nevertheless, most politicians and policy analysts accepted the structure of the debate as given. The problem of economic policy coordination was the context. The strategy for convergence was the instrument. And the creation of the euro was the goal.

Since the start of EMU in January 1999—and the introduction of physical notes and coins in January 2002—the debate has shifted to macroeconomic governance and not convergence. The questions facing policymakers concern what policies they should pursue across those countries which have adopted the single currency taken as a whole—the Eurozone. In this new debate, the euro is not the objective. It is the context. Within the context of EMU the focus for attention lies on the structure for macroeconomic policy making and on the goals to which macroeconomic policies should be directed.

This change in tack is not a complete departure from the past. Some EU member states—such as Denmark, Sweden, and the United Kingdom—do not yet participate in the euro. By the same token, none of the ten countries invited to join the European Union at the December 2002 European Council summit in Copenhagen will be given automatic entry into EMU. For those politicians and policymakers outside the Eurozone, discussion continues to focus on the merits of joining the single currency as an objective.

More important, perhaps, many of the institutions and commitments made during the process of convergence leading up to EMU continue to shape the pattern of macroeconomic governance now that the single currency has come into being. The reference values for "excessive" fiscal deficits and public debts are only the most obvious of such institutional holdovers. In monetary integration as elsewhere, the influence of the past is strongly felt.

This chapter examines the debate about macroeconomic governance in Europe today. My objectives are more descriptive than analytic. Because it takes place over multiple levels of analysis—supranational, national, and subnational—European debate over macroeconomic governance is unprecedented and therefore deserving of attention in its own right.

If there is an analytic claim in this chapter it is only an implicit one. The debate about macroeconomic governance in Europe signals the fundamental stability of EMU as a policy framework. Most EU member states have moved beyond questioning whether the single currency should exist. Instead they are considering how the single currency can be used to serve the best interests of the European Union. By implication, they are also considering who can and should determine what the "best interests" of the EU are.

The chapter is organized in four sections. The first introduces the concept of "macroeconomic governance" and explains why it has emerged at the center of policy debates today. The second outlines the structure of macroeconomic policy making in three areas—monetary, fiscal, and employment-related. The third debates derivative dimensions of macroeconomic policy making—wage bargaining, distributive conflict, and exchange rates. The fourth section evaluates prospects for the future.

Macroeconomic Governance and Monetary Union

The concept of "macroeconomic governance" is rarely invoked in national political debate. Politicians and pundits may argue over the direction of macroeconomic policy or the state of macroeconomic performance, but they are unlikely ever to combine the terms "macroeconomic" and "governance" in framing their polemics. This is not to imply that macroeconomic governance is irrelevant at the national level. Rather it reflects the fact that within an existing nation-state, both the "macroeconomy" and "governance" can be taken for granted. The macroeconomy is the national economy and governance is national governance. By implication, talking about macroeconomic governance is much the same as talking about government control over the national economy. It is too obvious to be worth mentioning.

By contrast, there is nothing obvious about macroeconomic governance within Europe's single currency. The irrevocable fixing of exchange rates between countries changed both the structure of the "macroeconomy" and the pattern of governance. For those countries participating in EMU it is no longer accurate to equate the national economy and the "macroeconomy"—at least not in policy-relevant terms. By the same token, it would be premature to expand the macroeconomy to encompass the whole of the Eurozone. For policy-makers, the euro has transformed the macroeconomy into a strange hybrid of the national and the European—at times favoring one level of analysis over the other.

The governance of this macroeconomy is hybrid as well. Some institutions are purely national, some predominantly European, and some blend the influences of the two. Even the policymakers involved appear to play multiple roles. For example, the heads of state and government act as both "poachers and gamekeepers" in the various procedures through which the single currency is administered and supported; they must abide by their commitments and they must enforce them.

The change to the macroeconomy is perhaps the most subtle and the most difficult to appreciate, primarily because the macroeconomy is itself so abstract. Macroeconomics is the study of relations between statistical aggregates. When macroeconomists talk about supply and demand, they mean *aggregate* supply and *aggregate* demand. Concepts like price inflation, employment, and unemployment are similarly aggregated. So is output and so is output growth. More complicated data are often just combinations of aggregates. Hence "productivity" is output given employment. "Real" output is output given inflation. "Real" growth is the change in output given inflation. And "real" productivity growth is the change in output given inflation and employment.

The crucial assumption operating behind these concepts both in relation to one another and in combination is that the level of aggregation is the same. It makes little sense to speak about the meeting of supply and demand when supply is aggregated at one level and demand at another. Likewise, it would be unusual to deflate national income by European price increases or to calculate productivity using European employment and only national output. Such calculations can be done, but their usefulness for feeding back into the standard models of macroeconomics would be open to question. By the same token, macroeconomists can operate across different frames of reference—regional, national, European, even global. There is nothing sacrosanct about the use of national data in macroeconomic analysis. However, it is essential that macroeconomists make explicit what level of aggregation they are using at any given point in time.

The introduction of the euro made it impossible to assume that the "national" level is always—or even usually—the most policy-relevant level of aggregation for analysis. For monetary policymakers, now it is more useful to aggregate data for price inflation at the European level. Hence economists working in the member states and at the European Commission had to devise a "harmonized index of consumer prices" (HICP) with which they could aggregate price developments across the different member states. Meanwhile concepts like output growth and unemployment remain more persistently national in scale. Policymakers may allude to aggregates for these data across the Eurozone as a whole, but they are more likely to act upon data for national growth and national unemployment.

The logic behind these multiple levels of aggregation is institutional. The responsibility for monetary policy operates at the European level (through the European System of Central Banks [ESCB] and its attendant European Central Bank [ECB]). By contrast, fiscal policy remains firmly in the control of the member state governments. This division of labor makes it difficult for policy-makers and politicians to explain their macroeconomic prescriptions to the public. In part, confusion has increased as a result of the greater abstraction implicit in ever higher levels of data aggregation. Put simply, European inflation data are less likely to reflect changes in local prices than national inflation data. Hence, for example, German consumers should be forgiven for their confused response to pronouncements about the threat of European inflation during the summer of 2002—a time when prices in Germany were actually falling and not rising.

Cognitive dissonance is not the only problem that results from having multiple levels of aggregation in the macroeconomy. The implicit threat of policy competition or policy conflict across levels of aggregation is important as well. Continuing with the German example from the summer of 2002, monetary policymakers at the European level expressed concern that deficit spending on fiscal policy would stimulate aggregate demand and so exacerbate the threat of future inflation. At the national level, meanwhile, policymakers argued that efforts to avoid fiscal deficits would tip the German economy back into recession and might even encourage a sustained round of price deflation reminiscent of the Great Depression of the 1930s. Both arguments have merit, depending upon the perspective that is taken in the analysis—national versus European. The problem is that there is no objective principle for determining which perspective or which level of aggregation is the "most appropriate" for policy making. Within EMU, the macroeconomy exists at both levels at once.

The politicians and policymakers who framed Europe's economic and monetary union were well aware of the prospect that the single currency would give rise to policy competition between national and European institutions. Their response was to try and settle such conflict before the fact by establishing rules and guidelines for acceptable behavior. The thinking at the time was that if the member states could forge binding commitments in anticipation of EMU there would be no basis for competition or conflict once the single currency came into being. The agreement to avoid excessive debts and deficits is one such commitment. The goal of achieving a medium-term fiscal position close to balance or in surplus as set out in the 1997 Stability and Growth Pact (SGP) is another. And the injunction that the ECB pursue absolute price stability without political interference from the member states or other policy institutions is a third. When added together, these commitments and others were meant to provide a framework for the achievement of macroeconomic stability even after the single currency expanded the macroeconomy to encompass multiple levels of data aggregation and policy action.

This rule-based solution is not limited to the single currency alone, and policy competition has long been a problem for Europe's policymakers. Hence the single currency exists within a larger body of rules established by the European Union as a framework for solving economic problems in a coordinated fashion. Many of the rules would have been adopted whether or not EMU came into being. The member states committed themselves to a wide range of objectives in the Maastricht Treaty on European Union (TEU) and in the Treaty Establishing the European Community (TEC), of which monetary union was only one—and an instrumental one at that. (The relevant treaty articles are reproduced in Box 3.1.) Moreover, virtually all of the countries of Western Europe had to respond to the deterioration of public finances and to the growth of unemployment during the 1980s and 1990s whether or not they were in the European Union and whatever they decided about the merits of irrevocably fixed exchange rates.

In order to illustrate the operation of European commitments beyond EMU, it is useful to consider the case of Great Britain. Although long skeptical of the single currency, the British government not only agreed to undertake the medium-term fiscal commitment to achieving a budgetary position close to balance or in surplus, but also played a role in the elaboration of the European

Box 3.1   The Economic Objectives of the European Union

Article 2, Treaty on European Union

The Union shall set itself the following objectives: to promote economic and social progress and a high level of employment and to achieve balanced and sustainable development, in particular through the creation of an area without internal frontiers, through the strengthening of economic and social cohesion and through the establishment of economic and monetary union, ultimately including a single currency in accordance with the provisions of this Treaty.

Article 2, Treaty Establishing the European Community

The Community shall have as its task, by establishing a common market and an economic and monetary union and by implementing common policies or activities referred to in Articles 3 and 4, to promote through the Community a harmonious, balanced and sustainable development of economic activities, a high level of employment and of social protection, equality between men and women, sustainable and non-inflationary growth, a high degree of competitiveness and convergence of economic performance, a high level of protection and improvement of the quality of the environment, the raising of the standard of living and quality of life, and economic and social cohesion and solidarity among Member States.

response to the jobs crisis (through the Cardiff process). Furthermore, the British government, like all member state governments, is responsible for following the "broad economic policy guidelines" elaborated at the European level and it is also responsible for helping to enforce the compliance of other member states. The nature of these commitments is elaborated below. For the moment, suffice it to say that the single currency is only part and not parcel of the EU policy framework.

In their efforts to establish a rule-based framework for macroeconomic policy coordination, EU policymakers faced three problems. First, the economic issues to be addressed—such as excessive indebtedness or rising unemployment—are difficult to resolve under the best of circumstances. At a minimum, policymakers who hope to resolve conflicts through the promulgation of fixed rules must be able to anticipate the challenges, obstacles, or contingencies that the future will hold. Such foresight was beyond the architects of Europe's monetary union. They did not plan for the threat that might be posed by falling prices rather than rising prices. They did not anticipate the profound fluctuations in oil prices and in the euro–dollar exchange rate. They (perhaps) underestimated the persistence of European unemployment and the aging of Europe's population. And these are just the most prominent developments that have occurred since the start of EMU, let alone others that may occur in the years to come.

Second, most of the "solutions" available to individual member states have the effect of complicating matters for the rest. Here it is useful to consider an example from the time before EMU. If France were to try to eliminate unemployment by devaluing the French franc against the German mark, the results might be good for France but they would be bad for Germany (and for any other country that attempted to stabilize its currency against the mark). The depreciation of the franc would lower the prices of French products in Germany and so increase the volume sold and the amount of employment in French manufacturing. By contrast, German goods sold in France would become more expensive, decreasing the volume sold and putting pressure on employment in Germany.[2] In this example, the single currency is part of the solution and not part of the problem. The irrevocable fixing of exchange rates between countries combined with the substitution of the euro for separate national currencies eliminates the danger that member states will attempt to engineer a competitive devaluation. France cannot reduce the value of the franc relative to the mark because neither currency exists.

As suggested above, however, the creation of a monetary union does not eliminate all possible forms of policy competition or policy conflict. Quite the opposite, the single currency gives rise to problems of its own. Continuing with the hypothetical Franco-German example, the French government might be tempted to create jobs by subsidizing wage costs (and so underpricing German exports) or by offering generous tax incentives to foreign industries (and so luring away German investment). A single currency does little to prevent this type of competition between member states. Instead, a single currency raises the prospect that actions taken at the member state level would interfere with the conduct of a common monetary policy. The fiscal deficits created by subsidizing wages or foreign direct investment—and by exacerbating unemployment in Germany—might undermine the price stability of the European single currency.

Third, Europe's policymakers could not agree on rules for all facets of the macroeconomy. They could establish a framework for combining monetary and fiscal policy and even for outlining a collective approach to tackling the jobs crisis. However, they had greater difficulty establishing rules for dealing with the common euro exchange rate, for governing collective bargaining over wages and working conditions, and for the management of distributive conflict more generally. In this way, their macroeconomic framework could never be comprehensive and would always be vulnerable to shocks emanating both from outside the Eurozone and from within.

The result, then, is that the rules are counterproductive. In effect, the rule-based framework that was established to avoid competition between policies adopted at the national and European levels has itself become a source of conflict. At issue is not only how to change the rules that govern macroeconomic policy making in the Eurozone, but also whether such rules can be reformed without bringing down the whole macroeconomic framework. The danger is that if the rules are removed or their legitimacy is brought into question, then the competition between policies at the national and European levels or between member states will only intensify. It is unsurprising, therefore, that the debate over macroeconomic governance in Europe has become the focus for attention in the single currency.

EMU and the European Union
Policy Framework

The first step in untangling this debate is to understand the rules themselves. The EU policy framework addresses the need for economic policy coordination by mitigating the incidence of conflict in two dimensions: across policy types (monetary, fiscal, and regulatory, i.e., market-structural) and across policy levels (European, national, regional). Some of the rules are explicit in enjoining particular action. Monetary policy, for example, should be focused on the promotion of price stability. Some of the rules circumscribe unacceptable behavior. Hence, fiscal policy should not result in "excessive" deficits. And some of the rules promote broadly compatible objectives, such as a medium-term budget balance, competitive markets, a skilled and flexible workforce, and a dynamic and responsive industrial base.

This section sketches out the rules that constitute the EU policy framework as they apply to the monetary, fiscal, and employment-related policy domains. The subdivision across policy domains ignores many of the important micro-economic considerations related to international trade, state aids to industry, or inter-firm competition in product markets. In keeping with the focus on macroeconomic governance, the subdivisions are primarily macroeconomic in their ambit. Hence the employment-related measures deal with regulatory structures that might ordinarily be regarded as within the purview of microeco-nomics, and yet the goal of these measures is the manipulation of aggregate statistics for employment and unemployment.

The subdivision across policy domains is also primarily institutional. The monetary rules operate according to common principles and through European institutions (the ECB and ESCB). The fiscal rules operate according to com-mon principles but through member-state institutions. Meanwhile, employment-related rules describe the means through which national leaders develop national principles for implementation at the national and subnational levels. In this sense, the three policy domains constitute separate but overlapping re-gimes. The extent of the separation between the different regimes should not be exaggerated. The individual rules and policy domains are not so important as the system as a whole. It matters less whether monetary policy should always be directed to the promotion of price stability than whether—taken together—stable prices, sound finances, and competitive markets help to resolve the prob-lems of economic policy coordination across the fifteen (and soon more) differ-ent EU member states.

MONETARY RULES

The monetary elements of the policy framework are the most clearly deline-ated. According to Article 105, Paragraph 1 of the Treaty Establishing the Euro-pean Community (TEC):

> The primary objective of the ESCB shall be to maintain price stabil-ity. Without prejudice to the objective of price stability, the ESCB shall support the general economic policies in the Community with a view to contributing to the achievement of the objectives of the Community as laid down in Article 2.

This article is unambiguous. Only two terms, "price stability" and "prejudice," provide room for interpretation. And the power to interpret these terms lies within the sole jurisdiction of the ESCB. Paragraph 2 of the same article lists the obligation "to define and implement the monetary policy of the Commu-nity" as the first of "the basic tasks to be carried out through the ESCB."

Meanwhile, Article 108 enjoins all parties to the European Union to respect the independence of the ESCB in the exercise of its duties. (The organizational structure of the ESCB is provided in Box 3.2.)

In practice, the ESCB has displayed both dogmatism and pragmatism in the management of its responsibilities. Much of the ESCB's dogmatism can be found in its explicit interpretation of the price stability mandate. One of the first actions of the "Governing Council" of the ESCB was to define price stability as an annual rate of change of less than 2 percent in the HICP for those

Box 3.2   The Organization of Monetary Authority in Europe

The European System of Central Banks (ESCB) unites all central banks of the member states of the European Union (EU) and is the central authority responsible for defining and implementing the common monetary policy of the Eurozone—meaning those countries that have adopted the single currency (the euro). The ESCB consists of the member state central banks (MSCBs) and a European Central Bank (ECB).

The ECB serves as the executive to the ESCB and is governed by an "executive board," which includes a president, a vice president, and four regular board members. The ECB prepares the policy decisions of the ESCB—both monetary and otherwise; it collects and analyzes data about economic performance across the Eurozone; and it represents the ESCB in international and European fora.

Within the ESCB, the MSCBs are represented by their governors or presidents. The MSCBs implement the policy decisions of the ESCB; they collect and analyze data about economic performance within the member states; and they represent the ESCB at the member state level.

The two decision-making bodies of the ESCB are the "Governing Council" and the "General Council." The Governing Council is responsible for the monetary policy of the Eurozone and for the general operation of the single currency. It comprises all six of the Executive Board members of the ECB, plus the governors or presidents of those MSCBs that that have adopted the single currency. The Governing Council meets twice monthly although (as of November 2002) it takes monetary policy decisions only in the first of its bimonthly meetings. The minutes of Governing Council meetings are not published, but the president of the ECB holds a press conference immediately after the first meeting in each month.

The "General Council" is a transitional decision-making body that is responsible for relations between the Eurozone and those member states outside the single currency, including enlargement. It is transitional in the sense that once all EU member states participate in the single currency, the mandate of the General Council will have been fulfilled. The General Council comprises the presidents or governors of all central banks in the ESCB plus the president and vice president of the ECB. The four regular members of the ECB executive board may attend meetings of the General Council, but they do not have voting rights.

countries participating in the monetary union—the new aggregate being called the Monetary Union Index for Consumer Prices (MUICP). This action set off an immediate round of criticism from national politicians and from central bankers outside the monetary union. These critics argued both that the 2 percent ceiling is too low and that it is asymmetrical insofar as it sets a ceiling for price movements but not a floor. Both criticisms point to the same weakness: followed closely, the ESCB's interpretation of price stability poses the risk of deflation, or falling prices. Even where deflation is avoided, a too-restrictive conception of price stability would inhibit growth. For his part, the ECB president, Wim Duisenberg, responded on behalf of the ESCB by noting that the goal of European monetary policy is not to manage growth but to stabilize prices. Referring to the qualification that monetary policy could be set to contribute to other objectives "without prejudice to . . . price stability," Duisenberg suggested simply that price stability *is* the ESCB's contribution to the EU's other objectives. Finally, he argued that the predominant threat to price stability lies in unchecked inflation.[3]

The dogmatic side of the ESCB also emerged in relation to its institutional independence. When Duisenberg announced in October 1998 that monetary policy would rest on two pillars—the monitoring of broad liquidity growth and the estimation of future inflation—he offered little insight into how, precisely, the Governing Council would use these sources of information in making its policy decisions. He resisted releasing the precise models with which the European Central Bank would generate its own estimates for future price inflation across the monetary union. And he refused to release the minutes of Governing Council meetings even months after the fact. Over time, Duisenberg has yielded on some of these issues—most notably when he conceded to pressure from the European Parliament to release the specifications of the ECB's forecasting models. However, he has remained a staunch defender of the independence of the ESCB and its interpretation of the price stability mandate throughout the first years of EMU.

The pragmatic side of the ESCB has been more procedural than rhetorical. The two-pillar strategy for basing monetary policy decisions is one example. When EMU started in January 1999, the aggregates for liquidity growth and price movements (M3 and MUICP) were both new and difficult to interpret. Europe's monetary policymakers had trouble understanding the underlying relationship between liquidity growth and economic activity, they had difficulty predicting future price movements, and they had little concrete basis upon which to anticipate how changes in monetary policy would work their way across the member state economies. Faced with such uncertainty, using two monetary aggregates seemed preferable to relying upon just one (namely, expected inflation). Over time, it became clear that the reference value for liquidity growth was less useful as a basis for monetary policy decisions than predicted inflation. Not only did M3 repeatedly overshoot the reference value of

4.5 percent, but it did so for a variety of different and yet theoretically "exceptional" reasons. The ESCB has not abandoned either its two-pillar strategy or its 4.5 percent reference value for M3 growth, but neither has it let actual performance of the monetary aggregates interfere with the rational conduct of policy.

The pragmatic side of the ESCB can even be seen in the policy decisions of the Governing Council. Despite the rhetorical commitment to a monolithic objective of price stability, the Governing Council has made interest rate decisions that could be interpreted as pro-growth. One of these decisions occurred in April 1999, when the Governing Council eased interest rates by one half of one percent, in the first relaxation of monetary policy since the founding of the monetary union. At the time, M3 growth was declining but remained above the reference value of 4.5 percent. Meanwhile, actual inflation was low (about 1 percent per annum) and yet even the ECB admitted that adverse energy price rises and exchange-rate movements threatened to put upward pressure on prices in the future. Hence, while there was some justification for a reduction in interest rates, it was ambiguous. By contrast, the ECB's move was large and decisive. At the time, the widespread belief among market analysts was that the ECB was lowering interest rates in order to aid the member states in their efforts at structural reform. A number of journalists at the press conference where the decision was announced tried to get the ECB president to admit that he was acting in favor of structural reform rather than price stability. Duisenberg refused. And yet when one correspondent queried Duisenberg as to whether this interest rate reduction was in effect a sop to the member states so that they would make greater efforts to tackle unemployment, Duisenberg responded: "I do not have that much difficulty with your words."[4]

Another "pragmatic" decision occurred in December 2002. Then too, the Governing Council of the ESCB decided to lower interest rates by one half of one percent. However, M3 growth was well above the reference value (at 7.2 percent compared to 4.5 percent per annum) and actual MUICP inflation was running ahead of 2 percent per annum. Duisenberg's explanation for this relaxation of monetary policy was that, while actual inflation was high, output growth was low and expected to remain so into the coming months. Hence the contribution of economic activity to future inflation should be expected to diminish—making it possible for the ECB to cut rates without fear of undermining price stability. This logic is far removed from the dogmatic assertions that the contribution of the ECB is to stabilize prices. Nevertheless, four years into EMU, the journalists who participated at the press conference accepted the justification almost without question.[5]

ECONOMIC (FISCAL) RULES

The juxtaposition of dogmatism and pragmatism is recurrent in the rule-based framework for macroeconomic policy making. But nowhere are the two tendencies—the dogmatic and the pragmatic—so tightly intertwined as in the realm of economic (read "fiscal") policy.[6] On the dogmatic side, the rules are clear: the "member states shall regard their economic policies as a matter of common concern and they shall coordinate them within the Council [of Ministers],"[7] they "shall avoid excessive government deficits," and they shall "respect the medium-term budgetary objective of close to balance or in surplus."[8] The near-religious compulsion embedded in these rules is most evident in transgression. Any member state that fails to operate within the framework is self-interested (pride), excessive (gluttony), and indolent (sloth). By contrast, member-state actions in compliance with the fiscal rules express solidarity, moderation, and self-discipline.

On the pragmatic side, the rules governing the fiscal policies of the member states are wrought with ambiguity. This point is best explained within the context of institutional development. Therefore, it is useful to begin with the structures set down in the amendments to the TEC agreed at Maastricht in December 1991. That framework for economic policy coordination included only two procedures—one for multilateral surveillance and one for excessive deficits. Because these procedures are still in use, the descriptions are in the present tense.

The "multilateral surveillance procedure" derives its force from the general commitment of the member states to treat their economic policies as a matter of common interest. The procedure focuses on the elaboration of "broad economic policy guidelines" (BEPGs) by the Council of Ministers for the member states and for the EU as a whole. Following that, both the Council and the European Commission are involved in monitoring the policies of the member states in order to determine whether they are actually following the guidelines. Where the Council decides that a member state has failed to live up to its obligations under the BEPGs, it may make appropriate recommendations and it may even decide to make those recommendations public (as a form of rebuke).

The "excessive deficit procedure" derives from a more specific commitment to avoid excessive deficits on fiscal accounts. The logic behind this commitment is derivative. Excessive deficits are bad because they undermine monetary conditions across the single currency. In this sense, the commitment to avoid excessive deficits is nested within the commitment to treat economic policy as a matter of common interest. By the same token, the excessive deficit procedure follows much the same outline as the multilateral surveillance procedure—but with three important exceptions. First, the commitment to avoid excessive deficits operates as a permanent feature for policy coordination and so does not need to be written into the BEPGs in order to have force. Second, the reference values for "excessiveness" are fixed in a protocol to the Maastricht treaty—being "3 percent for the ratio of planned or actual government deficit to gross domestic product [GDP] at market prices [and] 60 percent for the ratio of government debt to gross domestic product at market prices."[9] By implication, the commitment to avoid excessive deficits is not only permanent but also difficult to change without changing the TEC. Third, the excessive deficit procedure has a wider range of sanctions to be applied in its enforcement. As with the multilateral surveillance procedure, the Council can make recommendations to errant member states and it can also make those recommendations public. However, unlike the multilateral surveillance procedure, the council may encourage compliance with the commitment to avoid excessive deficits by issuing credit advisories, by restricting member state access to the resources of the European Investment Bank, by requiring the member state to make a substantial non-interest bearing deposit, or by levying a fine "of an appropriate size."

The ambiguities arise primarily in the relationship between these two procedures. The Maastricht amendments to the TEC do not clarify either priority or timing. Hence, unless prima facie evidence for an excessive deficit exists, it is ambiguous which procedure comes first and where one procedure lets off so that another can take over. Such ambiguities were less important during the period of convergence leading up to EMU—if only because most member states had excessive deficits. However, in a hypothetical world where almost every member state is close to fiscal balance, which procedure would the Council use to guard against a sudden deterioration? Similarly, could a member state accused of running an excessive fiscal deficit escape the more punitive sanctions embedded in the excessive deficit procedure by shifting the focus of attention to its compliance with the BEPGs under the rubric of multilateral surveillance? The ambiguity of the Maastricht framework for economic policy coordination is suggested in Figure 3.1.

The Stability and Growth Pact (SGP) adopted by the European Council at its June 1997 Amsterdam summit eliminates some of the ambiguity in the framework for economic policy coordination. The SGP includes three elements: a resolution committing the member states "to respect the medium-term budgetary objective of close to balance or in surplus" (as mentioned above) and to use the whole panoply of enforcement mechanisms available under the excessive deficit procedure; a Council regulation (No 1467/97) "on speeding up and clarifying the implementation of the excessive deficit procedure"; and a Council regulation (No 1466/97) "on the strengthening of the surveillance of budgetary positions and the surveillance and coordination of economic policies." This

Figure 3.1   Maastricht Coordination Framework

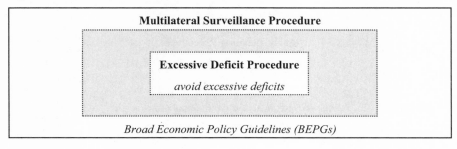

third element introduces a new "early warning procedure" through which the Council of Ministers can react to the threat that a member state will fail to comply with the BEPGs or with the obligation to avoid excessive deficits. In this way, the member states have an incentive to correct problems before they become manifest.

The revised Amsterdam framework for economic policy coordination is depicted in Figure 3.2. What has changed from the Maastricht framework is that the provisions of the SGP fill in the ambiguous relationship between the procedures for multilateral surveillance and for excessive deficits. The point to note in this diagram, however, is that both of the Maastricht procedures are strengthened as a result. Council action under the excessive deficit procedure is more timely and decisive. And Council action under the multilateral surveillance procedure is more timely and decisive as well. Moreover, the procedures remain nested. The BEPGs derive from the most general commitment and operate through the wide-ranging multilateral surveillance procedure. The medium-term objective of budget balance or surplus is more specific and is reinforced with the early warning procedure. The 3 percent deficit ceiling is more specific still and remains subject to the (clarified) excessive deficit procedure.

Despite the changes introduced in the SGP, however, recent experience suggests that ambiguity continues to arise both in the application of the procedures and in their effectiveness. The Council of Ministers had to resort to each of the three procedures—multilateral surveillance, early warning, and excessive deficit—during the first four years of monetary union. However, despite the strength of the rhetoric surrounding the process of fiscal policy coordination, the results were at best mixed. Some of the countries sanctioned by the Council—such as Ireland and France—simply refused to comply. Others—such as Germany and Portugal—assented to the Council's recommendations and then failed to implement them.

The Irish case arose first. Throughout the year 2000, the Irish government ran an impressive fiscal surplus (equal to almost 5 percent of GDP) and yet Irish output growth (also running at about 5 percent) far outpaced the rest of the European Union. Although Ireland fell well within the obligations of the

Figure 3.2   Amsterdam Coordination Framework

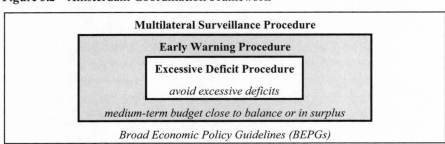

SGP, the fast pace of Irish growth threatened to add inflationary pressure to the monetary union as a whole. As a result, the Council instructed the Irish government to tighten its fiscal policy in order to put a brake on the economy as part of the BEPGs for 2000. The Irish government chose to ignore this recommendation, and instead passed a modest tax concession that was expected to reduce the government surplus to something closer to 4 percent of GDP. When the Council reviewed this action in February 2001, its response was unyielding:

> The Council finds that the planned contribution of fiscal policy to the macroeconomic policy mix in Ireland is inappropriate. The Council recalls that it has repeatedly urged the Irish authorities, most recently in its 2000 broad guidelines of the economic policies, to ensure economic stability by means of fiscal policy. The Council regrets that this advice was not reflected in the budget for 2001, despite developments in the course of 2000 indicating an increasing extent of overheating. The Council considers that Irish fiscal policy in 2001 is not consistent with the broad guidelines of the economic policies as regards budgetary policy. The Council has therefore decided, together with this Opinion, to make a recommendation . . . with a view to ending this inconsistency.[10]

This decision was published with a formal reprimand of the Irish government. The result was far less than expected. The Irish government refused to change its policy. Irish public opinion temporarily soured regarding EU membership—which may have contributed to the June 2001 rejection of the Nice treaty in a popular referendum. And a general weakening of economic activity across Europe (together with the tragic events of September 11, 2001) slowed down the pace of Irish growth in any event. Not only was the Council's action under the multilateral surveillance procedure both ineffective and unpopular, but it was also irrelevant.

The next cases to arise concerned Germany and Portugal. During the late Autumn of 2001, the European Commission indicated that both countries risked running government deficits beyond the 3 percent threshold. In its January 2002 recommendation to the Council of Ministers, the Commission argued that both countries should be given an early warning under the SGP. The Council's reply in both cases was the same. On the one hand, it accepted that the Commission was correct in its recommendation. On the other hand, it was persuaded by the commitments made on the part of Germany and Portugal to ensure that they did not breach the deficit threshold of 3 percent. Hence the Council decided not to issue the early warnings. Both decisions were unanimous. Both were also in error.

By the end of 2002, it was clear that Germany and Portugal would fail to stabilize their deficits below the 3 percent threshold. Even worse, much of the data reported by the Portuguese government greatly underestimated the size of the deficit that already existed—above 4 percent. The Council entered Portugal into the excessive deficit procedure in November 2002, and it initiated the procedure with respect to Germany the following January. In turn, both countries made solemn undertakings to resolve their fiscal imbalances, and they agreed to make public the recommendations of the Council. What is unclear is whether such commitments will prove any more effective than those made a year earlier.

Whatever the outcome, the Council of Ministers appears to have learned from the experience of its initial decision not to issue an early warning to Germany and Portugal. Faced with the prospect that France would exceed the 3 percent deficit threshold, the Council chose a firmer line. At the same time that the Council started the excessive deficit procedure for Germany it issued an early warning to France. The result was reminiscent of the Irish reprimand of 2000. Where Germany agreed to the publication of the Council's recommendation, France did not. The German government's contrition contrasted sharply with the French government's resistance. What is unclear is whether the Council's strong stance will alter the final result. As in the Irish case, the Council may find its actions not only unpopular, but also overtaken by external events.

EMPLOYMENT-RELATED RULES

The fiscal rules for economic policy coordination reveal the limits of European influence. The employment-related rules reveal the potential. The point here is easily overstated. When the Amsterdam European Council formally introduced responsibility for employment as part of the TEC in June 1997, few commentators expected much from the results.[11] More than five years later, these low expectations have been greatly surpassed. Europe remains beset by the problem of unemployment. Nevertheless, the member states have worked out a program through which they have begun to address that in a coordinated fashion.

The framework for employment-related policy operates through a series of parallel "processes" (as opposed to procedures)—each named for the European Council summit at which it was initiated. The Luxembourg process was started in November 1997 and encourages the promotion of active labor market policies—that is, policies to create jobs, to retrain workers, and to improve the matching between actual job vacancies and potential applicants for employment. The Cardiff process was added in June 1998 and emphasizes the market structural reform both for products and for inputs to production (such as labor and capital). Finally, the Cologne process was initiated in June 1999 as a means for involving employers and trade unions in a "macroeconomic dialogue" with policymakers both in the member states and at the European level. In turn, these processes are united in the March 2000 Lisbon "strategy" and its "open method of coordination."

One strength of this part of the European macroeconomic framework lies in the fact that it is flexibly adapted to the needs of the separate member states. Through these processes, the member states themselves rely on the support of European institutions and of each other in the implementation of the various reform measures. At the center, the "open method of coordination" described in the Lisbon strategy is contingent upon a variety of factors, such as individual targets, collective benchmarks, and shared "best practices." Such things are unlikely to solve the jobs crisis in Europe. But they may help. And they were largely unavailable before they were introduced through the European Union.[12]

A further strength of the employment-related framework is that it is readily identifiable as a common endeavor. Hence both the ESCB and the Council of Ministers rely on information about member-state unemployment and market structural reforms when making macroeconomic policy decisions. Such information is important for two reasons: First, it helps to explain the data—for example, why inflation is rising or falling, or why government expenditures are in deficit or surplus. Second, information about labor-market performance and market structural reform helps macroeconomic policymakers to predict how the aggregates they observe will likely move in the future and how the member states will respond to a change in policy.

The existence of a common framework for employment-related policies also makes it possible for macroeconomic authorities to recommend action that could forestall unpopular policy moves or that could justify more popular ones. Such considerations are manifest in the actions of the Council of Ministers. They are evident in the behavior of the ESCB as well. Recalling the ESCB decision to lower interest rates in April 1999, the focus for concern across Europe lay in the importance of using the benefits of a period of relatively favorable performance in order to tackle unemployment and market rigidities. Moving forward to the decisions of the Council to initiate an excessive deficit procedure against Germany in January 2003, the criticism was that the German government had not taken advantage of the opportunities with which it had been presented.

External Factors

The German government might be forgiven for not having tackled the problems of unemployment and market structural reform with the vigor expected by the European Central Bank or even the Council of Ministers. Despite the many facets of the framework for European macroeconomic coordination, there are a number of elements that remain beyond the control of individual member states or even the European Union as a whole. To illustrate this point, it is necessary only to move backward through the catalog of processes, procedures, and prescriptions just described. For example, macroeconomic dialogue cannot

control wage bargaining. Market structural reform and active labor-market policies cannot eliminate distributive conflict—which is to say, conflict over taxes
and other fiscal resources between organized groups in society. And no efforts
to consolidate fiscal accounts or to stabilize prices can determine the exchange
rate between the euro and the rest of the world. Fiscal and monetary policy may
be used to target exchange rate performance, but they cannot fulfill a domestic
objective at the same time.

Such omissions are potentially critical. Wage bargaining can undermine
macroeconomic performance. Distributive conflict can prevent market structural reform. And exchange rate movements—or other international price
movements—can thwart the achievement of both fiscal and monetary objectives.

Nevertheless, it would be unrealistic to expect that either the member states
or the European Union could eliminate the influence of such factors. No country—and no arrangement between countries—can ever lay claim to complete
control. Consider, for example, three illustrations from successive United States
presidencies. At the start of the 1970s, Richard Nixon struggled to put a cap on
price and wage movements, and yet even his direct controls could only forestall
(and not eliminate) an explosive price-wage spiral. Later that same decade,
Jimmy Carter struggled to reform the basic structures for Social Security, only
to incur the wrath of innumerable special interest groups and most notably the
elderly. And at the start of the 1980s, Ronald Reagan's "supply-side" fiscal reforms collided with a dollar appreciation that crippled the competitiveness of U.S.
manufacturing and sparked widespread concern about the "de-industrialization of
America."[13]

Yet the ubiquitousness of forces beyond the control of macroeconomic
policymakers does not mean that vulnerability to such forces is everywhere the
same. Here three comparisons are relevant to the European Union: between the
same member states before and after joining the single currency; between different participating member states; and between the Eurozone and those member
states which remain outside. Are countries more or less vulnerable after having
joined the single currency? Do all participating member states share the same
risks and to the same degree? Is the Eurozone as a whole more or less vulnerable than a given member state?

The analysis in this section is necessarily abbreviated, given the scope of
these questions. My goal is twofold: First, it is to illustrate the vulnerabilities of
the European Union to factors beyond the influence of policy rules both inside
and outside the single currency. Second, it is to suggest that the nature of vulnerability within the single currency is unique—particularly with respect to
distributive conflict. The conclusion to this section can be offered in advance
and, indeed, has already been anticipated: The creation of the monetary union
constitutes a trade-off. It eliminates some vulnerabilities and solves some problems, but it creates others as well. Moreover, the single currency is not alone in

Table 3.1   External Factors Affecting the Macroeconomic Policy Framework—A Comparative Overview

	Over Time	*Across Participants*	*Inside versus Outside*
Wage Bargaining	Two new risks: coordinated wage norms; decreased national discipline	Coordinated bargaining countries most affected	More diverse and more decentralized within Eurozone than outside (implies less vulnerable to wage bargaining but more vulnerable to distributive conflict)
Distributive Conflict*	More constraints ("hand-tying") during the convergence process than after	High degree of idiosyncratic variation	
Exchange Rates	No intra-European exchange rates: less volatility but less room for adjustment	Varies with trade patterns and with manufacturing structure	Lower level of trade exposure and fewer important exchange rates

* "Distributive conflict" refers to conflict over the distribution of resources, specifically conflict between interested groups over the level of taxation and the payment of benefits via the welfare state.

this regard. The broader collection of rules constituting the EU's macroeconomic policy framework has a similar effect. Table 3.1 provides an overview of the argument.

WAGE BARGAINING

Wage bargaining influences macroeconomic performance for two reasons. First, wages are an important part of prices because labor is an important part of production. Hence when wages increase, so do production costs and so do prices—and that means higher inflation. For some manufacturers, however, it is not possible to raise prices to match higher wages. Foreign competitors may be able to provide similar products more cheaply or consumers may not be willing to pay the higher price. As a consequence, those firms that cannot raise prices will respond to higher wages by laying off workers. In this case, the result of higher wage claims is seen in terms of unemployment rather than inflation. Unfortunately, the two results are not necessarily exclusive. The experience of the 1970s revealed that inflation and unemployment can increase at the same time. Wage bargaining was not wholly responsible for this unfortunate combination, but it did contribute on both sides.

Despite its importance, however, wage bargaining lies outside the EU policy regime. Europe's heads of state and government have made numerous statements about the necessity to bring the social partners—meaning representatives of labor and industry—into line with the broader macroeconomic framework.[14] However, apart from the Cologne "macroeconomic dialogue," they have made little progress in establishing effective control over wages. The easy explanation is that the area is too diverse. National trade unions are organized along different principles and have different rights and responsibilities accorded by national legislation. National bargaining patterns are different as well, with some countries (such as France) emphasizing negotiations at the firm level, others (such as Germany) focusing more on national industrial sectors, and still others (such as Belgium) relying upon cross-sectoral national bargains. Such diversity belies easy coordination at the European level, at least in the sense of generating an effective price-incomes policy. The European Council and the ECB can admonish the social partners to act responsibly, but they cannot force them to do so.

The creation of a European single currency suggests two different problems. The first is that trade unions across Europe will take advantage of the fact that wages are denominated in the same currency from one country to the next in order to encourage wage negotiators in different member states to coordinate their bargaining efforts. This is a problem insofar as the different countries of Europe have different productivity levels and different cost structures. Coordinated bargaining would benefit some of these countries by restricting competition from previously low-wage producers. However, coordinated wage bargaining would hurt other countries by making their workforce too expensive. During the early days of monetary union, there was some evidence that such coordination might take place. The national unions of Belgium, Germany, Luxembourg, and the Netherlands agreed to coordinate their bargaining efforts at a September 1998 meeting in the Dutch city of Doorn. Three months later, the European Metal Workers Federation established a European coordination rule.[15] The effectiveness of these agreements remains unclear.

The second problem with wage bargaining in the single currency is that countries that have relied on price-incomes policies during the period before monetary union will no longer be able to do so. The classic example here is Germany. As Peter Hall has argued, the willingness of trade unions to accept instructions (or signals) from the German central bank (the Bundesbank) is a cornerstone of the country's historic price stability.[16] Now that the Bundesbank is no longer in control of monetary policy, however, there is a danger that the trade unions will cease to bargain in a disciplined fashion. This danger is not limited to Germany. A number of European countries, such as Belgium and the Netherlands, have traditionally relied on patterns of wage bargaining coordination that may no longer be available under EMU. Even more countries, such as Ireland, Italy, and Portugal, developed coordinated bargaining precisely in order to stabilize inflation rates during the convergence process leading up to EMU.[17] Should such coordination mechanisms break down, it is unclear how the governments of these countries will be able to restrain their unions from pricing themselves out of the European marketplace. Indeed, evidence from Ireland and the Netherlands suggests that such adverse bargaining may already be under way.

Wage bargaining is potentially problematic in Europe's single currency. Nevertheless, it is less problematic than it can be for any given member state. Short of the threat of Europe-wide coordination, the Eurozone does not risk having its macroeconomic conditions disrupted by wage bargains in the manner that most European countries experienced in the 1970s. The diversity of bargaining regimes from one member state to the next is far greater than the internal diversity of wage bargaining in any European country. As a result, the likelihood that aggressive trade unions could hold European macroeconomic policymakers hostage is only marginal. By contrast, the British government must contend with its firefighters, the French with their air-traffic controllers, and the Italians with their public transport unions. The ECB has the luxury of standing above such an affray. Wage bargaining can pose national problems more readily than European ones.

DISTRIBUTIVE CONFLICT

The problem of distributive conflict is more closely related to fiscal policy than to monetary policy. In its simplest form, government resources are limited but the demands that different groups place upon those resources are not. The motivations of these groups may be immediate (as when drought affects farmers) or they may be permanent (as with old-age pensioners). The groups may organize according to ideology or religion (as with church schools); they may represent economic sectors (export manufacturers), functional divisions (trade unions), demographic categories (retired persons), ethnic identities (minorities), social structures (single mothers), or lifestyle choices (the National Rifle Association). All that matters is, first, that such groups act collectively in order either to demand resources from the government or to resist government efforts at taxation, and second, that the government cannot satisfy all their desires at once.

This notion of distributive conflict is useful because it helps us to understand two different problems of government. First, governments may run fiscal deficits because they try to satisfy more groups than they can with available resources—borrowing from the future in order to make up the difference. Second, governments may have difficulty changing the structure of taxes and expenditures (or other regulatory benefits such as job protection legislation) because existing institutions are defended by organized groups—in what Paul Pierson has called the "new politics of the welfare state."[18] Adding these two elements together, the notion of distributive conflict also helps us to understand why governments in Europe run "structural deficits"—meaning institutionalized spending that exceeds tax resources no matter how well the economy is performing. To the extent to which such structural deficits put upward pressure on prices, distributive conflict can help us to understand the persistence of European inflation as well.

The process of convergence leading up to monetary union was designed to force member states to overcome the problems of domestic distributive conflict in order to reduce public debts and fiscal deficits and so make it possible to decrease the level and persistence of price inflation. For many countries—such as Italy—the challenge was formidable. However, the goal of participating in EMU made it possible to overcome the opposition of vested interests and to rally support around often draconian reform measures.[19] For those countries which have succeeded in becoming members, however, the threat of exclusion from the single currency is no longer relevant. All that remains is the threat of sanction by the Council of Ministers under the terms of the SGP. And while this is a serious threat, it is less imposing than exclusion from EMU. Hence it is possible to suggest that participation in the single currency has had the effect of releasing an important constraint on the management of distributive conflict.

Within the single currency, all member states have problems with conflict between vested interests. Importantly, however, these problems are all different from one country to the next. The groups that are potent in Italy, for example, are not the same as those which are powerful in Germany or Portugal. Many of the issues are similar—and relate to pensions or labor-market protection—but the constellation of political forces is different. Hence it is difficult to determine a priori which countries are likely to be most affected and when. The fact that the German government was the driving force behind the excessive deficit procedure and the Stability and Growth Pact is sufficient to suggest that any country could find itself facing a difficult battle for structural reform.

Viewing the Eurozone as a whole, however, what is striking is the diversity of distributive conflict in evidence from one member state to the next. This diversity is in part a function of the extreme decentralization of the EU as a political system. So long as the focus for government resource allocation lies at the member-state level, it will be necessary for interest groups to remain organized at the member-state level as well.[20] It is also in part a result of past commitments and past institutions that were created at the member-state level. The member states are very different in structure, so it only stands to reason that the groups that would emerge at the member-state level are different as well.[21] This diversity of conflicts across the Eurozone contrasts sharply with the relative coherence of distributive conflict within a given country. Where national politicians can persuade their electorates to support an overarching objective, such as membership in the single currency, Eurozone politicians have much greater difficulty establishing a common objective. This explains the "openness" of the

Lisbon strategy. It also explains the difficulty that macroeconomic policymakers in the Eurozone must face in encouraging structural reform. Without an overarching objective, Eurozone politicians must rely on national leaders to tackle distributive issues. And, as in Germany, it is unsurprising that many of these national leaders would have difficulty living up to the challenge.

EXCHANGE RATES

The influence of exchange rates operates in two ways: through the level (that is, through the value of the domestic currency in terms of foreign currency) and through the size and frequency of changes in that level (that is, through the volatility of the exchange rate). When the domestic currency is relatively cheap in terms of foreign currency, then export manufacturers benefit from a relative price advantage but import consumers suffer from the high cost of goods from abroad. When the domestic currency is relatively expensive in terms of foreign currency, then the calculus is reversed and export manufacturers suffer from uncompetitive prices while import consumers benefit from the low cost of goods from abroad. Finally, when the exchange rate is volatile, almost everyone suffers, except for those financial institutions that profit from selling hedging instruments.

The creation of the single currency irrevocably fixed the level of the exchange rate between participating countries and so eliminated intra-European exchange rate volatility. Some groups benefited from the levels chosen for particular countries and some suffered. However, virtually all participants gained from the elimination of volatility. This benefit is not one-sided. All groups may have lost from the inability of participating countries to alter their intra-European exchange rates in order to facilitate economic adjustment. The evidence that exchange rates are effective in promoting adjustment is disputed.[22] Nevertheless, in countries such as the United Kingdom, the bulk of academic and policy opinion is that the cost of surrendering the exchange rate as a policy instrument is potentially high.

The single currency did not eliminate the importance of external exchange rates—particularly between the dollar and the euro. Moreover, although the euro–dollar exchange rate is the same for all participating member states, the implications of that exchange rate are not. Those countries which are heavily dependent upon U.S. export markets (such as Germany) are correspondingly more vulnerable than countries that trade less with the United States (such as Austria). Similarly, member states that import most of their energy resources from outside the Eurozone (such as Italy) are more sensitive to changes in the euro–dollar exchange rate than member states that have substantial domestic supplies (such as the Netherlands). In this sense, the euro–dollar exchange rate introduces a new source of asymmetry into the economic performance of the Eurozone member states.

It would be inaccurate, however, to regard the asymmetries induced by the euro–dollar exchange rate as unique to the Eurozone. All EU member states experience this asymmetry. The difference for countries outside the Eurozone is that they must contend with movements in the exchange rate between their domestic currency and the euro as well. Here it is useful to consider the case of the United Kingdom. When the single currency began in January 1999, the pound traded at 1.45 euros and 1.64 dollars. Within two years, the euro fell dramatically against the pound while the dollar rose. On January 2, 2001, the pound stood at 1.58 euros and 1.50 dollars. By implication, British manufacturing exports to the Eurozone suffered greatly both from the cost of a strong pound and from the unexpectedness of this appreciation. This situation held constant through 2001, but it changed again in 2002. By January 2, 2003, the pound traded at 1.54 euros and 1.60 dollars.[23] However, it would be a mistake to conclude that this modest reversal in the pound–euro exchange rate could compensate for the damage done to British manufacturing over the preceding years. Not only did the industry suffer from the loss of markets and profits, but it also was forced to cut back on its investments in productive equipment, workforce training, and brand recognition. Such lasting effects of movement in the pound–euro exchange rate provide powerful ammunition for those who argue in favor of an early British entry into the single currency.

The Problem of Macroeconomic Governance

External factors such as wage bargaining, distributive conflict, and exchange rates all work to emphasize differences between the member states, both in terms of their economic structures and in relation to their macroeconomic performance. Moreover, it is unrealistic to assume that these differences will diminish over time. Such convergence was never part of the process leading up to monetary union, and it is not part of the Lisbon strategy that predominates today. The member states are different, and they should be expected to remain so. But does this difference belie the usefulness of monetary integration or of the EU's rule-based macroeconomic policy framework as a whole?

The temptation is to argue that no single rule—or collection of rules—can bind diverse political economies at the same time. Whether the focus of attention is the "one size fits all" monetary policy, the stability and growth pact, or the regulations embedded in the welfare state, the argument that different countries should follow different policies has strong intuitive appeal. Indeed that argument is the strongest arrow in the quiver of objections that the Euroskeptics in Britain have to joining the single currency.

The point to note, however, is that the rule-based framework is predicated on a series of trade-offs rather than a series of out-and-out constraints. Monetary union eliminates exchange rate volatility at the cost of a common exchange rate and a common monetary policy. Fiscal coordination eliminates policy competition between countries and between levels, but at the expense of some freedom of maneuver at the member-state level. Employment-related policies provide encouragement and inspiration (through, for example, shared best-practice standards), but at the expense of intrusive monitoring and at times politically embarrassing admonishments for poor performance. On balance, those member states participating in the single currency have accepted implicitly that the trade-offs are favorable. Even Britain embraces most of these rules despite its skepticism toward the single currency per se.

What the EU policy framework lacks is some mechanism for generating flexibility when the trade-offs implied become less favorable. After all, the rule-based system is made up of rules and it offers little opportunity for discretion over when the rules should apply. This lack of opportunity for discretion is easily explained. The member states are different, and so the trade-offs they face under the rule-based system are different as well—at least in specific terms. In general terms, the member states can agree on the need for rules and even on their constitution. But in specific terms they cannot agree on the impact at any given point in time of the common monetary policy, the 3 percent deficit rule, the coordinated drive for welfare state reform, and so on. For discretion to work, the member states must not only agree on how to amend, adapt, or avoid the rules but they must also be able to sell that discretion back to the electorates, wage negotiators, and other interest groups that are active in their home countries.

Such precise agreement is beyond the decision-making capacity of the European Union. And hence the member states are left with rules but no discretion. This regrettable impasse is still superior to the alternative of uncoordinated macroeconomic policies at the member-state level. But it is not the *optimum optimorum*. The European Commission president, Romano Prodi, made this concession explicitly in a much-misunderstood interview that he held with the French newspaper *Le Monde*. Essentially he argued that the EU framework for macroeconomic policy coordination is "stupid" because it affords no intelligent discretion. Yet he insisted that the framework is necessary. The relevant part of his interview is translated in Box 3.3.

If the EU is to make its macroeconomic policy framework more intelligent and less "stupid," then it will have to institutionalize some mechanisms for discretion over the rules. This is more challenging than it seems. And as the European Union expands to include the countries of Central and Eastern Europe, it will become only more challenging still. This is the problem of macroeconomic governance, and it will remain at the center of political debate in Europe for the foreseeable future.

Box 3.3   An Interview with Romano Prodi

October 18, 2002

Question: The French Minister of the Economy, Francis Mer, has said that budgetary politics should be decided in the [national] capitols. What do you think?

Prodi: With the euro, if you have economic divergences between countries, it is not possible to modify interest rates or to devalue the currency. In that context, the idea of having different economic policies is completely crazy. When you have the same money, you can have different inflation rates for one year but not for three or four years. The stability pact is the means for being together in the same currency.

Question: Should the stability pact evolve with growth?

Prodi: But we have proposed new flexibility in putting off from 2004 to 2006 the date for balancing public finances, and in asking in return that the member states reduce their structural deficits by 0.5 percent of GDP per annum. It is not possible to have diverging policies. I am convinced that the coordination of economic policies will soon be desired by all member states. But the reality today is the stability pact. We have made it more intelligent. But if there is not a limit of 3 percent on public deficits, we will not be able to avoid large uncontrolled increases in public deficits.

Question: Before the euro, a country with little discipline endured a rise in interest rates and risked a devaluation of its currency. Today, who is the policeman in the system?

Prodi: It is the coordination of economic policies, it is the stability pact. That is the minimum of the minimum. The stability pact is imperfect, that is true, because we should have a tool that is more intelligent and more flexible, but you know well that if you want flexibility and intelligence, you need authority.

Question: Do you have it?

Prodi: No, that is clear that no, no one has the authority. That is the problem.

Question: The financial markets no longer have the authority?

Prodi: Yes. In the euro, it is not logical to have the direction without having the guide to follow it. We cannot have a Europe that is flourishing, strong, and growing, without the power to adjust its decisions according to the times. I know very well that the stability pact is stupid, like all decisions that are rigid. If we want to adjust it, we need unanimity, and that does not work. The intelligence that we have is insufficient. We also need the power to decide.

Source: Interview by Arnaud Leparmentier and Laurent Zecchini, "La France sera en minorité si elle n'est pas le levain de l'Europe," *Le Monde*, October 18, 2002 (author's translation).

Notes

I would like to thank Julien Halfon for his help on the translations. The usual disclaimer applies.

1. This chapter is a "second edition" in the sense that it adds to the discussion provided in the first *Europe Today*. See Erik Jones, "The Politics of Monetary Union," in Ronald Tiersky, ed., *Europe Today: National Politics, Integration, and European Security* (Lanham, Md.: Rowman & Littlefield), 273–303. For a more comprehensive treatment of these arguments, see Erik Jones, *The Politics of Economic and Monetary Union: Integration and Idiosyncrasy* (Lanham, Md.: Rowman & Littlefield, 2002).

2. See, for example, Erik Jones, "Liberalized Capital Markets, State Autonomy, and European Monetary Union," *European Journal of Political Research* 42, no. 2 (March 2003): 111–36.

3. See, for example, the exchange between Willem Buiter, "Alice in Euroland," *Journal of Common Market Studies* 37, no. 2 (June 1999): 181–209, and Otmar Issing, "The Eurosystem: Transparent and Accountable or 'Willem in Euroland'?" *Journal of Common Market Studies* 37, no. 3 (September): 503–19. The comments attributed to Duisenberg are recurrent and can be found in his monthly press conferences, which are reproduced at www. *ecb.int.*

4. The ECB press conference cited here was held on 8 April 1999.

5. ECB press conference, 5 December 2002.

6. In the jargon of the European Union, the terms "economic" and "fiscal" are often used as close synonyms. Hence, economic policy is fiscal policy. I have followed that usage here.

7. The relevant composition for the Council of Ministers here includes those ministers of economics and finance—the ECOFIN Council. When only those ministers for member states participating in the Eurozone are in attendance, this organization is referred to as the "Eurogroup." Importantly, the Eurogroup does not have the same legislative authority as held by the ECOFIN Council and so acts only informally to coordinate the positions of the Eurozone countries within ECOFIN. In my analysis here, I have tried to avoid excessive specificity in this area and refer instead only to the "Council." Readers looking for a more institutionally detailed account should consult Chapter 2 of Jones, *The Politics of Economic and Monetary Union.*

8. The first citation is taken from Article 99, Paragraph 1 of the TEC. The second refers to Article 104, Paragraph 1. The third citation is taken from the "Resolution of the European Council on the Stability and Growth Pact" in European Council, "Amsterdam European Council, 16 and 17 June 1997—Presidency Conclusions," Brussels: European Council Secretariat SN 150/97 (June 17, 1997), Annex 1, p. 4.

9. The citation is taken from the "Protocol on the Excessive Deficit Procedure," Article 1.

10. The citation is taken from the minutes of the 2,329th Council meeting dated 12 February 2001. These minutes are hosted on the Council's website and can be accessed through the principal gateway for the European Union at *europa.eu.int.*

11. See, for example, Christopher Pierson, Anthony Forster, and Erik Jones, "The Politics of Europe: (Un)Employment Ambivalence," in *Industrial Relations Journal:*

European Annual Review 1997, ed. Brian Towers and Michael Terry (Oxford: Blackwell, 1998), 5–22.

12. Dermot Hodson and Imelda Maher, "The Open Method as a New Form of Governance: The Case of Soft Economic Policy Coordination," *Journal of Common Market Studies* 39, no. 4 (November 2001): 719–46.

13. David P. Calleo, *The Bankrupting of America: How the Federal Deficit Is Impoverishing the Nation* (New York: William Morrow, 1992).

14. Erik Jones, "Economic and Monetary Union: Playing for Money," in *Centralization or Fragmentation? Europe before the Challenges of Deepening, Diversity, and Democracy*, ed. Andrew Moravcsik (Washington, D.C.: Brookings Press for the Council on Foreign Relations, 1998), 59–93.

15. Paul Marginson and Thorsten Schulten, "The Europeanization of Collective Bargaining," *European Industrial Relations Observer* TN9907201S (28 July 1999) [www.eiro.eurofound.ie].

16. Peter A. Hall, "Central Bank Independence and Coordinated Wage Bargaining: Their Interaction in Germany and Europe," *German Politics and Society* 31 (Spring 1994): 1–23.

17. Erik Jones, Jeffry Frieden, and Francisco Torres, eds., *Joining Europe's Monetary Club: The Challenges for Smaller Member States* (New York: St. Martin's Scholarly and Reference, 1998).

18. Paul Pierson, "The New Politics of the Welfare State," *World Politics* 48, no. 2 (January 1996): 143–79.

19. James I. Walsh, "Political Bases of Macroeconomic Adjustment: Evidence from the Italian Experience," *Journal of European Public Policy* 6, no. 1 (March 1999): 66–84.

20. Simon Hix takes the opposite view and argues that the EU and the European Parliament are developing as coherent systems for resources allocation and therefore also for distributive conflict (or distributive politics). See, for example, Simon Hix, *The Political System of the European Union* (Basingstoke: Palgrave, 1999). Even were I to concede this point, however, it would still remain true that the EU as a political system suffers from more diverse forms of distributive conflict than any of the member states.

21. Erik Jones, "Idiosyncrasy and Integration: Suggestions from Comparative Political Economy," *Journal of European Public Policy* 10, no. 1 (February 2003): 141–59.

22. Daniel Gros, "External Shocks and Labor Mobility: How Important Are They for EMU?" in *The New Political Economy of EMU*, ed. Jeffry Frieden, Daniel Gros, and Erik Jones (Lanham, Md.: Rowman & Littlefield, 1998), 53–82.

23. These exchange rate data are available for download from the Bank of England at *bankofengland.co.uk*.

Suggestions for Further Reading

Crouch, Colin, ed. *After the Euro*. Oxford: Oxford University Press, 2000.

Dyson, Kenneth. *The Politics of the Euro-Zone: Stability or Breakdown?* Oxford: Oxford University Press, 2000.

Dyson, Kenneth, ed. *European States and the Euro: Europeanization, Variation, and Convergence*. Oxford: Oxford University Press, 2002.

Howarth, David, and Peter Loedel. *The European Central Bank: The New European Leviathan?* Basingstoke, UK: Palgrave, 2003.

Kaelberer, Matthias. "Ideas, Interests, and Institutions: The Domestic Politics of European Monetary Cooperation." *Comparative Politics* 35, no. 1 (October, 2002): 105–23.

CHAPTER 4

NATO

European Security and Beyond?

Jeffrey Simon and Sean Kay

NATO's Twenty-First-Century Challenges

On September 12, 2001, the nineteen European and North American members of the North Atlantic Treaty Organization (NATO) declared the terrorist attacks against New York City and Washington, D.C., as an attack on them all. These political ties that bind NATO members are the essence of this multipurpose European security institution. However, despite this political statement of unity in the face of new threats, NATO's operational utility for managing such new and severe threats has been increasingly questioned. Could the institution maintain its ongoing post–Cold War adaptation while simultaneously assuming a new and broader mission of counterterrorism? For the United States, NATO's key member, it initially seemed that the answer was no—as Washington failed to utilize offers of military assistance from its European allies in the war in Afghanistan. Indeed, under the administration of U.S. president George Bush, the United States seemed to be increasingly moving away from binding multilateral commitments. Meanwhile, low defense investment in Europe, combined with a growing political role for the European Union as an alternative to NATO, raised questions about the strength of the transatlantic partnership. Consequently, when its heads of state met in Prague in November 2002, NATO's relevance seemed to rest in the balance. Concerns about NATO's future were hardened during the deep transatlantic rift that emerged over the 2003 Iraq war.

NATO is a political-military institution that serves the security interests of its member states, which by 1999 included the United States, Canada, and seventeen European countries. In November 2002, NATO invited seven additional countries to negotiate membership, raising the total number of NATO allies to twenty-six. NATO's core function is collective defense; in principle, any aggression against a member state would be seen as an attack against all members. This underlying purpose is bolstered by multilateral political consultation, military planning, and exercises.

NATO's origins lie in the beginning of the Cold War as it was founded in

April 1949 in response to the Soviet domination of Eastern Europe. Over time, the alliance served three main functions: engaging the United States in European security, protecting against the Soviet-led Warsaw Pact in the east, and integrating postwar (and post–Cold War) Germany into the western community of nations. With the end of the Cold War, NATO was looked to by its members, and by nonmembers as well, as the core foundation of a new institutional design for European security cooperation. Subsequently, NATO has played a critical role in shattering the artificial division of Europe drawn at the end of World War II.

After the end of the Cold War, NATO served to promote transparency in multilateral defense planning, civilian control of the military in Central and Eastern Europe, and peace operations in the Balkans, and to integrate Russia and Ukraine into western concepts of international security. NATO also deals with new security challenges such as the proliferation of weapons of mass destruction.

While basic theory of international relations would predict that, as an alliance, NATO would disappear in the absence of a threat, the combined values and institutional mechanisms of cooperation have served to sustain NATO. NATO persists because its member states have continued to see a shared interest in both sustaining and adapting its institutional functions. Institutions should change when the reasons that gave birth to them change. A military alliance should change when the threat facing it changes. In the early twenty-first century, Europe emerged as one of the most peaceful continents on earth. Nevertheless, Europe also has found itself challenged by a new era of instability, with fragile democratic transition in the east combined with rapid and often destabilizing economic transitions from communist to free-market economies to challenge the sustainability of democracy in central and eastern Europe. Horrific ethnic cleansing in the Balkans propelled NATO into an assertive peacekeeping operation in Bosnia-Herzegovina and eventually into its first war over Kosovo in 1999.

NATO's first decade of transition was far from complete when the general threat perception changed radically after the terrorist attacks on New York City and Washington, D.C., on September 11, 2001. NATO already had a full agenda, including its plans for ongoing enlargement. However, NATO was now challenged to meet a new threat to the collective defense of its members—international terrorism, possibly operating eventually with weapons of mass destruction. If the NATO members carefully calibrate their security strategies by building on the decades of trust and cooperation established in the transatlantic relationship, then the institution can once again effectively adapt to new security challenges. However, if not carefully managed, NATO risks a significant challenge to its relevance. This chapter assesses NATO's post–Cold War transformation by surveying NATO's efforts to stabilize the East, engage in the Balkans, and restructure to meet the new security challenges of the twenty-first century.

Stabilizing the East

Since the fall of the Berlin wall and the expansion of democratic revolutions throughout central and eastern Europe, NATO members have consistently sought to utilize multilateral institutional mechanisms to meet emerging post–Cold War security challenges. For NATO, this meant extending the "hand of friendship" to former Warsaw Pact countries—and implementing its first post–Cold War enlargement with the former German Democratic Republic (East Germany) integrating with the Federal Republic of Germany (West Germany). As a result of German unification, NATO's area of responsibility quickly extended eastward—and thus so did NATO's interest in the countries to Germany's east increase. Because East Germany was virtually collapsed into the West, its membership in NATO became an obvious outcome and was eventually accepted by the Soviet Union as a prerequisite for German unification. The essential role of NATO as the critical mechanism of ensuring that the growing power of Germany would be locked within western institutions was established.

Nevertheless, stabilizing German unification would be only a first step for NATO's post–Cold War adaptation. Quickly recognizing that the positive geopolitical dynamics of the collapse of the Soviet Union, the dissolution of the Warsaw Pact, and the end of the Cold War could be lost if the region were subsumed with instability, NATO embarked on a gradual process of extending its multilateral institutional functions to include nonmembers to the east. Initially, NATO focused on building a relationship with other international institutions, such as the Organization for Security and Cooperation in Europe (OSCE). As the only European institution that included literally all the states ranging from Vancouver to Vladivostok, the OSCE was seen as a useful mechanism for building cooperative relationships to the east without simultaneously creating a sense of encirclement around Russia. Nonetheless, the OSCE was a largely toothless organization—a security institution with few organizational attributes that stressed broad principles and norms of international relations but had no enforcement mechanisms. While the OSCE would, over time, eventually undertake very important grassroots efforts to promote stability throughout eastern Europe, it was not a satisfactory mechanism for managing the major challenges confronting post–Cold War Europe.

For the countries of eastern Europe, emerging from the shadow of communism and returning to Europe both in terms of their political identity and security commitments became a dominant factor of international relations in the 1990s. Absent any better alternative, countries ranging from the Baltic to the Black Sea began pressuring NATO to establish direct relationships with them—

eventually including membership. NATO's early response was intellectually ambitious but operationally gradual. NATO began in 1991 by establishing the North Atlantic Cooperation Council (NACC). A U.S. initiative, the NACC was a new institution of consultation and cooperation on political and security issues open to all of the newly independent members of the Warsaw Pact. The NACC states consult on issues including national defense planning, principles and key aspects of strategy, force and command structures, military exercises, management, and the conversion of defense production to civilian purposes.

While symbolically important, the NACC never achieved the operational utility that its advocates had hoped for. Indeed, the NACC quickly lost effectiveness when it became clear how the sheer number of states present would hinder decision making even at the consultative level. At an NACC ministerial meeting in Istanbul, Turkey, in June 1994, for example, the Russian delegation haggled for five hours over the language of the final communiqué, to forestall discussion of the question of NATO enlargement.

Meanwhile, key NATO members began to consider enlarging the alliance. This was rejected by the U.S. administration under President George Bush and then, at first, by President Bill Clinton.

Germany was the first NATO member to advocate enlargement. In 1993, German officials—particularly Minister of Defense Volker Ruhe—quietly pushed NATO to open its membership as a way to stabilize both Germany's eastern border and the economies of the region. The idea was now greeted favorably by some American officials.

However, major bureaucratic opposition remained. Senior State Department officials were concerned about strong Russian opposition. Officials from the Department of Defense and Joint Chiefs of Staff worried about the risk of military dilution by bringing in, too fast, countries that were not prepared to be contributors to alliance security as well as the collective defense worries in an expanded membership. Other concerns focused on the costs of enlargement and the impact on NATO's decision making. Could an institution that makes its official decisions by unanimous consensus work effectively with as many as ten new members?

Nonetheless, the compelling arguments for NATO enlargement would persist. Three counted most heavily: filling a strategic void between the rising power of Germany and the declining power of Russia; linking NATO membership to political, economic, and diplomatic reform; and expanding American engagement in European security.

The divergence between risks and benefits of enlargement forced an alliance-wide compromise in 1994—the so-called Partnership for Peace (PFP). The PFP was approved by the NATO heads of state meeting in Brussels in January 1994 and was utilized to delay enlargement—out of deference to Russia and because of the lack of preparedness among candidate countries—while creating a functional means by which countries could associate with NATO to the degree they wished, short of receiving direct security guarantees. For those countries seeking NATO membership, the PFP would be the road map to guide them in that direction. PFP became an extremely important tool for shaping the post–Cold War security environment in central and eastern Europe, because the program required participants to adhere to the protection and promotion of fundamental freedoms and human rights and the safeguarding of freedom, justice, and peace through democracy. Operationally, the PFP allowed participating countries to identify ways in which they could work with NATO and what assets they might contribute to joint planning for noncollective defense missions such as peacekeeping and other forms of crisis management. Through a planning and review process, participating states would work to develop NATO-compatible methods and procedures and toward developing interoperability for various kinds of noncollective defense NATO operations.

Those countries most enthusiastic about joining NATO initially saw the PFP as a "policy for postponement." Only direct assurances from Washington that the PFP could lead to eventual membership in NATO encouraged investment of resources in the program by partners. Yet the PFP became a success that went far beyond initial expectations, growing to include nearly thirty individual partnership programs. These partnerships with NATO have been formed with a diverse group of countries—from the former Soviet republics and former Yugoslavia to former Warsaw Pact and neutral states as well. Eventually, even Russia saw value in the PFP and joined in 1995—although only after considerable prodding by the United States and NATO.

NATO Enlargement

By 1997, a number of central and eastern European countries were being seriously considered for membership in NATO, with Poland, Hungary, and the Czech Republic emerging as the consensus candidates to be invited at a summit held at Madrid, Spain. NATO enlargement was an important, and logical, extension of the adaptation already under way within NATO since the end of the Cold War. In retrospect, NATO's first historic success was overseeing and guaranteeing the reconciliation between Europe's two former great adversaries—Germany and France. By providing a secure environment for these longstanding rivals, NATO helped facilitate European economic union, which has proceeded to a point where it is unthinkable that these two countries could go to war. Beyond this first political reconciliation, NATO's institutionalization of transparent defense budgeting and force planning; common defense resources management; and communications, command, and interoperability standards also have contributed mightily to building confidence and security among European allies. The secular European battleground largely has been pacified. Even the smaller NATO members—such as the Netherlands, Belgium,

Luxembourg, Denmark, and Norway—today feel more secure in the shadow of their large German neighbor because of NATO. Thus, at a strategic level, NATO enlargement helps alleviate concerns over relative German strength and about historical fears of Russia.

NATO's great challenge for the opening of the twenty-first century is to expand that zone of confidence, security, and stability to Europe's eastern half through enlargement. Indeed, by enlarging, NATO is fulfilling a founding mission, as Article 10 of the NATO treaty states: "The Parties may, by unanimous agreement, invite any other European state in a position to further the principles of the Treaty and to contribute to the security of the North Atlantic Area to accede to this Treaty."

NATO has indeed enlarged a number of times. During the original treaty negotiations in 1948, the core group of the United States, Canada, and Great Britain grew to include France, Belgium, Luxembourg, and the Netherlands. This group then added Italy, Portugal, Denmark, Norway, and Iceland as founding members. Following the treaty signing in 1949, NATO enlarged three more times, adding Greece and Turkey (1952), West Germany (1954), and Spain (1982). Generally, Cold War enlargement was based on pragmatic strategic criteria and had little to do with advancing any specific principles other than collective defense. For example, strategically located Portugal, despite being under Salazar's dictatorship, was allowed to join NATO at its foundation in 1949. Spain, ruled by another dictator, Franco, was left out because of European objections, but it still benefited from a unilateral U.S. security commitment. Greece underwent a coup in the 1960s, which NATO did nothing to prevent or end, and Turkey has witnessed repeated extraconstitutional changes of government and suppression of minority populations. Nonetheless, it can be argued that the fact that such members were able to remain in NATO was a matter of choosing between bad and worse at the same time. The overriding necessity was the immediate task of remaining firm against the security dangers of communist pressure.

Nevertheless, the post–Cold War political and strategic environment provided an atmosphere in which NATO could be used more effectively both as a strategic tool and as a vehicle for spreading the principles that had come to represent the core foundations of the West. NATO's path to enlargement was gradual, transparent, and ultimately a largely political process, with minimal attention paid to the military requirements. In 1995, NATO began the process by completing a formal study explaining the "how and why" of enlargement. Members agreed that enlargement should be used for:

1. encouraging and supporting democratic reforms, including civilian and democratic control over the military;
2. fostering in new members of the alliance the patterns and habits of cooperation, consultation, and consensus building that characterize relations among current allies;

3. promoting good-neighborly relations, which would benefit all countries in the Euro-Atlantic area, both members and nonmembers of NATO;

4. emphasizing common defense and extending its benefits and increasing transparency in defense planning and military budgets, thereby reducing the likelihood of instability that might be engendered by an exclusively national approach to defense policies;

5. reinforcing the tendency toward integration and cooperation in Europe based on shared democratic values and thereby curbing the countervailing tendency toward disintegration along ethnic and territorial lines;

6. strengthening the alliance's ability to contribute to European and international security, including through peacekeeping activities under the responsibility of the OSCE and peacekeeping operations under the authority of the United Nations Security Council, as well as other new missions; and

7. strengthening and broadening the transatlantic relationship.

New NATO members would be expected to conform to the purposes and principles of the Charter of the United Nations, and the safeguarding of the freedom, common heritage, and civilization of all alliance members and their rule of law.

According to NATO, enlargement would avoid drawing new divisions in Europe after the Cold War, and thus a NATO-Russia relationship was expected to form another cornerstone of a new, inclusive, and comprehensive security structure in Europe. NATO concluded that integration into NATO would be costly and burdensome. However, it also noted that there would be no a priori requirement for the stationing of either conventional forces from current NATO countries or nuclear weapons on the territory of new members in the existing security environment. New members would both contribute to, and receive, full Article 5 benefits of collective defense. However, in the absence of pre-deployed troops, collective defense would be provided by a reinforcement of nation-state forces, thus making the decision to implement security guarantees highly political and contextual rather than automatic. On the other hand, no candidate country for NATO membership faced any serious conventional external security threat during the 1990s.

During this same period, the United States shaped alliance consensus toward enlargement by articulating its own priorities for membership criteria. President Bill Clinton's speeches and Secretary of Defense William Perry's "five principles" emphasized that new members should conform to basic political principles: democracy and the rule of law; economic liberty and free markets; OSCE norms concerning treatment of ethnic minorities and social justice; resolution of territorial disputes on the basis of good neighbor relations; and democratic, civilian control of the military. Because NATO does not have a procedural mechanism for sanctioning or expelling a member whose democracy fails, civilian control over the armed forces would be a critical component of NATO membership. Officially, the NATO enlargement study defined "effective" democratic control of the military as transparent defense planning, resource allocation and budgeting, and parliamentary and public accountability, adding the stipulation of some level of military capability and NATO interoperability. Thus, for NATO enlargement to succeed, the organization would have to use a calculated incentives-based approach to affect relations both among states and within them.

These principles and the various practical rewards of both the Partnership for Peace and NATO enlargement have contributed to post-communist political reform and international stability among the former Warsaw Pact countries of central and eastern Europe. The prospect of NATO membership has provided building blocks for developing genuine mutual confidence and geopolitical security in this region. At the same time, the political basis of NATO's enlargement contributes to a general sense of European stability, which is also in the interests of a stable, democratic, and west-leaning Russia. Similar to the historic Franco-German reconciliation, Europe has seen an equally significant historic rapprochement between Poland and Germany—solving Russia's traditional concerns over relative German power and ambitions to its east. This has been embedded in a treaty agreeing upon borders, trade, and combined Polish-German military activities and cooperation. Poland, in turn, has expanded this new zone of European confidence-building and security to Lithuania and Ukraine, with the Polish-Lithuanian and Polish-Ukrainian militaries working together. Russian and Polish officials mutually acknowledge that their bilateral relationships have improved significantly since Poland joined NATO. A few other examples nurtured by NATO enlargement include treaties between Hungary and Slovakia and between Hungary and Romania. These treaties not only recognize existing borders but also establish principles for the treatment of ethnic minorities. In fall 2002, voters in Slovakia voted resoundingly against a political party headed by an authoritarian ruler whose leadership would have eliminated Slovakia's prospects for NATO membership.

In July 1997 NATO invited Poland, Hungary, and the Czech Republic to negotiate membership in NATO, and they entered as NATO members in March 1999—just ahead of NATO's fiftieth anniversary. The decision to limit the first round of NATO membership to these three most democratic and prosperous countries to the east was not without controversy. A majority of European states had lobbied hard for Romania and Slovenia to be included as well. Moreover, in spite of their political credentials, the three invitees were not well prepared at the military level to uphold the serious commitments that they would be making as NATO members to the collective interests of the organization. Perhaps most significantly, NATO needed a means of assuaging concerns from the remaining "failed suitors" who had not received invitations as a way to keep their reform programs on track. Consequently, NATO promised to keep the door to future membership open and specifically mentioned Romania,

Slovenia, and the three Baltic countries of Lithuania, Latvia, and Estonia as serious candidates for future membership. NATO promised to review membership criteria and in April 1999 began an aggressive review process of aspirants' candidacies through a NATO "Membership Action Program" (MAP), which would include country reports to NATO on efforts states were making to meet membership criteria and analysis from NATO, in response, on their progress to date.

NATO would thus have the experience of the first round of NATO membership enlargement to judge future rounds by, in addition to the information and experiences gained via the MAP. In terms of NATO's initial experience with Poland, Hungary, and the Czech Republic, the early track record was not promising. Each of these new members experienced significant and ongoing integration difficulties. Each shared a common burden of a Warsaw Pact culture, and each inherited inappropriate armed forces that were too large and equipment-heavy, had decaying Soviet military technology, and needed to reduce infrastructure. To varying degrees, Poland, Hungary, and the Czech Republic have each failed to implement their defense investment and budgetary goals that were initially promised to NATO upon their membership ratification. This has been especially true in Hungary, where NATO officials privately lectured officials in Budapest as to their responsibilities in being NATO members. In addition to their budgetary shortcomings, all three new NATO members have had significant planning failures and problems in restructuring their military personnel, have encountered difficulties in establishing an effective division of executive and parliamentary relationships with the military, and have failed to produce real-world national security concepts in defining force requirements. Consequently, all three countries have shown major incompatibilities between their national planning processes and those of NATO. Basic obstacles, such as the lack of English-language-trained personnel, have proven very difficult to overcome. For each new member, these difficulties have been compounded by a general public decline in public/social support for the military as a national institution.

For NATO, the most important first-round lesson has been that, as an institution, NATO exerts leverage on states only when they are aspiring to NATO membership. Once a country joins NATO, the incentive to invest in capabilities and demonstrate a capacity to contribute to collective interests quickly diminishes. Since 1999, the MAP experience suggests even more serious challenges lie ahead for NATO as it integrates seven new countries following the 2002 Prague Summit. Rather than move in a slow, step-by-step process based on a careful assessment of membership criteria, NATO chose a large-end political option of inviting Estonia, Latvia, Lithuania, Slovakia, Slovenia, Romania, and Bulgaria. Despite the grandiose nature of NATO's ongoing enlargement, the problems begin when one considers that all of the invitees are substantially weaker than NATO's three new members. While Romania and

Bulgaria offered substantial territorial and geostrategic gains for NATO, they were the weakest in terms of political and economic stability. Meanwhile, Estonia, Latvia, Lithuania, and Slovenia offer very little in terms of military or geostrategic gains, but they are the most politically and economically advanced of the new members.

The functional contributions of the new NATO allies can be summarized in the following way:

Bulgaria: With a population of 7.9 million people, Bulgaria has an active armed force of 68,450 personnel and spends 2.8 percent of GDP annually on defense. Nevertheless, Bulgaria's armed forces are in serious need of modernization and professionalization. Bulgaria's primary contribution to NATO will be its strategic location on the Balkan peninsula and as a bridge to Turkey and the Black Sea. Despite its geostrategic benefits, Bulgaria is not at the expected level of political and economic standards for NATO membership. Bulgaria has to reform its intelligence apparatus to ensure the safe-keeping of secrets within the NATO intelligence-sharing process.

Estonia: With a population of 1.4 million people, Estonia has an active armed force of 5,510 and defense spending set at 1.7 percent of GDP. Estonia has minimal contributions to bring to NATO, and its primary asset is its relative political and economic success among former Soviet republics. Estonia lacks transparency in appointments to public posts and continues to have tensions with its Russian minority—especially in terms of needing to naturalize its ethnic-Russian citizens.

Latvia: With a population of 2.4 million people and an active armed force of 5,500, Latvia spends about 1.2 percent of its GDP on defense. Latvia has more to do in tackling corruption and has problems with guaranteeing the security of intelligence-sharing capabilities in NATO.

Lithuania: With a population of 3.75 million, Lithuania has an active armed force of 13,510 and spends 1.8 percent of its GDP on defense. Lithuania continues to struggle with defense reforms but offers a strategic benefit as extending the west toward Ukraine. Lithuania's main contribution is its relative success, among post-Soviet states, in political and economic reform.

Romania: With a population of 22.5 million, an active armed force of 99,200, and defense spending at 2.5 percent of GDP, Romania brings significant military capabilities to NATO. Furthermore, its geostrategic location on the Black Sea and border with Ukraine further enhance Romania's geostrategic contributions. Romania has also sent considerable international forces (400) to Afghanistan. Nevertheless, Romania is not at NATO's political and economic standards for membership. Additionally, Romania has significant ongoing challenges in reforming its intelligence apparatus to ensure the protection of intelligence-sharing within NATO.

Slovakia: With a population of about 5.4 million, Slovakia has an active armed force of 26,200 and spends about 2 percent of GDP on defense. Slovakia serves as a land-bridge to Hungary and also further extends the west to the Ukrainian border. Slovakia's membership invitation had been placed in some doubt by the possibility of a return to government of its authoritarian former prime minister, Vladimir Meciar, in September 2002. Meciar was defeated but did still gain considerable popular support. Slovakia also has lagged behind economically and needs to pursue an active antifraud drive, fight money laundering, and discourage discrimination against its Roma minority.

Slovenia: Slovenia has a population of 2 million people and an active armed force of about 4,000, with defense spending at about 1.5 percent of GDP. Slovenia has sought to specialize its armed forces for special forces operation as well as alpine activity. It also offers a land-bridge to Hungary and might help project stability into the Balkan region. Slovenia's main dilemma as a new NATO member is very low public support for its membership which, prior to its invitation, rarely rose far above 40 percent.

Slovenia illustrates the dilemma for NATO. Slovenia's primary strategic value to NATO would be to serve as a land-bridge to Hungary and at the same time demonstrate a positive future for former Yugoslav states. However, despite its recent Yugoslav heritage, Slovenia is for all practical purposes a very central European state. Its population of 2 million people sees virtually no external security threat. Consequently, its leaders have devoted very little interest, energy, or resources to defense. Public support for NATO membership rarely rose above 40 percent before the Prague invitations. When U.S. president George Bush suggested to the leadership of Slovenia in summer 2001 that they needed to do more to invest in defense capabilities, the Slovene leadership responded that they would not be pressured and that NATO membership was not that important to them. Realizing that NATO membership had become a mostly political activity, the Slovenian leadership had every reason to expect that they could gain admission to NATO with as little actual effort as possible beyond a good public relations package. Yet for all of its weaknesses as an ally, Slovenia will have a fully weighted capacity to impact NATO decision making.

Ultimately, NATO enlargement has played a critical strategic role in helping maintain a western orientation among central and eastern European states and facilitating a bridge to Russia. NATO enlargement has not run its course, but as a major intellectual issue the act of enlargement has lost its initial controversy. Now, larger questions arise as to whether enlargement to the east dilutes

NATO's military effectiveness, complicates NATO's already complex decision-making procedures, and thereby risks accelerating an American withdrawal from European security. Meanwhile, there remain states in Europe that are out of NATO's security sphere but would likely benefit most from actual security guarantees—Albania, Macedonia, and Georgia. Indeed, these three countries, plus Croatia and Ukraine, remain official candidates for NATO membership. Larger-end questions about the future role of security outliers such as Belarus and the integration of Serbia and Montenegro into Western institutions, and—significantly—the future role of Russia in NATO, remain to be permanently settled. It would be ironic if, in the end, the result of NATO enlargement were to be a military dilution of NATO, institutional ineffectiveness, and a diminution of American engagement in European security—all historically long-term Russian strategic objectives.

NATO and the Balkans

While NATO's role in reaching out to the east via the Partnership for Peace and enlargement was a steady and carefully crafted approach, NATO's ride through the Balkans has been anything but stable and has often been highly inconsistent. Nevertheless, NATO can claim extraordinary accomplishments in meeting the most immediate and clear threat to European stability since the end of the Cold War. But as with NATO enlargement, it might be that NATO's reach into the Balkans went further than the institution was prepared to manage effectively. In Kosovo, NATO might have fought its first—and last—war. Doubts about the future of NATO have been growing ever since. Some concerns are legitimate, while others often ignore the major contributions that NATO has made to international peace and stability in the Balkans. Like NATO enlargement, the Balkans engagement has been primarily a test of the values that NATO seeks to represent. The ultimate challenge for the organization, however, now lies in whether or not the institution has reached past the point where it can sustain its core geostrategic foundations.

NATO's post–Cold War institutional engagement of eastern Europe via partnership and enlargement was largely successful on its own merit. However, by 1995 this adaptation was fundamentally challenged by war in the Balkans, which at this stage had included wars in the former Yugoslav republics of Slovenia, Croatia, and, most significantly, Bosnia-Herzegovina. In 1992, NATO began a process of developing peacekeeping capabilities and rapid reaction forces while signaling threats toward the warring parties in the region. In practice, however, there was no consensus on how and when to use military power. By early 1993, the leading European nations and the United States were using political action in institutions as a feeble substitute for taking responsibility to intervene in a conflict that most likely could have been resolved much sooner than it was.

The western states were well-intentioned in seeking to limit the conflict and at least prevent it from spreading to neighboring states. Nevertheless, at times international organizations—including NATO—became obstacles to ending the Balkan war. For example, the United Nations imposed an arms embargo on all parties in the former Yugoslavia in 1991. Enforced by NATO, the embargo exacerbated an imbalance of power favoring aggressive Serb forces (which had inherited most of the military apparatus of the Yugoslav National Army), allowing them to make territorial gains against Muslims and Croats and carry out a policy of "ethnic cleansing"—or more accurately, genocide. In the United States, there was significant support to lift the embargo—even unilaterally if necessary. However, lifting the arms embargo became politically impossible once the UN had deployed peacekeepers on the ground in 1992. Contributing states, particularly NATO members Britain and France, worried that their troops would get caught up in increased fighting if more weapons flowed into the region. Because they had a veto in the institutions that were responsible for managing the crisis, the result was institutional paralysis.

NATO remained supportive of UN humanitarian efforts and agreed to enforce a no-fly zone over the region. By 1994, the NATO mission in Bosnia-Herzegovina included protection of heavy weapons exclusion zones and so-called safe havens for civilians around major population centers. Yet, rather than guaranteeing safety, these areas became military targets as Serb artillery shells dealt out death and destruction with impunity.

By 1995, its members gradually increased NATO's operational role in the Balkans. The United States advocated a "robust" use of NATO air power against violators of UN resolutions combined with a lifting of the arms embargo against the Bosnian Muslims, but European countries with forces on the ground continued to block those proposals. When in May 1995, NATO did launch a more assertive bombing campaign against Serb ammunition depots, Serb forces responded by taking several hundred peacekeepers hostage—even chaining some to likely NATO bombing targets. By summer of 1995, NATO appeared on the verge of complete ineffectiveness.

Refusing to let NATO be a victim of the Bosnian war, the United States gained consensus for a bold action plan among the NATO allies beginning in July 1995. On August 28, Bosnian Serbs shelled Sarajevo once more, killing thirty-nine civilians. NATO responded with Operation Deliberate Force in early September. This was a major air campaign with narrow political objectives: to end the shelling of Sarajevo, to open the airport and the roads around Sarajevo for safe transit, to remove all Serb heavy weapons from a 12.5-mile radius around Sarajevo, and to deter attacks on other safe havens. The air power, along with Muslim and Croat territorial gains, pushed the Bosnian Serbs toward a negotiated settlement—formalized later that fall at the Dayton peace conference sponsored by the five-power contact group (the United States, Great Britain, France, Germany, and Russia).

The preconditions for peace in Bosnia-Herzegovina, however, went deeper than NATO's engagement. There had been dramatic shifts in the balance of power on the ground, and the Yugoslav patrons of the Bosnian Serbs in Belgrade needed to gain favor with the west to end devastating UN economic sanctions. Most importantly, NATO's limited air campaign complemented what emerged as a major Croat-Muslim ground offensive, which rapidly overturned many Serb territorial gains. The combined NATO air power and Croat-Muslim ground offensive proved sufficient to bring the Serbs to negotiate a peace. The Dayton accord—which created an integrated federal state of Bosnia-Herzegovina —depended on NATO's earlier institutional planning to provide for a climate of peace. Without strong and credible peacekeeping forces in place, the agreement might have unraveled. Rapid deployment was necessary to reassure the Muslims and Croats, who feared that the Bosnian Serbs might negotiate a cease-fire only to regroup in the hope that the Serb-led Yugoslavia would intervene and annex eastern Bosnia in the name of "Greater Serbia." Such Serb actions might have prompted Croatia to annex western Bosnia.

The peace in Bosnia-Herzegovina was less than perfect, and NATO members were especially reluctant to take risks in hunting down indicted war criminals—a necessary precondition for a lasting peace. Indeed, there is a strong possibility that any removal of international peacekeepers from Bosnia-Herzegovina could lead to a new round of violence and war. Nonetheless, NATO's intervention through the Bosnia Peace Implementation Force (IFOR) and the subsequent follow-on force (SFOR) in the Balkans show that the alliance had become more flexible, could field new and creative command structures, and could use force to back up diplomacy. NATO's role also validated the Partnership for Peace. Eager to show their willingness to contribute to a NATO operation, thirteen PFP countries and sixteen non-NATO states joined the effort. Earlier, PFP exercises with NATO paved the way for quick integration of contingents from PFP countries, which provided some 5,200 personnel of the 51,300 total. The PFP also provided a framework to bring Russia into IFOR under a NATO command while serving alongside U.S. troops in some of the most dangerous areas of operation.

NATO demonstrated its significant potential for post-crisis engagement in that it completed its military tasks as mandated by the Dayton accords within six months. Warring parties were successfully separated, thereby creating an environment in which the nonmilitary aspects of rebuilding could begin. NATO's role in rebuilding Bosnia-Herzegovina was formally limited but informally significant. NATO was mandated to help to create secure conditions for the conduct, by others, of nonmilitary tasks, including the conduct of free and fair elections. NATO was also directed to support the UN High Commissioner for Refugees and other international organizations in humanitarian missions as well as to aid movement of civilian populations, refugees, and displaced persons. NATO also would help in clearing minefields.

In this basic mission, NATO contributed to nonmilitary operations as well by providing four hundred civil affairs personnel to a program uniting active and reserve civil affairs officers from around the world. Their duty was to help rebuild civil infrastructure. NATO military and civilian representatives worked in conjunction with the World Bank and a variety of nongovernmental organizations to identify over two hundred projects. NATO rebuilt bridges, repaired roads, and found staff for similar projects such as power, natural gas, water, and telecommunications. NATO also provided security when cargo of a strategic nature, such as electrical transformers or hydroelectric turbines and turbine shafts, was transported over disputed territory. By March 1996, NATO had helped to open 80 percent of Bosnia's major roads for use.

By summer 1998, it was clear, however, that while the Balkans had gained an uneasy peace, there was no lasting security. NATO's mission was only a partial success, as the sources of conflict remained unresolved. NATO military commanders were reluctant to hunt down indicted war criminals or assume other risky responsibilities for attaining long-term security. Yet without any sense of security, the region's ongoing instability threatened to undermine NATO's other programs in the east. Most significantly, the unfinished nature of the Balkan peace soon became painfully transparent with a growing crisis within Yugoslavia—in Kosovo.

Kosovo is a provincial area within Serbia which—along with Montenegro—came to represent what was now left of the country of Yugoslavia. Kosovo is an area with about 1.2 million people, including a 90 percent ethnic Albanian, Muslim population and about a 9 percent Serb population. Kosovo is a place where Serbs have deep sentimental ties; it is often referred to as the cradle of Serb civilization, and it bears emotional Serb sentiments dating back to the fourteenth century. Nationalist Serb leaders—in particular Slobodan Milosevic—used the Serb sentiment toward Kosovo as a rallying point to gain political support during the 1980s. During the 1990s, Milosevic gradually stripped the Albanian majority in Kosovo of the political, cultural, and ethnic autonomy that had sustained its ongoing quest for independence. More radical elements involved in that quest became the Kosovo Liberation Army (KLA), which began an extended campaign—including terrorist attacks—against Serbs in Kosovo. Refusing to concede Kosovo, Milosevic responded with a brutal oppression of ethnic Albanians there. By late summer 1998, several hundred thousand ethnic Albanians had been internally displaced or forced out of the country into neighboring Albania and Macedonia.

Increasingly through 1998, NATO saw Kosovo as a growing threat to stability in the Balkans—and possibly even beyond. The risk was geostrategic, in that a heavy influx of ethnic Albanian refugees into Albania and Macedonia could lead to severe economic destabilization in these very unstable Balkan countries. Such an outcome could prompt intervention by the Albanians or Macedonians and eventually draw in larger neighboring countries, including Greece and Turkey. Equally important, NATO leaders also felt a historic sense of guilt for not having intervened early in the Bosnia-Herzegovina conflict, when they could have acted to prevent what became a genocide. Nevertheless, in its determination to avoid repeating the mistakes of the past, NATO pushed forward toward a war that would, instead, create an entirely new set of institutional and strategic dilemmas.

Through March 1999, NATO leaders sought to combine a threat of force with aggressive diplomacy to compel Milosevic into a political settlement that would provide for a high degree of autonomy for Kosovo but still retain the overall territorial integrity of Serbia. In the end, neither the Kosovar Albanians nor Serbs were satisfied with this approach, and diplomacy failed. In late March of 1999, NATO thus engaged in its first war—and, rather than acting as a defensive institution, NATO was acting offensively. However, in waging a war for values, NATO would soon become exposed to a variety of internal contradictions regarding what would become its new strategic concept of operations: securing values. In sum, NATO went to war, and it eventually won. Milosevic's ethnic cleansing of Kosovo was halted, and by 2002 Milosevic was on trial for war crimes in the Hague. However, NATO's first war could have been its last because of a variety of key decision-making and institutional shortcomings.

NATO sought to use military force as a tool of spreading Western values into the former Yugoslav area. During the Kosovo war, NATO approved a new strategic concept that declared that its new mission was to "stand firm against those who violate human rights, wage war and conquer territory" and that NATO would seek to "contribute to building a stronger and broader Euro-Atlantic community of democracies—a community where human rights and fundamental freedoms are upheld; where borders are increasingly open to people, ideas and commerce; where war becomes unthinkable." In the end, NATO emerged from the Kosovo war with its campaign for Western values eventually affirmed. Nevertheless, when NATO went to war it did so absent a legal mandate from the United Nations. Russian and Chinese opposition to the use of force prevented the UN Security Council from playing its role under international law as the only institution that can legally authorize the use of force. Technically, this action was also legally problematic for NATO's own founding treaty, which states in Article 1 that the members must "refrain from the use of force in any manner inconsistent with the purposes of the United Nations." Article 7 of the NATO treaty requires its members to respect "the primary responsibility of the Security Council for the maintenance of international peace and security." The NATO allies reasonably concluded that the UN was not living up to its own responsibilities regarding guarantees for the protection of human rights and the maintenance of international peace and security.

Concerns over the absence of an international legal mandate, which were largely European, combined with alliance-wide domestic political constraints to impact the operational concepts that NATO would deploy in war. When NATO bombed, it did so only above fifteen thousand feet to protect allied pilots and aircraft. NATO members seemed to signal that the lives of hundreds of thousands of ethnic Albanians were not worth risking the lives of western pilots or airplanes. Scores of innocent civilians were accidentally killed by NATO bombs because of poor target identification—including a large convoy of misidentified Albanian refugees. NATO's bombing strategy eventually led it to target and bomb civilian infrastructure, particularly electric power grids, damaging civilian drinking water in the process. Attacking civilian targets was strategically necessary to pressure Milosevic and his political allies in Belgrade. However, critics asserted that this strategy was a technical violation of the Western principles regarding the international law of war. NATO thus found itself in an institutional conundrum created by a divergence between its humanitarian mission and the military requirements of strategy for winning a war.

Militarily, NATO leaders failed to learn the full military lessons of the 1995 success that compelled a peace in Bosnia-Herzegovina. Some allied decision-makers believed that it was the limited NATO bombing that had forced the Serbs to negotiate. Thus it was assumed that the same would occur in any engagement with Yugoslavia over Kosovo: that a limited use of air power would force the Serbs to capitulate and negotiate an internationally negotiated settlement. Limited air power could have impacted Serb forces, but a ground threat was also necessary—as it had been in the Croat-Muslim offensive in Bosnia-Herzegovina. Yet NATO's political leaders denied their military this essential tool while putting their faith in the political impact of a few days of air attacks. One of NATO's key institutional functions is to facilitate effective information exchange so that appropriate military strategies can be developed. However, in the case of Kosovo, NATO's political dynamics did not reflect a successful process of information development within the institution. Indeed, senior American and NATO officials predicted on the eve of the war that a campaign against Milosevic would take only a matter of days—and indeed only a few days' worth of initial target sets were approved by NATO's political leaders.

Once war over Kosovo began, allied leaders had to balance the gains of effective warfare against the risk of a collapse of NATO's fragile political consensus. Of the NATO allies, only Britain was enthusiastic about a ground campaign to liberate Kosovo. Several NATO members told U.S. president Bill Clinton that their governments might fall if a ground war option were even discussed. In Greece, over 90 percent of the public opposed the war. It was also unclear if American congressional and public support could be sustained in the event of a ground attack. NATO's internal decision-making rules appeared to have had a major impact on the organization's capacity to fight an effective war.

NATO works through a simple decision-making process; all members must be in consensus before any agenda item becomes official policy. Any member can veto NATO policy in the agenda-setting or consensus process. Often, NATO policy reflects the lowest common denominator of international security decision making, and such was the case in the procedural outcome of NATO's engagement in Kosovo. NATO's procedures allowed the institution to instigate military planning in summer 1998. However, at the political level, NATO leaders refused to let NATO military planners officially move forward with operational planning for ground forces. Absent consensus in NATO on a serious ground threat, Serb leaders largely concluded that NATO's threats were a bluff and that, even if NATO did bomb, they could weather the attack and hope to see the alliance divide politically.

Maintaining political cohesion in NATO thus became more important than selecting a military strategy that would actually lead to a fast victory against Yugoslavia. NATO's political role was often criticized as a "war by committee" and did not resonate well with American military planners. This was especially true because, while the war had shown that European countries could have an equal say over political objectives, there was a major divergence in actual capabilities that they could bring to fighting a war. During the war, the United States dropped 90 percent of the high-tech precision weapons, dropped 90 percent of cruise missiles, and supplied 90 percent of all electronic warfare and intelligence/reconnaissance capabilities. The Americans did not need the Europeans to fight this war, and many U.S. military planners concluded that NATO created major costs in terms of strategy and operational efficiency. Conversely, the Europeans were increasingly frustrated with the notion that, in terms of boots on the ground, it was their forces that were providing about 80 percent of all peacekeeping and peace-support operations in the Balkans. Structurally and functionally, a major divide was growing within NATO.

This divergence between political consensus and military strategy and capabilities severely tested the relationship between American military planners and their European allies. In Europe, the general belief was that the military should focus the attention of its air power primarily on the Serb forces in the field that were responsible for the conduct of ethnic cleansing. Europeans were highly uneasy about bombing raids undertaken deep inside of Yugoslavia that might cause civilian casualties. Conversely, American military concepts would have focused primarily on strategic "centers of gravity" in Belgrade that would use overwhelming force rapidly to show that NATO was serious about its objectives. As the war went on, Serb forces expelled over 800,000 Albanians from Kosovo. In terms of its stated objectives of deterring Serb attacks on civilian Albanians, NATO was losing.

Three months into the war, NATO had eventually agreed to a far more aggressive use of air power. However, the key to victory likely had more to do with the likelihood that individual NATO allies—especially the United States and Britain—would eventually undertake a land invasion of Yugoslavia. Growing signs that a land invasion was inevitable appeared to combine with Russian diplomatic pressure on the Serbs to force them to negotiate a settlement favorable to NATO's objectives.

NATO did, in the end, prevail over Milosevic. Its objective of spreading Western principles was validated. Milosevic soon was sent to the Hague as an indicted war criminal. However, the war took a major toll. Leading NATO member states concluded that the primary lesson of Kosovo was not to do this again.

By 2000, NATO had been demoted in U.S. military planning. When the United States went to war in Afghanistan, NATO's political support was welcome, but its operational support was rejected. Because military planning and cooperation are NATO's political architecture, its relevance as an institution came into doubt. This trend, a consequence of the Kosovo war, accelerated significantly after the terrorist attacks of September 11, 2001. Nevertheless, NATO's engagement in the Balkans has, overall, been extraordinarily successful and the organization's most direct contribution to security in post–Cold War Europe. Whether NATO can build on that success and simultaneously adapt its institutional structure for the new mission of counterterrorism is its most important challenge in the twenty-first century.

Transforming NATO for a New Century

After becoming NATO secretary general in late 1999, Lord George Robertson began a mantra of "capabilities, capabilities, capabilities" as the key to rectifying the widening gap in transatlantic relations. However, by the time NATO leaders met in Prague in November 2002, the gap increasingly seemed to widen beyond mere capabilities. The United States, it appeared to many observers, was increasingly pursuing a unilateralist foreign and security policy. As U.S. Secretary of Defense Donald Rumsfeld opined, the core concept now would be that multilateral operations are useful, but the coalition should be shaped by the mission—the mission should not be shaped by the coalition. In other words, no more Kosovo-type operations for the United States. Increasingly, the transatlantic divide seemed to grow over specific policy issues such as the Kyoto accord on global warming, creation of an International Criminal Court, and Middle East policy. But a more fundamental divergence of values also appeared to emerge between European public opinion and the administration of U.S. president George W. Bush. Increasingly, Europeans seemed to view the United States as an out-of-control superpower too quick to resort to force, while Washington viewed the Europeans as overly focused on their internal affairs and unwilling to engage forcefully in global politics.

Answering the question of whether NATO could adjust to meet new transatlantic security challenges would have to begin by recognizing that at its core, NATO is a military alliance. Alliances must address threats effectively or alternative means of meeting such threats will be found. NATO must prove itself adaptable to these new challenges if it is to have value for the future. While NATO can survive on bureaucratic inertia and on secondary programmatic activity such as engaging countries from Central and Eastern Europe, its core foundations will not remain strong unless a clear and focused mission can be achieved for the institution. If NATO's core security foundations are not solid, then the political house that is built upon it will also lose value. A NATO that is politically unmanageable, militarily ineffective, and strategically irrelevant will be of no value to anyone other than those who might seek to exploit transatlantic differences and decrease the sense of security in the Euro-Atlantic area. A NATO that examines the creation of new capabilities—without first understanding what these capabilities will be for—will be a NATO without a mission. A NATO without a purpose is one which will not endure.

THE NEW SECURITY THREAT: INTERNATIONAL TERRORISM

In 1994, NATO placed the issue of proliferation and delivery of weapons of mass destruction on the official agenda, but took it little further at the time. When NATO invoked its Article 5 clause of collective defense on September 12, 2001, NATO's future threat agenda was immediately clarified. To the degree that NATO had been searching for a mission bridging the twenty-first century, its members found one: global terrorism. Suddenly, concepts like enlarging NATO to hedge against a future Russian threat seemed very outdated. Indeed, in the early campaign against terrorism, countries like Russia and former Soviet states in Central Asia would be operationally more crucial to the United States–led antiterror coalition than traditional NATO allies.

While the declaration of September 12 was politically important, operationally, NATO was in fact sidelined. American officials said that if European members wanted to contribute, they would have to increase their capabilities.

The transatlantic defense spending gap had become, by 2001, devastating. The United States was spending an average of 3.5 percent of its GDP on defense, while many European nations spent less than 2 percent. Collectively the United States spent more than all the other NATO members combined. Europe spent collectively about two-thirds of what the United States spent—but got only about one-third the capability because they spent so much on salaries for a conscript-based military. The American increase in defense spending in 2001 of $48 billion was more than the total defense budget of any individual NATO ally. America's total defense spending would be greater than the next fifteen closest military powers in the world combined. However, at a political level, any increase in capabilities might give the Europeans more leverage over American policy and thus also make working through NATO unpalatable for the United States. Either way, it looked to many NATO observers that the United States had gradually begun a withdrawal from the military priority it had traditionally placed on NATO. Indeed, in his two most important speeches in 2002—the State of the Union in February and the address to the United Nations in September—U.S. president George Bush never once mentioned NATO. This was unprecedented for a post–World War II American president.

NATO was not completely left out of the early campaign against terrorism. NATO forces broke up al Qaeda terrorist cells in Bosnia-Herzegovina. NATO also provided a rapid deployment of AWACS airplanes to help control airspace over the United States. Moreover, while not conducting a formal NATO operation, fourteen NATO allies and many of its PFP members assisted Operation Enduring Freedom in Afghanistan and the follow-on International Security Assistance Force. Indeed, the Partnership for Peace had, once again, demonstrated its extremely high value. Years of direct dialogue, exchanges, and training between the NATO allies and the countries of Central Asia, for example, helped to pave the way for the deployment of American troops into the region.

But in the end, Europe and America have different perceptions of the risks associated with terrorism. Europeans largely view terrorism as a civilian–police challenge and not a military priority. Europeans also have come to live with terrorism over several decades and generally accept it as a marginal but acceptable risk to daily routines. Some also point out that while America suffered immensely on September 11, 2001, these attacks pale in comparison to the sixty million killed on their continent during two world wars in the twentieth century. Such comments fall largely on deaf American ears who are eager to be proactive against terrorism and to attack it on a global basis. Most significantly, the notion of an "axis of evil"—states that sponsor terrorism combined with the development of weapons of mass destruction—that was espoused by President Bush was largely rejected by continental European countries. This divide became especially clear in fall 2002 and early 2003 when key NATO allies—particularly Germany, France, and Turkey—expressed not only reservations but opposition to any U.S. attack on Iraq. NATO was even paralyzed into inaction over a request from Turkey to prepare for any collective defense needs that might come from a war in Iraq. Meanwhile, the United States appeared to seek to provoke divisions in Europe by isolating its traditional "old" European allies in favor of the "new Europe" in Central and Eastern Europe, which was more supportive of America's Iraq policy. In reality, however, public opinion across Europe strongly opposed American policy toward Iraq. In sum, while the allies in NATO tend to agree that there is an existential threat of international terrorism, they do not agree on the degree of strategic importance attached to it.

MILITARY CAPABILITIES

Assessing what NATO collectively needs in order to be militarily relevant requires explaining first what NATO is for. If, for example, NATO is for traditional collective defense, then it would need traditional land-air-sea–based capabilities. However, as the traditional cold-war model is no longer valid, NATO must be prepared for a new set of military requirements organized less around territorial defense and deterrence and more around high-end military capabilities and rapid deployment. In this context, numbers matter less than attaining the right mix of interoperable equipment and highly trained personnel. Such an advance for NATO is also essential because a perpetuation and deepening of a burden-sharing relationship, in which the United States does the heavy war fighting and the European allies fulfill the mopping up and peacekeeping functions, is not sustainable for the long-term.

NATO's military structure required a major overhaul in light of new challenges for several reasons. First, targeting decisions during the 1999 Kosovo Air Campaign became so contentious that some NATO planners came to see NATO as better employed in preparing military forces for collective action, rather than actually commanding them directly. Second, a new strategic purpose for NATO derived from a campaign against terrorism will require defense requirements different from those currently existing within NATO. NATO does not have a command capability for significant non-European power projection missions. Absent this capacity, the United States will likely continue to prefer to organize coalitions of the willing that avoid NATO altogether. Third, NATO would need to adapt and adjust its operational concepts to include the nonmilitary/civilian dimension of security, particularly by organizing for effective operations working in conjunction with the European Union—especially its tried and expanding multinational police capability.

At its Prague summit, NATO took a major political step toward revitalizing its capabilities for a new era and officially identified counterterrorism as a major component of its evolving mission. Subsequently, its members agreed to create a NATO Response Force consisting of technologically advanced, deployable, interoperable, and sustainable forces, including land, sea, and air elements ready to move quickly to wherever they might be needed. While it would not be fully operational until October 2006, such a force was also seen as providing the catalyst for a major reinvestment in military capabilities among the NATO allies. Conceptually, this would mean that NATO would, through its defense planning cycle, identify the requirements for organizing a force that would include about twenty-one thousand troops and associated logistics, transportation, command and control, and intelligence needs, etc. Then, NATO would survey its member states and see what they might contribute in targeted areas of specialization to the force.

By streamlining force contributions into a multinational spearhead force, the NATO allies would not need to individually boost their defense spending. Instead, they would have to commit to rationalizing their military investment in terms of the collective requirements of NATO. In that context, NATO also approved a "Prague Capabilities Commitment," which would require the members to improve their ability to operate in a high-threat environment, targeting new challenges such as chemical, biological, radiological, and nuclear defense; intelligence, surveillance, and target acquisition; air-to-ground surveillance; command, control, and communications; combat effectiveness (including precision-guided munitions and suppression of enemy air defenses); strategic lift and sea-lift; air-to-air refueling; and deployable combat support and combat service units. NATO also agreed to implement work on civil emergency planning and to develop its institutional capacity for managing the challenge of the proliferation, and possible use by terrorists, of weapons of mass destruction.

While such declarations are vital steps to reorganizing NATO for the future, there is no guarantee that NATO members will adequately invest in these programs. The risk for NATO is that, as it enlarges to include twenty-six countries, it will evolve into a three-tier military institution with the United States at one end, Britain, France, and Turkey in the middle, and the rest basically picking up the pieces. It is possible that some new NATO members who are going to have to rebuild their militaries from scratch will eventually find it easier to adapt to new NATO criteria. Moreover, while NATO itself does not formally require contributions from new members to the actual Article 5 mission of the day, some of the new members have contributed significantly to the international coalition against terrorism. Romania, for example has established requirements for increased cooperation among state agencies, increased intelligence capabilities, and homeland defense, while also seeking to balance civil liberties. Romania sent four hundred troops to participate in Operation Enduring Freedom in Afghanistan and another forty-eight to the post-crisis International Assistance force there. Romania also supports a new interpretation for NATO's Article 5, arguing that the alliance should not wait for attackers but rather to preempt and take the initiative. On the other hand, Slovenia's response to the international war against terrorism has been mild, and no major changes have been made in its armed forces.

Whether or not new NATO members contributed in the early months after September 11, 2001, it remains to be seen whether such contributions are sustainable and whether they will be translated into long-term contributions to NATO's Rapid Deployment Force. If the new members continue to be concerned primarily about their own territorial defense, or find it politically unpalatable to professionalize fully their armed forces, then these new NATO members will struggle to find their place in NATO. Additionally, NATO will have to perfect a means of exercising and financing new military operations, as the new NATO members themselves may not be prepared to sustain large-scale investments in their integration to high-end NATO activities on their own. On a larger scale, some analysts have questioned the seriousness of NATO's interest in fundamentally transforming its mission given that, while new members are expected to show they can contribute to NATO's collective defense, there was never any post–September 11 reevaluation of NATO's enlargement criteria to reflect a serious commitment to the actual collective defense threat facing the organization. Even more problematic for NATO remains the fact that its traditional members have continued to resist significant investment in new defense capabilities. Generally, the traditional western European NATO allies view counterterrorism as a civilian police function and, aside from peacekeeping, would like to move away from the principle of force as a means of projecting power. A key question as to the new members of NATO is whether they will continue to support the American concept of military investment, or whether, now that they have attained the invitation ticket to NATO, they will prioritize their aspiration to join the European Union and thus affiliate more closely with its strategic culture.

NATO might eventually need to examine how this operational force relates to the European Union. NATO and the EU struggled through the 1990s to find ways to work together so that their missions would not duplicate each other and would, instead, be mutually reinforcing. Inside the EU, there has been a growing political effort to enhance its Maastricht pillar of shaping a common Foreign and Security Policy. Initially this effort focused on building up the Western European Union as a means of creating a European security and defense identity that would be separable, but not separate, from NATO. The means to bridge the relationship between the two institutions would be to create combined Joint Task Forces headquarters inside NATO but which could be managed by non-American leaders should the European Union choose to run its own operation. By 2000, the European Union had opted to abandon the WEU, and instead create a direct EU Rapid Reaction Force that would cover a broad spectrum of operations independent from NATO. Such missions, however, would largely focus on low-end peacekeeping operations and would ultimately have to borrow significant command, control, and logistical assets from NATO. This force, intended to be in place by the year 2005, would spur the EU to becoming a political counterweight to the United States and give the European nations a capacity to manage crises in their own backyard. Given America's global security responsibilities, Washington has been gradually warming over time to the idea of an independent European force so long as it does not duplicate NATO activities or discriminate against NATO members that are not part of the European Union.

How the NATO and the EU forces relate to each other without duplicating their efforts remains to be developed. As it developed its own concept for a Rapid Deployment Force, NATO did not elaborate on specific linkages to the European Union in the conceptual design of its new force capabilities. In the end, the absence of such linkage risks removing the incentive that the traditional

European NATO member might have from investing in the NATO force. More problematic, a failure to sufficiently link the military capabilities available in NATO with the civilian—especially multinational police—components of the European Union might not adequately reflect a comprehensive approach to combating terrorism. Such a NATO-EU approach might include the sharing of interior (police and border control) and finance (banking) information and thus involve home and interior ministries in joint NATO-EU planning mechanisms. In the end, the Prague summit established goals for NATO. Whether they will be met remains to be seen.

POLITICAL REFORM: IS NATO A NEW LEAGUE OF NATIONS?

It is one thing for NATO to have capabilities to act. It is another for NATO to decide to act. At the Prague summit, NATO agreed to support United Nations efforts to disarm Iraq. NATO did not, however, agree as an organization to do anything about it. This approach reflects the realities of the way NATO makes decisions—by consensus. NATO's basic rules require that all members agree on an issue before it becomes policy. Actually, there is no "official" affirmative vote in the NATO process. Rather, a policy is placed on the agenda. Then a period of time is given in which member states have a right to "break silence" and declare their opposition to discussing the issue at hand. If states are actively pursuing an agenda item, they will lobby each other to build consensus to the point where no country will break silence and block discussion. The consensus process is slow and difficult. Consensus often means that policy is basically the lowest common denominator upon which all of its members will agree. The lack of consensus to intervene in the Balkans from 1991 to 1995 led to NATO inaction at a time when up to 250,000 people were killed or missing in ethnic cleansing in Bosnia-Herzegovina. The Kosovo war was carried out with consensus, but only to a point, as there would be no agreement on a ground option. Indeed, the measure of success in NATO during the war became maintaining consensus even at the expense of success in waging war. NATO began the process of enlargement in 1993—but agreed to implement the policy only in 1996 and came to full consensus on whom to invite only in 1997.

During the Cold War, consensus meant preapproving military plans that would automatically be implemented if there were an attack on any NATO member. Time then would have been of the essence, and NATO's top military commander, the Supreme Allied Commander Europe (SACEUR), would not have had the luxury of time to consult all the allies. While this process worked well in a time of high agreement on the external threat, the end of the Cold War allowed divergent member-state interests to be more aggressively articulated in the NATO decision-making process. Two very fundamental challenges now confront the consensus process: (1) can an organization with twenty-six or more members make effective decisions; and (2) will Russia's new relationship with NATO transform NATO's identity? In both cases, the question is whether, as NATO grows, it will become more political and thus less capable of action. Will NATO begin to look like the failed League of Nations of the 1920s?

The Prague summit decision to invite Estonia, Latvia, Lithuania, Slovakia, Slovenia, Romania, and Bulgaria to negotiate membership in NATO poses the first significant challenge to NATO's decision-making effectiveness. Central to this challenge is a basic notion that, as the institutional membership gets so large, effective consensus-based decision making becomes more difficult. This challenge is compounded by the fact that there is no rule in NATO that allows the institution to punish or expel any member that does not adhere to the basic principles of international or domestic behavior expected of NATO members. Indeed, the consensus process would allow any NATO member to veto the consideration of any such punishment, and even placing the issue on the NATO agenda for discussion would likely be opposed by key traditional NATO allies.

The second round of invitations to join NATO places enormous stress on its political institutions. As the decision-making body, the North Atlantic Council (NAC), enlarges from nineteen to twenty-six, the relative "weight" of consensus formation will change. Of the present nineteen NAC members, there is the "giant" United States, seven large members (Germany, Turkey, France, United Kingdom, Italy, Spain, and Poland), and seven medium-sized members (Canada, the Netherlands, Belgium, Portugal, Greece, Hungary, and the Czech Republic). The NAC prior to Prague had only four small states, Denmark, Norway, Iceland, and Luxembourg. The Prague enlargement adds six more small states, plus medium-sized Romania, that alter the balance toward these smaller allies who each can veto NATO consensus. Of course, many of the traditional NATO members might have problems meeting the criteria set for NATO enlargement. However, this only proves the point that it was in the preaccession period that NATO had the maximum leverage over NATO members. Once they are in, there is no guarantee that they will maintain preaccession defense commitments of political and international standards expected of NATO members.

In the end, NATO's enlargement was mostly a political act and thus reflected the growing political nature of the institution. While this change would have important symbolic value in helping these long-suffering countries of the east "return to the west" and was thus, ultimately, highly justifiable in principle, it remained in practice a challenge for NATO to ensure that enlargement served as a net contributor to NATO's lasting relevance. It might even become necessary to take another step in its institutional reform in order to protect against any faltering new member—or even old member—from failing to contribute to NATO. The basic problem for NATO is that its leverage to promote international and domestic reform among countries exists when countries are trying to become members. Once inside NATO, the institution loses its political leverage. One reform scenario would therefore be for NATO to create a committee to monitor members' adherence to NATO criteria and report each year to the North Atlantic Council. Then, the NAC would have within its power the ability to sanction the member—to include a suspension of its membership rights or even face expulsion from the alliance. The problem with this scenario is that even getting such an institutional rule reform on the agenda for consideration would likely be blocked in the consensus process. Some current NATO members even now might not meet some of NATO's articulated membership criteria. Thus both old and new members would resist being exposed in this manner.

Short of the ability to suspend members or expel them, the broader question of the consensus rule within NATO therefore remains. Twenty-six countries in NATO will have to agree for consensus to be achieved. While some observers argue that an enlarged NATO will have no problem attaining consensus, there is no obvious reason to suggest that this is true. Some reform scenarios might include the nation of "constructive abstention" in which states will choose not to block activity but at the same time not participate in a particular NATO action. In this scenario, NATO would lose its "all for one and one for all" quality, but it could nevertheless act. Another scenario would be for the North Atlantic Council to establish a general political principle or mandate, but then to allow NATO countries to establish a "coalition of the willing" organized around the benefit of NATO assets but not necessarily involving NATO as a formal action-based institution. Another scenario would allow the NAC to expand its decision-making influence to include nonmembers who might contribute substantial forces to a NATO-authorized operation not involving collective defense—for example, including countries like Sweden or Finland. NATO also might establish a principle of basing actions on "consensus minus one" in the event that a NATO member itself is the source of an international problem, thereby ensuring that this member could not use NATO rules to block action against itself. Finally, NATO could form an elite council consisting of its primary military contributors, including the United States, Britain, Germany, Turkey, and France (should it return to the NATO military committee, which it left in 1966). Such a committee could have rotating members of several smaller NATO allies, similar to the framework of the UN Security Council. All of these options seem very good in theory, but the practice of instituting decision-making change would be extremely difficult.

NATO's new strategic agenda will require a sharper focus on security and stability in Central Asia and the Middle East, which will also create a need for further institutional adaptation. Indeed, it may be that, if Europe wants to sustain its influence with the United States, it needs to focus on increasing its capability to operate with the extension of American power into these regions. Moving in this direction, NATO agreed in spring 2003 to begin providing the command structure under the United Nations for the peace support operations in Afghanistan. Some observers even envisioned NATO eventually taking over peace operations in Iraq and in the Israeli-Palestinian areas. If NATO is to play a significant role in such regions, it will have to pay up and look close.

Two circumstances threaten an adequate response. First, as an example of the U.S. preference for bilateral engagement, American troops moving into Georgia for antiterrorism training were organized unilaterally through its European Command and not through the PFP. Second, NATO expansion means that significant attention and resources must go to these new members. Indeed, there are now more members in NATO than in the PFP. There is a risk of "integration fatigue" at the moment when PFP needs the most attention. Meanwhile, many of the Mediterranean Dialogue countries have not demonstrated interest in working with NATO but are interested in the European Union. Consequently, NATO could use a direct relationship between the PFP and the European Union, to coordinate Middle East and PFP countries in a comprehensive engagement with the key European security institutions.

These questions of institutional reform also hinge very much on the future development of relations between NATO and Russia. In 1997, NATO and Russia established a permanent Joint Council, largely to engage with Russia and signal a desire to work simultaneously with Moscow as NATO enlarged. Unfortunately, the Russians never fully took advantage of this institutional mechanism, and during the Kosovo war in 1999 they withdrew from direct engagement with NATO. In spring 2002, NATO and Russia went a step beyond consultation and created what amounts to an NAC-plus-Russia relationship that would involve Russia fully in decision making on specific issues such as peacekeeping, crisis management, counterterrorism, and nonproliferation. On these issues, Russia would, if it chose to engage effectively, have the weight of a full NATO member, while at the same time NATO would preserve the right to act independently if its members deemed it necessary.

Russia now has a very significant voice in the NATO consensus process. The degree to which Russia plays a positive or negative role in this process will also significantly impact the ability of NATO to reform effectively for future missions. But most importantly, there is a great historical irony awaiting NATO if it cannot effectively reform. If the end result of NATO's inability to adapt to its enlarged membership and new missions is that it becomes a purely political institution and is militarily ineffective, this will affirm one of Russia's long-term goals: to see NATO diminished as the primary security institution in Europe. If the political trends in NATO continue, then at some future date the actual membership of Russia—along with many of the other former Soviet republics—might be seriously considered. This would complete NATO's evolution from an alliance to a political talking shop. Then the question becomes, Can NATO succeed where the League of Nations failed?

What Next For NATO?

Students and future practitioners of European security can point to extraordinary successes for NATO. The organization served as the mechanism for a sustained engagement by the United States in Europe during and after the Cold War. It has helped to lock Germany into the institutional framework of western security architectures. NATO has first successfully deterred the Soviet Union and now bridged the artificial barrier between east and west imposed by Stalin on the people of central and eastern Europe, both through the Partnership for Peace and NATO's enlargement. Perhaps most importantly, NATO has helped to end ethnic cleansing and war in the Balkans. These are not small achievements. However, as an institution struggling for a new-found relevance, NATO cannot afford to rest on its laurels. If NATO cannot be adequately reformed, then in the end it may be necessary to reopen the founding Washington Treaty for amendment. Or it may be necessary to pursue the creation of a new institution to meet whatever challenges NATO is unable to adapt to effectively. However, neither of these worst-case outcomes is necessary if creative leadership of the alliance is sustained via a new generation of strategic thinkers on both sides of the Atlantic.

Suggestions for Further Reading

Asmus, Ronald. *Opening NATO's Door: How the Alliance Remade Itself for a New Era.* New York: Columbia University Press, 2002.

Daalder, Ivo H., and Michael E. O'Hanlon. *Winning Ugly: NATO's War to Save Kosovo.* Washington, D.C.: Brookings Institution, 2000.

Drew, S. Nelson. *From Berlin to Bosnia.* Washington, D.C.: National Defense University Press, 1995.

Eisenhower, Susan, ed. *NATO at Fifty: Perspectives on the Future of the Atlantic Alliance.* Washington, D.C.: Center for Strategic and Political Studies, 1999.

Goldgeier, James. *Not Whether, but When: The U.S. Decision to Enlarge NATO.* Washington, D.C.: Brookings Institution, 1999.

Kelleher, Catherine. *The Future of European Security.* Washington, D.C.: The Brookings Institution, 1995.

Kaplan, Lawrence S. *NATO and the United States: The Enduring Alliance.* New York: Twayne Publishers, 1994.

Kay, Sean. *NATO and the Future of European Security.* Lanham, Md.: Rowman & Littlefield, 1998.

Mandelbaum, Michael. *The Dawn of Peace in Europe.* New York: The Twentieth Century Fund, 1996.

Michta, Andrew, ed. *America's New Allies: Poland, Hungary, and the Czech Republic in NATO.* Seattle: University of Washington Press, 2000.

Papacosma, S. Victor, Sean Kay, and Mark Rubin, eds. *NATO after Fifty Years*. Wilmington, Del.: Scholarly Resources, Inc., 2001.

North Atlantic Treaty Organization. *NATO Handbook*. Brussels: NATO Office of Information and Press, 2000.

Serfaty, Simon. *Stay the Course: European Unity and Atlantic Solidarity*. Washington, D.C.: Center for Strategic and International Studies, 1997.

Simon, Jeffrey. *Hungary and NATO: Problems in Civil-Military Relations*. Lanham, Md.: Rowman & Littlefield, 2003.

———. *NATO and the Czech and Slovak Republics: A Comparative Study in Civil-Military Relations*. Lanham, Md.: Rowman & Littlefield, 2004.

———. *Poland and NATO: A Study in Civil-Military Relations*. Lanham, Md.: Rowman & Littlefield, 2004.

Simon, Jeffrey, ed. *NATO Enlargement: Opinions and Options*. Washington, D.C.: National Defense University Press, 1996.

Sloan, Stanley R. *NATO, the European Union and the Atlantic Community*. Lanham, Md.: Rowman & Littlefield, 2002.

Sperling, James, ed. *Europe in Change: Two Tiers or Two Speeds?* Manchester, UK: Manchester University Press, 1999.

Szayna, Tomas. *NATO Enlargement: 2000–2015: Determinants and Implications for Defense Planning and Shaping*. Santa Monica, Calif.: Rand Corporation, 2001.

Wallander, Celeste A. *Mortal Friends, Best Enemies*. Ithaca, N.Y.: Cornell University Press, 1999.

CHAPTER 5

EU Enlargement

The Return to Europe

John Van Oudenaren

Introduction

The collapse of communism caught the European Community by surprise. At the time of its third enlargement in January 1986, few politicians in Brussels or the national capitals would have predicted that within five years they would be debating membership for ten candidate countries from central and eastern Europe, three of which were then still part of the Soviet Union. It was assumed that with the accession of Portugal and Spain, the Community more or less had reached the limits of its expansion in western Europe and that the challenge of the future was to "deepen" cooperation among existing members rather than "widen" to new members. The outlook changed dramatically as Soviet power withdrew from Europe and the newly democratic countries of central and eastern Europe looked westward for help in bolstering their political systems and their newly established market economies.

Change in the region began in the late 1980s, after the coming to power in the Soviet Union of Mikhail Gorbachev in March 1985. Gorbachev, preoccupied with his own country's internal economic problems, made clear that he would not interfere with reforms that fellow "socialist" countries might undertake to revive economic growth and close the widening technology and productivity gaps with the West. Gorbachev was a reformer, not a revolutionary. He intended to improve and streamline the communist system, not dismantle it. However, by 1989 the process he had helped to unleash had largely spun out of his control, as popular movements in the countries of central and eastern Europe rose up against their communist leaders.

Partially free elections took place in Poland in June 1989, resulting in a resounding victory for the opposition Solidarity movement. In the same month, roundtable talks between government and opposition began in Hungary, aimed at fundamental change in the political system. By mid-1989, there was reason to hope that at least these two countries were on a path that would lead to the establishment of market economies and pluralist political systems.

Western governments felt a strong need to respond to these signs of change and to support them with external aid. At the July 1989 Paris summit of the seven largest industrialized democracies (the G7), the leaders of the West and Japan issued a declaration of support for economic and political reform in eastern Europe and called for an international conference to coordinate western aid to Poland and Hungary. In December 1989, the EC Council of Ministers approved PHARE (*Pologne Hongrie: Actions pour la Reconversion Economique*), an EC-funded program of technical assistance to encourage the development of private enterprise and the building of market-oriented economies.

By the fall of 1989 the reform process was accelerating, turning into a full-fledged albeit largely peaceful revolution against the communist order. In September, Hungary opened its border with Austria, allowing thousands of East German citizens to travel through Czechoslovakia and Hungary to West Germany. After months of mass demonstrations in Leipzig, Dresden, and other cities, on November 9 the Berlin Wall was thrown open by an East German government that no longer could control its borders. In November and December, opposition rallies led to the ouster of the communist regime in Czechoslovakia. In December, roundtable talks between government and opposition began in Bulgaria. For the most part these revolutions were peaceful, but they culminated in late December with bloody fighting in Romania between opposition and security forces and the execution, on Christmas Day, of former dictator Nicolae Ceausescu and his wife, Elena.

The most immediate political challenge facing Western governments was German unification. West German Chancellor Helmut Kohl quickly seized the initiative on this issue, putting forward, in November 1989, a ten-point plan for creation of a German confederation. The United States supported unification, but Britain and France were skeptical. The Soviet Union had taken a hands-off attitude toward the changes in eastern Europe, but it vigorously opposed unification. The Soviet Union still had several hundred thousand troops in the GDR, and as a World War II victor power it had certain legal rights in Germany. In the GDR itself, it initially was unclear whether the voters would opt for rapid absorption by West Germany or whether they would seek to maintain some kind of separate identity within a German confederation.

By the fall of 1990, these uncertainties were resolved. In July, Kohl and Gorbachev met at a Soviet retreat in the Caucasus and reached agreement on the external aspects of German unity. Germany would remain in NATO, Soviet troops would be withdrawn, and a special bilateral treaty of friendship and cooperation between Germany and the Soviet Union would be signed. On August 31, the two German states signed a treaty on unification, and on September 12, the four victor powers concluded a treaty on the "final settlement with regard to Germany." On October 3, less than a year after the breaching of the Berlin Wall, Germany was united.

Unification had major implications for the EC. Most directly, it entailed the enlargement of the Community through the addition of the five states of the former GDR. By becoming a part of the Federal Republic, these states automatically joined the Community without the complex, formal accession process that other new members faced. With the addition of sixteen million new citizens, Germany became by far the largest EC member state but one that was less affluent, on a per capita basis, than it had been before unification. The eastern states immediately became eligible for EC regional aid funds traditionally earmarked for southern Europe and depressed regions of the Community. Indirectly, the challenge of anchoring a larger Germany in the west encouraged France and Germany to work together to reform and strengthen the EC, culminating in the conclusion in February 1992 of the Maastricht treaty, establishing a new entity, the European Union, that incorporated the existing Community along with new mechanisms for cooperation in foreign and security policy and justice and home affairs.

The Europe Agreements

While focusing on the immediate question of Germany, the Community and its member states took up the broader challenge of stabilization in central and eastern Europe as a whole. Grant aid, loans, expanded trade, political dialogue, and support for selective admission to western organizations all became elements in the Community's approach. At an extraordinary session of the European Council in November 1989, French president François Mitterrand proposed the establishment of a special bank to help finance economic transition in the central and east European countries. The other member states embraced Mitterrand's idea, which led to the founding of the European Bank for Reconstruction and Development in 1991. In July 1990, the Community extended its PHARE program to Bulgaria, Czechoslovakia, and Yugoslavia. Assistance to Romania was temporarily delayed, owing to the post-Ceausescu government's suppression of student demonstrations in the spring of 1990, but in 1991 Bucharest became eligible for PHARE grants.

Responding to requests for increased access to west European markets, the Community also set about negotiating new trade arrangements to replace those that had been concluded in the 1980s with the then still-communist countries with their centrally planned economies. In August 1990, the European Commission proposed the conclusion of what it called "Europe agreements" among the Community, its member states, and Hungary, Poland, and Czechoslovakia. The name was chosen to underline the difference between these agreements and the Community's association agreements with many countries outside Europe, notably in North Africa and the Middle East.

These agreements provided a legal framework to facilitate the expanding economic, commercial, and human contacts between the EC and countries that were rapidly emerging from communism. In addition, they offered an interim response to the requests from many of the countries of central and eastern Europe for rapid admission to the Community as full members. The EU was neither economically nor politically prepared to admit new members at this time, and few experts believed that the fragile central and eastern European economies were ready to cope with the competitive pressures and demanding regulations that would come with full membership. The Europe agreements thus were intended to establish a form of association that would help to prepare the central and eastern European countries for membership, as well as provide concrete and symbolically important links to the Community that, while falling short of membership, reflected a commitment on the part of western Europe's major economic bloc to take responsibility for its eastern neighbors. The preambles to the agreements noted the aspirations of the central and eastern European signatories to join the Community, but they stopped short of guaranteeing that membership was assured.

The key economic provision of the Europe agreements was the establishment, within a ten-year period, of free-trade arrangements between the Community and the associated countries. Expanded market access was controversial in some member states, where protectionist lobbies sought to maintain tight quotas on the import of iron and steel, textiles, and agricultural goods—the very items these countries had to sell. At one point Hungary and Poland threatened to suspend the negotiations unless they received a better offer from the Community negotiators. The deal was improved, and in December 1991, these two countries and Czechoslovakia concluded the first of the Europe agreements. (The agreement with Czechoslovakia later was replaced, following the breakup of that country in 1993, by separate agreements with the Czech Republic and Slovakia.) Europe agreements also were reached with Romania (February 1993), Bulgaria (March 1993), Estonia, Latvia, and Lithuania (June 1995), and Slovenia (June 1996).

Under the terms of the agreements, the central and eastern European states were required to align their laws with those of the EU countries and to adopt EU rules on competition and many technical standards. In the forty years since the founding of the European Coal and Steel Community, the EU had passed some one hundred thousand pages of legislation. These laws, in turn, often required national legislation or rules to ensure their implementation. For the central and eastern European states to cooperate successfully with their western neighbors and especially to aspire to eventual membership, they had to undertake the arduous task of replacing communist (or nonexistent) laws with legislation compatible with that developed over the course of decades in the rest of Europe.

Under the provisions on financial cooperation, the Europe agreements reaffirmed the availability of grant assistance under the PHARE program and made the central and eastern European states eligible for loans from the European Investment Bank, the EC's Luxembourg-based bank that supports infrastructure projects in the Community itself. Reflecting the concern in western Europe about possible surges of immigrants from the economically distressed east, the agreements were cautious with regard to the movement of workers. Their liberalizing effect in this sensitive area was rather modest, because, rather than facilitating new flows of people, they improved the lot of central and eastern European workers already in EU countries.

Outside the economic sphere, the Europe agreements provided for expanded political dialogue and cultural cooperation. High officials were to meet at regular intervals to discuss topics of common interest and to aim at achieving convergence in the foreign policy positions of the central and eastern European states and the EU. Many cultural and educational exchange programs funded by the Community were extended to central and eastern Europe. To monitor implementation, each Europe agreement provided for the establishment of an association council consisting of representatives of the EU, the member states, and the associated states. These councils were to meet at the ministerial level at least once each year to review progress and to take decisions regarding further action. The Europe agreements were to remain in effect until superseded by treaties of accession between the associated countries of central and eastern Europe and the fifteen member states of the EU and to serve as the legal framework for the "preaccession process" designed to prepare the central and eastern European countries for enlargement.

The Debate on Enlargement

The negotiation and early implementation of the Europe agreements proceeded in parallel with a vigorous debate on enlargement throughout the Continent. Almost immediately after assuming power, the new leaders of central and eastern Europe began to push for admission as quickly as possible, to the EU and to other western institutions such as NATO. These suggestions evoked an ambivalent response in western Europe. On the one hand, political leaders were concerned about instability: the spread of ethnic conflict such as had erupted in the former Yugoslavia, surges of refugees and migrants, environmental disasters, and political extremism. Membership in a strengthened European Union was probably the only way to ensure, over the long term, that upheaval and reversion to dictatorship were banished from the region. In addition, many in western Europe felt a strong sense of obligation to their neighbors in central and eastern Europe—especially to those who had led the fight against communism. Welcoming these people into the European family was clearly the right thing to do.

On the other hand, the costs and complications of enlargement promised to be enormous and could well derail the ambitious plans of the 1980s to deepen—to create a Union with a single currency, a common foreign and security policy, and increased powers for its central institutions. There also was the difficult question of where to draw the line: Even if the decision in principle to admit former communist countries was taken, it still was necessary to decide which countries, how many, and according to what criteria. It was not too difficult to envision Germany's eastern neighbors, Poland and the Czech Republic, becoming members, but what about the countries in the unstable Balkans? The question of membership became even more acute when, at the end of 1991, the Soviet Union dissolved into fifteen constituent states, raising the prospect that the Baltic countries or Ukraine or even Russia might apply.

Moreover, the former communist states were not the only candidates for membership. In May 1992, the EU and the **European Free Trade Association (EFTA)**, a grouping that included Austria, Finland, Norway, Sweden, and Switzerland, agreed to create a European Economic Area in which nearly all EU-EFTA barriers to trade were eliminated. Although the EFTA states were affluent democracies with market economies, most had refrained from joining the EU out of concern that doing so would compromise their political neutrality and antagonize the Soviet Union. However, with the Cold War ending, this reason was no longer valid. Most of the major EFTA states decided to apply for EU membership. In addition, two smaller Mediterranean states, Cyprus and Malta, had applied already in 1990. Finally, there was the problem of Turkey: It had an association agreement with the EU that dated back to the 1960s and also had applied for membership. Many political leaders in western Europe were doubtful that Turkey, with its size, relative poverty, and cultural distance from Europe, would ever become a member, but it was important not to reject it out of hand, given Turkey's strategic importance and long-standing record as a loyal member of NATO.

In the debate on enlargement, British prime minister Margaret Thatcher and her successor, John Major, were among the most enthusiastic proponents of enlargement. They tended to favor the earliest and broadest possible expansion. As Thatcher later wrote, "Having democratic states with market economies, which were just as 'European' as those of the existing Community, lining up as potential EC members made my vision of a looser, more open Community seem timely rather than backward."[1] At the other pole of the debate were the federalists (such as European Commission president Jacques Delors) who, although they recognized that something had to be done for central and eastern Europe, were concerned that a broader and more diverse membership would undermine progress toward a more cohesive union. Skeptical about the admission of even the EFTA countries, Delors warned that it would take fifteen to twenty years before the central and eastern European countries would be ready for membership.[2]

The most decisive voice in the debate was probably that of Kohl, who favored enlargement to central, eastern, and southeastern Europe—including the three Baltic states—but ruled out membership for Russia, Ukraine, and other states of the former Soviet Union. Kohl's position was somewhere between that of the British, who were accused by many of favoring indiscriminate and hasty enlargement, and that of Delors and many in the southern European countries, who sometimes were suspected of wanting to postpone enlargement indefinitely. The German view therefore tended to emerge as the compromise position.

The June 1993 Copenhagen meeting of the European Council was the first occasion on which the EU member states formally declared enlargement to the central and eastern European countries as an explicit goal. Although they did not set a timetable, the EU leaders stated that accession would "take place as soon as an associated country is able to assume the obligations of membership by satisfying the economic and political conditions required."[3] The associated countries were those countries with which the EU had concluded or planned to conclude agreements. Poland, Hungary, Czechoslovakia, Romania, and Bulgaria already had signed such agreements, and the European Council had signaled its intention to negotiate Europe agreements with the three Baltic states and Slovenia. Negotiations aimed at concluding so-called Partnership and Cooperation Agreements with Russia and the non-Baltic states of the former Soviet Union were under way or planned, but these agreements were not intended as a prelude to membership, which was not mentioned in their preambles. Thus, by the time of the Copenhagen Council, the future shape of the European Union had been decided: It would include ten or more states in the Baltic to Black Sea region, but it most likely would not include Russia, Ukraine, or other countries in the former Soviet Union.

The European Council further specified four criteria for determining whether an associated country was ready for membership: (1) stability of institutions guaranteeing democracy, the rule of law, human rights, and respect for and protection of minorities; (2) existence of a functioning market economy; (3) capacity to cope with competitive pressures and market forces within the Union; and (4) the ability to take on the obligations of membership, including adherence to the aims of political, economic, and monetary union. The "obligations of membership" meant acceptance of what in the EU lexicon was known as the *acquis communautaire*, a term used to denote the sum total of the Community's achievements in harmonizing legislation, creating a single market, and forging common policies.

Membership had to be comprehensive; there could be no "à la carte" acceptance of some areas of integration and rejection of others. Recognizing that the *acquis* itself was expanding as the EU became involved in new policy areas, the European Council did not insist that the new members meet all EU standards and participate fully in all areas of integration from day one of membership. They were not, for example, expected or required to adopt immediately the EU's single currency. But they had to commit to eventual participation in monetary union. Similarly, they were expected to participate in the Union's Common Foreign and Security Policy, and to cooperate in the development of a European Security and Defense Identity.

Although it was up to the central and eastern European applicants to meet these political and economic criteria, the European Council established one condition for the EU itself to meet, stipulating that "the Union's capacity to absorb new members, while maintaining the momentum of European integration, is also an important consideration in the general interest of both the Union and the candidate countries."[4] This condition later was interpreted to mean that negotiations regarding the admission of additional candidates—apart from the EFTA countries, three of which were admitted in January 1995— would not begin until at least six months after the completion of the Intergovernmental Conference (IGC) that was scheduled to convene in 1996 and that would take up the question of institutional reform of the European Union.

With the Copenhagen decision, the EU committed itself to admitting ten countries with a combined population of 105 million. Measured at purchasing-power standards, per capita gross domestic product (GDP) in these countries as a group was less than one-third the then current EU average (see Table 5.1). In addition to its relative poverty, central and eastern Europe was highly diverse, with different languages, religions, and historical traditions. The magnitude of the enlargement challenge facing the EU thus called for an effective pre-accession strategy to prepare these countries for membership, along with an overhaul of the EU's own policies and institutions to enable it to function with a larger and more diverse group of members.

Table 5.1   Central and Eastern Europe: Basic Data

	Area (1000 sq mi.)	Population (millions)	GDP ($ billion at PPP)	GDP per capita ($)
Hungary	35.9	10.2	73.2	7400
Poland	120.7	38.6	280.7	7250
Romania	91.7	22.7	114.2	5300
Slovakia	18.9	5.4	46.3	8600
Latvia	24.7	2.5	10.4	4260
Estonia	17.4	1.5	9.3	6450
Lithuania	25.2	3.7	15.4	4230
Bulgaria	42.8	8.4	35.6	4100
Czech Rep.	30.4	10.3	119.9	10,800
Slovenia	7.4	2.0	19.5	10,000
EU (current member totals)	1250.4	371.6	7699.8	20,693

Source: Adapted from European Commission, *Agenda 2000: For a Stronger and Wider Union* (Brussels: European Commission, 1997).

PPP = purchasing power parity.

Preaccession Strategy

THE INTERNAL MARKET

Joining the European Union entails a process of market integration that is deeper and more intrusive than that necessitated by other kinds of free-trade arrangements. As defined by the Treaty of Rome, the internal market is "an area without internal frontiers in which the free movement of goods, persons, services and capital is ensured."[5] Other provisions in the EU treaties prescribe certain social and employment standards that members are expected to maintain as they operate the single market and place strict limits on state aid to industry and on cartels and monopolies that hinder competition.

At the request of the European Council, in 1995 the Commission issued a white paper that spelled out the demands that participation in the internal market places on the member states: "An internal market without frontiers relies on a high level of mutual confidence and on equivalence of regulatory approach. Any substantial failure to apply the common rule in any part of the internal market puts the rest of the system at risk and undermines its integrity."[6] It went on to note that "any systematic checks and controls that are necessary to ensure compliance with the rules take place within the market and not when national borders are crossed." To operate the internal market, a member state must adhere to the general principles contained in the EU's founding treaties and to a large body of secondary legislation, most of which takes the form of directives that are passed by the Council of Ministers (with the co-decision of the European Parliament) that are then transposed into national laws and regulations that vary from country to country, depending upon legal and administrative traditions and other circumstances. Compliance with EU directives and with other sources of Community law is monitored by the Commission and is subject to the jurisdiction of the European Court of Justice.

In addition to the translation of directives into national legislation, the internal market relies heavily on the principle of mutual recognition. Beginning with the famous *Cassis de Dijon* ruling of 1979 (see Chapter 7), the European Court of Justice has held that any good circulating legally in one member state also must be free to circulate in any other part of the Union, except in certain special circumstances in which a member state can prove that some danger to health or safety might result. In the late 1980s and early 1990s, the member states, making a virtue of necessity, completed the Single European Market program by using mutual recognition, rather than the more time-consuming and politically difficult harmonization of national law.

Under the mutual recognition principle, any product that Poles lawfully produce or import must be available to Germans, Spaniards, Belgians, and everyone else in the Union. Belgian consumers thus want to be assured that

Polish-made products are safe and reliable. This system places a heavy premium on establishing adequate standards and effective regulatory and inspection bodies in the acceding countries. As the white paper noted, "structures [needed to operate the market]—be they testing laboratories, metrology institutes, or customs posts at the external border of the Community—all need to win the confidence of the Community as a whole if the principle of mutual recognition is to be applied." Similarly, Belgian companies that compete with Polish producers in the same single market must be confident that they are competing on a level playing field: that Polish firms, particularly state-owned firms left over from socialism, are not benefiting from hidden or open subsidies, tax concessions, and other advantages that contravene EU norms.

POLICY INTEGRATION

In addition to market integration, joining the European Union entails extensive policy integration in such areas as transport, the environment, and, most important for the countries of central and eastern Europe, agriculture and cohesion. Policy integration is in some respects even more challenging than market integration, if only because of the large costs involved, notably in the **Common Agricultural Policy (CAP)** and in the Structural Funds.

Agriculture has long been a problem area for the EU. Originally intended to ensure food security for Europe and an adequate standard of living for its farmers, the CAP accomplished this objective by maintaining EU agricultural prices above world market levels and buying surplus products from farmers that then were stored or dumped on world markets. The result was a huge burden on the EU budget, high food costs for European consumers, and disputes with many of the EU's leading trading partners, including the United States and Canada. Governments and outside experts were concerned that extension of the CAP to new countries in central and eastern Europe, all with large agricultural sectors and many small, inefficient farms, would overburden the EU budget and lead to new international trade frictions.

The European Commission attempted to allay these concerns, stressing that agriculture would be a problem for enlargement only if the EU failed to carry through with planned reforms of the CAP. Launched in 1992, CAP reform's key element was a phased decoupling of income support for farmers from price support in the markets. Instead of maintaining farm incomes through the ruinous policy of maintaining high overall price levels, after 1992 the CAP allowed prices to move toward world levels while giving farmers direct compensatory payments to maintain their incomes. The Commission calculated that because preaccession agricultural prices and farm incomes in central and eastern Europe were by EU standards already low, the CAP funds that would flow to farmers in these countries would be much less than often was suggested. The Commission also noted that there was scope in these countries for integrated rural development, that is, for new economic activity in rural communities that would not result in added production of unneeded milk, grain, and meat (e.g., food processing and packaging, tourism, national parks and forests, and handicrafts). Demographic factors also were expected to ease the burden of integrating central and eastern European agriculture into the CAP, as the children of farmers nearing retirement age chose not to continue farming and took up other jobs in the industrial and service sectors of the economy.

Structural or cohesion funds were another sensitive area of policy integration addressed by the Commission. As part of a long-term effort to narrow income disparities in the Union, the EU provides these funds to poorer countries and regions for infrastructure and other economic development projects. Relatively wealthy countries such as Sweden and the Netherlands are net contributors to the cohesion funds, while Greece, Ireland, Portugal, and Spain have been the main beneficiaries. It was obvious that if the same formulas that were used for disadvantaged regions in the existing Union were applied to the much poorer countries of central and eastern Europe, the demands on the EU budget would be unsustainable. The Mediterranean countries made clear that they would resist attempts to divert regional aid from the south to the east to underwrite enlargement. The candidate countries thus were advised to be realistic in the expectations of how much direct assistance they would receive as members from the EU budget. For their part, the European Commission and the EU member states recognized that, as with agriculture, enlargement provided a strong rationale for the EU to improve the efficiency of its cohesion policies and to adopt measures to ensure that funds were provided only to those countries and regions that really needed and could effectively use such assistance.

The Accession Process

Admission of new member states is governed by the Maastricht treaty, which stipulates that any European state that respects the principles of "liberty, democracy, respect for human rights and fundamental freedoms, and the rule of law" may apply to become a member of the Union. According to the procedure set forth in the treaty, applications are addressed to the Council of Ministers. The Council then asks the European Commission to prepare an opinion on the candidate's suitability for membership, after which the Council must decide unanimously on whether to open accession negotiations. Negotiations are carried out by the Commission and the presidency of the Council and are aimed at producing draft treaties of accession between the applicant countries and the members of the Union. Once the negotiations are completed, a draft treaty is submitted to the Council and the European Parliament for approval. The

Council must approve the treaty unanimously, the Parliament by an absolute majority. The member states and the applicant country then formally sign the accession treaty, which is submitted for ratification by all parties in accordance with national constitutional provisions. In most cases this means a simple vote by parliament, but it also can involve a national referendum. (In 2003, candidate countries held referenda on joining the Union; no current member state did so.)

Between March 1994, when Hungary became the first of the central and eastern European states to apply formally for membership, and June 1996, when Slovenia filed its application, all ten associated countries completed this step in the process.

The Commission began working on its opinions shortly after receiving the membership applications from the candidate countries, relying upon experts from its own bureaucracy and on information gathered from the countries themselves. The prospective members were asked to complete long and detailed questionnaires to determine how much convergence with EU norms and legislation had been achieved and to identify remaining problem areas. At its December 1995 Madrid session, the European Council asked the Commission to prepare a "composite paper" that would include opinions on all ten central and eastern European countries. As already decided shortly after Copenhagen, negotiations on enlargement would not begin until six months after the completion of the post-Maastricht IGC. With the conference expected to conclude during the Dutch EU presidency in the first half of 1997, the summer of that year became the target date for the Commission to complete its opinions on all of the applicant countries.

As expected, the Commission delivered its long-awaited report in July 1997, a little less than a month after the Amsterdam summit closing the IGC. Entitled *Agenda 2000*, it gave a detailed assessment of each of the eleven candidate countries—the associated countries and Cyprus.[7] It also recommended steps that the European Union needed to take to be ready for enlargement. In judging the preparedness of the candidate countries for membership, the Commission referred explicitly to the political and economic criteria established by the European Council at Copenhagen. As measured against these criteria, it recommended that five central and eastern European states were ready to begin accession negotiations: the Czech Republic, Estonia, Hungary, Poland, and Slovenia. In addition, it reiterated an earlier opinion that Cyprus was ready to start accession talks. It rejected one applicant—Slovakia—for political reasons, namely, the lack of democracy and respect for human rights under Prime Minister Vladimir Meciar. It concluded that four other countries—Bulgaria, Latvia, Lithuania, and Romania—needed to make greater progress with economic transformation before accession negotiations could begin.

At the December 1997 European Council in Luxembourg, the EU heads of government endorsed the Commission's recommendation in favor of Cyprus and five central and eastern European countries, but they also put in place certain mechanisms intended to minimize any sense of exclusion on the part of the other five central and eastern European candidates. They announced that the accession process would begin on March 30, 1998, at a twenty-six-member meeting in London. The participants would be the fifteen EU member states, the ten associated states, and Cyprus. This meeting would set the overall framework for accession talks with the candidates and symbolically underline that all eleven had the same status and the same theoretical chance to achieve membership. Within this framework, the EU proposed to establish an "enhanced preaccession strategy" based on a new mechanism, the "accession partnership," and to begin the first accession negotiations. The EU stressed that those countries not asked to begin negotiations in 1998 were not necessarily being left permanently behind: They could catch up by improving their economic and, in the case of Slovakia, political performance. The Commission was asked to make annual reports to the Council and to recommend when additional countries were ready to begin accession negotiations.[8] Following a positive report on progress issued by the Commission in the fall 1999, at the December 1999 Helsinki summit the European Council backed the start of accession negotiations with six additional countries: Bulgaria, Latvia, Lithuania, Malta, Romania, and Slovakia. Negotiations with these countries thus began in early 2000.

The Accession Negotiations

In principle, a country joining the EU is asked to accept the *acquis communautaire*. There thus would not seem to be all that much to settle in the accession negotiations. In practice, however, candidate countries often try to negotiate transition periods for the phasing in of EU rules and policies on their territory, or even to secure permanent derogations from certain EU policies or legal provisions. In such negotiations, the current EU member states and the Commission generally try to minimize all such derogations and to keep transition phases relatively short, so as to preserve the unity and coherence of the Union and especially its single market. The acceding countries, on the other hand, may have incentives to delay the adoption of certain costly standards or to seek other exceptions to the *acquis* in response to particular domestic economic or political circumstances. The negotiations also deal with budgetary, policy, and institutional questions: how much each new member state will pay into and receive back from the EU budget, production quotas and subsidy levels under the CAP, and how many seats it will receive in the European Parliament, votes in the Council of Ministers, and so forth.

As was predicted by many in the early 1990s, agriculture was the most difficult issue in the enlargement negotiations. The basic framework for the negotiations was set at the Berlin European Council in March 1999, where the fifteen, generally following the guidelines established in *Agenda 2000*, adopted a budgetary framework for the period 2000–2006 based on the assumption that as many as six new member states could join the Union in 2002. In the agreement, CAP spending in the current member states in the first post-enlargement year was set at EUR 39.4 billion, while comparable spending for six new member states was set at EUR 1.6 billion. There was no provision for direct income support for farmers in the new member states—a decision taken on the grounds that such payments were a replacement for earlier indirect supports, which farmers in the new member states had never received.[9]

When negotiations on the agricultural chapter opened in June 2000, the Berlin framework quickly became a sticking point. In their opening positions, all of the candidate countries requested that direct payments be granted to their farmers at the same level provided to farmers in current member states. The 1999 Berlin budget agreement did not provide for such payments, which some member states argued were not part of the *acquis* and should not be extended to new members. Differences over production quotas were equally stark. The Commission proposed that quotas be based on past performance levels during the 1995–1999 reference period. The candidate countries argued that in recent years their agricultural production had been hit by the collapse of communism, falling export markets, and adverse weather. They therefore generally opposed any agreement based on current output levels.

Reacting to the strong political response in Poland and other candidate countries to its position on direct payments, in early 2002 the Commission revised its initial approach and proposed that direct payments to farmers in the new member states be set at 25 percent of EU levels upon enlargement and rise to 100 percent over a ten-year period, a stance that the candidate countries still argued was unacceptable and would put their farmers at a competitive disadvantage.[10]

After agriculture, the item in the accession negotiations with the greatest financial implications was the structural and cohesion funds. The Commission outlined its proposed approach to the negotiation of the structural funds chapter in January 2002, staying roughly within the Berlin framework (after allowing for adjustments in the enlargement scenario).[11] It proposed that structural operations funds be phased in over a three-year period from 2004 to 2006 to take account of the absorption capacity of the new members. Aid would be capped at 4 percent of GDP, considerably below the levels received by Portugal and Ireland in the 1990s. The ten new member countries would receive some EUR 25.567 billion in 2004–2006. EU aid per capita in the new member countries would reach EUR 137 in 2006, compared with EUR 231 in the four current member-state cohesion countries. Additional structural funds would be allocated for nuclear safety projects (closing Soviet-built plants in Slovakia and Lithuania), for infrastructure in northern Cyprus, and for a special fund for institutional capacity building in the new member states.

Another difficult issue in the accession negotiations was the free movement of people. Movement of labor within the EU is one of the four freedoms (along with free movement of goods, services, and capital) guaranteed in the Treaty of Rome and made the centerpiece of the program in the late 1980s and early 1990s to complete the European Union's internal market. But free movement of labor with central and eastern Europe also has been highly controversial in the current member states, provoking widespread fear, particularly in Germany and Austria, about waves of cheap labor moving westward and exacerbating unemployment and depressing wages. In view of the sensitivity of this issue, the free movement of labor was an area in which the Union itself, departing from its usual stance that the *acquis* should be kept intact and that transition periods and derogations be as limited as possible, insisted upon an extensive transition regime and a delay in the full application of the *acquis* for at least five years.

Another important issue in the accession negotiations was the "Schengen" system of border controls, named for the Luxembourg town where it was decided. Begun in 1985 as an intergovernmental arrangement among five member states of the then EC, Schengen was incorporated into the *acquis* with the 1997 Treaty of Amsterdam and was expected to be implemented in full by the candidate countries from day one of membership (even though Britain and Ireland have opt-outs and do not participate in Schengen). The need to tighten the external borders of the Union is seen in Brussels and the national capitals as an inevitable counterpart to the removal of barriers to the flow of goods and people within the Union. With internal border controls dismantled, crossing the external borders of the Union to enter one member state means in effect legal entry into all member states of the Union. Governments in EU capitals thus insist that the new EU members control their external borders, especially since the candidate countries already have become important transit points for nationals of "third," or outside, countries seeking to enter the Union. To comply with Schengen, the candidate countries were required to impose visa restrictions on visitors from Russia, Ukraine, Belarus, Moldova, and other countries of the former Soviet Union, a move that caused tension with some of these countries, particularly with Russia over access to Kaliningrad, an exclave of Russia that after enlargement will be surrounded by EU member states (Lithuania and Poland). They also were required to take practical measures to improve the control of their external borders, including hiring additional and more professional border guards, building additional fences and watchtowers, and improving surveillance by aircraft and helicopter.

Although at times difficult, the negotiations on these and the other enlargement-related issues proceeded relatively smoothly. Beginning with the easiest and least controversial areas, the negotiators "closed" successive chapters with the candidate countries, as the latter continued to make progress in adapting their economic and political systems to EU norms. In the crucial area of the single market, the Commission largely prevailed in its insistence on ac-

ceptance of an undiluted *acquis*. With the important exception of free movement of labor, remarkably few transitional arrangements were granted in the
three most relevant chapters. The free movement of goods chapter was closed
with the ten leading candidate countries with a mere six transitional arrangements, all relatively short in duration and dealing with marketing authoriza-
tions for pharmaceuticals and, in one case, medical devices. Similarly, there are
only a few transitional arrangements in the chapter on freedom to provide services, all having to do with the financial sector and such issues as the status of
credit unions in various accession countries. In the chapter on free movement
of capital, there are eleven agreed transitional arrangements, but they deal with
the politically sensitive issues of the purchases of secondary residences and farm
and forest land in the accession countries rather than the movement of capital
for general business purposes.

The one area in which the single market *acquis* was affected by transition
arrangements is the free movement of labor, which was done largely at the insistence of the current member states. Under the terms of the provisions for free
movement of persons to be included in the accession treaties, for two years following accession each of the member states in the existing Union may apply
national measures to limit access to their labor markets from the new member
states. Following this period, there will be reviews of the access that new-
member-state labor markets have to the old member states. The old member
states may keep transition arrangements in place for another three years. The
transition period should end after five years, but member states in the old
Union will have the right to prolong transition arrangements for another two
years if there are serious disturbances of the labor market or the threat of such
disturbances. These provisions will limit the flow of labor from east to west,
but they are in part a political gesture, aimed at assuaging concerns in countries
such as Austria and Germany about unemployment and competition for jobs
from workers in the new member states. Most experts believe that immigration
pressures after enlargement will be modest, as workers in the accession countries will be encouraged to stay where they are (or even return from western
Europe) by the rising incomes and increased job opportunities in their own
countries after enlargement (much as happened in Portugal and Spain when
they joined the EC in 1986).

In view of the steady progress being made in the accession negotiations, at
the European Council meeting in Göteborg in June 2001 the fifteen set the end
of 2002 as the target date for concluding accession treaties with those countries
judged ready for membership, a timetable that would allow these countries to
join the EU in 2004 and to take part as members in the elections to the European Parliament set for June of that year.[12] At the Laeken European Council in
December 2001, the fifteen confirmed this timetable and named the ten countries that they regarded as on track for membership in 2004: Cyprus, the Czech
Republic, Estonia, Hungary, Latvia, Lithuania, Malta, Poland, Slovakia, and

Slovenia. The stage thus was set for a "big bang" enlargement that among the negotiating candidate countries would leave out only Bulgaria and Romania, whose economic performance and progress in adopting the *acquis* still lagged behind that of the other candidate countries.[13]

However, as 2002 began, there still were many unresolved issues relating to agricultural payments and production levels, the EU budget, and certain rules and regulations for which various candidate countries sought exceptions or transitional arrangements. Because the negotiations with the candidate countries on agriculture were linked to the EU's own internal discussions on the reform of the CAP, finalization of this issue was deferred from the initial target date of the spring of 2002 to the fall of that year, after the scheduled national elections in France and Germany. The stage thus was set for an intense round of negotiations during the Danish presidency in the second half of 2002, aiming at a finalization of the accession terms at a December summit in Copenhagen.

Endgame

In October 2002 the European Commission delivered its long-awaited recommendations on which countries were ready to finalize accession negotiations by the end of the year. It reaffirmed the choice of the "Laeken 10" and stated that although Bulgaria and Romania were not ready for membership, they could join the main group by 2007.[14] Meeting in Brussels in late October, the heads of state and governments of the fifteen made the final decisions about the financial terms to be offered to the new member states upon accession. In the compromise final offer on agriculture to the candidate countries, the fifteen agreed to start direct payments at the 25 percent level and raise them to full EU levels only by 2013—an arrangement that was not essentially different from the deal on offer in the spring and that was criticized by candidate country governments as unfair and possibly endangering prospects for approval of the accession treaty in national referenda. The October European Council also settled on the amount of aid under the structural and cohesion funds to be given to the new member states in 2004–2006, cutting assistance from the EUR 25.567 billion level agreed at Berlin to EUR 23 billion.

These decisions paved the way for an intense final round of negotiations with the ten lead candidate countries, aiming toward conclusion at the December Copenhagen summit. Acting on its own initiative, in late November the Danish presidency put forward a supplementary package intended to win final accession country acceptance of the deal. It called for additional spending of EUR 2.45 billion beyond the levels agreed by the European Council in October, to be devoted to agriculture, improving border security, and, for Slovakia and Lithuania, nuclear dismantling. Following continued hard bargaining in the days leading up to the Copenhagen summit, the Danish package became the basis for the final accession deal. It was agreed that some EUR 40.4 billion would be paid by the EU to the accession countries in 2004–2006, half of it to Poland. This was a gross figure, not counting payments into the EU coffers from the accession countries. Net of such payments, total transfers to the new members in the remainder of the budget period were projected to be about EUR 12 billion. The EU stuck to its original position that direct payments to farmers in the new member states would be set at 25 percent of EU levels, but the accession countries won the right to transfer money from long-term EU aid funds and their own national budgets to direct payments, with the effect that such payments could reach 60 percent of EU levels by 2004. These terms ultimately were accepted by all ten of the candidate countries in the days leading up to the summit, resulting in a triumphant outcome in Copenhagen.

Apart from the terms of the accession deal, one of the most noteworthy aspects of the enlargement endgame was the set of final premembership checks that the EU put in place to ensure that the candidate countries would follow through on implementation before May 1, 2004, the target date set by the EU Council of Ministers for formal entry following the completion of all ratification procedures. At the insistence of member-state governments that were skeptical of the degree of real convergence with EU norms in the candidate countries or worried about their own domestic public opinion, the accession process includes final checks in the period between signature of the accession treaties and the official entry into the EU following ratification. If one or more candidate countries backslides or fails to complete agreed preaccession tasks, formal admission to the Union could be delayed. The accession treaties also contain safeguard clauses that can be invoked by the existing member states after accession and that allow for the temporary suspension of full market access in the event of economic crisis.[15]

CYPRUS

The most suspenseful issue in the enlargement endgame concerned the question of Cyprus. The Cypriot government had applied for membership already in 1990, and in June 1993 the Commission had issued a favorable opinion on the application of Cyprus for membership, noting the relative strength of the Cypriot economy and the progress that Cyprus had made in using its association agreement with the EU to align itself with many EU laws and practices. Under pressure from Greece, in June 1994 the Corfu European Council confirmed that the next phase of the enlargement process would include Cyprus. This meant that the EU was pledged not to proceed with any eastward enlargement without also taking up the Cypriot application, either simultaneously or beforehand. The Cyprus candidacy thus was at least tacitly linked with those of the central and east European countries. Greece subsequently warned repeatedly that it would veto any enlargement that did not include Cyprus. For its part, Turkey argued that any move to incorporate Cyprus into the EU would run counter to the 1960 Treaty of Guarantee signed by Greece, Turkey, and Britain, which bars Cyprus from joining any international organization of which Greece and Turkey are not both members. The Turkish government further warned that if the Greek Cypriot government joined the EU against its wishes, it would incorporate the northern part of the island into Turkey. The EU rejected this interpretation of the 1960 treaty and argued as a matter of principle that Turkey could not wield a veto over the actions of the legally recognized government in Nicosia.

Throughout the 1990s, EU policy toward Cyprus rested on the hope that the prospect of EU membership would soften the differences between the Greek and Turkish communities, much the way EU membership for Ireland and the United Kingdom helped to defuse conflict over the status of Northern Ireland. Per capita income in the Turkish sector of Cyprus is only one-third the level of that in the south, and the Turkish minority stands to benefit enormously from the structural aid and market access that would come with enlargement. By the time the EU began accession talks with Cyprus in March 1998, however, there was little sign that this approach was working. The Turkish community turned down an invitation to participate in the talks and repeated its threats to accept an offer to merge with Turkey.

At the December 1999 Helsinki European Council, the fifteen expressed support for a comprehensive political settlement on the island, to be negotiated under UN auspices, that would allow a united Cyprus to enter the EU. However, they also stipulated that if no settlement was reached by the completion of the accession negotiations, the Council would decide on accession without a settlement being made a precondition. The Helsinki decision subsequently became the standard EU formulation on this issue—the last word, in effect, to which the Turkish community and Turkey were expected to respond.

Eleventh-hour hopes that a settlement could be reached that would enable a united Cyprus to enter the Union were concentrated heavily on the initiative put forward by UN Secretary-General Kofi Annan in the fall of 2002. It called for the establishment of a loose confederation that then would enter the EU. Accepted by the Greek Cypriot government but rejected by Turkish Cypriot leader Denktash, the UN offer remained the basis for negotiations that were to extend beyond the December 2002 Copenhagen decisions into the period before Cyprus accedes in May 2004 and possibly into the membership period itself. Absent an agreement, however, the EU was determined to admit a divided Cyprus into the Union, a prospect that was certain to heighten tensions with Turkey and that will create certain practical problems with regard to trade and the free movement of people.

TURKEY

Of even greater significance for—and clearly linked to—the Cyprus question for the long-term future of the EU is the fate of Turkey, which has applied to become a member of the Union but about which many Europeans remain profoundly ambivalent. Turkey and the EC signed an association agreement in September 1963, similar to the 1962 agreement between the European Community and Greece that helped to pave the way to eventual membership of that country. The 1963 agreement referred to "the accession of Turkey to the Community at a later date."[16] It was followed in 1970 by the conclusion of an additional protocol to the 1963 agreement that came into effect in January 1973 and stipulated that the two sides were to establish a customs union within a twenty-two-year period, or no later than the end of 1995. In April 1987 Turkey formally applied for EC membership, but its candidacy was not taken very seriously in Brussels or the member-state capitals, given Turkey's poverty and such complicating issues as Turkey's relatively poor record on democracy and human rights, its disputes with Greece, and the Cyprus problem.

Despite deteriorating political relations between the two sides over human rights and other issues, Turkey and the EU concluded the long-awaited customs union in March 1995, along with an accompanying package of financial aid. The European Parliament threatened to reject ratification of the agreement over Turkey's human rights record but, under heavy prodding from the Commission and member-state governments, finally approved it in December 1995, allowing the customs union to begin on January 1 of the following year. Many in western Europe saw the 1995 agreement as a substitute for EU membership. Turkey, in contrast, regarded the customs union as a step toward EU membership, which remained a key objective.

In *Agenda 2000*, the European Commission affirmed Turkey's eligibility for membership, but it drew attention to the many economic, political, human rights, and foreign policy problems that came with Turkey's candidacy. In the December 1997 Luxembourg decisions, Turkey was not invited to begin accession negotiations along with the six leading candidate countries, nor was it given the prospect of rapidly catching up with the other candidate countries, as were the second-wave central and eastern European countries. This decision in effect placed Turkey in a separate category and provoked a severe crisis in Turkish-EU relations. The fact that western Europe seemed to be backing away from earlier pledges regarding membership contributed to a deep sense of betrayal in Turkey.

Relations between the two sides finally took a turn for the better in December 1999, when the Helsinki European Council, endorsing the recommendation in the Commission's October 1999 progress report, formally upgraded the status of Turkey to candidate member. The heads of state and government declared that "Turkey is a candidate state destined to join the Union on the basis of the same criteria as applied to the other candidate states."[17] To lend substance to this claim, the EU agreed to develop a preaccession strategy for Turkey and to conclude an accession partnership agreement on the same basis as those negotiated with the other candidate countries. Turkey also was granted the right to participate in certain EU programs and in multilateral meetings among the EU member states and the candidates for membership.

While the Helsinki decisions mitigated the previous tensions, they by no means resolved the underlying issues. Turkey faces economic, political, and security problems that distinguish it from the rest of Europe. Per capita GDP is only one-third the EU average. According to current projections, Turkey's population will surpass even that of Germany by 2015, making it the largest country in the Union were it to become a member. Internally, the struggle with the Kurdish independence movement has resulted in thousands of deaths and harsh criticism in western Europe about violations of human rights by the Turkish government and armed forces. Above all, there are doubts in both Turkey and the EU about whether Turkey ever can become a member state and whether, even if it were to make all the requisite political and economic reforms, it would be accepted in the European family by the historically Christian nations of the West.

This point was dramatically underscored in November 2002 when former French president and European Convention president Valéry Giscard d'Estaing, in a move seen as a tactic to delay scheduling accession talks with Ankara at the upcoming Copenhagen summit, spoke out against membership for Turkey, telling *Le Monde* that it had "a different culture, a different approach, a different way of life." "Its capital is not in Europe, 95 percent of its population live outside Europe, it is not a European country." In his view, Turkey's entry into the EU would lead to demands to admit other Middle Eastern and North African states, starting with Morocco. Ultimately it would mean "the end of the European Union."[18]

Giscard's foray clearly backfired, however, and the reaction to it was a factor—albeit probably a secondary one—in the remarkable turn of events that led to decisions at the Copenhagen summit that, while they fell short of Turkey's maximal demands, dramatically advanced its prospects for membership. Turning aside intense pressure from Turkey and the United States to set a definite date for the start of the accession negotiations, the European Council declared that it would take a decision on negotiations in December 2004 (following the European Commission's regular report on the progress of the candidate countries), but that if it was satisfied that Turkey met the Copenhagen political criteria, the EU would open accession negotiations "without delay." From Turkey's perspective, the failure to secure a guaranteed date was a setback for pro-EU sentiment within Turkey and raised the prospect that Cyprus, which would participate in the December 2004 decision as an EU member, could block its candidacy. However, the fairly mild response of the Turkish government (in dramatic contrast to its reaction to the 1997 Luxembourg decisions) seemed to confirm a widely held view that an informal guarantee had been extended and that, if Turkey continues on its present trajectory, negotiations indeed will begin in 2005.

An Enlarged Union and a Wider Europe

The accession negotiations at the December 2002 Copenhagen summit ended amid deepening intra-European and transatlantic tensions over the post–September 11 international situation and in particular over the U.S.-UK project to drive Iraqi dictator Saddam Hussein from power on the grounds that his possession of weapons of mass destruction posed a grave threat to regional and global security. France and Germany led the opposition to U.S. policy, backed by Belgium and several other smaller European countries and the overwhelming majority of European public opinion, while Britain, Spain, and Italy were more supportive of U.S. policy. The divisions among the EU member states and across the Atlantic placed the candidate countries in an awkward position, forcing them to choose between solidarity with the United States or with key European countries.

The crisis came to a head in January 2003, as France took the lead in opposing the United States in the UN Security Council. Asked to comment on the growing opposition to U.S. policy in Europe, U.S. Secretary of Defense Donald Rumsfeld provoked a storm of controversy by claiming that the opposition was centered in "old Europe" and that the "center of gravity is moving east." A week later, the leaders of Spain, Portugal, Italy, the UK, Denmark, and three accession countries—Hungary, Poland, and the Czech Republic—published an open letter in the European edition of the *Wall Street Journal* in which they declared their commitment to solidarity with the United States. The "Letter of Eight," as it became known, was followed by a second declaration by the "Vilnius Ten" declaring their support for Washington. Both letters had been drafted and approved in ad hoc consultations among the governments concerned, without involving the EU machinery in Brussels or Greece (the EU presidency country). French president Jacques Chirac was furious at these apparent breaches of intra-European solidarity and claimed that the accession countries had "missed a good opportunity to keep quiet." This remark in turn caused deep offense in the accession countries and raised questions about whether "old" member states such as France in fact were prepared to welcome the new member states as equals.

Although these developments severely strained political relations in Europe, they did not derail the enlargement process, which went ahead as planned. Under the auspices of the Greek presidency, the leaders of the ten accession countries met in Athens on April 16, 2003, with their member-state counterparts to sign the accession treaty. Moreover, despite the earlier controversies over agriculture and finance, voters in the acceding countries overwhelmingly approved the accession treaty: 84 percent for and 16 percent against in Hungary, and respective percentages of 93 and 7 in Slovakia, 77 and 23 in Poland, 77 and 23 in the Czech Republic, 54 and 46 in traditionally Euroskeptic Malta, 90 and 10 in Slovenia, and 91 and 9 in Lithuania. In most of these countries, the only shadow over the referenda was low turnout: only 46 percent of eligible voters cast their ballots in Hungary and only 52 percent in Slovakia, suggesting more indifference and ignorance than outright opposition.

With ratification assured, the key question for the EU was what kind of Europe would emerge in the future. The EU and the accession countries still face years of hard work and difficult economic, political, and institutional adaptation to fully overcome the division of Europe. Income levels in the accession countries still range only from 33 percent (Latvia) to 80 percent (Cyprus) of the EU per capita average, and convergence to EU levels may take decades. While the accession countries have adopted nearly all of the *acquis* in the accession negotiations and transposed it into national law, developing all of the ingrained habits of trust and cooperation that have grown over decades in the western part of Europe still will take time.

The EU also will face some important challenges relating to the "leftovers" and "left outs"—countries that are slated to become members of the Union but are not yet ready, as well as countries that are unlikely ever to become members but are nonetheless still part of Europe and will need to find ways to relate to an expanded EU. Bulgaria and Romania are expected to join the EU in 2007, but only if they use the intervening period to make up the deficiencies that prevented them from joining with the other ten candidate countries in 2004. The fate of Turkey also remains a question mark for the Union. Whether it can make the reforms needed to launch accession negotiations in 2005 and whether the EU itself can hold true to its promise, politically unpopular in many places, to make Turkey a member will be key issues for the future.

The Western Balkans—Albania, Bosnia-Herzegovina, Croatia, Macedonia, and Serbia and Montenegro (the loose federation that replaced Yugoslavia in 2003 and technically includes the province of Kosovo)—also are likely to become members of the EU at some point, as these countries are virtually surrounded by present and future EU member states. The task of actually preparing these poor, war-torn, and crime-ridden countries to rejoin Europe is likely to be long and difficult, however, and will require large amounts of political and financial capital from the international community and, above all, from the EU itself. Farther east, there is the question of Russia, Ukraine, Belarus, and Moldova. Given its size, diversity, and great-power traditions, Russia is unlikely ever to become a member of the EU, but building a solid and cooperative Russia–EU relationship, probably in the form of a free-trade agreement, is in the interests of both sides. Ukraine, Belarus, and Moldova—the new "lands between"—

might at some point become members or very close associates of the Union, or they could drift back into closer association with Russia. Either way, their ultimate path will be of huge significance for the EU and the wider international community.

Perhaps the biggest question looming on the horizon is how the EU itself will change as a consequence of enlargement and of the important institutional changes that are being driven by the enlargement process. The accession countries have rejoined Europe only to find "Europe" itself engaged in a vast debate about how Europe should be defined, where its ultimate borders lie, and how it can be made to work efficiently with an expanded and more diverse set of members—all issues that were being addressed in the European Convention and the ensuing Intergovernmental Conference (IGC) of 2003–2004. By fully participating in both the Convention and the IGC, however, the central and eastern European countries had received confirmation, if any were still needed, that after decades of separation, they indeed had returned to Europe.

Notes

1. *The Downing Street Years* (New York: HarperCollins, 1993), 769.
2. Charles Grant, *Delors: Inside the House that Jacques Built* (London: Nicholas Brealey, 1994), 143.
3. *The European Councils: Conclusions of the Presidency 1992–1994* (Luxembourg: Office for Official Publications of the European Communities, 1995), 86.
4. *The European Councils: Conclusions of the Presidency 1992–1994* (Luxembourg: Office for Official Publications of the European Communities, 1995), 86.
5. *European Union: Selected Instruments Taken from the Treaties* (Luxembourg: Office for Official Publications of the European Communities, 1995), vol. 1.
6. Commission of the European Communities [hereinafter, CEC], *White Paper: Preparation of the Associated Countries of Central and Eastern Europe for Integration into the Internal Market of the Union*, COM(95) 163, May 3, 1995, 8.
7. CEC, *Agenda 2000*, 3 vols., Strasbourg, DOC/97/6–8, July 1997.
8. "Luxembourg European Council, 12 and 13 December 1997: Presidency Conclusions," SN 400/97, 4.
9. "Presidency Conclusions: Berlin European Council, 24 and 25 March 1999," DOC/99/1.
10. CEC, *Enlargement and Agriculture: Successfully Integrating the New Member States into the CAP: Issues Paper*, SEC(2002) 95 final, Brussels, January 30, 2002. Online at europa.eu.int.
11. CEC, *Communication from the Commission: Information Note—Common Financial Framework 2004–2006 for the Accession Negotiations*, Brussels, SEC(2002) 102 final, January 30, 2002. Online at europa.eu.int.
12. "Presidency Conclusions: Göteborg European Council, 15 and 16 June 2001," SN 200/1/01. Online at europa.eu.int.

13. "Presidency Conclusions: European Council Meeting in Laeken, 14 and 15 December 2001," SN 300/1/01. Online at europa.eu.int.

14. CEC, *Towards the Enlarged Union: Strategy Paper and Report of the European Commission on the progress towards accession by each of the candidate countries*, Brussels, COM(2002) 700 final, October 9, 2002. Online at europa.eu.int.

15. "Presidency Conclusions: Copenhagen European Council, 12 and 13 December 2002," SN 400/02. Online at europa.eu.int.

16. *Agreement Establishing an Association between the European Economic Community and Turkey*, Ankara, September 12, 1963, *Official Journal of the European Communities*, 3687 (1964).

17. "Presidency Conclusions: Helsinki European Council, 10 and 11 December 1999," SN 300/99.

18. "Pour ou contre l'adhésion de la Turquie à l'Union européenne," *Le Monde*, November 8, 2002.

Suggestions for Further Reading

Much information is available on the website of the European Union, europa.eu.int, and in particular the home page of the Directorate-General for Enlargement of the European Commission, online at europa.eu.int/comm/enlargement/index_en.html.

Avery, Graham, and Fraser Cameron. *The Enlargement of the European Union.* Sheffield, UK: Sheffield Academic Press, 1998.

Baun, Michael. *A Wider Europe: The Process and Politics of European Union Enlargement.* Lanham, Md.: Rowman & Littlefield, 2000.

European Commission. *Towards the Enlarged Union: Strategy Paper and Report of the European Commission on the progress towards accession by each of the candidate countries*, Brussels, COM(2002) 700 final, October 2002. Online at europa.eu.int.

Van Oudenaren, John. *The Changing Face of Europe: EU Enlargement and Implications for Transatlantic Relations* (Washington, D.C.: American Institute for Contemporary German Studies, 2003).

CHAPTER 6

Keep Out! Protectionism, Migration Control, and Globalization

Jochen Lorentzen

November 15, 2002: In the early morning hours a small fishing vessel from Mazara del Vallo in Sicily trawls the waters some thirty-five nautical miles south of the island of Pantelleria in search of its catch. Suddenly the crew of the *Giove* spot another vessel. The twelve-meter boat has engine damage and is drifting, helpless in the choppy sea. Aboard are 129 migrants or, as the media will later refer to them, *clandestini,* illegal immigrants. The captain of the *Giove,* Gaspare Giaccalone, informs the coast guard in Pantelleria. The local commander dispatches two patrol boats. The two officers, Francesco Nicolosi and Toni Casano, reach the ship, abandoned by its crew. The wind from the nearby deserts in North Africa that the locals call *scirocco* whips up the sea. The rescuers realize that it is too dangerous in these weather conditions to transfer the shipwrecked migrants onto the coast guard vessels. They decide to tug the vessel into port at Pantelleria together with the *Giove.*

The four boats arrive at destination at a quarter to seven in the evening. One can see that the people who leave the boat are not from nearby Morocco or Tunisia. Their skin color gives away their origins farther south. Most turn out to be from Liberia. There are men, women, and children. The youngest, Milton, is no more than two years old. He is traveling with his mother, a housekeeper, and his father, a painter and decorator. The migrants are exhausted from the strenuous trip, scared, and cold; some suffer from hypothermia. A few are too weak to walk by themselves. One man faints and is assisted by Dr. Nagar of the local hospital. The police accompany the migrants to buses that take them to a refugee center next to a military barrack. The local authorities provide the migrants—most of whom have no money on them—with blankets, clothes, and food.

The fate of these people in Europe is uncertain. But they were relatively lucky. Every year people who try to get illegally into Europe face horrible ends to their journeys: they drown in the Mediterranean; they freeze to death crossing the mountains in Romania or the woods that separate Russia from the Baltics; they suffocate in unventilated truck trailers; or they are killed by unscrupulous traffickers along the way.

Why do people entrust their lives, and that of their children, to unsafe passages to distant destinations where they will officially not even be welcome? People try to come to Europe for many reasons. One reason that almost all of them share is the hope for a life better than what prevails in their home countries. There are, in turn, many reasons for life being difficult at home. Many, perhaps most, are homemade. This essay first focuses on one that is not, namely, rampant protectionism by a blatantly hypocritical EU against the very products that poor countries are good at making. If you cannot sell what you produce, you can sit back and either despair or fantasize that divine intervention may rain milk and honey on you. Or you consider your options, get up and leave in search for something to do, including a job abroad, that allows you to take care of your family. In short, market access and migration are linked, albeit not always in intuitively obvious ways. Protectionism sheds light on the difference between the ideology and the practice of globalization, or between what it promises and what it actually delivers.

The second focus of the essay is on the causes, mechanisms, control, and consequences of migration itself. Most of the readers of this book are in principle likely to have the required identity papers and the financial resources to go to pretty much any place in the world, be it for work or for pleasure—if not immediately, then at some not-too-distant point in the future. They have that in common with the increasing volume and variety of cross-border flows of goods, services, and capital which, along with rapid technological innovation, we tend to think of as globalization. But the freedom to travel is the privilege of a relatively small elite. The vast majority of the world's population could not simply hop on a plane to Paris or London even if they could afford the ticket. The reason is that their request for a visa would be turned down. To them, globalization means putting up with more international competition at home while not being able legally to offer their labor abroad. If circumstances make them go anyway, they become illegal migrants and subject to legal and other sanctions. They are also likely to come in contact with one of the fastest-growing and most heinous forms of organized crime, namely, human trafficking. If they make it to a destination country, their illegal status affects how they work, where they stay, and if they can integrate into the local society, including the official labor market.

The contradiction between the progressive liberalization of the markets for (most but not all) goods, services, and capital on the one hand, and the retention of severe restrictions on the mobility of labor on the other, is the third and final focus. The liberalization of the world economy makes it necessary for individuals, firms, and countries to adjust to often dramatic changes. The benefits and the costs of this process are not distributed evenly. By keeping labor mobility off the globalization agenda, rich countries deprive poorer countries of benefits.

This is brutally selfish, curiously shortsighted, and totally inconsistent with growing economic interdependence in the world.

Global Trade Liberalization and (EU) Market Access

The EU is a major player in the world trading system. In 2001, 18.4 percent of the world's exports originated in the EU, and it was the destination for 18.2 percent of its imports. Of exports from developing countries, 29.2 percent went to the EU in 2000, slightly more than to the United States. The EU is also one of the most influential members of the World Trade Organization. Issues it pushes are likely to receive attention, even if controversial, and not much happens in world trade negotiations unless the EU is on board. The EU regards itself both as a champion of global trade liberalization and a staunch defender of developing-country interests. On December 16, 2002, Pascal Lamy, the European Commission's chief trade official, declared, after submitting the Commission's ideas for agricultural negotiations in the current world trade round:

> The message today is we are pushing the Doha development agenda forward across the board. We are ready to put our money where our mouth is, and we have now put forward ambitious but realistic proposals in all sectors, including agriculture, one of the most challenging for the EU. This is a win-win proposal. It is fair to others, particularly developing countries, as it takes into account their development needs.

To many farmers and producers of labor-intensive products like textiles or clothes in developing countries this must have seemed a bad, old joke. Bad because EU trade policies are inimical to giving poor countries a fair chance to compete in the global economy. All rich countries are hypocrites when it comes to protectionism. The EU has merely the dubious honor of being *primus inter pares* of the bad guys. In a report entitled *Rigged Rules and Double Standards*, the British charity Oxfam ranked the EU first in the Double Standards League of free-trade rhetoric and protectionist practice, ahead of the United States, Canada, and Japan.[1]

The joke is also old. Global trade negotiations take place, until 1994 under the auspices of the GATT and from 1995 through the WTO, in so-called rounds. EU intransigence on farm sector reform is proverbial and almost derailed the Uruguay Round of trade negotiations in the early 1990s. Ten years on, in the curiously named Development Round of world trade negotiations launched in Doha, Qatar, in November 2001, the EU was again holding up progress in agricultural liberalization, by and large the single most important potential outcome of global trade talks for the large majority of developing countries.

This section describes EU trade policy vis-à-vis developing countries in the context of commitments under the WTO Uruguay Round Agreement.[2] It points out where the EU has not honored the spirit of the agreement and what consequences this has had for developing country producers. It also looks at the ongoing new world trade talks in which the EU is again showing little inclination to entertain demands for farm sector reform. Finally, it discusses the reasons behind this sorry state of affairs.

EU TRADE POLICY VIS-À-VIS DEVELOPING COUNTRIES

Agriculture

Many of the world's poorest people eke out a living by working the land. In the forty-nine poorest countries, from Afghanistan to Zambia, three-fourths of the labor force work in agriculture, producing 30 percent of GDP.[3] So one of the grand bargains underlying the Uruguay Round negotiations was to bring agriculture for the first time into the multilateral discipline of the WTO. In exchange, the developing countries agreed to the inclusion of issues close to the heart of multinational firms, namely, services (GATS), trade-related investment measures (TRIMS), and trade-related intellectual property rights (TRIPS).

The Agreement on Agriculture required the EU to replace nontariff barriers such as quotas with more transparent tariffs and to reduce average tariff levels. Yet tariffs applied by rich countries on farm goods on average remained four to five times higher than those on industrial products (see Table 6.1); more than a third of EU agricultural tariff lines that denote the import taxes individual products face had duties above 15 percent.[4] Products of particular export interest to developing countries, such as in food processing, regularly run into tariff peaks that, for example, for meat products, can go as high as 250 percent. The

Table 6.1   Uruguay Round Tariff Rates of OECD Countries

Sector	Bound rate %	Applied rate %
Agriculture	15	14
Textiles and clothing	11	8
Other manufactures	4	3

Source: Kym Anderson, "Developing-Country Interests in WTO-Induced Agricultural Trade Reform," in Developing Countries in the World Trading System: The Uruguay Round and Beyond, ed. Ramesh Adhikari and Prema-Chandra Athukorala (Cheltenham: Elgar, 2002), 40–67, table 3.1.

Note: Bound rates refer to the maximum applicable rates as opposed to those that are effectively applied. The higher bound rates may be invoked in times of distress.

world's other major traders are no angels, either—Canada protects its meat industry with tariffs of 120 percent, while the United States charges 121 percent
on ground nuts and Japan 170 on raw cane sugar. Tariff escalation, a practice
whereby products at higher levels of processing attract higher tariffs than the
upstream inputs, essentially allowed rich countries to engage in import substitution of more profitable downstream activities. In plain language, this means
that a poor Colombian coffee farmer can export coffee beans without facing
tariffs. This is essentially because rich countries need the beans but cannot grow
them. But tariffs would hit him hard were he to try to export roasted or soluble
coffee. Rich countries prefer to keep the only lucrative part of the coffee value
chain for their own producers. Under these circumstances it is pretty difficult
to increase local value added, which is what needs to happen for incomes in
poor countries to grow. Ironically, if poor countries tried to do the same thing
by raising tariffs on, say, machinery to build up their own equipment industry,
the international financial institutions would harangue them for applying the
wrong policy. Finally, developing-country producers continued to attract the
misguided wrath of EU bureaucrats, who subjected them to anti-dumping investigations or countervailing action. In the former, the European Commission
accuses foreign producers of selling their wares in the EU market below cost to
gain an unfair competitive advantage. In the latter, it charges that foreign firms
benefit from government subsidies that give them an edge vis-à-vis their competitors in the EU. The economic logic behind these actions is dubious at best,
and the administrative practice is ludicrous in its bias in favor of vested domestic
interests—of producers, that is, because consumers would obviously only benefit from cheap imports.

The Agreement on Agriculture made at the Uruguay Round also committed the EU to reducing domestic and export subsidies. But EU countries every
year still subsidize the farm sector with more than $300 billion, roughly twice
as much as the value of agricultural imports from developing countries.[5] For
good measure, most of these subsidies are concentrated on commodities ex-
ported to the south. In the current trade talks, the EU has agreed to negotiate
reductions—not eliminations—of export subsidies, but not a cut in the overall
level of subsidies.

All of this is bad news for farmers in developing countries, except for those
in some former colonies who enjoy privileged trading relationships with the
EU. In short, EU farm trade policy has three effects. First, high average tariffs
make it difficult or outright impossible to penetrate the EU market. Tariffs on
meats, cereals, and dairy products range between 50 percent and more than 100
percent. Second, subsidies (both export and non-) allow EU producers to dump
their products at artificially deflated prices on developing-country markets.
Handouts from the CAP amount to between one-half (wheat) and three-
quarters (beef and veal) of the income of export producers. This allows EU
exporters to offer their fare at between a quarter (white sugar) and one-half

(skimmed milk) of production costs and pushes more competitive local producers out of the domestic market.[6] Third, the glut of EU exports also reduces
the contestability of (e.g., non-sugar-producing) third-country markets both in
high- and low-income countries simply because nobody can beat the subsidized prices of EU exporters.

The cost of refined cane sugar from South Africa, Mozambique, Malawi,
and Zambia is considerably less than one-half of the cost of refined beet sugar
from Europe. Yet in 2001 EU sugar exports accounted for 40 percent of the
world market. Both farmers and refiners such as Germany's Südzucker, Italy's
Eridania, and the UK's British Sugar enjoy guaranteed prices. The life of these
companies resembles the best tradition of Soviet planning. The EU market is
protected by tariffs up to 140 percent while these *de facto* monopolists over-
charge European consumers, who pay three times the world price for their
sugar, and swamp third-country markets.[7] Poor farmers in poor countries pay
a high price for these instances of organized and officially approved market dis-
tortion. Often they have no choice but to give up farming because they cannot
cover their costs.

Textiles and Clothing

Textiles and clothing are another important sector for developing countries.
Traditionally the EU, along with the United States, Canada, and Norway, had
protected its textile and clothing markets through the Multifibre Arrangement
(MFA). Under the MFA, industrial countries negotiated bilateral quotas with
important textile producers such as China, Hong Kong, India, and Korea, as
well as with marginal exporters like the Fijis and Slovenia. These quotas set
upper limits on exports from developing countries. In the Uruguay Round, developing countries obtained a commitment, through the Agreement on Textiles
and Clothing (ATC), from advanced importing countries to start liberalizing
the sector in 1995 and to phase out quotas, gradually but completely, over a
ten-year period.

What the EU has done during this transition period, in the good company
of the United States (which has an even worse record in textile protectionism),
is to follow the letter of the ATC while giving its spirit short shrift. Under the
ATC each importing country was free to decide which products it wanted to
include in quota-free imports in the three liberalization stages—1995, 1998,
2002—provided for by the agreement. Since the product coverage of the ATC
is more extensive than that of the MFA, countries were in principle allowed to
integrate products that were never affected by quotas in the first place. Like
picking one's nose in public, this was not strictly illegal but clearly neither was
it generally regarded as correct behavior. It is exactly the course of action taken
by the EU. Until the end of 2001, the EU had eliminated only fourteen of its
219 quotas, affecting a mere 5 percent of total restrained imports and concen-

Table 6.2   Import-Weighted MFN Average Tariffs by Product Group (percentage)

	Manufactures	Textiles	Clothing
Developed countries	3.1	8.1	12.2
EU	3.5	8.2	11.7
U.S.	3.0	8.1	12.0

Source: UNCTAD, Trade and Development Report 2002 (Geneva: UN, 2002), table 4.3.

trating on lower-value-added commodities such as yarns and fabrics. It plans to drop only a further thirty-eight quotas in the third stage, thus leaving the bulk of liberalization of clothing—almost four-fifths of all restrained products—for the very end of the transition period in 2004.[8] Even then things are not going to be easy for textile exporters. Tariffs on clothing are two to three times as high as those on other industrial products (see Table 6.2). In addition, just to compound the bad news, the EU resorts to tariff escalation, much as in agriculture, and when imports surge despite all this armory, imposes antidumping measures that pretty much amount to penalizing foreign producers for being more efficient than their EU counterparts. Unfortunately, while the Uruguay Round Antidumping Agreement clarified the procedures under which antidumping cases can be pursued—for example, injury to the claimant industry must be shown for action to be taken—it did nothing to address the weird logic upon which antidumping investigations are based.[9]

The implication of all this is that the more important the EU is as an export market and the more important textiles and clothing are in a developing country's export composition, the worse the ATC's effects—or, more precisely, the liberty the EU has taken in interpreting it—would appear to be.

The Political Economy of Trade Policy Making

It is not surprising that uncompetitive businesses ask for import protection. But it is a little harder to understand why farm businesses or manufacturers of textiles and (non-luxury) clothing, not exactly the powerhouses of advanced economies, are successful in obtaining protectionism. Economic theory teaches two things. The first is that liberalization creates winners and losers. The second is that, on balance, because of the efficiencies associated with letting people do what they do best, the gains to the winners outweigh the costs to the losers so that liberalization brings net benefits. Clearly, if global farm trade were radically liberalized, many European farmers would land on hard ground. But competitive farmers the world over would benefit, and so would European consumers, both because it would lower their taxes and because they would get a liter of milk for approximately half of what they pay under the current system. The International Monetary Fund estimates that world farm liberalization would generate static benefits to the tune of $128 billion, of which the developing countries would roughly get a fifth.

So if the EU's leaders decided on the basis of economic rationality, they would scrap the current system. Of course, politics is about more than just the most efficient possible resource allocation. For example, it is about a fellow called Stoiber trying to win a federal election in Germany in 2002, and another fellow called Chirac trying to avoid losing an election in France in 2002. Both of these men are beholden to farm interests even though agriculture accounts for little in terms of output and employment in either of these countries. Farm interests have been so successful in lobbying EU governments because humoring them is politically easier than standing up to their blatant subsidy seeking. It would be different if every packet of butter carried a label advising the consumer that, thanks to her purchase, the owner of a large agro-industrial complex (with a financial net worth many multiples of her own) was yet again a little richer. But trade and subsidy policies are rarely if ever that transparent. In most EU countries, the farm ministry is firmly in the hand of the farm lobby, a bit like ministries of defense representing the armed forces rather than defending national security.

The EU's intransigence vis-à-vis developing-country interests in farm goods and labor-intensive commodities in the global trade talks suggests that it is trying to get away with reaping as many benefits as possible from globalization while having others foot the associated bill. Even where laudable attempts were made—for example, with the 2001 Everything-But-Arms (EBA) initiative aimed at allowing the world's forty-nine poorest countries tariff- and quota-free access to the EU—producer lobbies succeeded in obtaining exemptions for big-ticket items such as sugar, rice, and bananas. If this strategy of malign neglect of developing-country interests plays out—as it did for pretty much all advanced economies in the aftermath of the Uruguay Round—the EU is doing a marvelous job at furthering its unenlightened self-interest.

However, on current standing it does not look as though the EU strategy will play out at all. There is hope that the EU, short of letting the Doha Round collapse, will eventually have to compromise.

MARKET ACCESS AND MIGRATION

The link between trade and migration is complex. For example, obviously, all people who cannot make a living by selling their products do not become migrants. Some are simply too poor to have the option of trying their luck in a different place. Yet it is also clear that the impossibility of making a livelihood in one location contributes to the pressure to look for alternatives in another, regardless of whether this eventually translates into a move or remains an unrealized aspiration.[10]

Although the link between trade liberalization and migration is not straightforward, it is pretty obvious that keeping competitive exports such as textiles and farm goods from poor countries out of rich-country markets begets people packing their bags and leaving home. It is also obvious that EU farm subsidies have the same effect.[11] Trade integration per se is unlikely to change this; income levels may continue to diverge across factors, sectors, or regions. This means that the dynamics and pressures associated with globalization would put immigration on the agenda even if protectionism were a foreign term in the world economy. Liberalizing labor flows would likely bring benefits much higher than what the world can hope for from the current Doha trade negotiations. The next section shows why.

Migration and Immigration

If the 1990s saw globalization make big strides, they were also the decade in which countries the world over adopted more restrictive immigration regimes than previously. In 1976, only some 7 percent of UN members had restrictive policies in place. At the time of this writing, their numbers had risen to 40 percent in a substantially larger UN. Advanced economies are at the forefront of this development. This throws up the question of why people do not enjoy the freedoms accorded to goods, services, and capital. This section attempts to answer this question. It first gives an idea of the scale of migration worldwide. Next it discusses theoretical explanations of why people move and contrasts them with empirical findings. The following section again takes up linkages between trade and migration. Then it describes the economic and political rationales underlying immigration policy in the EU and its structure and content and discusses the implication of the current regime.

SCALE AND SCOPE

Migrants are people who live permanently or for long periods outside their countries of origin.[12] Estimates differ as to how many people fit this definition worldwide. For anyone interested in a frank discussion of the relative merits of immigration, it is convenient to drop conservative estimates in favor of higher numbers. This is because, in any controversy with those who envision mass invasions by the world's poor, belittling the extent of the phenomenon is bound to fail.

Worldwide some 150 to 200 million people are migrants with regular papers. It is obviously more difficult to be sure of the extent of irregular migration, but observers attach a similar ballpark figure to people like the shipwrecked arrivals in Pantelleria. All told, fewer than 7 percent of the world population are migrants.[13] The 56 million regular migrants in Europe compare to 50 million in Asia, 41 million in North America, and 16 million in Africa. Almost two-thirds of these people are concentrated in just fifteen rich and poor countries.[14]

Of course, the concentration of migrants varies widely across countries. In Europe, one out of three inhabitants of Luxembourg is a foreigner, and one out of five in Switzerland. The share of foreigners in Germany and Austria is relatively high at 9 percent; by contrast, it is rather low in Italy and Spain, at below 2 percent. But two-thirds of foreigners in Europe are actually other Europeans, although intra-European migration represents less than 0.2 percent of the EU population (see Figure 6.1).[15] In 1999, this meant that for every one thousand inhabitants, 27 foreigners arrived in Luxembourg, and fewer than 2 in France, Finland, Hungary, and Portugal.[16] Some 223,000 seasonal workers were employed in Germany; France admitted about eight thousand. In places like Brussels or London, one in four inhabitants is foreign.[17] Documented Africans and Asians numbered three and two million, respectively, in 1996.[18] New arrivals of *clandestini* are estimated at 500,000 per year. To bring these figures into perspective, Iran and Pakistan alone host some three million Afghans.[19]

In discussions about whether these numbers mean that there are—by whatever standards—"too many" immigrants in Europe, convenient use is made of an old myth, namely, that Europe has traditionally not been an immigration target and, by implication, could or should not become one, either. In *Guests and Aliens* Saskia Sassen picked the myth apart and set the historical record

Figure 6.1   Share of Nonnationals in the EU-15, 1985–1998

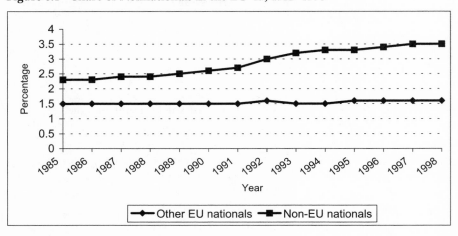

Source: Eurostat, *European Social Statistics. Migration* (Luxembourg: Office of Publication of the European Communities, 2000), table A-5.2.

straight. Immigration has always existed, even to traditionally out-migration countries like the EU's southern members.[20] It materialized because the supply of migrants was met by demand for labor and thus conditioned on the operation of the economic system in receiving countries. Historical evidence also shows that when opportunities are saturated, migrant flows eventually adjust downward, although this may take time and be incomplete.

Thus, when mass out-migration from Greece in the 1960s led to seasonal or longer-term labor shortages on fields, construction sites, and dockyards, Africans arrived to fill the vacancies with official blessing. Around the same time, Tunisians settled in western Sicily to help in the fishing fleet, as grape harvesters, or on construction sites.[21] And while the majority of these immigrants hailed from nearby African countries such as Egypt or Morocco, others came later from as far away as Sri Lanka, Cape Verde, or Peru.[22] Apart from the obvious answer that migrants are somehow in search of a better life, the question remains what exactly causes people to migrate, who they are, where they go, and how long they stay.

WHY DO PEOPLE MOVE?

Very few people move because they think it's fun. The vast majority of humans prefer to spend their lives close to where they were born. When people hit the road, it is mostly for negative reasons. Often life at home is hard or perhaps unsustainable. Wars, famines, or altogether failed states and the attendant consequences of poverty and economic stagnation are among the more extreme causes.

Theories of migration differ in terms of what they consider the key unit of analysis.[23] Standard neoclassical economics focuses on individuals; they decide to move if the expected net return from migration is positive over a certain period of time. This calculation depends mainly but not exclusively on economic considerations such as job opportunities. Individuals try to get a job abroad if the cost of making it to the foreign country is lower than the expected wage differential. In other words, once international wage differentials equal the costs of labor movement, the migration process stops.

More recent work looks at related groups of people, such as households or extended families. They insure themselves against unexpected income losses due to crop failures or commodity price declines by sending members abroad to provide them with remittances. The government of the Philippines sponsors this kind of migration. It looks after the welfare of Filipino migrants abroad, has approved legislation to allow them to vote in the 2004 elections, and annually honors outstanding migrants through Bagong Bayani (new heroes) awards.[24] According to IMF estimates, worker remittances and employee compensation accruing to developing countries annually run to about $60 to $70 billion. Thus the official figure alone exceeds the approximate $50 billion of development aid flows. Obviously, unofficial figures are much higher, because migrants from countries with underdeveloped banking systems or untrustworthy institutions rely on money-transfer channels that do not show up in official statistics. When remittances are invested visibly, they may become symbols of migration success and set in motion cumulative causation by encouraging others to follow the good example.

Migration, especially over large distances, is resource-intensive. It is clearly easier for people with means to afford these costs. But migration is also an option to the poor. They can sign a bond to repay the debt they owe a trafficker in exchange for bringing them into a destination country.[25] Increasingly, this is becoming a form of modern slavery. The issue of trafficking is taken up in more depth below.

Globalization, too, contributes to migration. When backward areas are brought into the global economy, existing societal structures are often disrupted, so that previous ways of living become unviable. For example, foreign direct investment (FDI) by multinational firms into modern agro-industrial complexes tends to displace small farmers who have little choice but to try and become wage laborers. Unless their home cities provide employment opportunities, they look for jobs abroad.

Or take a western multinational electronics company that invests in an export-processing zone in a developing country. It tends to hire young women who give up traditional unwaged employment in, for example, subsistence farming. Having abandoned their fields, they can rarely return to their previous activity, even if their jobs in the factory don't work out. Household production for internal consumption or for the local market also ceases, making food security more precarious. The feminization of the workforce means that men suddenly face more competition from women. Also, when women, along with the extensive support they provide, are absent from traditional households, traditional employment opportunities for men tend to fall. All of this may raise unemployment and contribute to a migration push, first into local cities, and then into cities abroad.[26]

It takes two to tango, and migration flows also depend on pull factors in the recipient countries. Investment bankers in New York and London entrust their kids to nannies from Latin America and the Philippines.[27] The vegetable harvests in Italy's Apulia or Spain's Andalusia wouldn't happen without seasonal workers from Morocco. Small and medium-sized manufacturing firms in central and northeastern Italy, in industries as diverse as apparel and agricultural machinery, have resorted to immigrant labor to cope with increasing competition from East Asian tiger economies since the 1970s.[28] Sweatshops power both high-tech and downgraded manufacturing sectors. Leather accessories for the world's most renowned fashion houses are assembled right under our noses by migrant workers cramped into damp and dark basements, toiling away long hours for abysmally low pay. In Los Angeles's garment district or Milan's Chinese quarter, enormous wealth and highly rewarded employment in professional services coexist with and/or exploit underground industries that operate in third-world conditions.[29] The point is that unskilled jobs can be part of the most modern sector of the economy, and backward sectors can be part of major growth trends.[30] This phenomenon is not exclusive to rich countries. With long-term growth rates in eastern Europe likely to be higher than in western Europe, countries like Poland are likely to experience the same tight labor markets as some sectors in its neighboring countries.[31]

The so-called black economy in the EU is estimated at 16 percent.[32] Much of it consists of "3D" (dirty, difficult, and dangerous) jobs that resident workers refuse to accept. Migrant workers fill these jobs because they are willing to and because their unofficial status makes them attractive to employers. If they become specialists in certain occupations, demand for them will rise as economic opportunities expand. Thus economic misery in one part of the world is not a sufficient condition for migration; it works only in conjunction with organized recruitment in the other. Empirical evidence shows that when demand falls, both legal and illegal migration flows adjust.[33]

In sum, migration and settlement are multifaceted phenomena that are best understood by examining economic changes in the sending country that induce people to leave; the opportunities in the destination region; and the linkages between the two areas through international production systems, informal networks developed by the migrants themselves, and mediating mechanisms such as the budding migration industry of lawyers, recruiters, traffickers, and the like.[34]

The next question is why and how long people stay. The populist answer is that immigrants regard their host countries as the incarnation of heaven on earth and are hell-bent on staying forever. Politicians who bring such a charge are clearly given to hyperbole in that they belittle the objective differences between heaven on the one hand and Carinthia and Padania on the other.[35] They are also curiously ignorant of what we know about the determinants of migrants' relative return decisions. The section on immigration regimes below discusses this in some detail.

LINKAGES BETWEEN TRADE AND MIGRATION

The section on market access to the EU in the context of global trade liberalization described how EU protectionism prevents producers in poor countries from selling their goods on EU markets. Trade barriers obviously make it more likely that people will move, and they are one of the reasons behind migration decisions outlined in the section on why people move. Yet trade integration need not reduce the push factors behind migration. Simply put, while liberalization makes the world as a whole better off, it does not do the same for every individual. In the aggregate, globalization is a positive-sum game. However, it also produces losers. The real challenge is how to help the losers cope with their predicament. In other words, trade liberalization and migration management are not alternative policy strategies. Unless this insight informs EU policy vis-à-vis developing countries, frictions between Europe and its neighbours and between policy goals and outcomes are bound to grow.

As an illustration, take the EU's relationship with its North African and Middle Eastern neighbours. On the whole the countries from Morocco to Egypt have abundant cheap labor. The EU, by contrast, is specialized in capital-intensive production. If the EU dropped its protectionism against farm and simple manufactured goods, Tunisian footwear producers and Moroccan vegetable growers would benefit and consequently have less incentive to move. In this case, exporting indeed substitutes for the decision to migrate, and there are only a few losers.[36]

But this is a highly simplified model. When made more realistic, it yields a completely different outcome. Let's say Morocco uses its cheap labor in making textiles while the EU produces capital-intensive machinery. Theory tells us that if trade is liberalized, commodity prices converge. Machinery in Morocco and textiles in the EU become cheaper, and thanks to their export success workers in these two industries get higher wages. However, this also means that relative wages of farmers fall. Hence they have an incentive to migrate. So in this case there are more losers, and trade liberalization and migration become complements.

A similar outcome pertains if we compare vegetable cultivation in Morocco and in Andalusia. The Spanish growers employ better technology in this labor-intensive sector, such as larger plots, greenhouses, and the like. If migration is restricted, Spanish wages are higher. If controls are relaxed, Moroccans move to Spain to take advantage of the higher wages, raising Spain's labor/capital ratio—and, thus, specialization in horticultural production—leading to more exports. Thus an increase in migration leads to more, not less, trade, which in turn may act as a pull factor on further inward migration because Moroccan farmers have a hard time competing against vegetable exports from Andalusia.

These models do not always produce clear predictions. Let's say a Moroccan employee of a print shop has skills that in principle allow him to work in a footwear factory, too. But the entrepreneur who owns the print shop cannot really move his equipment because it is specific to the task. If trade liberalization allows international publishing houses to compete in Morocco and consequently lowers the price of printed material, the worker will have to reduce his wage demands or risk getting laid off. Hence it will become more expensive for him to buy shoes. At the same time, his newspapers get cheaper. At the end of the day, what happens to his real wage depends on how important newspapers are in his consumption basket and whether he can find a job in another sector.

Moroccans are just across the sea from Spain and can literally get into a boat to try to make it into the EU. Extremely poor people in the world's least developed countries, for example sugar-cane farmers in Zambia or Mozambique, do not have that option. But if the EU abolished its subsidies on sugar exports and tariffs on sugar imports, the wages of those farmers would go up over time. Thus, at least in principle, migration would become affordable. Again migration might then complement liberalization.[37]

What this discussion shows is that the dynamics of globalization simultaneously contain and promote the push and pull of migration. In theory we manage to specify the conditions under which more market access alleviates migratory pressure. In practice this is a messy affair, and there is not enough knowledge about the exact empirical linkages between trade and migration across sectors and countries. In any event, it is important to underline that a more enlightened trade policy by itself is not going to do the trick of making migratory pressure or the demand for migrant labor disappear. Hence a world economy based on à la carte globalization that liberates all factor flows except labor is a fundamentally flawed concept.

Immigration Regimes in the EU

EU policies on immigration are rather restrictive. This does not mean that all migrants are unwelcome. It means that, compared to its own regime in the 1960s or compared to North American practices, the EU has been trying to keep migrants out, certainly those that are unskilled. Motives for this policy are to be found in two sets of arguments. The first charges that immigrants steal jobs from locals and are a burden on the welfare system. The second is rooted in notions of state sovereignty and national identity that in a direct sense have little or nothing to do with economic costs or benefits. Hence, this section treats economic and political justifications for restrictive immigration separately. Furthermore, it looks at the structure and delivery of immigration policy. Finally, it analyses the consequences.

LABOR-MARKET EFFECTS OF IMMIGRATION

When the owner of a riding stable in Italy hires a farm hand from Albania and pays him his market wage, the additional output increases, albeit only by little, the average incomes of Italian citizens.[38] Hence, they are better off. Even though he makes less than his employer and the other stable owners, the immigrant is better off, too; indeed, this is the reason he migrated in the first place. The news of his success breaks back home and more willing laborers follow, until each livery stable in Italy employs an immigrant from Albania.

After a couple of years the Italian government decides to grant the Albanians citizenship. (This hypothetical situation is so unrealistic that it requires considerable powers of imagination from the reader. Please try.) In principle this gives them the right to buy land and set up their own stables. But since the new government policy took them completely by surprise, none of them have yet done so.

The good news again reaches the homeland and motivates more Albanians to seek positions as stable hands in livery stables, which are doing a budding business. After a while every stable's personnel consists of the owner (who may not muck out the boxes but does work full-time in the establishment), a naturalized citizen-laborer, and a new immigrant laborer. The newcomer is just as qualified for the job as his first-arrived cousin (reportedly almost everybody in Albania is a cousin of almost everybody else). But while the two may help each other with heavy tasks, they will also on occasion be in each other's way, so that the incremental output of the new immigrant is slightly lower than that of the first. This means that the new arrival's market wage is lower, too. The owner reduces his long-time employee's wage as well because—since the two cousins are doing the same job—he can always hire a second new arrival to replace the first. The outcome is that the owner makes more profit, the new immigrant is happy, and the old immigrant is upset.

But what if he takes his savings and buys half the farm from the original owner with whom he splits the proceeds? The two owners pay themselves and the new immigrant the latter's market wage. Now the former citizen-laborer is no longer worse off because he compensates his lower wage through earning profits from the operation of the stable.

The key difference between the two alternative endings of the story lies in who appropriates the return from capital. As the first ending shows, in the short to medium run, workers may lose out from additional immigration if they do not own productive assets. This ownership may be indirect—for example, through pension funds. In the long run, what happens to native workers also depends on the effects of immigration on productivity, whether immigrants make demands on social security, and how much they pay in taxes. In essence, these are empirical questions.

There is no specific empirical evidence to support the link between immigration and labor-market conditions of unskilled workers.[39] This obviously defies everybody's intuition, especially that of the directly concerned. It is a shame, therefore, that governments in the EU do not make much use of these insights and bring them to the attention of the wider public.

A study commissioned by the British government found that, far from being a burden on the public purse, immigrants have a net positive effect on prosperity and little or no effect on wages and job prospects of locals.[40] This also goes for their contribution to sustaining pension systems in the context of ever-aging populations (see Table 6.3).[41]

Table 6.3   Share of Population over 65 in Total Population

	1980	2000	2010	2030	2050
World	5.9	6.9	7.6	11.8	16.4
More developed	11.6	14.4	15.9	22.6	25.9
Less developed	4.1	5.1	5.8	9.9	15.0
Least developed	3.1	3.1	3.2	4.5	8.1

Source: ILO, *World Employment Report 2001* (Geneva: ILO, 2001), table 1.6.

Immigrants also create jobs. People who get off their butts in search for work halfway round the world are unlikely to be couch potatoes. Their youth and entrepreneurial dynamism are clearly exceptional and even perhaps more conducive to the EU's lofty (and, judging by its performance to date, somewhat ridiculous) aspiration of becoming the world's most competitive economy by 2010. When Rahma el Mouden arrived in the Netherlands in 1975, the girl from Morocco was fifteen years old. Some twenty years later, with substantial experience as a cleaning woman, she started a company called MAS, Multicultural Amsterdam Cleaners. In 1999, she employed seventy-five workers, mostly immigrants, and generated a million dollars in sales. Foreigners in the EU earn at least $461 billion a year and pay $153 billion in taxes, roughly $60 billion more than immigrants receive in welfare benefits.[42]

It does happen, of course, that immigrants bid down wages or take over a native's job. Much textile parts manufacturing in the Italian town of Prato, a traditional textile center, has been taken over by Chinese businesses. But if they had not come, there would be no native workers doing their jobs, either. Instead, productive capacities associated with a large part of the textile value chain would have closed for good because locals are unwilling to work at the low wages dictated by fierce international competition in this sector. Clearly, painful economic change regularly happens, but it is seldom migrants that drive this process. The demise of farming as a way of life, the disappearance of many heavy and engineering industries in the 1970s, or the IT meltdown in 2000 have nothing to do with immigration.

The point is that immigrants—especially illegal immigrants, who of course pay no taxes and are ineligible for welfare benefits—mostly take up jobs that no one else is prepared to do. It is obviously easier for less competitive firms and sunset industries to get away with irregular employment and tax avoidance if they can rely on migrant labor. In the early 1990s, some 200,000 or so illegal immigrants lived in 38,000 dwellings just outside of Lisbon. They stayed in overcrowded shacks made from timber and corrugated iron and had to put up with awful sanitary conditions. Approximately 15,000 of them were slave laborers sold by intermediaries to factories or construction companies in Lisbon,

Northern Portugal, or the Algarve.[43] It is preposterous to argue that Portuguese citizens would tolerate any of this. Indigenous workers prefer situations of semi-employment or unemployment if confronted with what amounts to hard work for lousy pay. Short of completely dismantling Europe's welfare system and fragmenting informal family support systems, this attitude is not going to change.

The alternative to such abuses would be properly organized contract labor migration. But when such systems are politically inopportune to set up, governments may tacitly accept illegal movements to accommodate the need of employers for cheap workers without taking any political heat.[44] It is fair to say that such practices make them accomplices to abuse and, in the worst case, slavery. Native unskilled workers would best be protected by properly managed and regulated migration. When, officially, governments cite the plight of the local poor as a justification for keeping migrants out, while letting them in unofficially to keep unviable businesses afloat, they are being cynical. They certainly do not have a good economic reason for restricting immigration.

HANG-UPS OVER SOVEREIGNTY, NATIONAL IDENTITY, AND THE "OTHERS"

The international norm for exit from countries is (or should be) freedom; for entry it is privilege. Control over which and how many foreigners get into a country is a traditional right of the nation-state. States try to exercise this right by granting or denying access to individuals at their borders. Before globalization, when the idea that societies largely corresponded to economic systems was a lot easier to implement, states were responsible for cushioning the weak against the adverse effects of international competition that resulted from increasing openness. But states have been less and less able (and willing) to honor the redistributive social compact of the postwar era.[45] This weakens their legitimacy. Successful immigration control, by contrast, could help strengthen legitimacy because it projects the image that states defend the entitlements of welfare and distributive justice against outsiders.[46] The traditional perception is that a state unable to keep out undesirable elements is not worth its salt. But the current emphasis on "control" suggests that state sovereignty walks on short legs because illegal migration is on the rise and there is no indication of any letup in this development.

In an attempt to strengthen their border-control capabilities, EU member states have instituted before-the-border regimes of immigration control. Thus borders no longer refer just to the physical installations that correspond to the demarcations drawn on political maps but may mean a foreign airport, a refugee center in a migration transit country, an embassy—in short, any space in which the state requires document checks, processes visa applications, or otherwise rejects demands for entry. From a control point of view, the advantage of this buffer zone is that, at least in part, it is not subject to domestic legal or international human rights norms that otherwise constrain the administrative effort of keeping out migrants deemed undesirable. The geographic extension of access control to European countries is a curious antidote to the EU's recognition that a true single market implies borderless travel. If European integration cannot be realized unless a traveler from Madrid can disembark at Helsinki airport without having to produce an ID, how is a global economy supposed to function when borderless travel for a majority of the world's population is becoming less, not more, achievable?

The focus on borders is thus problematic per se because it is fundamentally at odds with both the rhetoric and the practice of globalization. The notion of sovereignty on which it is based reflects the conception of a world that no longer exists. And the focus on individual migrants as the principal subject of the control effort is problematic because it ignores the fact that migrants' decisions to leave sending countries are largely matched by some sort of demand for their labor in the receiving countries.[47]

A majority of Europeans are concerned that immigrants (and other minorities) threaten social peace and welfare and exacerbate unemployment. Natives without higher education and with experience of unemployment have more critical views of immigrants and are more skeptical of multiculturalism.[48] Not surprisingly, therefore, people less likely to have benefited from globalization are more hostile toward one of its more visible manifestations, namely, people come from afar. What makes the latter different is, apart from their origin, what they look like, whom they worship, which social practices they honor, how affluent they are, and so on. Diffuse notions of national identity and cultural integrity become a defensive reflex that makes "the others" a scapegoat for social ills.

Table 6.4 shows that the traditionally strongest immigrant communities—for example, Turks and North Africans in Belgium; Turks and citizens of the former Yugoslavia in Germany and Switzerland—still account for the majority of the non-naturalized population from outside the high-income part of Europe. But they are increasingly joined by others from much farther away. Thus, 7 percent of all Africans in Germany are from Ghana; Brazilians account for 1 percent of the non-EEA foreign population in Switzerland (more than the Swiss in either Belgium or Germany); and there are growing communities of Chinese, Vietnamese, and Sri Lankans. In Italy, Morocco and Albania have replaced the United States and Germany as the most important sending country (see Table 6.5). The more ethnically, racially, or culturally diverse the foreign population is, and the more the indigenous national identity is built upon ideas of ethnic or racial superiority and prejudices born out of ignorance, the more conflict potential exists that can be fomented, propagated, and instrumentalized.[49] We know, of course, that migrants did not invent globalization, and that

Table 6.4 Global Diversification of Migration Flows in Select European Countries (total population by citizenship, 1 January 1998)

From/to:	Belgium Number	Percent	Germany Number	Percent	Switzerland Number	Percent
Total	10,192,264	100.0	82,057,379	100.0	7,096,465	100.0
Nationals	9,289,144	91.1	74,691,546	91.0	5,721,307	80.6
Non-nationals	903,120	8.9	7,365,833	9.0	1,375,158	19.4
Non-nationals not from EEA *of which*	339,863	3.3	5,506,417	6.7	554,704	7.8
EAST. EUROPE	14,945	4.4	1,999,408	36.3	339,716	61.2
Poland	6,034	1.8	283,312	5.1	4,327	0.8
Ex-Yugo.	1,309	0.4	1,269,606	23.1	316,607	57.1
OTHER EUROPE	82,882	24.4	2,109,027	38.3	80,574	14.5
Turkey	73,818	21.7	2,107,426	38.3	80,333	14.5
AFRICA	171,124	50.3	305,595	5.5	31,345	9.2
North	146,364	43.1	143,618	2.6	13,208	2.4
West	3,297	1.0	79,469	1.4	5,340	1.0
Horn	—	—	36,494	0.7	3,145	0.6
Sub-Saharan	14,590	4.3	44,157	0.8	9,460	1.7
AMERICA	22,035	6.5	194,371	3.5	42,285	7.6
USA	12,592	3.7	110,105	2.0	12,989	2.3
ASIA	25,677	7.5	781,034	14.2	58,336	10.5
Top 5	15,280	4.5	384,395	7.0	31,764	5.7

Source: Eurostat. *European Social Statistics. Migration* (Luxembourg: European Communities. 2000). table B-2.1.

Note: EEA (European Economic Area) = EU-15 + (EFTA—Switzerland). Top 5 Asian migrant source countries for Belgium = China, India, Japan, Philippines, Pakistan; for Germany = Afghanistan, Iran, Lebanon, Sri Lanka, Vietnam; for Switzerland = Sri Lanka, Vietnam, India, China, Philippines.

globalization without migration—and, hence, more cultural diversity—is impossible. Yet the very concept of migration control neglects this insight.

Paradoxically, migration control also worsens the disproportionate incidence of crime among immigrants. Illegal immigrants are overrepresented among criminal immigrants and also among the immigrant population at large. Offenses range from petty theft to very serious forms of organized crime. The rise in crime coincides with the beginnings of more restrictive immigration regimes from the mid-1970s. This obviously unintended consequence results from a selection bias in terms of which type of potential migrant is willing to challenge restrictive immigration regimes and accept illegal ways to enter desti-

Table 6.5   Stock of Foreign Population in Italy by Nationality
(percentage of total population)

	1985	1990	1995	1999
Morocco	.6	10.0	9.5	11.9
Albania	.0	.0	3.5	9.2
Philippines	1.8	4.4	4.4	4.9
Yugoslavia	3.3	3.8	5.7	4.4
Romania	.0	1.0	2.5	4.1
United States	12.1	7.4	6.1	3.8
China	.4	2.4	2.2	3.8
Tunisia	1.0	5.3	4.1	3.5
Senegal	.1	3.2	2.4	3.0
Germany	8.8	5.3	4.0	2.8
Sri Lanka	.6	1.5	2.0	2.4
Egypt	1.6	2.5	2.2	2.3
Poland	.0	2.2	2.2	2.2
Peru	.0	.7	1.0	2.1
India	1.2	1.4	1.5	2.0
Other	68.4	48.9	46.8	37.5
TOTAL	100.0	100.0	100.0	100.0
Of which: EU	—	19.0	16.5	11.6

Source: OECD. Trends in International Migration (Paris: OECD. 2001), table B.1.5.

nation countries.[50] Drug runners from Kosovo and North Africa and pimps from Nigeria have fewer qualms about maneuvering their way around immigration authorities to run their rackets on the streets of Milan and Turin than a tailor from Vietnam who hopes for a job in an Italian textile firm.[51] Thugs clearly have a higher risk tolerance than law-abiding people, be they residents or migrants.

Crimes committed by some immigrants turn at least part of the resident population against all immigrants. The way governments deal with these fears tends to make matters worse. Those on the right follow their law-and-order reflexes and promise yet more migration control, which in turn attracts more of the people societies can happily live without. Those on the left seldom confront the objective security problem head-on for fear of raising the ugly specter of xenophobia and racism. This is the wrong policy, because it does not sufficiently differentiate between foreigners and criminals. The thugs prey on everyone regardless of status. Hence, resident aliens and illegal immigrants are in need of protection, too. Also, as long as parts of the electorate feel unsafe walking the streets, multiculturalism will lose out to national homogeneity and thus make globalization much more difficult to manage. This is all the more unfortunate as it threatens to waste promising social capital and goodwill; the majority of Europeans are actually optimistic about multiculturalism.[52]

THE "NEW" EU IMMIGRATION POLICY

Traditionally, immigration policy has been the exclusive prerogative of the member states. This changed in 1999 when the Treaty of Amsterdam stipulated that the EU, over a period of five years, should assume responsibility over a range of issues, from internal movement of third-country nationals to common asylum procedures and a comprehensive system to combat illegal immigration. However, because of the real or imagined significance of immigration to state sovereignty, how many migrants each member state would accept and how long these people would be allowed to stay was to remain its own decision. In late 1999 the European Council mandated political guidelines to set up a so-called Area of Freedom, Security and Justice—a sort of EU equivalent to national justice and home affairs legislation, procedures, and practices.

Under the new system, immigration is both European Community and national responsibility. Prior to the adoption of the Treaty of Amsterdam, third-country nationals working in one member state had, in principle, no right to travel freely to another. In practice, they still don't. Freedom of movement inside the EU is thus a privilege accorded only to citizens. It is controversial whether this practice violates international human rights. But clearly the EU has not covered itself in glory in this respect.[53] The current situation is as though an Algerian violinist working with the Boston Symphony Orchestra had to apply for a visa to visit the opera in New York or Chicago. The new treaty at least offers the perspective that this will change in the foreseeable future if the European Commission manages to formulate harmonized policies and procedures and navigate them through the Council. The Commission's draft directive for the admission of third-country nationals proposes the establishment of a single residence and work permit.[54] Overall, lifting immigration out of the nonjustifiable twilight zone of ill-defined intergovernmental cooperation under the Maastricht treaty and introducing a single constitutional base and more democratic control through the involvement of the European Parliament is welcome per se. But it is, of course, the content of these emerging policies that matters most.

The commission has tabled a number of proposals emphasizing that business as usual is not an option in immigration policy. In its communication on a community immigration policy it acknowledged the economic reality of push and pull factors and argued that "the existing 'zero' immigration policies which have dominated thinking over the past thirty years are no longer appropriate."[55] The report also recognized that migrants generally have a positive effect on economic growth without burdening the welfare state or exacerbating unemployment. It implicitly admitted the perverse incentives that restrictive policies contain. In Nigel Harris's words, "[p]reventing people working so that they could not become citizens forced them to become citizens in order to work."[56] The commission proposed that migrants be allowed to visit their home countries without losing their status in the host countries, and that all these rules apply to unskilled as well as skilled workers.[57] In conclusion, lest it forget, it put the council on notice that "a shift to a proactive immigration policy will require strong political leadership and a clear commitment to the promotion of pluralistic societies and a condemnation of racism and xenophobia."[58]

But it may well happen that member states will have none of this and, instead, exploit the strengthened effectiveness of the new framework to justify policies that regard immigration as essentially a law-and-order problem and "securitize" its management.[59] In the minds of national executives pondering the implications of a borderless Europe, immigration ranks right next to drug trafficking and organized crime, arguably a pretty weird assortment of apples and pears that suggests that policymakers have a rather limited understanding of the effects of their actions.[60]

Even if the Commission's relatively enlightened approach carries the day, the ultimate emphasis in immigration management remains on control. The idea is that we rich European countries are happy to rescind some of the more knee-jerk attitudes toward immigrants, including those that are visibly different from us in that they are not white, because we realize that we benefit economically from their presence. Even in hard times we know that migrants are much more likely than citizens to set up a corner shop and employ the whole family to keep it open to business as long as our medieval regulations on opening hours allow. Settling for long-term unemployment is simply not their typical reaction.

But we do not trust markets totally. If we did, we would acknowledge that people do not travel immense distances, shouldering very considerable costs and high risks, unless work prospects in the destination countries are reasonably realistic. Inward migration to Japan has been lower than to the United States not just because the Japanese prefer to keep their society homogeneous but because, if given the choice, only fools would opt to go to a country that has not grown for some ten years over one that has, on balance, done very nicely.[61] So we insist on a system that allows us to filter those we deem worthy from those that we don't.

In trade, not trusting markets totally is the exception rather than the rule. A WTO member that declared a systematic preference for *Made in Germany* over *Made in Taiwan* would be treated like a bishop trying to convince the pope to retire the Almighty from the Holy Trinity. To be sure, protectionism is alive and well, but the long-term trend since World War II has been one of progressive liberalization. When trade officials announce protectionist measures, they do not swagger into the press conference to brag about their achievements. They employ defensive, convoluted rhetoric because they know that what they are doing is not right. The same is true for capital and services. Some of this is schizophrenic, but at least we acknowledge our shortcomings.

No such recognition informs our thinking about immigration. There is a powerful residual of us-and-them sentiment that gives rise to idiotic fears of hordes of unskilled desperados going for the good life in Aalst, Peterborough, Hvidovre, or Pésaro. Nobody has calculated the total costs of trying to intercept the 500,000 illegal immigrants Europol estimates arrive in Europe every year. Control measures include actions in the source countries, the creation of buffer zones in eastern Europe replete with funding to improve border surveillance, detention, police raids, penalties on employers, repatriation, and so on. They increasingly involve private actors—for example, airline carriers or security services—that states use to extend migration control to deterrence-before-entry.[62] In principle, any public policy should stand the test that benefits outweigh costs and that the intervention leads to the desired outcome. The first question is hard to answer, because people evidently disagree about what constitutes a "benefit." But we do know that immigration policy does not work—remember the *clandestini* from the beginning of the essay.

CONSEQUENCES

The number of *clandestini* is on the rise both because governments of destination countries try to restrict their legal entry and because they are evidently unable to do so completely. Their lack of full control over illegal migration is no more surprising than their inability to rein in the drug or the arms trade. When demand and supply are outlawed, a black market emerges. This is not an argument in favor of the over-the-counter availability of weapons-grade plutonium. It merely cautions that migration control is no longer merely about an individual wanting to get into a country and a government at destination granting or refusing access. Indeed, restrictive migration control leads to a migration industry which, in the words of a long-time observer, "may be more powerful in shaping population flows than the policies of states."[63] It also suggests that the criminal networks active in the migration industry must be included in any attempt to assess the relative costs and benefits of migration control. These networks are among the nastiest constituent elements of global crime, and dealing with the consequences of their presence does not come cheap.

Their business is human trafficking or, even more chilling, the body trade. It works like this.[64] Tirunaukarasu Shadacharan runs a travel agency in Colombo, Sri Lanka. Kent Tours & Travels fronts for what really is a business that offers to get Sri Lankans to western Europe (in 2000), for about $10,000. Mr. Shadacharan first obtains travel documents for his clients, who might be young Tamils from the war-torn Jaffna peninsula in the north. They go to Egypt by ship, holding a passport and a letter of appointment from an Egyptian cargo company, both of which are fake. Upon arrival in Egypt they apply for a transit visa, which is easily granted. While the migrants stay in Cairo safe houses, the traffickers prepare counterfeit documents for their onward journey by washing old visas, forging stamps, or using genuine visas from someone else's passport. Then the migrants fly to Amsterdam from where, in principle, they can reach other EU destinations. They might claim refugee status, go underground, and take menial jobs. If they were unable to finance the whole trip by themselves, they might end up indebted to the smugglers.

Not everybody needs upwards of $10,000 to make it to western Europe. In 1999 Albanian *clandestini* paid just $540 for the short ride by power boat across the Mediterranean. Middlemen in Tirana offered "package tours"—guaranteeing multiple crossings in case of failed landing attempts due to police interference—for $2,000. That year Italian authorities picked up 2,600 illegals a month on the stretch of coast facing Albania and reckoned that two to three times this number made it into Italy.[65] Bringing merely one hundred people across covers the price of a boat—that's how profitable this investment is for the traffickers. In Europe alone revenue from trafficking was estimated at three to four billion dollars in 1999.

According to UN estimates, some four million people are trafficked each year. A quarter of these are employed (or, more often, exploited) in sex industries. The fate of women and children who are trafficked for sex purposes is among the saddest realities of the global economy.[66] Most of the prostitutes in western Europe come from eastern Europe and parts of the former Soviet Union, especially Russia and Ukraine. Many of these women are victims of the economic hardships that afflicted the transition economies and massively drove up inequality from Tallinn to Kiev. They lost their jobs as a result of necessary industrial restructuring. They also often lost their husbands, either literally or to alcohol, because many men were unable to cope with life in a market economy.

As with other migrants, they need to earn a living somewhere; this is the push factor. Western Europe's sex industry is worth some $9 billion; that is the pull factor.[67] What brings supply and demand together and establishes an equilibrium of sorts are organized gangs of traffickers. Most of the women they recruit are lured with promises of decent jobs. In reality they are sold to pimps who practically own them because they hold their identity papers. Women who do not submit to their fate are controlled through violence or murdered. To add hypocrisy to tragedy, even in EU countries such as Germany and the Netherlands, where prostitution is in principle legal, that status applies only to EU citizens. This is bad news for the women from third countries because it enhances their dependence on the men who exploit them.[68] This practice yet again underlines the predisposition of the EU to accord secondary status, lower protection, and less dignity to those it considers outsiders.

Conclusion: How Europe Fails the Developing World

Globalization has intensified relationships between the world's populations. The difference between the world economy and national economic systems is that the former is without the political institutions to (re)distribute the gains from integration and cushion against its costs. Migration is a response to this shortcoming; it "represents a claim to be included in systems for distributive justice."[69]

The governments of the EU are unwilling to entertain this claim. On the contrary, they are responsible for an unjust distribution of the costs of and benefits from globalization that fuels the push and perhaps also the pull behind migration. EU farm and trade policies make life harder for people in developing countries. In migration control, the EU exploits its influence by externalizing some of the dirty work while minimizing its costs. In its attempt to keep migrants at bay, the EU's use of its central European neighbors as a buffer zone effectively shifts the major burden to the transit countries.[70] This practice makes the rich EU a migration fortress and its poorer neighbours migration destinations of last resort. British prime minister Blair's proposal to punish developing countries unless they manage to stem outmigration to the EU by withholding EU aid is a telling example of rich-country hubris and a good illustration of making poor countries pick up the tab for the dislocations in rich countries caused by economic change.

Migration control is needed, some right-wingers argue, because the boat is full. They have a point in that there are obviously physical limits to how many people Europe can accommodate. It is also obvious that these limits will be exhausted in a densely populated country such as Holland long before they would be felt in Canada. If driving through the Scottish Highlands became just as much a nightmarish experience as being in London traffic during rush-hour; if visiting the cafés of Budapest implied a three-year waiting period; if the density of airline traffic darkened our skies; if siblings had to take turns going to school because average class sizes in elementary school had grown to five hundred without any concomitant expansion in building facilities; if plumbers started fixing our teeth because dental practices were too busy issuing new appointments before summer 2007; and so on, the boat would indeed be full. No new passengers should be accepted lest it sink. Needless to say, Europe is nowhere near this situation.

The upside of liberalizing immigration and the downside of restricting it are clear, certainly in economic and business terms. It is hardly a coincidence that the *Economist*, the *Financial Times*, and the *Wall Street Journal* are in support of free immigration and against racism. So why does it not happen?

It does not happen because of the sorry moral and mental state of Europe's political leaders. At issue is not so much the disgraceful rant by populists such as Kjærsgaard (People's Party, Denmark), Haider (Freedom Party, Austria), Bossi (Northern League, Italy), Hagen (Progress Party, Norway), and Le Pen (National Front, France). Hopefully they are but a passing stage act in Europe's political theater of the absurd. The real culprits are smack in the political mainstream, both left and right. They are guilty of avoiding a rational debate on the relative merits of a more open immigration policy because keeping out migrants and asylum seekers, much like being tough on crime, is a vote getter. Much to our shame, racism is still socially acceptable in Europe. That makes foreigners, especially those who come from afar, easy scapegoats for all the problems that our politicians do not have the guts to address. What they should do is go out and educate a largely uninformed electorate. Instead, they play fiddle to our xenophobic instincts. There is no excuse for this.

Of course, while political leaders bear the principal responsibility for the current state of affairs, European citizens have their share of hypocrisy. For example, many people will oppose official immigration for fear of increased competition in domestic labor markets. At the same time, they will happily condone illegal immigration because it provides them with the cheap builder from eastern Europe who renovates their summer home for a fraction of what they would normally pay.

German or French tourists visiting the sights around Mazara del Vallo in Sicily might admire the temples in the nearby Greek settlement of Selinunte or the remnants of a Phoenician trading outpost on the island of Mózia. In Pantelleria they would find *dammusi*, Arab-inspired architecture. Elsewhere they might come across traces of Jewish or Lebanese trading activity. In the past, migrants contributed to the creation of societies. The extraordinary vibrancy of classical and early medieval Mediterranean culture is a good illustration. It is shortsighted not to take inspiration from history for modern migration policy.

Open markets require open minds. It is unrealistic to expect that everybody is prepared to live with the consequences. But those who do not should not hold public office unless they are prepared to bite the bullet and go on record advocating nationalism, mercantilism, and a general retreat from globalization. A more open approach to immigration would help convince skeptical developing countries that they can reap some of the gains from globalization. If they continue to be skeptical, the emerging global environment of free markets and accountable governments is likely to suffer.

Notes

Zdenka Lomanova cheerfully provided very able research assistance. The 2002 graduate class of the MScIB Programme at Copenhagen Business School animatedly debated a couple of provocations drawn from a very first draft of this text and encouraged me to let it loose on a wider audience. My colleague Steen Thomsen carefully read the text and provided helpful comments and constructive criticism. My parents and my brother put up with my (ultimately elusive) search for the captain of the *Giove* during a family Christmas outing to the port of Mazara del Vallo. My thanks go to all of them.

1. Oxfam, *Rigged Rules and Double Standards.* Online at www.maketradefair.com, 2002.

2. For an overview, see Paul Brenton, "The Changing Nature and Determinants of EU Trade Policies," in *Globalizing Europe*, ed. Thomas L. Brewer, Paul A. Brenton, and Gavin Boyd (Cheltenham: Elgar, 2002), 205–41.

3. UNCTAD, Least Developed Country Report 2002: Escaping the Poverty Trap, (Geneva: UN, 2002), Annex Table 3.

4. WTO, "Market Access: Unfinished Business," Special Studies no. 6. Online at www.wto.org, 2001.

5. OECD, Agricultural Policies in OECD Countries (Paris: OECD, 2002).

6. CAFOD, "Dumping on the Poor." Online at www.cafod.org.uk, 2002.

7. Oxfam, "The Great EU Sugar Scam," Briefing Paper no. 27. Online at www.oxfam.org, 2002.

8. Paul Brenton, "The Changing Nature and Determinants of EU Trade Policies"; Hanaa Kheir-El-Din, "Implementing the Agreement on Textiles and Clothing," in *Development, Trade, and the World Trade Organization*, ed. Bernard Hoekman, Aaditya Mattoo, and Philip English (Washington, D.C.: World Bank, 2002), 186–94.

9. J. Michael Finger, "Safeguards," in *Development, Trade, and the World Trade Organization*, ed. Bernard Hoekman, Aaditya Mattoo, and Philip English (Washington, D.C.: World Bank, 2002), 195–205.

10. Cf. Peter Stalker, *Workers without Frontiers* (London: Lynne Rienner, 2000).

11. Gregory White, "Encouraging Unwanted Immigration: A Political Economy of Europe's Efforts to Discourage North African Immigration," *Third World Quarterly* 20, no. 4 (1999), 839–54.

12. Stephen Castles, *Ethnicity and Globalization* (London: Sage, 2000), chapter 5.

13. To be sure, this is a very high estimate. Many serious observers such as the UN Population Division speak of about half this figure.

14. United States (35m), Russia (13.3m), Germany (7.3m), Ukraine (6.9m), France (6.3m), India (6.2m), Canada (5.8), Saudia Arabia (5.2), Australia (5.5), Pakistan (4.2m), UK (4.0m), Kazakhstan (3.0m), Hong Kong (2.7), Ivory Coast (2.3), Iran (2.3m). See United Nations Population Division, *World Population Monitoring 2002* (New York: UN, 2002).

15. OECD, *Trends in International Migration* (Paris: OECD, 2001), 35.

16. OECD, *Trends in International Migration*, 18.

17. OECD, *Trends in International Migration*.

18. John Salt and James Clarke, "International Migration in the UNECE Region: Patterns, Trends, Policies," *International Social Science Journal* 52, no.165 (2000), 313–28.

19. United Nations Population Division, *World Population Monitoring 2000* (New York: UN, 2001).

20. Saskia Sassen, *Guests and Aliens* (New York: New Press, 1999).

21. A part of Mazara del Vallo's old port district from which the *Giove* hailed is tellingly (and officially) named *La Kasbah*.

22. Russel King, "Migration and Development in the Mediterranean Region," *Geography* 81, no.1 (1996), 3–14.

23. Dirk J. van de Kaa, "International Mass Migration: A Threat to Europe's Borders and Stability?" *De Economist* 144, no. 2 (1996), 259–84.

24. *Migration News*, vol. 9, no. 12. Online at www.migration.ucdavis.edu/, 2002.

25. Bimal Ghosh, "Towards a New International Regime for Orderly Movements of People," in *Managing Migration*, ed. Bimal Ghosh (Oxford: Oxford University Press, 2000), 6–26.

26. Saskia Sassen, *The Mobility of Labor and Capital: A Study in International Investment and Labor Flow* (Cambridge: Cambridge University Press, 1988); Castles, *Ethnicity and Globalization*, chapters 5 and 8; Stephen Castles and Mark J. Miller, *The Age of Migration*, 2nd ed. (London: Macmillan, 1998), chapter 7.

27. Cf. Benjamin Jones, "An Ecuadorian in Madrid," *Europe* (November 2001), 11.

28. Cf. King, "Migration and Development in the Mediterranean Region."

29. See for example, Vincenzo Ruggiero, "Trafficking in Human Beings: Slaves in Contemporary Europe," *International Journal of the Sociology of Law* 25 (1997), 231–44.

30. Sassen, *The Mobility of Labor and Capital*; see also Castles and Miller, *The Age of Migration*, chapter 7.

31. Krystyna Iglicka, "Migration Movements from and into Poland in the Light of East-West European Migration," *International Migration* 39, no.1 (2001), 3–32.

32. Ghosh, "Towards a New International Regime for Orderly Movements of People."

33. Sassen, *Guests and Aliens*, 137.

34. Castles and Miller, *The Age of Migration*, chapter 2.

35. Carinthia and "Padania" are regional strongholds of two of Europe's most xenophobic elected politicians, Jörg Haider from Austria and Umberto Bossi from Italy.

36. Cf. White, "Encouraging Unwanted Immigration."

37. For an in-depth treatment, see Riccardo Faini, Jaime de Melo, and Klaus F. Zimmermann, "Trade and Migration: An Introduction," in Riccardo Faini, Jaime de Melo, and Klaus F. Zimmermann, eds., *Migration: The Controversies and the Evidence* (Cambridge: Cambridge University Press, 1999), 1–20.

38. The idea of this section draws on a neat parable by Julian Simon, *The Economic Consequences of Immigration*, 2nd ed. (Ann Arbor: University of Michigan Press, 1999), chapter 1.

39. Faini, Melo, Zimmermann, "Trade and Migration."

40. Stephen Glover, Ceri Gott, Anaïs Loizillon, Jonathan Portes, Richard Price, Sarah Spencer, Vasanthi Srinivasan, and Carole Willis, "Migration: An Economic and Social Analysis," RDS Occasional Paper no. 67 (London: Home Office, 2001).

41. Jonathan Coppel, Jean-Christophe Dumont, and Ignazio Visco, "Trends in Immigration and Economic Consequences," Economics Department Working Papers no. 284 (Paris: OECD, 2001).

42. William Echikson, "Unsung Heroes," *Business Week*, 6 March (2000), 92–100.

43. M. Eaton, "Foreign Residents and Illegal Immigrants in Portugal," *International Journal of Intercultural Relations* 22, no. 1 (1998), 49–66.

44. Castles, *Ethnicity and Globalization*, chapter 6.

45. The points of tension between multiculturalism and social citizenship are often exaggerated. The postwar experience from OECD countries shows that ethnolinguistic diversity and social redistribution may well be at odds. But how this relationship exactly played out varied from country to country because it was contingent on the structure of political institutions. In general, consociational democracies like Belgium and the Netherlands, with centralized institutions and a tradition of consensual decision making, handled the friction better than liberal welfare states such as the UK with less extensive entitlement programs. Social democratic and corporatist welfare states of the Scandinavian or continental European variety to this day appear to succeed to reconcile cultural diversity with more ambitious welfare programs, albeit increasingly at the price of restrictive immigration and naturalization policies. Just to put things in perspective, a much more formidable challenge to inclusive social rights results from substate nationalisms like the Flemish, Catalans, or Basques. See Keith G. Banting, "Looking in Three Directions," in *Immigration and Welfare*, ed. Michael Bommes and Andrew Geddes (London: Routledge, 2000), 13–33.

46. Bill Jordan and Franck Düvell, *Irregular Migration* (Cheltenham: Elgar, 2002), chapters 1 and 10.

47. Saskia Sassen, "The De Facto Transnationalizing of Immigration Policy," in *Globalization and its Discontents* (New York: New Press, 1998), chapter 2.

48. Eva Thalhammer, Vlasta Zucha, Edith Enzenhofer, Brigitte Salfinger, and Günther Ogris, "Attitudes towards Minority Groups in the European Union," (Vienna: SORA, 2001).

49. Cf. Helga Leitner, "International Migration and the Politics of Admission and Exclusion in Postwar Europe," *Political Geography* 14, no. 3 (1995), 259–78; Jim Mac Laughlin, "Racism, Ethnicity and Multiculturalism in Contemporary Europe: A Review Essay," *Political Geography* 17 no. 8 (1998), 1013–24; Thomas F. Pettigrew, "Reactions towards the New Minorities of Western Europe," *Annual Review of Sociology* 24 (1998), 77–103.

50. Virginie Guiraudon and Christian Joppke, "Controlling a New Migration World," in *Controlling a New Migration World*, ed. Virginie Guiraudon and Christian Joppke (London: Routledge, 2001), 1–27.

51. Marzio Barbagli, *Immigrazione e criminalità in Italia* (Bologna: Mulino, 1998).

52. Thalhammer et al., "Attitudes towards Minority Groups in the European Union." For a discussion of the situation in the United States, see Peter H. Schuck, "Immigration at the Turn of the New Century," *Case Western Reserve Journal of International Law* 33, no. 1 (2001), 1–11.

53. Jacqueline Bhabha, " 'Get Back to Where You Once Belonged': Identity, Citizenship, and Exclusion in Europe," *Human Rights Quarterly* 20, no. 3 (1998), 592–627; Theodora Kostakopoulou, "The 'Protective Union': Change and Continuity in Migration Law and Policy in Post-Amsterdam Europe," *Journal of Common Market Studies* 38, no. 3 (2000), 497–518; Ian Ward, "Law and the Other Europeans," *Journal of Common Market Studies* 35, no. 1 (1997), 79–96.

54. Commission of the European Communities, "Communication from the Commission to the Council and the European Parliament on a Community Immigration Policy," COM(2000) 757 final.

55. Commission of the European Communities, "Communication from the Com-

mission to the Council and the European Parliament on a Community Immigration Policy," 6.

56. Nigel Harris, *Thinking the Unthinkable: The Immigration Myth Exposed* (London: I.B. Tauris, 2002), 31.

57. Commission of the European Communities, "Communication from the Commission to the Council and the European Parliament on a Community Immigration Policy," 8, 17.

58. Commission of the European Communities, "Communication from the Commission to the Council and the European Parliament on a Community Immigration Policy," 22.

59. Virginie Guiraudon, "European Integration and Migration Policy: Vertical Policy-making as Venue Shopping," *Journal of Common Market Studies* 38, no. 2 (2000), 251–71; Jef Huysmans, "The European Union and the Securitization of Migration," *Journal of Common Market Studies* 38, no. 5 (2000), 751–57.

60. Cf. Kostakopoulou, "The 'Protective Union.'"

61. Cf. Harris, *Thinking the Unthinkable*, chapter 2.

62. Gallya Lahav, "Immigration and the State: The Devolution and Privatisation of Immigration Control in the EU," *Journal of Ethnic and Migration Studies* 24, no. 4 (1998), 675–94.

63. Castles, *Ethnicity and Globalization*, 126; cf. John Salt and Jeremy Stein, "Migration as a Business: The Case of Trafficking," *International Migration* 35, no. 4 (1997), 467–94; John Salt, "Trafficking and Human Smuggling: A European Perspective," *International Migration* 38, no. 1 (2000), 31–56.

64. The following account is based on a real example described by Charu Lata Joshi, "The Body Trade," *Far Eastern Economic Review*, 26 October (2000), 100–103.

65. "Europe's Borders: A Single Market in Crime," *Economist*, 16 October (1999), 23–28.

66. Cf. Donna M. Hughes, "The 'Natasha' Trade: The Transnational Shadow Market of Trafficking in Women," *Journal of International Affairs* 53, no. 2 (2000). 625–51.

67. "In the Shadows," *Economist*, 26 August (2000), 38–9.

68. Cf. Hughes, "The 'Natasha' Trade."

69. Jordan and Düvell, *Irregular Migration*, 243.

70. Cf. Marek Okólski, "Recent Trends and Major Issues in International Migration: Central and East European Perspectives," *International Social Science Journal* 52, no. 165 (2000), 329–41.

CHAPTER 7

The Making of a Supranational Rule of Law

The Battle for Supremacy

Karen J. Alter

The European Union has the most effective international legal system in existence, standing in clear contrast to the typical weakness of international law and international courts. In most international legal systems, international courts hear few cases, violations of international law are not pursued, and the most important legal disputes are resolved out of court. But in Europe, the **European Court of Justice (ECJ)** hears many cases, and its jurisprudence shapes state behavior. There is an international rule of law that truly works in Europe. It functions much like a domestic rule of law, where violations of the law are brought to court, legal decisions are respected, and the autonomous influence of law and legal rulings extends to the political process itself.

The European legal system was not always so effective at influencing state policy and compelling compliance. The legal system designed at the founding of the European Community in 1957, and seemingly desired by the member states, inherently was limited and weak. Indeed the ECJ had little political influence in the 1960s and 1970s—the European Court heard few cases of political significance, and its most important doctrines were not widely accepted in national legal and political communities. It was a system through which few cases made it to the Court, and through which the largest infractions could easily and without repercussion persist until the political will to rectify the situation emerged.

The transformation of the original legal system was orchestrated by the ECJ through bold and controversial jurisprudence. The critical change involved the preliminary-ruling mechanism, which allows a national court to stop domestic legal proceedings and send a legal question to the ECJ for interpretation. In key decisions, the ECJ took this relatively obscure legal mechanism and turned it into a means to ensure that states respect European law. It did this by empowering individuals to raise national violations of EU law in national courts and by making European law hierarchically supreme to national law. In the transformed European system, private litigants challenge national policies that violate European law, national courts send these challenges to the ECJ as preliminary ruling references, and national courts apply European law over conflicting national law—thus holding European governments accountable for implementing and complying with their European obligations.

The European Court's actions in transforming the EU legal system were extremely controversial. The ECJ based its provocative interpretations on the "special" and "original" nature of the Treaty of Rome, arguing that unique features of the treaty implied that national sovereignty had, in certain areas, been irrevocably transferred to the EU level and that European law created rights for individuals that national courts had to protect. But nowhere did the Treaty of Rome actually say that European citizens could draw on European law in national courts to challenge national policy. Nowhere did it say that national courts were to enforce European law over national law. Few politicians or legal scholars saw the Treaty of Rome as anything more than a traditional international treaty. Indeed the whole idea that it created a "new legal order of international law" was really nothing more than an assertion of the European Court.[1] How, then, did what started as bold assertions of an obscure court in Luxembourg become a reality that transformed national legal systems and limited state sovereignty?

The court's bold jurisprudence had to be accepted by national judiciaries and national governments in order for the "new legal order" to become a reality. Both had significant reasons to reject the Court's edicts. For national judiciaries, accepting the Court's new legal order meant becoming agents of the ECJ at the national level, giving up some of their own interpretive autonomy, and taking on the confrontational task of enforcing international law against their own governments. It also required national judges to reinterpret key constitutional clauses and reconsider fundamental issues: What are the limits of national sovereignty? Does the executive have the power to make policy at the EU level, circumventing democratically elected national parliaments? What is the highest law of the land? Is it the proper role of the judiciary to police compliance with international agreements? For countries such as France and Britain, where courts traditionally played a subservient role in the political process and were not allowed to asses the validity of a national law for any reason, the ECJ was asking for nothing short of a legal revolution.

European governments had perhaps even more reason to oppose this change. It meant ceding national sovereignty to an activist international tribunal that interprets EU law expansively. ECJ decisions have gone well beyond the intentions and expectations of states, which have come to find themselves constrained in ways and in policy areas they had not imagined. For example, the Court told a conservative British government that it had to restrict the workweek to forty-eight hours, despite the British claim that such a law exceeds the European Community's authority. It ordered the German government to pay fines to beer importers, even though EU rules do not authorize courts to award damages for violations of European law. It implied that the Irish government had to tolerate the advertising of abortion services in Britain as part of the free movement of services. It may be true that national policymakers in the 1950s wrote the European policies and texts without recognizing the future implications of their decisions. But clearly the Court's actions went well beyond what member states thought they had agreed to. How did the European Court escape the limits put on it at its creation? Once it had escaped, why didn't the member states, the "masters of the treaty," not reclaim their sovereign rights and reassert political control over the legal process?

This chapter explains how the European Court's controversial declarations of new powers came to be accepted within national systems, by national judiciaries, and by national governments.

The Transformation of the European Legal System

To understand how the EU legal system was transformed, we must first understand what the ECJ was intended to do. Courts serve a variety of functions in the political process. Some have constitutional powers to practice judicial review, that is, to review whether laws and practices of the government are constitutional. Courts also are forums for resolving disputes between private parties, and they are part of the process through which governments enforce their laws. Courts exercise their power through direct review; that is, cases brought to it by disputants. In some European countries, unlike the United States, some courts have the power of abstract review, which means the case does not arise out of an actual dispute. For example, they can hear challenges to the constitutionality of laws raised by members of parliament or leaders of the government. The European Court practices both abstract and direct judicial review. Member states and other EU institutions can raise cases against each other (direct review) and challenge the validity of EU policy (abstract review). Only in a few rare circumstances can individuals bring cases directly to the ECJ. Instead, they gain access through national courts, which then use the preliminary-ruling procedure to refer the issue to the European Court.

A CHECK ON EU INSTITUTIONS

The Council of Ministers is the EU's main legislative body, and the European Commission is the executive body that oversees the implementation of and compliance with EU policies. The ECJ is the constitutional court of the European Union, reviewing the validity of EU laws and European Commission decisions to make sure that the Council and Commission do not violate the founding treaties or exceed their authority. Challenges can be raised in national courts and referred to the ECJ or brought to the Court by member states or one of the EU institutions. There are many reasons why an EU law or a Commission decision might be found to be invalid. The law could be "ultra vires," exceeding the authority of the EU institutions under the treaties. The law could violate basic rights guarantees of national constitutions or the European Convention of Human Rights. Or a Commission decision could have lacked due process or been based on insufficient or incorrect information.

DISPUTE RESOLUTION BETWEEN COMMUNITY INSTITUTIONS AND MEMBER STATES

The European Court also hears disputes among its constituent parts: the member states and the different institutions of the European Union. A national government or the Commission can challenge a Council decision if it believes that the decision was adopted under the wrong voting rule or that policy making in the area under question is best handled at the level of the national, regional, or local government. In light of amendments to the Maastricht treaty, the European Parliament now can challenge a Council policy if it believes that its prerogatives in the policy-making process have been infringed. Through these challenges, the Court helps mediate the separation of powers between EU institutions, and the Union and its member states.

ENSURING NATIONAL COMPLIANCE WITH EUROPEAN LAW

Member states also wanted the Court to help ensure compliance with European law, but at the same time they wanted to protect their national sovereignty.

Box 7.1. The European Court's Three Basic Functions

In hearing cases, the European Court fills three main functions: (1) It ensures that EU institutions do not exceed their authority, (2) it helps resolve disputes between community institutions and between member states, and (3) it helps to ensure national compliance with European law. In all of these roles, the ECJ is the highest authority, and its decisions are binding and final. The first two functions of the ECJ have remained unchanged, thus they are not part of the transformation of the EU legal system. They are part of the system of checks and balances within the European Union, and they remain relatively uncontroversial. However, the third function, in which the EU asserts federal power over its constituent states, is hotly contested, as member states want to ensure that national sovereignty is not compromised.

Thus, they allowed only the Commission or other member states to raise issues of member-state noncompliance in front of the Court, and they denied the Court the power to levy fines or penalize states for noncompliance with EU law. The Commission remains the primary monitor of member-state compliance with EU law. It gathers and investigates complaints from individuals, firms, and other member states and raises infringement cases before the ECJ if it suspects a violation of European law. Member states also can raise infringement suits, but they usually let the Commission pursue the issue.

In the original EU legal system, national courts were not supposed to consider issues of national compliance in cases raised by individuals. The treaty, it was thought, created obligations for states vis-à-vis other states and EU institutions but not toward their own citizens. In other words, citizens had no right to force their government to comply with EU rules, just as Americans have no right to force the U.S. government to follow the rules of the World Trade Organization, arms control treaties, or international environmental accords. The main transformation of the EU legal system was to create a right for European citizens to have their government comply with EU rules. The ECJ, through its jurisprudence, created legal standing and a means for individuals to challenge in front of national courts those national laws that conflict with EU law.

The European Court did this by altering the preliminary-ruling procedure (Article 177), which was designed to allow individuals to challenge EU law and policy in national courts and to help national courts interpret complex EU directives and regulations. National courts could stop legal proceedings to send a question of interpretation to the ECJ. Thus, a national court could ask the ECJ how to interpret the rules for awarding export licenses or for recognizing the diplomas of individuals trained in other countries. What national courts could not do, however, was ask if a national policy was in violation of European law or if a government was failing to live up to its obligations under European law.

In the transformed preliminary-ruling system, national courts can challenge the compatibility of national policy with EU law, and individuals can demand that their government implement EU legislation in full. The procedure works as follows: Before a national court, an individual argues that a national law or policy conflicts with European law. If there is a question about the meaning of the European law, the national judge can make a "preliminary-ruling reference" to the Court asking for an interpretation of the EU law. The parties in the case are allowed to submit arguments to the ECJ, as are EU institutions and national governments. The EJC's advocate general suggests to the Court what it should do based on an analysis of the arguments, the case law of the Court, and the laws in question. The Court issues its decision, and the national judge applies the ECJ ruling to the case at hand. Alternatively, the national court can resolve the dispute on its own, based on previous ECJ jurisprudence. The U.S. equivalent of this would be if an anti–death penalty group appealed the federal death penalty law to the U.S. Supreme Court, which then asked the International Court of Justice whether the U.S. policy violated inter-national human rights conventions. Based on such a convention, the International Court of Justice might then tell the U.S. Supreme Court that the policy was indeed in violation of this agreement, and the U.S. Supreme Court would tell Congress to change the law. This is unthinkable in the U.S. setting, and it was unthinkable in Europe where few courts had powers of judicial review. Yet it now exists.

Let's look in more detail at how the European Court constructed such a revolutionary change in the structure of the EU legal process, a change that has limited the power of European governments at home and compromised na-tional sovereignty. The institutional foundations for the current EU legal sys-tem were judicially created in the early 1960s. As Joseph Weiler has shown, the ECJ essentially "transformed" the preliminary-ruling process, creating a legal basis for national courts to enforce European law in the national realm.[2] The two key institutional transformations were the "doctrine of direct effect" and the "doctrine of EU law supremacy." The doctrine of direct effect declared that European law creates individual rights that can be claimed in front of national courts and must be protected by national courts. The doctrine of EU law su-premacy declared that EU law absolutely prevails over national law and that national courts have an obligation to apply supreme EU law over conflicting national law. Together, these two doctrines expanded access to the ECJ and cre-ated a means for EU law to be enforced in the member states, independent of politicians' will to comply. They have fundamentally altered the enforcement system for EU law and put the ECJ in the position to influence national and EU policy.

The Doctrine of Direct Effect

The legal cases leading to the key ECJ decisions were quite technical, and their actual material and political impact were not particularly significant. But from a legal perspective, the decisions were monumental. The doctrine of direct effect was declared in 1963, in a case known as *Van Gend en Loos*. The case evolved when the Dutch government reclassified urea-formaldehyde under a new tariff category and raised its tariff rate. The firm Van Gend en Loos brought suit in the Dutch Tariff Commission, claiming that when the Dutch law reclassified urea-formaldehyde, it resulted in an increase in the tariff rate in violation of Article 12 of the Treaty of Rome, which prohibits member states from increas-ing tariffs on goods from other member states after the coming into force of the treaty. The Dutch Tariff Commission used the preliminary-ruling procedure to send the issue to the ECJ, asking if an individual may invoke Article 12 before a national court and if the reclassification of urea-formaldehyde constituted a violation of the treaty.

The European Court took the relatively novel view that the treaty could indeed create direct effects, and it defended its position on rather disputable grounds (see Box 7.2). The *Van Gend* decision meant in essence that citizens have a right to have international treaties adhered to by their government, and to this end they can, in certain circumstances, have legal standing to demand that their government stick to their international obligations. After the first case, national courts sent the ECJ a host of other references asking if different provisions of the treaty created direct effects. Private litigants can always question the validity of EU laws themselves, but only where EU law creates direct effects can EU law be invoked to challenge national policy. The Court's doctrine allows it selectively to expand individual rights to different provisions of the treaty on an article-by-article, directive-by-directive, legal-provision-by-legal-provision basis.

From a legal perspective, the ECJ's *Van Gend* decision was radical. Traditionally, international treaties are interpreted narrowly, sticking closely to the

Box 7.2.   The Doctrine of Direct Effect: Van Gend en Loos

To ascertain whether the provisions of an international treaty extend so far in their effects, it is necessary to consider the spirit, the general scheme, and the wording of those provisions.

"The objective of the EEC Treaty, which is to establish a Common Market, the function of which is of direct concern to interested parties in the Community, implies that this Treaty is more than an agreement that merely creates mutual obligations between the contracting states. This view is confirmed by the preamble to the Treaty that refers not only to government but to peoples. It is also confirmed more specifically by the establishment of institutions endowed with sovereign rights, the exercise of which affects Member States and their citizens.

"In addition the task assigned to the Court of Justice under Article 177, the object of which is to secure uniform interpretation of the Treaty by national courts and tribunals, confirms that the states have acknowledged that Community law has an authority that can be invoked by their nationals before those courts and tribunals.

"The conclusion to be drawn from this is that the Community constitutes a new legal order of international law for the benefit of which the states have limited their sovereign rights, albeit within limited fields, and the subject of which comprise not only Member States, but also their nationals. Independent of the legislation of Member States, Community law therefore not only imposes obligations on individuals but is also intended to confer upon them rights that become part of their legal heritage. These rights arise not only where they are expressly granted by the Treaty, but also by reason of obligations that the Treaty imposes in a clearly defined way upon individuals as well as upon Member States and upon the institutions of the Community."[3]

wording of the text. But the ECJ interpreted lacunae in the treaty as a license to fill in gaps; although the treaty did not say that EU law created individual rights that could be claimed in national courts, the Court took strength from the fact that it didn't say that the EU law *did not* create such rights, either. Nor, ECJ justices later would argue, did it say that EU law *did not* take precedence over national law. The Court's approach has been called a "teleological approach" to legal interpretation where, as ECJ Justice Robert Lecourt put it, "Law [is] in the service of an objective. The goal is the motor of the law."[4] The ECJ's goal was to further European integration and increase the effectiveness of the European legal system. This meant, at times, creatively interpreting the treaty.

The Doctrine of EU Law Supremacy

The *Van Gend* decision was amplified with the creation of the doctrine of supremacy, which was declared in the 1964 *Costa v. ENEL* decision. The *Costa* case was contrived by its lawyer in order to probe the supremacy of EU law over subsequent national acts, a principle directly implied by the *Van Gend* decision. Refusing to pay his electricity bill of roughly $3.00, the lawyer in a small-claims court challenged the validity of the 1962 Italian nationalization act that created the state-run electricity company ENEL. The Italian small-claims court sent preliminary-ruling references simultaneously to both the Italian Constitutional Court and to the ECJ. Imagine the situation. A small-claims court judge was asking the foreign European Court to strike down the Italian government's decision to nationalize the electricity industry! Materially, the entire case was absurd, but it raised a very important legal issue. At stake was the principle of whether a government could void an EU obligation simply by passing a new law at the national level. In legal terms, the question was whether EU law took precedence over national law passed both before and after the coming into force of EU law, thus whether EU legal obligations were unalterable through unilateral national action.

In its decision, the Court argued that the EU law must be seen as supreme over national law adopted both before and after the coming into force of EU law. It supported this position on the following grounds:

> By contrast with ordinary international treaties, the EEC Treaty has created its own legal system, which, on entry into force of the Treaty, became an integral part of the legal systems of the Member States and that their courts are bound to apply. By creating a Community of unlimited duration, having its own institutions, its own personality, its own legal capacity and capacity of representation on the international plane and, more particularly, real powers stemming from the

limitation of sovereignty or a transfer of powers from the States to the Community, the Member States have limited their sovereign rights, albeit within limited fields, and have thus created a body of law that binds both their nationals and themselves. . . . It follows from all these observations that the law stemming from the Treaty, an independent source of law, could not, because of its special and original nature, be overridden by domestic legal provisions, however framed, without being deprived of its character as Community law and without the legal basis of the Community itself being called into question.[5]

This decision was revolutionary: The European Court indirectly was asserting the authority to rule a national law inapplicable and was granting EU law supremacy over subsequent national acts. Thus, the doctrine challenged the tradition of *lex posterior derogat legi apriori* (last law passed trumps all previous laws), a fundamental component of many countries' legal doctrine on the relationship of international law to national law.

In addition to making EU law hierarchically superior to national law, the newly created supremacy doctrine instructed national courts to accord EU law supremacy in their *application* of law.[6] The instruction already was present in the *Costa v. ENEL* decision, but it was made even more explicit in the 1978 *Simmenthal* decision. After restating the principle of EU law supremacy, the Court said:

> It follows from the foregoing [argument supporting the primacy of EU law] that every national court must, in a case within its jurisdiction, apply Community law in its entirety and protect rights of individuals and must accordingly set aside any provision of national law that may conflict with it, whether prior or subsequent to the Community rule.
>
> Accordingly, any provision of a national legal system and any legislative, administrative or judicial practice that might impair the effectiveness of Community law by withholding from the national court having jurisdiction to apply such law the power to do everything necessary at the moment of its application to set aside national legislative provisions that might prevent Community rules from having full force and effect are incompatible with those requirements which are the very essence of Community law. . . . [Thus] a national court which is called upon, within the limits of its jurisdiction, to apply provisions of Community law is under a duty to give full effect to those provisions, if necessary refusing of it its own motion to apply any conflicting provision of national legislation.[7]

Thus, the supremacy doctrine implied that national courts must, in their application of national law, apply the supreme EU law.

It bears repeating that these two decisions were extremely controversial, not just because they challenged traditional international law interpretations, but because the interpretive arguments underpinning the ECJ's interpretation were not widely shared. The ECJ based its decisions on the "special" and "original" nature of the Treaty of Rome, but few politicians or legal scholars saw the Rome treaty as anything more than a traditional international treaty. Although the Court pointed out many supposedly original features, it is questionable if these elements actually are that unusual as far as treaties go; and even if they are extraordinary, it would not necessarily mean that EU law creates direct effects or is supreme over national law. Some legal scholars argued that the ECJ was putting too much weight on the preamble, which mentioned the "peoples of Europe," a preamble tacked on at the end of the negotiations when each country was allowed to add one statement reflecting their view of the treaty's goal.[8] Others questioned whether there was any sound legal basis for the ECJ's decisions. German legal scholar Hans Heinrich Rupp called the ECJ's legal argumentation "wishful thinking."[9] Writing later in the 1970s and 1980s, observers continued to note national judicial resistance to the doctrine of EU law supremacy despite the years of campaigning by the ECJ and its proponents. As late as 1989, Ronny Abraham still was asking if "in effect, . . . the court has not exceeded its authority in pretending to dictate to national judiciaries the attitude to adopt in the case of a conflict between two norms."[10]

The ECJ has used the opportunities presented by national courts' referrals to make many important legal expansions of EU authority, or—as some might say—to change the Treaty of Rome in order to build a common market and make European law more enforceable.

Another important European Court precedent was set by the *Francovich* decision, which held governments financially liable if they failed to implement European directives into national policy.[11] This meant that an individual could sue the government for damages if the government's failure to correctly incorporate a European directive into national policy created hardship for the individual. For the first time, citizens could claim a right to have their government follow their European legal obligations—and win compensation for a government's refusal to implement European directives.

Under the transformed EU legal system, preliminary-ruling references have been used to challenge national policies that serve as barriers to the free movement of goods, people, services, and capital, such as health and safety rules designed primarily to keep out products produced in other countries. Preliminary-ruling references also have been used to challenge national policies that seemingly have little to do with the free movement of goods, people, services, or capital. For example, Irish student groups challenged an Irish ban on the advertisement of abortion services, and the British Equal Opportunities Council challenged British gender-equality laws. Clearly, Ireland did not intend membership in the EU to affect its abortion policy, nor did the United Kingdom

Box 7.3.   Expanding the Reach of European Law

Crème de Cassis, the black currant elixir which transforms white wine into Kir, also transformed the nature of Europe's common market. It is largely due to a famous European Court case involving this liqueur that the 1992 single-market initiative has been able to do so much to restore progress to the European Community, but also to arouse such unease in Member States about loss of sovereignty.

Quote from "Message in a Bottle That Changed Europe," *The Independent*, May 6, 1990

The French liquor *Cassis de Dijon* was behind one of the ECJ's most well-known decisions. A German law banned importation of the liquor because it did not fit into the legal categories the Germans had for alcohol. It had too much alcohol to be considered beer or wine, but not enough to be considered a spirit like whiskey. Defending their law on health grounds, the German government claimed that the law helped avoid the proliferation of alcoholic beverages with low alcohol content, products that could "more easily induce a tolerance towards alcohol" than more highly alcoholic beverages. This argument was absurd considering the amount of beer the Germans drink, and considering that Germans drink plenty of Kir when they travel. More likely is that Germany wanted to preserve the market for its own berry alcohol.

The ECJ struck down the German law as a hidden trade restriction. After dismissing the German government's arguments, the Court went on in its decision to state a general principle, now the most often-cited part of the ruling:

There is therefore no valid reason why, provided that they have been lawfully produced and marketed in one of the Member States, alcoholic beverages should not be introduced into any other Member State.[12]

This sentence introduced the criterion of a product being lawfully produced in one member state as the basis for its admittance into the market of another member state. In reality, the clause carried no legal weight; the German law had been overruled earlier in the decision on the basis of well-established jurisprudence. But the Commission seized on this language and asserted that the ruling implied that national regulations governing how a good was produced had to be recognized as equivalent to the regulations of the exporting member state. This interpretation was refuted, but the ensuing battle led to the principle of *mutual recognition* being inscribed into the Single European Act.[13]

envision that membership would mean that it had to work harder to ensure equal pay for men and women or to swallow a rule agreed by other member states regarding the number of hours employees could work per week. These were considered issues of national policy, to be decided by democratically elected governments—not by intergovernmental bargaining in Brussels. Especially in cases such as these, the Court has been accused of overstepping its authority and meddling in the affairs of member states.

The institutional consequences of the doctrine of direct effect and doctrine of EU law supremacy were the fundamental transformation of the European legal system's enforcement mechanism and the harnessing of the national courts to enforce European law at the national level. Without the doctrine of direct effect, the ECJ had few cases and thus few opportunities to pronounce a breach of EU law. But armed with the doctrine, individual citizens became the new monitors of compliance with EU treaties and EU law. Self-interested individuals were much more likely than either member states or the Commission to bring cases. In addition, in the past member states had been able to convince the Commission not to bring suit in politically contentious cases—through delaying tactics, compromises, and even threats; individuals and national courts were much harder to influence, and a member state's political control over the Court's docket correspondingly weaker. The doctrine of EU law supremacy allowed the ECJ to "dialogue" with national courts about the meaning of European law and thus to influence national legal interpretation. Finally, the transformation of the preliminary-ruling procedure turned national courts into enforcers of European law in the national realm, making ECJ decisions harder to circumvent. Whereas it was not very costly politically and financially to ignore the ECJ, it *was* costly for national politicians to ignore their own national courts. National judicial support added both important moral force to ECJ decisions and coercive power through the imposition of fines.

The ECJ's doctrines also led to a fundamental change in the political relationship between the ECJ and the member states. Before, if politicians did not like an ECJ decision, they could simply ignore it. Fearing that noncompliance with ECJ decisions would make them dead letters, the Court's judges were rather meek in demanding change in the 1960s and early 1970s, finding technical ways to limit the substantive impact of their decisions.[14] However, as national courts became more willing to apply ECJ decisions against their governments, the Court responded in the 1970s and 1980s by issuing bold decisions with significant political and material impact. Now if politicians did not like an ECJ decision, they had to fight actively to have it reversed at the EU or the national level, which took much more effort and mobilization than simply ignoring a decision. Because reversing an ECJ decision was politically and institutionally difficult and because national courts would enforce ECJ jurisprudence, the Court gained political leverage over national governments with its ability to enforce compliance.

The transformed system depends on the willingness of national courts to send cases to the ECJ and to apply ECJ jurisprudence. Private litigants cannot raise issues directly in the European Court of Justice, and if the national judge refuses to make a reference or follow European Court jurisprudence, there is little the private litigant can do except to appeal to a higher national court. If the highest court refuses to make a reference, the litigant is out of luck; she cannot appeal the case to the ECJ herself. The system also depends on politicians' ultimate acquiescence in the face of unpopular decisions. Neither national judicial nor political support is guaranteed, and there are limits on both.

Winning the Support of National Courts and National Governments

The ECJ's interest in the supremacy and direct effect of EU law was clear. The transformed preliminary-ruling procedure gave the Court more opportunities to issue influential decisions, more legal tools, and access to the moral, coercive, and political power of national judiciaries. The vast majority of ECJ decisions, and especially influential ones, usually come through preliminary-ruling cases. The transformed system helped promote the ECJ's political agenda of promoting European integration, "constitutionalizing" the Treaty of Rome, and creating the legal foundations for a European federation.

Less clear, however, is why national courts would want to facilitate the expansion of ECJ authority and the penetration of EU law into the national legal system. In countries without a tradition of judicial review, the ECJ was asking national courts for nothing short of a legal revolution. In order to accept a role enforcing EU law supremacy, national judges would have to change how they interpreted their constitutions, alter entrenched national legal precedents regarding the relationship of international to national law, and embrace a new judicial role as an enforcer of international law. Although the objections to EU law supremacy usually were stated in legalistic terms, underlying the doctrinal differences were different conceptions of the role of the judiciary in the political system.

Within almost every European country, the Court's supremacy doctrine raised fundamental issues of political authority. The doctrine touched on the limits of parliamentary sovereignty, the sanctity of the national constitution, the separation of authority between the parliament and the executive, the separation of authority between regional and federal governments, and the role the judiciary should play in the political process. For the French and the British, applying EU law supremacy went against the very essence of democracy as embodied in the notion of parliamentary sovereignty. Lachaume explained French judicial reservations, saying:

> The national judge should not have doubts in the face of a statute posterior to a treaty that contradicts it, because this statute expresses, if one dare say, the latest state of the general will. He would therefore . . . apply [the law]. If the law contradicts the treaty, and without saying that it is inconceivable that a legislature did not know what it

was doing, it is the general will that—right or wrong—is decisive. The
judge cannot but yield. His function as judge consists of applying the
law, not of judging it. Above all, . . . in establishing the incompatibility of a law with a previous treaty, the judge must disregard the law.[15]

The Germans had different concerns. Having experienced what could happen when judges did not supervise adequately what politicians did, they feared
that EU law supremacy could undermine their national courts' ability to ensure
respect for the German constitution and for democracy. A judge in Rheinland-
Pfalz argued:

> The most important aim of the Constitution is to avoid a repetition
> of the developments that, in the Weimar Republic, led to the abolition
> of the separation of powers, and thus to the collapse of the rule of
> law. The path to the complete surrender of the doctrine of the separa-
> tion of powers through the Special Powers Act of 24 March 1933 took
> its first open form in the excessively wide interpretation of Art. 48
> (2) of the Weimar Constitution in favor of the executive. As early as
> this, the thinking of leading academic lawyers had reached the highly
> dangerous stage, in which an inadequately circumscribed clause in
> the Constitution had itself become a gap in the Constitution. The un-
> dermining and destruction of the rule of law for a second time can be
> avoided only by the courts opposing every attempt to interpret an-
> other inadequately circumscribed constitutional provision so as to
> weaken the Constitution's protection of the principle of separation
> of powers, and reduce the significance of the rule of law to a sham.[16]

National high courts also were concerned about ceding interpretive authority to the European Court of Justice. Reluctant to admit that they were looking
out for their own institutional interests, high courts cloaked their concerns in
legalistic arguments about respecting the constitution, protecting constitutional
guarantees and legal certainty, and respecting parliamentary prerogatives. Although the arguments were not wholly without merit, many legal scholars
found them exaggerated and legally inconsistent, revealing ulterior motives behind the legal arguments.

Finally, there were political factors that judges had to consider. The transformed EU legal system implied a significant loss of national sovereignty; a foreign court could rule on national law and policy in areas seemingly only tan-
gentially related to creating a common market. National judges were sensitive
to issues of sovereignty and were accustomed to deferring to national parliaments while leaving foreign policy to the government.

The ambivalences of national judiciaries were widespread in the 1960s and
1970s, and many of their well-founded fears have become realities. Pioneering
national courts that enforced EU law over the will of politicians were de-

nounced and their independence threatened. ECJ jurisprudence also has directly encroached on high-court prerogatives, providing ample fodder for high courts concerned that they would lose authority to the ECJ. The ECJ instructed lower courts to ignore the jurisprudence and rules of higher courts if they hindered the lower courts from applying EU law supremacy; indeed, certain national high courts have, for all practical purposes, become subjugated to the jurisprudence of the European Court. A former German tax court judge argued that, given the advanced development of EU taxation law, "the Chamber of the Bundesfinanzhof, that is the five judges who are in charge of VAT jurisdiction, would hardly be needed any more."[17]

Given the controversy surrounding the legal reasoning offered by the ECJ in support of the supremacy of EU law, and given its incompatibility with national legal doctrine and traditions, there was ample legal basis for national judges to reject the ECJ's doctrine of EU law supremacy. Although most national judges were not hostile to the European Court and did not want to create legal barriers to the political decision to integrate Europe, at the same time they did not want the ECJ stepping too far on their legal turf or upsetting the national administration of law. As some high-court judges argued, politicians' failure to create an adequate enforcement mechanism for the Treaty of Rome did not mean that national judges must take on a role in enforcing EU law supremacy.

During the years following the ECJ's supremacy declaration, a virtual battle over legal interpretation was waged at the national level. Many national courts refused EU law supremacy, sticking to established constitutional interpretations. But some national courts accepted EU law supremacy, reinterpreting national constitutional provisions to support their position. As national courts went different ways on the issue of EU law supremacy, a variegated pattern of national judicial adherence and nonadherence emerged.

THE BATTLE WITHIN NATIONAL JUDICIARIES

The legal concerns about EU law supremacy and the challenges to ECJ authority often were given their strongest voice by higher national courts. This is not so surprising when one considers that they had the most to lose by the extension of ECJ jurisdictional authority over national legal issues. As courts of last resort, high courts traditionally enjoyed dominant influence over the development of national law and were the final interpreters of national law. Whenever a new area of EU law was declared to create "direct effects," the supreme interpretive authority over that area of law became part of the European Court's jurisdictional authority. Higher courts were also concerned with policing the overall functioning of the national legal system, making them inherently more conservative than lower courts. Their concerns are manifest in their jurisprudence regarding EU law supremacy, in which some high courts reject ECJ legal arguments, refuse the authority of the ECJ, try to limit the reach and scope of ECJ jurisprudence, and try to keep lower courts from making referrals to the ECJ. Their resistance also is manifest in the referral patterns of high courts to the ECJ. Even though high courts, as courts of last instance, must refer questions of EU law to the ECJ, the constitutional courts in Italy, Belgium, Germany, and France never have made a referral. Other national high courts have sent relatively few referrals compared to the number coming from lower courts. More important than the number, however, is the type of referrals being made. High-court referrals to the ECJ are much more likely to be narrow technical questions about EU law—questions that do not allow the ECJ to expand the reach or scope of its jurisprudence. Reserving for themselves difficult questions about the relationship of European law to national law is a sort of "don't ask and the ECJ can't tell" policy, which limits the ECJ from expanding its jurisdictional reach at the expense of national high courts by denying the ECJ the opportunity to do so. It is not, however, universally true that high courts do not send issues of substance to the ECJ or accept its jurisprudence. Sometimes high courts embrace EU law to further their own competitive battles with other high courts or political bodies.

Although EU law supremacy posed a threat to the influence and authority of high courts and implied a significant compromise of national sovereignty, lower courts found few costs and numerous benefits in making referrals to the ECJ and applying EU law. As first-instance courts, lower courts were used to having another court hierarchically above them and to having their decisions reversed by courts above them. Neither did they have to worry about how their individual actions might upset legal certainty or the smooth functioning of the legal system. Thus, they were more open to sending to the ECJ broad and provocative legal questions about the reach and effects of European law on the national legal order. There also were many benefits for lower courts in seizing the ECJ and invoking EU law. It allowed lower courts to circumvent the restrictive jurisprudence of higher courts and reopen legal debates, achieving legal outcomes they preferred for either policy or legal reasons. For example, appealing to EU law allowed pro-women industrial tribunals in Great Britain to circumvent the Employment Appeals Tribunal and the Conservative government, and to get legal outcomes that helped promote equal pay for men and women.[18] Having an ECJ decision also magnified the influence of the lower-court decisions in the legal process, as the decision became part of established legal precedent and sometimes led to journal articles on decisions that otherwise would not have been reported publicly and could decisively contribute to the development of national law. Having an ECJ decision behind a lower-court decision also lessened the possibility of reversal by a higher court, thus actually bolstering the legal power and influence of the lower courts.

For the lower court, the ECJ was like a second parent whose approval wards off punishment. When the lower court disagreed with the decision—or potential decision—of one parent (the higher national court), it would ask the other parent (the ECJ). Having the other parent's approval decreased the likelihood of a sanction for challenging legal precedence or government policy. If the lower court, however, did not think that it would like what the other parent might say, it would follow the "don't ask and the ECJ can't tell" policy and not make a referral.

The different strategic calculations of national courts vis-à-vis the European Court of Justice created a "competition-between-courts" dynamic that fed the process of legal integration and came to shift the national legal context out from under high courts. The limitations created by high courts on interpretation of national law provoked lower courts to make referrals to the ECJ so that the lower courts could deviate from established jurisprudence or reach new legal outcomes. By using EU law and the ECJ to achieve their own ends, lower courts created opportunities for the ECJ to expand its jurisdiction and jurisprudence; in some cases they actually goaded the ECJ to expand the legal authority of EU law. In this respect, one can say that lower courts were the motors of legal integration, driving legal expansion through their referrals to the ECJ and bringing ECJ jurisprudence into the national legal order.

Higher courts tried to stop lower courts from referring cases to the ECJ so as to keep EU law from encroaching on their legal domain. In Britain, the Court of Appeals and the House of Lords developed narrow guidelines about when a lower-court referral to the ECJ was justified;[19] and in Italy, the Constitutional Court said that all issues of the validity of European and national law were constitutional issues, so that only it could decide if EU law was supreme with respect to subsequent national law.[20] In other cases, high courts issued their own narrow interpretations of EU law to limit its applicability in the national realm and ward off referrals to the ECJ. Sometimes high courts even quashed lower-court decisions to refer a case to the ECJ or directly challenged ECJ jurisprudence. But the ability of higher courts to stop lower-court referrals was limited. The decision to refer a case to the ECJ had to be appealed to the higher court in order for a high court to be able to quash a referral, and often decisions were not appealed. In some cases, lower courts also ignored the rulings of the higher courts and made referrals anyway, to provoke the ECJ to issue an alternative interpretation.

THE ECJ'S ROLE

The ECJ, for its part, encouraged the competitive dynamic between lower and higher courts. It defended the right of lower courts to refer any question they wanted and encouraged them by giving serious evaluations of their questions, while dismissing higher-court refutations of lower-court authority. In direct challenge to the Italian Constitutional Court, the ECJ even instructed lower courts to ignore the constitutional rules, guidelines, or jurisprudence of higher courts if such rules would lead the lower court not to give effect to EU law.[21]

Lower-court actions allowed EU law to expand into new issue areas and to influence national law. As all it takes is one court referral for the ECJ to expand its jurisdictional authority, the possibilities presented by the preliminary-ruling system were abundant. As we have seen, the influence of EU law spread to areas never envisioned by national politicians, such as the provision of education grants to nonnationals, the provision of equal pay to men and women, industrial relations, and the advertisement of British abortion services in Ireland.[22] As legal questions were appealed up the national judicial hierarchies, higher courts were put in the position of either quashing ECJ doctrine or accepting it. High courts freely accepted ECJ jurisprudence as long as it did not encroach on their own authority, but when the ECJ strayed onto their territory, high courts rejected ECJ doctrine. The often confrontational responses of high courts were likened by legal commentators to a "state of war" between the ECJ and higher national courts, and in some cases analysts baldly concluded that the latter deliberately chose war over cooperation.[23] Because ECJ jurisprudence did not affect all high courts equally, there was seldom a unified opposition to any given ECJ decision. Thus, a varied pattern of acceptance and refusal of ECJ jurisprudence and jurisdictional authority by national high courts emerged within and across national legal systems.

Lower courts referred to the ECJ questions that high courts would not have asked, and the actions of the lower courts came to shift the national legal context out from under the high courts. First, the acceptance of EU law supremacy by some courts and the rejection of ECJ legal authority by others within the same national system created problems of legal consistency, which, for legal communities committed to legal logic and legal reasoning, was alarming. Second and perhaps even more important, at a certain point it became clear that high courts had failed in their efforts to stem the legal tide of EU law or to decisively control the development of national law. As the French Commissaire du Gouvernement argued in the famous *Nicolo* case: "It cannot be repeated often enough that the era of the unconditional supremacy of internal law is now over. International rules of law, particularly those of Europe, have gradually conquered our legal universe, without hesitating furthermore to encroach on the competence of Parliament. In this way certain entire fields of our law such as those of the economy, employment or protection of human rights, now very largely originate genuinely from international legislation."[24]

It was not merely the fact that there was more EU legislation but, rather, that ECJ doctrine had made more areas and types of EU law directly binding. As ECJ doctrine expanded and was applied to more issues, a much wider range of national law came to be influenced by EU law and the ECJ. Pinpointing the ECJ's doctrine as the source of legal expansion, former House of Lord's judge

Lord Denning reconfigured his famous metaphor of EU law as an incoming tide, arguing:

> Our sovereignty has been taken away by the European Court of Justice. It has made many decisions impinging on our statute law and says that we are to obey its decisions instead of our own statute law. It has put on the Treaty an interpretation according to their own views of policy. The European Court has held that all European directives are binding within each of the European countries; and must be enforced by the national courts; even though they are contrary to our national law. No longer is European law an incoming tide flowing up the estuaries of England. It is now like a tidal wave bringing down our sea walls and flowing inland over our fields and houses—to the dismay of all.[25]

Because so much national law touched on EU law and so many lower courts were following the ECJ rather than their own high courts, opposition to ECJ jurisprudence lost its influence and effectiveness. National high courts repositioned themselves to the new reality, reversing decisions that had challenged EU law supremacy and adjusting national constitutional doctrine to make it compatible with enforcing EU law over national law. But they did not accept the legal reasoning offered by the ECJ. By basing the supremacy of EU law on national constitutions rather than on the ECJ's legal reasoning, high courts left open legal avenues through which they could refuse the authority of the ECJ in the future without contradicting their jurisprudence on EU law supremacy.

THE COMPETITION DYNAMIC IN LEGAL INTEGRATION

The legal process in general, and legal integration more specifically, is not only about courts competing against each other. Clearly, judges also care about policy outcomes, legal logic, and legal certainty, and the relationships between courts are not so adversarial that judges mainly want to challenge each other. But because EU law supremacy involved the question of who decides and who is the highest authority, it was more contentious than most EU legal issues. The competition dynamic was instrumental in establishing the supremacy of EU law over national law, and it continues to be central to the development of EU doctrine and the process of legal integration in Europe.

Without the competition dynamic, it is difficult to understand why national legal doctrines shifted from *lex posterior derogat legi priori* to doctrines compatible with the supremacy of EU law. The debate over the relationship of national to international law was an old one, and although tensions still remained by the time the ECJ declared EU law supremacy, the national legal debates in many countries had settled into an equilibrium around the principle *lex posterior derogat legi priori*. Given that there was no clear legal basis for EU law supremacy, and there *were* solid and entrenched legal reasons to refuse to enforce the supremacy of international law, there was seemingly no reason to reverse this long-standing doctrine. Indeed, many national courts refused to change national doctrine in light of ECJ rulings for many years, picking apart the legal arguments proposed by supporters of EU law supremacy.

At the same time, to the extent that national courts had an interest in enforcing international over national law—either because it empowered them or because they thought it was the right thing to do—they had all the tools they really needed long before the ECJ told them they could. In many European countries, the new postwar constitutions created legal opportunities to make national law compatible with international law, and the failure of the legal profession during fascist rule made judicial review particularly acceptable in Germany and Italy. But it took lower-court referrals and invocations of ECJ jurisprudence for national doctrine to shift. Had the ECJ not been there as a willing actor to support the deviations from national legal precedent, it is highly unlikely that national courts supporting EU law supremacy would have been so bold in their challenges. Had supporting courts not incorporated EU law, seized the ECJ, and ignored existent national jurisprudence, it also is unlikely that higher courts would have overturned historic traditions and doctrines and accepted a role enforcing international law in the national realm. Without the ECJ as a common reference point for national court competition dynamics, it also is doubtful that the national legal systems of all the member states would have evolved to similar doctrinal positions regarding the supremacy of European law over national law.

Competition between courts continues to be an influence as concerns about European legal integration and jurisdictional authority make some national courts more reluctant—and lower courts more willing—to refer questions to the ECJ. Competition also is involved in high-court threats of noncompliance with ECJ jurisprudence, which they use to influence the development of EU law.

In trying to establish a federal system in the United States, it took decades before the U.S. Supreme Court's authority to review state law and state-court decisions was accepted by the state supreme courts. In Europe, the process of establishing the supremacy of EU law over national law took less than twenty-five years. The competition dynamic in legal integration could well explain the rapidity through which this fundamental legal transformation came about.

GAINING POLITICAL ACQUIESCENCE—AND POLITICAL SUPPORT?

The idea that national courts would become enforcers of EU over national law was unforeseen by negotiators and politicians in the 1950s and 1960s. The decision to create a relatively weak enforcement mechanism for the Treaty of Rome must be seen as a political choice. Other models of potentially more effective systems were on the negotiating table, and it would have been possible to make the Court's rulings enforceable.[26] Indeed, by removing the sanctioning powers of the Court and the Commission, member states actually made the enforcement mechanism for the Treaty of Rome weaker than that of the Coal and Steel Community. Stronger enforcement mechanisms were rejected because they would have infringed on national sovereignty and given too much power to supranational institutions.

Extending the supremacy and direct effect of EU law fundamentally changed the union's legal system. It transformed the preliminary-ruling procedure from a mechanism designed to allow national courts to question EU law into a means for individuals to challenge national law. This transformation has decreased the ability of politicians to keep issues in the political realm and out of the legal realm. National courts send questions and issues to the ECJ that member states and the Commission would not dare to raise, thus involving the ECJ in all sorts of unforeseen issues. Because national courts are applying ECJ jurisprudence, all of the enforcement mechanisms of national law can be brought to bear on politicians disobeying EU law. The supremacy of EU law also has meant that national parliaments can be overruled by the ECJ and by national courts. This is not just an abstract possibility, it is a reality—as national parliaments have found on numerous occasions. When Lord Denning declared, "Our sovereignty has been taken away by the European Court of Justice," he was not so wrong.

Why didn't politicians react more vigorously to the ECJ's declaration of EU law supremacy? Part of the answer lies in the ECJ's judicial strategy in the 1960s, which made it hard for politicians to use their legislative tools to respond to the ECJ's doctrinal declarations. Politicians care most about the material and political impact of court decisions, and the ECJ was following a well-known judicial practice of expanding its jurisdictional authority by establishing legal principles rather than applying the principles to the cases at hand. In a move similar to that of U.S. Supreme Court Justice Marshall in *Marbury v. Madison*,[27] the ECJ declared the supremacy of EU law in the *Costa* case, but it found that the Italian law in question did not violate EU law. Given that the Italian law was still valid, what was there for politicians to protest or reverse? With ECJ jurisprudence unenforceable, the ECJ also was careful to temper its decisions to encourage voluntary compliance. The ECJ's jurisprudence in the 1960s showed clear signs of caution, and the ECJ seemed to intentionally avoid issuing decisions that would agitate politicians into action. One analyst observed of the Court's early jurisprudence that "by narrowly restricting the scope of its reasoning, [the ECJ] manages to avoid almost every question in issue."[28] It also was unclear that national courts would accept the ECJ's supremacy doctrine. In the very same *Costa* case in which the supremacy of EU law was declared, the Italian Constitutional Court refused the validity of EU law supremacy.[29] And four years later the French Conseil d'État found itself incompetent even to ask if national law conflicted with a previously passed international law.[30] Thus, not only were ECJ decisions not creating discomfort for politicians, its supremacy declaration was more hypothetical than actual in the 1960s.

For the 1960s and early 1970s, one could argue that ECJ jurisprudence did not create significant political concern because its impact was minimal. But arguments about clever judges, politicians not understanding legal implications of decisions, or unwarranted complacence go only so far. By the late 1970s, the ECJ clearly had crossed over the comfort zone of politicians. In 1979, former French prime minister Michel Debré launched the attack, saying, "once again, the attitude of the Court [leads to a] usurpation of the sovereignty of the member states." He was followed in the 1980s by Helmut Kohl, who assailed the ECJ and its jurisprudence in an address in the Bundestag;[31] French president Giscard d'Estaing, who called on the Council to do something about "the Court and its illegal decisions";[32] and an outraged British member of parliament, who argued that a ruling of the ECJ had "set aside the British constitution as we have understood it for several hundred years."[33]

The early failure to oppose judicial activism does not imply political support. Indeed, it is clear that politicians did *not* support the transformation of the EU legal system and that legal integration proceeded despite the intention and desire of national leaders. As Joseph Weiler has pointed out, the largest advances in EU legal doctrine at both the national and the EU level occurred at the same time that member states were scaling back the supranational aspirations of the Treaty of Rome and reasserting national prerogatives.[34] The supremacy of EU law was declared in 1964 shortly before France began its "empty chair" policy to block EU policy making and the expansion of European Commission authority and before the "Luxembourg Compromise" in which all national politicians agreed to stop the advancement to qualified majority voting in order to protect national sovereignty. Indeed, when the issue of the national courts enforcing EU law first came to the ECJ, representatives of the member states argued strongly against any interpretation that would allow national courts to evaluate the compatibility of EU law with national law.[35] Again in the 1970s, while politicians were blocking attempts to create a common market, EU law supremacy was making significant advances within national legal systems. With politicians actively rejecting supranationalism, it is hard to argue that they actually supported an institutional transformation that greatly empowered a supranational EU institution at the expense of national sovereignty.

Even today there is no indication that the member states on the whole actively support the system of having national courts enforce EU law. The European Council has continued to refuse attempts formally to enshrine the supremacy of EU law in a treaty revision or formally to give national courts a role in enforcing EU law supremacy. Indeed, the latest changes toward bolstering the enforcement system for EU law have focused on the infringement procedure of the Commission and the member states. Although the Maastricht treaty reform gave the ECJ the powers that politicians had been unwilling to grant when they negotiated the Treaty of Rome, it did nothing to reinforce the enforcement mechanisms of the preliminary-ruling procedure. National leaders also continue to threaten to sanction the ECJ politically. The question, then, is, Why did politicians fail to stop an institutional transformation they clearly did not want?

There is much evidence that politicians did try to stem judicial activism. At the national level, politicians instructed and even ordered domestic actors not to follow ECJ decisions with which they disagreed. In 1968, the German Finance Ministry issued an edict saying, "We hold the decision of the European Court as invalid. It conflicts with well reasoned arguments of the Federal government, and with the opinion of the effected member states of the EU," and it instructed customs officials to ignore the ECJ decision in question and to reject all claims based on the ECJ decision.[36] In 1978, in response to an unwanted ECJ decision, a law was passed in the French National Assembly making it a punishable offense for anyone holding public office in France to follow the Court's doctrine announced in the contested opinion.[37] Just one year later, the Assembly tried to sanction the Cour de Cassation (France's highest court of appeal) for accepting EU law supremacy by reiterating a prohibition against French courts' setting aside national law.[38] A bill sanctioning national courts for accepting EU law supremacy also passed the Belgium legislature in 1973.[39]

National legislatures also have tried to overturn some national-court and European-law decisions, but the supremacy of EU law trumped their actions. In one notable exchange, the French National Assembly tried to pass a law to avoid refunding illegally collected car registration fees, but on the basis of the supremacy of EU law the Cour de Cassation awarded a refund despite the new French law. In response, the National Assembly transferred some of the Cour de Cassation's authority over tax issues to the jurisdiction of the Conseil d'État. The Cour de Cassation was not intimidated, and a few years later new powers were transferred from the Conseil d'État to the Cour de Cassation after extensive lobbying by Paris lawyers.

In the end, all of their attempts ended with politicians backing down from confrontation with national courts. There seemed to be two reasons for their retreat. First, many of the attempts to sanction the judiciary politically were seen as unconstitutional. Following constitutional principles was an embedded norm for national politicians, many of whom had formal legal training; moreover, it was a position with significant domestic political support. Political efforts to sanction courts were rallying cries for the supporters of a rule of law to come to the defense of the national courts. This combination of influences undermined the will of politicians to engage in a constitutional battle over the separation of powers.

Second, the executive branches of the national governments had an incentive to keep other branches of government from interfering too much in EU policy making, and they worked to quell domestic disputes over EU law. In France, the executive branch circumvented parliamentary revolts, either by ignoring them, outmaneuvering them, or encouraging other branches of government to let the issue die. In Germany, the national government devised legal strategies to circumvent unwanted ECJ jurisprudence and opposition to EU law as well. It even went so far as to buy off plaintiffs who threatened to raise EU legal disputes that were bound to provoke conflict. These attempts to mitigate the effects of contested ECJ jurisprudence while formally complying with EU law often worked, quelling the dispute but leaving the legal principle intact.

Unable to stop national courts from applying unwanted ECJ jurisprudence, politicians turned to the EU level to stem the encroachment of European law. But institutional constraints at the EU level kept politicians from credibly threatening the Court into quiescence. Legislating over ECJ jurisprudence may require only a qualified majority if the ruling in question is based on an EU regulation or directive, but clarifying legislation in light of an unwanted interpretation of a vague text is hardly a sanction of judicial activism. To reverse an ECJ decision based directly on an EU treaty or to attack the ECJ's independence or authority, member states would have to amend the treaty itself. Any amendment requires unanimity as well as ratification by national parliaments. Even if all governments agreed that the ECJ has been overly activist and perhaps even issued illegitimate decisions that compromised their national interests, in any given substantive dispute member states usually have differing interests that undermine efforts at political consensus building. There also are pockets of political support for the Court even when its decisions compromise supporters' interests. States with strong domestic political support for a rule of law often have opposed obvious political attempts to circumvent or create a political control over the ECJ. And, unsurprisingly, small states have been big supporters of increased ECJ authority and autonomy. Common EU institutions magnify the political power of small states; within the EU legal system, small member states have equal say in the interpretation of EU law, and in front of the Court the power differential of member states is equalized.

The impact of institutional rules on attempts to sanction the ECJ are clear in the pattern of political response to the Court. Frequently within the Council, initiatives to expand the authority of EU legal institutions are blocked, while calls to sanction the ECJ go nowhere. Given the well-known disagreements among member states over what to do about the Court's activism or unwanted jurisprudence, threats by angry politicians to sanction the ECJ usually ring hollow. With no credible threat of action against it, the Court can be comfortable—as long as national courts will go along with it—and national governments will acquiesce, bringing their policies into accordance with EU law.

But politicians still can use the appointment process to influence judicial positions. Each state appoints a judge to the ECJ for renewable six-year terms, which in theory allows politicians significant control over ECJ appointees. But because ECJ decisions are issued *unanimously*, national judges have significant protection from wrathful politicians because of their own governments' ECJ judges. To avoid this hint of national veto, all states would have to use the same criteria in selecting judges, which is unlikely, given that governments disagree about whether they like or dislike ECJ rulings. Furthermore, the appointment process to the ECJ and to national high courts is very complex, involving party politics, legislative politics, and other issues, so that EU legal positions are seldom the most salient issue influencing the selection criteria. Even if an activism litmus test was created, the U.S. experience shows that, once appointed, judges often do not behave as expected.

It is, however, not impossible to mount a credible threat against the ECJ. After numerous failed attempts, member states have for the first time seemingly achieved their goal. Stuck into the Maastricht treaty was the "Barber Protocol," which limited the impact of a recent ECJ decision on equal pay in pension programs for men and women. During the Maastricht negotiations, the ECJ also was excluded from two of the new pillars of the treaty. The ECJ was given some new jurisdiction in the Treaty of Amsterdam, but the right of lower courts to make referrals was limited in new areas, and the treaty prohibits new EU provisions in the areas of justice and home affairs from creating direct effects.[40]

Yet, politicians still will find it difficult to control judicial activism. The European Court continues to make controversial decisions and to expand its power to issue compensation for violations of European law.

Politicians have many constraints that limit their ability to control judicial activism, but political acquiescence still was critical for the Court's controversial legal doctrines to take hold. Early on, national courts waited to see which way political and legal consensus would develop on the issue of EU law supremacy. This was the time politicians could have acted effectively. During this critical period, when the ECJ's doctrines were not well established, the Court's early strategy to avoid political controversy was important. As politicians remained silent, national courts went ahead on their own. In the end, the ascendance of Community law was assured through the evolution of national judicial decision. Once national courts accepted EU law supremacy, it was very difficult for politicians to reverse the outcome, as we have discussed earlier. To use a metaphor of Joseph Weiler's, once politicians let the toothpaste out of the tube, it was quite difficult to get it to go back in.

The Influence of the European Court of Justice on European Politics

The acceptance of EU law supremacy by national judiciaries created an institutional basis for an effective rule of law in Europe, providing the opportunity for the ECJ to influence many areas of EU and national policy. It is doubtful that the EU legal system could have become effective if it had had to rely on infringement challenges initiated by the Commission or a member state. But once the ECJ had national courts to implement its jurisprudence, its largest political threat—noncompliance—was gone, giving the Court more latitude in its decision making. Because the ECJ knew that politicians probably would not be able to build consensus to reverse activist jurisprudence or to attack the Court for its excesses, it was emboldened to make decisions with more significant material and political impact. In these respects, national judicial support was indispensable to the legal and political authority of the European Court.

Because of the alliance between the ECJ and the national judiciaries, judicial politics in Europe has been transformed. National sovereignty has been fundamentally redefined so that national parliaments and governments are no longer necessarily the highest authority. The ECJ has become an important and influential actor in Europe, and courts have become political players in all sorts of policy areas.

CHANNELS OF INFLUENCE

There are several ways the ECJ can influence politics and the policy-making process. It can (1) provide a medium for individuals to pursue their own and domestic political agendas, (2) provoke a political response and lead states to change EU or national policy, and (3) shift the focus of political debate by creating definitive interpretations of EU law and policy.

The Court as a Medium for Individuals to Challenge National Policy

Individuals and groups have used the EU legal system to force their government to change national policy. An example of this is equality policy in the United Kingdom. The British Labour government of the 1970s passed laws regarding equal pay and equal treatment of men and women and created the Equal Opportunities Commission (EOC) to pursue cases of gender discrimination. When Margaret Thatcher came to power, she did not share the Labour government's interest in equal pay issues and was in general opposed to state regulation of the activities of business. She cut funding to the Equal Opportunities Commission and interpreted existing legislation extremely narrowly, making it difficult for women who faced discrimination to pursue a legal claim. The EOC sought redress for women in the British legal system, but the British courts also interpreted the law narrowly. The EOC then turned to a European litigation strategy, targeting friendly lower-court tribunal chairs who would make a referral to the ECJ. The European Court granted direct effect to the provision of the Treaty of Rome that states that men and women must receive equal pay for equal work, and it expanded upon this provision and some EU directives to develop a doctrine regarding the responsibility of governments to ensure equal pay for equal work. Using the EU legal system, the EOC won a number of legal victories, which it could then turn into policy victories through negotiation and the collection of copycat cases.[41]

Even without actually bringing a case, groups can use the threat of a legal suit in negotiation with other actors. For example, European law guarantees the maximum of a forty-eight-hour workweek, the creation of work councils in firms of a certain size, and proper notification of employees before they are fired. These laws, enforceable through the EU legal system, have shaped labor relations in European countries by influencing negotiations between firms and unions.

The Court as a Provoker of Political Responses

The ECJ often jars the policy-making process by provoking political responses to its decisions. When the ECJ makes a decision that the states or certain interest groups do not like, they will mobilize to encourage new legislation at the European or national level. For example, the Court recently applied a very clear directive in European law to strike down a German affirmative-action policy designed to promote businesses owned by women. The ECJ made this decision because the German law ran afoul of the EU statute on equal pay for men and women and because the judges wanted to show that they would apply EU law fairly regardless of whether the plaintiff was a woman or a man. Women's groups and national governments were dismayed and mobilized to create a legal basis for affirmative-action policies, enshrining the right to promote woman-owned firms in the Treaty of Amsterdam.

This process is entirely appropriate. The ECJ is not a democratic body, nor is it the forum where important social policy should be made. Political decisions are best taken by political bodies accountable to their constituents. Thus, the Court limits its policy role to ensure that European rules are democratically accountable to the people of Europe, while at the same time provoking political responses through its jurisprudence.

The Court as an Interpreter of EU Law and Policy

In addition to provoking political responses, the Court focuses political disputes. An analogy to this role might be the U.S. debate on abortion, which is significantly shaped by U.S. Supreme Court jurisprudence. Those who want to legislate in the area of abortion rights must do so in its shadow, making sure that whatever law they pass will be acceptable to the Supreme Court. Thus, antiabortion groups do not advocate making abortion illegal, as they know the Supreme Court will not accept such a policy. Instead, they propose cooling-off periods and banning certain abortion practices, while hoping that the political climate in the United States and in the Supreme Court changes so that eventually abortion itself will be illegal.

There are no judicial-political issues as charged as abortion in the European Union. But the European Court's jurisprudence still affects the political process. ECJ interpretations of the treaties create a framework defining what types of EU and national legislation are possible. Of course, states could always change the treaty if they do not like the ECJ's interpretations, just as Congress could try to change the U.S. Constitution. But such a change is not easy. In the EU, it would require new intergovernmental negotiations, unanimous consent of all national governments, and ratification of the new text by national parliaments in all member states. This threshold is very high, and it might not be possible politically to change the text of the treaty. It might be easier, however, to change a law, as in the affirmative-action case discussed earlier. Knowing that new policies must pass muster with the ECJ shapes how actors think about their policy options. Negotiations take place in the shadow of ECJ interpretations. As Alec Stone argues, the political process itself becomes judicialized.[42]

At the European Union level, the ECJ influences the rules of the policy-making process and policy outcomes. By resolving disputes about policy-making procedure, the Court shapes negotiations by allowing different institutions and member states greater or lesser influence in decision making. In addition, when the ECJ decides on the validity of an EU regulation or directive, it influences what policies EU institutions can pass and how EU law is interpreted and implemented. Usually, the Court becomes involved in EU policy issues when a national government, EU institution, or interest group disagrees with a policy or is concerned about its lack of influence over the policy-making process and turns to the legal realm to challenge the status quo. But the ECJ also engages in its own activist policy making, reading into EU treaties meanings that were not fully intended by national governments in order to direct the process of European integration. At the national level, the Court of Justice has influenced the domestic policy of member states in areas as diverse as education, industrial relations, gender equality, and the advertising of abortion services. In these cases, the European legal system was used by individuals and domestic groups to challenge national policies with which they disagreed, in hopes of achieving policy outcomes that were unattainable through national channels.

There are of course limits to the role the ECJ can play in the policy-making process. A significant constraint is built into the legal process itself. The Court must wait for cases to be raised; thus it must be invited by a national government, European institution, or national court into a policy debate. The ECJ also must stick to the legal method and the language of law lest it undermine its legal legitimacy or lose the support of national courts. In addition, public opinion and political concerns also impose limits. Still, the Court has shown itself quite capable of acting independently and influencing policy at the EU and national level. In many respects, judicial politics is part of the EU policy-making process, and the opinion of the ECJ can be important in shaping politics and policy.

Legal experts and ECJ judges have expressed significant doubt that the EU legal system could have become effective if it had had to rely on an infringement procedure initiated by the Commission or a member state. But the transformed preliminary-ruling system allowed the ECJ to create its own political constituency, indeed its own political power base: the national judiciaries. Because of this alliance between the ECJ and the national judiciaries, judicial politics in Europe has been transformed. Given that national judiciaries in Europe historically have played a much less significant role in policy making than they have in the United States, this transition is especially significant. How the ECJ will use its position and authority to influence EU and national politics in the future remains to be seen. But its success in establishing the political and legal authority of an international court is unprecedented. No longer can it be said that an international court cannot influence significantly national and international politics.

Notes

This chapter is based on Karen J. Alter, "The European Court's Political Power," *West European Politics* 19, no. 3 (1996), 458–87. I have used the term "European Union" throughout to avoid confusion, but the European Union was called the European Community during much of the time discussed in this article, and technically the law remains European Community law, not European Union law.

1. *Van Gend en Loos v. Nederlandse Administratie Belastingen*, Case 26/62 (1963), ECR 1. The ECJ later dropped the label of "international law" and argued that the EC legal order was sui generis and that EC law was not international law but supranational law.

2. Joseph Weiler, "The Transformation of Europe," *Yale Law Journal* 100 (1991), 2403–83.

3. *Vand Gend en Loos.*

4. Robert Lecourt, *L'Europe des juges* (Brussels: Etablissement, Emile Bruylant, 1976), 309.

5. *Costa v. Ente Nationale per L'Energia Elettrica (ENEL)*, Case 6/64 (1964), ECR 583.

6. Bruno De Witte, "Retour à 'Costa': La primauté du droit communautaire à la lumière du droit international," *Revue Trimestrielle du Droit Europèene* 20 (1984): 425–54.

7. *Amministrazione delle Finanze dello Stato v. Simmenthal SpA (II)*, Case 106/77 (1978), ECR 629.

8. Hjalte Rasmussen, *On Law and Policy in the European Court of Justice* (Dordrecht: Martinus Nijhoff, 1986).

9. Hans Heinrich Rupp, "Die Grundrechte und das Europäische Gemeinschaftsrecht," *Neue Juristische Wochenzeitschrift Heft* 9 (1970): 353–59.

10. Ronny Abraham, *Droit international, droit communautaire et droit français: Le politique, l'economique, le social* (Paris: Hachette, 1989), 184.

11. *Francovich v. Italy*, Cases C-6, 9/90 (1991), ECR 1991.

12. *Rewe Zentral AG v. Bundesmonopolverwaltung für Branntwein*, Case 120/78 ECR 1979, 649.

13. Karen J. Alter and Sophie Meunier-Aitsahalia, "Judicial Politics in the European Community: European Integration and the Pathbreaking *Cassis de Dijon* Decision," *Comparative Political Studies* 24, no. 4 (1994): 535–61.

14. Clarence Mann, *The Function of Judicial Decision in European Economic Integration* (The Hague: Martinus Nijhoff, 1972).

15. Jean-François Lachaume, "Une victoire de l'ordre juridique communautaire: L'arrêt Nicolo consacrant la supériorité des traités sur les lois postérieures," *Revue du Marché Commun* (1990): 384–94.

16. Andrew Wilson Green, *Integration by Jurisprudence* (Leyden: A. W. Sijthoff, 1969), 391.

17. R. Voss, "Federal Republic of Germany National Report," in *Article 177 Experience and Problems*, ed. Henry Schermers, Christian Timmermans, Alfred Kellermann, J. Watson, and Stewart Watson (Oxford: Elsevier Science Publishing Company, 1987), 239–52.

18. Karen J. Alter and Jeannette Vargas, "Explaining Variation in the Use of European Litigation Strategies: EC Law and UK Gender Equality Policy," in *Comparative Political Studies* (forthcoming).

19. *H. P. Bulmer LTD. v. J. Bollinger S. A.*, English Court of Appeal decision of 22 May 1974 (*Common Market Law Review*, 1974), 291.

20. Italian Constitutional Court decision of 30 October 1975 (n. 232), no. 28 July 1976 (n. 205) and 29 December 1977 (n. 206).

21. *Amministrazione delle Finanze dello Stato v. Simmenthal SpA (II)*, Case 106/77 (1978), ECR 629.

22. *Casagrande v. Landeshauptstadt München*, Case 9/74 (1974), ECR 773, CMLR 158/423; *Society for the Protection of Unborn Children Ireland Ltd. v. Grogan*, Case C-159/90 (1991), CMLR 3 849.

23. P. J. G. Kapteyn, National Courts–Conseil d'État (Assemblé), Decision of 22 December 1978, *Cohn-Bendit, Common Market Law Review* (1979), 701–703.

24. Despite what the name would imply, the Commissaire du Gouvernement is not a representative of the government. He/She is a member of the Conseil d'État who offers a reasoned opinion to the Conseil to consider. Since Conseil d'État decisions are short and cryptic, the argument of the Commissaire is often printed along with the Conseil's decision and used to help interpret the legal basis for Conseil judgments. *Raoul Georges Nicolo and another*, Conseil d'État decision of 20 October 1989, M. Frydman, Commissaire du Gouvernement, *Common Market Law Report* 1 (1990), 173–91.

25. Lord Denning, introduction to *The European Court of Justice: Judges or Policy Makers?* (London: The Bruge Group Publication, 1990).

26. Based on interviews with national representatives from Luxembourg, France, and Germany who negotiated the articles of the Treaty of Rome relating to the ECJ. For

more on the original intent of the EC legal system, see Karen J. Alter, *The Making of a Rule of Law: The European Court and the National Judiciaries*, Ph.D. dissertation in Political Science, Massachusetts Institute of Technology, 1996.

27. *Marbury v. Madison,* U.S. Supreme Court 5 U.S. (1 Cranch) 137, 2 L.Ed. 60 (1803), 904; and ECJ's *Costa* decision (op. cit.). I am indebted to Anne-Marie Slaughter for this insight.

28. Clarence Mann, *The Function of Judicial Decision in European Economic Integration* (The Hague: Martinus Nijhoff, 1972), 413.

29. Italian Constitutional Court decision of 7 March 1964, *Foro Italiano* 87(I), 465.

30. *Syndicat general de fabricants de semoules de France*, Conseil d'État Commissaire du Gouvernement, 1 March 1968, *Common Market Law Report* 9 (1970), 208.

31. Federico Mancini and David Keeling, "Democracy and the European Court of Justice," *Modern Law Review* 57, no. 2 (1994), 175–90; and Hjalte Rasmussen, *On Law and Policy in the European Court of Justice* (Dordrecht: Martinus Nijhoff , 1986).

32. Rasmussen, *On Law and Policy*, 354.

33. Deirdre Curtin and Kamiel Morelmans, "Application and Enforcement of Community Law by Member States: Actors in Search of a Third Generation Script," in *Institutional Dynamics of European Integration*, ed. Deirdre Curtin and Ton Heukels (Dordrecht: Martinus Nijoff, 1994), 423–65.

34. Joseph Weiler, "The Transformation of Europe," *Yale Law Journal* 100 (199), 2403–483.

35. Eric Stein, "Lawyers, Judges and the Making of a Transnational Constitution," *American Journal of International Law* 75, no. 1 (1981), 1–27.

36. 7 July 1966 (IIIB.4-V 8534–1/66). Republished in *der Betrieb* (1966), 1160.

37. Rasmussen, *On Law and Policy*, 352.

38. Guy Isaac, "A propos de l'amendement Aurillac: Vers une obligation pour les juges d'appliquer les lois contraires aux traités?" *Gazette du Palais II* (1980), 583–85.

39. Hervé Bribosia, "Report on Belgium," in *The European Courts and National Courts*, ed. Anne-Marie Slaughter, Alec Stone Sweet, and Joseph Weiler (Cambridge: Hart Publishing, 1998).

40. Karen J. Alter, "Who Are the Masters of the Treaty? European Governments and the European Court of Justice," *International Organization* 52, no. 1 (Winter 1998), 125–52.

41. Karen J. Alter and Jeannette Vargas, "Explaining Variation in the Use of European Litigation Strategies: EC law and UK Gender Equality Policy," *Comparative Political Studies* (June 2000).

42. Alec Stone, "Where Judicial Politics Are Legislative Politics: The French Constitutional Council," *Western European Politics* 15 (1992), 29–49.

Suggestions for Further Reading

Alter, Karen J. "The European Legal System and Domestic Policy: Spillover or Backlash." *International Organization* 54, no. 3 (2000): 489–518.

Alter, Karen J. *Establishing the Supremacy of European Law: The Making of an International Rule of Law in Europe.* Oxford: Oxford University Press, 2001.

Conant, Lisa J. *Justice Contained : Law and Politics in the European Union*. Ithaca: Cornell University Press, 2002.

Dehousse, Renaud. *The European Court of Justice: The Politics of Judicial Integration*. New York: St. Martin's Press, 1998.

Mattli, Walter, and Anne-Marie Slaughter. "Revisiting the European Court of Justice." *International Organization* 52, no. 1 (1998): 177–209.

Pollack, Mark. *The Engines of Integration? Delegation, Agency and Agenda Setting in the European Union*. Oxford: Oxford University Press, 2003.

Sandholtz, Wayne, and Alec Stone Sweet. *European Integration and Supranational Governance*. Oxford: Oxford University Press, 1998.

Slaughter, Anne-Marie, Alec Stone Sweet, and Joseph Weiler. *The European Court and National Courts*. Oxford: Hart Publishing, 1998.

Stone Sweet, Alec, and Thomas Brunell. "Constructing a Supranational Constitution: Dispute Resolution and Governance in the European Community." *American Political Science Review* 92, no. 1 (1998): 63–80.

Talberg, Jonas. *European Governance and Supranational Institutions: Making States Comply*. London: Routledge, 2003.

Weiler, Joseph. "The Transformation of Europe." *Yale Law Journal 100* (1991): 2403–83.

PART TWO

COUNTRIES

CHAPTER 8

Unified Germany

The Desire for Stability and the Need for Change

Helga A. Welsh

Germany

Population: 82.4 million
Area in Square Miles: 137,830
Population Density per Square Mile: 598
GDP (in billion dollars, 2001): $2,167.3
GDP per capita (purchasing power parity in dollars, 2001): $26,321
Joined EC/EU: January 1, 1958
Joined NATO: 1955
Political Parties:
Alliance 90/The Greens
Christian Democratic Union or CDU
Christian Social Union or CSU
Free Democratic Party or FDP
Party of Democratic Socialism or PDS
Social Democratic Party of Germany or SPD

Sources: "Organisation for Economic Co-operation and Development," at
www.oecd.org/home/ (accessed August 5, 2003); "2003 World Population
Data Sheet," at www.prb.org/pdf/WorldPopulationDS03_Eng.pdf
(accessed August 5, 2003); "The World Factbook," August 1, 2003, at
cia.gov/cia/publications/factbook/index.html (accessed October 6, 2003).

North
Sea

DENMARK

Baltic Sea

SCHLESWIG-
HOLSTEIN

•Rostock

MECKLENBURG-
WESTERN POMERANIA

HAMBURG

•Hamburg

BREMEN

Bremen •

BRANDENBURG

POLAND

LOWER SAXONY

BERLIN
⊛ **Berlin**

Potsdam•

NETHERLANDS

NORTH RHINE-
WESTPHALIA

•Magdeburg

SAXONY-ANHALT

•Cologne

•Leipzig

Dresden
•

Bonn

Rhine

HESSE

THURINGIA

•Erfurt

SAXONY

BELGIUM

Frankfurt
am Main
•

CZECH REPUBLIC

LUX.

RHINELAND-
PALATINATE

SAARLAND

FRANCE

Stuttgart
•

BAVARIA

BADEN-
WURTTEMBERG

Rhine

Munich
•

AUSTRIA

N

0   100 Miles

0   100 Kilometers

SWITZERLAND

LIECH.

ITALY

Introduction

After more than four decades of separation, in 1989–1990 the formerly communist East Germany and democratic West Germany unified. Questions were immediately posed as to how successful the new nation would be in attaining political and economic stability. How would the profound desire for stability, born out of the dramatic upheavals of the twentieth century, mesh with the need to adjust to new domestic and international circumstances? How would Germany continue to learn from the past, while finding ways to live in peace in its shadow? To this day, old and new generations of Germans struggle with a special sense of responsibility and the challenging task of unifying the two very different Germanys that emerged after World War II.

The first major transformation of the twentieth century came in 1918–1919. As a result of defeat in World War I and the collapse of the Second Reich (1871–1918), an authoritarian monarchy was overturned and replaced with the democratic parliamentary system of the Weimar Republic. The beginnings were inauspicious, associated with defeat and humiliation, widespread political violence, and severe economic and social problems. The optimistic assumptions of the Weimar constitution about the balance of power among president, chancellor, and parliament were tested to the limits by extreme party fragmentation and polarization; economic deterioration after 1928 added to the sense of instability. Democracy had only shallow roots in the public and the elites, and it was rather quickly abandoned. The Nazi party, one of many marginal radical groups in 1928, with 2.6 percent of the vote, received 37.8 percent in the 1932 elections. Once at the helm, Adolf Hitler ruthlessly and with amazing speed consolidated his power.

Under his leadership, Nazi Germany instigated World War II. Hitler's geopolitical goal of building a "Thousand-year Reich" resulted in Germany's expansion into most of Europe; Nazism's racist claim of "Aryan" superiority and anti-Semitism, homophobia, anticommunism, and eugenic views led to the murder of millions of people in what came to be known as the Holocaust and to totalitarian rule in Germany itself. The lessons of the Weimar Republic's breakdown and the Nazi smashing of constitutional parliamentary government continue to inform German politics to this day. Weimar has come to symbolize political instability and democratic breakdown.

Soon after World War II, Germany experienced two different kinds of transformation: in the western part, a stable democracy evolved, whereas in the east, under Soviet tutelage, a communist dictatorship took hold. While apparently stable, the latter slowly regressed and collapsed in 1989. The final major regime change began in late 1989 and culminated in October 1990, when the promise of unification, kept alive in Western Germany as a constitutional prerogative, finally and unexpectedly became a reality.

In one short century (1914–1991), to use Eric Hobsbawm's term, Germans experienced the collapse of three forms of dictatorship and one democratic political system. Regime transformations are extraordinary and trying times; they involve a change in the government's structure, main representatives, and underlying ideology. For some among both the mass public and the elites, the new order's novelty will appear frightening; for others, its apparent resumption of familiar features will be reassuring or depressing. Uncertainty infiltrates political realms and the everyday life of individuals.

It is no wonder, then, that contemporary Germans treasure the stability and security of the system of the Federal Republic that has brought them democratic rights and freedoms, prosperity, and peace. The search for political and economic stability was a hallmark of German politics after each regime transformation, including the fall of communism in the German Democratic Republic. Moreover, it left an important legacy; institutional and policy changes have been marked by a distinct preference for cautious piecemeal approaches and consensual conflict-solving mechanisms, rather than radical transformation.

The Quest for Normality

History is a combination of evidence and interpretation, which may allow for both delusion and understanding but, in any case, shapes the identity and the institutions of nations. The horrors inflicted by the Third Reich forced Germans toward a critical and open confrontation with their past.[1] The process started in 1945 as part of the Allied denazification and democratization programs, but after the onset of the Cold War swift political and economic consolidation took precedence. Nevertheless, however much more important the future seemed then, the past would not go away. Challenged by a new generation, the silence muffling German involvement and collusion with Hitler's regime was shattered in the 1960s, and, step by step, a historical consciousness emerged that informs the public discourse to this day. No interpretation of German history can avoid confronting Auschwitz. It pervades debates ranging from abortion and political asylum to reparations for Nazi victims and foreign military involvement and explains the heightened sensitivity to right-wing activities at home and abroad.

Its past may have made Germany, in the words of poet C. K. Williams, a symbolic nation;[2] Germans are usually defined not in terms of what they are or do but what they represent. This perception undercuts the nation's quest to become normal. Germany is admired for its cultural and scientific achievements and reviled for horrible crimes. The first eighty years of German history as a nation-state were, in many ways, defined by authoritarianism, militarism, and nationalism. Yet German history also stands for the promise that political culture can successfully change. The overwhelming majority of today's Germans are democratic, pacifist, and not nationalistic, except for an occasional patriotic exuberance at soccer games and other sport events. Compared to that of other nations, Germany's national pride continues to rank low and is mostly associated with social peace and economic performance. In 1999, when Germans were asked to identify their feelings on the Federal Republic's fiftieth anniversary, 33.2 percent mentioned pensiveness, and 28.5 percent could not think of anything in particular.[3]

What is normality for a nation-state? An important precondition of normality is the acceptance of, and identification with, the domestic and international position. The fall of communism ended Germany's division, granted full sovereignty to the country, and made obsolete its role as the front line between hostile ideological camps. Whereas international developments worked unambiguously in favor of a "normal" position for Germany in Europe, the American historian Fritz Stern and others have repeatedly pointed to the importance of "inner peace" as a precondition for a democratic (or normal) Germany. Religious and class conflicts that had riddled the Weimar Republic no longer plague German society and politics, and a broad consensus regarding the virtues of democratic institutions has replaced ambivalence or even hostility. The commitment to stability and democracy has not derailed despite continued differences in political culture between eastern and western Germans and incidences of xenophobic violence that were particularly unsettling at the beginning of the 1990s.

Unification increased Germany's room for political maneuvering in the international arena, yet, at the same time, it demonstrated the continued constraints imposed by history. One can *feel* normal but not be recognized as such by others. While Germany may be the undisputed giant in Europe as measured in population and economy, its actions are still vigilantly scrutinized. Are its leaders reliable and predictable and willing to take on international responsibilities? Can Germany exhibit national interests and pride, like other nations, without arousing their fears? Is it a sign of normality that Germany is no longer the European model but has to struggle with economic and financial woes just as other countries do? Is it normal for foreign observers to worry about Germany's current economic malaise and uncertainty about its evolving new international role, or is it another sign of caution and mistrust? Will normality remain forever elusive? Answers to these questions are far from simple, and they can differ depending on the nationality and even the age of the respondent. Germans and their international partners search for ways to absorb and to adapt to the country's evolving status.

STABILITY AND CHANGE

"Bonn is not Weimar"—the determination not to repeat the instability that led to dictatorship—informed the writing of the West German constitution, the creation of its political parties, and its particular economic system after World War II. All these steps were aimed at avoiding the mistakes of the past by defending democracy and establishing political, economic, and social conditions that would provide security for individuals and the country as a whole. Germany's division was an early by-product of the emerging Cold War. With the hope of eventual reunification, and from a position of strength, western allies and western Germans sought to secure democracy and buffer against Soviet expansion. In May 1949, the Federal Republic of Germany was created. The sleepy town of Bonn was chosen as the temporary capital and seat of government; similarly, the constitution was named the Basic Law to emphasize its transitory character. Soviet and eastern German communists followed suit in October 1949 and founded the GDR. Once Germany was officially divided into two separate states, West Germany promulgated the Federal Republic as the official successor state of the defeated Germany; international recognition of the GDR was denied until the 1970s. The building of the Berlin Wall in August 1961 eliminated the last escape valve for eastern Germans; the ensuing diplomatic ice age between the two German states melted only gradually in the 1970s and 1980s.

Initially, both German states—supported by their respective allies— pursued the goal of unification. However, in response to West German chancellor Willy Brandt's 1969 announcement that there are two German states but one nation, eastern leaders developed a policy of strict demarcation and separate identity. For them, unification was no longer on the agenda. In the West, with the passage of time, unification started to resemble a national myth more than a practical policy goal. When, after forty-one years, it occurred, no new constitution was written. Article 23 of the Basic Law expeditiously allowed the former GDR to join the constitutional framework of the Federal Republic of Germany. The more cumbersome path of renegotiation of a new constitution, based on Article 146 of the Basic Law, was never seriously considered.

Time pressure, combined with various controversies, forced the postponement of specific decisions during negotiations for the Unification Treaty between the two German states. Should Berlin be not only the capital of Germany but also the seat of government? History provided arguments on both sides. National and international observers heralded the Bonn Republic as a beacon of German stability and democracy. The darker sides of German history, they argued, with its goose-stepping and mass demonstrations of nationalism and militarism, are forever tied to Berlin. For some, Bonn's provincial character seemed a virtue, while others hoped for a renaissance of Berlin's earlier glamour in the arts and sciences. Berlin recommended itself as the traditional center of power and, because of its geographical position, as a potential bridge between eastern and western Germany and between eastern and western Europe. In June 1991, a heated parliamentary discussion narrowly decided in favor of Berlin (338 in favor; 320 against). In 1999, when parliament and government finally moved to Berlin, the earlier controversy seemed to belong to a bygone era. Neither the glamour nor the goose-stepping have resurfaced; another aspect of normality has returned to Germany.

The campaign slogans of the Christian Democratic Union (CDU) in 1957, "No Experiments" and "Prosperity for All," capture the essence of post–World War II German politics. To rise above societal divisions that proved fatal in the first attempt toward democratization, German political elites had a strong interest in finding a consensual and stable model. The desire to prevent another dictatorship on German soil led to an institutional structure that entails multiple elements of power sharing and decentralization. Institutions can only provide a framework, and they come to life through actions.

In all democratic settings, politics is the art of getting things done and therefore requires bargaining and compromise. For the German "negotiation democracy" to take hold, a complex system of checks, balances, and conflict-solving mechanisms emerged. Some of the features of consensual decision making were intentional; others evolved through cultural preference and political stipulation. Consensual decision-making features secure high levels of acceptance once new policies are formed, but they also slow down or even block policy-making processes. Such blockages have become more frequent and cause considerable concern among the policy establishment.

Three aspects of German politics and policy making will be highlighted to give a better understanding of the functioning of the system: (1) the power balance among the major parties and the need for coalition building; (2) regionalism and the division of labor between the federal government and the individual states, or *Länder*; and (3) the characteristics of the German social and economic system and the call for change.

GOVERNANCE AND POLICY MAKING: POLITICAL PARTIES, ELECTIONS, COALITION BUILDING

Germany's political system is commonly called a party democracy or party state. Both characterizations emphasize the central role of political parties. Functions and organizational principles for political parties are explicitly set out in Article 21 of the Basic Law, but the extent of party influence goes far beyond representing the will of the people. Over the years, representatives of the main parties have become an integral part of federal, state, and even public institutions, such as the public television stations; the staffing of many leadership positions is characterized by power sharing among the main political parties. Since the 1960s, generous federal financing of parties—between 30 and 35 percent of their funds—acknowledges their public role and assures greater independence from private donations. Still, financial scandals remain a matter of concern. For example, between 1993 and 1998, approximately 2 million German marks were secretly given to the CDU and deposited in illegal party accounts. The extent to which the donors may have received political favors in return for their money captured the public's attention in late 1999 and 2000. The finance scandal led to the formation of a parliamentary investigative committee, the resignation of top politicians, heavy electoral losses for the CDU in 2000, substantial monetary fines for the party, and the tainting of former chancellor Helmut Kohl's reputation. The exposure of illegal finance practices may have been the tip of the iceberg for the CDU, but it was not an isolated incident, either. Financial scandals have contributed to public cynicism and mistrust toward the political parties.

Through its rulings, the Federal Constitutional Court has reinforced the central role of the main political parties and given meaning to the principle of "militant democracy" by banning two parties. In the early days of the Federal Republic, one party on the right, the Socialist Reich Party, and one party on the left, the Communist Party of Germany, were declared illegal on the basis of their antidemocratic ideology.[4] Since then, a more relaxed attitude toward questionable fringe parties has prevailed. Legal precautions have given way to trusting that the policy establishment and the electorate will reject extremism.

Unlike right-wingers in many of its western European neighbors, Germany's radical right-wing parties have not been represented in the national parliament, notwithstanding their sporadic success at *Länder* levels and in elections to the European Parliament. The reasons are manifold: the particular historical sensitivity to fringe parties on the right—after all, Hitler's National Socialist Party had modest beginnings—have alerted the public and the elites, and the media go out of their way to expose their weaknesses. The majority of Germans consider a vote for right-wing parties objectionable. In addition to historical factors, the current amalgam of several right-wing parties has undermined its appeal to potentially disgruntled voters by their mutual opposition and by their lack of charismatic leadership, disciplined party organization, and a membership base. Finally, the dismal, heavily publicized behavior of right-wing parties at the state and European level has dissuaded voters.

In 1949, sixteen parties and seventy independents competed for seats in the first postwar parliament. Eight parties and three independents were elected, raising the specter of fragmentation, an all-too familiar feature of the Weimar Republic. In response, the electoral system of the Federal Diet (*Bundestag*) was modified in 1953; most of its features are still in place today. They mix elements of personalized voting (single-member district) with a vote for party lists (proportional representation). For parties to be represented in the parliament as a party group or faction, they have to gain at least 5 percent of the vote or win three district (direct) mandates. The particular characteristics of the electoral system have been a point of reference or even emulation for several countries, including New Zealand, Venezuela, Portugal, Italy, and South Africa. The electoral system is credited with achieving a successful balance between excluding marginal parties and incorporating newly emerging parties; thus, instead of paralysis, it combines political stability with a capacity for moderate change.[5]

Starting in the 1950s, a rapid process of consolidation laid the foundation for a three-party system, comprising the CDU/CSU,[6] the Social Democratic Party of Germany (SPD), and the Free Democratic Party (FDP). These parties dominated the political landscape from the 1960s until the 1980s. Since then, two additional parties have been elected to the national parliament. The Greens (after unification called Alliance 90/The Greens) have brought "new politics" issues, such as gender, environment, peace, and grassroots participation, to the forefront. Following unification, the political representation of the Party of Democratic Socialism (PDS) in the Federal Diet, state parliaments, and local councils has been a point of contention. However, it can be argued that it facilitated the incorporation of eastern interests into the German policy process and mitigated fragmentation that might have favored the political right. Despite different agendas and origins, both parties have placed high value on the political inclusion of women; their party rules mandate that at least 50 percent of electoral candidates on the party ballot lists must be women. These party quotas have had important spillover effects on the remaining parties, and their overall impact on female representation in the Federal Diet is undeniable. Between 1983 and 2002, the number of female members of parliament increased from 9.8 to 32.2 percent, making Germany one of the highest-ranked countries in number of women in a national parliament on a global scale.

The core parties, CDU/CSU on the one hand and SPD on the other, vie for voters in the center of the political spectrum. Both portray themselves as catchall and social welfare parties; that is, as parties with appeal to a wide electorate. After World War II, CDU/CSU and SPD represented clear ideological choices and strategies, ranging from economic to military policy. For many years, the strength of the SPD was based on a strong membership, whereas the CDU was seen as the party with a built-in electoral majority; for forty-two out of fifty-three years, it was at the helm of government. Today, the ideological positions of the major parties have converged in many areas, including foreign, security, and economic policies. The incremental narrowing of the ideological gap has contributed to shifts in electoral strength, membership base,[7] and a growing number of voters who switch between parties. These trends contributed to a neck-and-neck race between CDU/CSU and SPD in the September 2002 election; in the end, fewer than seven thousand votes separated them. A map of voting preferences locates SPD strongholds in the north and CDU/CSU dominance in the south.

A recurring feature of German politics involves the need to form coalitions. Only once, in 1957, was one party, the CDU/CSU, able to garner a majority of the votes, and, even then, it engaged in a coalition government. In Germany and elsewhere in Europe, coalition governments most often take the form of minimum-winning coalitions; that is, one major party aligns itself with a minor party or parties to achieve a majority. For most of postwar West Germany, the Free Democratic Party of Germany, rooted in classic European liberalism, had the luxury of choosing its coalition partner; a small party acted as the power broker. Traditionally, the FDP favored the CDU/CSU, but, in 1969, it switched and aligned with the SPD. That coalition lasted until 1982, when the FDP rejoined the CDU/CSU in a coalition that survived several elections and ended in 1998. Alliance 90/The Greens has transformed from its roots as an antiparty party to a governing party: in 1998 and, once again, in 2002, it joined the SPD in "red-green" coalition governments.

Table 8.1   Federal Elections, Coalition Governments, and Chancellors (1949–2002)

Election Year	Coalition Parties	Chancellor
1949	CDU/CSU, FDP, and DP (German Party)	Konrad Adenauer (CDU)
1953	CDU/CSU, FDP, DP, and GB/ BHE (All-German Bloc/Federation of Expellees and Displaced Persons)	Konrad Adenauer (CDU)
1957	CDU/CSU and DP	Konrad Adenauer (CDU)
1961	CDU/CSU and FDP	Konrad Adenauer (CDU)
		Oct. 1963: Ludwig Erhard (CDU)
1965	CDU/CSU and FDP	Ludwig Erhard (CDU)
	Dec. 1966: CDU/CSU and SPD	Kurt Georg Kiesinger (CDU)
1969	SPD and FDP	Willy Brandt (SPD)
1972	SPD and FDP	Willy Brandt (SPD)
		May 1974: Helmut Schmidt (SPD)
1976	SPD and FDP	Helmut Schmidt (SPD)
1980	SPD and FDP	Helmut Schmidt (SPD)
	Sept. 1982: SPD	
	Oct. 1982: CDU/CSU and FDP	Helmut Kohl (CDU)
1983	CDU/CSU and FDP	Helmut Kohl (CDU)
1987	CDU/CSU and FDP	Helmut Kohl (CDU)
1990	CDU/CSU and FDP	Helmut Kohl (CDU)
1994	CDU/CSU and FDP	Helmut Kohl (CDU)
1998	SPD and Alliance 90/The Greens	Gerhard Schröder (SPD)
2002	SPD and Alliance 90/The Greens	Gerhard Schröder (SPD)

Source: Adapted from Forschungsgruppe Wahlen e.V., *Bundestagswahl. Eine Analyse der Wahl vom 22. September 2002* (Berichte der Forschungsgruppe Wahlen e.V., 108), Mannheim 2002, 85.

In the last two decades, more frequent divided majorities in the two houses of parliament have made the cooperation between CDU/CSU and SPD necessary for passing legislation. However, "covert" cooperation among them is one thing, and establishing formal, grand coalitions—a formal governmental alliance—another. Such an arrangement was in place at the national level between 1966 and 1969, and, ever since, reference to grand coalition governments has aroused quite different reactions. Some highlight their "undemocratic" nature, since any meaningful parliamentary opposition is removed. Others emphasize that, during crises, grand coalition governments can overcome political hurdles to move along the policy agenda from initiation to implementation. Critics and advocates agree that grand coalitions should be enacted for only limited periods in times of duress. The 1960s coalition between CDU/CSU and SPD is generally conceded to have set important precedents for new forms of consensual policy making that have shaped the functioning of the political system ever since. Coalition governments are the norm at the state level as well; here, however, greater flexibility regarding the choice of partners prevails. For example, in 2001, the SPD was engaged in coalitions with the CDU, the FDP, the PDS, and Alliance 90/The Greens, whereas the CDU relies mostly on alliances with the FDP and SPD.

Whether likely coalition partners are announced before an election, or the final composition is determined afterwards, differs from place to place and time to time. What has become increasingly common at the national level is the wording of detailed coalition agreements in which specific goals for governance bind the parties. (See Box 8.1.) Coalition governance requires compromises; in most cases, one major and one minor party coalesce, and the profile and political clout of smaller parties is elevated.

Finally, the German electorate—consistent with its preference for stability—tends to favor continuity over change. No coalition government was ever voted out of office after just one term. Indeed, the Federal Republic has witnessed only three changes in administration (1969, 1982, and 1998), and only the last resulted from the outcome of elections and not the maneuvering of the political parties. As is true for all parliamentary systems, the head of government is responsible to, and dependent on, his or her party. Political parties and not the electorate have been the prime movers and shakers in the replacement of chancellors. The one exception was Helmut Kohl, whose sixteen-year tenure ended at the voting booth in 1998.

By definition, negotiation and bargaining often take place behind closed doors and include non-elected advisors and experts. This kind of informality is a built-in feature of all democracies and, in particular, coalition governments. In recent years, these informal features have acquired new meaning and importance in German politics. Chancellor Helmut Kohl (1982–1998) first elevated informal politics to new importance; his "coalition committee" became a vehicle to control unruly *Länder* and his coalition partner, the FDP. Later, when his administration lost the majority in the upper house of parliament, he extended

Box 8.1   Coalition Agreement 2002–2006 (Summary)

On 16 October 2002, representatives of the SPD and the Green Party signed a coalition agreement setting out the legislative program for the years 2002 to 2006. The following issues were spelled out in considerable detail:

MORE EMPLOYMENT, A STRONG ECONOMY AND SOLID FINANCING
    Labor Market
    Economic Policy
    Financial Policy

REGENERATION OF EASTERN GERMANY
A CHILD-FRIENDLY COUNTRY AND BETTER EDUCATION FOR ALL
    Education and Families, Schools and Childcare
    Vocational Training
    Higher Education
    Research, Innovation and Sustainability

ECOLOGICAL MODERNISATION AND CONSUMER PROTECTION
    International Environment Policy
    Withdrawal from Nuclear Energy

MOBILITY FOR THE 21ST CENTURY
CONSUMER PROTECTION—HEALTHY FOOD—MODERN AGRICULTURAL POLICY
    Healthy Food and a Modern Agriculture
    Agriculture

SOLIDARITY AND RENEWAL OF THE WELFARE STATE
    Social Security
    Health

EQUAL OPPORTUNITIES
SECURITY, TOLERANCE AND DEMOCRACY
    Justice and Home Affairs

FAIR GLOBALISATION—GERMANY WITHIN EUROPE AND THE WORLD
    Foreign and Defence Policy
    European Integration
    Reform of the CAP
    International Development

© 2003 SPD.de

informal politics to include opposition and social partners, that is, labor unions and employer associations. Chancellor Gerhard Schröder (1998–) has changed strategies and emphasis but not the idea; indeed, during his first term in office, he was dubbed the "consensus chancellor," since he sought the participation and consent of a variety of policy actors through new and old informal means that sidelined parliament and cabinet.

Why do we see this increase in the importance of informal politics? When established channels of consensus no longer work smoothly, politicians look for innovative ways to circumvent barriers to decision making. More than ever, most major policy initiatives have involved commissions and so-called rounds of consensus. They exist at all levels of the political process: the federal government, the federal parliament, and the federal presidency. While given less attention, they are also prominent at the *Länder* level. Overall, according to some estimates, approximately six hundred consulting bodies exist at the federal level and an additional thousand at the *Länder* level. In recent years, some of the most visible reform initiatives were first discussed in these commissions, including the reform of the armed forces, labor market, health, pension and nursing insurance, higher education, immigration, and the integration of foreigners.

Informal policy-making bodies bring together widely diverse political and academic actors; their political role is limited in time and scope, but their potential to shape the policy agenda is worth noting. They have been criticized for circumventing democratic accountability and transparency at the expense of the parliament, yet they have been defended as a way to bridge ideological differences, to propose innovative ideas, and to undermine existing political barricades.

In recent years, fueled by the 2002 parliamentary election, when the chancellor candidates of SPD and CDU dominated the campaigns, the alleged Americanization of politics has received widespread attention. Americanization refers to a focus on the personalities running for office rather than their parties and the greater role of the media, in election campaigns specifically. For example, for the first time in the 2002 election, the two challengers debated on television, and campaigns were tailored to highlight top politicians. Even Alliance 90/The Greens, a party whose roots defy leadership principles, took advantage of its most prominent politician, Joschka Fischer. A vote for "Joschka," according to campaign slogans, was a vote for Alliance 90/The Greens.

Although the talk of Americanization identifies an important trend, the terminology oversimplifies. The exposed role and greater variety of the media in German politics have favored the individualization of politics and the transmission of sound bites over complex party programs. Despite these trends, Germans predominantly vote according to party and not chancellor preference. In the 2002 election, 64 percent of those surveyed considered parties more important for their electoral choice than their leading politicians. Recently, "Americanization" has also been connected to the dominant role of the chancellor, whose powers allegedly resemble more and more those of the U.S. president. However, in the parliamentary history of the Federal Republic, stronger and weaker chancellors have alternated, and their role remains much more constrained than that of the chief executive in presidential systems. Finally, the principle of chancellor democracy and the emphasis that it places on the head of government are not recent inventions but trace their roots to Konrad Adenauer (1949–1963), the first politician in that position.

COOPERATIVE FEDERALISM AND REGIONALISM

Different folkloric traditions and dialects demonstrate Germany's regional cultural variety. They are accompanied by political manifestations of regionalism. Strong regional attachment may seem surprising, since the boundaries of the *Länder* were redrawn after World War II and some new entities created; in the case of eastern Germany, they were recreated in 1990, after they had been abandoned in 1952. Even if these geographic loyalties have limited historical sources, regionalism has been a persistent feature of German politics. It has been reinforced by the division of the country into a Catholic south and Protestant north, and it contributed to the late creation of a German nation-state in 1871. The impact of the regions manifests itself in, among other things, the *Länder*'s leadership role in asserting regional rights vis-à-vis the European Union, the training and recruitment of national leaders through state offices, the division of labor between the federal government and the individual *Länder,* the reciprocal influence of *Land* and national elections, and the eminent role of the Federal Council *(Bundesrat)* in Federal Republic policy making.

With respect to the making of policy, the writers of the Basic Law institutionalized regional participation and created multiple checks and balances. Decentralization is based on a complex division of power; the interests of the *Länder*, initially eleven and after unification sixteen, are represented in the second house of parliament, the Federal Council. Depending on the size of its population, each *Land* varies in its electoral weight from three to six votes. State governments select their regional representatives and instruct them how to vote; thus, each *Land* casts its vote as a unit. The interconnectedness of the federal and state levels has reinforced multilevel bargaining, with cooperative federalism as its result.

The national government's increasing power in directing state affairs and its role in unification enhanced centralized decision making to the point that Germany is often referred to as a unitary federal system. Far from weakening regional representation, however, the trend toward centralization is partially counterbalanced by the legislative powers of the Federal Council: its participation is necessary for the passage of 50 to 60 percent of all bills. This development has been reinforced by the greater frequency of divided majorities in the two houses of parliament; that is, from 1972 to 1982, 1991 to 1998, and again since 1999, different parties controlled the Federal Diet and Federal Council. In the process, the Federal Council's mediation committee, which is composed of equal numbers of members from the Federal Diet and the Federal Council, has acquired a prominent role. Under divided majorities, the main opposition party in the lower house of parliament has the majority in the upper house; thus, the chamber can be, and has been, used as a tool of the opposition party.

German federalism is built on sharing the fiscal burden. To reduce economic inequities, funds are transferred from richer to poorer states. Although givers and takers have changed during the life of the Federal Republic, the west is more prosperous than the east, and shifts in employment and industrial patterns have made the south now economically better off than the north. Until 1994, uniformity (*Einheitlichkeit*) of living conditions in the different parts of Germany had been the constitutionally prescribed goal, but, as part of constitutional reform, the term was replaced with equality (*Gleichwertigkeit*). The political message is clear: the economic strains associated with unification have necessitated a rethinking of constitutional goals. In addition, the superimposition of the east-west divide on the existing north-south gap has added new levels of competition and conflicts over the distribution of funds. Today, in the political struggle for influence, who is rich and who is poor matters more than ever. Financial strength and weakness have led to alliances between east and west and between the major political parties. In addition, the needs of the states have opened up new possibilities for the federal government to garner votes in the Federal Council in return for financial assistance.

A similar superimposition of the east-west gap on the existing north-south gap is evident in voting behavior. The most glaring example has been the success of the PDS in the East. After 1989 the communist parties in eastern Germany and the rest of eastern and central Europe seemed destined for extinction, but a redrafting of their ideologies, a solid organizational background and membership base, and the takeover by skilled younger politicians led to the rejuvenation of most. In the so-called new *Länder* of the Federal Republic—that is, those in the eastern part of Germany—the PDS has emerged as a strong regional and local party. Electoral success partly derives from its role as a voice for eastern interests and against West German dominance. With the passing of time, however, eastern Germans' separate identity may also fade. In 2002, for the first time since 1990, the PDS was no longer able to garner sufficient votes for party representation in the Federal Parliament, but two individual candidates who won district seats are present. Although the PDS shares many characteristics with other formerly communist parties, unification imposed circumstances that are specific to Germany. Strong polarization of forces for and against former communist parties has been common across central and eastern Europe, but the dominance of the traditional western German party system has isolated the PDS. To this day, a coalition with the PDS at the national level—but not at the regional and local level—is unacceptable to all parties, and the appeal of the PDS to western voters, with about 1 percent of the vote, remains marginal.

A SOCIAL MARKET ECONOMY: STILL A MODEL?

After World War II, the vision of a social market economy won out over competing ideas of capitalism and socialism. Its realization was anything but defined, yet the message of economic and social stability was important. A high level of employment and social protection, extensive participatory rights through codetermination, collective bargaining, and close cooperation between labor unions and employer associations became the cornerstones of "model" Germany. Codetermination refers to the equal role of workers and employees on companies' supervisory boards, while collective bargaining elevates the role of labor unions by including nonunion members in wage deals. The so-called social partners—that is, labor unions and employer associations—are privileged in their access to, and role in, managing the economy. For many years *Modell Deutschland* performed extremely well. It contributed substantially to domestic social peace, the legitimacy of the political system, and international prestige. Bargaining and compromise emerged as the pillars of the economic system, just as they did in the political system.

In addition to their role as mediator, governmental institutions set the legal framework, yet many functions of policy implementation are handed to semi-public institutions, such as the Federal Agency for Labor. Thus, state intervention is circumscribed; the economic and social system, including the social welfare system, relies mostly on a regulatory culture and transfer payments. Germany is classified as a conservative welfare model: most of its social benefits are based on insurance payments that vary according to income. The system offers a comprehensive social safety net but not the equalization of payments or benefits; it differs substantially from both the social-democratic (Scandinavian) and liberal Anglo-Saxon models. It is conservative in its emphasis on family values. Many of its policies reinforce the traditional role of women as mothers and caregivers, for example, in the provision of extended maternity leaves, the tax code that favors married couples and families, and child allowances. It protects wage earners but makes it more difficult, in particular for women, foreigners, and older people, to enter or reenter the labor market.

The economic and social system emphasizes the principle of social solidarity through its inclusive provision of services; no citizen is left without generous social benefits. The benefits of the social market economy have extended to all Germans, but differences in living standards and economic performance persist. Unemployment in the eastern part of Germany continues to be approximately twice as high as in the west, and, although wages and salaries in the east have doubled since unification, in most sectors, they still have not reached the western level. After initial high increases immediately following unification, economic growth in all of Germany has stagnated; the per capita gross domestic product still favors western productivity 2 to 1. Between 1990 and 2002, approximately eight hundred billion euro were transferred to eastern Germany, and in June 2001, the so-called Solidarity Pact II assured the continued flow of funds until 2019. Funds have been used mostly for infrastructure projects and social transfer payments.

Pressure for change in the areas of health care, pensions, the labor market, and immigration built up in the 1980s but, as a consequence of unification, have increased now to the point that reforms can no longer be delayed. In international comparison, performance indicators ranging from education to economic growth have fallen further behind. Although Germany's economy is still by far the biggest in Europe, its economic performance indicators are at best mediocre. In fact, its economic growth rate has been below par on the European level and, in recent years, it no longer fulfilled the criteria of the stability and growth pact that it imposed on other European nations as a precondition for adopting the euro. Structural unemployment has remained high for much of the last decade. The rapid aging of the population, combined with low birth rates, jeopardizes the viability of the pension and health care systems. Signs of crisis are plentiful.

Yet, reforming the system has been painful and slow. Any reforms that have occurred have been incremental and, in most cases, fell short of altering the basic structures of the system. Piecemeal approaches repeatedly have soon necessitated a "reform of the reform" and no longer seem adequate. In the public discourse, terms such as *policy paralysis* and *stalled Republic* have commonly been used to describe the German malaise.

The difficulty of initiating and implementing important policy reforms has been explained by the role of institutions and the level or lack of elite and societal support. Germany provides a perfect example of a society in which, for most people, the status quo appears more attractive than change; particular policies, such as extensive job protection, long vacations, and generous health-care provisions, have been so successful that citizens have become attached to them—indeed, identify with them. Many have become accustomed to the structure and benefits of the established system and associate change with a worsening of their situation. Consequently, resistance to change has characterized the political landscape in recent years. In 1997, then federal president Roman Herzog used the soft power associated with his office to "jolt" fellow citizens into action. He identified entitlement thinking, lack of courage, and a pattern of discourse that focuses on crisis as major barriers to reform and described the steps that lead from proposing a policy to killing it. Problems, he concluded, are adjourned rather than tackled.

Others have pointed to the institutional disincentives of the German political system, including a large number of veto players that block policy initiatives.

They range from the Federal Council to the Federal Constitutional Court, whose potential as tools of the opposition is significant. Veto players also encompass powerful interest groups, in particular the labor unions. Whether Germany is indeed a "stalled" society will be determined in the immediate future; the calls for leadership—and greater courage in tackling problems and fighting entrenched interests—can no longer be ignored.

A CHANGED SOCIETY—CHANGED POLITICS?

German demographic composition, lifestyle, and political attitudes and orientations have changed dramatically since the inception of the Federal Republic in 1949. While continuous and almost silent, their overall effects are startling and important for an understanding of German politics. Germans of today are better educated, are more secular, live predominantly in cities and no longer in small towns, and, on average, have a much lower rate of fertility but a higher life expectancy than their grandparents. In addition, society has become much more heterogeneous and solidly democratic.

POPULATION AND MIGRATION

In terms of population, Germany, with its slightly more than 82 million people, clearly surpasses its powerful neighbor France (59 million) and the United Kingdom (60 million). Population density remains quite distinct; in 2000, it amounted to 267 per square kilometer for the western part and 140 for the eastern part. After World War II, West Germany quickly emerged as the major magnet for Germans expelled from eastern territories of Europe. Soon 8 million expellees, comprising 18 percent of West Germany's population in 1950, were joined by 2.6 million refugees from the communist East Germany. Furthermore, about 3.6 million ethnic Germans from eastern Europe and the former Soviet Union resettled in Germany between 1962 and 2000.

The successful integration of ethnic Germans remains one of the major postwar achievements; the integration of foreigners, however, has turned out to be more difficult. Between 1961 and 2000, at one point or another, 25 million foreigners resided in Germany, of which 18.7 million returned to their homelands. The overall increase in foreign population is nevertheless substantial; after labor shortages in the 1950s opened the doors to so-called guest workers, the number of foreign-born residents climbed to 690,000 in 1961. In 2000, the number of foreigners in Germany had increased to 7.4 million, or 9 percent of the population. Many had turned from temporary migrants to permanent residents; in fact, almost half have lived in Germany for more than ten years and 30 percent for more than twenty years. Seven million foreigners live in the western part of the country, predominantly clustered in the major cities. By far the largest group consists of approximately 2 million Turkish residents.

The long road toward normalizing Germany's relations with foreign-born residents is blocked by multiple obstacles. They include the legacy of an imagined homogenous society; the combined inflow of asylum seekers, ethnic Germans, and labor migrants; and an economic dynamic that changed from labor shortages to high levels of unemployment. Path-dependent processes, based on earlier policies, made it impossible to halt immigration.[8]

The opening of the borders among European Union member countries, set in place with the Schengen Agreement (1985) and followed up by the Dublin Convention (1990) and the Maastricht Treaty (1992), added new layers of differentiation. On the one hand, European Union policies encouraged and protected the free movement of people from one member state to another. On the other, as Europe is a favored immigrant destination, it also introduced new levels of exclusion for those outside the borders of the European Union. The process of European integration enhanced the pressure on Germany to come to grips with an altered international environment. Finally, German unification and the fall of communism eliminated the need to protect the special citizenship status of Germans under the Basic Law. Thus, external and domestic pressures facilitated a reevaluation of German immigration policies.

- In the 1990s eight out of ten people who asked for political asylum in Europe came to Germany. The asylum law was substantially altered in 1993. A new provision that potential applicants had to ask for asylum in any so-called safe country en route to Germany limited the inflow into Germany; the yearly number of asylum seekers has since declined from a high of more than 438,000 in 1992 to 118,000 in 2001.
- After a heated domestic debate, the 2000 New Citizenship Law facilitates naturalization and allows dual citizenship until age twenty-three.
- In 2000, a ground-breaking green-card initiative for foreign computer specialists revealed educational and labor shortages in key sectors of the economy, despite overall high unemployment; more than ten thousand people took advantage of this opportunity.
- An immigration and integration law, passed in 2002, was declared unconstitutional on procedural grounds; it was reentered into the legislative process at the beginning of 2003. All parties realize that such a law is necessary, even if their interests differ, and the details are disputed.

Döner kebab, pizza, and cevapcici have become part of the German cuisine, but the adaptation of foreign eating preferences says little about the political climate for foreigners. In often painful and lengthy debates, two opposing myths finally had to be laid to rest. The Conservatives' argument that Germany is not a country of immigration became untenable. The optimistic multicultural vision of the political left was also dismantled; high unemployment rates, lower educational achievement, and crime among foreigners, along with upsurges of xenophobic violence, have made integration measures—for example, in the provision of language courses—as important as immigration regulations. Hardly any other issue in Germany is as emotionally charged, and none has greater potential to mobilize voters, than immigration. However, reluctantly, Germany has become a country of immigration.

The Search for "Inner Unity": Eastern and Western Germans

On October 3, 1990, the formerly communist GDR and the democratic Federal Republic of Germany unified. Less than a year earlier, on November 9, 1989, the Berlin Wall—symbol of the division of the country and Europe into two ideologically hostile camps—had started to crumble. Within a short time, in cities across the GDR, protesters' chants turned from "We are the people"—that is, demanding their rights to democratic participation—to "We are one people"—that is, requesting national unity. The outcome of the March 1990 democratic elections in East Germany seemed to confirm the message: those parties that had advocated a swift move toward unification won with ease. The stage was set. With record speed, eastern and western Germans negotiated the Unification Treaty, outlining the parameters of the unified country.

The onset of the Cold War after World War II had prevented the negotiation of a peace treaty for Germany; thus, no matter how much Germans advocated unification, it could only happen with the consent of the former Allies: the United Kingdom, the United States, France, and the Soviet Union. The so-called Two-plus-Four Treaty negotiations brought their foreign ministers and those from the two Germanys to the bargaining table. The successful outcome of the treaty negotiations suggests a smooth and predictable process; in reality, it was riddled with uncertainties and suspicion. The United States gave active (and crucial) encouragement to the right of self-determination for Germans, whereas the other Allies were more circumspect. Helmut Kohl, the "Chancellor of Unity," skillfully used the window of opportunity that opened in spring and summer 1990 to bring unification to fruition. It secured him a safe place in history books, victory in the December 1990 elections, and again in the 1994 elections. Paradoxically, the difficulties of unification also contributed to his downfall in 1998; the promised "flowering landscapes" in the eastern part of Germany did not materialize quickly enough.

Champagne corks popped on October 3, 1990, the Day of German Unity. If the festivities associated with this national holiday lack the deeply rooted sense of patriotism that French citizens or Americans exhibit on similar occasions—German unification was a matter of business, not emotions—it does not mean that Germans were and are not supportive of unification. In 1999, on the fiftieth anniversary of the Federal Republic of Germany, eastern and western Germans overwhelming agreed that the decision to unify had been a good thing (90 and 83 percent, respectively).[9] However, when asked whether they associated joy or concern with unification, 45 percent felt predominantly joy and 50 percent, concern.

In the years immediately after unification, fractures between eastern and western Germans turned to a carefully maintained distance. By the middle of the 1990s, the steady repetition of economic, cultural, societal, and political differences had done precious little to break down old perceived barriers and, in fact, had created new ones. Today, although the legacies of unification are still prominent, they are no longer the center of public attention. In the past, media coverage highlighted differences between the two parts of Germany; since the middle of the 1990s, for good political reason, Germany as a whole is emphasized. Yet the facade of normality is deceiving.

Individual memory, historiography, and public discourse do not always coincide, and cleavages are even more pronounced when two parts of a nation merge after forty years of separation. Eastern and western Germans have very different recollections of the postwar experience, especially that in the communist East. The coming together of the German population has been delayed by the proclivity of some western German politicians to portray the development of the Federal Republic as a complete success story and that of the Communist East as a complete disaster. Even under a dictatorship, a certain degree of normality exists; sacrifices and compromises as well as professional and private achievements shaped private lives. Often eastern Germans feel that their individual biographies have been devalued. Part of the irritations might have been predicted: forty years of separation take time to mend, and the numerical, economic, and political asymmetry between the two parts of Germany—at the time of unification the population ratio was 4 to 1—remains important.

Will unification be achieved when eastern Germans act and feel like western Germans, or should it be based on mutual recognition and respect?

> . . . the project of German unification contains a built-in tension. It requires attention to the differences between East and West, while at the same time, it intends to eliminate them. Eastern Germans insist on being different. Thus, it requires the recognition of different biographies, special needs, and special milieus and cultures, and, at the same time, easterners' desire to share the same economic, political, and social status as their western compatriots. Western Germans, on the other hand, would prefer political attitudes, behavior, and identity that mirror their own, but they can live with continued inequality in social, political, and economic relations.[10]

Hopes and expectations were high and hard to fulfill. For example, the desire to bring justice to those who had been persecuted under the communist regime led to restitution of property, reparations, access to secret police files, and (limited) punishment of those who had been responsible for some of the crimes. These measures could only attempt to redress some of the wrongs; they could not and cannot undo them, and they remain imperfect.

Before and after unification, the speed and efficiency of decision making and the safeguarding of cherished institutions and policies that had been tried, tested, and found successful in West Germany were more important than reform. At first glance, the unification superimposed the West German model onto the former German Democratic Republic, but in reality, the merging of the two Germanys has challenged and influenced German politics in numerous intended and unintended ways.

Unification amplified the economic burden imposed by global economic challenges, and, together, these processes have undermined some of the basic tenets of the "old" system. For example, neocorporatist arrangements and the power of the labor unions, as well as the principle of collective bargaining that guaranteed equal wages across the nation, are under fire. In 2000, only 45 percent of all jobs in the eastern part of Germany were covered by those agreements; in the west they had declined to 63 percent. Membership in the German Trade Union Federation has decreased from 9.7 million in 1994 to 7.9 million in 2001.

The difficulty of transferring institutions extended to the political and social realm as well. Successful institutional transfer, according to Wade Jacoby, is more likely when it is supported by active segments of society and when flexibility in adaptation is part of the strategy. He denies the presence of the latter in the instance of German unification: "To put it metaphorically, although the East Germans were allowed to order their own meal, the menu was limited, substitutions were not welcome, and the chefs were easily insulted if the specials were ignored."[11] This situation added to misunderstandings and misgivings.

Equally challenging has been the dramatic change in the workforce. Three-fourths of East Germany's industrial workers lost their jobs in the aftermath of unification. The western-imposed shock therapy may have been economically rational, yet, the favorable exchange rate mechanism for the eastern German currency was clearly politically motivated and, from an economic point of view, much less rational. Whatever the causes, the economic restructuring has been painful for many easterners, and misunderstanding and resentment are common. "They do not enjoy being told that 8,000 people now produce the same amount of steel in the east as 86,000 did a decade ago, or that the 40,000 Saxons still working on the land now grow more farm produce than 200,000 did in 1990."[12] The imbalance of migration between east and west—which increased again in 1998 after a considerable decline—can be partly attributed to the unabated high unemployment in the east, which floats around 17 to 18 percent.

Although the democratic stability of Germany is not questioned, political attitudes and orientations continue to differ between the east and the west. Persistent discrepancies exist in trust toward political institutions and the evaluation of German democracy; eastern Germans are more detached from both. An overwhelming majority of western and eastern Germans consider democracy the best form of governance, but eastern Germans are much more skeptical about the German version. Whereas 80 percent of citizens in the west identify with their democracy, only 49 percent of eastern Germans agree; 27 percent favor a different form of democracy. Not surprisingly, satisfaction with democracy also varies greatly: on average, 62 percent in the west but only 30 percent in the east are satisfied with the functioning of democracy in Germany; the gap in attitudes has persisted without major alterations since unification.[13] Compared to citizens in the "old" Federal Republic, eastern Germans rely more on a "strong state" (for example, in managing the economy) and place greater value on social justice and less on freedom. The effects of these differences are most obvious in divergent voting behavior. The eastern part of Germany features less party attachment and thus dramatic electoral turnarounds, greater skepticism toward political engagement—for example, in the form of membership in political parties and interest groups—and a lower voter turnout. In view of the dominance of western Germans in the political process and in political representation, the perceived lack of political voice reinforces the distance that many eastern Germans feel toward the political system.

The forced secularization of the GDR has left legacies that show no sign of lessening. In 1991, 11 percent of western Germans did not belong to any religious organization; by the year 2000, the number had increased slightly to 13 percent. During the same time period, the figures for the eastern part of Germany not only remain higher but increased even more rapidly than in the West; the number of those without religious affiliation rose from 65 to 71 percent. The religious distance between East and West is equally evident when church attendance is considered: in 2000, 24 and 63 percent, respectively, never attended religious services.

Unification was a jump into cold water, and its consequences have played out in many ways. Some of the goals associated with the merging of the two states have been fulfilled. Others, in particular the economic recovery of the eastern part, have remained unfinished. Germans in East and West live in a democratic society whose core foundations are accepted, but the growing together of what belongs together, to use the words of former chancellor Willy Brandt, has taken longer than anticipated. There is pride in what has been accomplished since 1989 and concern about what remains to be done. The feeling of ambivalence best summarizes any assessment of the process of German unification.

The Merging of Old and New: Foreign and Security Policy

Probably in no other policy area is the collective memory of Germany's past more persistent and relevant than in its foreign and security policies. Before unification, Germany was widely considered an economic giant but a political dwarf, because of its limited international role. After World War II, membership in international organizations provided an opportunity to reenter world affairs and to fend off potentially resurgent nationalism. The history of the Federal Republic is the history of a network of international cooperation.[14] Its integration into the European community began with the establishment of the European Coal and Steel Community in 1952. The Western Allies' aspiration to control (West) Germany, while simultaneously integrating it into the international community of democratic nations, contributed to the creation of the North Atlantic Treaty Organization in 1949, which, after a heated domestic debate regarding remilitarization, Germany joined in 1955. The notion that NATO was formed in order to keep the United States in (Western Europe), the Russians out, and the Germans down captured the prevailing concerns. From the beginning, and to this day, Germany renounces possession of nuclear, biological, and chemical weapons, long-range combat aircraft, and missiles; furthermore, it has no general staff apart from NATO troops. Unification did not change German leadership's steadfast support for NATO, emphasizing its role as a defensive military alliance and, more and more with time, as an alliance of values.

James Sperling captures the basic sentiment of foreign policy analysts when he remarks that the "debate surrounding German power inevitably invokes a confrontational logic,"[15] focusing on the readiness or reluctance to use it. For foreign observers, the doubt and, at times, the fear, of Germany's potential power influence the assessment of German foreign policy. Germany has been called a "reluctant power," the "central power in Europe," the "leading European power," a "global economic power," a "permanently reformed civilian power," or a "re-emerging military power."[16] However, to what extent power can be translated into influence depends on many variables, including the willingness to use economic and other resources, the preferences of domestic and international actors, and more intangible considerations, such as bargaining skills and the constraints and possibilities that are conditioned by institutional factors.

Whether German actions are ascribed to soft power or structural power, their analysis depends on who is doing the interpreting and the particular questions asked. Are we interested in Germany's influence on concrete foreign policy agendas and outcomes or more concerned about its role in shaping specific policy environments? Is Germany's role in central and eastern Europe the question, or are we wondering how it fits in the European Union or in international organizations, such as the United Nations or the World Trade Organization? Has Germany been staunchly multilateral in security and military affairs but more self-interested and aggressive in economic policies?

GERMANY AND EUROPE

The German constitution explicitly authorizes the federation to "transfer sovereign powers to intergovernmental institutions," including a system of mutual collective security and the European Union. From the outset, Germany was an enthusiastic supporter of European integration. It was considered a way to assure reconciliation and lasting peace between the rivals and former enemies, Germany and France; now and then, the two countries are considered the "motor" that drives the process of European integration. More broadly, the project of an integrated Europe provided an avenue for peace, economic prosperity, and international recognition.

The spread of integration from economic areas to include, among other things, foreign and defense policies, justice and home affairs, and the environment has significantly changed the dynamics of European Union member states; the Europeanization of its members' national politics has evolved as a major postwar trend. Europeanization emphasizes (1) the interdependency of national and supranational governance; (2) regulations and prohibitions regarding policy areas; and (3) feedback mechanisms that can impose EU legislation on national member states.[17] Only a few policy areas remain outside the realm of European policy making; as a result, it has been estimated that at least 50 percent of all rules and regulations that are in force in Germany have their origin in the European Union.

Research on Germany's role in the European Union has focused on questions about how "good a European" it really is and how much it influences European Union affairs. Foreign observers' initial worries that a unified Germany might be less committed to European integration were quickly laid to rest. In fact, while its supportive attitude may have been understandable in the early days of European integration, some scholars are at times puzzled by Germany's continued enthusiasm. To explain it, they have emphasized aspects of political culture, political structure, and policy style. Once again, history provides the starting point. After World War II, European integration provided a vehicle for international recognition; it was also widely seen as contributing to the economic miracle of the 1950s. Among political elites, the interconnectedness of national and European politics is undisputed; German and European interests are seen as compatible, if not identical. Commitment to Europe is also part and parcel of a strong attachment to multilateralism as an idea and as a means to pursue national interests; according to Klaus Goetz, it has become part of the elites' "genetic code."[18]

The complementary nature of its institutional structure has been cited as an important factor in Germany's pro-European attitude. The highly decentralized political system, coalition governments, and the principle of delegation to semipublic institutions have made the interaction with European institutions, in the words of one observer, a "warm bath" instead of the "cold shower" that many British elites and citizens may feel.[19] In addition, a bureaucratic culture of rules and regulations is part of both European and German policy making. Finally, lengthy negotiation and bargaining that allow package deals and aim at achieving consensus are key elements of both German and European policy making. In other words, German politicians are at ease with the institutional and policy-making environment of the European Union.

Institutional features may also partially explain why a reluctant or negative attitude toward European integration has remained a "dark matter" in German politics. Charles Lees argues that reservations expressed toward European Union policies and the election of small right-wing parties with an anti-European agenda have given "soft Euroskepticism" a limited outlet at the *Länder* level. Thus, Euroskepticism could be articulated and contained at the same time. In general, however, the adoption of an anti-European attitude by parties on the far right may have discredited Euroskepticism "by association."[20] Despite pockets of anti-European attitudes, cross-party consensus in the Union's favor has remained stable. More than in some other member countries, where public referenda on major treaty ratifications, such as the Maastricht or Nice treaties, are common, the German political elite has reserved the right of approval.

Some attribute Germany's advocacy for both widening and deepening integration and its major financial contribution to the European Union budget to its willingness to consistently play the "good European." However, Germany's attitude toward Europe can not be measured solely with regard to its commitment to integration—where it scores high—but must consider concrete domestic policy implementation as well. Here, the picture is more ambivalent. Germany's infringement of European Union law has been quite frequent and defies the unqualified notion of the "good European." Recent research has also questioned the "fit" of specific European Union policies to the German national setting; considerable "adaptational pressure" to adjust to European policy initiatives has been the result.[21]

The Schröder government has become more outspoken about conditions that, in its view, no longer adequately reflect the changed European environment. Despite Germany's weakened economic position, it contributes far more to the EU's budget than any other member country. The status of the German language in European Union affairs has not been raised. And although its population increased with unification to make it by far the most populous country, the number of German votes in EU decision making has only modestly increased. Its share of members in the European Parliament is higher than that of other member countries, but its votes in the much more important Council of Ministers have remained equal to those of other "large" countries.[22] The resistance of other member states to changing the status quo in these areas exposes the intangibles of German influence.

One way to interpret the reluctance to redistribute votes and to revise the appropriation of funds is simply to look at the national interests of other member states. While arguing against changes that might make Germany more powerful and diminish their own influence and interests, they have successfully renegotiated their own positions. Thus, other factors have to be at play. For example, in interviews conducted with European Union officials, Germany's influence in determining outcomes ranks behind that of France and the United Kingdom. For some, the discrepancy between Germany's formal and informal powers can be attributed to weaknesses in its bargaining skills, including the staffing of crucial portfolio positions, or a lack of coherent bargaining positions due to its multiple political power centers.[23] Bargaining associated with the federal structure familiarizes German politicians with multilevel governance. It may also hamper the effectiveness of German negotiating, since the *Länder*—who are represented with offices in Brussels—and the national government both clamor for attention and influence.

Although in some areas Germany has been unable to use its power potential to the fullest, in others, its influence in shaping concrete outcomes has been substantial. It has been very successful in dictating the conditions under which countries could join the European currency and in setting the tone and pushing for enlargement of the European Union into central and eastern Europe. Germany also played a crucial role in framing and implementing the **Stability Pact for South Eastern Europe** which, to date, is one of the European Union's most important foreign and security policy initiatives. The Stability Pact intends to bring democratic stability and economic growth to the region and holds out the promise of greater cooperation with, and eventual membership in, the European Union as an important incentive.

No straightforward answer neatly delineates Germany's strengths and weaknesses; instead, a complicated network of institutional interactions and trajectories, depending on situation and interpretation, can advance or hamper national influence at the European Union level.

German citizens support European integration but somewhat less enthusiastically than their leaders; most see both advantages and disadvantages. When compared to other member countries, Germany falls into the mid-range—not as Euroskeptic as the British or some of the Scandinavians, but also not as supportive as some of the smaller countries and, in particular, southern European countries. German citizens predominantly associate the common European currency, free movement of people, cultural variety, peace, and greater participation in the world with European Union membership. They have remarkably little specific knowledge about the workings of the Union's institutions, in line with the other "big countries" in the European Union, although they think they are well-informed. They widely endorse common European security measures, defense policy, and foreign policy. Divisive topics include EU enlargement, but no EU move was more opposed by the German electorate than the introduction of the common European currency, the euro. A few months before the official introduction of euro coins and banknotes in January 2002, only 45 percent of western Germans and 27 percent of eastern Germans considered replacing the German mark a good thing. For the political elites, on the other hand, giving up the "sacred cow" of the national currency was unambiguously the price for unification; Germany had to sacrifice its lead financial role in Europe to compensate for its increase in population and status. Neither of the major political parties veered from completing the project.

Germany still is the primary net contributor to the European Union budget, although accession of the eastern *Länder* has also made it a noteworthy beneficiary of funds. In view of the recent economic downturn, the role of the "paymaster" of the European Union has received greater attention. Since by far the greatest share of the budget goes to the Common Agricultural Policy (CAP)—of which France is the greatest benefactor—Germany and France in the 1990s have disagreed on the terms and timing of overdue reforms to the agricultural market.

The relationship between France and Germany and its function as the engine of European integration have been the subject of much reflection. For most of the postwar period, the two countries set the timing according to which European integration moved or stalled. Cordial and close relations between French and German leaders covered up occasional bilateral conflicts of interest. The friendships between Konrad Adenauer and Charles de Gaulle, Helmut Schmidt and Valéry Giscard d'Estaing, and Helmut Kohl and François Mitterrand are legendary. The early greater personal distance between Jacques Chirac and Gerhard Schröder was noteworthy not only in comparison to the past, but because the words of former president Mitterrand rang particularly true: "The Franco-German friendship is neither natural nor automatic; it is under constant construction and supported at every moment by a political will."[24]

Depending on their point of view, observers emphasize either ties that bind or degrees of separation. Independent of recent controversies and their outcome, farming policy, enlargement of the European Union into central and eastern Europe, the reweighing of votes in the European Council to account for Germany's larger population, the appointment of individuals to particular offices (for example, the head of the European Central Bank), or defense policy, the changed power balance between Germany and France is central to the discussion. Recent international developments have favored a more influential Germany and weakened the special position of France. France's national identity is closely tied to its prominent role in European and world affairs; thus, a shift in the balance of power between the two nations remains an important reference point for French politicians. What remains undisputed, however, is that, after three German invasions of France between 1870 and 1940 alone, military conflict between the two has become unthinkable. Independent of official spats, they remain each other's most important trading partners, and thousands of educational exchanges and partnerships between towns and villages reinforce bonds at the grassroots level.

Franco-German relations do not exist in a vacuum but are influenced by other international actors. For example, when British politicians are more engaged in continental affairs, France and Germany try to use them to strengthen their own position within Europe. If the British are more distant or play up the Anglo-American special relationship, then France and Germany tend to rely more on each other. The latter tendency reemerged with force up to and during the Iraqi conflict in 2002 and 2003. The deadlock in negotiations of the Common Agricultural Policy was resolved, bilateral initiatives in the area of the European security and defense policy took off, and the two nations cooperated on controversial issues in order to bring the draft treaty establishing a constitution for Europe to a timely conclusion in June 2003. In handling the Iraqi crisis and the effort to strengthen Europe vis-à-vis the United States, France and Germany not only catapulted common interests to the forefront but also unearthed frictions with other European countries.

The pro-U.S. attitude in the Iraqi conflict of Prime Ministers José María Aznar López of Spain and Silvio Berlusconi of Italy and of governments in central Europe may be partly explained by the wrestling for position caused by the impending 2004 enlargement of the European Union. The engine that drives or slows European integration may still be cranked predominantly by French and German leaders, but one thing is already clear: neither the special relationship nor their role in Europe can continue unchanged once the European Union encompasses twenty-five members. The Iraqi conflict may have been the last hurrah of a policy style that served Europe and German-French relations well for more than four decades. But what will replace it is, as of now, still undefined.

One particular area of concern for many European countries—and in particular for France—has been the specter of Germany's dominance in central and eastern Europe, particularly in view of the enlargement into much of the region in 2004. Germany's potential hegemony in post–Cold War eastern Europe is based on a long historical trajectory of influence. Germany is the region's main foreign source for direct investment and maintains a multifaceted and high level of trading relations with it. Germany provides it with substantial aid and assistance and a model for institutions, ranging from banking to electoral regulations. Last but not least, its geographical position in the heart of Europe links the extremities to the trunk.

Václav Havel, president of Czechoslovakia and, later, the Czech Republic from 1990 to 2003, eloquently summarized the dilemma:

> Germany is both our inspiration and our pain; a source of under-
> standable traumas and many prejudices and misconceptions, as well
> as the standards against which we measure ourselves; some see Ger-
> many as our greatest hope, others as our greatest danger.[25]

In contrast to widespread public perception, scholarly assessments consistently
reject claims of hegemony or even disproportional influence based on economic
and/or political power. Instead they emphasize the intrusive power of the past
and past policies that inform bi- and multilateral relations.[26]

Germany supported central and eastern Europe's inclusion in both NATO
and the European Union. Its backing was in no small measure due to its wish
to be surrounded by peaceful and democratic neighbors. Enlargement was not
only a way to speed up the process of democratization but also to compensate
for the price that the central and eastern European countries had to pay when
Europe was divided after World War II. Germans, in particular, understood
those legacies very well. In the process, the nation has also shown a clear preference toward those countries that made significant progress toward economic
and political consolidation and that are in close geographic proximity—the
Czech Republic, Hungary, and Poland are foremost among them. In view of
public concern about high unemployment at home, German leaders were particularly apprehensive about the potential impact of labor migration from central and eastern Europe as part of the EU's policy of free movement of people,
whereas some central Europeans, in particular, Poles, were concerned about the
potential financial impact on land purchases by western Europeans, especially
Germans. Transition periods were introduced to ease in the new policies.

The "return to Europe" for countries that used to be communist governed
and under Soviet influence necessitated a reworked relationship with a weakened Russia and the newly independent states of the former Soviet Union. Germany was in a unique position, since it could build on a long-standing and close
relationship. Although, with the final withdrawal of Russian troops from eastern German territory in 1994, an important chapter in postwar history was
closed, over the years, Germany kept Russia engaged and informed. It has remained Russia's closest partner in the West and, through multiple economic and
political linkages, acts as gatekeeper to Europe. Germany's involvement in eastern Europe surpasses that of other nations, but the focus of its international
relations has remained the West.

TRANSATLANTIC RELATIONS AND THE IRAQ WAR

The significant role of the United States in shaping postwar Europe is undisputed, and nowhere more acutely than in Germany. There is widespread ac-
knowledgment that West Germany was lucky to have had such a benign princi-

pal occupation power. It benefited greatly from U.S. support in military, economic, and political matters during the Cold War and, finally, in bringing about German unification when the opportunity presented itself in 1989–1990. The network of cultural, economic, and political exchanges is dense and has reached a level that is normally reserved for countries that are members of integration schemes, such as the European Union. With record speed, the occupation power turned into a trusted friend and ally.

It is against this backdrop that the distinct downturn in relations during 2002 and 2003 created such a shock and has led to intense soul-searching among elites and public. To be sure, with joint responsibilities and tasks come competition, and conflicts did emerge in the past as well, yet the level of disharmony and distrust evident during the Iraqi conflict revealed a new and different climate. Although the adage "all politics is local" may explain Chancellor Schröder's outspoken anti-Iraq war rhetoric during the electoral campaign of 2002, exchanges between him and U.S. president George W. Bush were, at times, emotional and tense. What made matters almost worse from the U.S. point of view was the fact that the chancellor's strong opposition to any German military involvement in Iraq—shared and reinforced by the pacifist coalition partner, the Greens—may have earned crucial additional votes that made it possible for the so-called red-green Social Democrat–Green Party coalition—by a very narrow margin—to stay in power.

In the months leading up to the Iraq War, Germany remained strongly in the antiwar camp. The government could count on the overwhelming support of the German people; shortly before the parliamentary election of September 2002, popular support for German participation in a war against Iraq that would not be sanctioned by a United Nations mandate amounted to a mere 4 percent. This position remained largely unchanged even after the war had begun and ended: in May 2003, 72 percent condemned the war against Iraq. In tandem with the conflict's escalation, the perception of U.S.-German relations worsened considerably. In May 2002, 88 percent of Germans considered those relations very good or good; one year later, the number had declined to 36 percent.[27]

Is the changed climate in U.S.-German relations a sign of increasing anti-Americanism in Germany? Not so, say most Germans. The position taken in the Iraqi war is fostered by strong and widespread pacifism but also by criticism of the Bush administration's policy style. In explaining the deterioration of relations, however, the German government does not remain unscathed. Some criticize the unusual—and, by implication, unnecessarily harsh and undiplomatic—tone of SPD politicians during the electoral campaign and afterwards. Others point to the failure of Germany—and Europe more generally—to shoulder international responsibilities, including military, which has disillusioned the U.S. presidential administration.

As of summer 2003, the foreign policy establishment in Berlin works diligently at "normalization." There is wide agreement that emotional exchanges must become more businesslike but friendly and that mechanisms to deal with commonalities and differences in the relationship between the two countries must be created or redefined. The discourse about how significant and deep-seated the differences are is more controversial. Has a paradigm change toward hegemonic unilateralism under President Bush taken place, and does it have staying power for the foreseeable future? A lively public debate exposes uncertainties in interpretations and concerns about how the relations can be repaired. Apart from disagreement about remedies, however, Germans and their government agree that the United States remains the most important alliance partner. Ironically, the Iraqi conflict has reinforced the conviction among major European powers, Germany included, that their role, in particular, their military role, has to be strengthened if the transatlantic alliance is to function better. This increasing participation has been a long-standing goal of various U.S. administrations. That it is discussed with greater urgency and resolve in Berlin and elsewhere now may be one of the lasting legacies; future assessments of German military and security policies may see the Iraqi controversy as just one more crucial catalyst on the road to a greater international role that had begun a decade earlier.

Civilian Power and Military and Security Policies

Maybe nowhere is the change in Germany's international role more apparent than in its security and military policies. Up until the 1990s, the preferred way to show international solidarity and responsibility was checkbook diplomacy. Based on Article 87a of the Basic Law, Germany shied away from direct involvement in military conflict in "out-of-area" operations and instead provided financial assistance to defray the cost of military involvement. However, with the passing of time, first the Gulf War in 1990–1991 and then the conflicts in the former Yugoslavia rendered this position increasingly untenable. Pressure on the Kohl government mounted to engage members of the armed forces in humanitarian and crisis management. According to Adrian Hyde-Price, "the idea behind these 'salami tactics' was to gradually prepare public opinion for an out-of-area role."[28] The Federal Constitutional Court's 1994 ruling on Article 87a of the Basic Law opened the door for possible "out of area" military deployment, provided that it would take place as part of multilateral operations and had the blessing of the United Nations and the approval of the Federal Diet. Burning villages and ethnic cleansing in Bosnia and Kosovo catalyzed a moral policy of "never again" (Auschwitz) and reinforced the prevailing notion of "never alone."

In 1999, the postwar taboo of German military involvement was broken when the German Air Force engaged in the Kosovo conflict. Since then, Germany has rapidly widened its scope of military operations. In January 2003, it assumed a role as nonpermanent member on the United Nations Security Council. Although it has not pressed for a permanent seat, it has stepped up efforts in peace missions under the aegis of the United Nations. Germany provides approximately 10 percent to the UN's regular budget and, at the end of 2001, participated in seven of the eighteen UN or UN-mandated missions. In 1998, about two thousand soldiers were engaged in humanitarian and peace-keeping operations abroad. By the beginning of 2003, the number had risen to nearly 8,500 and the troops were spread from Georgia and Macedonia to the Horn of Africa and Afghanistan, second only to the United States in deployment of soldiers in such missions.

Germany's widening military engagement has not been accompanied by a reform of the armed forces. The reluctance to increase military spending is based on ideological and financial grounds, and the modernization of the armed forces, including a decision on continuing or abandoning conscription, has run into many bottlenecks. The overall goals include a reduction of the armed forces from over 320,000 to 277,000 by the year 2006, with 150,000 of them trained for deployment in peacekeeping and humanitarian missions abroad. Concerns about Germany's ability to provide security, humanitarian, and peacekeeping assistance also affect the future of the envisioned European Security and Defense Policy (ESDP). Germany has committed 18,000 soldiers to the Rapid Reaction Force of 60,000, with an additional 12,000 available for rotation. In other words, personnel and materiel are stretched to their limits, but recent international developments have also driven home the need for action.

FOREIGN AND SECURITIES POLICIES: AN INTERIM ASSESSMENT

Germany's international position is evolving, and occasional anticipated and unanticipated tensions among alliance partners are part of the process. They are the result of mutual expectations that, in turn, are built on, and influenced by, long memories and conditioned by a quickly changing international environment. In the eyes of many Germans, including many of its leaders, Germany has finally come of age and should be allowed to speak on behalf of its interests. In the eyes of some foreign governments, a more docile Germany is preferable to a more assertive one. Ever since unification, French governments have been apprehensive about Germany's new role in Europe, in light of its manifold economic and political ties to central and eastern Europe. Americans have come to expect German leaders to emphasize friendship and appreciation and to criticize, if at all, subtly and mostly behind closed doors. In 2002, when voters expressed a strong pacifism, the outspoken attitude of the Schröder administration against a potential war in Iraq and the response in Washington, D.C., were a case in point. Recent strains in the countries' bilateral relations reflect broader concerns about policy style and substance—for example, between unilateral and multilateral strategies and in the interpretation of security threats and environmental concerns—between Europe and the United States; what has changed is that Germany has taken a more visible role in expressing those concerns than in the past.

The strategic triangle of Berlin-Paris-Washington remains the cornerstone of German foreign policy, even if the style of the discourse and the perception of influence have changed. European integration as a prerequisite for peace, France as Germany's most important ally in Europe, and the United States as a close, trusted partner reinforce the imperative for stability in German foreign policy. It continues to be shaped by the collective memory of the past, and by interests and institutional arrangements that emphasize multilateral decision making, that is, a team approach to solving international problems. A high premium is placed on peace and diplomatic conflict resolution. Furthermore, broad consensus on foreign policy is reflected among elites and the public, and this identification emphasizes the concept of civilian power.

In the last twelve years, the percentage of those in the Federal Diet who were born and/or socialized under the Third Reich has consistently declined. Today, only thirty of the 603 members were born before 1940, compared to about one-third even ten years ago. In addition, with the advent of the red-green coalition in 1998, a new generation of political leaders came to the helm of the German government. In their youth, most of them had been active in critically examining Germany's past; as members of the 68ers, the rebellious student movement of the 1960s, their "antifascist" credentials are beyond dispute. In particular, Alliance 90/The Greens has its roots in the peace movement. Joschka Fischer, the respected foreign minister in both cabinets under Schröder, uses his personal and his party's pacifist credentials to legitimize the greater engagement in foreign and security policy. Pacifism and antifascism provide the basis for a new self-confidence; the role history plays in determining German interests remains a sine qua non of foreign policy. In Chancellor Schröder's words, "Germany owes it to its history to emphasize the alternatives to war." Auschwitz, once again, serves as the major narrative. Many have argued that the acceptance of Germany's increased role in foreign and security policies at home and abroad owes much to the red-green leadership; only a government of confirmed pacifists could have broken the taboo of military involvement. The Nixon-goes-to-China syndrome may have found its parallel in German foreign and military policy.

The German government tries to maintain a careful balance between its past and its role as a major European power that cannot and should not avoid international responsibility. Linking *Realpolitik* with morality and vision remains a

Box 8.2   Speech by Federal Foreign Minister Joschka Fischer

At the "Weimar Lectures on Germany," April 10, 2002 (excerpts)

The process of European integration, the chance to repeat in the east what was achieved in the west after 1945, globalization, the instabilities of a world in upheaval, and the new world-wide challenges including international terrorism cannot but affect German foreign policy. The need for reevaluation, for greater involvement within and also beyond Europe's borders, cannot be denied, and must take account of the increased weight of our country and the high expectations of our partners. Since reunification, Germany's importance has increased more than many Germans realize, even today. As Foreign Minister, I am reminded of this time and again. To deny that this objective potential has increased would be foolish and dishonest and would promote mistrust, not trust.

The question, then, is how the united Germany can deal with this increased influence as wisely and responsibly as possible. The starting point of my thoughts is that Germany, on account of its history, is not in a position to make independent initiatives or to play its own proactive world politics. Our constants must remain prudent self-restraint, a clear rejection of any kind of renationalization of foreign policy and, in particular, dedicated commitment to completing European integration. It is obvious, too, that in the future Germany will be called upon more frequently when massive human rights violations occur and when peace and security are endangered. Military assistance can be called upon from Germany as a last resort. We have debated this point often and hard in the last few years. Yet Germany's key contributions must be political, and above all it must be made within the European framework. . . .

Nothing has changed the development of Germany or of Europe so profoundly and with such lasting effect as European integration, which began 50 years ago among the ruins of the Second World War. With it began an entirely new era in Europe, or, to be more precise, in Western Europe. It is even possible to say that European history underwent a complete about-turn.

* * *

The foreign policy of the EU will never have as strong a military orientation as that of the USA. Our experiences of history—centuries of bloody wars and civil wars in very small areas—are very different to those of the United States and they will continue to be characterized by a greater reticence towards military action. We will always look first for a political solution, but without excluding the use of force as a last resort. . . . Clearly, Europe will never be able or want to rival the United States militarily, but alongside a civilian crisis management capability it must also possess its own self-sufficient, independent military capabilities, if it wants to be in a position to practice effective conflict prevention and to secure or even enforce peace, alone if necessary.

challenge to the foreign policy establishment. The ambivalence in pursuing foreign and security objectives is reflected in some accounts of German foreign policy and actions. What bothers some foreign and domestic observers, including many members of the German foreign policy establishment, is not the vision of German interests but the occasional lack of adequate strategy in pursuing those interests.

Outlook

A few months after the electoral victory of the red-green coalition in 2002—and amidst heavy criticism regarding the wobbly beginning of its second term in office—Chancellor Schröder referred to three policy principles that he considered of particular importance for his administration. He wanted to pursue a foreign policy based on sovereignty and alliance responsibilities but one that "develops strength and courage of differentiation." Economic dynamism should not lose sight of the need for social solidarity. Finally, society should remain enlightened and tolerant, while respecting the law-and-order responsibilities of the state.[29] The third guideline hinted at Germany's role in fighting terrorism and managing the challenges associated with immigration; the first combined traditional foreign policy objectives with a call for greater self-confidence in articulating German international interests. Economic reinvigoration, without neglecting social responsibility, remains a cornerstone of any domestic policy. The three guidelines reflect a broad consensus of all the major political players in Germany and are not controversial, yet they present challenges that will shape the policy discourse for years to come. They are interwoven, since economic strength or weakness is invariably linked to Germany's status, particularly in European affairs but also in its ability to fulfill international obligations.

As Germany's international and domestic agenda influence its path toward greater normality, the impact of its past will keep the question of normality in the political discourse. The debate about Germany's international role will be more lively and more controversial outside of Germany; at home, the restructuring of Europe at the end of the twentieth century has led to more settled and widely accepted foreign and security policies. For the German elite and citizens alike, the urgency of reforming many aspects of their domestic policies, including health care, pension, labor market, immigration, and education, has top priority.

Notes

1. *Economist,* December 21, 1996.
2. C. K. Williams, "Das symbolische Volk der Täter," *Die Zeit* 46/2002 (Internet version).

3. *50 Jahre Bundesrepublik Deutschland. Ergebnisse einer repräsentativen Bevölkerungs-umfrage* (Mannheim: IPOS, May 1999), 4.

4. For an elaboration of the principles of the party state, see Michaela W. Richter, "The German Party State: A Reassessment," in *Transformation of the German Political Party System*, ed. Christopher S. Allen (New York and Oxford: Berghahn Books, 1999), 62–98.

5. For detail regarding the electoral system, see Giovanni Capoccia, "The Political Consequences of Electoral Laws: The German System at Fifty," *West European Politics*, 25, 3 (July 2002): 171–202.

6. Various Christian-based political groups organized in 1945 but party consolidation across zones of occupation soon led to the emergence of the Christian Democratic Union (CDU). Political leaders of the Christian Social Union (CSU) in Bavaria decided to remain separate; the anomaly of two conservative parties that share many programmatic similarities but are regionally divided persists. The CDU is the main center-right party in all parts of Germany except Bavaria; its so-called sister party, the CSU, exists only as a regional party in Bavaria. The two parties are being treated as one in the remainder of this chapter, since they almost always act in unison at the federal level, occasional tensions notwithstanding.

7. Recently, the two major parties share the plight of membership losses, and, in contrast to the past, their overall membership base no longer differs greatly in numbers (2001: CDU 604.135; SPD: 717.513).

8. Cf. Randall Hansen, "Globalization, Embedded Realism, and Path Dependence," *Comparative Political Studies*, 35, 3 (April 2002): 259–83.

9. *50 Jahre Bundesrepublik Deutschland*, 14.

10. Helga A. Welsh, "East-West Electoral Encounters in Unified Germany," in *Power Shift in Germany: The 1998 Election and the End of the Kohl Era*, ed. David P. Conradt et al. (New York and Oxford: Berghahn Books, 2000), 196.

11. Wade Jacoby, *Imitation and Politics. Redesigning Modern Germany* (Ithaca and London: Cornell University Press), 189.

12. "An Uncertain Giant. A Survey of Germany," *Economist*, December 7, 2002, 14.

13. Statistisches Bundesamt et al., eds., *Datenreport 2002. Zahlen und Fakten über die Bundesrepublik Deutschland* (Bonn: Bundeszentrale für politische Bildung, 2002), 607–8.

14. Beate Kohler-Koch, "Europäisierung: Plädoyer für eine Horizonterweiterung," in *Deutschland zwischen Europäisierung und Selbstbehauptung*, ed. Michèle Knodt and Beate Kohler-Koch (Frankfurt and New York: Campus Verlag, 2000), 11.

15. James Sperling, "Neither Hegemony nor Dominance: Reconsidering German Power in Post Cold-War Europe," *British Journal of Political Science* 31 (2001): 410.

16. The list is adopted from Gunther Hellmann, "Precarious Power: Germany at the Dawn of the Twenty-First Century," in *Germany's New Foreign Policy. Decision-Making in an Interdependent World*, ed. Wolf-Dieter Eberwein and Karl Kaiser (New York: Palgrave, 2001), 293.

17. Manfred G. Schmidt, "Die Europäisierung der öffentlichen Aufgaben," in *50 Jahre Bundesrepublik Deutschland. Rahmenbedingungen–Entwicklungen–Perspektiven*, ed. Thomas Ellwein and Everhard Holtmann (Opladen and Wiesbaden: Westdeutscher Verlag, 1999), 386.

18. Quoted in Simon J. Bulmer, "Shaping the Rules? The Constitutive Politics of the European Union and German Power," in *Tamed Power: Germany in Europe*, ed. Peter J. Katzenstein (Ithaca and London: Cornell University Press, 1997), 67.

19. Bulmer, *Shaping the Rules,* 50.

20. Lees, "'Dark Matter': Institutional Constraints and the Failure of Party-based Euroscepticism in Germany," *Political Studies* 50, 2 (2002): 244–67.

21. Cf. Carl Lankowski, "Germany: A Major Player," in *The European Union and the Member States,* ed. Eleanor Zeff and Ellen Pirro (Boulder and London: Lynne Rienner, 2001), 89–114; and Maria Green Cowles et al., eds., *Transforming Europe: Europeanization and Domestic Change* (Ithaca and London: Cornell University Press, 2001).

22. The importance and political sensibility of voting rights in the Council of Ministers became glaringly evident during the December 2003 meeting of EU leaders. Under the proposed "double majority" principle EU laws would pass if backed by a majority of the twenty-five member countries, representing at least 60 percent of the population. More populous countries (in particular Germany) would have benefited from this switch but medium-sized countries such as Poland and Spain resisted the move, and the negotiations aimed at finalizing the draft treaty establishing a constitution for Europe failed.

23. Gerald Schneider and Stefanie Bailer, "Mächtig, aber wenig einflussreich: Ursachen und Konsequenzen des deutschen Integrationsdilemmas," *Integration* 25, 1 (2002), 49–60.

24. Quoted in "Scenes from a Marriage," *Economist*, March 24, 2001, 30.

25. Quoted in Wayne C. Thompson, "Germany and the East," *Europe-Asia Studies* 53, 6 (2001): 947.

26. Cf. Ann L. Phillips, *Power and Influence after the Cold War: Germany in East-Central Europe* (Lanham, Md.: Rowman & Littlefield, 2000); and Jeffrey Anderson and Celeste A. Wallander, "Interests and the Wall of Ideas. Germany's Eastern Trade Policy after Unification," *Comparative Political Studies* 30, 6 (December 1997): 675–98.

27. The data are taken from various reports of *Forschungsgruppe Wahlen,* Mannheim, September 2002 to May 2003.

28. *Germany and European Order: Enlarging NATO and the EU* (Manchester and New York: Manchester University Press, 2000), 147.

29. "Notfalls auch mit Zwang," *Die Zeit* 49/2002 (Internet version).

Suggestions for Further Reading

Allen, Christopher S., ed. *Transformation of the German Political Party System: Institutional Crisis or Democratic Renewal?* New York and Oxford: Berghahn Books, 1999.

Anderson, Christopher J., and Carsten Zelle, eds. *Stability and Change in German Elections: How Electorates Merge, Converge or Collide.* Westport, Conn.: Praeger, 1998.

Brady, John, et al., eds. *The Postwar Transformation of Germany: Democracy, Prosperity, and Nationhood.* Ann Arbor: University of Michigan Press, 1999.

Bulmer, Simon, et al., eds. *Germany's European Diplomacy: Shaping the Regional Milieu.* Manchester and New York: Manchester University Press, 2000.

Conradt, David P. *The German Polity.* 7th ed. New York: Longman, 2001.

Conradt, David P., et al., eds. *Power Shift in Germany: The 1998 Election and the End of the Kohl Era.* New York and Oxford: Berghahn Books, 2000.

Dettke, Dieter, ed. *The Spirit of the Berlin Republic.* New York and Oxford: Berghahn Books, 2003.

Harding, Rebecca, and William E. Paterson, eds. *The Future of the German Economy: An End to the Miracle?* Manchester and New York: Manchester University Press, 2000.

Harnisch, Sebastian, and Hanns Maull, eds. *Germany as Civilian Power? The Foreign Policy of the Berlin Republic.* New York: Palgrave, 2001.

Helms, Ludger, ed. *Institutions and Institutional Change in the Federal Republic of Germany.* New York: St. Martin's Press, 2000.

Jacoby, Wade. *Imitation and Politics: Redesigning Modern Germany.* Ithaca and London: Cornell University Press, 2000.

Katzenstein, Peter J., ed. *Tamed Power: Germany in Europe.* Ithaca and London: Cornell University Press, 1997.

Maier, Charles S. *Dissolution: The Crisis of Communism and the End of East Germany.* Princeton, N.J.: Princeton University Press, 1997.

Markovits, Andrei S., and Simon Reich. *The German Predicament: Memory and Power in the New Europe.* Ithaca and London: Cornell University Press, 1997

McAdams, A. James. *Judging the Past in Unified Germany.* Cambridge: Cambridge University Press, 2001.

Müller, Jan-Werner. *Another Country: German Intellectuals, Unification, and National Identity.* New Haven: Yale University Press, 2000

Patton, David F. *Cold War Politics in Postwar Germany.* New York: St. Martin's Press, 2001.

Phillips, Ann L. *Power and Influence after the Cold War: Germany in East-Central Europe.* Lanham, Md.: Rowman & Littlefield Publishers, 2000.

Schissler, Hanna, ed. *The Miracle Years: A Cultural History of West Germany, 1949– 1968.* Princeton and Oxford: Princeton University Press, 2001.

Schmidt, Manfred G. *Political Institutions in the Federal Republic of Germany.* Oxford and New York: Oxford University Press, 2003

Zelikow, Philip, and Condoleezza Rice. *Germany United and Europe Transformed: A Study in Statecraft.* Cambridge, Mass.: MIT University Press, 1995.

SPECIALIZED SCHOLARLY JOURNALS

German Politics (Frank Cass Publishers)

German Politics and Society (Berghahn Books)

Internationale Politik. Transatlantic edition (in English; published by the German Council on Foreign Relations)

CHAPTER 9

France
Ending the Gaullist Era?

Robert Graham

France

Population: 59.5 million
Area in Square Miles: 212,394
Population Density per Square Mile: 279
GDP (in billion dollars, 2001): $1,594.5
GDP per capita (purchasing power parity in dollars, 2001): $26,177
Joined EC/EU: January 1, 1958
Joined NATO: 1949
Political Parties:
Citizen and Republican Movement or MCR
Democratic and European Social Rally or RDSE
French Communist Party or PCF
Left Radical Party or PRG (previously Radical Socialist Party or PRS
    and the Left Radical Movement or MRG)
Liberal Democracy or DL (originally Republican Party or PR; now
    merged into the UMP)
Movement for France or MPF
Rally for France or RPF
Rally for the Republic or RPR (merged into UMP)
Socialist Party or PS
Greens
Union for French Democracy or UDF (coalition of DL, CDS, UDF,
    RP, and other parties)
Union for a Popular Movement or UMP (including RPR, DL, and a
    part of UDF)

Sources: "Organisation for Economic Co-operation and Development," at
www.oecd.org/home/ (accessed August 5, 2003); "2003 World Population
Data Sheet," at www.prb.org/pdf/WorldPopulationDS03_Eng.pdf
(accessed August 5, 2003); "The World Factbook," August 1, 2003, at
cia.gov/cia/publications/factbook/index.html (accessed October 6, 2003).

Introduction

Two monuments are impossible to miss on a stroll down the Champs-Elysées, the vast elegant avenue that acts as the spinal cord of Paris, the French capital. At one end, at the Place du Général de Gaulle, is the Arc de Triomphe, an imposing nineteenth-century copy of the kind of triumphal arch erected to honor victorious Roman emperors. At the other, the Place de la Concorde, is an ancient Egyptian obelisk brought back as booty by Napoleonic troops.

For a nation that prides itself on the uniqueness of its own heritage and invented the word *chauvinism*, the French have expropriated symbols from other peoples' cultures and histories to reinforce their own identity to a surprising degree. Even the Champs-Elysées, seen as so quintessentially French—and Parisian—has a name borrowed from classical times.

However, the most important aspect of these monuments is how they underscore the way French rulers—whether monarchs, emperors, or latter-day presidents—have used architecture and urban planning over the centuries as a projection of France's *gloire* and *grandeur*. This is not only a statement of how France wishes to be seen in the world, but also how its rulers perceive themselves as the embodiment of this glory and grandeur. Attachment to this quite un-American idea of grandeur explains how, even after the French Revolution, France and its rulers have preferred a monarchical concept of power.

The Fifth French Republic, which began in 1958, created a presidential system under General Charles de Gaulle that has been frequently referred to as a "republican monarchy." The most recent, and arguably the last, French president to project himself in an imperial manner was François Mitterrand. During his fourteen-year reign from 1981 to 1995 he became known as "the last Pharaoh" because of his addiction to *grands projets*. The results of Mitterrand's grandiose vision are evident in three of his huge undertakings: the remarkable expansion of the Louvre, which houses the world's largest museum collection; the giant new national library (after his death named the "François Mitterrand Library"), designed around four L-shaped towers modeled on open books; and the modernistic hollow square "Arche de La Defence," a monumental construction that extends the natural east-west perspective of the Champs-Elysées another two miles to a towering set of glass-fronted office buildings in the neighborhood of La Defence.

Even President Jacques Chirac, the successor of Mitterrand, could not resist the temptation to indulge in *grandeur*. He has ordered the construction of a new *Musée de l'homme* (the Museum of Human Civilizations) on the banks of the quintessential Parisian monument, the Eiffel Tower. Paris was without doubt already overflowing with museum exhibition space, but President Chirac, like his predecessors, wanted to leave his own mark on this center of world culture.

Curiously enough, Charles de Gaulle, the man who has done the most to shape the destiny of modern France, showed the least interest in the projection of such grandeur through monuments. He preferred words and deeds to relight the flame of French influence and French independence on the world stage. Halfway up the Champs-Elyseés, he is now commemorated by a statue on a twenty-foot-high plinth. The general's tall, ungainly figure is caught in full stride on the day he was mobbed by jubilant crowds as he savored his finest hour—walking down the Champs-Elysées to celebrate the Liberation of Paris in August 1944.

De Gaulle's triumphant return to Paris was the vindication of a lonely and courageous role as leader of the French Resistance in wartime London. Then, even in the darkest moments when he felt sidelined by Roosevelt and Churchill, he never lost faith in a free France or doubted his own sense of destiny as a savior of France. This lasting belief in his own destiny ensured that the nation turned to him in 1958 as savior at the height of the demoralizing colonial war in Algeria.

The projection of his heroic role in the Resistance, alongside de Gaulle's own obstinate battle to preserve the independence of the Free French forces based in London, was essential to the "Gaullist" ideal. This portrayed France plowing a lone furrow in postwar Europe: clinging to the beauties of the French language and the universal values of "Liberty, Equality and Fraternity" to demonstrate "the French Exception"—the insistence that France, when she was "being herself," was somehow different from other countries.

In practical terms this saw France striking an independent path on the world stage by insisting on the possession of her own nuclear deterrent, distancing itself from the NATO alliance while trying to retain cordial relations with both Moscow and Washington during the Cold War. However, by the turn of the century this "historic" Gaullist stance had drifted into the realms of nostalgia.

Three main developments were to undermine Gaullism: (1) the collapse of communism and the fall of the Berlin Wall; (2) the increasing integration of the European Union against the backdrop of globalization; and (3) the hegemonic position of the United States.

The implosion of the Soviet empire and the end of the Cold War meant France could no longer play off the United States against the Soviet Union. French independence vis-à-vis the United States also carried less weight because a contrarian position in Paris quite simply mattered less. This partly reflected the success of the American economic model of free-market capitalism and enterprise culture in generating growth and prosperity. Equally, the projection of American military power was so overwhelming—first in the 1991 Gulf War, then in the Kosovo conflict, and more recently in Iraq—that the French independent nuclear deterrent became more a status symbol than a tool of international diplomacy. Throughout the 1990s France wound down its military spending, falling well behind Britain both in terms of readiness and rapid reaction capability. Chirac when reelected in 2002 sought to reverse this trend but budgetary constraints made it highly unlikely defense spending could be raised to match Britain's 2.2 percent of GDP even by the end of the decade.

Within Europe, France was disoriented by enhanced German power following reunification of Germany in 1989–1990. France had always held the upper hand, even though Germany was economically stronger. France played upon its permanent seat at the United Nations Security Council, upon its possession of nuclear weapons, and, in the last resort, upon Germany's World War II guilt and its desire to make amends for the horrors of Nazism. A reunified Germany overnight made Germany more populous—80 million inhabitants against France's 60 million. French leaders found it more difficult to play the old game of European superiority in front of a new generation of German politicians following the 1998 election of Chancellor Gerhard Schröder. The latter felt no need to apologize for Germany's past and was therefore less susceptible to exploiting German guilt for diplomatic advantage. Reunification also shifted the geographical focus away from the Rhine, much farther east to Berlin.

The rise of the new Germany coincided with a realization among the French political establishment that their endorsement of European integration—often no more than halfhearted—had led France to surrender large swaths of sovereignty to Brussels regulation. The process began with the creation of the European Union's single market and accelerated with the embrace of the monetary union. Further changing the European balance of power, dominated by the Franco-German axis, was the advent of a more assertive Britain under Tony Blair during the mid-1990s. Britain came to play a much bigger role in setting the agenda in Brussels; and English became the lingua franca within the EU commission, pushing aside the long-standing primacy of French as the working language. By 2000, 55 percent of all EU commission documents were drawn up in English as opposed to 33 percent in French.

The erosion of the Gaullist nationalist stance extended to the economic sphere. The limits imposed by Brussels on state aids to business and industry, combined with increased cross-border competition, opened up the French economy to a hitherto unprecedented degree. By the turn of the century foreign investors—led by U.S., British, and Scandinavian investment funds—controlled on average over 40 percent of the shares of the leading companies in the CAC 40 (the main bourse index). Monopolies like those of telephones and electricity were being unbundled by a combination of privatization and EU-led market liberalization.

Within France, the gradual weakening of the Gaullist legacy was reflected in the political career of current president Jacques Chirac. He had founded the RPR (Rassemblement pour la République) in 1976 as a vehicle for his presidential ambitions. Chirac presented himself as the rightful heir to de Gaulle's inheritance. Yet when he had gained the presidency in 1995, Chirac felt immediately obliged to forgo his Gaullist skepticism toward closer European integration for fear that France would be left in the cold. He also endorsed far more liberal economic policies than de Gaulle would have ever contemplated. By the time of his reelection in May 2002, Chirac was perfectly happy to see his RPR merge into a broad center-right movement, the UMP. The movement contained no reference to the founding father of the Fifth Republic.

When he had unveiled the de Gaulle statue in 2001, Chirac said: "The inheritance of de Gaulle is the dream of a France with an individual role on the world stage yet resolutely open to embrace Europe and the World." In other words, France's willful individualism could only have impact if expressed in the context of broader alliances.

It is tempting, therefore, to see Chirac's role in championing the opposition within Europe and at the United Nations to the United States–led invasion of Iraq in the early months of 2003 as a resurgence of old-style Gaullism. In deliberately challenging American-imposed regime change in Iraq, Chirac insisted this was not French anti-Americanism. Instead he evoked a vision of a "multipolar" world functioning under the umbrella of the UN's legitimacy that contrasted with Washington's "unilateralist" approach as a global policeman. This stance certainly reflected the traditional Gaullist fear of France being forced to pursue an American policy that it disliked yet could not influence.

However, de Gaulle had always acted in the context of playing off the two superpowers. Chirac's behavior during the Iraqi crisis, on the other hand, was in a post–Cold War context, opportunistic by nature and reactive in form, and once U.S. troops invaded Iraq, he lacked a coherent policy on how to resolve poisoned relations with Washington other than to seek to renew the ties of friendship. Chirac's stand on Iraq was also very much dictated by the politics of a new evolving intra-European power balance as the EU faced enlargement from fifteen to twenty-five members. The French president sought to exploit the Iraqi crisis to retain the initiative as the main EU driving force by clinging to a close alliance with Germany and seeking to outmaneuver the leadership ambitions of Britain's Tony Blair. That this helped split the EU and alienate the accession countries like Poland, who felt strong loyalty to Washington, ultimately undermined the domestic and international popularity of Chirac's opposition to the war.

More importantly, in the more than three decades since de Gaulle relinquished power, the Fifth Republic had acquired a remarkably different social complexion, with over five million Muslims—representing close to 10 percent of a once essentially Christian and predominantly Catholic population. A prime reason for Chirac's opposition to the war was a domestic political concern: the fear of social instability among this new Muslim community of largely North African origin, angered by the prospect of France being party to the invasion of a fellow Arab country.

A Republican Monarchy

The institutions of the Fifth Republic, which Chirac inherited, were tailor-made for de Gaulle's authoritarian instincts and the need for strong government during the colonial crisis in Algeria. The system, enshrined in the 1958 constitution and confirmed by subsequent referendum, was shaped round a strong presidency—precisely to ensure, rather to re-create, order. Among the president's most potent weapons was the power to dissolve the National Assembly. The National Assembly for most of the past four decades was little more than a rubber stamp for government policy. The executive itself could often bypass parliament by resorting to decrees, rather than laws, on a wide area of topics. The system reflected France's preference for strong rulers, whether hereditary monarchs like Louis XIV or popular heroes like the Emperor Napoleon. Not for nothing was the Fifth Republic dubbed a "republican monarchy."

Unlike the United States, the French presidential system lacks proper checks and balances. The judiciary was politically appointed and subject to political interference, and the presidency could exercise effective control over the executive and legislative branches, while also influencing the main media through subsidies, advertising deals, and favoritism. The sole check on presidential power was found under a government of *cohabitation*—when parliamentary elections returned a legislature controlled by a color different from that of the presidency. Since the 1980s this has happened three times. The longest episode was the most recent, from 1997 to 2002, when President Chirac dissolved parliament early, misread the electoral mood, and had to face a left-wing coalition under Lionel Jospin, the austere Socialist prime minister.

Executive control over the country was reinforced by a highly centralized public administration whose authority was extended to the provinces via state-appointed prefects, not elected officials like American governors but senior civil servants running the ninety-six different administrative departments. The structure of the civil service was highly pyramidal, with small decisions requiring approval from the top and little delegation of responsibility. However, the absence of checks and balances in the French presidential system was exposed by Chirac's resounding reelection victory in May 2002 and by the subsequent victory in the June general elections of the center-right alliance backing him. As president, Chirac took control of all aspects of the executive. He plucked Prime Minister Jean-Pierre Raffarin from virtual obscurity; Raffarin, in theory the head of the government, was a sort of appointee to do his bidding. Both arms of the legislature—national assembly and the senate—were thus beholden to Chirac. His nominees headed the intelligence and security services, as did the key prefects as well as key members of the judiciary. In the media, public television was generally subservient, and the main private station, TFI, was owned by the Bouygues industrial group, whose family were keen Chirac supporters.

The Trauma of Decolonization

When de Gaulle was recalled in 1958 as a providential figure, the nation will-ingly entrusted him with the wide powers described above. Apart from restor-ing national morale and imposing stability after the Fourth Republic's unstable experiment with parliamentary democracy, his prime task was to end the bitter colonial conflict in Algeria.

Algeria was the pride of the French nineteenth-century colonial ventures. The prospect of starting a new life in Algeria attracted thousands of settlers to this rich North African territory, which became an extension of metropolitan France and the flagship of *la mission civilisatrice de la France* (i.e., the alleged "civilizing" spread of French culture). However, by the 1950s, two incompati-ble forces confronted each other—the desire of the French to stay in a land, Algeria, they had made theirs; and an indigenous population of Arabs and Ber-bers determined to assert their identity as an independent nation. Unlike Brit-ain and the Netherlands, who began their decolonization process immediately after World War II, France proved far more resistant to handing over its colo-nies. This had much to do with France's postwar psychology of being anxious to compensate for the humiliation of German occupation. Possession of colo-nies was a reaffirmation of the French global presence. They stretched from Indochina to the Maghreb and from West Africa across to the Caribbean and Pacific.

The fight to keep Algeria in French hands sometimes carried the Cold War banner of anticommunism. Mostly France was defending its self-esteem. The humbling defeat at Dien Bien Phu in 1954 at the hands of the Vietminh, and the subsequent "loss" of Indochina, had made the French military ever more determined to prove they could "win" in Algeria. The more fanatical officers fighting in Algeria even attempted a putsch to prevent de Gaulle from decoloni-zing. Indeed, this group helped form a right-wing terrorist organization, the OAS, whose members and sympathizers were behind no fewer than six at-tempts on de Gaulle's life between 1961 and 1964.

The final casualty toll of civilians and military in this colonial war, which lasted from 1954 until 1962, was never established. The Algerians claimed one million lives lost. The French military engaged two million men in all: con-scripts, professionals, and locally recruited militia. The French death toll in ac-tion and through accidents was 24,614 in a conflict called a "law-and-order op-eration," until the National Assembly finally accorded it in 1999 the status of a "war."

De Gaulle and successive governments went to great lengths to avoid antag-onizing the military by any admission that the Algerian anticolonial struggle represented a defeat or that the conduct of the fighting was morally wrong. As late as 2002, 490 senior French officers published a pamphlet defending the

Algerian war and protesting the idea that France should make some sort of official statement of regret. They also rejected suggestions that the widespread use of torture on Algerian nationalists and the civilian population was morally wrong; rather, they insisted that circumstances justified such an abuse of human rights.

The national trauma caused by having to negotiate a handover after having done so much to keep Algeria French was compounded by the aggressive assertion of independence by the tough new masters of this ex-colony. French property was nationalized, French citizens were effectively declared persona non grata, and the Muslim "collaborators" with the colonial administration were victimized. Within less than a year, almost 1.2 million *pieds noirs* (French *colons*) abandoned Algeria for a new life, mostly in France but some in Spain or southern Africa. The enforced departure from Algeria was the single biggest colonial exodus seen in the last century, much larger than that of Portuguese citizens from Angola and Mozambique. It was to have a profound impact on France's social structure and political stability, to say nothing of the economic burden. The sense of betrayal was shared by a large section of the military, who believed they had won the war in Algeria but lost the peace, thanks to the politicians. The smoldering resentment of these two groups toward the political establishment was to become an important component in the electoral support garnered by Jean-Marie Le Pen when he formed his extreme right National Front in 1972. Le Pen himself was a former paratroop officer who had served in Algeria.

The Algerian conflict also was to have a lasting impact on the sizable North African immigrant community living in France. The latter had begun coming to France to fill menial service and factory jobs as early as the 1920s. The independence of its North African protectorates, Tunisia and Morocco, and then Algeria, had left these immigrants with a split personality—leaving them neither fully assimilated as French nor wholly identified with their countries of origin. However, they clearly preferred to remain in France and encouraged family and relatives to join them, despite the consequent problems of integration and assimilation. Furthermore, the instability of post-independence Algeria made France a beacon of safety and opportunity. By 1990 over 40 percent of foreigners residing in France, excluding those already with French or dual nationality, were accounted for by Algerians, Moroccans, and Tunisians. This hard core of the immigrant population was composed of 614,000 Algerians, 572,000 Moroccans, and 206,000 Tunisians.

Energy Dependence and Nuclear Independence

Although General de Gaulle realized that France could not win the political battle against Algerian nationalism, he was reluctant to forgo strategic French assets in Algeria. The peace negotiations dragged on for two years until 1962 in the hope of retaining French sovereignty over vast tracts of the Saharan desert. French engineers had discovered highly promising oil and gas fields in the Saharan desert. Access to this oil and development of a French nuclear deterrent touched the very heart of de Gaulle's sensitivity about France's independence vis-à-vis Europe and the United States.

France lacked independent sources of energy for its expanding economy in the postwar era. Coal was less and less competitive to mine in France, and, unlike Britain with its British Petroleum and half share in Shell, the Anglo-Dutch group, France had failed to develop a big multinational oil company with access to adequate supplies from its own oil finds. The international oil business was still dominated by the so-called Seven Sisters—the seven major oil companies. Unfortunately, the finds of light crude oil and high quality gas in the Algerian Sahara gave France only short-lived control over its own hydrocarbons resources. By 1970 French oil interests had been nationalized—prompting a renewed search for oil sources by France first in Libya, then in Iraq and Iran.

De Gaulle's obsession about France's energy dependence was instrumental in a political decision to opt for a huge investment in nuclear power. As a result, France came to rely on nuclear reactors for over 70 percent of its power generation. Even after a freeze on new nuclear power plants in 1997, France possessed fifty-five nuclear reactors and was the sole major European nation so heavily committed to nuclear energy.

Hand in glove with this emphasis on energy independence came the doctrine of self-reliance in defense so as to protect French sovereignty. France, which had participated in the Manhattan Project, began its own atomic weapons program in the aftermath of World War II. Possession of first atomic and then nuclear weapons technology was the ultimate guarantee against any failure in the reliability of the U.S. defense umbrella. Nuclear weapons furthermore helped confer Great Power status and confirmed France's all-important permanent seat in the UN Security Council. Abortive talks on nuclear cooperation with the United Kingdom in 1962, and de Gaulle's conviction that London was Washington's "Trojan horse," led the independent nuclear deterrent to become a central feature of the Fifth Republic's security. De Gaulle's frustration over the failure to forge a Franco-British-American axis to manage Europe's defense also led him to quit the military structure of NATO in 1966. His strategic doctrine envisaged that the French nuclear deterrent could be used "against all comers," that is, in theory including even the United States. The hope was to give Paris greater leverage in relation to both Moscow and Washington. In fact, it simply made France an awkward partner for the United States while never seriously putting into question French acceptance of American protection of Europe in the last resort against any Soviet incursion.

The Gaullist nuclear doctrine remained in place until the fall of the Berlin Wall. Even thereafter, the nuclear rationale was not seriously challenged, from within or without the French political establishment. President Mitterrand made the first gesture of change toward the end of his second term in 1992 when he suspended live testing. He had earlier ridden out a storm in 1985 over the action of French intelligence services who blew up in a New Zealand harbor the *Rainbow Warrior,* a ship hired by activists from Greenpeace to protest France's nuclear testing in the Pacific.

Immediately after winning the 1995 presidential election, Chirac sought to show his Gaullist colors by resuming France's tests in the Pacific. An international outcry led to the tests being cut to six from eight; and in 1998 France signed the Comprehensive Test Ban Treaty. Since then France has relied upon laboratory simulation—in discreet association with the United States—for its nuclear warheads.

The Transatlantic Divide

The collapse of the Soviet Bloc facilitated France's participation in multilateral military actions initiated by the United States. Paris's studied distance from the NATO-alliance military structure, in place since 1966, served little purpose once there was no opposing Warsaw Pact.

The first instance of these un-Gaullist reflexes emerged when President Mitterrand accepted that France should join the U.S.-led alliance in the 1991 Gulf War against Iraq. The action to evict Iraq forces from Kuwait was backed by NATO and supported by Iraq's Arab neighbors. Even this left-wing French president realized that France gained little by standing on the sidelines and trying to take the moral high ground over a war in the Middle East.

His decision to make a French military contribution was nevertheless opposed by an important section of the left and right, using the old Gaullist argument that France had no interest in a conflict whose objectives and conduct were determined by Washington. Such sentiments were subsequently instrumental in France's refusing to be part of the Anglo-American campaign to continue overflights of Iraq—and bombing—to keep the Saddam Hussein regime in check. Eight years later some French leaders questioned France's participation in a smaller but not dissimilar venture to eject the Serb regime from Kosovo. The logic of intervention was more clear-cut in the 1999 Kosovo conflict, since it was located in the Balkans, Europe's backyard. Premier Lionel Jospin and President Chirac required no arm-twisting from Washington to provide a major French contribution to a war that pushed Russia dangerously into the pro-Serb camp defending the Milosevic dictatorship in Belgrade.

The French military contribution consisted of air strikes, battlefield intelligence gathering, and a naval blockade in the Adriatic. On occasion President Chirac challenged and sought to interfere with the American-controlled program of air strikes, notably regarding political targets in Belgrade. But the

French public never wavered in its backing for France's contribution, and in France the strong pro-Serb lobby, with its sympathies for the Milosevic regime, barely protested.

More remarkable was the wholehearted endorsement by the mainstream political parties of the U.S.-led action in late 2001 in Afghanistan to oust the Taliban and its Islamist allies in the al Qaeda terrorist movement of Osama bin Laden. This was an awkward moment for politicians who were preparing for the presidential and parliamentary elections that occupied almost the entire first half of 2002. But the decision to participate went unchallenged. That the Afghan venture inaugurated the operational life of the *Charles de Gaulle,* the nation's sole nuclear-powered aircraft carrier, was rich with symbolism. Here was the first vessel named after the general whose baptism of fire consisted of acting as a backstop in a multinational fleet in the Arabian Sea. Later the *Charles de Gaulle* took orders from an American command based in Florida for an operation prompted by the terrorist attack on New York's Twin Towers in September 2001. Over thirty French warships and supply and support vessels took part in the naval operation. Meanwhile French special forces were involved in helping the U.S. military inside Afghanistan, and Mirage jets found themselves based in Uzbekistan, the first such operational base in a former Soviet republic. This was the biggest non-U.S. contribution to the Afghan campaign, and it also served as an important diplomatic gesture of solidarity toward the United States in the fight against international terrorism.

However, the French military capability highlighted the accelerating gap with U.S military power after the collapse of the bipolar world. Not for nothing was it a Frenchman—Hubert Védrine, foreign minister from 1997 to 2001— who coined the term "hyperpower" for the new, unrivalled muscular might of the United States on the world stage. Of all America's European allies, France felt most threatened by such military hyperpower, which provided the shield for further Anglo-Saxon dominance in the cultural, diplomatic, and economic domain at the expense of French *grandeur*. At the UN General Assembly the number of delegations speaking in French, the language of international diplomacy for two centuries, dwindled sharply. Between 1992 and 2000, delegations using French dropped from thirty-one to twenty-one.

France also found itself on the other side of the fence from the United States in opposing the use of genetically modified organisms (GMOs)— especially over the introduction of GMO maize seeds and the import of modified soya. Although this position was shared with the rest of the EU, France was among the EU countries in which the GMO debate became most intertwined with—and impassioned by—the antiglobalization debate. The defense of French culture and the French way of life was exemplified by the romanticized image of *le paysan* (the small farmer) producing genuine produce, unpolluted by capital-intense agriculture. These sentiments were incarnated by José Bové, a media-wise former protester in the 1968 student movement who had gone back to his roots in central France, running a small farm. Heading a radical farmers organization, Bové was in the forefront of agitprop actions like uprooting American-style genetically modified crops. He was then catapulted to international notoriety, becoming the French antiglobalizationist par excellence when he led a group to tear down a McDonald's fast-food site at Millau in 1999. He went on to play a prominent role in the Seattle protests.

Another important antiglobalization group emerged on French soil in the form of ATTAC. This was an association largely formed by leftist intellectuals lobbying for the introduction of a globally raised tax on all international financial transactions—the "Tobin Tax" (named after the academic who first floated the idea and subsequently dismissed it as impractical). From humble origins in 1999, ATTAC swiftly acquired a web of international associations and sympathizers, aided by the Internet. It won 128 signatories among the deputies in the 1997–2000 legislature, obliging both the Conservative President Chirac and Socialist Premier Jospin to lend a sympathetic ear to their views. Nevertheless, both the right and left establishments maintained an ambivalent attitude toward the antiglobalization movement. Condemning the violence of protests like that at the G7 summit in Genoa in 2001, Chirac, in a Clintonesque mode, added: "I hear what you are saying." French governments, more or less sincerely, have also sent representatives to the antiglobalization meetings at Porto Alegre, Brazil.

The antiglobalization movement tended to play to all the visceral anti-American reflexes of the French left, which flowered in the vehement opposition to the American war in Vietnam in the 1960s. This one-time rejection of U.S. imperialism had become, by the late 1990s, an ill-defined, all-embracing cry of alarm against the corrupting influence of the "American way of life": an attitude containing a strong element of hypocrisy and contradiction. McDonald's, the very symbol of the abhorrent fast-food culture, proved enormously popular in France, and its franchises not only generated catering jobs but underpinned the livelihoods of over thirty thousand French farmers from whom it bought meat. Thus, on the one hand, the mustachioed figure of Bové was feted as the man who dared to shake his fist at fast-food culture. Simultaneously, a highly successful nationwide advertising campaign featured national soccer hero goalkeeper Fabien Barthez, balancing a McDonald's hamburger on his polished bald pate.

To round off the contradiction, France could not be portrayed solely in terms of its fine food traditions, with every main street full of boutique butchers, bakers, and caterers. It also was the first country in continental Europe to develop big American-style out-of-town shopping centers with hyper-supermarkets. Groups like Carrefour were European leaders in the field.

Where the transatlantic divide cut deepest was on a moral issue. Capital punishment laws in a significant number of states in the United States are viewed in France with a mixture of puzzlement and repulsion. Moreover, the continued existence of the death penalty in the United States served to justify a conviction that the French and their European colleagues lived in a more "civilized" society. This in turn fed a French, and European, sentiment of moral superiority. Curiously the Europe-wide criticism of U.S. capital punishment was most vociferous in France, the last EU member to abolish the death penalty in 1982.

All these elements made up a volatile cocktail of anti-Americanism that often required only minor incidents to ignite passions. Matters were aggravated by a perception in Washington among Democrats and Republicans that these French national sensitivities reflected a broad-based anti-Americanism rather than a genuine disagreement about policy. Often it was hard to tell from newspaper articles and the rhetoric of officials whether Washington was anti-French or France anti-American.

America was partner and ally, but also competitor and rival.

The Iraqi Crisis

The French clash with Washington over policy toward the Saddam Hussein regime in Baghdad that developed in late 2002 was only in part the product of the aforementioned underlying frictions. Chirac's impetuous character, his enhanced presidential powers, and the influence of Dominique de Villepin, his new foreign minister with a propensity to take risks, were key ingredients. De Villepin, as chief of staff in l'Elysée (the French White House) throughout Chirac's first term, had been the person who ill-advisedly counseled Chirac to dissolve parliament early in 1997, thereby allowing the left to seize control of the legislature from 1997 to 2001, leaving the president an impotent figure.

In the summer of 2002 Chirac had finally rid himself of the awkward *cohabitation* with the left. The pent-up frustrations of this enforced five-year inactivity on the international stage resulted in a burst of diplomatic activity as Chirac reasserted himself. Seventy years old, he was determined to demonstrate his credentials as the most experienced statesman on the world stage. He had, after all, been around with the likes of Nixon and Brezhnev, and had dealt with George W. Bush's father.

Ironically, in the light of subsequent events, he put a premium on improving strained relations with the United States, priding himself on his knowledge of the country in which he had worked as a student in a Howard Johnson chain and courted a Southern belle. De Villepin, whom he trusted implicitly and regarded as the son he never had, felt even more familiar with the United States, having spent time as a press attaché in Washington. With his good command of English and flamboyant manner, de Villepin immediately created a good impression with the Bush administration. As a result Chirac believed he could do business with Washington despite the strong influence of the neoconservatives in the Bush team and France's concern over the growing talk in Washington of a military initiative against Iraq's weapons of mass destruction (WMD).

Encouraged by de Villepin, Chirac felt he could influence Washington's policy toward Iraq while simultaneously giving France a higher profile on the world stage. However, he misread the mood in Washington by not appreciating the degree to which the Bush administration had been traumatized by the events of September 11 and not understanding how the Bush administration saw the United States threatened by rogue-state leaders like Saddam Hussein. He also failed to see how he antagonized Washington with his vision of a "multipolar" world—that is, a world that did not just revolve round the United States but had several alternate and balancing poles of power. These elements sowed the seeds, on the French side, for subsequent confrontation.

When Bush addressed the UN General Assembly in September, Chirac concluded that a diplomatic solution to Iraq was possible. Indeed, so confident was the Chirac/de Villepin duo of locking Bush into a UN-led solution that they were willing to risk U.S. irritation by dragging out discussion of resolution 1414 for over seven weeks. When the Security Council unanimously approved this resolution on November 8, Chirac saw this diplomatic success as the triumph of his multilateral approach against U.S. unilateralism. He then envisaged three scenarios: (1) the new UN weapons inspection mission would prove that Iraq had WMD and so legitimize military action via a second resolution; (2) the Iraqi regime would quickly prove uncooperative, thus obliging a military response; (3) the inspectors would demonstrate the threat from WMD was nonexistent and so render military action unnecessary. Of these possibilities, Chirac and his advisors viewed it more likely that Saddam would be obstructive. Hence Chirac insisted that it would be necessary for the Security Council to convene at a subsequent date to consider what action to take, a military response being the last resort. From the outset, therefore, France was ambiguous about any ultimate involvement in a U.S.-led military coalition. In the French legalistic mindset, the UN path once chosen had to be pursued even though the Pentagon hawks were already committed to a military buildup in the Gulf whose logic was war.

Until early January, Chirac and his advisors believed the UN path had the backing of Secretary of State Colin Powell and Bush. France had reviewed plans to field over fifteen thousand ground troops and was cooperating in letting United States special forces use its military facilities in Djibouti. But just when the United States military buildup acquired critical momentum, Paris felt that the inspections were beginning to bear fruit after a shaky start. Here the positions began to move in opposite directions. Following a mission to Washington on January 13 by Maurice Gourdault-Montagne, Chirac's diplomatic advisor, Paris was convinced that the U.S. administration had dropped a diplomatic solution and was bent on regime change instead. Yet despite the war signals from Washington, France felt the UN inspections might work, given more time—by destroying the WMD and in so doing undermining the Iraqi dictatorship's credibility, perhaps leading to regime change from within. Chirac was certain the UN route had to be fully pursued since the alternative of an externally imposed regime on this complex Middle East oil-producer was so uncertain and dangerous. Where Chirac saw risks and dangers only acceptable within the multinational framework of the UN, Bush and his colleagues saw opportunities for demonstrating U.S. military muscle and redrawing the broader Middle East map.

The transatlantic split emerged at the UN on January 20 when de Villepin told a press conference that France "would resume all its responsibilities" in the event of a resort to war. This veiled threat to use France's Security Council veto should any war resolution be presented in the near future was a clear breach of the previously united front at the UN in dealing with Iraq. But at this stage France's position represented a genuine disagreement over tactics and aims—not an orchestrated outburst of anti-Americanism. This also applied to the Franco-German opposition, with Belgian support, to a United States request in mid-January for NATO to guarantee backing for Turkey in the event of an Iraqi attack. For Chirac such a gesture prejudged the failure of the UN weapons inspections in Iraq.

Unexpectedly entering this delicate diplomatic equation was the renewed Franco-German entente. Chirac had from the outset of his second term sought to give a special significance to the fortieth anniversary of the Elysée treaty, which formalized France and Germany's post–World War II reconciliation. He used the elaborate treaty celebrations on January 22 as a lever to enhance France's visibility in Europe. In doing so, he made two mistakes. First, on such a public occasion that trumpeted the closeness of French ties with Germany, he felt obliged to identify with Chancellor Gerhard Schröder's overt opposition to military action in Iraq. Unlike Schröder, Chirac had never previously excluded the use of force against Iraq; he had merely said that it was the "ultimate resort." His identification with the Schröder position locked him into the antiwar camp, later to be joined by Russia's Vladimir Putin.

Second, by explicitly claiming that the Franco-German axis would continue to be the driving force for an enlarged Europe, he not only antagonized EU members like Britain, Italy, and Spain (already strongly committed to backing the United States over Iraq) but also irritated the accession countries in Eastern Europe, like Poland, who were also close allies of Washington. In direct response to Chirac's apparent arrogance in speaking for Europe came two open letters challenging this assumption. Although the immediate context of these letters was support for the Bush administration's policy on Iraq, the broader European message was clear: other voices had a right to speak for Europe, and they represented a majority. The first letter bore the signatures of the leaders of eight EU member and accession countries, including those of Britain, Italy, Poland, and Spain. Those in Blair's entourage were the main actors here, the British prime minister having his own ambitions to set the European agenda. The second letter, encouraged by Washington lobbyists, came from the "Vilnius Ten," a group of central and east European former Soviet satellites, who endorsed the United States' position over Iraq.

Chirac was incensed. He had not been consulted about either of these two letters; and his leadership of Europe, with Schröder in tow, had been challenged. Furthermore, he felt the letters failed to reflect public sentiment throughout Europe that still saw no justification for a U.S.-led regime in Iraq. Chirac vented his anger by publicly chiding the signatories, especially those in the accession countries, whom he accused of being bad-mannered and childish. The school-masterly scolding almost went as far as questioning the latter's credentials to join the EU club. Such intemperance from Chirac widened the divisions in Europe and played into the hands of hawks in the U.S. administration like Secretary of Defense Donald Rumsfeld, who bluntly categorized Europe into the "old" and " new"—the old being France and Germany.

Instead of seeking to mend fences, Chirac hardened his position against an early resort to war in a joint Franco-German-Russian stance, insisting that the UN inspections continue. By now Bush was too committed to beginning military action in Iraq before the summer heat set in at the end of March. Yet by so openly opposing the invasion of Iraq, Chirac enabled the Bush administration to present France as traitorous, a traditional ally who had undermined Western solidarity on a matter of international security.

The intra-European clash was further exacerbated by Britain's Blair insisting on tabling a second resolution at the end of February to obtain UN Security Council backing for the invasion. The United States had never felt that this was necessary but agreed to help Blair, whose domestic opinion demanded a fresh resolution to authorize war. Chirac warned Blair there would be no majority for the resolution, and he privately told the Bush administration it would be better to attack Iraq without a second resolution. France would then simply issue a statement regretting military action once it occurred. But as Blair persisted, so Chirac was determined to prove publicly that the UK resolution could not muster a majority among the fifteen Security Council members. He also said in a television interview that he would use a French veto if pressed to vote while the inspections were incomplete. Thus when the second resolution was eventually dropped and the war began on March 19, the divide was ever more apparent.

Throughout the Iraqi crisis the level of debate in France was remarkably slim. The opinion polls showed more than 70 percent backing for the Chirac/de Villepin diplomacy. The left was most enthusiastic in supporting Chirac's antiwar stance, the ruling parties of the right more troubled. Many on the right were deeply uneasy about Chirac's histrionic behavior. Despite misgivings about the Bush administration's case for toppling Saddam Hussein and imposing a pax americana on Iraq, right-wing politicians questioned the wisdom of

---

Box 9.1   French TV Interview of President Jacques Chirac

On the Second Iraq Resolution at the UN, March 10, 2003

Chirac: I am convinced this evening that this resolution, which contains an ultimatum giving the international green light to a war, does not have a majority of nine votes [in the Security Council]. . . .

My position is that whatever the circumstances, France will vote no because it considers this evening there is no reason to go to war to achieve the objective we have fixed, which is the disarmament of Iraq.

Interviewer: Mr. President, some call the right of veto the diplomatic equivalent of the atomic bomb: even among the ranks of your parliamentary majority some consider this would be shooting your allies in the back.

Chirac: One shouldn't be influenced by such polemics. I repeat: War is always the worst of solutions. And France is not a pacifist country that rejects the principle of war—proof of this is in our being the main contributor to NATO forces now in the Balkans. . . . France considers war as the last step in a process in which all means should be used to avoid it for the very reason that the consequences of war are so dramatic.

Interviewer: Is not use of the veto in this manner virtually unprecedented against the United States?

Chirac: The right of veto has been frequently used. France has employed it 18 times since the beginning, the last being in 1989 at the time of the Panama crisis. Britain has used it 32 times and the United States 76 times. Thus what you call the right of veto, saying no to the majority, is not an exceptional phenomenon, it's in the nature of things, it's international law.

---

breaking ranks with such an important ally, with whom France shared fundamental values. Even on the left figures like Bernard Kouchner, the popular ex-Socialist minister and founder of Médecins sans frontières (Doctors without Borders), said France should not be seen opposing the United States when the latter's aim was to get rid of an evil dictatorship. The French business community was the most vociferous in expressing alarm at the possible consequences of anti-French sentiment in the United States provoked by Chirac. The subsequent coolness toward France and things French served to confirm these concerns. Chirac and Bush were able to shake hands at the G8 summit on the shores of Lake Geneva at Evian at the beginning of July 2003, but this marked a very formal and incomplete reconciliation. Chirac backed a UN resolution on helping with the reconstruction of Iraq, but he remained convinced that the United States had bitten off more than it could chew in Iraq. In the week before he met Bush, Chirac told the *Financial Times,* "A war that lacks legitimacy does not acquire legitimacy just because it has been won."

The Franco-German Engine at the Heart of European Integration

That France chose Germany as its main ally was not surprising.

The mutual suspicion between France and the United States dated back to de Gaulle's wartime sense of hurt for being excluded from the Churchill–Roosevelt axis. It reemerged over Eisenhower's refusal to commit large-scale U.S. military aid to fend off French defeat in Indochina in 1954, and yet again two years later when the United States stood back from supporting Britain and France's Suez venture. De Gaulle was also to be deeply unhappy about the Kennedy administration's tolerance, even indulgence, toward Algerian nationalism.

With Britain regarded as too Atlanticist and faced with Washington's unwillingness to treat France as a trusted partner, a reinforced relationship with Germany became a diplomatic and political necessity. The Franco-German alliance was carried forward on the wings of the visionary ideals for European integration proposed by Jean Monnet, the effective father of the European Union. Monnet recognized that only by working together and creating a community of interdependent economic interests could the terrible scars of Nazism begin to heal and peace be assured for future generations. The combination of France's international weight and military strength alongside Germany's revived economy provided an unquestioned force for leadership in continental Europe. Sentiment did not enter this entente. Both recognized it was a marriage of reason, not the heart.

The 1963 Elysée treaty sealed this pact. It allowed Germany to shake off its wartime guilt and reinforce the democratic credentials of the Bonn-based Federal Republic through closer alliance with France. In return, France could play the senior diplomatic partner and set the agenda of the nascent European Community. The marriage of interests between the oddly paired imperious de Gaulle and the worldly-wise Konrad Adenauer, the German chancellor, set the tone for their successors. The political balance would have altered had de Gaulle allowed the UK to become a player. But he vetoed British entry into what was then the European Economic Community (EEC). France kept Britain out until 1973, when President Georges Pompidou, convinced of the need to have the UK inside the EEC, negotiated a deal with Edward Heath, the unusual fiercely pro-Europe Conservative British prime minister. Yet self-interest did not erase French misgivings about Germany. Each of the 36,000 towns and villages in France remained silent witness to the ravages of the recent past in the form of war memorials in central sites to those who died in the two world wars. The Alsace region in eastern France had changed hands three times in less than 150 years through wars.

French military industries, for example, were located in sites as far away as possible from the threat of German invasion—notably in the Massif Centrale round Clermont Ferrand (where the main mint was also to be found) or deep in the southwest, at Bordeaux, Toulouse, or around Pau and Tarbes next to the Pyrenees. The French military was even wary for strategic reasons of allowing a fast train line (the TGV, for *très grande vitesse*) to connect Paris to Strasbourg on the German frontier right up until the late 1980s.

The Franco-German entente was facilitated by the postwar division of Germany making East Germany a separate state within the Soviet Bloc. West Germany's population was similar in numbers to that of France, and the Iron Curtain obliged German leaders to look westward toward Brussels and Paris. Where differences arose, Germany was usually willing to cede to a France ever ready to raise its voice. From the outset, de Gaulle viewed the European Community as a loose association of independent states bound together by the Franco-German alliance. However, de Gaulle did not renege on the 1957 Treaty of Rome he had inherited from the Fourth Republic. Instead he exploited the treaty to serve French interests with uncompromising obstinacy.

For a whole year in 1965–1966 he boycotted European institutional meetings in Brussels, eventually gaining acceptance of the principle that, when key national interests were at stake, a state could invoke a de facto veto. The deal in effect obliged the Treaty of Rome adherents to continue negotiating on any issue blocked by veto until a consensus was found. The spirit of consensus enshrined in this "Luxembourg Compromise" was to condition the negotiating environment on all subsequent sensitive issues.

France was not alone in exploiting the veto threat. But French officials and national leaders became adept in its use, ensuring that both the Brussels bureaucracy and the policies pursued by European governments reflected a French-directed agenda—notably regarding agriculture, where the system of subsidies and rebates for farming was heavily weighted in favor of France's large dairy and meat industry as well as its cereal and sugar-beet producers.

While de Gaulle was a reluctant European, his two immediate successors—Georges Pompidou and Valéry Giscard d'Estaing—felt ideologically much more at ease with integrating France more closely. Pompidou, in particular, who was de Gaulle's dutiful prime minister and whose presidential career was tragically cut short by cancer, laid less emphasis on the exclusiveness of the Franco-German axis. In the case of the aristocratic Giscard d'Estaing, he was to find common ground with Helmut Schmidt, Germany's Social Democrat chancellor. Both former finance ministers, the two men understood the need to develop a system that avoided sharp swings in their currencies. As an increasingly high proportion of trade and investment developed between Treaty of Rome states, common tools were essential to reduce competitive devaluations and poorly aligned national currencies. Coordinating closely with the Brussels commission, Giscard d'Estaing and Schmidt were instrumental in the 1979 creation of the European Monetary System (EMS)—the forerunner of the single currency introduced two decades later.

The EMS agreement proved that when France and Germany worked together, their combined weight acted as a catalyst for change and innovation in Europe. Thereafter, French and German politicians referred to this axis as the Franco-German "motor"—driving the European engine. While European integration benefited from this bipartite directorate, the behind-the-scenes Franco-German horse-trading marginalized the other players and caused resentment.

The Franco-German motor was much in evidence over the creation of EMS, which involved French recognition of the supremacy of the Bundesbank, the German central bank. Thereafter the D-mark became the benchmark currency and the Bundesbank took the lead on interest rate policy. Indeed, the Banque de France was obliged to maintain a strong franc to keep in line with the German mark. The "strong franc" policy was unpopular with politicians and the business community because it reduced room for maneuver of interest rates. But the interlinkage between the French and German central banks proved an essential ingredient in Europe's currency stability in the move toward the euro in the late 1990s.

France obtained numerous compensations for accepting German economic leadership. For instance, the site of the nascent European parliament was awarded to Strasbourg. The city's location on the Rhine frontier between France and Germany in the center of northern Europe justified the choice as a symbol of European unity. Strasbourg's abysmal transport links made Euro deputies think otherwise. By the turn of the century European members of parliament were still not reconciled to the inconvenience of travel to Strasbourg, preferring their other home in Brussels.

The ideology of the respective French and German leaders mattered less than might have been imagined. When François Mitterrand won the French presidential elections in 1981 as the candidate of the left, his nationalization policy ran counter to the trend in every main European economy. This did not prevent him from enjoying a close relationship with German chancellor Helmut Kohl, who was a conservative Christian Democrat. Deeply marked by his wartime experience, first as a young prisoner of war, then, after his escape, as an official in the Vichy government, and finally as a Resistance leader, Mitterrand profoundly believed in the fashioning of a new European identity based on the stability of the Franco-German axis. While he took an Olympian view of European affairs, he entrusted much of the practical hard work to Jacques Delors, whom he promoted from being French finance minister to head the European Commission in 1985. The latter was to be instrumental in providing the input first for the creation of the Single Market and then the 1991 Maastricht treaty, which prepared the ground for European Monetary Union (EMU) and the euro. Mitterrand did not share old Gaullist reservations about the loss of sovereign control over monetary policy. Rather by bringing all the EU members under the monetary union umbrella, he saw this as the final step in binding Germany to European democracy.

In the wake of the fall of the Berlin Wall, Mitterrand reacted negatively to Kohl's plan for immediate incorporation of East Germany into an expanded Federal Republic. Like Margaret Thatcher, the then British prime minister, he disliked the inevitable increase in Germany's weight in Europe and toyed with ways to either prevent or at least stall reunification. But when he saw that Kohl's enterprise could not be stopped, he decided that the best policy was to ensure that the complex reunification operation worked.

The two men's firm commitment to monetary union provided a route map for Europe during the 1990s. It survived Mitterrand's 1995 departure from his fourteen-year tenure in the presidency and made the Franco-German motor appear to be still driving Europe. However, behind this façade the Franco-German relationship underwent a profound mutation that could not be easily compensated by personal chemistry between leaders.

Shifts after German Reunification

France was to be affected by German reunification in six main ways:

1. French politicians could no longer pretend that France and Germany were more or less the same size in population. Germany had acquired an additional sixteen million people, bringing its total population to eighty million against the sixty million in France. Sooner or later this population difference had to be reflected in voting rights within the European Union's institutions.
2. France's geostrategic position in relation to the fifteen members of the European Union began to change. The collapse of the Soviet Bloc and the incorporation of East Germany directly into the EU—coupled with the demands of other eastern European countries to join this club—shifted the focus eastward. The move of the German capital to Berlin, not so far from the Polish frontier, almost automatically shifted the center of European gravity—even before the EU enlargement process began.
3. The end of the four-power military presence in Berlin united the divided city, closed the book on postwar occupation, and marked the coming of age of the new democratic Germany. Four decades after the defeat of Hitler, Germany had paid its dues to Europe, especially to France, and was ready to play a less guilt-ridden role. France for its part could no longer leverage this guilt to its diplomatic advantage.
4. Reunification required a huge transfer of resources from West to East Germany. The sums involved were so large that Germany could no longer bankroll the EU's budget as it had done since the Treaty of Rome. The chief beneficiary of German largesse over the years had been French agriculture. The Germans therefore became advocates of reforming the Common Agricul-

tural Policy (CAP) and reducing their own budgetary contributions—putting the French on the defensive as guardians of the status quo.

5. Heavy German spending to modernize and incorporate a backward former communist state enormously complicated the task of macroeconomic management for the French authorities who had agreed to follow German monetary policy. At the Central Bank level, the Bundesbank and Banque de France shared similar views on the pursuit of orthodox monetary policies. But while French leaders disliked the rigidity dictated by the Bundesbank philosophy and wanted some form of political control over monetary policy, the Germans readily accepted policies that were long familiar to them.

6. German domestic budgetary constraints were to prove a major handicap in enhancing Franco-German military cooperation in terms of joint armaments programs and of developing a Rapid Reaction Force. With democratic Germany limited by its constitution to NATO theater defensive action, the collapse of communism tended to enhance antimilitarist sentiment, notably after the Greens entered government in 1998. In contrast, France remained committed to a global projection of its power, albeit on a much more modest scale than the United States. As French diplomats liked to say, Germany subscribed to the view of Europe being a "grand version of a greater Swiss Federation," essentially neutralist regarding the outside world. This was the precise opposite of how French politicians on both the right and left viewed Europe's role. Instead, they envisaged the EU evolving from being the world's largest economic grouping into a political and military power capable of balancing the United States.

While Mitterrand remained in office, his long-standing personal relationship with Kohl kept the Franco-German alliance going with only limited tensions. Mitterrand was, for instance, dismayed when Germany pressed ahead in 1991 with the recognition of Croatia and Slovenia as independent states, thereby destabilizing Yugoslavia—France's main ally in the Balkans. Chirac's presidency in 1995 signaled the end of an era. By formation Chirac was a Gaullist with limited enthusiasm for European integration. He shared little affinity with the visionary approach to building a better Europe believed by both Mitterrand and Kohl. Nevertheless he was quick to bury his Gaullist instincts when confronted with the decision whether or not to endorse monetary union. Very pragmatically he accepted the move toward a single currency. He realized that his predecessor's policies were too complicated to undo and could envisage no valid alternative.

Franco-German frictions surfaced after 1997, when the left-wing Socialist-led coalition under Lionel Jospin won the French general elections, forcing Chirac to surrender all but nominal executive power to Jospin. The German partner now had to deal with an awkward left-right *cohabitation* lasting five full years. French protocol dictated that the first point of contact by a German leader (or any other) be with President Chirac. Yet without control over parliament, Chirac was empowered to deliver nothing unless there was prior agreement with Jospin. As a result the German chancellor had to conduct an uneasy diplomatic ballet between the president and prime minister, who were bitter political rivals. On informal get-togethers, this would mean a dinner with Chirac and a pre-dinner meeting with Jospin, or vice versa. The protocol of *cohabitation* and the need to accommodate both Chirac's and Jospin's sensitivities would have been comic but for the duplication of the rounds of talks and the difficulty of establishing a proper rapport with either of the two politicians.

The frustrations of *cohabitation* were fully exposed when Gerhard Schröder, the German Social Democrat, became chancellor in 1998. In theory Jospin's left-wing coalition government was politically close to that of Schröder's: both contained Greens for the first time and each was committed to a social policy agenda. Yet the two men could never develop a relationship. Jospin, a onetime Trotskyite, adhered to a socialism of the old school that deeply distrusted capitalism. He welcomed the Greens as partners because they provided valuable votes, but he had no time for their political views. Schröder carried no such ideological baggage. When confronted with Jospin's dogmatic plans to introduce the thirty-five-hour workweek, Schröder felt more in tune with Britain's Tony Blair, advocating a "third way" that would adapt socialism to the triumphal march of the American-style market economy.

Left alone, the Frenchman Jospin and the German Schröder might well have developed a better relationship. But President Chirac could not resist the temptation to interfere. At crucial EU summits, the French president never failed to pull rank as head of state to act and speak in the name of France. Chirac remained marked by the snub he received as a prime minister from Mitterrand at a G7 summit in Tokyo. Mitterrand would not let him sit with the heads of state, arguing that this was his prerogative. Where G7 summits were concerned Chirac made sure that this privilege applied to the *cohabitation* during his presidency, and Jospin never attended one of these meetings.

In a similar vein, President Chirac—grudgingly supported by Jospin—was determined to preserve French parity with Germany. This was particularly evident at the EU summit in Nice in December 2000 when France held the presidency. EU leaders were preparing the ground for institutional reform to make way for an enlarged European Union that would expand its fifteen-country membership to an eventual twenty-seven countries. In practical terms EU leaders had to find a formula that permitted a revised weighting of states' votes in the European Council, the key executive institution. This meant ensuring that a large group of small states could not club together to outvote the big members. It also meant recognizing Germany's greater weight, as the EU's most populous state, both within the Council and in seats at the European Parliament.

No one but France disputed such logic. For France, and Chirac in particular, who took command at Nice, recognizing Germany as first among equals in an enlarged EU undermined French supremacy in continental Europe. President Chirac was so anxious to prevent this that he badly misread the mood of his colleagues at Nice. The result was one of the EU's biggest summit fiascoes: the French presidency had to backtrack on its parity proposals and accepted with ill grace that Germany should have greater weighting in the system of voting in the council than France, Italy, or the United Kingdom—the other big countries.

Elections Clear the Air

The French elections of 2002 swept away *cohabitation*. Chirac's reelection to a new five-year presidential term allowed him to inject new life into French foreign policy. Central to this was Chirac's aim to reinvigorate the Franco-German axis, as he stated in his August 2002 annual foreign policy address to French ambassadors:

> An agreement between France and Germany is not on its own sufficient to make Europe advance, but experience has continually shown that it was a necessary condition for such advancement. It is certainly going to be under the drive and initiative of our two countries that tomorrow's Europe will be mapped out. I have thus decided that the fortieth anniversary of the Elysée treaty in January 2003 will be the occasion for France and Germany to conclude a new founding pact.

Chirac's EU colleagues treated such reemphasis on the Franco-German axis with skepticism. Nevertheless, following a narrow reelection victory, Schröder was ready to make common cause with Chirac. French diplomatic support allowed him to devote more time to his domestic problems caused by an enfeebled German economy and a fractious coalition. This curious mutual need led the two men to address their deepest differences with pragmatism. For instance, in November 2002, Chirac persuaded Schröder to drop support for a major overhaul of spending in the notoriously French-weighted and German-paid EU Common Agricultural Policy (CAP). Although serious change in the financing of the CAP was effectively postponed for another decade, at one stroke the biggest potential thorn in the French-German relationship was removed.

This breakthrough encouraged the two men to tackle other divisive issues, such as the German emphasis on a federalist approach in the European convention redefining the EU architecture to accommodate enlargement. The agreements reached were often a minima but they were nevertheless deals that other EU members could not ignore. Even where they disagreed, especially over eco-

---

Box 9.2   Press Conference Held by Jacques Chirac in Nantes

Following the 78th Franco-German Summit, November 23, 2001

Sometimes the Franco-German motor irritates people (in Europe). And one hears or reads such and such a criticism on the subject as though there was a will to act in a hegemonic way, forcing everyone else to accept what France and Germany decided together. This could not be further from our thoughts and behavior. Since the creation of the European Union, when we began as six member states, experience has always shown that when France and Germany got along together, the construction of Europe progressed—with greater or less difficulties. But it nevertheless developed. On the other hand, if France and Germany could not get along, the construction of Europe quite simply stopped. Our partners could see this perfectly well for themselves. Thus while they sometimes were upset to see the Franco-German motor acting in too dynamic a fashion, once this motor ran out of steam or broke down for one reason or another, they would rush to us saying: "But why are you letting this happen? It's your responsibility. You can't do this!" . . . The construction of Europe stops if we can't get along.

---

nomic governance of the Eurozone, their differences tended to be papered over: such was the new entente.

On the important issue of European defense plans, the two started out far apart but gradually came closer together. Germany had agreed in the late 1990s to create a joint Rapid Reaction Force with France but had been slow in implementing its side of the deal. Even after 2000 when other EU members, including Britain, had agreed to mold this into a European project, Germany had little to say about how the projected new military force would, or could, be used. French politicians wanted a truly "European" command structure separate from NATO, so as to be free from United States stewardship. However, the German government, always a strong NATO supporter, was lukewarm to such a separation from the alliance. Like other EU members of NATO, the Germans preferred the European Rapid Reaction Force to be part of the Alliance and simply change hats when the occasion required—that is, when the United States did not wish to become involved in an affair that purely concerned Europe. Only in this way would it be compatible with the construction of a "European" force that would also retain the benefits of the United States' global military umbrella. Neither Schröder nor those German leaders before him were willing to place their faith solely in the protection offered by France's nuclear strike force of submarines. But having been reelected in September 2002 on a platform that included outright opposition to military action in Iraq, Schröder broke with Germany's long-standing transatlantic loyalty. As a result Schröder dropped his previous reservations about a European defense identity separate from NATO and embraced the French position despite strong criticism from the conservative German opposition and reservations from within his coalition.

Who Needs Nuclear Weapons?

Cross-party attachment to France's independent nuclear deterrent remained constant despite the new post–Cold War international environment.

At the time of the fall of the Berlin Wall, France devoted a third of its defense budget to nuclear weapons. Over the next decade the nuclear program's share of defense spending fell but still accounted for a substantial 20 percent. The "peace dividend" from the end of the Cold War was limited as France sought to protect its sovereignty from all comers. Even when Chirac briefly decided to resume nuclear testing in the Pacific in 1995, the polemic was more international than domestic. The nuclear doctrine has been pretty constant.

Over the years French officials discussed with their British counterparts sharing nuclear technology, pooling resources, and, more broadly, ways to dovetail a common strategic approach in the use of their respective nuclear arsenals. But two fundamental barriers prevented substantive cooperation. First, neither country wished to surrender the world-power status still accorded the possessors of a nuclear strike force. Second, British technology and intelligence sharing were so deeply intertwined in the transatlantic relationship with the United States that the UK was never willing to risk getting into bed with France at the cost of a break with Washington. French leaders, on the other hand, wanted only one bride at the altar. They also feared that a closer military alliance with Britain might provide the back door for greater U.S. military control over France. The best example here was the French-led Helios satellite intelligence project, which the UK declined to join because it felt no overriding need to break long-standing cooperation with the United States in this field.

The 1998 Franco-British agreement reached at St. Malo marked a key departure from the two nations' mutual wariness over defense cooperation. For the first time under the Fifth Republic, France accepted that Britain was willing and able to play its part in developing a Europe-level defense. France recognized that without the inclusion of Britain, whose forces were the best equipped and prepared in Europe, the EU would never develop a credible foreign and security policy. For its part, Britain accepted for the first time the possibility of a European defense policy that was linked to—but not an integral part of—the United States' strategic interests in Europe. The development was only possible after both Britain and France had measured the consequences of the EU being completely unable to cope on its own with the Kosovo crisis, which was a European problem par excellence. The significance of St. Malo was all the greater because it occurred during the Chirac–Jospin co-habitation with

Box 9.3   Defense Commission Discussion of the Military 2003 Budget

National Assembly, October 15, 2002

The threat from the East has disappeared and the main areas of concern are the proliferation of weapons of mass destruction and ballistic missiles able to deliver them. Faced with this, our system of deterrence has reacted. . . . France very quickly drew the lessons of the end of the Cold War with a halt to testing and a switch to simulation . . . and the complete halt to the production of fissile materials. No other nuclear power has gone so far in making such adjustments. The current dispositions are coherent both technically and in terms of strategic doctrine. . . . Our doctrine of deterrence envisages two types of situation. Although our frontiers and those of our European union partners face no direct threat, the emergence of an aggressive power in the medium and long term cannot be completely ruled out. Important nuclear arsenals remain. In this context deterrence remains the ultimate guarantee of our survival against a major hostile power possessing the means to threaten us. . . . The (traditional) French concept of the weak being able to deter the strong no longer applies. But one cannot exclude that future developments in proliferation will allow regional powers to threaten our vital interests. As the president of the republic says . . . in such a case "the choice would not be between total annihilation and inaction. The damage risked by any potential aggressor would be primarily targeted at the centers of political, economic and military power." The modernization of our nuclear arsenal is thus designed to maintain its credibility while also increasing the range of possible responses. . . . The combination of strategic doctrine and technical capacity in place should last well beyond 2015. As it is already operating on the basis of strict necessity, it would be dangerous to raise questions about . . . cuts in this and that program since any such gains would be more than offset by a loss of deterrence credibility.

a conservative president and a Socialist premier both backing the agreement. The disappointing follow-up to St. Malo resulted from the residual suspicions and differing strategic perceptions of the two nations. In the end this boiled down to Chirac's desire to build up a European defense capability more to offset the "hyperpower" of the United States rather than to complement the latter's unchallenged military capability in the opening years of the twenty-first century. Britain, on the other hand, conceived a European defense capability as wholly complementary to the United States–dominated NATO, evolving toward a more global role following the incorporation of former East Bloc nations and the twenty-first-century challenges of terrorism and WMD. These differences were highlighted by the Iraqi crisis. Yet even at the height of spats between Blair and Chirac in February 2003, the two countries were ready to examine practical measures of defense cooperation, notably over the construction of new aircraft carriers and military aircraft transporters.

Colbert, Cartels, and Competition

The French decisions to back the creation of the single market and then monetary union were essentially taken for political reasons. However, Chirac, Mitterrand, and even Giscard d'Estaing—the most pro-European of all the Fifth Republic presidents—underestimated the impact of these decisions on domestic policy.

A large and strong public sector had lain embedded in the French body politic since the days of Colbert in the seventeenth century. Colbert championed state interventionism as the catalyst for economic development. This spirit was very much present in the reconstruction of postwar France. It also suited de Gaulle in the founding of the Fifth Republic, especially as he had to deal with the complex task of quickly resettling the million or so *pieds noirs*, descendants of the former French colonists, being ejected from Algeria.

Neither de Gaulle nor his immediate successors saw reasons to interfere with the state-controlled monopolies in public transport, electricity, gas, telephones, and tobacco. Nor was there any move to disturb the protected business environment afforded the few private-sector barons like Dassault in aviation or Bouygues in construction. Being business-friendly meant allowing the cartels and monopolies to prosper.

Mitterrand resorted to the heavy hand of state interventionism through his nationalization policies in the early 1980s. The Ministry of Finance, whose rehousing he oversaw in new headquarters at Bercy in the southeastern end of Paris, even had its main building named after Colbert.

Despite these instincts to retain a large role for the state and protect national champions from external competition, French leaders found themselves on the defensive during the onset of the 1990s. The cumulative effect of EU regulations, liberalizing trade and imposing tough competition policy rules, began to radically alter the nature of the French economy.

Initially, the pressures for change manifested themselves in the Brussels-imposed curb on state aid for failing businesses. No longer could failing companies be bailed out by the state without a tough clearance process conducted by the EU commission. Companies that came under the Brussels microscope for benefiting unfairly from state assistance included such flagship names as Air France, the national carrier; Renault, the state-controlled automotive group; and Crédit Lyonnais, the big commercial bank, following its near collapse in 1992–1993.

Even where Brussels approved such state handouts, they were granted on a once-off basis. Thus the government was left with no alternative but to seek fresh funds through opening up the capital, setting in motion a process of partial privatization.

Alternatively, whole sectors were threatened by exposure to global competition and had to be radically restructured because the state could no longer intervene to prop them up as in the past. This was the case of the coal and textile industry, largely located in northeast France around Lille and the Pas de Calais region.

The drive by the EU commission to end monopolies and increase cross-border competition was another important pressure imposing change on the structure of the French economy. The breath of competition was most obvious in the opening up of the telecom sector, which began with the grant of mobile phone licenses, allowing fresh operators to enter the fast-expanding telecom sector.

Admittedly the old protectionist reflexes did not disappear once the mobile licenses went to French companies and not outsiders. But France Telecom was partially privatized to face competition with the end of its fixed-line monopoly in 1999.

The next big state-run monopoly to be undermined was the energy sector. Here the process of change was both material and psychological, as Brussels imposed a progressive opening of the French electricity and gas market monopolized by EDF and Gaz de France. EDF had been a pillar of postwar reconstruction, had pioneered the large-scale development of French nuclear power, and had become the world's largest electricity group. It was also a household name for reliability and seen as a benign employer whose workforce was the fortress of the Communist-controlled CGT, the biggest of the three main trade-union federations in France. EDF paid for 3,500 workers who were allowed to be full-time union employees. EDF was forced to open up 20 percent of the industrial energy market to competition. Even this relatively small dent in EDF's monopoly obliged the electricity giant to compensate for the loss of market share by boosting its presence outside France. The purchase of overseas groups in turn forced EDF to adopt greater financial transparency and a capitalistic approach to management.

The search for funds to finance investment inevitably led EDF down the path of privatization. Despite strong union protests, who feared their privileges would be compromised—notably, their generous pensions—Chirac decided to proceed with privatization plans in the wake of his 2002 reelection. A similar tale on a smaller scale applied to Gaz de France.

Less visible but part of the same Brussels-imposed liberalization was the shake-up in the auctioneering business. French auctioneers—known as *commissaires priseurs*—possessed a professional status controlled by the Ministry of Justice, dating back to the late seventeenth century. It was a closed shop, with no outsider permitted to hold auctions in France. The *commissaires priseurs* fought a dogged rear-guard action to hold on to their monopoly against the onslaught of Christie's and Sotheby's, the slick international art auction houses.

The French auction monopoly should have ended in 1998 according to the timetable laid down by Brussels, but the necessary changes in legislation were delayed by a parliament in no hurry to let foreigners break this closed shop. In the event, the French auction business was not fully open to competition until four years later. By then French financier François Pinault had already become owner of Christie's and a major reorganization was taking place among the groups of *commissaires priseurs*, the bigger ones merging to be more competitive.

In the banking and insurance sector, whose privatization was set in motion earlier, a process of consolidation took place. The 1998 battle for the control of investment bank Paribas saw the first hostile takeover with an unseemly fight between BNP and Société Générale, who eventually triumphed. But those liberals who hoped to see the consolidation of French banking as a prelude to a cross-frontier concentration at the European level were disappointed. The Banque de France, backed by the finance ministry, insisted that no foreign bank could acquire a controlling stake in a French bank unless the center of decision making remained in France. Consolidation stopped at the French frontier.

Budgetary Pressures and the Stability Pact

Another set of pressures on France's economic structure came from the budgetary discipline imposed by the single currency.

Under the terms of the 1991 Maastricht treaty, and reinforced by the 1996 Stability Pact agreed in Dublin, EU member states were bound to observe strict guidelines in their budgetary policy. The budget deficit had to be kept below a ceiling of 3 percent of GDP save in exceptional circumstances and at the risk of a fine. The debt stock was also limited to a ceiling equivalent to 60 percent of GDP.

France had begun the 1990s with budget deficits well above 3 percent of GDP and was hard-pressed to comply with these strictures. Necessity overruled ideological objections as politicians hunted for means of raising money without making unpopular cuts in public spending. For instance, the annual demands of servicing the huge debts of the French national railways, a national icon with its high-speed trains, alone presented a major problem.

One of the simplest resorts was to sell state assets to ease the budgetary squeeze. From 1997 to 2002 a left-wing government with four Communist ministers presided over the Fifth Republic's largest sustained sell-off of state assets. The Jospin government steered clear of using the word "privatization." To the left this seemed too much like selling the crown jewels.

Such sensitivities led to restrictions on winding down the state stake in France Telecom: a parliamentary law was necessary should the state wish to go below a 51 percent controlling stake. This half-and-half approach to privatization proved the undoing of France Telecom. Unable to use its shares in paper transactions for its ambitious program of external acquisitions because this would dilute the state stake below 51 percent, France Telecom was obliged to borrow instead. When the international telecom bubble burst in 2001, France Telecom was landed with a mountain of debt to the tune of 70 billion euros. The government then struggled to find a formula that did not involve renationalization.

Overall, the Jospin administration obtained close to 40 billion euros in receipts from state asset sales over the five-year period, almost double that during the combined years of the Balladur (1993–1995) and Juppé (1995–1997) governments. More assets would have been sold during 2001–2002 had stock market conditions not deteriorated sharply. To protect the special status of EDF, Jospin battled his EU colleagues to defend the concept of such entities enjoying a special status by virtue of being a public service. He argued that they required the steady hand and support of the state to be able to offer a proper "service." The right-wing administration that emerged after the 2002 general elections did not feel the same compunction to defend EDF as a public service. Rather, the Raffarin government saw its overhaul and partial privatization as an important example of how the state should slim down its presence in the economy.

At a broader macroeconomic level, the single currency led to a sea change in the traditional role of French governments in formulating fiscal policy. By imposing budget-deficit constraints and debt ceilings, the Stability Pact removed a large part of the freedom governments had enjoyed in deciding the levels of taxation and borrowing. In political terms, it severely circumscribed the use of an essential electoral weapon: the promise of tax cuts and spending increases.

The Stability Pact strait jacket became a major issue for the center-right government after it won the 2002 parliamentary elections committed to honoring Chirac's pledges of tax cuts and defense spending increases. With a 2002 budget deficit likely to breach the 3 percent of GDP limit, the Brussels Commission and several Eurozone partners criticized the new government's budgetary proposals as irresponsible. The commission argued that in the Eurozone the irresponsibility of one member prejudiced all the others. Should the European Central Bank judge there to be inflationary risks from such fiscal laxity, then the likely response was raising interest rates—and so increasing the cost of debt service.

At first Chirac instructed the government to ignore these complaints, provoking a major confrontation with France's EU partners over the workings of the pact. Then in late 2002, faced with the prospect of a formal warning and a possible subsequent heavy fine, the government appeared willing to make budgetary adjustments in 2003. This incident, which also involved Germany and Portugal in differing forms, raised serious questions about the rigidity of the Stability Pact based on Bundesbank orthodoxy. But the political moral was that in future governments were not free to make electoral promises and pursue policies that were at odds with the strictures of a collective European endeavor to make a success of the euro.

A second aspect to euro-induced changes was a move toward tax harmonization across borders to prevent "tax-dumping"—that is, one nation unfairly profiting from widely differing tax levels. France had long been a country with heavy taxes. A large volume of tax receipts was necessary to pay for an expensive state machine and a high level of public services ranging from health to pensions and subsidized public transport.

Throughout the 1990s French governments had limited room for tax cuts. They were inhibited by the high built-in costs of the state machine that gave employment to almost one in four of the active workforce. Overall fiscal pressure did not fall below the equivalent of 45 percent of GDP—high in relation to the EU average. The big tax burden was mainly felt through heavy corporate taxes, a high rate of Value Added Tax (a consumption and sales tax, in France averaging 19.6 percent, against the lower EU norm of 17 percent), and big social security contributions. In contrast, individual income tax was relatively light. Remarkably, only seven million persons have to pay income tax, since low incomes are exempted.

Conflicts also emerged with Brussels over cuts in particular taxes. Chirac promised in his 2002 reelection campaign to cut the VAT applied to the restaurant business—in France a vociferous lobby accounting for a sizable part of employment in the services sector. However, the EU commission opposed selective VAT adjustments, arguing that it was better policy to reduce VAT levels across the board.

In the case of France, this was easier said than done. The VAT consumption and sales tax revenues, as opposed to income tax, accounted for an amazing 40 percent of total tax receipts. Any French government would obviously have to struggle to find an alternative source of revenue for even a general reduction in the rate of one percentage point. More generally, the advent of the single European currency, the euro, provided an increasingly level playing field across Europe, with a clear comparative display of prices in the individual countries. French governments thus became aware of the need to compete aggressively to attract inward investment. Competitive advantage became a complex equation of wage costs, tax incentives, infrastructure, and investment climate.

France remained attractive in the short term. It boasted a central location within the EU; public transport was modern and efficient; the workforce was well-educated, well-trained, and productive; and the quality of life ranked high. These trump cards ensured that France consistently gained the largest volume of inward investment in continental Europe from the mid-1990s onward while the EU economies were growing fast and adapting to the Internet-led technology boom.

But the investment climate was clouded by bureaucratic red tape, high corporate taxes, and labor rigidities. A further burden was added by the introduction of the thirty-five-hour week, phased progressively after 1998. Thus labor-intensive industries began to shift their focus toward lower-cost Eastern Europe and developing countries like China. Even the traditionally patriotic Renault announced in 2002 that its next car production plant would be in Eastern Europe.

Another phenomenon was France's growing inability to retain the "best and brightest." Mathematicians and computer experts were snapped up by Silicone Valley, and a new younger school of executives sought experience in the United States. Meanwhile some two hundred thousand French men and women moved across to London in the 1990s—to work in easy-to-find service jobs, to learn English, or to work in the City. This was a wake-up call to Paris, feeling the effects of the new mobility of labor attracted abroad by higher salaries, lower taxes, less rigid hierarchies, and greater opportunity for individual initiative. This movement also marked a break in the closed "hexagonal mentality"—one of seeing everything in terms of what happens within France's six-sided borders, and believing it to be best.

In corporate governance, keeping abreast of competitors' innovations began to be the order of the day with a not-always-healthy willingness to adopt what worked best. For instance, the quotation of big French companies on Wall Street, and the need to satisfy international investors and analysts with the publications of quarterly results, would have been unthinkable in Paris boardrooms as late as the mid-1990s. But by the turn of the century, the metamorphosis of French capitalism was such that these practices were readily incorporated.

Even stock options, branded by the left as the unacceptable face of Anglo-Saxon capitalist greed, found their way quietly into the system of corporate remuneration. Indeed, the prospect of earning better salaries with more challenging jobs began to tempt a growing number of high-flying civil servants—the so-called "enarchs"—away from promising careers in the administration and into business. When Laurent Fabius became finance minister in 1999 this one-time Socialist premier found difficulty in recruiting his staff. Working on the staff of France's most powerful ministry was traditionally one of the most coveted posts. But several of the talented people he wished to recruit had already moved to the private sector, and others were planning to make the jump.

The Weakening Ideological Debate

Hand in hand with a narrowing of government policy initiatives, the 1990s saw a gradual erosion of both the ideological divide and political ideologies themselves. The mainstream political parties experienced increasing difficulty in finding programs that differed from their adversaries yet squared with the strait jacket imposed by Brussels regulations and the demands of monetary union.

The violent upheavals of the May 1968 student protests were long forgotten. The Trotskyites of then—including a youthful long-haired Lionel Jospin (Gerhard Schröder had been a similar, if less radical, student protestor)—had become respectable political figures; several even had turned 180 political degrees to rest on the right. Voters increasingly adopted the view that governments could do little to improve their lot and abstention rates rose sharply.

By the 2002 presidential and parliamentary elections those going to the polling stations fell to a record low of 60 percent compared to 75 percent at the outset of the Fifth Republic. In tandem, the protest vote rose sharply: either in the form of spoiled and blank votes or votes being cast for parties that were antiestablishment.

The ideological confusion of the French electorate began during the fourteen-year Mitterrand presidency as the old left-right struggle for ideas waned. The political agenda on the left ceased to be dominated by the Communist Party, whose credibility was undermined by its slavish alignment with Moscow throughout the Cold War. On the other side of this divide gathered an ill-assorted group of right-wing parties who generally managed to bury their rivalries to fight elections. Yet their programs were based round the ambitions of their leaders, and their success lay in understanding the innate conservatism of the majority of the French voters.

That the French electorate naturally sympathized with the parties of the right was shown by the Fifth Republic's electoral record. In the twelve general elections held between 1958 and 2002, the right won nine. Of the five presidents, only Mitterrand was from the left. Mitterrand's dogged leadership in the 1970s eventually brought the non-Communist left more or less united under the Socialist banner and pushed the Communists from the ideological driver's seat. This success, coupled with divisions on the right, provided Mitterrand with the political respectability to win the 1981 presidential elections. On the back of this victory, the left swept to power in parliament for the first time since the 1936 Popular Front government.

But what did Mitterrand and the Socialists stand for? The initial policies marked Mitterrand as a man leaning toward the Marxists when he immediately embarked on a program of wide-scale nationalization. The nationalized companies included banks, chemical conglomerates, insurance groups, and steel concerns. Yet within four years nationalization had proven an economic and financial failure, and he was ready to reverse this policy. Such a speedy turnabout suggested that Mitterrand had introduced his nationalization policies to co-opt the Communists rather than out of any deeply felt ideological belief.

By the end of Mitterrand's second presidential term in the early 1990s, France had begun to open up its markets and reprivatize. The Socialist label had become almost impossible to define, blurring with a national consensus on a basic set of commitments shared by the moderate left and right. These encompassed a strong endorsement of the French welfare state with a comprehensive national health service; generous unemployment benefits; protection of labor and (belatedly) an enlarged right to strike; free public education; and generously funded state-run pensions. The right also shared the left's commitment to state-run public transport and a large budget supporting cultural activities.

The ideological confusion was again apparent on the left when Jospin unexpectedly won the general elections at the head of a Socialist-led coalition in 1997. Like Mitterrand, he felt the need to plant a leftist label at the outset. So he pressed ahead with the introduction of a controversial thirty-five-hour working week.

The idea of shortening the working week from thirty-nine to thirty-five hours had been floated in vague terms during the election campaign as a means of creating more jobs. In theory, if people worked fewer hours, businesses would recruit more workers to make up for the productivity thus lost. But neither the application of a reduced workweek nor its cost had been thought through. Jospin faced a wall of hostility from French employers, and the trade unions were dubious about the job-creation potential. But he still persisted with the measure, turning it into his flagship policy. Significantly, no other EU government, not even the left-wing governments, followed Jospin's left-wing lead, and the actual impact of the thirty-five-hour workweek on job creation was highly contested. Above all, the sharp fall in unemployment in the three-year period 1998–2000 occurred during sustained annual average economic growth of 3 percent when companies boosted recruitment to meet expanding demand. Jospin later explained his thinking at the time (see Box 9.4).

The French right must also share blame for sowing ideological confusion. Chirac won the presidency in 1995 on a simple theme. He promised he would end *"la fracture sociale,"* the social divide in society. His program was phrased to sound like that of the Socialists. It was aimed at appealing to the moderate left disillusioned by an ailing Mitterrand's feeble grip on the nation's pulse and the Socialists' corrupt control of state-owned companies. Yet within months Alain Juppé, his prime minister, was pursuing liberal economic and social policies that emphasized precisely this divide in society. Out of office again in 1997, the right proved unable to develop a coherent platform of new ideas.

The right's appeal in the 2002 general elections was less its own merits than the failings of the outgoing Jospin left-wing government. President Chirac's single most important election-winning pledge was to crack down on crime. His tough law-and-order platform deliberately stole a long-standing theme from the extreme right and placed it where the Socialists had seemed least credible. The latter were accused of having been too lax on immigration, which had led to a surge in the crime of big city suburbs.

But the real cause of the confusion and disillusion among the electorate was *cohabitation*, the conjunction of a president of one political color and a government of another. Who was really responsible for policy?

Chirac was the leader of the French right and therefore, although the presi-

Box 9.4   Lionel Jospin on the Thirty-Five-Hour Workweek

We inherited more than 3.1 million people out of work, of whom 1.1 million were long term unemployed. It was therefore evident that unemployment had to be attacked on all possible fronts, that of growth, confidence, that of business investment, of sustaining household consumption, and also on that of reducing the amount of time worked. This reduction in working time seemed to me to fit into the logic of technological developments and was made possible thanks to improved productivity. The 35-hour week also responded to a medium and long term economic logic. This measure also contained an element of symbolism: The government wanted to demonstrate its will to break with the fatalism concerning unemployment.

But why impose the change by a law? Above all, because it was a pledge made during the elections to the French electorate. It was not a question of coming to government and announcing this emblematic measure would be handed over to be debated . . . especially since the top business organization, the *Patronat,* was opposed in principle. We could not just wait while the matter was debated. The promise would have lacked credibility and the French people would say: "They are just like the others. They make promises . . . but never keep them." I was thus absolutely determined to pass this legislation as we had previously promised.

Source: "Le Temps de réponder, Paris," *Stock*, 2002, p. 120.

---

dent, de facto head of the parliamentary opposition opposed to the left-wing majority that had the government. But as head of state he could not play an overtly partisan role against the government. If he did so it would create permanent tension between president and prime minister with the risk of blocking the government process. Parliament, too, was caught up in the same dilemma. The solution in both instances was an unsatisfactory modus vivendi based on surface mutual restraint punctuated by occasional bursts of ill-temper between Chirac and Jospin.

Jospin sought to eliminate *cohabitation* with legislation that cut the presidential term from an overlong seven to five years and by fixing presidential elections six weeks before the parliamentary vote. This major constitutional change turned France's presidential system more presidential. This was evident in Chirac's 2002 reelection and the subsequent rejection of *cohabitation* in the vote for a unified movement of center-right parties, the new UMP, the president's party.

In theory these changes also encouraged the emergence of an alternating bipolar political system where right and left needed to differentiate their policies to win elections. Cast in opposition by their defeat in the presidential and parliamentary elections, the Socialists and their allies were forced to consider how to return to power. Should they try to move away from the center with a more leftist platform? Or to regain power should they become more social democrat and Blairite? The initial temptation was to move further to the left without being able to persuade other groups already occupying this space to join them in a convincing alliance.

Here the formation of the UMP movement to fight the 2002 elections and its subsequent victory marked a political turning point. The main component of the UMP was Chirac's Gaullist RPR party founded in the early 1970s. But the policy platform was infinitely more liberal than anything associated with this latter party or indeed the statist ideas of de Gaulle himself. Thus, even if a Gaullist trumpet still echoed in foreign policy during the Iraqi crisis, in domestic politics France had moved beyond Gaullism—and under a system more presidential than that enjoyed by the general.

Fringe Groups

The blurring of the distinctions between mainstream left and right had two significant repercussions on the electoral process.

It fostered a growing disinterest in politics that was reflected in low voter turnout. It also encouraged a protest vote to be cast in favor of parties representing the extremes at either end of the political spectrum. Both phenomena gained by France's system of a two-round vote in the presidential and parliamentary elections. Since the first round was rarely decisive, the voter could express a vote "from the heart." Having done so, this voter then became more difficult to persuade either to participate in the second round or to cast a ballot that was "useful" for electing a politician.

In the past, the prime beneficiary of the protest vote had been Jean-Marie Le Pen's extreme right National Front. Mitterrand had cleverly used this ex-paratrooper to split the vote on the right with his appeals to latent xenophobia and fear of France losing its identity within the new Europe. His inflammatory rhetoric was openly racist, seeking to curb the wave of North African–led immigration. Yet he resonated with those who felt excluded from the system—small shopkeepers, retirees, the unemployed.

By the 2002 presidential elections, Le Pen had to soften his racist tone and switched his appeal to being an antiestablishment candidate, the champion of the marginalized. He never saw himself as a winner but, rather, as someone stirring the political soup to the discomfort of the establishment. In the first-round vote he scored a remarkable 16.9 percent—beating Jospin to second place. This led Le Pen to take part in an unusual second-round runoff against Chirac in which the left called for a "republican" vote to support Chirac to preserve French democracy from electing a neofascist head of state. Chirac polled an unprecedented 80 percent plus. It was a remarkable turnaround for a man who had entered the presidential race in a weak position, discredited by a string of corruption scandals related to his days as a free-spending mayor of Paris in the late 1980s and early 1990s.

Overall the first presidential round in April 2002 saw more than a third of the votes going to candidates either on the extreme right or the extreme left. None of the programs of these candidates contained serious policy details. Three Trotskyite candidates, each one advocating an end to the French bourgeois-run state, polled almost 11 percent, while Communist leader Robert Hue gained less than 4 percent. Polls revealed part of the traditional Communist vote had switched to Le Pen as their champion.

Certainly there were more similarities than differences in the socioeconomic profile of those voting on the extremes. All were victims in one form or another of a fast-changing world that they resented and in which they felt their grievances went unheard, whether over employment, immigration, or rising crime. The common element was being "anti"—antiestablishment, anti-Europe, anti-immigration, antiglobalization. The basic forum for these "anti" grievances was extraparliamentary.

Violence lurked at the edges of this anger against society and its institutions. This was underlined by a bungled attempt to assassinate Chirac during the annual Bastille Day parade in 2002. Police investigations showed the preparations to be amateurish and the product of a lone, grudge-driven venture. Nevertheless, the youthful would-be assassin belonged to a fringe student movement linked to a breakaway segment of the National Front; and at least one shot from his .22 rifle was fired at Chirac before the gunman was overpowered by alert members of the crowd.

The Centralized State

Amid the external pressures working change on France, the one seemingly immutable element was the organization of the French state. The Fifth Republic followed the principle of previous constitutions in endorsing a highly centralized state.

When the Fifth Republic started out, France was not alone in this respect. Of the larger countries, Britain and Spain were also then highly centralized. Yet democratic Spain initiated an experiment in regional autonomy that led from the early 1980s to a major devolution of power from Madrid to the regions. Britain under the premiership of Tony Blair embraced, a decade later, a milder form of devolution with regional parliaments in Scotland and Wales.

Alone within the EU, France clung to a model of the state whose structure looked increasingly rigid and at odds with the decentralization trend. Brussels had come to see regions as efficient instruments of development, and a more general political view held that regional government closed the democratic gap between rulers and ruled.

Aware of this change in sentiment, Jospin took an important step in July 2000 to breach the principle of the centralized state. He proposed that the Mediterranean island of Corsica be granted a limited degree of autonomy.

Jospin acted out of exasperation. Previous governments had unsuccessfully tried a variety of carrot-and-stick approaches in an attempt to head off terrorist actions by a small group of hard-line Corsican nationalists seeking independence while simultaneously appeasing moderate nationalist demands to recognize the island's special status within the republic. On each occasion the issue of autonomy had been avoided because it clashed with the principle of the "indivisibility" of the republic.

The Jospin proposal envisaged merging the island's two administrative departments into a single unit and creating a new Corsican assembly with the right to legislate on specific issues relating to the environment, economic development and tourism; the teaching of Corsican in kindergartens and primary schools; and a phasing out of special Corsican inheritance laws. The grant of this highly circumscribed autonomy was conditioned on an end to violence on the island and a four-year phase-in period.

Traditionalists on the right and convinced republicans on the left reacted with hostility to this breach of the centralist taboo. Jean-Pierre Chevènement, the outspoken interior minister with a reputation for quixotic gestures, resigned in protest. President Chirac showed his displeasure in February 2001 by refusing to allow the draft Corsican law to be placed on the agenda of the weekly formal cabinet meeting over which he presided. This was the first instance during the Fifth Republic of a head of state blocking discussion of an item in cabinet.

Chirac then called on the constitutional council to rule on the proposal's validity, resulting in a considerable watering down of the text. In particular, the constitutional council decided that the new Corsican assembly could not initiate laws; it could merely "modify" existing parliamentary legislation within the limited range outlined by Jospin. The final law was an unsatisfactory compromise. But this experiment was endorsed in the opinion polls and the right was split. Two former prime ministers—Eduard Balladur and Raymond Barre—as well as ex-president Valéry Giscard d'Estaing backed the legislation. More importantly, it set a precedent for other regions to claim greater individual recognition. The special status accorded Corsican (a corruption of Italian and Genoese dialect) raised questions about how France's other minority languages be treated. Breton nationalists, for example, had long been pushing for increased use of Breton. In the Basque country the growing radicalism of Spanish Basque nationalism had spilled over into France with a determined, and at times aggressive, move to encourage more native Basque speakers. At the other end of the Pyrenees, the Catalan autonomous government with its dynamic center in Barcelona financed the revival of Catalan in the Languedoc region—lost to French cultural influence in the seventeenth century. In the North of France, around

Lille, the removal of formal frontiers with Belgium under the Schengen agreement on EU internal movement also fostered a new sense of identity among local Flemish speakers.

Jospin in 1998 promoted legislation that would have France belatedly adopt the Council of Europe's charter on the treatment of regional languages. "Respect for and promotion of pluralism means accepting the contribution to our heritage of regional languages and cultures," he said. But this ran up against the unequivocal nature of Article 2 of the Republic's constitution: "The language of the Republic is French." As a result, the status of France's minority languages—Alsatian, Basque, Breton, Catalan, Flemish, and Provençal (Occitan)—remained unresolved. The sole exception was Corsican. Even so, 335,000 students in kindergarten and primary schools, controlled either by the state or privately financed, received some form of lessons in a regional language. Each year the demand for such lessons has increased.

One way of reconciling French constitutional objections to regional autonomy was dressing up the change and presenting it as decentralization. This approach was proposed by Jean-Pierre Raffarin, an astute provincial politician chosen by Chirac to be premier after the center-right had won the 2002 general elections. Instead of making Corsica an exception to the rule of the unitary state, Raffarin argued it was more consistent to permit a generalized decentralization of power. He sought to do this by allowing local authorities the right to "experiment." This was shorthand for allowing them space for new initiatives in education, regional development, transportation, and coordination with neighboring authorities.

His twofold aim was laudable. He sought to use devolution of power to local authorities as a means of cutting the size of the state bureaucracy and to bring decision making closer to the electorate, who in turn would demand greater accountability. But he, too, ran into constitutional objections when he tried to introduce the idea into Article 1 of the constitution that the French state had "a decentralized organization." This contradicted both the spirit and letter of the article that declared France as an "indivisible" republic. Other objections focused on the existing bureaucratic infrastructure, which was already overloaded. Mitterrand initiated a modest decentralization process in 1982 by creating a new system of regional government, obliterating the role of the prefects in the departments.

The regions had been given a lukewarm reception by the general public, since they reflected neither historic boundaries nor identities. For instance, the Burgundy region bore scant relation to historic Burgundy. The regions were run by elected councils and given control over broad economic development plans like infrastructure, plus management of secondary education and professional training. But they were essentially an extra layer of government, with little to justify their staff costs or the pay for their elected politicians. A total of

550,000 people held elected local office; and in the two decades since the regions were created local authority staff doubled to 1.5 million.

The regions received only 10 percent of treasury transfers to the local authorities, a good 30 percent went to the departments, and the lion's share went to the municipalities that were both politically more important and could tap local rates and business taxes. Raffarin himself had been president of the Poitou-Charentes region in southwestern France and knew the issues at stake. But his plans of enhancing the regions' role, especially in economic development, ran up against objections from the prefects—the most powerful members of the civil service. They believed the regions could acquire a higher profile only at the expense of the *départements* that they themselves controlled. Civil servants who opposed any change in their status were also well aware that effective decentralization—of necessity—entailed a problematical shake-up of the public administration. Here huge vested interests were at stake.

INSEE, the official statistics institute, assessed the strict civil service and military payroll at 3.1 million in 2000. Of these 1.2 million alone were employed by the education ministry. But the overall number was closer to double that figure if people working in hospitals, local administrations, and state-controlled companies were included. This six-million-strong bloc within the national workforce constituted an enormously complex and powerful set of lobbies opposed to virtually any change in the status quo. The essential fears were job losses and curtailment of pension privileges that allowed people to retire earlier on higher benefits and lower contributions than the private sector. Resistance to any loss of these *acquis* (acquired rights) benefited from the fact that the public sector remained the one area where trade unions had muscle, through the threat of disruption to vital services. The government in 1993 deliberately steered clear of touching the public sector privileges when Balladur introduced a phased increase in pension contributions and the retirement age.

It therefore required sharp political antennae and great determination to bring about change in this civil service culture. The first two attempts at reform in the 1990s were abject failures. The Juppé government tried to overhaul public sector pension privileges, beginning with the railways in 1995. Under pressure to bring the budget deficit down to meet the Maastricht criteria, Juppé rushed at reform and was undone by his arrogant, confrontational tactics, which allowed striking railwaymen to enjoy a high degree of public sympathy.

Acutely conscious of the Juppé failure, Jospin made a timid and more selective stab at cutting back the public administration. In early 1999 he sanctioned a reform of the finance ministry centered on merging tax assessment and tax collection operations that had been separate arms since the Napoleonic era. The unions correctly realized that the merger was a prelude to a wider shake-up with consequent job losses, and immediately the finance ministry civil servants went on strike. After less than two months' protest, Jospin made a scapegoat of

Christian Sautter, his finance minister, and sacked him for the fiasco. Serious reform was shelved for the remainder of the legislature.

Raffarin was even more haunted by the Juppé experience, since this was suffered by a government in which he was a junior minister. But by now, the budgetary pressures to begin structural reform of the state apparatus were far greater. His tactic lay in pursuing reform through stealth and consensus. A window of opportunity lay in a policy of nonreplacement of retirees. Between 2002 and 2015, 60 percent of the civil service were due to retire, with the numbers beginning to accelerate from 2005 as the baby boomer generation left the workforce. The value of the Raffarin reforms therefore hinged on the percentage of jobs that the government chose to leave unfilled, coupled with the subsequent improvements in labor flexibility and productivity. The start was not promising. The 2003 budget provisioned for a net cut of a mere twelve hundred jobs. Yet without a more radical nonreplacement policy, the budgetary burden of such a large public sector would be reflected in future pension liabilities. By the year 2000, over 3.3 million people were receiving public-sector pensions of one sort or another. These pensions were not capitalized (i.e., not based on a system of savings) and not properly funded, since individual contributions were on a pay-as-you-go basis.

All the governments of right and left during the 1990s realized that France was building up unfunded future liabilities of enormous proportions. The OECD showed as early as 1994 that France, without a system of private pension funds to back up state pensions, had net liabilities equivalent to double the gross domestic product (216 percent of GDP), against 43 percent in the United States and 100 percent in the UK. The best the Jospin government could do was to commission three reports that merely highlighted the problem and the unpalatable choices ahead. One of these reports, released in 2000, revealed that if the system of civil service pensions remained unchanged, by 2020 it would account for 60 percent of all annual pension payments. With unquestionable statistics like these, Raffarin was able to proceed with a limited but unprecedented overhaul of public-sector pensions in June 2003. Against strong union opposition, parliament pushed through a law extending retirement age requirements for civil servants to the level of the private sector by 2008.

Pensions were one side of the coin of the changing demographic profile of France. The other was the aging population itself. The percentage of people in the active workforce was shrinking, while over the next few decades the retirement numbers would rise sharply. Between 1980 and 2000, life expectancy rates rose by five years for men and four years for women, to seventy-five and eighty-two, respectively. INSEE projects that 20 percent of the French population would be over sixty by 2020. The proportion was expected to reach a third of the population by the 2030s, representing a huge increase in the cost of caring for the health of this aging population as well as covering the pension charge.

Conclusion

The successful passing of public-sector pension reform laws in mid-2003 demonstrated that the French right could introduce structural change, for once without being intimidated by street protest. But the measures were so limited and the funding so insufficient that the pension debate will dominate the socio-economic agenda in the short and medium term. The softly-softly approach to reform of the present center-right administration means that France has yet to make up its mind on two key interrelated domestic questions. Do people want to continue with the big state apparatus? If so, are they ready to pay its very considerable cost? If the answer to both questions is yes, then the politicians have little room for maneuver. But, equally, if they demand the same level of services while the state spends less, the political choices risk unpopularity.

The prime pressure for a slimmer state and further liberalization of the economy will continue to come from outside France. The main forces of change will be Brussels regulation, EU enlargement, peer group pressure within the Stability and Growth Pact, and the requirements of global competition. France will retain a strong industrial base but in the medium term changes in EU agricultural funding will affect the heavily protected farming sector. The damage caused to business confidence by the introduction of the 35-hour week is being rectified, but France cannot easily reduce its high labor overheads due to the need to fund the expensive social security system.

The constitutional changes shortening the presidential term from seven to five years have sharply reduced the likelihood of a future *cohabitation*. The ultimate check on presidential power lies in the voters opting for another *cohabitation*. But this situation could lead to a constitutional stalemate between president and parliament, each claiming equal popular legitimacy. The smoother functioning of the executive certainly places a dangerous amount of power in the hands of the president. The enhanced and highly personalized presidential system lacks sufficient checks and balances for its own good, and in particular undermines the vigor of parliamentary debate and initiative. This constitutional development also risks widening the gap between the politicians and the electorate, in turn creating more space for the extremes of the right and left to operate. The increasing disaffection with politics is already making it harder to build a consensus on sensitive issues like immigration, and it encourages protest. It also plays into the hands of the extremists on the left and right who denounce the dangers of EU enlargement.

Foreign relations will remain conditioned by the conviction that France's diplomatic weight in Europe is reinforced by acting in concert with Germany. The strong emphasis on the Franco-German axis is not without risks. France could be linking itself to a partner who proves much weaker than expected, both diplomatically and economically. But the importance of the Berlin–Paris axis is only likely to change if and when Britain makes up its mind whether to join the Eurozone. If Britain were to embrace the single currency, France might be constrained to consider an informal tripartite directorate to steer the EU. Such a directorate would add greater equilibrium to the heart of Europe as the United States increasingly disengages militarily, and even politically, from the Old Continent. However, Britain does not share Chirac's view of a "multipolar" world—a vision that ultimately means dissociating from a close transatlantic alliance. The rivalries and divisions that surfaced within Europe during the Iraqi crisis can be papered over but will not be so quickly forgotten. The extraordinarily complex process of trying to make EU enlargement work will also test France's relations with the former Eastern Bloc countries.

France will continue to play a high-profile role on the international stage by virtue of its former colonies, the huge geographic spread of its overseas *départements*, its Security Council membership, and its determination to defend the French language against the onslaught of English. The defense of the French language—and, by extension, French culture—remains a national imperative. Thus, as English makes further inroads in all spheres of life, the issue will become more sensitive, making France more complex in its dealings with the Anglo-Saxon world. Yet it is questionable how much mileage Chirac can wring from his doctrine of a multipolar world. Shaping policy around a strategy that is designed to contain America's freewheeling use of its hegemonic power sounds appealing to many nations worried about Washington's unchecked behavior. But can France set itself up either as Washington's intellectual and diplomatic sparring partner or its open critic and opponent? Such an influential role is possible only if the United Nations remains a central institution in the preservation of world order. If the United States decides that working through the UN limits its autonomy to act militarily and politically on the global stage, then the value of this institution diminishes. Chirac may well be proven right in his warnings before the Iraqi conflict about the dangers of invading and occupying that country. But he failed to prevent the war and subsequently was obliged to endorse a United States–sponsored UN resolution on Iraq's postwar reconstruction. This suggests that France will seek gain where it can, punch above its diplomatic weight whenever allowed by its European partners, and avoid a lasting break with Washington. The danger in Franco-American relations lies in a failure of the two administrations to understand their respective national cultures and how their very different institutions work. When France rows with its European partners, each knows the other's history. The EU link, moreover, compels daily cooperation across a huge and complex canvas. Neither of these considerations necessarily applies in dealings with the United States.

Suggestions for Further Reading

Fenby, Jonathan. *On the Brink: The Trouble with France*. London: Little, Brown, 1998.
Hoffmann, Stanley. *Decline or Renewal? France since the 1930s*. New York: Viking, 1974.

Jack, Andrew. *The French Exception: France Still So Special?* London: Profile Books, 1999.

Johnson, Jo, and Martine Orange. *The Man Who Tried to Buy the World: The Rise and Fall of Jean-Marie Messier.* New York: Penguin, 2003, in press.

Jospin, Lionel. "Modern Socialism." Pamphlet. London: Fabian Society, 1999.

Lacouture, Jean. *Mitterrand: Une histoire de Français.* 2 vols. Paris: Seuil, 1998.

Ross, George. *Jacques Delors and European Integration.* Oxford: Oxford University Press, 1995.

Sa'adah, Anne. *Contemporary France: A Democratic Education.* Lanham, Md.: Rowman & Littlefield, 2003.

Schmidt, Vivien. *From State to Market: The Transformation of French Business and Government.* Cambridge: Cambridge University Press, 1996.

Simmons, Harvey. *The French National Front.* Boulder, Colo.: Westview, 1996.

Tiersky, Ronald. *François Mitterrand: A Very French President.* Lanham, Md.: Rowman & Littlefield, 2003.

———. *France in the New Europe: Changing yet Steadfast.* Belmont, Calif.: Wadsworth, 1994.

Védrine, Hubert (with Dominique Moisi). *Les cartes de la France: à l'heure de la mondialisation.* Paris: Fayard, 2000.

CHAPTER 10

Britain

In and Out of Europe?

Michael Mannin

Britain

Population: 60.2 million
Area in Square Miles: 94,548
Population Density per Square Mile: 637
GDP (in billion dollars, 2001): $1,550.2
GDP per capita (purchasing power parity in dollars, 2001): $26,369
Joined EC/EU: January 1, 1973
Joined NATO: 1949
Political Parties:
Conservative and Unionist Party
Democratic Unionist Party (Northern Ireland)
Liberal Democrats
New Labour Party
Party of Wales (Plaid Cymru)
Scottish National Party or SNP
Sinn Fein (Northern Ireland)
Social Democratic and Labour Party or SDLP (Northern Ireland)
Ulster Unionist Party (Northern Ireland)

Sources: "Organisation for Economic Co-operation and Development," at
   www.oecd.org/home/ (accessed August 5, 2003); "2003 World Population
   Data Sheet," at www.prb.org/pdf/WorldPopulationDS03_Eng.pdf
   (accessed August 5, 2003); "The World Factbook," August 1, 2003, at
   cia.gov/cia/publications/factbook/index.html (accessed October 6, 2003).

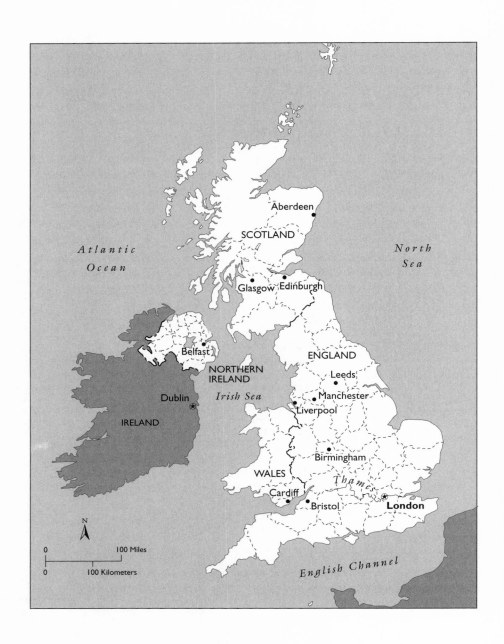

Introduction

The words "political earthquake" are used rather too often in journalism to describe events that prove ultimately rather more mundane than newspapers and TV news would like them to be. In Britain on May 2, 1997, however, a new door in British politics had opened with startling and, it was perceived, great consequences for British politics and society as it faced the twenty-first century. The election of a "New Labour" government with the massive legislative majority of 179 and the collapse of the Conservative Party after eighteen years of continuous rule indeed qualified as a political earthquake in British electoral history. Somewhat symbolically the sun shone throughout the British Isles on the Friday after that election, as many families celebrated what seemed a new political dawn for politics in the UK.

Some four years later, in 2001, there appeared to be a ringing endorsement of New Labour in the shape of another resounding electoral victory for Prime Minister Blair's "Third Way" government and another potential five years in power. No other Labour prime minister had secured a large enough second-term majority to achieve the opportunity for a radical impact on policy making. As Table 10.1 shows, Labour governments since 1945 had achieved only two six-year periods in office, while the Conservative party had dominated the sec-

Table 10.1   UK Governments, 1945–2001

Elections	Governing Party	Parliamentary Majority	Time in Office (years)
1945	Labour	147	5
1950	Labour	6	1
1951	Conservative	16	5
1955	Conservative	59	4
1959	Conservative	99	4
1964	Labour	5	2
1966	Labour	97	4
1970	Conservative	31	4
1974 (Feb)	Labour	None	(8 months)
1974 (Oct)	Labour*	4	6
1979	Conservative	44	4
1983	Conservative	144	4
1987	Conservative	102	4
1992	Conservative	21	5
1997	Labour	179	4
2001	Labour	167	Ongoing to 2006

* Including a short Labour-Liberal Parliamentary Pact (1978).

ond half of the century as the party of government, with long terms of office lasting from 1951 to 1964, from 1970 to 1974, and then from 1979 to 1997, the Thatcher–Major period—a remarkable electoral achievement.

The brief description of British postwar politics that follows places the Blair government in a broader context than merely its large parliamentary majorities. Here we introduce the larger themes of this chapter that make for the "exceptionalism" of the British relationship with continental Europe. These themes are:

- the salience of British contemporary history as a powerful factor in shaping political pathways;
- the various attempts at modernization—economic, institutional, and social;
- the significance of national identity and the evidence of disintegration within the four-nation United Kingdom; and
- the Europe–Atlantic dilemma that has faced both Conservative and Labour administrations since 1945.

The Post-1945 Legacy

The choice of the year 1945 to commence an explanation of contemporary British politics is apposite to the aim of this volume: to set national politics within its broader European context. The end of World War II meant the collapse of prewar world order as well as fascism and the rise of new phenomena—particularly the international involvement in European (and world) affairs of two previous allies but soon to be protagonists, the United States and USSR. As well as the rigidity imposed by ideological and military rivalries of the western and eastern blocs, the end of World War II also hastened in the demise of the Empire, an adjustment that Britain's politicians and public acknowledged with difficulty. The Cold War ran through to the last decade of the century, and its impact on British domestic politics and foreign policy was a major determining factor throughout the period.

This, together with an associated decline in Britain's position as a world economic player, needed to be reconciled with the triumphalism of a successful war outcome—for Britain had stood "alone" for two years before the welcome military support of the United States became available—and the shared view of elites and population that Britain remained a world player in the postwar international scenario. These factors continue to color attitudes and behaviors within the British political system and constituted a problematic cultural legacy during later adjustments to regional (European) rather than global views of Britain's international position and future.

Post–World War II triumphalism helped to shape domestic politics in a rather more direct manner. The electorate, with high expectations of peacetime, returned a Labour government to take up the task of social and economic re-newal with a Commons majority not matched for forty years until another tri-umphalist "postwar" era—the Falklands/Malvinas Thatcher period (1983–1990). Peace ushered in social democracy and a Keynesian political economy that was to last through to the mid-1970s; this was shared in both Labour and Conservative "consensus" politics. The "welfare state" established during the 1945–1951 Labour governments was consolidated under subsequent Conserva-tive and Labour administrations and was to give sacred-cow status to such ser-vices as a comprehensive National Health Service, universal family allowances, wide-ranging social security, and free secondary education. The nationalization of important industries such as coal, steel, and rail transportation in this period completed a genuine revolution in domestic policies when compared to the pre-war situation. This continuity, even after the return of a Conservative adminis-tration, which was to last until 1964, placed Britain firmly in the mainstream of a European mixed-economy philosophy that existed in each of the nation-states destined to join the European Union. That philosophy, translated into votes, meant that until 1970 Labour and Conservative parties regularly polled close to 90 percent of the votes cast in British general elections. (See Table 10.2.)

The postwar Labour government, however, was far less radical when con-sidering its foreign policies and domestic institutional reform. As we have sug-gested, historical and cultural factors, together with postwar external realities, set boundaries within which a radical British government had to work. Several European countries—notably France, Italy, and, inevitably, West Germany—made serious institutional changes to their structures of government in response to their prewar and wartime experiences. Others, like Poland, Czechoslovakia, and Yugoslavia, created political systems in response to the military and eco-nomic strictures of their dominating neighbor, the USSR. Uninvaded and victo-rious, Britain thought no significant changes to British political institutions were necessary, apart from reducing the delaying powers of the House of Lords as a second chamber, and no such changes were seen as politically feasible. In consequence, the monarchy; the status of Scotland, Wales, and, significantly, Northern Ireland; the prevailing electoral arrangements; and subnational gov-ernment were all left broadly untouched until the 1960s, when a second Labour administration in a piecemeal and generally halfhearted manner began to tackle the question of institutional reform. The British political system in the postwar era administered a massive welfare program and mixed economy through a cen-trally directed, London-based unitary government; power concentrated on the leaders of either the dominant Labour or Conservative party in the House of Commons, thus ensuring political legitimacy on the majority party—until the next general election. (See Box 10.1.)

While strong government was on face value a major advantage of this West-minster model,[1] the dangers of an "elected dictatorship," ineffectual mecha-nisms of parliamentary accountability, and elite domination of the decision-

Table 10.2   Seats and Votes in General Elections since 1945

Elections	Conservative Seat No	Conservative Vote %	Labour Seat No	Labour Vote %	Liberals (Now Liberal Democrats) Seat No	Liberals (Now Liberal Democrats) Vote %	Others Seat No	Others Vote %	Total Number of MPs	Electoral Turnout
1945	210	39.6	393	48.0	12	9.0	25	3.4	640	75.5
1950	298	43.4	315	46.1	9	9.1	3	1.4	625	83.6
1951	321	48.0	295	48.8	6	2.6	3	0.6	625	84.0
1955	345	49.7	277	46.4	6	2.7	2	1.2	630	76.0
1959	365	49.4	258	43.8	6	5.9	1	0.9	630	78.7
1964	304	43.4	317	44.1	9	11.2	0	1.3	630	77.1
1966	253	41.9	364	48.0	12	8.6	1	1.5	630	75.8
1970	330	46.4	288	43.1	6	7.5	6	3.0	635	70.0
1974 (Feb)	297	37.9	301	37.2	14	19.3	23*	5.6	635	81.0
1974 (Oct)	277	35.8	319	39.2	13	18.3	26	6.7	635	72.8
1979	339	43.9	269	36.9	11	13.8	16	5.4	635	78.0
1983	397	42.4	209	27.6	23**	25.4	21	4.6	650	72.7
1987	376	42.3	229	30.8	22**	22.5	23	4.4	650	75.3
1992	336	41.9	271	34.4	20	17.8	24	5.9	651	77.7
1997	165	30.7	418	43.2	46	16.8	30	9.3	659	71.4
2001	166	32.7	412	42.0	52	18.8	29	6.5	659	59.4

* Northern Irish MPs are counted as "others" from 1974.
** In 1983 and 1987 "Liberal" includes the SDP/Liberal Alliance.

making process, and thus the marginalization of some socioeconomic and geographically peripheral groups, were inherent in such a system. A nineteenth-century parliamentary system had grafted upon it a massive twentieth-century welfare state, and, though able to operate through the discipline of national political parties, it was to prove wanting in the delivery of a pluralist democracy as an effective check on the executive and its administration.

Equally, the economic problems—of industrial decline, technological obsolescence, uncompetitively priced exports, and a vulnerable international currency (the pound sterling)—invited radical economic policies that the consensus style of welfare politics of both Labour and Conservative governments was unable to deliver. The 1950s and 1960s were the era of stop-go policies—where successive governments would attempt to manipulate economic conditions prior to an election to their electoral advantage and inevitably to the detriment of the economy. Attempts to replace Keynesian "demand management" with more balanced budget approaches were thwarted by strong labor union repre-

Box 10.1   British Government

The Westminster Model

Britain is a parliamentary democracy whose national politicians are elected to the House of Commons by a first-past-the-post, single-member-constituency electoral system. There is also a second chamber, the House of Lords, whose members are primarily appointed by party leaders in the House of Commons. The second chamber is currently under reform. While the Lords plays a formal, revising role in the process of legislation, the Commons is in practice the most politically powerful chamber. Its constitutional authority to legislate on any matter (parliamentary sovereignty) is enhanced by its role as the major source of the British executive—the prime minister, Cabinet, and departmental ministers. The government is created from the ranks of the party able to command a majority in the Commons. Formally the government survives as long as it commands the support of the Commons—in practice the majority party, or until a Parliament ends (maximum 5 years). The final choice of an election date is with the Prime Minister. Parliamentary parties provide the opportunity for majoritarian government; a majority party will not share power with opposition parties, whose task it is to oppose—and wait its electoral opportunity. There is thus no separation of legislative–executive functions; but while senior judges have seats in the Lords, there is in practice a clear separation of the judicial from the political process. However, the creation of an independent supreme court is currently under consideration. While the PM and cabinet have a collective responsibility to the Commons, a series of factors have enhanced the status of government and weakened that of Parliament. Powerful majority party discipline, extensive policy initiatives, direct appeal to the electorate, and international responsibilities and treaties, not least those associated with the EU, have reduced parliamentary powers. At best the Westminster model delivers responsible Cabinet Government: in the second part of the twentieth century many commentators have suggested a better epithet for a British government is prime ministerial dictatorship. However, the myth if not the reality of parliamentary sovereignty is often utilized by politicians to challenge any reduction in the decision-making powers of British government by moves toward further EU integration.

sentation often culminating in bitter strikes, such as the miners' strikes of 1972 and 1974 against the Conservative Heath administration and the "Winter of Discontent" of 1978–1979 during the Labour Callaghan government. In these circumstances both institutional and economic reforms were limited by short-term government reactions mainly concerned with responding to economic crises and attempting to reconstitute electoral fortunes. These domestic circumstances were exacerbated by the rise in oil prices and the collapse of the postwar Bretton Woods system which had, till 1973, provided a degree of certainty for the international currency and trading activities that were so significant to the UK's economy and international standing.

One response to this catalog of problems was a reluctant recognition that Britain's economic future might well be better protected by joining the European Common Market. Initial attempts in 1961 and 1967 were thwarted by a mixture of British government miscalculation and French reluctance to admit a halfhearted partner. It was not until 1972 that a more confident and positive application led by the EU enthusiast Edward Heath proved successful. A subsequent Labour administration endorsed this major step in a different direction by referendum, in 1975.

Membership in the EU did not solve Britain's domestic ills. A spent Labour administration was replaced in 1979 by the first Thatcher government, which was to create new parameters for economic policy—the Thatcher "revolution"—which fundamentally challenged most of the consensus assumptions established in the period following World War II. Her revolution brought with it the conditions for profound economic and, eventually, political change in the late 1990s and is worth our attention in seeking an explanation of the nature of current UK politics and the proclaimed "Europeanism" of New Labour.

The Thatcher Revolution

There is considerable debate in British political and academic circles as to whether the extended period of Conservative government led by Margaret Thatcher and subsequently by John Major (1990–1997) was indeed revolutionary. Box 10.2 compares the characteristic of consensus politics, 1945–1976,[2] with that of Thatcher's brand of market-driven conservatism.

Superficially, the changes within the context of the relatively stable nature of British postwar consensus seem to represent "blue-water thinking." After a first parliamentary term and with the popularity of the victory in the 1982 Falklands/Malvinas war behind her, Mrs. Thatcher commenced a controversial political journey that has continued long after her loss of office in 1990. The UK economy was indeed refitted by the end of the 1980s. The denationalization of the gas, water, and electricity industries and their sale on the open market (privatization) proved electorally popular, as members of the public were encouraged to invest in these and other new companies on the stock market. This, together with the establishment of generous "right to buy" for tenants in public housing, who formed a substantial voting minority, was designed to create a "property owning democracy" of individuals with a share in "the market." Full employment as the main goal of macroeconomic policy was abandoned, in favor of supply-side policies devoted to containing inflation. Monetarism with its emphasis on control of the supply of money via interest rate manipulation and, later, the search for stable exchange rates via Britain's entry to the European Exchange Rate System (1990) provided a market "hidden hand" solution to inflation, and thus price and wage levels.

Box 10.2   Consensus Politics versus Market-Driven Conservatism

Welfare Consensus, 1945–1976

Neoliberalism and Market Economics, 1979–97

1. Principles
- macroeconomic policy (e.g., fiscal and monetary policy) used to create demand and stimulate growth
- microeconomic policy (e.g., incomes policy) to restrain inflation

1. Principles
- reverses Keynes by using macroeconomic policy to control inflation and microeconomic policy to create supply-side incentives for growth

2. Characteristics
- principle of equality
- growth of the public sector
- government incentives and controls on industry
- improvement of government tools for control (e.g., statistics, expanded government borrowing)
- commitment to full employment

2. Characteristics
- social and economic inequality seen as stimulus
- replaces full employment commitment by the control of inflation
- monetarism (controlling the money supply) partly by reducing government expenditure
- reliance on the free market (deregulation) rather than government regulation
- privatization rather than nationalization
- curbing of trade union power seen as causing unemployment

3. Government controls by:
- fiscal policy (expenditure and taxation)
- lending decisions
- close cooperation with main economic groups (corporatism)

3. Change of Policy
- Control of money supply had to be replaced by use of interest rates to control inflation
- Sale of public corporations to create popular capitalism

4. Problems
- exaggerated view of government power (neglects influence of foreign trade, cooperation of other governmental organizations, large business organizations, etc.)
- assumes continuing economic growth
- high level of social expectation not always economically viable

4. Problems
- difficulties in defining and controlling money supply
- some public spending cannot be cash limited (e.g., many social security payments)
- politically difficult to make substantial cuts in many benefits and services (e.g., health services)
  a. cuts that are made create wide economic disparities and social difficulties (e.g., unemployment, cuts in social security, underclass)
  b. difficulty of controlling demand (e.g., savings levels)
  c. influence international economy, IMF, and World Bank
- policy of deregulation implies government has no other instrument except interest rates to control inflation

Such a change in economic goals and mechanisms was to have radical and, indeed, lasting consequences for consensus politics and the corporatist collaboration with trade unions and employers that was a feature of postwar governments. A miners' strike—the bitterest confrontation that the UK had experienced since the general strike of 1926—lasted for twelve months, 1984–1985, and polarized the UK electorate between those who gave support for Thatcher's revolution and those who wished to sustain the corporatist-consensus politics. The miners' arguments were roundly defeated; further legislation reduced the bargaining power of trades unions, and the Labour Party, despite limited attempts to move away from its corporatist-socialist roots, was once again defeated in the 1987 election by a still substantial vote in favor of "Thatcherism." But the Thatcherite search to end the "dependency culture" was not so successful; radical changes to the welfare state were to prove more electorally problematic. The public continued to demand free access to health and education, and the worst aspects of unemployment continued to be ameliorated by a still generous (by U.S. standards) benefits system. Spending on social security increased by almost two-fifths in real terms (1979–1990).

But what did Thatcherism mean, and what were its consequences and logical outcomes? It must be pointed out at the outset of such an evaluation that Mrs. Thatcher's revolution has had as great an impact on her own party—the Conservatives—as it has had on the Labour Party. British Conservatism has its own ideological divisions loosely characterized by the terms of "one-nation" Toryism, and as a counterpoint, "market-individualism" or "neoliberalism." Both have roots in the nineteenth century. Toryism, the dominant paradigm from 1945 to the late 1970s, springs from an organic "one nation" view of the British state, one that is class structured and elite led. Conservative leaders such as Churchill, Eden, Lord Home, and Macmillan represent this paternal, pragmatic, and consensus-searching vision of the party's role. In contrast, neoliberalism springs from a belief in individualism and thus implies a limited role for the state in the lives of its citizens, whose engagement with the free market through their resourcefulness (or lack of it) would shape their destinies. Mrs. Thatcher's oft-quoted aside, "There is no such thing as society," illustrates a fundamental difference between the extent of intervention that neoliberal Conservative governments are willing to engage. Despite a failed attempt by Edward Heath (1970–1972) to introduce more market-oriented values to government, it took Mrs. Thatcher's political vision and parliamentary and national authority from 1983 to 1990 to begin "decoupling" the dominant welfare state attitude of voters.

These two strands of British Conservatism are linked, however, not just by a shaped desire for the exercise of power in a dominant two-party system but also by a strongly stated nationalism supported by a world vision of Britain's external presence. This international vision was and is shared by Labour governments, but it has been most forcefully expressed through Conservative values and significantly by the reassertion of Britain's role in the world under Mrs. Thatcher. This was to have a significant bearing on the European and world views of the current Blair government and is worth contextualising. It is also a salient factor in discussing the issue of a British identity that in turn provides us with a link between the external and internal determinants of Britain's policy toward the EU.

External Legacies and Domestic Realities: Changing Images of Britishness

By the late 1960s, save for the embarrassing problems of Southern Rhodesia (Zimbabwe), Britain's imperial role in Africa was over, with both Conservative and Labour governments giving way to what Howard Macmillan termed "the winds of change." Only Hong Kong, to be returned to Chinese administration in 1997, Gibraltar, and a few disparately placed islands remained as colonial dependencies; Empire had been transformed into Commonwealth—a free association of independent countries once part of *pax Britannica*. Political and economic dependency was replaced by historical bonds and cultural affinities— especially that of a shared language: English. This postimperial diaspora was also symbolically linked by the estate of the British Crown—the Monarch, Elizabeth II, remaining head of the Commonwealth and, for the remaining mainly white dominions (Canada, Australia, and New Zealand) and some ex-colonies, also head of state. Periods of migration during the second half of the century, to and from Britain, together with sporting links in the shape of cricket and rugby tours, the Commonwealth Games, and royal visits contributed to maintaining the image of Britain as a mother-country to a vast multicultural hinterland. The adaptation of empire to commonwealth affected the pace of change and direction of British foreign policy, especially when combined with the more strategically threatening problem of the Cold War, in which Britain was expected to play not just a role in the defense of Western Europe through NATO but a world role in policing and defending other parts of the world from communism wherever, traditionally, British forces were stationed.

The reinforcement of a vision of Britain as a world player is also evident in the nature of the relationship that has existed between the United States and Britain since the 1940s. This will be examined in depth later but suffice it to say that during, and indeed after, the Cold War period that "special relationship," personified in the close wartime ties between President Roosevelt and Prime Minister Churchill, was replicated in similar close associations between the Kennedy/Macmillan, Reagan/Thatcher, and more recently Clinton/Blair—and more recently still, Bush/Blair—administrations. In reality Suez, Vietnam, and the South African anti-apartheid sanctions strained U.S.-UK relations, as periodic disagreement over international trade interests have led to a U.S.-EU (and thus British-U.S.) confrontation. But the perception of a close affinity between two English-speaking democracies is a powerful factor in reinforcing a public and elite perception of Britain as an "equal" partner to the United States as a world player. This was never more evident than in the events leading to the 2003 Iraq war, when British government support for U.S.-led intervention gave Prime Minister Blair the opportunity for "world status" as the major ally to President Bush.

The external perception of Britain as a world player is conceptualized by Churchill's "three overlapping circles" model of British world presence—in the Commonwealth/Empire, in the "English-speaking world," and in Europe—which summarizes established conventional interpretations of Britain's postwar foreign policy. As seen later, while the prioritization of these spheres altered during the second half of the twentieth century, putting the "great" back in Great Britain by external involvement above its economic or military capacity has been a preoccupation of British political leadership in the search for external and domestic success. (See Table 10.3.)

British identity therefore includes this external dimension as part of its character, and all postwar prime ministers have attempted to embrace a positive external image to their domestic electoral advantage. Thatcher's Falklands "success" and her initial hard-line position on many EU issues, together with a strident anti-Soviet stance in support of President Reagan, produced the Iron Lady image that she used to some considerable domestic advantage. John Major's popularity peaked after his staunch support of U.S.-led NATO involvement in the Gulf (1991). Tony Blair continues to play a full role in such international crises as Kosovo (1999) and Afghanistan (2001), and, more controversially, Iraq (2003), to gain domestic political advantage by asserting a British world presence.

But, examined from a domestic perspective, British identity presents a more complex phenomenon when related to internal cultural divisions that belie the notion of a "United Kingdom." Its complexity begins with the misunderstandings that abound regarding the terms used to describe Britain as a geographic and political entity. Spatially, "the British Isles" encompass the two main islands and many others in their vicinity. The largest island is Great Britain, and the smaller one is Ireland, which comprises the Republic of Ireland (Eire) and Northern Ireland. Politically there are two nation-states: the Irish Republic and the rather pompously titled United Kingdom of Great Britain and Northern Ireland. The latter consists of the historic nations of England, Scotland, and Wales and the still-disputed area of Northern Ireland, whose population contains both a nationalist group seeking to join a greater Irish Republic and "loyalists" who wish to reinforce their connection to the existing nation-state of the United Kingdom.

The "Irish question" is not the only problem in identifying the concept of a British nation-state. England and its motley collection of monarchs from Anglo-Saxon, Nordic, Norman, French, Welsh, Scottish, Dutch, and German origins has dominated its Celtic fringes of Wales, Scotland, and, until 1922, Ireland. This domination is political, economic, and military and, through the spread of English, also cultural. In consequence the terms "England" and "English" are often confused by outsiders to refer to Great Britain or the British, respectively, or are used casually and sometimes arrogantly by the English when referring to Britain as a nation-state. Thus British nationalism (as a bundle of ideas and beliefs within a community leading to a clearly bounded nation-state) becomes a disputed concept when the dominance of England as a hegemonic nation is challenged or weakened. British nationalism, conversely, is strongest when there exists a common enemy to the nations and islands of Britain, and for reasons associated with its historic world and imperial role, Britain has had enemies aplenty.[3]

The concept of Britishness and the idea of a United Kingdom rested relatively unchallenged into the late 1960s. Welsh, Scottish, and Irish nationalism and their counterparts in regional England were little in evidence, at least electorally. The national parties, Labour and Conservative (with their Unionist allies in Northern Ireland), dominated British politics from a London base. No significant secessionist movement challenged this centralized hegemony. Parliamentary sovereignty, time-limited but centralized party government, a redistributive welfare state, and the constitutional monarchy as a symbol of this sociocultural nexus presented the British with a significant and a tangible set of shared experiences to leave unquestioned any parallel, less hegemonic, factors. These were to emerge gradually during the last thirty years of the century, both as challenges to the concept of a United Kingdom and as opportunities, first under Thatcherism and later under Blair's "New Labour" governments, for major structural and institutional changes to the postwar consensus.

By 1972 the Catholic minority in Northern Ireland had launched its struggle for civil rights. This soon became a rebellion against the British state. "Stormont," the Unionist-dominated Northern Irish parliament, was dissolved outright by the British Conservative government in 1972. Scottish separatists, organized by the Scottish Nationalist Party (SNP), commenced a long campaign for independence on the strength of the discovery of oil and gas resources in the North Sea (Scottish oil, according to them). In 1974, eleven SNP members were returned to the House of Commons and forced through legislation to grant limited powers to a Scottish Parliament. A plan for a Welsh Assembly was also drawn up. Both plans were subsequently rejected in referenda (1979). Nationalist MPs played a salient role in the Commons defeat of the Labour government under James Callaghan and in the subsequent general election of 1979, but were all but swept away by Mrs. Thatcher's Conservative victory. Irish nationalism, an altogether more violent phenomenon, sought solutions

Table 10.3 Main Events in Britain's "Three Circles" of Influence

	Britain and World Events	Britain and Europe	Britain and Empire/Commonwealth
1946	Foundation of UN.		
1947/8		Berlin airlift, Cold War commences; *Marshall Aid* (U.S.): assists economic recovery.	Indian/Pakistan independence.
1949	*NATO* founded. UK leading role.		
1950	*Korean War:* British troops involved.	*Schuman Plan* (ECSC): Britain rejects membership.	
1953	Britain develops nuclear capability.		
1956	*Suez crisis:* British/French/Israeli invasion aborted.		
1957		*Treaty of Rome:* Britain rejects membership.	
1960			Commencement of African-Caribbean colonial independence process.
1961	Purchase of Polaris missiles from USA.	1ˢᵗ British EEC application; rejected.	
1962	Devaluation of pound sterling.	2ⁿᵈ British EEC application; rejected.	
1967			Northern Ireland Civil Rights Movement.
1968	Refusal of Wilson to commit troops to Vietnam.		Withdrawal of troops "east of Suez."
1972	Discovery of North Sea oil resources.	Britain joins EC with Eire, Denmark.	Direct rule for Northern Ireland imposed. IRA campaign commences.
1976	World recession: Britain borrows from IMF.		
1982			Falklands/Malvinas Intervention.
1986		Single European Act: Actively supported by Britain.	
1987		Mrs. Thatcher's Bruges speech: (negative analysis of political integration).	

Year			
1989		Collapse of communism: curtailment of Cold War.	
1990	Britain joins EMS: Mrs. Thatcher resigns.		
1991		Gulf War: Britain actively supports U.S. within NATO.	
1992	Major government signs *Treaty of Union*, opts out of Social Charter and EMU; Britain and Italy forced out of EMS. Bosnia: NATO intervention (1992–95).		
1996	BSE (beef crisis); Britain isolated in EU; splits within Conservative Party over EU.		
1997	Blair government signs *Treaty of Amsterdam*, joins Social Charter; referendum on EMU promised.		Return of Hong Kong to Republic of China.
1998			Good Friday Agreement, N. Ireland: Armed decommissioning commences. Power sharing through Northern Ireland Assembly.
1999	Blair government actively supports Kosovo intervention.		
2001	Reelected Blair government, promising EMU referendum again.	9/11 Destruction of World Trade Center.	
2002			Power sharing process breakdown (N. Ireland).
2003	Evaluation of 5 EMU tests by British Treasury: British entry postponed.	Iraq War: Britain is a vocal member of coalition and provides troops for invasion.	

through the terrorist activities of the Provisional Irish Republican Army and other paramilitary groups in Northern Ireland, the British mainland, and occasionally in Europe, where British military targets existed. In effect the 1970s and 1980s presented a much less sanguine picture of the United Kingdom than when Enoch Powell, a Conservative and later Northern Ireland Unionist MP, presented his controversial views regarding English domination within a united Great Britain in 1961 (see Box 10.3).

Powell's reference to Welsh (the leek) and Scottish (the thistle) identities grafted upon a hegemonic English history and culture springs from a romantic and narrowly contrived patriotism that nevertheless rears up in sporting affiliations around English national soccer, rugby, and cricket but more insidiously in the often racist terminology of the extreme right. There is, however, little room for Europeanism in this parochial view of Britain as a showroom for English independence and cultural supremacy. Churchill, in his "Humble address to the Sovereign" in 1945, presents what David Marquand terms the whig-imperialist view of the British state, characterized by a grand worldview within a confident national-statehood, founded on free government that can adjust to change over time. This view, argues Marquand, still exists today despite the unraveling of the imperial characteristics on which it is founded. Policies associated with Europe of both left- and right-wing governments were colored by these perceptions during the postwar consensus period to the end of the 1970s.[4] The perceptions do not reject an association with European ventures but rest on an expectation that European supranational structures should be relatively loose-fitting and, as both prime ministers Major and Blair have opined, that Britain should be "at the heart of Europe" (and thus in control!).

William Hague, a Thatcher-approved leader of the Conservative Party (1997–2001), presented an altogether more realist view in his 1998 address to a French business school. Hague stressed the considerable differences in World War II experiences which, he argued, underscore a confident sense of British identity that will not permit anything more than an appreciation of the European federal tendencies of Britain's continental neighbors. He went on to praise the EU for its postwar achievements but warned of the danger of a "fortress Europe" that would fly in the face of global (and thus British) economic and security interests. National identity, alongside a neoliberal view of the role of the state and economy, thus precluded any further moves toward integration such as economic and monetary union or a common foreign and security policy. Such was the position of the Conservative Party during the 1997–2001 Parliament.

Tony Blair and the European policies of New Labour are dealt with at length later. His perspective on a British identity (as offered in Box 10.3) is in marked contrast to that of William Hague. In his speech, delivered in French to the Assemblée Nationale in 1998, he seems to reject Hague's separatist view of British national identity and so adopts a more inclusive post–Cold War analysis

Box 10.3   The Identity Conundrum

Differing Views of British Nationalism

It is the golden circle of the Crown which alone embraces the loyalties of so many states and races all over the world. The wisdom of our ancestors has led us to an envied and enviable situation. We have the strongest Parliament in the World. We have the oldest, the most famous, the most secure, the most serviceable monarchy in the world. King and Parliament both rest safely and solidly upon the will of the people expressed by free and fair election on the bases of universal suffrage. Thus the system has long worked harmoniously both in peace and war.

—Winston Churchill, 1945

From this continuous life of a united people in its island home spring, as from the soil of England, all that is peculiar in the gifts and the achievements of the Island nation. All its impact on the outer world—in earlier colonies, in the later Pax Britannica, in government and lawgiving, in commerce and in thought—has flowed from impulses generated here. And this continuing life of England is symbolised and expressed, as by nothing else, by the English kingship. English it is for the leeks and thistles grafted upon it here and elsewhere. The stock that received these grafts is English, the sap that rises through it to the extremities rises from roots in English earth, the earth of England's history.

—Enoch Powell, 1961

For those on the continent of Europe who had lived under Nazi tyranny, nationalism became understandably tainted by fascism, collaboration and war. Britain's experience had been quite different. It was our national identity . . . which had helped see us through our darkest days of the war. For us, patriotism was the focus of our resistance against Nazi tyranny. We have never been as nervous of our national feelings as our continental neighbours and, as a result I believe we have never really understood, let alone shared, the fears and ambitions of European Federalism.

—William Hague, 1998

The first vote I cast was in favour of Britain entering the Common Market. As I watch my children grow up now, I want them to live in a Europe in which they feel as at home in the glory of Paris, the beauty of Rome, the majesty of Vienna as they do in their own London . . . because men like Monnet and Schuman and yes Churchill, had a vision to declare that the world they found was not going to be the world they would leave to future generations. I believe that you, in France, share that vision with the British.

—Tony Blair, 1998

Box 10.4   Tony Blair's Speech to the French National Assembly

March 24, 1998 (extracts)

I talk of a Third Way or New Labour. My conviction is that we have to be absolute in our adherence to our basic values, otherwise we have no compass to guide us through change. But we should be infinitely adaptable and imaginative in applying those values. There are no ideological preconditions, no pre-determined veto on means. What counts is what works . . . I believe in one nation and in Britain for some, the objective is to get back to the old days. But it is an illusion, as indeed many of the best political lines are. In [my] constituency, in those old days were 25 local mines. Everyone knew each other. People worked together. At night in the pub or club they socialised together. The communities do not have that powerful glue to bind people together . . . By reinventing the machinery of government we can begin to reconnect the governed and those that govern them . . . Power should be exercised as close as possible to the people whose lives it affects. We are passing legislation to develop power to a Parliament in Scotland and to an Assembly in Wales, and we will do the same in Northern Ireland where we will continue to work for peace. . . .

I believe in a Europe of enlightened self interest and happen to share European idealism. I am by instinct an internationalist. But even if I weren't, I should be an internationalist by realism. The forces of necessity are driving us to cooperation. . . . But we politicians must constantly explain, and justify, our vision. For me the spirit of Europe's development is the idealism of practical people; high ideals pursued with new realism . . . We integrate where it makes sense to do so; if not we celebrate the diversity which subsidiary brings.

---

of Europeanism in light of the future of British children, including his own. The supranational ideals of the European founding fathers are seen as potentially achievable and not necessarily incompatible with Britishness. A more careful analysis of his speech (Box 10.4) illustrates the more calculating pragmatic approach typical of successive British governments, who have struggled with the conflicting messages emanating from a disputed concept of identity and therefore of what British interest might amount to in European venues as against other international arenas.

Europe as a Problem: Conservative Party Dilemmas in the 1990s

A brief examination of the contemporary struggles of the Conservative Party with regard to the European Union reveals the fault line in British politics that runs through Britain's problems of establishing a consistent European policy.

This analysis is also important in explaining the changing perspectives of New Labour on the issue and in making a more general evaluation of the direction of British politics in the twenty-first century.

During the last few years of her premiership, Mrs. Thatcher took an increasing anti-EU line on many issues. This was in part because of her perception that the EU was coming increasingly under the control of federalists, like Jacques Delors, then president of the European Commission, and President Mitterrand of France. She was also encouraged by the increasingly strident position of the neoliberal wing of her party after the 1987 election and the nationalist neoconservative line on many issues that emerged earlier in the 1980s after the Falklands intervention. Moderate Conservatives, whose pro-European proclivities did not stress this Atlanticist free-trade vision, were forced to resign from her cabinet.[5] The resignation of Geoffrey Howe in 1990, after a particularly problematic European Council meeting in Rome, provoked a leadership contest that she was to lose narrowly. Though other issues associated with local taxation and her authoritarian style of leadership also contributed to her unpopularity, it was the issue of "Europe" and Britain's increasing isolation from EU partners that triggered a revolt in the parliamentary party.

Ironically, Mrs. Thatcher's stridency came just at a time when the British public was beginning to look with a slightly less jaundiced eye at the EU. The Single European Act, the security of the exchange-rate mechanism, and the Social Charter, together with the uncertainties of a postcommunist central and eastern Europe, seemed to suggest to some of the British public and its elites that closer ties with the EU were now important. The reunification of Germany and the need for economic and political stability in Europe revived a more cooperative spirit. "In such circumstances," suggested the commentator Alex May, "Thatcher's prejudices seemed not only out of place, but distinctly dangerous."[6]

Her successor, John Major, elected ahead of the Europhile Michael Heseltine, sought to unite the party with a pragmatic and less antagonistic style of leadership. Thrown into the Maastricht negotiations for further political and economic union, the new Conservative government offered conciliation with the aim of putting Britain "at the heart of Europe." But at the EU economic and political intergovernmental conferences (1990–1991) the Major government differed little in its policy preferences from the previous administration. Early enlargement of the union to include the "new" democratic states of central and eastern Europe (CEE), an opt-out from the single currency with a preferred option of a hard (parallel) currency, and a rejection of moves toward extended qualified majority voting (QMV) for the Council of Ministers gave little evidence of a new approach to Britain's EU partners.

The subsequent Maastricht treaty confirmed Britain's continued exceptionalism in several matters. Prime Minister Major returned from the negotiations to declare that Britain has won "game, set and match." His successes included the removal of any reference to a federal goal for the European Union, an opt-out from the Social Charter of the treaty[7] and the final stage of the EMU, and a weaker version of a Common Foreign and Security Policy (CFSP) than desired by France and Germany. However, prime ministerial elation could not disguise the fact that the Maastricht treaty (1992) represented a considerable triumph for those who sought a supranational EU. Qualified majority voting was extended in the Council of Ministers, economic and monetary union was (eventually) to be reached within seven years, embryo foreign policy machinery had been established, the European Parliament (EP) was to enjoy an extension of its powers, and, even if mostly symbolically, the concept of European citizenship was created. In effect neither pro- nor anti-EU lobbies were impressed by John Major's claims.

In a parallel series of events during the Maastricht process, the Major government was to suffer a body blow to its economic policies and political credibility that was to have lasting repercussions. In October 1990, Mrs. Thatcher had, somewhat reluctantly, joined Britain to the EU's International Exchange Rate Mechanism (ERM). Out of power, she publicly denounced this decision, which she claimed was forced upon her in the last days of her premiership. In the autumn of 1992, Britain's then overvalued currency and worsening economic condition resulted in international speculation against the pound. Despite costly attempts to maintain the pound's value by the British treasury, Britain and Italy were unable to stay within the narrow ERM band and were forced to leave the mechanism (Black Wednesday, September 16, 1992). This was received by the government and importantly by the British press, as both an ignominious defeat and an illustration of the danger of European integration. In particular the Bundesbank was castigated by the British government for not offering more support for the pound. In other EU member states, the failure of the ERM was seen as a reason to move rapidly toward the closer economic union that the conditions of EMU offered. For the Conservative government, the lesson was different, and it ushered in a period of even deeper Euroskepticism, thereby increasing the party division that was to contribute to its massive defeat in 1997.

John Major's difficulties with his EU colleagues were compounded by the growing strength of Euroskeptical opinion within his cabinet as well as on his back bench.[8] His 1992 majority over other parties dwindled from twenty-one to a handful of votes by 1997 through by-elections (special elections) and desertions to the opposition. The BSE (bovine spongiform encephalopathy, or mad cow disease) crisis, during which British beef was designated by EU veterinarians as potentially dangerous and unfit for human consumption (1996 onwards), and the subsequent ban on British beef exports to EU member states resulted in bitter recriminations between the British and other EU governments. The 1996 Intergovernmental Conference (IGC) on further institutional reform was all but derailed by the intransigence of the British in negotiations. By then the

Major government was playing to a domestic audience made up not only of his skeptical back bench, but also of a xenophobic press, particularly that of the Murdoch group newspapers (*Sun* and *Times*). Major's own more pragmatic views were consequently suppressed in a continual battle with his own party. As one commentator suggested, Britain's negotiation positions during this period "are explicable and rational only as manoeuvres designed to buy off Conservative factions at home."[9] In sum, a number of factors combined to create a British exceptionalism during the 1990s that resulted in a reputation for "European deviance" not seen since the years prior to the signing of the Treaty of Rome in 1957.

Helen Wallace, writing on the cusp of New Labour's victory in 1997, compares the European trajectory of several EU member states at the time and conceptualizes Britain's pathway as having five dimensions. The *symbolic dimension* of strong attachment to the EU in terms of ideas and values associated with the integration project is absent or negative for large sections of British public opinion. NATO and Atlanticism attract a more positive response. Because of attachment to the concept of "Britishness," a perceptual distance from "Europe" and the institutions of integration is much more evident among the British than among, for example, German, Irish, or Finnish publics.

Second, the *substantive dimension* showed support for free trade and market deregulation policies but much less commitment to state-sponsored social policies. Similarly, commitment to the CFSP and Justice and Home Affairs, pillars two and three of the TEU, caused "discomfort." Finally, the growing significance of EMU produced an antagonistic reaction by significant sections of the Conservative Party's public and media.

A third dimension, *issue linkage*—the extent to which a government views policies and pathways as separate or as a series of arenas leading toward integration—is again less evident in British EU policy perspectives than in other member states, which adopt the more neofunctional view of inevitable "spillover" from one policy to another. A case-by-case pragmatic approach to policies has long been a characteristic of both political and administrative culture in British government. During the Conservative period of applied neoliberalism, EU policies were evaluated more by the extent that they fitted market philosophy than by general views of mutual interests.

Such a piecemeal approach was also encouraged by a fourth dimension, *option availability*, when considering an EU future. For most member states the Atlanticist or go-it-alone option was not perceived as viable. During the 1980s and early 1990s a sense of national confidence presented Conservative governments with the potential of alternatives to an EU future.

Finally, Wallace points to a *contingent dimension*—the impact of everyday domestic politics on policy formation and debate. Battles over Britain's payments to the EC budget (1980s), the ERM and later EMU in the 1990s, BSE, the Social Charter, employment legislation, and the whole debate over sovereignty overwhelmed the Thatcher and Major governments, "subjecting the European policy debate to political short-termism, complicated Parliamentary arithmetic and the electoral cycle."[10] Unlike some other member states where EU policies were perceived as a welcome aspect of modernization, EU policy issues were controversial and, for many Conservative politicians, dangerous. It is against this background that a reformed New Labour Party assessed its European policies as part of its march back to power in June 1997.

The Emergence of New European Labour

Previous Labour governments had faced criticisms and often outright opposition to EC membership from the socialist left of the party and from important sections of the Trades Union movement. Divisions over European policy contributed to the formation of a breakaway Social Democratic policy in 1981, led by Europhile moderates. In the 1983 election, with a predominantly left-wing manifesto that included withdrawal from the EC, the party was defeated. Inevitably, issues of modernization of party machinery and policies included a reconsideration of Labour's perception of the EC, at base, as a "rich man's club." Much of the credit for this reconsideration must go to Neil Kinnock, who between 1983 and 1992 led the party from a position of withdrawal to positive endorsement of a European Union. Kinnock is currently deputy president of the European Commission.

By 1992, a coincidence of organizational change, ideological reconstruction, and positive leadership led to a radical reevaluation of Labour's destiny as a party of UK government within Europe. The first and most significant factor was the diametrical shift of most trade unions at the 1988 Trades Union Congress (TUC), toward what Ron Todd, of the huge Transport and General Workers' Union, called "the only card game in town . . . in a town called Brussels."[11] By then Jacques Delors had thrown a lifeline to the battered British Trades Union movement in the shape of emerging EU "mechanisms" of "social solidarity" and "social cohesion" emanating from Single European Market (SEM) compensatory mechanisms, which in more concrete terms meant the opportunity of new forms of workers' rights and legal protection.[12] For the first time in its postwar history, a previously skeptical British Trades Union movement had come out in favor of "Europe."

The second event, Labour's 1989 success in the European parliamentary elections (40.1 percent vs. 34.7 percent for the Conservatives), produced an optimistic view of Labour's electoral chances against a previously rampant Conservative Party. This success, coming a few months after Mrs. Thatcher's Euroskeptical Bruges speech, brought forth no evident public reaction against a manifesto text that included federalist proposals for social and economic harmonization. The third event, the resignation of Margaret Thatcher (November

1990), boosted Labour's oppositional confidence to take a pro-European stance on such issues as the Social Charter, the ERM, and the extension of qualified majority voting (QMV) for the Council of Ministers.

Labour's growing Europeanization was also apparent in the Maastricht debates in the UK, which were concluded in May 1992. Despite the disappointing though narrow electoral defeat a month earlier, Labour outflanked the Conservatives in the debate by demanding a Social Charter opt-in (rather than out), a move supported not only by the center of the Party but by its socialist left. The subsequent leadership election of the pro-European John Smith signaled "the end of significant opposition to Labour's [new] European policy."[13]

In accounting for this turnabout from the 1983 position of EC withdrawal, several observations are in order. As part of its long search for electoral legitimacy, the party in the late 1980s and early 1990s sought ideological hope in the success of "European social democracy" exemplified in the long-lived Swedish social model, Mitterrand's mostly successful reinvention of the Partie Socialiste, or until 1990, German social democracy. Following its 1989 policy review, the Labour Party reconciled itself with liberal politics and capitalist society and in doing so opened up the potential of a dialogue and eventual alliance with continental social democratic parties within the framework of the European Union. However short-lived—for we shall argue later that Blairism has veered away from this path with the sleek "Third Way" model—ideological barriers to the development of a positive European policy had been lowered. The left of the party, even before the shock of the 1992 election defeat, thus reconsidered its position in the light of the reanalysis of the EU by the Trades Union movement and its dwindling political influence within the party.

As socialism throughout Europe began to adjust to the post–Cold War era, the EU with its broad post-Maastricht policy agenda, which included such "new social movement" arenas as equal opportunity, the environment, sexual and minority rights, and obligatory management consultation with labor representation on a wide variety of issues, commanded at least the interest if not the wholehearted support of radical groups previously encased in socialist orthodoxies. Added to this was the disputed role of the EU in a globalized economy. The neoliberal/monetarist triumph of the 1980s seemed to have brought with it the death knell of nationally applied, Keynesian demand-based policies. Despite the evident neoliberal message of the SEM and the emerging monetarist project of economic and monetary union, "left parties warmed to the process of European construction, seeing the possibility of transferring to the supranational level the control decreasingly available at the national level."[14] There was, in effect, only one show in town for late-twentieth-century European social democracy and socialism, and if there was to be a choice between global capitalism and a Rhineland version, apparent in much of the new European project, then the Labour Party of Neil Kinnock, and from 1992, of John Smith, saw little room to maneuver.

Blair, Europe, and a Third Way

The sudden death of John Smith in 1994 and the selection of Tony Blair as leader marked a further change in Labour's path to modernization. The process of organizational restructuring had commenced under the leadership of Neil Kinnock in the mid-1980s and included rebalancing the party's trades union links and legitimizing relationships with business via a macroeconomic policy of monetary stability. Others perceived this path as only a recast of social democracy that, as the 1992 election result illustrated, did not convince the British voter of Labour's ability to govern.

Blair's "Third Way" took no chances with Britain's voters in attempting to challenge the low-tax, deregulated, stable-price economic environment that they had come to expect from the Thatcher–Major years. Such elements of the Third Way program—the radical center, the active civil society, the "new" mixed economy, equality as inclusion, positive welfare, the social investment state, and more[15]—sprang as much from what had become politically and economically possible during the 1990s as from any radical, challenging, and new set of values. Fortuitously, Tony Blair attained the Labour leadership at a time when Conservative Euroskeptics began their persistent guerrilla campaign against the "Eurorealist" views of Prime Minister John Major, and during his period as opposition leader (1994–1997), Blair took full advantage of the prevailing political circumstances to advance a carefully constructed and positive European policy. With such easy targets, the Labour front bench promised a return of British influence and leadership in the EU on election, through a realistic and constructive reunion with EU political leaders. Through meetings with other social democratic parties within the fora of the Party of European Socialists and the Socialist International, as well as with bilateral meetings, Blair and others familiarized themselves with EU issues and built personal networks.

The 1992 general election and 1994 European election had gone some way toward purging the Labour Party of its Euroskeptical left. In effect, many of the political and ideological factors that had precluded the 1970s Wilson–Callaghan Labour administrations from adopting an evidently positive European policy had given way under Labour's drive toward modernization. The Labour Left–Trades Union anti-European alliance was no longer in evidence; the specter of a hard-line socialist condemnation had been lifted from the consciences of Labour's "soft" left regarding European association; the EU offered not just new-liberal market solutions but, through Delors's vision, a social dimension, excluded from British politics throughout the Thatcher period. Finally the division within the Conservative Party over EU matters permitted the Labour Party to present itself as the party not only best able to govern the British economy but to represent Britain in the increasingly powerful institutions of the EU. This was indeed a first for the "people's" party.

If these circumstances illustrated the new opportunities for European policy that New Labour seemed to enjoy, the 1997 general election manifesto commitments were positive but intergovernmentalist in character. Thus "retention of the veto on key matters of interest" to sustain the "vision of Europe of independent nations" and pressing for enlargement and the completion of the single market and reform of CAP were aims not dissimilar from the Conservative position under Major. However, willingness to sign the Social Charter and "lead Europe in reform" marked differences from the disengaging tone of the Conservative government to 1997. Options on the most contentious issue, whether to join the final stage of monetary union—adoption of the single currency—were to be left until conditions were "right" and approval via a referendum was achieved. (See Box 10.5.)

Labour in Power: Grappling with the European Agenda

At the June 1997 Amsterdam summit, Labour's new commitment seemed evident enough. The Social Charter signed, Blair made much of his contribution to the creation of an employment provision in the treaty. Support for strengthening the powers of the European Parliament (EP), increasing qualified majority voting (QMV) in several policy areas, and strengthening EU human rights provisions were in marked contrast to the position of the Major administration a few months earlier. As against this, a more traditional position of national interest first was taken on such matters as border controls (to be maintained in Pillar III); blocking QMV on Justice and Home Affairs cooperation; and limiting the extension of Common Foreign and Security Policy and a defense identity. Though deemed by Labour's spin doctors as a massive success for New Labour's fresh new Europeanism, aspects of the new government's performance were perceived as little different from those encountered in the worst days of the Major government's obstructionist period. Fallout from the mad cow disease and Common Fisheries disputes, obdurate resistance to European Commission criticism of a UK value-added fuel tax reduction, and objections to the further extension of the Social Charter reduced the risk of the Blair administration being criticized in the UK as "Brussels' poodle,"[16] as it was when Blair hectored his social democratic colleagues into accepting New Labour's perspectives on labor flexibility. This tendency to lead by lecturing was evident on several other occasions during Blair's first premiership.[17]

The British presidency of the EU (January–June 1998), like the Amsterdam summit, offered similarly mixed messages to fellow EU members concerning Labour's new Europeanization. Britain somewhat curiously excluded itself from the most serious objective of its own presidency—the effective launch of

Box 10.5   Labour Party Election Manifesto Statements on the EU, 1983–2001

1983 Manifesto
Withdrawal from EC within lifetime of Parliament.

1987 Manifesto
Work constructively in EC but reject EC interference in Labour program for national recovery.

1989 Policy Review
No withdrawal; facilitate cooperation, keep national veto, and improve Westminster scrutiny. EMS too "deflationary"; no membership of ERM unless linked to coordination of EC-wide growth policy. Acceptance of Social Charter.

1992 Manifesto
Unqualified support for Social Charter, "active part" in EMU negotiations. Reform Common Agricultural Policy.

Press enlargement of EC.

"Promote Britain out of the European second division."

1997 Manifesto
"Our vision of Europe is of independent nations' retention of the national veto over matters of key interest."

Press enlargement.

Completion of the single market (single currency): "the people would have to say Yes in a referendum."

Reform Common Agricultural Policy. Sign Social Charter, "promote employability and flexibility, not high social costs."

2001 Manifesto
Assessment of economic tests on euro within two years, followed by referendum if government recommends joining. Democratic reform, including European Parliament second chamber of national MPs Support European Defence Initiative.

Stage III of the EMU and thus progress toward the single currency. In keynote speeches leading up to the presidency, both Blair and then foreign secretary Robin Cook stressed the need for strong leadership to create a "citizens' Europe" and to push for deregulated labor markets and to consider the British conversion to the euro. It was apparent, however, that Britain's self-imposed isolation with regard to EMU left Blair and the British presidency effectively sidelined in shaping this fundamental aspect of increasing European integration. This fact dominated a subsequent internal review of Labour's European strategy ordered by Blair. Together with the British experiences in Kosovo, this

EMU dead end motivated Tony Blair's increasing emphasis on Europe in the St. Malo agreement that called for an Anglo-French-led EU defense force. This represented a complete change in the policy expressed by Robin Cook and Tony Blair at Amsterdam; it also signaled a search for an agenda-setting capacity to maintain a leadership role within the EU. While the tactic had already been reevaluated in the light of subsequent U.S. and NATO reservations, the events of September 11, 2001, have led to a reappraisal of an EU defense policy, to which the British government has contributed mixed messages.

Domestic Policies and Europe

The domestic institutional reforms undertaken by the first Blair administration may also contribute to this new climate. As suggested earlier, a number of features of late twentieth-century British policies, such as the practice of centralism, adversarial politics, and the mythology of parliamentary sovereignty, are scarcely conducive to the concept of European integration that is premised on some degree of supranationalism, consensus, and/or shared sovereignty on the part of member states. (Box 10.6 details these important changes.)

New Labour's policies toward Scottish and Northern Irish devolution and Welsh decentralization (1997–2001) and the current promise of a people-led regionalism in England attack assumptions of the historic, omnipotent British state that both Conservative and previous Labour administrations had used to justify British exceptionalism. Together with Lords reform and, at least in the first half of the 1997–2001 administration, a search for Commons consensus on constitutional issues, parliamentary sovereignty was similarly challenged. The creation of the Department for Constitutional Affairs in 2003 to oversee the implementation of decentralized government, as well as the proposal for a supreme court, may invigorate the debate on political change commenced in New Labour's first term. Though conflicting with the tenor of New Labour's "control freakery" (of party organization and policy presentation), these changes present an opportunity for the emergence of a new political sociology in Britain.[18] The inclusion of the European Convention on Human Rights into the UK domestic law may similarly allay the skeptical European perspectives of UK citizens. The sovereignty question remains, however, electorally unresolved and is a significant political football to be kicked to best advantage by the Blair administration or Conservative opposition in elections or a euro referendum.

Equally unresolved is the issue of British-U.S.-EU relations that remained throughout the second half of the twentieth century a complicating factor in Britain's relationship with its nearest neighbors. As much as parliamentary sovereignty, the "special relationship" is part of the metaphor of British exceptionalism in relation to its Euopean policy. Blair's easy relationship with President Clinton, the shared symbolism of "Third Wayism," the Kosovo experience, and

Box 10.6   New Labour's Constitutional Changes

As part of its 1997 manifesto, the Labour Party promised a series of constitutional reforms that were to provide the most radical aspect of its program through to 2001. These reforms, implemented during the first and second terms, were reinforced by the creation of a Department for Constitutional Affairs, 2003. Accompanying the announcement was the decision to abolish the post of Lord Chancellor, the symbolic link between the executive, legislative, and judicial branches of the constitution, and to create an American-style supreme court to replace the Law Lords. The new department will also take responsibility for relationships between central government and the Scottish and Welsh affairs. As a result, aspects of domestic policy are not nearly so centrally controlled as they were during the post–World War II era. The main reforms are listed below.

The Creation of Sub-Governments
Scotland

As of 1999 and for the first time since 1707, Scotland now has its own Parliament. While Westminster retains control over macroeconomic policy, the social security system, foreign affairs, and defense, all other domestic policies have been handed to a Scottish Parliament. Thus such policy as transport, education, environment, agriculture, policing , local governments, and economic development are the responsibility of the Scottish executive, which is responsible to Scottish members of Parliament (MSPs). MSPs are elected by a proportional representation voting system, similar to that of Germany, which has resulted in a coalition government of Labour and Liberal Democrat MSPs potentially very different from the Westminster "winner-take-all" model. The new Scottish government does not enjoy fiscal autonomy. It can only vary a British Treasury set income tax by 3 pence on the pound and still relies on a grant transfer to fund its policies. However, the Scottish executive has taken a different approach on several issues, notably in the funding of university education and in care for the elderly. While on issues of financial independence the position and role of Scottish Westminster MPs and Scottish EU relationships remain problematic, quasi-independence has resulted in an internal focus to Scottish affairs and a sense of purpose and nationhood that has underscored Scotland's identity as separate nation.

Wales

Concurrent with the creation of a Scottish parliament, Wales was offered its own elected assembly. The assembly, elected by the same voting system as in Scotland, delivered no overall majority in the first election, despite the high expectations of the Welsh Labour Party. Unlike the Scottish parliament, devolved powers were limited to secondary legislation (rules and regulations); primary legislation remains the responsibility of the Westminster parliament.

Wales remains completely dependent on a centrally delivered block grant. In effect the administrative functions of the Welsh Office have been passed to the Welsh Assembly. Since 1999, however, the Welsh Labour Party, in coalition with Liberal Democrats, has attempted to distance itself from messages emanating from the Labour Party in London on several occasions. Welsh devolution is a pale imitation of its Scottish counterpart, reflecting the closer association that Wales, especially in its southern and border areas, has with England. This association was evident in the narrow referendum majority (50.3 percent to 49.7 percent) in favor of the Welsh Assembly in 1997. However, coalition politics may remain the norm, and the development of a different detached political style, leading to a reinforcement of claims for further independence, is not implausible.

Northern Ireland

Following John Major's notable efforts to resolve the seemingly intractable problems of Northern Ireland, Tony Blair, together with a succession of heavyweight Labour Northern Ireland Ministers, forced through the Belfast Agreement, more familiarly called the Good Friday Agreement (April 1998). Support for this initiative came from President Clinton, former U.S. Senator George Mitchell, and General Jean de Chastelain of Canada, as well as the considerable efforts of the Irish government, which dropped their constitutional claim to the six counties. Though not giving up on their diametrically opposed views regarding the current sovereignty of Britain, Republicans and Unionists agreed to accept power sharing as a means to facilitate a political rather than a violent militant solution to the problem. A devolved administration springing out of a 108-strong Northern Ireland Assembly takes on domestic responsibilities similar to those of the Scottish Parliament. Members are elected through the mathematically proportionate single transferable vote system, from a wide range of political groupings; executive committees and ministerial positions are allocated so as to represent this wide range. A range of procedures ensures that minority positions can be protected.

The large Cabinet comprises both Republican and Unionist ministers. The agreement received massive referendum endorsements from the Republic (94.4 percent) and a 71 percent endorsement on an 80 percent turnout in Northern Ireland. Political divisions and flash points between the protagonists have resulted in the agreement's suspension, first in 2000 for three months and, more recently, in November 2002. However, the system of power sharing is important, as it represents a constitutional innovation capable of getting political opponents to work within political procedures that the traditional British winner-take-all system utterly precluded. Together with such factors as demographic change, changing perspectives of paramilitary groups (particularly the Provisional IRA), economic growth, and not the least the ideological exhaustion of the Northern Ireland Irish people, the agreement may have a life that even five years before its signing would not have been conceivable.

London Government

London, a "world class city," regained city-wide government in 2000, when the Greater London Authority (GLA) was established. Prior to this, its governance had been shared by several "functional" agencies, like the London Fire Service, Metropolitan Police or Transport Commission, and thirty-two London Borough Councils. A coordinated approach to the problems of the metropolis was lost when, in 1986, Mrs. Thatcher "streamlined away" the old Greater London Council (GLC) and six other conurbation governments (each under Labour control). Once again a referendum (with only a 34 percent turnout) endorsed the reestablishment of Capital City democracy (72 percent to 28 percent). Though limited in its functions to creating strategic plans to solve London's difficult transport, environmental, and land-use problems, the GLA has substantial influence in the activities of functional agencies running the police, transport, and emergency services. It has gained a constitutional significance in that the mayor is directly elected by a London-wide vote, the first such mayoral election in the UK. Several other conurbation governments have since followed London's example to create a democratic executive mayoral post.

The first GLA mayor, Ken Livingstone, is a radical, flamboyant, and controversial figure who left the Labour Party when not selected for the mayoral nomination. Subsequently he went on to win a substantial victory over all other party candidates and, as such, represents a new breed of local UK politicians not unlike the traditional U.S. strong mayor. Mayor Livingstone has already made his impact on London's groaning transport system by resisting central government–imposed solutions to the underground (subway) system and by introducing a controversial road pricing system for Central London. His election, unwanted by the Blair government, has produced a new dynamic in the heartlands of New Labour—the capital city.

Despite the political discomforts that these new arrangements have brought for the Labour government, their 2001 manifesto referred to the creation of elected regional assemblies in the English regions and also to a renewal of local-government independence for England and Wales. In effect, the British citizen is now experiencing a range of democratic pluralist systems that, it is hoped, will revive a flagging interest in political participation in recent years.

Parliamentary Reform: The House of Lords

With its origins in the thirteenth century, the Lords has been a bastion of tradition and hereditary privilege within the British political system. Until the Blair administration, Labour governments had done little to deal with this symbol of conservatism, despite a general and evident abhorrence in the party to the Lords' continuing representation of class-based politics in the British political system. Though its main constitutional power had been reduced to that of a one-year legislative delay, its conservative composition still proved unacceptable to all sections of the party. However, the pressure of other legislation and reluctance to "rattle the cages of the establishment" had left the Lords relatively unmodernized since a 1911 reform. New Labour's 1997 election manifesto boldly stated its intention to make the Lords more "democratic and representative" without altering its limited legislative powers.

By 1999 the hereditary principle for Lords membership had been abolished, though after all-party negotiations ninety-two hereditary peers were retained, albeit temporarily, as internally elected members. The size of the Lords was reduced, from thirteen hundred hereditary, life, judicial, and spiritual Lords, to 650. Although the hereditary link was broken, the government is not clear about what a new second chamber should look like. A Royal Commission, which reported in 2000, recommended such reforms as the establishment of gender equality, removal of prime-ministerial appointments, the creation of an independent appointments committee, and a system of "balanced" political representation to avoid single-party dominance. The commission did not recommend a wholly elected chamber, suggesting only a minority of elected members for the second chamber. Indeed, there was disagreement over the extent of direct and indirect representation that recurred in a joint parliamentary report of both houses (December 2002).

However, even with a small minority of directly elected representatives, a re-formed second chamber will enjoy both greater legitimacy and a more substantial and confident role in its activities, and if combined with some representation of regional interests (as they emerge), a "modernized" second chamber could play a substantial role in the redistribution of power within a previously over-centralized political system. Proposals to separate its judicial functions from its political role may also enhance its image as an institution with relevance to the twenty-first century.

The Human Rights Act

Before October 2000 and in keeping with the concept of parliamentary sovereignty, British courts were unable to review Acts of Parliament. After the passing of the Human Rights Act, they can now declare laws incompatible with the European Convention on Human Rights, most of which is now incorporated into British law. This means that British citizens may now approach their own courts directly, rather than appealing to the European Court of Human Rights in Strasbourg, if they feel their rights are violated by government action or incompatible legislation. Thus, for instance, part of the Anti-Terrorism Act of 2001, dealing with indeterminate detention without trial of foreign nationals, has been declared in breach of the European Convention. Despite criticism that the Act would release a torrent of ill-founded cases, there is little evidence of its misuse. While courts may not strike down legislation, as in the United States, merely by declaring that a particular piece of legislation violates the Convention's terms, it has meant that courts now play a greater constitutional role in Britain than previously. Also, the executive is not so dominant as it was prior to the Act's passing, now being subject to an international benchmark for citizens' rights.

Blair's support for Clinton's dire domestic position at various times may all be interpreted as part of a confident New Labour internationalism. In 1998 Blair set out Britain's world role as interpreting "the ideology that links Labour to the Democrats. I want to bring together the Anglo-Saxon definitions of those ideas and these policies with European ones."[19] The St. Malo defense initiative in December 1998 came out of (in part) that confident UK-U.S. relationship. As ex-president, Clinton was invited to give the keynote address at the October 2002 Labour Annual Conference, introducing himself to a captivated audience as "Clinton, Bill, Arkansas Constituency Labour Party."

Blair continues this identification with the Bush administration. After September 11 he reiterated his hope for a British future with feet in both the U.S. and EU camps through "the American spirit of enterprise: the European spirit of solidarity."[20] Full support for U.S. intervention in the Afghan and Iraq wars underscored this identification. The political limitations of such a position will be explored later. The point here is that the confidence to pursue this course of action emerges from Blair's undoubted international standing and good relations with both Bill Clinton and George W. Bush. It could also emerge as a serious obstacle to the European leadership aspirations that Blair set out as his aim for New Labour government.

There is sufficient evidence in the discussion so far to support the argument that Britain's engagement with the EU has moved from the reluctant support of the Wilson and Major eras to a pragmatically positive and in some cases positively enthusiastic stance during the first Blair government. However, the evaluation so far has omitted New Labour's ambivalence regarding the euro.

Betting on the Euro

> We should only be the party of the Single Currency if the economic conditions are met. . . . But if they are met, we should join and if met in this Parliament, we should have the courage of our argument to ask British people for their consent in this Parliament.
>
> —Tony Blair, Labour Party Conference, October 2001

> I will be the person who presents the economic assessment.
>
> —Gordon Brown, House of Commons, February 2002

A major problem for the successful implementation of welfare programs in previous Labour governments has been the periodic economic disasters that Labour chancellors have been forced to resolve as the external value of the pound impacted domestic policy plans with devastating effect. Three out of the four postwar sterling devaluations (1949, 1967, and 1977) were the work of Labour chancellors. The maintenance of a stable exchange rate represented, for all British governments and not least Labour, with its radical reputation and unknown qualities, a mark of orthodoxy, respectability, and commitment to an open economy.

The return of a Labour government in 1997 was premised on its ability to run the economy with competence, and therefore macroeconomic stability—with its emphasis on price stability—was to be the goal. Thus, only four days into the new administration, Gordon Brown announced the operational independence of the Bank of England, such being a requirement for any EU member state wishing to join Stage III of EMU. Rejoining the ERM at the same time, especially with its much more flexible exchange-rate tolerance, was also an option, as was full participation in the EMU. In this manner Labour and Britain would be locked into an EU institutional orthodoxy and international credibility never before attained. There were, however, economic arguments against such a move. The British economy looked in better shape than several continental economies, and there seemed no need to join a framework that was out of cycle with the British economy in 1997. However, such economic considerations were less important than political factors shaped by both the historic and contemporary experiences of the party.

In the mid-1990s the overwhelming desire for victory in the next election was shared throughout the party. New Labour sought to win the middle-class, Middle England vote, and Middle England viewed both the EU and especially the single currency with evident skepticism. On the other hand, Britain's isolation in the EU due to strident anti-European government policies was not acceptable, either. Blair's strategy, emerging from focus groups during 1995–1996 sought to square this circle. The aim was to support the advantages of the single market, to lead the EU to reform (and New Labour righteousness?), and to let the people decide the fate of the euro through a referendum—a position similar to that of the Wilson administration during 1974–1975. The New Labour policy thus outflanked Major's enforced position of ruling out entry for the period of the next parliament.

Public opinion on the euro, however, during 1997 ran 2 to 1 against joining and, but for short periods during 1998, remained at that level to the end of the parliament (June 2001). (See Figure 10.1.)

Other factors allowed more leeway. Opposition to the euro within the Parliamentary Labour Party (PLP) prior to 1997 was considerably less than in 1992. Subsequent elections have reduced anti-European sentiments to a rump of diehards (approximately 30 out of 461, now). While some union leaders remain skeptical, the Trades Union Congress is cautiously supportive. The Confederation of British Industry (CBI) offers lukewarm support for the single currency,

Figure 10.1   If there were a referendum now on whether Britain should be part of SEC, how would you vote?

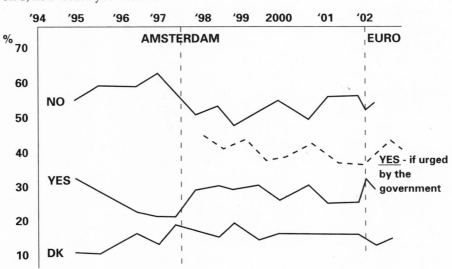

Source: Mori Opinion.

a factor that bears on the new and relatively successful relationship between New Labour and big business. Other organizations, especially those representing smaller business, have consistently taken a more skeptical stance. The British press remains similarly divided on the issue. New Labour's sensitivity to the *Mail*, *Sun*, and *Times* reportage of its activities makes their negativity a particular problem in establishing a positive line. (See Tables 10.4 and Box 10.7.)

Finally, within the Commons, the Labour government faces a Euroskeptical Conservative opposition, with its front bench, led by Michael Howard since October 2003, bereft of such Europhile heavyweights of the 1990s as Michael Heseltine, Ken Clarke, and Chris Patten. The Liberal Democrats, with sixty-one seats, are also critical but chiefly of New Labour's timidity to take what they believe to be the final leap to a federal Europe. As these are the forces aligned for and against the single currency, whither the agency of leadership: Which Blair project is for Europe?

Le Blair nouveau est arrivé?

The prime minister's speech to the Assemblée Nationale (March 1998) engaged with mainstream continental approaches to economic management. At the end of 1999 he endorsed an all-party campaign, "Britain in Europe," the subtext of which was inevitably the issue of the single currency and a British referendum. By January 2002, with a second landslide victory behind him, he was able to allow Europhile ministers to publicly announce support for the euro. One minister even gave out a possible timetable for British entry.[21]

However, enthusiasm for the euro was and remains guarded by two well-dug trenches: the five treasury "tests" and the promise of a referendum. Both techniques are part of Labour's European policy history. A referendum was promised by Harold Wilson in 1971, to placate a vicious left/right division on entry terms and, in reality, membership of the EC. By 1974 the concept had merit as an election platform, promising a people's vote on terms of entry after renegotiation; it also kept pro- and anti-Labour elites in the same boat during a difficult period of minority government. Despite negative public opinion as late as the spring of 1975, the referendum in June was won comfortably (60 percent to 40 percent) after considerable government intervention.[22]

The idea of a referendum on the single currency was born out of a similar anxiety. John Smith, during his brief period as leader of the opposition, had favored a referendum. In the light of Britain's withdrawal from the ERM, the Conservative government's discomfort with the issue of EMU, and a hostile press and public reaction to the single currency, such a policy looked electorally wise. By October 1994 Blair, now leader, saw the case to be constitutional and therefore appropriate as a discussion to "be taken very clearly by the British people."[23] Since Blair had recognized the need to win over the Murdoch press to the idea of a New Labour government, such a tactic was plausible and

Table 10.4 Newspaper Partisanship and Attitudes toward the European Union, 2001 and 1997

Paper	Circulation (000s) May	2001 EU Attitude	2001 Partisanship	1997 EU Attitude	1997 Partisanship
Daily Express	956	Sympathetic	Labour	Euroskeptic	Conservative
Daily Mail	2,415	Euroskeptic	Conservative	Euroskeptic	Conservative
Daily Star	694	Sympathetic	Labour	Euroskeptic	Labour
Daily Telegraph	1,020	Euroskeptic	Conservative	Euroskeptic	Conservative
Financial Times	487	Sympathetic	Labour	Sympathetic	Labour
Guardian	403	Sympathetic	Labour	Sympathetic	Labour
Independent	226	Sympathetic	not Conservative	Sympathetic	Labour
Mirror	2,787	Sympathetic	Labour	Sympathetic	Labour
Sun	3,447	Euroskeptic	Labour	Euroskeptic	Labour
The Times	707	Euroskeptic	Labour	Euroskeptic	Anti Euro

Circulation (000s):

	2001	1997
Euroskeptic	7,589 (58%)	9,714 (71%)
Sympathetic	5,553 (42%)	4,043 (29%)

Source: Anthony King, ed., *Britain at the Polls* (London: Chatham House Publishers), chapter 5.

Box 10.7   The Press, Political Parties, and Media Representation of the EU

Unlike TV and radio, the British press is partisan and often directly party political in its coverage of domestic events. The electronic media, both public service (the BBC) and commercial (the ITV and other channels), are required by convention and state to be balanced, impartial, and unresponsive to political pressures. The press however, is not subject to such stringency and has a tradition of political bias constrained only by laws of libel, a press complaints procedure, and the impact that their opinion may have on their daily sales. For this reason British political parties have shown far more sensitivity to their showing in print than on screen. Other factors contribute to that sensitivity: (1) with the partial exception of Scotland, newspapers are national in readership; (2) competition for advertising revenues has created a strident popular press prepared to present news in a sensational manner that can be dangerous or advantageous to party political image; (3) press barons have long sought political and business advantage through their ownership of the press and have been prepared to shape editorial policy to fit. Editors and politicians alike must court the press barons if they want editorial policy to favor them. The inevitable result has been a press favoring business over social interests; until recently, most newspapers have generally supported Conservative rather than Labour views. New Labour, mindful of the damage caused to Labour electoral performances during the 1980s, have adopted communication policies/procedures to improve their media image—raising cries of "control freakery" from within and outside the party.

British newspapers may be categorized into broadsheets (characterized as informed and analytical, with primarily an educated elite as readers) and tabloids (with a popular style geared to mass sales). The latter may be subdivided into "red tops" (downmarket populist) and "blue tops" (middle-market, populist). British newspapers, therefore, compete with both the electronic media and each other within a segmented reader market based on a complex set of socioeconomic characteristics.

With regard to issues associated with the EU, the combination of nationalist, sometimes xenophobic, tendencies; the Euroskepticism of media owners (especially the Murdoch, Black, and Rothemere empires); and the opaque, controversial, and occasionally idosyncratic nature of "Brussels bureaucracy" presents the press with almost daily opportunity for sensational and negative headlines, to inform a British public assumed to be antipathetic to European issues.

flexible. That the referendum was aimed at placating the press and electorate rather than Labour MPs may be seen as a mark of progress made within the party toward a settled European policy. Thus the promise of a referendum formed part of both the 1997 and 2001 election manifestos.

The use of "tests" also enjoyed a history longer than that of the concept of a referendum on EU policy. In 1961 Hugh Gaitskell had introduced the idea of preconditions for EC membership and as a way of distancing the Labour Party from what he perceived as the cavalier attitude of Harold Macmillan's application. Wilson applied "tests" in 1972 for similar reasons when responding to the terms of Edward Heath's negotiations over membership. By October 1997, five tests again emerged, alongside the promised referendum—a belt-and-braces strategy to maximize flexibility and credibility for EMU membership. The tests, however, only emerged after a somewhat bizarre set of internal maneuvers that illustrate New Labour's overriding concern with its public face, the division over EMU and other policies between prime ministerial and treasury camps, and the notion that the struggle to arrive at a clearly defined policy regarding EMU is, for Blair and others, a struggle for personal power within the government and party.

One of Blair's earliest problems after election in 1997 was establishing when a euro referendum might be held, with William Hague, the leader of the opposition, persistently inviting the PM to "come clean" on the issue. This pressure was to increase during 1998 as the date for the first cut of Eurozone members came nearer. In a response to a speculative newspaper article regarding an early sterling entry, confusion over the issue was evident in divergent responses from Number Ten and treasury press offices. In attempting to minimize a public relations disaster, Chancellor Brown plucked triumph from adversity by announcing the five "tests" through which membership would be decided—a "prepare and decide" strategy—and announced, "We are the first British government to declare for the principle of monetary union, the first to state there is no overriding constitutional bar to membership."[24]

The events leading to the emergence of the "five tests" say as much about New Labour's style of politics as they say about a new European policy. The tests—*sustainable convergence of the British and Eurozone economies; flexibility to cope with economic change; impact on investment; the impact on the City of London; whether it is good for employment*—can be flexibly interpreted. However, since their application remained in the hands of the Treasury and thus of Chancellor Gordon Brown, any decision on progress toward a referendum had to enjoy the chancellor's *impreinte* and be jointly shared by him *and* the prime minister.

Various factors precluded the application of the tests prior to the 2001 election. Brown's reported enthusiasm for early entry was blunted by the lack of preparation within the Treasury.[25] The National Changeover Plan sought to rectify this but would not be completed within the parliament's lifetime; resistance to an early decision also came from treasury advisors and the Bank of England governor, Eddie George, who warned, respectively, of the potential drain on public funds and the lack of British-EU economic synchronization. Public opinion in favor of joining rose only twice to a high point of 33 percent throughout the parliament, with the opposition and Euroskeptical press relentless in pursuit of political advantage. Since Blair's overriding objective was success in a second "historic" term for his New Labour project, the issue of the single currency remained wrapped up in its tests.

In June 2003 Gordon Brown presented a 1,700-page report (nineteen documents) to Parliament that formed the basis of his assessment of the "five tests." Only one "passed": the one related to the ability of the City of London to maintain its competitive advantage in global financial markets. The other four were deemed to have "failed." While joining the EMU would create better long-term investment opportunities and enhance productivity and thus employment opportunities, such benefits were conditional on the achievement of business cycle convergence with the Eurozone and clearer evidence of market flexibility to deal with economic problems. In effect the chancellor's verdict, delivered with considerable academic weight, postponed the single currency decision for reasoned, technical factors, but both maintained the principle of Britain joining and left the door open for a further test statement to be made in 2004. In the meantime a reinforced National Changeover Plan was presented, and Parliament was to consider a draft referendum bill in the fall of 2003, thus paving the way to a public vote on the issue—once the chancellor deemed that the "five tests" were clearly passed.

For the Euroskeptical opposition, this prepare-and-decide strategy was nothing more than an attempt to avoid the loss of a referendum before a general election—for Labour, a politically disastrous situation. The opposition shadow chancellor of the exchequer, Michael Howard, quoted in the June 10, 2003, *Guardian*, called the policy "a four-point briefing written on the back of an envelope that led to a five-point plan resulting in a six-year run around." Europhiles took heart from the suggestion that the tests could be revisited in time for a referendum prior to the next general election and were cheered by the sight of the prime minister and his chancellor together, endorsing the principle of euro membership and the need to move British policy toward a more positive and central role in EU affairs. This was reinforced by the mainly positive endorsement of a draft EU constitution by the British government as a good basis for negotiation over the future shape of an enlarged union. (Giscard d'Estaing's Constitutional Convention documentation was presented to the public a few days after Chancellor Brown's euro pronouncement.)

Inevitably the ensuing debate that surrounded this ambivalent position incorporated domestic, European, and international issues leading to convoluted discussion of Britain's political and economic future. Such factors as Britain's special relationship with the United States (especially after the Iraq war); the potential loss of national sovereignty; a federal versus intergovernmental EU; personal rivalry and the possible transfer of Labour Party leadership (from Blair to Brown); and, probably most tangible for a confused electorate, the impact of Eurozone membership on the cost of domestic housing loans—all formed part of a somewhat frenzied exchange that will be repeated in the next installment of the euro debate. As such, Blair's euro dilemma contains political, economic, idealistic, and personal dimensions and is therefore approached by him with the same caution demonstrated in the conduct of his domestic policies during the late 1990s. Far less caution is evident in his approach to foreign and security issues, to which this discussion now turns.

Britain's Security Posture: The Complementary Roles of EU and NATO

Winston Churchill's 1948 conception of British interests and thus, implicitly, security, encompassed three circles: Europe, the Commonwealth, and the "English-speaking world." Britain's influence in each of these spheres sprang from its being "at the very point of junction."[26] This model, adapted by subsequent Conservative and Labour foreign secretaries and prime ministers, remained influential through to the 1960s when, some commentators suggest, Britain's applications to join the EEC could be seen as an attempt to restore its position in each of the three circles.[27] However, given the rapidly declining role in Commonwealth interests from the 1960s to the early 1990s, a more realistic view of Britain's security in that period is in terms of the Cold War. Britain's security interests during those three decades fixed around the defense of Western Europe's eastern borders from the USSR's conventional forces, maintaining a capacity for deterrence against nuclear attack, and sustaining a military capability flexible and powerful enough to protect particular economic and postcolonial interests (of which the Falklands/Malvinas were the main example). Such interests were dependent on multilateral and bilateral relationships in which NATO and the United States played a pivotal role.

NATO, an organization constructed to defend western capitalism, was created in part by the considerable efforts of a Labour foreign secretary, Ernest Bevin, in 1949. The organization institutionalized a West European–U.S. defense interest and thus went some way in containing Britain's transatlantic-European dilemma; at least two of Churchill's spheres of influence interacted through its aims and structure. U.S. military power alongside European allies was successful in preserving the Cold War status quo and thus a European peace during the entire post-1945 existence of the USSR and NATO's military rival, the Warsaw Pact.

There was, however, no doubt that the United States was by far the major player within NATO political and military structures, and on several occasions British governments, whether from necessity or political choice, positioned themselves closer to the United States than some European allies would have wanted. The British perception of the U.S.-UK "special relationship" transcended even the political-organizational linkages that the NATO alliance provided. This was evident on several occasions. During the 1980s, Mrs. Thatcher's neoconservative nationalism, manifest in the Falklands/Malvinas dispute, revived a sense of Britain as a world player. UN and especially U.S. support were essential to the success of that operation. Similarly, Britain was the loudest of supporters when the United States decided, through NATO, to deploy cruise and Pershing II missiles in Western Europe. Similar support was offered for Reagan's "star wars" initiative and related and tough negotiations for U.S.-Soviet nuclear weapons reduction in 1981–1982. Again in December 1987, Mrs. Thatcher was to claim a mediator's role in reviving U.S.-Soviet negotiations on intermediate nuclear arms reductions. The Thatcher government also offered support for the U.S. bombing of Libya in 1986. Despite a less cordial relationship with President Bush, who saw Japan and West Germany as more powerful partners, Thatcher's and later John Major's support in the Gulf War of 1990–1991 again reinforced U.S.-Britain relationships.

By attaching British interests to those of the United States, Britain could punch considerably above the country's military weight and so might enjoy a world-class diplomatic status despite second-class economic performance. Britain's armed forces, dwarfed in comparison with those of the United States, the USSR, or China, were still the most powerful in Western Europe and, more significantly for the United States, were the most flexible to deploy. Defense expenditure reached a high point of 5.3 percent (1984–1985), falling to 4 percent in 1992. Larger than those of similar NATO partners (France, 3.4 percent; Germany, 2.2 percent; Italy, 2 percent), the UK's defense budget reflected the political will of successive British governments to fulfill international obligations. There was also the need to sustain an armaments industry, depending on a subsidized secure home market to recoup its research and developments costs and so compete successfully in the export market. Britain is currently the second largest world arms exporter after the United States.

Britain in the Post–Cold War Period, 1989–2001

The passing of the Cold War certainly disturbed many of the foreign and defense policy assumptions that British governments had shared for over forty years. By 1990, central and eastern Europe had become a diverse collection of new democratizing and potentially unstable neighboring states. Within two years, the USSR had ceased to exist and southeastern Europe had reverted to its unpleasant and historically inevitable path of ethnic and civil strife. World recession, on the one hand, and the Maastricht negotiations on the other, were the backdrops to the end of Cold War certainty. The first precluded the United States from providing the extensive economic support to the central and eastern European countries that was on offer to Western European countries at the end of World War II. With no new "Marshall Plan," the EU was encouraged by the United States to play a leading role in the economic development of its new neighbors. This reinforced long-term U.S. demands that European countries shoulder more of the financial and military responsibilities for European defense and also coincided with the collapse of the Yugoslav Republic and the emergence of European common foreign and security machinery in the Treaty on European Union. Added to these external pressures were Britain's own domestic economic difficulties and a public expectation of a "peace dividend" that had been encouraged by the findings of a 1990 defense review, "Options for Change," which recommended a 20 percent cutback in army expenditure and heavy piecemeal cuts in the RAF and Royal Navy.

The old and relatively simple model of Cold War security was complicated by challenges that now contained economic, environmental, societal, and political dimensions.[28]

Insecure East European boundaries, conflagration in the Balkans region, and the need to secure central European democracy implied a multilateral and multidimensional response on behalf of the European Union, the logic of which implied a closer linkage with EU rather than U.S. interests. However, NATO remained the only effective military organization capable of responding to system breakdown, as events in Kosovo were to show. Tony Blair's willingness to commit British ground forces contrasted with the United States' unwillingness to do so, and his experiences strengthened a new-found enthusiasm for the European Security and Defense Policy (ESDP) of October 1998.

However, the resilience of the three-circles model is evident in the response of Britain to the United States' powerful line on Iraq. The Conservative government offered the United States full support during the first Gulf War. Subsequently, Iraq's treatment of its Kurdish minority and later its prevarications over the full implementation of UN resolution 1137 on armaments inspection produced U.S.-British air strikes and the imposition of "no-fly" zones. British support for the United States came, however, in the face of criticism from its European allies, which was to be repeated before and during the 2003 Iraq War.

The opportunity to reposition British foreign and defense policies to emphasize the "European circle" of influence relied on attitudinal changes on the part of the British government toward the role of the EU and its nascent ESDP, as well as U.S. support for a more independent European presence—and thus new NATO arrangements to allow a separate European capacity to operate with U.S. assets. This in turn assumed a new entente between France and Britain and between NATO and France (since Britain and France were the more militarily powerful European NATO states). In 1996 France signaled its intention to rejoin NATO's military wing, and the British government supported the development of the Combined Joint Task Force concept, which would allow European-only forces to engage in military missions using NATO assets.[29]

The traditionally contradictory views of French and British governments over the role of NATO (the former seeking an independent European capacity, the latter maintaining an Atlanticist, or U.S.-led, U.S. vision of European security) was still evident when New Labour returned to power. At the Amsterdam council (1997) Tony Blair vetoed a Franco-German proposal to merge with the

West European Union, a postwar organization capable of providing a framework for an independent European defense capability within the EU. However, a year later the British-French St. Malo declaration seemed to present concrete proof of British willingness to accept an autonomous capacity for military involvement in peacekeeping (the Petersberg Tasks on behalf of the EU). There was every hope that at last there existed a will in British government to see that there was "no contradiction between being a good European and being a good Atlanticist."[30]

Even before the events of September 2001 unfolded, however, the problems of creating an effective European security system were evident. On several occasions, but most publicly at the Nice Council (December 2000), Tony Blair and President Chirac clashed on the level of independence that a European Rapid Reaction Force should have from NATO. Moreover, if the EU was to develop a credible military capacity, the need for massive increases in defense expenditure seemed inevitable. That implied a more integrated approach to European weapons procurement than had been achieved during fifty years of cooperation within NATO, and it did not fit easily into the budgetary plans of member states restricted by the Stability and Growth Pact agreed to facilitate Stage III of EMU. Finally, a new Bush-led U.S. administration, even prior to September 11, 2001, offered far less assurance that, in any new balance of NATO and EU security initiatives, the U.S. would be prepared to play its part in a multilateral framework.[31] There followed considerable efforts on the part of the Europeans to construct the European Security and Defense Policy, including development of institutional structures within the EU and commitment of forces to a 60,000-strong Rapid Reaction Force, declared operational at the Laeken Summit in December 2001. Before these efforts reached fruition, the Twin Towers were destroyed.

A NEW SPECIAL RELATIONSHIP?

The British government's and in particular Tony Blair's response to the tragedy of 9/11 and the subsequent Afghan war seemed unconditional. While Article 5 of the NATO Treaty was invoked for the first time on September 12, 2001, thus committing *all* NATO allies to the defense of the United States, in practice NATO was not called upon to act. Blair, however, pledged complete bilateral support for any U.S. military action to be taken on the war against terrorism. In Afghanistan the British presence, at least from the perspective of the British government and press, was seen as the most significant, and, in subsequent official statements of support, the case that Britain's interests are identical with those of the United States was openly broadcast. Thus the British defense secretary's pronouncement that he saw no divergence between U.S. and British security interests, "whether as part of close bilateral alliances or as within wider defence alliances such as NATO."[32] This statement, coming as it did prior to the November Prague NATO Summit (2002), demonstrates the British government's diplomatic commitment to its transatlantic ally, with all that might imply for future military support. The Prague Summit resulted in an invitation to six more eastern European states to join the alliance. If an enlarged NATO becomes unwieldy, there is new doubt of the effective military support that NATO might offer the United States in any crisis.

While remaining at the very point of junction of European and transatlantic circles of interest, the changing role of NATO and diminished U.S. commitment to the transatlantic alliance may see the further evolution of an EU-led security and defense framework that the British government will wish to support and attempt to lead. Conversely, and since 9/11, the Blair administration's headline prioritization of diplomatic and military support for the United States and its strategies against terrorism has produced tensions between Britain and its EU partners—as well as considerable domestic opposition in Britain, notably toward the 2003 military action in Iraq.

No other EU member state offered such unequivocal political and military support to the Bush administration in its uncompromising policy toward Iraq. Diplomatic support for the U.S. delegation at the UN and later military contributions to President Bush's call for a "coalition of the willing" seemed unswerving, with Blair often playing a leading role in the presentation of the U.S.-British stance. This was in direct contrast to the internationalist stance in favor of a resolution of the issues, taken by Germany, Russia, and, particularly, France. The rift between European states vocalized in Donald Rumsfeld's dichotomy of "new and old Europe" foreshadowed serious damage to the vision of the EU as a global actor. "Old Europe," characterized as protectionist and idealist, contrasted with a globalist-realist "New Europe" of which Britain seemed a leading member, alongside Spain and the central and some of the eastern European democracies, notably Poland.[33]

Not only did the Blair government find itself with few EU allies for the Atlanticist positioning, huge antiwar demonstrations and a divided parliamentary Labour Party resulted in a considerable downturn in public support for the government, two resignations from the cabinet, and a powerful backbench revolt in several parliamentary votes. Praised for his courage in much of the U.S. press, Prime Minister Blair was pilloried in most sections of the British media for adopting such a dangerous path. Apologists for the British government's stance could point to Blair's role in prolonging the search for a UN diplomatic resolution to the crisis, in mitigating the ferocity of the early assaults on Iraqi cities, and in contributing, after the war, to a Middle East "road map" for peace. In these terms the British role was little more than that of the Atlantic bridge or broker between U.S. and European international perspectives. Others saw in these events a painfully dogmatic and intransigent stance by the British government leading to irreparable damage to both Britain and the EU.[34]

In the aftermath of the immediate hostilities, events have been much less dramatic, with British contributions to the EU constitution debate and negotiations over reform of the Common Agricultural Policy and other ongoing EU matters receiving a "business as usual" reception. British postponement of adopting the euro in June 2003 was received with genuine regret by EU elites and most commentators.[35]

It may be that under the leadership of Tony Blair the British government is seeking to retain its "special relationship" with the United States to facilitate a new multilateralism in the post–9/11 unipolar international system, as well as encouraging new directions in European integration while the EU adjusts to enlargement and a new world order. U.S. security guarantees in these circumstances may be seen as a vital part of this policy. There is, however, no doubt that contemporary factors complicate what could, at St. Malo in 1998, have led Britain toward putting its European circle of interests above all others. Being "at the point of junction" offers Tony Blair opportunities to influence the U.S. administration as its closest ally; on the other hand, the potential of being seen as the stooge of U.S. foreign policy sits uncomfortably with the British government's search for the heart of Europe.

Conclusion: Europe and "Which Blair Project?"

The period 1997–2001 opened with what many considered to be a political earthquake in British domestic politics, with the election of a New Labour government, and closed with the collapse of post–Cold War hopes for a new international balance to which the United States and a more integrated European Union could make valuable contributions. During its six years in office, several factors have combined to suggest that Labour's European policy is proving less exceptional than its predecessors'—certainly when compared with the Conservative administrations of the Thatcher–Major years. Constitutional changes, yet to fully embed, have moved toward the decentralization of British government, which may result in a "new pluralism"; this, together with the adoption of the Human Rights Act, has begun to challenge the centralization of the British state and the omnipotence of parliamentary sovereignty and thus to facilitate the dispersal of power in the British political system. The potential of a new pluralism, it can be argued, deemphasizes the powerful historic symbolism of a sovereign British nation-state, so long a part of the exceptionalist view of Britain's position vis-à-vis European integration.

Politically, Britain is currently led by an avowed internationalist prime minister whose European "credentials" are publicly acknowledged. Parliamentary opposition to EU "integrationalist" policies in such fields as monetary union, social policy, and CFSP has been drastically curtailed with the reduction of mostly Conservative Euroskeptic MPs after the 1997 and 2001 elections. The

Labour government's majority in favor of a "positive" European policy contrasts with the political difficulties of the later Thatcher and Major administrations of 1989–1997. The Conservative opposition under its current leader Michael Howard remains divided over many EU policies, including, of course, the euro. Britain's most powerful corporate and labor union organizations play a constructive role in the shaping of British government–EU policies. Institutional interests, in the shape of local governments and regional consultative councils, play a full part in the emergence of European social partnership. Furthermore, as indicated in the previous section, the Blair government has played an active role in the development of an EU security presence as well as publicly supporting the enlargement process and its culmination at the Copenhagen Summit (December 2002).

This optimistic view notwithstanding, if the factors applied to Britain's "exceptionalism" in 1997 are applied to the current situation the conclusion is more pessimistic. A *symbolic attachment* to the integration project remains problematic for the British public and will be tested by debate, an eventual referendum, and a decision on the euro. A metaphor for acceptance of supranational rather than national values, the euro debate presents a challenge to New Labour's claim to understand the needs of the middle ground of British public opinion. A similar dilemma over support for U.S.-led rather than European solutions to global problems tests the extent to which British identity remains defined by external Atlanticist association or can be reoriented to accept an affinity with "being European." While the *substantive dimension*, i.e., acceptance of EU policy supremacy, remains uneven, it is probably true to say that, since 9/11, the British public has looked more positively on Europe-wide solutions in the fields of justice and home affairs and security policies. The single currency, along with taxation harmonization, fisheries and agricultural policies, and support for an EU constitution remain, however, largely unaccepted by significant elements of public opinion. With regard to the extent to which the Labour government sees EU policies as separate or linked—*issue linkage*—there is little evidence that the current administration is any more "neofunctional" (rather than traditionally pragmatic) in its approach to EU policy strategy than previous governments. The tendency to draw lines in the sand over potential spillovers in social policy, tax harmonization, Britain's budget rebate, and EU constitutional matters somewhat resembles the attitudes of Conservative administrations. One deregulation spillover that the social-market-oriented Blair administration promotes—labor flexibility—has, conversely, been opposed by some other member states, who see the uncomfortable neoliberal consequences for their electorates. The euro dilemma is the most salient example of a *contingent dimension* (the consideration of the domestic impact of EU policies) that is every bit as relevant to EU policy formulation under the Blair administration as the consequences of the Maastricht debates over the BSE crisis were for John Major. A further postponement of a euro referendum until after the next election, due in 2006, is possible if public opinion on the issue remains negative.

What is interesting and different from the EU dilemma facing the Major government in the 1990s is that, should he wish, Prime Minister Blair could call upon the majority of his parliamentary party, indeed the majority of Parliament, to support a pro-euro and thus prointegration stance. The jury remains out as to whether there exists, in the ostensibly prointegrationalist stance of New Labour's leadership, enough belief in a *European destiny* for a modernized Britain—that is, enough to change a public opinion that remains at best agnostic and, for the majority, obdurately skeptical of closer British involvement in a New Labour European project.

Notes

Thanks are due to my colleagues Charlotte Bretherton, Peter Gill, and Simon Lightfoot for their valuable comments on drafts of this chapter.

1. During the period 1945–1979 four governments (1950–1951; 1964–1966; 1974; and latterly 1976–1979) existed with virtually no parliamentary majority. Of these the 1964–1966 Labour government managed to present confident policy initiatives despite its electoral marginality in the Commons.

2. The period 1977–1979 ushered in public expenditure, cuts implemented by a reluctant Labour administration that presaged the more virulent attacks on welfare expenditure under the Conservatives in the 1980s.

3. Since 1945 British troops have fought in policing or antiterrorist actions in Palestine, Greece, Kenya, Malaya, Egypt, Borneo, Cyprus, Southern Arabia, Belize, and Sierra Leone, as well as in Northern Ireland; a short and bloody war against Argentina; and heavy involvement in UN and NATO engagements in Korea, Iraq, Bosnia, Kosovo, and latterly Afghanistan and Iraq. Of EU member states, only France has been so active.

4. David Marquand in *Insulting the Public: The British Press and the EU*, ed. P. J. Anderson and A. Weymouth (London: Longman, 1996), 6.

5. The resignation of the powerful minister Michael Heseltine (1986) and Nigel Lawson (1989) produced a divided backbench that sought to ameliorate and if necessary undermine her strongly anti-European stance.

6. Alex May, *Britain and Europe since 1945.* (London: Longman, 1999), 77.

7. The Social Charter was included as a protocol, rather than an integral part of the treaty, thus allowing the other eleven signatories to pursue common policies without British involvement.

8. In vain attempt to quell the disloyalties of his Euroskeptical back bench, John Major resigned his leadership (Summer 1995), subsequently defeating the challenge of one of his bitterest anti-European critics, John Redwood.

9. Helen Wallace, "At Odds with Europe,'" *Political Studies* 45:677–88.

10. Wallace, "At Odds with Europe," 687.

11. As quoted, Peter Broad, *Labour's European Dilemmas: From Bevin to Blair* (Basingstoke: Palgrave, 2001), 171.

12. When invited to the TUC annual conference (1988) the EU leader Delors was sung off the stage to a somewhat mumbled but nevertheless rousing chorus of "Frère Jacques"!

13. Broad, *Labour's European Dilemmas*, 187.

14. Ben Clift, "New Labour's Third Way and European Social Democracy," in *New Labour in Government*, ed. Steve Ludlam and Mike Smith (Basingstoke: Macmillan Press, 2001), 55–72 at 59.

15. Anthony Giddens, *The Third Way: The Renewal of Social Democracy* (Cambridge: Polity Press, 1998).

16. As quoted in Broad, *Labour's European Dilemmas,* 192.

17. At Malmo to fellow European Socialists (June 1997), in the mid-term report on Britain's presidency (Spring 1998) and on subsequent occasions, Blair infuriated colleagues by presenting Third Way social democracy as the only future for a successful Europe.

18. Thus Marquand: "When Newcastle sees a Scottish Parliament sitting in Edinburgh—when it realises that a Scottish minister is chief dealing directly with the Brussels Commission, cosying up to the German Lander and lobbying potential Japanese investors . . . it may well decide that it deserves an assembly too!" David Marquand, "The Blair Paradox," *Prospect*, May 1998, 4.

19. Speech, Labour Conference, October 2001.

20. Greenwood and Stancick, "British Business Managing Complexity," in *Britain for and against Europe*, ed. D. Baker and D. Seawright (Oxford: Oxford University Press, 1998).

21. Hugo Young, "Blair Must Come Out for the Euro . . . ," *Guardian*, February 26, 2002, 18.

22. David Butler and Uwe Kitzinger, *The 1975 Referendum* (London: Macmillan Press, 1976).

23. As quoted in Broad, *Labour's European Dilemmas,* 192.

24. Anthony Rawnsley, *Servants of the People: The Inside Story of New Labour,* rev. ed. (London: Penguin Books 2001), 87.

25. Rawnsley, *Servants of the People.*

26. May, *Britain and Europe since 1945,* 9.

27. May, *Britain and Europe since 1945,* 32.

28. Barry Buzan. As quoted in Charlotte Bretherton, "Security Issues in the Wider Europe," in Mike Mannin, *Pushing Back the Boundaries: The EU and Central and Eastern Europe* (Manchester: MUP, 1999),186.

29. Jolyon Howarth. "France, NATO and European Security: Status Quo Unsustainable; New Balance Unattainable," Center for European Studies, NYU, 2002.

30. J. Smith and M. Tsatsas, *The New Bilateralism: The UK's Relations within the EU.* (London: RIIA, 2002), 42.

31. Howarth, "France, NATO and European Security," 8.

32. Hoon Geoff as quoted; Richard Norton Taylor, "The U.S. will be legislator, judge, and executioner," *Guardian*, November 18, 2002, 22.

33. See Robert Kagan, "Power and Weakness," *Policy Review,* June/July, 2002, 3–28. Also Robin Harris, "The State of the Special Relationship," *Policy Review,* June/July, 2002, 29–43.

34. See Hugo Young, "WMD or Not, Blair Had Already Made Up His Mind," *Guardian,* June 4, 2003, 2. Also Martin Woollacott, "Never Mind Iraq, the Battle for Europe Is Much Bigger," *Guardian* June 6, 2003, 12.

35. Charles Bremner, "Europe Rues Blair's Missed Opportunity," *Times*, June 10, 2003, 15.

Suggestions for Further Reading

Anderson, Peter, and Anthony Weymouth. *Insulting the Public? The British Press and the European Union*. London: Longmans, 1999.

Budge, Ian, et al. *The New British Politics.* 2nd ed. Harlow, England: Pearson Education, 2001.

Dumbrell, John. *A Special Relationship: Anglo American Relations in the Cold War and After*. New York: St. Martin's Press, 2001.

King, Anthony, ed. *Britain at the Polls, 2001*. London, Chalham House, 2002.

May, Alex. *Britain and Europe since 1945*. London: Longman, 1999.

Marquand, David. "After Whig Imperialism? Can There Be a British Identity?" *New Community* 21, no. 2 (1995).

Rawnsley, Andrew. *Servants of the People: The Inside Story of New Labour*. Rev. ed. London: Penguin Books, 2001.

CHAPTER 11

Italy

A Society in Search of a State

Patrick McCarthy, with Mark Gilbert and Emanuela Poli

Italy

Population: 58.1 million
Area in Square Miles: 116,320
Population Density per Square Mile: 499
GDP (in billion dollars, 2001): $1,519.9
GDP per capita (purchasing power parity in dollars, 2001): $26,239
Joined EC/EU: January 1, 1958
Joined NATO: 1949

Political Parties:
Center-Left Olive Tree Coalition
Democrats of the Left, Daisy Alliance
 (including Italian Popular Party,
 Italian Renewal, Union of
 Democrats for Europe, The
 Democrats)
Sunflower Alliance (including Green
 Federation, Italian Democratic
 Socialists)
Italian Communist Party
Center-Right Freedom House
 Coalition
Forza Italia, National Alliance
The Whiteflower Alliance (includes
 Christian Democratic Center,
 United Christian Democrats)
Northern League
Christian Democratic Center or CCD
Democrats of the Left or DS
Democratic Center Union or UDC
Forza Italia or FI
Green Federation
Italian Communist Party or PCI
Italian Popular Party or PPI
Italian Renewal or RI
Italian Social Democrats or SDI
Socialist Movement-Tricolor Flame or
 MS-Fiamma
Socialist Party or PSI
National Alliance or AN
Northern League or NL
Southern Tyrols People's Party or SVP
 (German speakers)
The Democrats
The Radicals (formerly Pannella
 Reformers and Autonomous List)
Union of Democrats for Europe or
 UDEUR
United Christian Democrats or CDU

Sources: "Organisation for Economic Co-operation and Development," at www.oecd.org/
 home/ (accessed August 5, 2003); "2003 World Population Data Sheet," at www.prb.org/
 pdf/WorldPopulationDS03_Eng.pdf (accessed August 5, 2003); "The World Factbook,"
 August 1, 2003, at cia.gov/cia/publications/factbook/index.html (accessed October 6, 2003).

Introduction

In Italy, perhaps more than in any other European country, the divide between the domestic and the foreign was especially ambiguous up until the 1990s. Rather than treat these elements separately, then, this chapter weaves them together in chronological periods. First is the 1943–1954 era, which witnessed the birth of the party system in Italy and the influence of the Cold War. Second is the 1954–1992 period, during which the party system ran its course. Third is the post-1992 period, during which the party system has been characterized by great upheaval, and the pressure exerted by the ongoing process of European integration has greatly shaped Italian domestic politics.

Italy's political system changed significantly in the 1990s. From 1943 to 1992 it was dominated by the Christian Democrats (DC), who formed a succession of governments, and by the Italian Communist Party (PCI), which led the permanent opposition but was never considered a legitimate party of government. The uneasy relationship between the two "churches," Catholicism and communism, was moribund long before 1992, when the so-called *Mani Pulite* (Clean Hands) scandal broke. By proving numerous cases of corruption within the party system, Italian prosecutors destroyed much of the DC's power base. At roughly the same moment, in a not-unrelated development, the PCI was "liberated" by the fall of the Berlin Wall, by the collapse of the Soviet Union, and—most importantly—by its own internal changes. These developments might have led to genuine renewal in Italian democracy. They certainly have led to a period of innovation in the party system. On the political right, the billionaire media magnate Silvio Berlusconi formed a new political movement, *Forza Italia*, which proved capable, in company with the "post-Fascist" National Alliance and the Northern League, of winning both the 1994 and 2001 elections. The center-left, by contrast, has united in a coalition called the Olive Tree, whose founder, Romano Prodi, had been a president of the European Commission. The Olive Tree governed the country between 1996 and 2001, with Prodi as premier for the first two years.

In this chapter, we will discuss each of these three periods in turn, and each section will include a discussion both of Europe and of foreign and security policy. This is meant to simplify matters, but too much simplicity would represent a betrayal of Italy's remarkable gift for political complexity.

Italian Politics and the Pinocchio Problem

The most famous of all Italian children's books is *The Adventures of Pinocchio*.[1] But few of the generations of English-speaking or even Italian girls and boys who have read this classic have realized that it is a book about the Italian state.

Its author, Carlo Collodi, fought in the independence wars against the Austrians, who occupied much of what is now northern Italy. He published *Pinocchio* only eleven years after Italian troops wrested their capital, Rome, from the Pope in 1870.

This tale of a wooden puppet who manages to become a real boy is also a fable about becoming an Italian citizen. What must Pinocchio learn to do in order to become a real boy? He must speak the truth, obey his parents, and learn to read and write in school. The latter are also the duties of a citizen, as at that time people were allowed to vote only after demonstrating that they were literate.

At first Pinocchio tells lies and plays truant. But if he is not behaving like a citizen, the state (as "parent") is not keeping its side of the bargain, either. The police jail the innocent and allow the guilty to go free, while schools scarcely exist. Pinocchio shows resourcefulness in escaping from inside the whale and loyalty in rescuing his father. He teaches himself to read and write, substituting a twig and blackberry juice for pen and ink.

The inescapable conclusion was that in Italy there were Italians but no state. Why could not Pinocchio, why could not competent citizens, create a more just state than the authoritarian-absent state depicted by Collodi?

This nineteenth-century parable illuminates the "story" of the Italian political system from World War II to the present. In 1922–1924, after World War I, Benito Mussolini and his Fascist Party usurped power. They lasted until 1943; the final symbolic ending came two years later, with Mussolini's body left hanging in a Milan piazza. After the war, the task facing Italians, especially the new generation, was to construct a political system that was both democratic and efficient. Partially successful, they can take credit for maintaining a democracy, albeit one that did not allow alternation of opposing groups in government, and for a partial "economic miracle," which brought prosperity to the north and center of Italy, without widening or narrowing the gap with the south.

1943–1954: Catholics and Communists, Enemies and Allies

DOMESTIC POLITICS

The postwar period in Italy began with the overthrow of Mussolini on July 25, 1943, and in a sense ended only with the Clean Hands movement launched in February 1992. This long period was marked by three recurring traits: (1) Governments were always multiparty coalitions dominated by the Christian Democrats; (2) there was no significant alternation between right and left in power because the Communist Party was considered illegitimate, despite the preference of its leader, Palmiro Togliatti, for parliamentary rather than revolutionary activity; and (3) the electoral system was a highly complex form of proportional representation (PR) which, as opposed to the U.S. and British first-past-the-post systems, granted parliamentary seats to party seats according to the percentage of votes that a party received at the national level. This ensured that government coalitions were unstable and prone to internal squabbling.

On the economic front, a period of false starts was followed by a tough deflationary policy begun in 1947. It launched an "economic miracle" based on high industrial growth. The private sector led the way, but state industries, such as steel, were crucial also. In the countryside, a small-holding peasantry struggled to keep or acquire land, while at the same time many southerners left rural areas to seek work in the factories of Turin and Milan. The northern working class, while still better off than the peasants, was plagued by unemployment and by wages that were low by European standards.

Internationally, Italy sought legitimacy and prosperity by joining the stronger European countries in the European Coal and Steel Community (1951), the first successful piece of European integration. After hesitating, Italy joined the Western Alliance and the North Atlantic Treaty Organization (NATO). The United States exerted influence on Italian domestic politics via the Marshall Plan, NATO, and (perhaps most of all) Hollywood.[2] But the biggest single influence on Italian domestic politics was neither the United States nor the USSR, but the Catholic Church.

The Catholic Church in Italian Politics

The church had maneuvered cleverly during Mussolini's reign, first to work with him and then to separate itself from him. Pope Pius XII also won popular support by trying to limit both Allied bombing and the harsh German rule.[3] Churches, hospitals, and parish halls were opened to refugees as parish priests followed Pius's example. A propaganda film, *The Angelic Pastor*, depicted the pope dressed in white with his arms outstretched to God. Strong but gentle, Pius was, for many Italians, a new charismatic leader who would rescue Italy from defeat.

"How can you not be a Catholic if you are born in Italy?" Federico Fellini, the film director, asked (see Box 11.1). He was, of course, exaggerating, as Italy also has a strong secular tradition. Still, the majority of Italians had grown up with their imaginations permeated by the rituals, feasts, and discipline of Catholicism. Pius's church was authoritarian and fostered political as well as theological orthodoxy. Stalin was the anti-Christ and communists were ex-communicated. An emotional outlet was provided by devotion to the Virgin Mary, whose assumption into heaven was proclaimed official doctrine in 1950. Mary was not unmoved: during the 1948 elections, in Naples alone, thirty-six statues of her wept at the prospect of a communist victory.

Box 11.1.   Writing as Political Criticism

Postwar Italian culture was unusually rich, and film directors such as Federico Fellini and Michele Antonioni, as well as writers like Alberto Moravia, are well-known outside Italy. Aside from its aesthetic value, this culture also acts as a critical commentary on politics and society. Fellini's *Amarcord* ("I remember" in the Romagna dialect) depicts fascism as seen by a child growing up in Rimini, on the Adriatic. *La Dolce Vita* ("The Sweet Life") satirizes the prosperity that swept across Italy around 1960, bringing in its wake consumerism and corruption. Today the director Nanni Moretti, in films like *Caro Diario* ("Dear Diary"), broods on the end of political commitment and the disenchantment of the 1980s.

We may quote from four of the many writers who treat events or themes of this chapter. Salvatore Satta is best known for his novel about Sardinia, *Il Giorno del Giudizio* ("The Day of Judgment"), but he also published a short book about the breakdown of order in Italy in 1943. *De Profondis* is a severe commentary on how the disintegration of the state produces moral anarchy: "On each side of the shifting front of the battle, two quite separate Italies, or to be more accurate ten or twenty Italies, as many as there were citizens, waited, while other people fought to regain lost privileges or else, mouthing the word freedom, to obtain new privileges; in the general disintegration of the state, each person became her or his own state and issued laws that were dictated at best by hatred, at worst by greed and always without a trace of charity."

Giuseppe Tomasi di Lampedusa published *Il Gattopardo* ("The Leopard") in 1959 and in addition to Tancredi's remark, already quoted, here are the Leopard's pessimistic comments on Sicily: "Sleep, that is what Sicilians want, and they will always hate anyone who tries to wake them. All Sicilian expression, even the most violent, is really wish-fulfillment: our sensibility is a hankering for oblivion, our shooting and knifing a hankering for death; our laziness, our spiced and drugged sherbets, a hankering for voluptuous immobility, that is for death again." (translation by Archibald Colquhoun)

Leonardo Sciascia was another Sicilian with a different style and worldview from Lampedusa. A harsh critic of the DC and of the "historic compromise," his book on the Moro kidnapping, *L'affaire Moro*, satirizes the view that Moro was a great statesman and that to negotiate with the Red Brigades would have meant betraying the Italian state: "'One of the most eminent Italian statesmen' that's the expression that found its way into the press. It's a huge, grotesque lie, one of the many we heard in those hectic days. Neither Moro nor the party he led had ever had the slightest sense of the state. Indeed the ease with which one-third of Italian voters recognizes itself in the DC comes precisely from the absence, a reassuring and one might even say energetic absence, of any idea of the state."

Perhaps the most fascinating Italian intellectual of the postwar period was Pier Paolo Pasolini. In the 1950s, he collected dialect poetry from all across Italy as well as writing his own poems, of which the most famous is *Le Ceneri di Gramsci* ("The Ashes of Gramsci"), a reflection on the dead PCI leader. Pasolini also wrote two novels that re-create the world as seen by boys in the Rome slums. Although he was close to the Communist Party, Pasolini lost hope of revolution and became ever more a critic of modernity. He turned to the cinema, and in films like *Theorem* and *Canterbury Tales*, he depicted the exuberance of the human body. But Pasolini, who was a pederast and loved the "hunt" for slum boys in Rome, grew deeply pessimistic even about human vitality and beauty. Here are some judgments from one of his last books, *Lettere Luterane* ("The Lutheran Letters"): "It's not true that, whatever happens, we are moving forward. I do not believe in history or progress. Often the individual or society moves backwards or gets worse. . . . The press and television are terrifying forms of pedagogy. They present no alternative to what already exists. . . . You can always recognize what is considered today to be real: it is violent, a kind of active death that spreads itself over everything; old values are lost. The world is utterly and completely bourgeois. People feign ostentatiously to worry about democracy when all they care about is consumption; they hide behind a wild demand for tolerance, a disgusting, degrading conformity." Pier Paolo Pasolini was killed in 1975, supposedly by a boy he had picked up.

The Vatican had excellent diplomats who instructed their U.S. counterparts in the dangers that lay ahead. The first of these was communism. Pius, who had been less eager to condemn the Nazis, watched with horror as the Red Army advanced across eastern Europe, and his diplomats turned a deaf ear to President Roosevelt's argument that the Soviet Union could be persuaded to stop persecuting Catholics. The Vatican wanted western Europe free of communism; Italy must be turned into an anticommunist fortress where the Catholics should rule and the PCI should be shunted aside.

The Vatican was ready for battle. From its library emerged Alcide De Gasperi, who had been a leading light in the *Partito Popolare Italiano*, a Catholic mass party crushed by the Fascists when they came to power. De Gasperi established the *Democrazia Cristiana*. Rooted in the local parishes, the DC acquired a mass base without even trying. By December 1945, it was strong enough for De Gasperi to become prime minister. The Vatican urged the United States to support him, and the administration of northern Italy was duly handed over to the Italian government.

In June 1946, a referendum, in which De Gasperi wisely refused to take sides in order not to split his party, sent the monarchy into exile. The Vatican was displeased, but in the concurrent national elections the DC gained 35 percent of the vote to the PCI's 19 percent and the Socialist Party's 21 percent. The DC had grown rapidly, demonstrating its supreme talent for mediating among various groups and interests. It drew both ex- and antifascists, republicans, and monarchists, and it crossed class lines. Northern industrialists, who had never favored the party, were obliged nonetheless to deal with it. In return, the DC ceded important economic ministries to the Italian Liberal Party (PLI) and the Italian Republican Party (PRI), which were closer to business elites. The DC also had a major trade-union auxiliary, the Italian Confederation of Workers' Unions (CISL), and in agricultural regions the party mediated between landowners and peasants. It passed law for a moderate redistribution of land that, while offering ample compensation to landowners, built the DC's mass base among small farmers.

The DC had the defects of its merits: It mediated but could not lead; it was rich in different viewpoints but lacked vision; it was neither capitalist nor anticapitalist.

The Italian Communist Party, whether perceived as godless Bolsheviks or as selfless and heroic, never really challenged the DC. In effect it accepted Catholic rule in return for leadership of the opposition. The PCI's leader, Palmiro Togliatti, either genuinely believed that he could reach agreement with the Catholics or thought that the PCI had to placate them at any cost.[4]

The PCI: A "New Party"?

When Togliatti returned from exile in the USSR in March 1944, he was a legendary figure among Italian communists. A founding member of the PCI at its

Livorno congress in 1921, he had been in Moscow when in 1926 Mussolini arrested the leaders of the nonfascist parties, among them the PCI's leading theoretician, Antonio Gramsci. Togliatti had held important positions in the Third International (the worldwide communist organization dominated by the Soviets); he knew Stalin well, had avoided being murdered by him, and had fought in the Spanish Civil War. He bore some responsibility for the purge of the Polish Communist Party but had saved the PCI's clandestine ruling group.

Gramsci, by contrast, spent long years in prison before he died in 1937. Despite poor health, he had written his *Prison Notebooks*,[5] which contain a brilliant analysis of Italian society and assert that the Italian Communist Party must make alliances with other parties, penetrate civil society, and establish a new cultural hegemony before a revolution would be possible.

Togliatti took over Gramsci's general theme of a specifically "Italian road to socialism," which was somewhat dangerous vis-à-vis the Soviet Union. Yet Togliatti also considered Stalinist orthodoxy necessary. He surrounded himself with cultured young men generally of middle-class rather than proletarian backgrounds, including his best known successor, Enrico Berlinguer.

In his famous Salerno speech of April 1944, Togliatti told the Italian communists that the priority was to defeat nazism, not to attempt an Italian proletarian revolution. Moreover, the "new party" was not to be a Leninist-style revolutionary elite. To penetrate civil society and gain cultural hegemony, it had to be a mass party that would work by constitutional methods. These themes fit neatly into Soviet foreign policy, which implied a de facto division of Europe in which Italy belonged outside a postwar Soviet zone. The Italian and French Communist (PCF) parties were instructed not to foment revolution, because that would throw into question western acceptance of postwar Soviet domination of the eastern European countries. Thus, the PCI had to appear moderate, playing a waiting game that frustrated many Italian communists but also provided Togliatti with an edge of independence from Stalin.

There is an ongoing debate about Togliatti's ambiguity (*doppieza*). Did he speak parliamentary words while preparing for revolution? Or did he make the PCI permanently into a parliamentary party? At the time, many communist militants thought he was playing a double game and that soon the mythical hour of revolution would come. In fact the reverse was true. The "new party" was to be genuinely constitutional, but the rhetoric of revolution served to win over militants who had fought in the antifascist resistance.

Togliatti's strategy gave priority to the alliance with the Catholics. His plan was to remain inside the governing coalition, and to this end he diluted the partisans' plans for social reform. Still, the PCI's membership and share of the electorate increased significantly, as did its trade-union power and its influence among a generation of Italian intellectuals. Politically, Togliatti's strategy outdid the Socialist Party, making the PCI permanently the largest party of the left. This naturally worried the Catholic Church. Anticommunism grew along

with communism. Togliatti's "new party," while not revolutionary, had to oppose the choice of investment over consumption because the burden of sacrifice
fell on its main constituency, the working class. But the greatest cause of anticommunism was the PCI's identification with the Soviet Union. Once the
break between east and west became clear in autumn 1946, launching the Cold
War, the Italian communists had to quit or be pushed out of the governing coalition.

Yet Togliatti did his best to mollify the Catholics. In spring 1947, the PCI
voted in parliament to retain the Lateran Pacts, signed by the pope and Mussolini in 1929, giving the church much power over education and marriage. But if
Togliatti hoped to buy Vatican tolerance, he was mistaken. The church gra-
ciously allowed the communists to register their support for its privileged status
while simultaneously pressuring De Gasperi to drop them from the government. De Gasperi duly did so in April 1947. He had received some U.S. aid and
support and probably had been promised more. Togliatti appeared surprised
and reluctant to believe that the PCI was now condemned to lasting opposition.

The 1948 election confirmed the Cold War balance of power. The DC took
48.5 percent of the vote and an outright majority of seats, whereas the PCI and
PSI vote slumped to 31 percent. (See Table 11.1 for election statistics.) Catholic
rule of Italy was thus assured while the Communists were left with the consola-
tion of knowing they had outdistanced the Socialists by 22 percent to 9 percent
of the vote. Moreover, the PCI in parliament played an important role in designing the new constitution. So it was less a "counter-community" than the
French Communist Party.

Indeed, the DC and PCI had much in common. For example, the Veneto
(the Venice region), which was a Catholic stronghold, and Emilia-Romagna (the
PCI's showcase region in central Italy, with Bologna as its main city) showed
similar patterns of development: light industry spread through the countryside;
no large conveyor-belt factories; and cooperatives. The Communists and the
Catholics were equally suspicious, each in their own way, of the individualistic
strain in modern culture.

Both used the instrument of the mass party to democratize the political
participation in Italy. Unlike Britain, with its long parliamentary tradition and
successions of the right to vote in the nineteenth century, expanded democratic
participation came to Italy only in the twentieth century, via parties that had
deep roots in daily life. Therefore, political parties in Italy achieved a special,
almost sacred, quality, and followers identified more with them than with the
regime itself. Thus, the Vatican and Moscow weakened the legitimacy of the
Italian state, even as the DC and the PCI sought to strengthen it.

The Minor Parties

The other parties took their various places in the space left by the DC-PCI
condominium. The Socialist Party (PSI) was weak, although the prefascist so-

Table 11.1   Italy's National Elections, 1946–1996

Party	% of Vote Received															
	1946	1948	1953	1958	1963	1968	1972	1976	1979	1983	1987	1992	1994[a]	1994[b]	1996[a]	1996[b]
DC (Christian Democrats)	35.2	48.5	40.1	42.4	38.3	39.1	38.7	38.7	38.3	32.9	34.3	29.7				
PSI (Socialist Party)	20.7	9	12.7	14.2	13.8	14.5[c]	9.6	9.6	9.8	11.4	14.3	13.6		2.2		
PCI (Communist Party)	18.9	22	22.6	22.7	25.3	26.9	27.2	34.4	30.4	29.9	26.6					
UDN	6.8															
FUQ	5.3															
PRI (Republican Party)	4.4	2.5	1.6	1.4	1.4	2.9		3.1	3	5.1	3.7	4.4				
Bloco Nazionale	2.8	3.8														
Fronte Democratico Populare*		?														
Unita Socialista		7.1														
PNM		2.8	6.8													
PPI (Popular Party)														11.1		
MSI (Neofascists)	0.7	2	5.8	4.8	5.1	4.4	8.7	6.1	5.3	6.8		5.4				
Partito Socialista Democratico			4.5	4.6	6.1											
PLI (Liberal Party)	6.8	3.8	7	5.8	3.9	1.3	1.9	2.9	2.1	2.9						
Partito Nazionale Monarchico	3.0	3.5	6.9	4.9	1.7	2.0										
PNM				2.2												
PDIUM					1.7	1.3										
Partito Socialistica Unificazione						2										
PSIUP						4.4	1.9									
PSDI (Social Democrats)						14.5[c]	5.1	3.4	3.8	4.1	3	2.7				
Democrazia Proletaria								1.5		1.5	1.7					
Partito Radicale								1.1	3.4	2.2	2.6					
PDUP										1.4						
PDS (Democratic Party of the Left)**												16.1		20.4	21.1	
MSI/DN											5.9					
Lista Verdi											2.5	0.1		2.8		

Lega Lombarda	8.7			
RC (Rifondazione Comunista)***	5.6		6	8.6
Federazione dei Verdi	2.8		2.5	
La Rete	1.9		1.9	
Lista Pannella	1.2	3.5		
Alleanza Democratica	1.2			
Patto Segni		4.7		
Alleanza Nazionale (former MSI)		13.5	21	20.6
Forza Italia (Go Italy)			8.4	10.8
Lega Nord (Northern League)†			10.1	
La Rete/Movimenti Democratica		1.1		
Lista Pannella			1.9	
Progressisti	32.8			2.6
L'Ulivo (Olive Tree)				38.7
Polo della Libertà	22.8			
Polo del Buon Governo	16.7			
Patto per L'Italia	15.6			
Popolari/SVP/PRI			6.8	
L'Uliovo/Lega Aut. Veneta			0.9	2.7
CCD/CDU			5.8	
Lista Dini			4.3	
Movimento Sociale Tricolore‡				1.7

Data assembled by Gianfranco Pasquino. I wish to thank David Zammit for compiling this table.

Parties gaining under 1% not listed.

a = 75% of seats won by the "first-past-the-post" system.

b = 25% of seats decided by proportional representation.

c = 14.5% is PSI and PSDI combined.

*Socialists and communists.

**Ex-communists.

***Ex-PCI, remained communists.

†Ex–Lega Lombarda.

‡Movimento Sociale that refused to give up name.

cialist movement had not been forgotten. The PSI lacked the mystique possessed by the Communists and the Catholics. Moreover, its leader, Pietro Nenni, believed that Mussolini had come to power because the left was divided. Thus, the left must at all costs remain united. The Socialists left the government with the PCI in the 1947 Cold War breakup and did not return until the mid-1960s.

A social democratic party (*Unità Socialista*) was formed in 1947 by Giuseppe Saragat, winning a respectable 7.1 percent in the 1948 elections. Thereafter it took the name PSDI, but the social democrats failed to grow into a major force. Italy's social and cultural divisions were too great to permit the emergence of a reformist left that accepted capitalism. The PSDI became a useful but minor coalition partner for the DC and gave way easily to corruption.

The PSDI was balanced on the right by the Liberal Party (PLI), which had roots in the prefascist period. The Liberals, however, were a small elitist cadre that could not compete with the new mass parties. The northern industrialists quickly understood that the Liberal Party had no future and that they would have to bargain with the DC. The liberals had a southern wing that—as the Mafia quickly realized—could not compete with the DC.

In its northern incarnation, the PLI had to compete with the Republican Party (PRI), which, as a voice of republicanism, secularism, and socially progressive capitalism, had a mini-mass base in anticlerical Romagna. However, just as the PSDI did not create a strong social-democratic left, so the PRI was the party of a modern capitalism that postwar Italy never had. It won a mere 2.5 percent of the vote in 1948, becoming a perennial member of the DC-led coalitions and enjoying the approval of the United States, yet it never rose above 5 percent of the popular vote.

Initially, antifascism held the postwar Italian system together. In part a myth, it was useful because it protected the new republic against right-wing movements. Three such movements existed in the 1943–1954 period. The monarchists, who got about 3 percent of the vote in 1946 as in 1948, were concentrated in the south. By its very nature monarchism could not last, nor could *Uomo qualunque*, or the "Common Man" Party, a populist movement founded in 1946 by the journalist Guglielmo Giannini. It incarnated the traditional Italian resentment of the state, which the Northern League represents today.

The "Common Man" Party quickly declined as the neofascist *Movimento Sociale Italiano* (MSI), founded in December 1946, grew. The MSI's organization and doctrine enabled it to last. Led by left-wing fascists from the Salò Republic, its voters were mostly southern conservatives. In addition, its flirtation with violence appealed to young men stranded in the Naples or Rome subproletariat. The MSI survived into the post-1992 years, forming a tenuous link between the new period of reform and the old fascist regime.

Violence was widespread in the years after 1948. The DC minister of the interior, Mario Scelba, used force against striking workers and demonstrators.

The policy of giving priority to investment over consumption was correct, but it placed a heavy burden on the working class, which would submit its bill in the 1960s. As prime minister, De Gasperi shared the Vatican's view that the Catholic Party should be permanently in power, but he also understood the need for the DC and the fledgling republic to attain some independence from the Vatican. He argued that the DC should govern with non-Catholic coalition partners rather than on its own, and in this he widened the basis of support for the state.

In 1953, De Gasperi introduced an electoral law giving a bonus of extra seats to the winning coalition. Today it would be seen as an attempt to create more stable governments; then it was perceived as a "swindle"—*la legge truffa*. In the 1953 elections, the DC vote fell while the PCI and the PSI, running separately, together rose by 4 percent. De Gasperi resigned, and at its Naples congress of 1954 the DC elected Amintore Fanfani as leader. Permanent power was changing the party into the form it would assume until 1992.

ITALY IN EUROPE

Fear of subversion, communist or fascist, was one of many reasons Italy looked outward to Europe. The belief of a self-critical nation that other European countries were richer and stronger was the most important reason of all. In the late 1940s, to be European meant supporting federalism. Italy proposed turning the Organization of European Economic Cooperation (OEEC) into a political entity that could even discuss foreign affairs. Long after it became obvious that Gaullist intergovernmental cooperation rather than federation was more practical, Italian politicians rhetorically continued to propose pooled sovereignty. In practice, Italy dragged its feet when a particular step toward European unity displeased it, and it signed agreements that its weak state administration could not enforce. Meanwhile, the Italian state gained prestige and hence power over its own citizens by its role in European organizations.

Several of these traits emerge in the two European projects that were undertaken at the time. When the European Coal and Steel Community (ECSC) was formed in 1951, Italy was not consulted; yet De Gasperi told the Italian delegate, Paulo-Emilio Taviani, to agree to anything in order to show loyalty to the European idea. The shrewd Italians emerged with several victories, such as a longer transition period than other countries and a special subsidy for the Sardinian mines.[6]

The debate over the European Defence Community (EDC) in 1950–1954 revealed a subtle and healthy concern for national self-interest. After much hesitation, Italy decided that U.S. determination to rearm West Germany and France's plan to do this through a European multinational force, which avoided the re-creation of a German army, were good ideas. De Gasperi presented the

EDC as a step toward federalism, but the Italian parliament backed off, delaying its vote until after the negative French vote in 1954. The sigh of relief in Rome was audible: There would be no new military arrangements, but Italy was still a good European.

ITALY IN THE WORLD

Combining self-interest with loyalty to allies was the main trait of Italy's role in the Cold War. By autumn 1946, the Truman administration was convinced that the PCI's influence in Italy had to be reduced and the spread of communism in western Europe blocked. The PCI could do little to oppose the United States. Stranded in the western half of Europe, yet faithful to the USSR, the PCI had no chance of winning against the military might of the United States and the political skills of the Vatican. When De Gasperi dropped the PCI and the PSI from his government in 1947, Marshall aid was on its way.[7] In the run-up to the very Cold War 1948 elections it was arguable whether the Vatican or the United States played the greater role in the left's defeat. (In my view it was the Vatican.) In any case, U.S. interference in internal Italian affairs goes back to this period. "Secret" financing of Italian parties, the expansion of the CIA's role, and plans for armed intervention in the event of a communist takeover electoral victory became an integral part of Roman politics.

Never—from 1943 to 1989—did 51 percent of Italians vote for a left-wing government that included the PCI, which in any case the United States and its Italian partners would probably have blocked. In 1949, Italy joined the Atlantic Alliance and the North Atlantic Treaty Organization (NATO). Italy always sought to mediate transatlantic conflicts and produced no de Gaulle.

Yet there was a current of neo-Atlanticism that asserted Italian autonomy in indirect ways. One champion was Enrico Mattei. An ex-partisan and DC loyalist, Mattei began in this period to build up the state oil and gas giant, the *Ente Nazionale Idrocarburi* (ENI). His goal was to make Italy independent in the vital field of energy by striking deals with Third World producers. His dislike of the big U.S.-based oil multinationals irritated successive U.S. administrations. This was neo-Atlanticism: a combination of nationalism and Third Worldism that recurs in Italian foreign policy.

1954–1992: The DC Occupies the State
DOMESTIC POLITICS

Fanfani, who became DC secretary in 1954, distrusted market economics and believed in an interventionist state. But although the expanding public sector was often well run in the 1950s, state intervention in the economy offered the DC temptations that proved too strong. The weakness of a civil service that had no tradition of standing up to governments allowed the DC to develop a method of ruling called "systemic clientelism."

This took two main forms. First, the DC used government institutions to funnel resources toward DC supporters who repaid the taxpayers' "generosity" with votes and campaign contributions. The bank set up to finance projects in the south, *La Cassa per il Mezzogiorno*, helped the DC to dominate the region. The Gava family, which used the Rome government to control credit, building permits, and urban planning in Naples, wielded great influence. Farmers received subsidies and helped in creating funds for medical insurance and pensions. Banks whose presidents were appointed on political bases made loans based on the same criteria. Market forces were eluded, and it is no coincidence that the Bank of Naples, the Bank of Sicily, and the Sicilian Savings Bank all have encountered severe difficulties since 1992. The DC's coalition partners received their share of state patronage and created their own clientelistic networks. *Partitocrazia*, meaning government by the parties, was born.

The second form of systemic clientelism was even more insidious. It consisted of imposing a "tax," in the form of bribes, on private companies seeking public contracts. This undermined market effectiveness, making political affiliation more important than competence. Did private companies pay willingly or reluctantly? Either way, the result was the same. An uneasy truce, which each side violated frequently, was made between the DC and the northern industrialists. Meanwhile, the hopelessly overworked state grew bloated and incompetent. The political system looked weak from the outside because governments came, "ruled" for a year or less, and fell. This prevented long-term social or economic policies, which might have proved too divisive. Moreover, all governments were coalitions based on the DC. They included almost the same parties and almost the same politicians. So stasis rather than discontinuity was the key problem.[8]

Fascism left a legacy of distrust of the strong leader. The most emblematic figure of the postwar party system, Giulio Andreotti, understood this. He did not seek to accomplish great projects but rather accumulated power, which he loved for its own sake. A practicing Catholic, convinced of original sin but less sure about redemption, Andreotti joked that if one held the lowest possible opinion of one's fellow humans, one would commit a sin against charity but would rarely be wrong. Of all the DC leaders, Andreotti knew the workings of the state best. He was a perennial government minister who stacked the civil service with his clients. Since one of his favorite ministries was defense, the secret services held few secrets for him. A small man with hunched shoulders, Andreotti frequented the Rome salons and wrote many books about contemporary politics. He had many supporters in the Vatican, and he was a friend of Pope Paul VI. His faction inside the DC was particularly strong in Sicily, and in the 1990s he was accused, and eventually acquitted, of acting as the Sicilian Mafia's protector in Rome. For decades he was much favored by successive U.S. administrations for his anticommunism but, as foreign minister in the 1980s, he conducted a pro-Arab policy that the PCI liked but the United States abhorred.

The division of the DC into numerous factions prevented any one individual or faction from dominating and helped the party to penetrate most social groups and regions. The factions may be placed on a left-right spectrum: the Andreottiani were on the right while the "New Forces" group was on the left. But left and right usually meant less than the competition for control over patronage. The only faction whose ideological position was important, called the *Dorotei,* remained at the center and prevented the DC from drifting too far to the left or right.

The new kind of leadership was exemplified by Aldo Moro, who had neither De Gasperi's sense of the state nor Andreotti's cynical brilliance. Moro was the supreme mediator, whose method was to devise compromises first within his own faction, then among the other DC factions, and finally between the DC and the other parties. When the terrorists of the Red Brigades murdered him in 1978, Moro was working at his masterpiece—the "historic compromise" between the DC and PCI.

Personal loyalties rather than political opinions were at the core of the factions: A clan chieftain retained loyalty as long as he could deliver public goods. Yet it is a mistake to see Italian politics purely as the prerogative of a small group of people cut off from the nation. Politics often acted as a brake, but its very inactivity liberated the energies of other actors. The dynamic, job-producing small industrial firms of northern and central Italy grew quickly thanks to the benign neglect of the income-tax collectors and workplace inspectors.

Moreover, by including many factions and parties the system was protected against attacks from within. Nor could it be attacked from without, as its opponents, the PCI on the left and the MSI on the right, were illegitimate.

The last actor in the political system was the Italian secret services. Probably in alliance with right-wing terrorists, they hindered the PCI and warned the DC that it might be expendable. In 1964, an organized or perhaps merely threatened coup d'état, the Solo Plan, made the PSI settle for less than it might have in the center-left coalition. In 1969, a bomb that exploded at Piazza Fontana in Milan was a response—and warning—to worker and student protest movements. Protecting Italy from the Red Menace was eminently compatible with self-enrichment.

Although the political system did not change radically between 1954 and 1992, it did respond to developments in and outside Italy. One early case was the PCI's very limited reaction in 1956 to Khrushchev's "secret speech" revelations about Stalinism and, later the same year, to the Soviet invasion of its "comrade" country, Hungary. Togliatti did his utmost to delay and downplay the sad truth, well known to him, that Stalin had been a brutal tyrant. Instead, the PCI endorsed the Moscow line that the Budapest uprising was a capitalist plot.

This position lost the PCI both militants and intellectuals: The novelist Italo Calvino was only one of many who left the party. The PCI was, however, less aggressively Stalinist than the French communists, which helped it to limit the damage. Togliatti may have missed a historic opportunity to break with Moscow, but party members' faith in Stalin and in the USSR prevented cutting the umbilical cord.

As an immediate impact of the invasion of Hungary, the PSI broke its alliance with the PCI and increased to 14 percent in the 1958 election. In turn, this fostered the development of a DC-PSI coalition. The center-left opening was promising, giving the now more prosperous, less ideological Italian electorate a chance for a change in government. In Britain, alternation of parties in power could and did take place with the Labour government of 1964. But in Italy, the postwar formula of a DC permanently in power and a PCI permanently in opposition could not be abandoned.

The construction of the center-left took several years, and in retrospect one wonders whether it was worth the effort. The PSI's attempt to introduce reforms confronted the DC's attempt to co-opt the PSI into its clientelistic system of government. The DC eventually succeeded, which brought on the PSI the twin evils of decline and Bettino Craxi.

Accelerated Change

Important changes also were taking place in Italian society. In 1958, Pius XII died and was succeeded by Pope John XXIII. He was more open, theologically and politically, than his predecessor, and the Second Vatican Council, which he inaugurated, increased the role of the laity and emphasized the gentler, more human side of the church.

In a parallel development, students and workers began making their presence felt. Young workers from the south were not as politically sophisticated as older workers from Turin and Milan, but they were bolder and more direct. Their triumph came in the "hot autumn" of 1969, when strikes paralyzed industry, forced large salary increases, improved conditions on the shop floor, and won consultation rights. The established unions kept control of this movement, but at the price of ceding power to the shop stewards and of uniting the various unions around a common platform. The bill for the postwar method of economic development—investment before consumption—was presented.

The student strikers demanded better universities but also reform of the blocked political system. The militants of May 1968 believed in revolution, but "revolutionary" politics did not go beyond demonstrations, occupation of empty apartments, challenging right-wing or unpopular professors, and support of strikes. Some of this turned into spectacular battles with the police and with right-wing groups often linked with the MSI.

There was never more than a minority constituency for the revolution, although out of the 1968 upsurge came radical "groupuscules" such as *Lotta Continua* ("Continuing Struggle" or LC) and *Potere Operaio* ("Workers' Power"), which attracted marginals—LC's work with prisoners is an example—and "liberated" apartment and government buildings, which then were declared "free spaces." Frequently, this involved violence, ideologized as "exemplary" violence or as the "inevitable" violence to which a capitalist society would have recourse. When they began in 1971, the Red Brigades (*Brigate Rosse* or BR) chained unpopular managers to the gates of their factories and burned their cars.

These "exemplary" acts turned into the kidnappings and murders that the BR and other left-wing groups undertook in the 1970s, culminating in the 1978 kidnapping and murder of Aldo Moro. At its peak, the BR never exceeded about one hundred members living underground and perhaps a few thousand who gave various kinds of help, such as procuring false documents or sheltering a terrorist sought by the police.

The broader social trend that the turbulent late 1960s fostered was a demand for greater individual freedom. Young people had less sense than their parents of "belonging," whether to the church or to the Communist Party. Divorce was finally legalized in 1970. The *Partito Radicale* ("Radical Party" or PR), which began not as a party but as a civilian movement, promoted civil rights by nontraditional methods such as collecting signatures for referenda. The Italian women's movement grew steadily but was divided between groups linked to the mainstream, like the PCI-organized "Union of Italian Women" (UDI), and more radical groups that stayed away from what they considered a male-dominated political system. The demand for personal and civil liberties was bound to provoke a reaction in a country where modernity had come late and rapidly. Right-wing terrorism continued throughout the 1970s, culminating in the horrific bombing of the Bologna railroad station in August 1980.

A Great Communist Leader, but No Communist Rule

The center-left's failure was a counterpoint to the PCI's success. The communist vote went up at all three parliamentary elections between 1963 and 1972. Although it was too moderate to please the "revolutionaries" of May 1968 and although anticommunism helped keep the DC above 38 percent and sent the MSI up to 8.7 percent in the 1972 elections, the Communist Party was increasingly seen as the party of honesty, socioeconomic reforms, and political renewal. Demands for serious reforms were strengthened by the first oil price crisis in 1973–1974, which struck a severe blow at an economy reeling from the spiraling wage increases of 1969.

The PCI also had a new leader, Enrico Berlinguer. The son of a socialist parliamentarian who had opposed Mussolini's rise to power, Berlinguer studied law at Sassari University before he met Togliatti and went to work for the "new party." Although he made the obligatory visits to eastern Europe and heaped the obligatory praise on its communist leaders, Berlinguer was a great admirer of his fellow Sardinian, Antonio Gramsci, and hence believed in the Italian road to socialism. Reserved, taciturn, and industrious, Berlinguer was naturally austere. In a world of self-promoting, egotistical politicians, he was reluctant to talk about himself. When he became leader in 1972, he was little-known outside the PCI, and within the party many wondered whether he was too fragile for the job.

Over the next twelve years, however, Berlinguer took many bold stands, albeit with mixed political results. He brought the PCI to its highest-ever share of the vote in 1976 and—finally—into the governmental coalition in 1978. But his great project of a "historic compromise" between Communists and Catholics never came to be.

In the early 1980s, he emphasized what he called the Communist "difference": that the PCI was an island of honesty in a political system ravaged by systemic clientelism. Critics in the party argued that this insistence on difference worked to isolate the PCI. One might reply that the memory of Berlinguer's integrity helped his party to survive the "Clean Hands" investigation. Historians will remember Enrico Berlinguer as the last great Communist leader in western Europe. The rank-and-file sensed in him, in his lack of bourgeois self-indulgence, an aristocrat. When Berlinguer collapsed and died in 1984 at a Padova rally, having, characteristically, struggled to complete a speech, *all* of Italy, not just the Communists, mourned him.

The mid-1970s saw a string of Communist successes. The party defeated an attempt to repeal the divorce law in 1974, and in local elections of 1975 it took over almost all Italy's big cities, including Rome. In the 1976 parliamentary elections, the PCI jumped from 27 percent to 34 percent. However, many voters still feared the idea of the PCI as a national government party, which explains why the Christian Democrats, scandal-ridden and devoid of a coherent policy to solve the oil crisis, held steady at almost 39 percent. Furthermore, many new PCI voters wanted pragmatic reforms, not a Catholic-Communist alliance.

The outlines of a bargain were clear. The PCI would use its influence over the unions to moderate wage demands and reduce inflation. In return the Communists would be legitimized as a party of government, and a program of social reforms would be undertaken. The PCI kept its word: Domestic demand was reduced by 3 percent of GNP while the balance of payments moved into the black. With the DC leader Giulio Andreotti as prime minister, however, social reforms were few and slow. The practice of sharecropping, for example, was finally made illegal, although the law did not go into effect until 1982.

Berlinguer believed, as the current DS leader, Massimo D'Alema, argues today, that the PCI's task was to strengthen the Italian state. This led him to throw the PCI's weight behind the campaign against the left-wing terrorism that gripped Italy in the 1970s. During the Moro kidnapping, Berlinguer ruled out any negotiations with the Red Brigades, but politically it became too costly to pursue austerity, a tough line against the BR, and the alliance with the DC. The PCI quit the governmental coalition in spring 1979; in the elections that followed, its share of the vote went down by 4 percent.

The historic compromise was the last attempt that the postwar political system could make to reform itself, and it was now living on borrowed time. Signs that the regime was cracking came in the 1983 elections, when the DC vote dropped by 5 percent, and in the 1987 elections, where the PCI dropped by 3 percent to 26 percent.

Two forces kept the system alive. One came from outside: In autumn 1980, Fiat's management defeated its powerful unions and won back control of its shop floor. The swing toward monetarism and neoliberalism, which Margaret Thatcher carried out in Britain with sound and fury and which François Mitterrand engineered in France in his 1983 choice of austerity, took place in Italy outside the decaying political system.

The old regime had a final rhetorical flourish in the shape of Socialist leader Bettino Craxi's four years as prime minister from 1983 to 1987. Although Craxi made a few important reforms, such as cutting back wage indexation, he will be remembered for two other reasons: his defiance of the taboo, imposed by the memory of fascism, on charismatic—or, in his case, would-be charismatic—leadership; and his expansion of systemic clientelism. Craxi thus became one of the gravediggers of the old regime; another was Giulio Andreotti, prime minister from 1989 to 1992 and a genius in the art of remaining in power while doing nothing.

ITALY IN EUROPE

The main lines of Italy's European policy were continued throughout this period. Italian governments proclaimed universal enthusiasm for European integration and called on the population to make, in the name of "Europe," sacrifices that it would not make in the name of Italy. Ordinary Italians admired Europe because it did not resemble Italy. Italy continued to leave EC leadership to Germany and France. The French sometimes used Italy as an ally in the struggle to keep up with Germany, but equally often they ignored their "Latin sister."

Opposition to the European Community in the 1950s came mostly from the Communists. They feared, along with the Soviet leadership, that a united western Europe might be a threat to the USSR. They also argued that the large northern companies would profit most from the lowering of tariff barriers, and thus the north-south split would widen in Italy. Moreover, Italy was joining the EC with a lag in technological development, so it ran the risk of being limited to low-tech industries. However, the PCI knew its European policy was unpopular and gradually abandoned it.

Italy's lack of political clout in the EC was demonstrated by two issues. The first was the regional aid program, which financed development in poor regions in various countries. Southern Italy stood to benefit from this program, which was written into the Treaty of Rome in some detail, but regional aid remained a poor cousin until the 1970s when Britain, which also stood to benefit, joined the EC. The second issue was the Common Agricultural Policy (CAP), the largest single part of the EC budget. High prices were fixed for grain and meat, which France produced, but less money was allotted to producers of olive oil and wine, of whom Italy had many.

An example of Italy's ability to adapt to the EC was provided by the European Monetary System (EMS). Founded in 1979, the EMS was another Franco-German initiative. The EMS forced countries like Italy to hold the value of their money against the deutsche mark, the strongest EC currency. Italy did obtain the concession of a 6 percent currency fluctuation band, whereas the stronger currencies were limited to 2.25 percent. But Italian industrialists were not appeased. They had relied on regular devaluation of the lira against the mark in order to remain competitive. Thus, the EMS threatened both to cut Italian exports and to impose a deflationary bias on the economy. Yet, as if to demonstrate their flexibility (see Box 11.2), Italian exporters switched from the German to the U.S. market. The overvalued Reagan administration dollar of the 1980s made Italian goods cheap in the United States.

When a period of "Europessimism" ended and European integration was relaunched in the mid-1980s, Italy was once more in the public relations forefront. Craxi and Andreotti played an important role in the intergovernmental negotiations that led to the signature of the Single European Act in 1986. But although Andreotti blithely backed the subsequent 1992 Maastricht treaty introducing monetary union, this time Italian skill in adapting to EC requirements would not be adequate. Italy's huge accumulated national debt (well over 100 percent of GDP by the time Maastricht was signed) and its high public deficit (nearly 10 percent of GDP per annum throughout the 1980s) was not compatible with Maastricht's strict conditions for would-be entrants. Italians were going to have to choose between Europe and their longtime form of government. So European integration pressures were one cause of the 1992 political crisis.

ITALY IN THE WORLD

The Cold War was another force that had worked in favor of the old regime. Heretical as they might be in comparison with other communist parties, the

Box 11.2.   Small and Successful

Several allusions have been made to Italy's "small industries," which enabled the country to flourish despite its weak political system. Here is a description of small business in Bologna during the 1990s: "Between 1990 and 1997 Bologna entrepreneurs made a sustained effort, deploying all their caution, reason, reliability and vitality. They drew on their local roots and showed their sense of responsibility. They succeeded in achieving sustainable growth by re-organizing and adapting to a changed situation. They mastered many difficulties without the slightest support from the legal and bureaucratic structures of the government, without help from the banking system or assistance in retraining their workers. As so often happens, these structures, far from stimulating and promoting entrepreneurs, have isolated them and placed obstacles in their path."

This assessment emphasizes in a very characteristic manner the ability and especially the flexibility of small entrepreneurs (and, long before them, of Pinocchio!). It also dwells on their local ties. Conversely, it is critical of the state, which provides inadequate services. It goes on to make a judgment on small business in the global economy: "The small companies will have to draw on their elasticity and flexibility in order to compete with foreign firms, perhaps less creative or innovative but certainly sustained by a far better network of support by their governments." (This passage is drawn from the concluding pages of a report commissioned by the Association of Small and Medium-sized Industry of Bologna.)

PCI'S leaders remained loyal overall to the USSR. Togliatti's last word on the subject, the so-called Yalta Memorandum of 1964, argued that there were "many roads to socialism," and the PCI had built close ties with the leading European heretic, Tito's Yugoslav Communist Party. Yet when the PCI criticized the 1968 invasion of Czechoslovakia, it argued that crushing the Dubcek "Prague Spring" experiment in democratizing communism was an "error," not typical of Soviet policy.

Enrico Berlinguer's criticism was stronger, but precisely because he was innovative in domestic policy, he avoided an open split with the USSR in order to appease the PCI rank-and-file who had scant enthusiasm for the historic compromise. Berlinguer dared to state that NATO was a good thing because it would prevent the historic compromise from meeting the same fate as the Prague Spring. He even declared, a year later, that democracy was a "universal value," rejecting the old communist contention that "proletarian" democracy was superior to "bourgeois" democracy.

Berlinguer went further after the end of the historic compromise. In December 1981, he broke ranks with the Soviets over the imposition of military rule in Poland and the smashing of the Solidarity union movement. Meanwhile, the United States was even slower in changing its mind. U.S. leaders could not decide who would rule Italy, but they could decide who would not. They did not want the DC permanently in power, but they did want the PCI permanently in opposition. Neither the reassuring leadership of Berlinguer nor the PCI's services to the Italian state—supporting a new economic austerity and opposing the Red Brigades—made much difference in Washington. After a brief reevaluation at the outset of the Carter administration, the United States reaffirmed its adamant opposition to the PCI's presence in the government.

Whether the United States did more than make its views known is unclear. The Italian police were unusually inefficient in their attempts to rescue Aldo Moro; the Italian secret services, for their part, were headed at the time by members of a corrupt Masonic lodge, called the P2. Did the CIA know anything about the Moro affair?[9] It is not impossible.

Italian foreign policy continued to give priority to ties with the United States, even as it wanted to avoid clashes with the Eastern Bloc. Italy laid claim to a special role in the Mediterranean and the Middle East, a claim that represents a historic stand and that overlaps with the Catholic preference for Mediterranean over northern European culture.

As the postwar decades went by, Italy grew rather more independent of U.S. influence. For example, by the 1980s Italy was friendlier with the PLO (Palestine Liberation Organization) than the U.S. government desired. But it remained Italy's great protector, and Italian governments remained too weak to think seriously about a future in which the United States might withdraw, leaving Italy to construct a foreign policy of its own.

1992–2003: Into the Post–Cold War Era

DOMESTIC POLITICS

In 1992, Italy still was living in the postwar world. Italian political culture is skeptical about change. In *The Leopard*, Lampedusa's novel about Sicily and the unification of Italy, the aristocrat, Tancredi, goes off to fight for Garibaldi, whose aim is a united, democratic Italian republic. "If we want things to stay as they are, then things will have to change," says Tancredi. This is often seen as an example of *trasformismo* or "change without change." But the Sicily of *The Leopard* does change and present-day Italy is changing before our eyes.

The 1992 crisis had both socioeconomic and political causes. If we look at its purely social origins, several factors stand out. Socially, a lay middle class had developed from decades of prosperity in northern and central Italy. At the end of World War II, 70 percent of Italians attended Sunday mass. By the mid-1980s that figure had declined precipitously to 25 percent. Class differences were less distinct. In 1960, the average salary had been twice as high as the average wage; by 1983 it was only 1.3 times higher. In 1971, at the peak of trade union militancy, the working class represented 47 percent of the workforce, but by 1983 it had declined to 43 percent. Similar statistics for the urban middle class were 39 percent and 46 percent. The Italian electorate was becoming less "tribal" and more likely to switch their vote and to reward competence.

This sociocultural terrain is in several ways peculiar to Italy. In 1983, 40 percent of industrial workers were employed in plants with fewer than ten workers. The figure for France was 22 percent and for Germany, 18 percent. Small enterprises were profitable but insecure. They flaunted their industrial independence but resented having to borrow money from banks at twice the prime rate. They disliked the state, but they profited from its weakness to pay less than their share of taxes. Yet then they complained about poor infrastructure.

Another trait of the new period was the national debate about the state. This was not a rebellion of the poor against the rich—even if economic issues were important. Many groups—including skilled workers and entrepreneurs, but also lawyers, doctors, and other free professionals—were expressing their discontent with the way the Italian state was run. Four options existed: First, this coalition of social groups could try to reform the state, to obtain a greater share of public resources, or else to insist on greater efficiency. Second, the coalition could threaten to break with the south and establish a modern state in the north. Third, if reform efforts failed, the coalition could follow the old practice of avoiding the state. Finally, it could move from one to another of these strategies. Thus, it was hard to distinguish between innovators and conservatives, as every social category, every person, was both.

Why did this reform movement develop in the 1990s? One reason is that the Italian state was charging more for its services. By 1991 43 percent of gross domestic product (GDP) went to the state in taxes, 10 percent more than in 1980. Even so, the state was running annual deficits of nearly 10 percent of GDP and had accumulated a national debt that stood at 103 percent of GDP in 1992. To finance it the government sold bonds, which had to offer high interest rates that sent the debt ever higher, crowding out private-sector debt and slowing economic growth.

In the north, discontent found a political outlet in the Northern League.[10] When Umberto Bossi launched the movement in 1984, he tried to build a regional force that emphasized the dialect and culture of Lombardy. He soon realized that love of Lombardy was less strong than dislike of Rome. Bossi claimed to be a "federalist" opposed to the over-centralized Italian state and argued for the construction of a "Republic of the North" and the division of Italy into three "macroregions" for the North, the Center, and the South. But his federalism would eventually spill over into outright secessionism in the mid-1990s, when the *Lega* advocated the creation of the new state of "Padania." This initiative, which was accompanied by an improbable attempt to find the supposedly "Celtic" roots of northern Italians and by a number of theatrical political stunts, proved to be a wrong turn for the League. But Bossi did succeed in mobilizing millions of people to vote for an outright secessionist plank at the 1996 general elections. The League was a good litmus test of the intensity of the Italian political crisis in the 1990s.[11]

Perhaps most important of all for the collapse of the political system was the disintegration of the PCI in the wake of the collapse of the communist regimes of Eastern Europe in 1989. After the death of Berlinguer, the PCI stagnated both intellectually and electorally. In 1989, the party's new, relatively young leader, Achille Occhetto, began jettisoning the outmoded Marxist rhetoric of the party statutes. When, however, the PCI's process of modernization looked to be overtaken by events in Eastern Europe, Occhetto openly advocated creating a party "new even in name." This rejection of the PCI's identity as a communist movement was bitterly resisted by two substantial currents of opinion within the party, and it was not until March 1990 that the PCI was able to decide that it would in fact change its name. For the following year the PCI was unflatteringly known in the Italian press as *la Cosa* ("the thing") until it confirmed officially that it would become the *Partito democratico di sinistra* (PDS) in February 1991. The new party vowed it would be campaigning leftist force that would place women's issues, environmental concerns, and social policy questions at the heart of its agenda. Despite this clear progressive position, the symbolic attachment to communism proved to be too strong for a significant faction of pro-Soviet and pro-Cuban hard-liners within the party, who left to form *Rifondazione Comunista*—Communist Refoundation.

Despite the PCI's reluctant renunciation of its heritage, there is no doubt that the transformation of the PCI into the PDS had an electoral impact. Conservative Italians who were disenchanted with the workings of the party system, but who feared that a vote against the DC would be a vote for the Communists, suddenly found themselves free to vote for whomever they chose. The April 1992 general elections were to prove a watershed in Italian political history.

In the elections, the League was decisive in driving down the DC's vote to under 30 percent. The PSI, the DC's main coalition ally, saw its vote fall for the first time since the 1970s, and it failed to obtain more votes than the PDS, which held on to a 16 percent share, 10 percent less than in 1987. Even though the governing coalition was returned to office with a reduced majority of seats in the house—331 out of 624—nobody doubted that a major shift in the party system had occurred. The League's emergence as the second largest party in northern Italy, with almost 20 percent of the vote, and the largest party in such an important cultural and industrial center as Milan, could not be ignored. The DC's hold on power was being retained by virtue of its clientelistic hold over southern and central Italy. It no longer had a national mandate.[12]

The Arrival of "Clean Hands"

Then the earthquake finally did arrive—in the shape of investigating judges Antonio Di Pietro, Francesco Saverio Borrelli, and other Milan prosecutors who launched an investigation into corruption. They began with kickbacks exacted by Milan Socialists in exchange for state contracts. Soon they were exposing the "systemic clientelism" that had become the cornerstone of government. Here again one must ask the question, Why now? The system had been in operation for decades and many judges had been a part of it. What had changed was the growing unpopularity of the regime as a whole. If Andreotti and Craxi had won the 1992 elections by a large margin, they would have destroyed the Milan judges. Instead the magistrates in most of Italy rejected complicity with the politicians and relegitimized themselves as agents of reform.

At the same moment, the tacit agreement between the DC and the Mafia fell apart. After the condemnation of several leading mafiosi to long spells in prison at the beginning of 1992—an act which the Mafia regarded as a breach of their unwritten accord with the political elite—Mafia gunmen killed Salvatore Lima, Andreotti's closest henchman in Sicily. Behind this murder lay the rise to power within the Mafia of the Corleonesi family, led by Toto Riina. In May and July 1992, two judges active in the struggle against organized crime, Giovanni Falcone and Paulo Borsellino, were subsequently murdered at Riina's behest. The murders, however, triggered a wave of determined state activity against the Mafia. Many gang members were persuaded to break the *omertà* (vow of silence) and give evidence against their bosses. In 1993, the police captured Riina, and the Mafia chief was sentenced to life imprisonment. Many of Riina's accomplices and rivals were subsequently incarcerated. It would be unwise, however, to think that the Mafia is dead. There are many signs that it is reorganizing and is once again working with quiescent politicians to reestablish its power.

The murder of Falcone on May 23, 1992, was the last straw for public opinion. The death of this talented and courageous prosecutor, who had become a national hero for the skill with which he had conducted the fight against organized crime, blew away the last shreds of legitimacy possessed by the traditional parties. Andreotti and Craxi, who had hoped to become president and prime minister, now had to stand aside while Oscar Luigi Scalfaro, a veteran Piedmontese who although a member of the DC had an unblemished reputation for honesty, was elected president. Giuliano Amato, a technocrat associated with the PSI, was appointed prime minister. Amato was the first in a series of prime ministers who tried to reform the state. He imposed drastic austerity measures to cut the burgeoning budget deficit in the summer of 1992, although his premiership was marred by a dramatic collapse of the lira and by the judicial inquiries, which robbed his government of all legitimacy. Carlo Azeglio Ciampi, formerly head of the Bank of Italy, followed Amato as prime minister in the spring of 1993 and pursued similar policies. He helped bring about the July 1993 agreement that set up a permanent mechanism for management–union wage bargaining, which took into account the government's targets for inflation and money supply; he privatized two major banks, Comit and Credito Italiano;

and during his year in office the interest on a five-year government bond went down from 11.5 to 7.5 percent. Similarly, the 1995 Dini government reduced the government's annual deficit to 7.5 percent of GDP. The state's role in society and the economy was at last being brought under control and its role in everyday life was being diminished. This was a change—though whether it will prove a permanent change is an argument that divides academic opinion.

The slow pace of constitutional reform in the 1990s is another argument for the change-without-change thesis. It is easy to see why the political parties should have resisted innovation: Italy's constitution, which balances power between the separate branches of government, and the electoral law, with its rigid proportionality, were the heart of the old order. Therefore, proportional representation became the prime target of reformers. An April 1993 referendum provided a clear majority for the British winner-take-all method, although supporters of the old order succeeded in retaining 25 percent of the seats for distribution via PR to parties obtaining more than 4 percent of the vote.

Yet the March 1994 parliamentary election, the first held under the new rules, proved disappointing for the reformers. The widespread hope was that it would produce two stable, broad coalitions: one for the center-left and the other for the center-right. The larger would govern for five years while the smaller functioned as loyal opposition. However, it was unlikely that changing the electoral law would by itself immediately produce such a result. Voters and politicians need to learn how to use new institutions.

The Catholics had not learned the need for electoral alliances. The reformed remnants of the DC, which had by now revived the Catholic movement's first name, the *Partito Popolare Italiano* (PPI), ran on their own. With nearly 16 percent of the vote, they won a mere 7 percent of the seats. The left-wing coalition, based on the PDS, was defeated easily, winning just 213 seats in the Chamber of Deputies and taking only 32 percent of the vote. The PDS had still to acquire an identity of its own. As the ex-PCI, it was associated with the old regime even if it had been in opposition. Meanwhile, Communist Refoundation maintained its role as a vehicle of protest and won 6 percent.

The Berlusconi Phenomenon

Berlusconi's "Freedom Pole," by contrast, won over 49 percent in the March 1994 parliamentary election. It was an amalgamation rather than a coalition. Of its three main components, the Northern League's allegiance was purely strategic; and the second component, *Alleanza Nazionale* (AN), was the rebaptized MSI, whose legitimacy was also questionable.[13] The demise of the DC offered the AN the opportunity to become the new conservative party, especially in the south. Silvio Berlusconi's "Go Italy!" (*Forza Italia* or FI), conjured into existence in 1993, could have been the party of modern capitalism that Italy has never had. Alas, FI was and is a populist party, a tool for its charismatic leader.

The Berlusconi phenomenon is more complex than it seems. It is a natural part of the "politics of spectacle" and of "media democracy." Berlusconi could not have created an election-winning party in one year without owning the Fininvest Corporation with its three TV networks. The sales segment of the corporation, Publitalia, provided him with a skeleton base and plausible candidates. He already was known to the country, and he appeared often and well on TV during the campaign. Berlusconi had glamour, that promise of wealth and beauty that hangs around certain people who are involved with TV. He also owned Europe's finest soccer team, A.C. Milan, and the charisma of its star players, Ruud Gullit and Paolo Maldini, rubbed off on him.

Yet much more was involved. A close friend of Bettino Craxi, Berlusconi was an integral part of the old regime. Yet if this alienated many people, it may have reassured those who wanted continuity. Then, too, Berlusconi was a self-made businessman in a country that respects entrepreneurial talent. As unemployment grew, who could cope with it better than he? Berlusconi offered himself as a savior, the Pope Pius XII of 1993. His speeches were monologues in which he addressed not active citizens but "the people," whose role was to cheer on their leader as they cheered on Gullit. Berlusconi did not explain the problem of the public debt. Instead he set out to seduce the listener, to create the myth of a Berlusconi who incarnated "another" Italy, traditional in its emphasis on the family and anticommunism but new in its economic success.

In 1994, this appeal was hard to resist. FI edged out the PDS to become Italy's largest party, although with only 21 percent of the vote. It appealed to the young—winning nearly 40 percent of the age group under 25—and to the sophisticated, outvoting the Northern League in Milan by 29 percent to 16 percent.

The introduction of majority voting for 75 percent of the deputies was successful, or so it seemed. In the lower house the Freedom Party had an outright majority of seats, while in the senate it won a relative majority with twenty-nine more seats than the left and with the center holding thirty-one seats. For both chambers the Berlusconi government was, however, dependent on the wildly unreliable Northern League for a majority. Then, too, Berlusconi was a leading target of the Milan magistrates. Finally, could a crisis, at the core of which lay the state, be resolved by a prime minister whose TV networks competed with the public networks? Berlusconi was as much the problem as its solution.

And so he proved. Outside Italy, this supposedly strong "business" government was expected to cut government spending. But Berlusconi did not continue the austerity program of Amato and Ciampi. Once the financial markets realized this, they abandoned the lira and treasury bonds. The minister of justice issued a decree favorable to the politicians and businesspeople involved in corruption trials, thus making the investigating magistrates' task more difficult. The reaction of the public was outrage. The next day, July 14, the Milan magistrates resigned and Antonio Di Pietro read their statement on TV. Berlusconi's medium turned against him: Di Pietro convinced the viewers. Berlusconi at first took a tough line but then withdrew the decree on July 19.

In December 1994, Bossi brought down the government. Although he appealed to the people, Berlusconi had to recognize that the Italian constitution calls for a prime minister to have a majority in the House rather than a mystical populist bond with the nation. In January 1995, another central banker, Lamberto Dini, replaced Berlusconi at the head of a government of nonparty technocrats. An important episode in post-1992 politics had ended. Given its liking for populism of all kinds, the Italian electorate was bound to turn, at least once, to a charismatic leader. It was also probable, given the distrust that accompanies the liking, that the populist experiment would fail. With Dini, Italy was reverting to the Amato-Ciampi pattern of a technocrat as prime minister. Such a government would push ahead with the "European" policy of austerity, but it could be only a temporary solution.

Dini governed for just over a year. In the meantime, the center-left and center-right readied themselves for new elections. Innovation was greater on the center-left than on the center-right, which was hampered electorally by the defection of the by now secessionist Northern League. On the center-left, two new figures emerged: Romano Prodi, a Bologna economics professor and former industrialist, and Massimo D'Alema, who replaced Occhetto as leader of the PDS after the electoral defeat in 1994. Despite a troubled personal relationship, these two men both broke with the traditional political cultures to which they belonged. Prodi, a Catholic, nevertheless made a clear distinction between church and state.[14] Where the postwar DC distrusted the market economy, Prodi emphasized it, bringing the values of competition and competence into Catholic political culture. Massimo D'Alema, the former Communist, likewise expressly argued in favor of privatization and what he called "lo stato snello" (the slimmed-down state). He accepted the globalized economy as an opportunity as well as a constraint. In this sense, D'Alema resembled the British Labour prime minister, Tony Blair, although his stress on balancing monetary union by programs to reduce unemployment was akin to the policies of the French Socialist prime minister, Lionel Jospin. D'Alema even talked of carving out a stronger international role for Italy.[15]

The 1996 elections showed, moreover, that the left and center had learned how to use the electoral system. When Prodi began his campaign in early 1995, he presented himself as anti-Berlusconi. He brought together the majority faction of the PPI and the PDS as well as smaller groups on the left into a new coalition called the *Ulivo* (Olive Tree). Prodi's anti-Berlusconi motif was not merely a way of competing with a rival but also a critique of the cult of the charismatic leader. Berlusconi used his private plane, Prodi campaigned in a bus. Berlusconi spoke in a monologue, Prodi called for dialogue.

In the 1996 elections, the Olive Tree program of modernization with a human face was more appealing than the Berlusconi center-right's aggressive pro-market, anti-state language. The main reason for the center-left's victory was, however, its (relative) unity, which enabled it to win a majority of the seats (247 out of 475) awarded by first past the post. On the right, the Northern League chose to run alone and despite (or because) of its secessionist rhetoric was rewarded with its best-ever electoral result: a substantial 10 percent of the national vote—3.75 million votes—went to the League, and Bossi's movement even won 39 electoral districts outright. Had the League collaborated with the Freedom Pole, it seems probable that the right-wing parties would have swept the north and returned Berlusconi to the prime ministership. The Freedom Pole's parties took a much higher share of the votes cast in the PR part of the ballot (15.8 million to the 13.1 million accumulated by the *Ulivo*'s parties). The Olive Tree was thus dependent upon Communist Refoundation, and its mercurial leader, Fausto Bertinotti, for a majority in the Chamber of Deputies.

Despite the constraints provided by its precarious parliamentary majority, the Olive Tree government could boast some notable successes by 1998. Although a D'Alema-sponsored initiative to obtain all-party consent to constitutional reform fell victim to party infighting in the spring of 1998, the Olive Tree government did promote sweeping measures of privatization and impose austerity. It even successfully managed to squeeze Italy's public deficit within the 3 percent total permitted by the Maastricht treaty. In November 1996 Italy returned to the European Monetary System, from which it had been expelled in 1992, and in the spring of 1998 the EU declared Italy eligible to join EMU in 1999. This achievement was not obtained without sacrifice. The 1997 budget imposed austerity measures worth $41 billion on the Italian people. Nevertheless, the probable economic consequences of failure to enter EMU—which would have almost certainly provoked a currency crisis of Latin American dimensions—persuaded the Italians of the need to tighten their belts (and persuaded the rest of the EU to let Italy in).

The achievements of his government notwithstanding, Prodi paid a political price for his austerity policies. Communist Refoundation balked at a new round of cuts in the 1998 budget and brought down the government. By the narrowest of margins, Prodi was defeated in parliament and was replaced as prime minister by Massimo D'Alema, who tilted the center-left coalition toward the center even as he became the first ex-Communist to lead a western European country. Prodi soon found a new job—he has been president of the European Commission since June 1999—but he was angered by D'Alema's opportunistic exploitation of his defeat and has by no means ruled out a return to domestic Italian politics.[16]

D'Alema was less successful than Prodi as prime minister. His governing coalition, which included the full gamut of political opinion from Communists to anti-Berlusconi Conservatives, was litigious and ineffective. It limped on until the Spring 2000 local elections, at which the Olive Tree parties were soundly beaten by a resurgent Berlusconi. D'Alema resigned and was replaced by Giuliano Amato, who nursed the government for a year, but who was not chosen as the center-left's candidate for the premiership in the elections due in April 2001. That honor went to the mayor of Rome, Francesco Rutelli, whose film-star looks and polished style were held to be more attractive to the voters than Amato's sternly professorial persona. This may or may not have been the right calculation, but the move gave the impression that the center-left was running away from its record in government.

The Center-Right from Opposition to Government

In the meantime, Berlusconi had reorganized the Italian right into the "House of Freedoms" (*Casa delle libertà*). In a sense, this is the old "Freedom Party" under a new guise; however, the National Alliance, under the moderate leadership of Gianfranco Fini, has gradually shed its fascist past and successfully established itself as an authentic conservative party, while the coalition's Christian Democrat component, now named the "Democratic Union of the Center" (UDC), has established itself as a solid force, above all in the south. Most important of all, Berlusconi and Bossi, who had spent most of the late 1990s insulting each other (Bossi notoriously called Berlusconi "Berluscosa nostra" in a 1998 speech), realized in 2000 that they would never get back into government unless the League joined forces with the rest of the right.

The House of Freedoms is nevertheless firmly based on *Forza Italia*, or "Go, Italy!"—one of the most interesting new political phenomena in contemporary democratic politics. During its formative phase (1993–1996), *Forza Italia* was less a political party than an electoral committee that emerged in the last month of 1993 largely from Berlusconi's widespread network of private resources and connections developed through his commercial enterprise, Fininvest. Fininvest executives were involved in the recruitment of candidates, in setting up a broad, though loose, system of supporters' "clubs" on the ground, and establishing a market-research and polling agency, in running the media campaign.

In serving Berlusconi's purposes, *Forza Italia* had relatively little need for the organizational features of a traditional mass party. It did not need grassroots structures, as long as Berlusconi's appeal was channeled directly to the national electorate through privileged access to the media. It did not need a party bureaucracy, as long as Fininvest could supply the relatively small staff required for the organization of the campaign. Moreover, it did not need a membership base to legitimize the position of the leader, who was the founder and the "owner" of the party machine.

At the national election of March 1994, the high level of personal control Berlusconi exercised over all sectors of his electoral machine made *Forza Italia* an efficient and flexible instrument to assert his political will in a rapidly changing and unstructured political environment. Once the goal of government was

achieved, moreover, party organization and internal participation were relegated to a very low priority. In the months that followed the victory, *Forza
Italia*'s leadership made almost no effort to develop a centrally directed organization of local and intermediate party structures.

Berlusconi's preference for an elector-oriented party rather than for a
member-oriented party, and his consequent decision not to enroll members,
meant that *Forza Italia* lacked an upward delegation of political authority,
mechanisms of decentralization, and local and national congresses; intraparty
democracy was nonexistent and leadership accountability to the party base was
ruled out. All executive appointments, as well as candidate selection, were carried out by the party leader, who also controlled all decision-making processes
in relation to party strategies, policies, alliances, and drafting of the electoral
program. Fininvest personnel pervaded *Forza Italia*'s national leadership
group, its regional leaderships, and, to a lesser extent, the parliamentary party,
which was predominantly formed by inexperienced politicians at their first parliamentary mandate, lacking autonomous power bases in politics. *Forza Italia*
was essentially a "leader's" party, and it was, in this context, unusual in being
the first case of a major Italian party lacking strong participatory social roots.

Such an ultra-light and nonparticipatory organizational model, however,
soon revealed its shortcomings. In regional and local elections, *Forza Italia* always under-performed compared to its national electoral performance, and
weaknesses were particularly evident in municipal elections. Moreover, the
weakness of party structures at the local level and the poor horizontal and vertical linkages also penalized the party during the parliamentary elections of April
1996. As a result, *Forza Italia* spent five years (1996–2001) engaged in a deep
restructuring of the party: strengthening and maintaining the organization became imperatives in order to survive in opposition and regain electoral competitiveness.[17]

By the end of 1998, *Forza Italia*'s organization had become more consistent
and permanent throughout Italy, and it had started measuring its forces in a
number of national demonstrations against government policies, in nationwide
thematic rallies and in a series of elections. The real test for the party's stability,
however, was represented first by the European elections of 1999 and then by
the regional election of 2000. In both cases, *Forza Italia* gained 5 percentage
points compared to the 1996 parliamentary elections, passing from 20.6 percent
gained in 1996 to 25.1 percent in 1999 and 25.6 percent in 2000. *Forza Italia*
had established itself as the largest party in Italy. Equally important, it had established its primacy on the right: both the League and the National Alliance
have seen their support erode since 1996. *Forza Italia*, despite its somewhat
cloudy ideology (a combination of traditional Christian Democrat rhetoric
about the family and generic appeals to the virtues of the free market) and the
troubles of its leader (Berlusconi by 2001 was on trial for several serious crimes,

including fraudulent accounting and corruption), was, for good or for ill, the point of reference for right-wing voters in Italy.

During the 2001 election campaign, this revitalized right fought a media-savvy campaign that focused on the Berlusconi "rags to riches" personal success story (a copy of a lavishly illustrated 130-page hagiography was sent to every Italian family) and on explicit promises of rapid economic progress. In a TV program conducted by a friendly journalist, Berlusconi signed a five-point "Contract with the Italians" that promised accelerated growth rates, higher pensions, lower taxes, more infrastructure spending on public works, and the creation of 1.5 million jobs. He pledged to resign if he had not achieved at least four out of five of these objectives by the end of his government's mandate.

The Olive Tree, despite Rutelli's reasonable showing as leader, could not match this brilliant (and cynical) marketing strategy. It appeared deeply divided, at odds with its record in government, and lacking in ideas. The relationship between the center-left's two largest forces, the "Democrats of the Left" (as the former PDS had been known since 1998) and the "Daisy" (the informal alliance of ex–Christian Democrats, liberals, and assorted moderates led by Rutelli), was never less than tense. Neither Communist Refoundation nor "The Italy of Values," a personal movement headed by the former prosecutor, Antonio Di Pietro, made an electoral pact with the Olive Tree, which weakened the center-left's chances in the seats awarded by FPTP.[18]

The "House of Freedoms" accordingly won a clear electoral victory in the elections held on May 13, 2001 (see Table 11.2). This sweeping victory gave Berlusconi and his allies the chance to make good on their promises. They have, however, run into significant difficulties. First, parliamentary activity has been dominated by Berlusconi's own personal problems. During the electoral campaign, a number of foreign newspapers, notably *The Economist* and the Spanish conservative daily *El Mundo*, charged Berlusconi with being "unfit to govern" Italy.[19] The massive conflict of interest inherent in having a billionaire media mogul in charge of the state, in addition to Berlusconi's numerous pending trials, seemed incompatible with his being premier. During the campaign, Berlusconi promised to divest his holdings, a promise he has signally failed to keep, and his government has promoted the passage of a new law regulating the media which will, in the opinion of many critics, permit Berlusconi to retain an unchallenged monopoly over the private media in Italy. Berlusconi has solved his legal problems, meanwhile, by the simple expedient of retrospectively decriminalizing some of the laws he is alleged to have broken and by obtaining (a possibly unconstitutional) legal immunity from prosecution while in office. Months of parliamentary time have been taken up since May 2001 with the passage of these "made-to-measure laws."[20]

Second, it has become apparent that the economic promises made by Berlusconi during the campaign will only be realized with difficulty. Italy, now that it is no longer able to rely on a declining lira to maintain competitiveness,

Table 11.2 Italian Parliamentary Elections—May 13, 2001

	Chamber of Deputies				Senate			
Coalition and Parties	Votes (%)	No. proport. seats	No. majority seats	Total number of seats	Votes (%)	No. proport. seats	No. majority seats	Total number of seats
House of Freedom	**49.5**	**86**	**282**	**368**	**42.5**	**24**	**151**	**175**
Forza Italia	29.4	62	133	195		10	73	83
National Alliance	12.0	24	75	99		6	40	46
Catholic Centrists	3.2	0	41	41		7	21	28
Northern League	3.9	0	30	30		1	16	17
New Socialist Party	1.0	0	3	3		0	1	1
Independent						0	1	1
Olive Tree	**35.5**	**58**	**192**	**250**	**39.2**	**51**	**79**	**130**
Democrats of the Left	16.6	31	107	138		27	36	63
The Daisy	14.5	27	49	76		16	25	41
Greens	2.2	0	17	17		6	10	16
Italian Communists	1.7	0	8	8		1	1	2
Olive Tree–SVP	0.5	0	5	5		0	3	3
SVP		0	3	3		0	2	2
Independent		0	3	3		1	2	3
Communist Refoundation	5.0	11	0	11	5.0	4	0	4
European Democracy	2.4	0	0	0	3.2	2	0	2
Italy of Values	3.9	0	0	0	3.4	1	0	1
Bonino's List	2.2	0	0	0	2.0	0	0	0
Social Movement	0.4	0	0	0	1.0	0	1	1
Others	1.1	0	1	1	3.7	1	1	2
Total	100.0	155	475	630	100.0	83	232	315

is struggling to achieve even moderate levels of economic growth. Growth in both 2002 and 2003 has been less than 1 percent of GDP. The two classic devices in the hands of governments for overcoming slow growth—tax cuts and increased public spending—are ruled out in the case of Italy by its commitments to the EU's so-called Stability and Growth Pact, which limits public sector borrowing to just 3 percent of GDP per year. In the case of Italy, which has to deal with the legacy of fifty years of open-handed government and a national debt of over 100 percent of GDP, this means that Italy is obliged for the foreseeable future to run a permanent primary surplus (i.e., a surplus before interest payments on the national debt) in its public accounts. Italy could export its way out of trouble—but here, too, Europe and the legacy of Italy's overworked state are causing problems. Italian industry is not geared to using a strong currency for trade. Moreover, Italy's costly and inefficient state imposes a high permanent cost (both in terms of taxes and inefficient performance) on businesses that are having to cope with global competition in fields (footwear, ceramics, sporting goods, certain kinds of machine tools) where Italy is a world leader. The small businesses of the northeast are increasingly locating production in eastern Europe as a way to cut costs. Last but not least, Italy could attempt to provide for long-term growth by reducing the structural costs of the state. This, however, is a recipe for conflict with the unions and with middle-class pensioners who enjoy one of the most generous pension regimes in the world. Writing in 1997, the eminent Italian economist Michele Salvati argued that the euro would impose a "Copernican revolution" on the Italian economy.[21] It is fair to say that the rightness of Salvati's argument is now plain for all to see.

Third, the tenants of the "House of Freedoms" are a litigious bunch. The League backed Berlusconi in 2001 because Berlusconi promised Bossi "devolution"—the transfer of all health care, educational, and local police functions to the regional governments and a constitutional law to transform the senate into a chamber representing the regions. Together with powers already transferred by the Olive Tree government in 1999–2000, such a decisive shift of responsibilities would enable the League to claim that it had finally succeeded in imposing a federalist organization upon the Italian state. This measure, however, is anathema to both the National Alliance and the UDC, which have stalled the measure in parliament by insisting on the inclusion of a clause allowing the central state to assert the primacy of the "national interest." On this, and a raft of other issues, the "House of Freedoms" is split with dissent. In June–July 2003, the deep divisions within Berlusconi's majority brought the government to the edge of a crisis. In this respect at least, *trasformismo* lives on unperturbed and the new parties are very much like the old.

ITALY IN EUROPE AND THE WORLD

Berlusconi was able to avoid a government crisis in July 2003 and to get the law suspending the trials against him, because Italy was taking over the presidency of the European Union at a delicate moment in the EU's history (the intergovernmental conference to decide the EU's constitution will take place during Italy's presidency). The president of the republic (since 1999, Carlo Azeglio Ciampi) and public opinion were desperate to avoid the humiliation of Berlusconi's either being condemned for corruption or having to desert crucial appointments in Europe for bargaining sessions with his coalition partners in Rome. This was not least because Berlusconi's government had already achieved the reputation of being somewhat skeptical toward the EU. Berlusconi's first foreign minister, Renato Ruggiero, a staunch supporter of the EU who was president of the World Trade Organization in the 1990s, resigned in

January 2002 to protest the anti-European attitudes of many of Berlusconi's ministers.

As it happened, Berlusconi's opening speech to the European Parliament in July 2003 ended in farce, when the Italian premier lost his temper with hecklers on the Socialist benches of the parliament and compared a German member of the parliament to a concentration camp "Kapo." This scarcely credible gaffe provoked a major rift between Italy and Germany and confirmed most of Europe in its belief that Berlusconi was not only unfit to run Italy but was unfit to run Europe, too.

Such folkloristic incidents aside, Italy's determination to cut a good figure on the European stage illustrates the central point about its relationship with the EU since the Maastricht treaty. Europe has become an integral part of Italian *domestic* politics. If one looks back over the previous section, one sees that Italian politics has been shaped at every step by the requirements of European integration. The necessity of participating in the euro acted as a *vincolo esterno* (external constraint) throughout the 1990s, imposing unpopular austerity policies upon the governments of Amato, Dini, Prodi, and now Berlusconi.[22] While European unity has always been an issue capable of mobilizing great idealism in Italy, it is now seen as more of a vital issue of national well-being. Unlike its counterparts in Britain, Norway, and Switzerland, the Italian political class believes, with good reason, that Italy could not maintain its enviable standards of living outside of the European Union. "Europe" acts as a tool for modernizers of all kinds, and all would-be reformers appeal to "European" standards as a justification for policy change.

This "Europe" is often a figment of Italian politicians' imaginations. The EU itself, as the events of the last decade have shown, is hardly a model of clean and efficient government; other countries, notably France and Belgium, have had comparable problems of political corruption to Italy; still other countries— Germany springs to mind—have creaking systems of public welfare, inefficient universities, and grave disparities in regional living standards. There is a sense in which Italy is eminently European already—or, perhaps, Europe now has many of the same shortcomings as Italy. The psychological importance of European integration, however, is a major and undeniable factor in Italian domestic politics. It has been a source of great pride that several leading Italian politicians, most notably of all Romano Prodi, have occupied top European jobs with distinction since the 1990s.

As the European Union evolves into a more closely integrated political unit with foreign policy ambitions, Italy, rather like Britain, has found its traditional foreign policy orientation being called into question. Italy, under any government, would hate to have to choose between the United States and the European Union. Its behavior during the Iraq crisis was symptomatic of its embarrassment over this issue. Berlusconi, like Tony Blair, Spanish premier José María Aznar, and several premiers from Central and Eastern Europe, backed the

United States' hard line during the crisis. But unlike Britain, Italy did not commit fighting troops and immediately worked to mend fences with France, Germany, and Belgium in the aftermath of the crisis. Italy's behavior during the Iraq crisis was, in fact, paradigmatic. In every crisis of the 1990s, whatever the political orientation of the government of the day, Italy has backed the United States after a tormented domestic debate in which the anti-Americanism of large swaths of public opinion was very vocal. This was true of the first Gulf conflict in 1991, when the then Andreotti government supported Desert Storm and even made a token military contribution to the coalition; it was also true of the Kosovo crisis in 1999, when the D'Alema government was initially reluctant about the use of force and distinctly skeptical of the idea of an independent Kosovo. When NATO intervened militarily, however, Italy fell into line immediately. Still, Italy was far from enthusiastic over NATO enlargement in the 1990s, not least because all Italian governments since 1992 have worked hard to better relations with Russia. Berlusconi, to the irritation of some of his European partners, has even proposed that Russia should join the EU. The creation, in May 2002 in Rome, of a NATO-Russia Council owed much to Italian diplomacy, and it is clear, in general, that Italy wishes to see an empowered EU, Russia, and the United States acting in concert in world affairs, rather than seeing each other as potential rivals.

In the 1990s, Italy has achieved a high reputation for its skills in peacekeeping missions. Italian peacekeepers are at work in southern Iraq; this is just the latest of a series of missions in Afghanistan, Somalia, and elsewhere that have occupied thousands of Italian troops every year throughout the 1990s. After the United States and the UK, Italy is the third largest contributor to UN-sponsored peacekeeping operations. In the spring of 1997, when Albania collapsed in the wake of a financial scandal and a wave of Albanian migration threatened to spill over into Italy, Italy initiated and led an EU "coalition of the willing" that restored order in Albania and brought about some measure of economic and political reconstruction. Italy sees fulfilling such tasks in the Balkans and the Mediterranean as the essential task for a common European foreign policy and believes that the EU could become an active regional player without jeopardizing its relations with the United States.

Last, but not least, at any rate for the Italians, Italy has argued that its high profile in peacekeeping actions, together with its obvious economic importance, justifies its being included as a permanent member of the UN Security Council. Britain and France's possession of permanent seats at the UN rankles Germany, Japan, Brazil, and India as well as Italy, but there is no sign that Britain and France will decide to relinquish their places in favor of a single EU seat. In 1998, Italy successfully opposed a plan to enlarge the Security Council by including Germany, Japan, and three other places assigned permanently to Africa, Asia, and Latin America.[23]

Italy's ambitions for a greater world role for herself and for Europe, how-

ever, only underscore the central theme of this chapter: Italy's Pinocchio problem. Italy's economic achievements have been unquestionable in the postwar
years; its diplomacy is inventive and talented; it has shown a tremendous and
durable commitment to European integration. Nevertheless, it does not command the automatic respect that Britain, France, Germany, or even the Netherlands, Spain, and Sweden do. Why not? The answer surely is that Italy's political class and the Italian state inspire little confidence, either within Italy or
without. Italy's postwar achievements have been immense in many fields, but
its democracy since 1945 has been a distinctly tormented one. Moreover, it appears that the collapse of the political system based upon Christian Democracy,
far from being a new beginning for Italian democracy, has merely ushered in a
new era in which Italy's political elite will continue to use the state as an instrument for the pursuit of their own interests, not any conception of the collective
good.

Notes

I wish to thank Lisa Handy, who worked as my research assistant on this chapter,
Emanuela Poli, who helped with some initial revisions, and Mark Gilbert, who completed the revision process of this chapter.

1. Carlo Collodi, *The Adventures of Pinocchio* (Oxford: Oxford University Press,
1996).

2. Stephen Gundle, *Between Hollywood and Moscow: The Italian Communists and
the Rise of Mass Culture* (Cambridge: Cambridge University Press, 1995).

3. Aurelio Lepre, *Storia della prima repubblica* (Bologna: Il Mulino, 1993).

4. Giorgio Bocca, *Palmiro Togliatti* (Rome: L'Unità, 1992), 405.

5. Antonio Gramsci, *Selections from the Prison Notebooks* (New York: International
Publishers, 1992).

6. F. Roy Willis, *Italy Chooses Europe* (Oxford: Oxford University Press, 1971),
20–31.

7. John Harper, *America and the Reconstruction of Europe* (Cambridge: Cambridge
University Press, 1986).

8. Gianfranco Pasquino, "Italy: A Democratic Regime under Reform," in *Political
Institutions in Europe*, Josep M. Colomer, ed. (London: Routledge, 1996), 138–69.

9. Claudio Gatti, *Rimanga tra noi* (Milan: Longanesi, 1990).

10. Ilvo Diamanti, *La Lega* (Rome: Donzelli, 1993).

11. For the *Lega Nord*, see Anna Cento Bull and Mark Gilbert, *The Lega Nord and
the Northern Question in Italian Politics* (London: Palgrave, 2001).

12. Gianfranco Pasquino, *La nuova politica* (Bari: Laterza, 1992).

13. Piero Ignazi, *Postfascisti* (Bologna: Il Mulino, 1994).

14. See Romano Prodi, *Governare l'Italia* (Rome: Donzelli, 1995).

15. For D'Alema's ideas, see Mark Gilbert, "In Search of Normality: The Political
Strategy of Massimo D'Alema," *Journal of Modern Italian Studies* 3, no. 3 (Fall 1998),
307–17.

16. See Sergio Fabbrini, *Tra pressioni e veto: Il cambiamento politico in Italia* (Bari-Roma: Laterza, 2001) for an account of the significance of Prodi's downfall.

17. For an account of FI's structural development, see E. Poli, *Forza Italia: struttura, leadership e radicamento territoriale* (Bologna: Il Mulino, 2001).

18. Accounts of the May 13 election include I. Diamanti e M. Lazar, "Le elezioni del 13 maggio 2001" in *Politica in Italia*, ed. P. Bellucci and Martin Bull (Bologna: Il Mulino, 2002), 71, and Sergio Fabbrini and Mark Gilbert, "The Italian General Election of 13 May 2001," *Government & Opposition* 36, no. 4 (Autumn 2001), 519–36. Readers of Italian should also consult Gianfranco Pasquino, *Dall'Ulivo al governo Berlusconi* (Bologna: Il Mulino, 2002), and Itanes, *Perché ha vinto il centro-destra* (Bologna: Il Mulino, 2001).

19. *Economist*, 28 April 2001.

20. David Hine, "Silvio Berlusconi, i media e il conflitto di interesse" in *Politica in Italia Edizione 2002*, ed. Bellucci and Bull (Bologna: Il Molino, 2002), 291–307.

21. Michele Salvati, "Moneta unica, rivoluzione Copernicana," *Il Mulino* n. 1 (1997).

22. For the effects of European integration on Italian domestic politics, see Maurizio Ferrera and Elisabetta Gualmini, *Salvati dall'Europa* (Bologna: Il Mulino, 1999).

23. For a useful survey of recent Italian foreign policy, see Osvaldo Croce, "Italian Security Policy after the Cold War," *Journal of Modern Italian Studies* 8, no. 2 (Summer 2003), 266–83.

Suggestions for Further Reading

Bufacchi, Vittorio, and V. Burgess. *Italy since 1989: Events and Interpretations*. London: Palgrave, 2001.

Cento Bull, Anna, and Mark Gilbert. *The Lega Nord and the Northern Question in Italian Politics*. London: Palgrave, 2001.

Gilbert, Mark. *The Italian Revolution. The End of Politics, Italian Style?* Boulder, Colo.: Westview, 1995.

Ginsborg, Paul. *A History of Contemporary Italy: Society and Politics 1943–1988*. London: Penguin Books, 1990.

Ginsborg, Paul. *Italy and Its Discontents 1980–2001*. London: Allen Lane, 2001.

Gundle, Stephen. *Between Hollywood and Moscow: The Italian Communists and the Rise of Mass Culture*. Cambridge: Cambridge University Press, 1995.

Harper, John. *America and the Reconstruction of Europe*. Cambridge: Cambridge University Press, 1986.

Hellman, Stephan. *Italian Communism in Transition: The Rise and Fall of the Historic Compromise in Turin*. Oxford: Oxford University Press, 1989.

Hine, David. *Governing Italy: The Politics of Bargained Pluralism*. Oxford: Oxford University Press, 1993.

McCarthy, Patrick. *The Crisis of the Italian State*. New York: St. Martin's, 2001.

Miller, James E. *The United States and Italy, 1940–1950*. Chapel Hill: University of North Carolina Press, 1986.

Newell, James. *Parties and Democracy in Italy*. Aldershot: Ashgate, 2000.

Pasquino, Gianfranco. "Italy: A Democratic Regime under Reform," in *Political Institutions in Europe*, ed. Josep M. Colomer. London: Routledge, 1996.

Pasquino, Gianfranco, and Patrick McCarthy, eds. *The End of Postwar Politics: The Italian Elections of 1992*. Boulder, Colo.: Westview, 1993.

Pasquino, Gianfranco, and Carol Mershon, eds. *Italian Politics Ending the First Republic*. Boulder, Colo.: Westview, 1995.

Zamagni, Vera. *The Economic History of Italy 1860–1990: Recovery after Decline*. Oxford: Clarendon Press, 1993.

CHAPTER 12

Spain

"Middle Power" or "Major Player"?

Paul Heywood

Spain

Population: 41.3 million
Area in Square Miles: 195,363
Population Density per Square Mile: 211
GDP (in billion dollars, 2001): $861.4
GDP per capita (purchasing power parity in dollars, 1996): $21,393
Joined EC/EU: January 1, 1986
Joined NATO: 1982
Political Parties:
Basque Nationalist Party or PNV
Canarian Coalition or CC (a coalition of five parties)
Convergence and Union or CiU (a coalition of the Democratic
　　Convergence of Catalonia or CDC and the Democratic Union of
　　Catalonia or UDC)
Galician Nationalist Bloc or BNG
Party of Independents from Lanzarote or PIL
Popular Party or PP
Spanish Socialist Workers' Party or PSOE
United Left or IU (a coalition of parties including the
　　PCE—Communist Party—and other small parties)

Sources: "Organisation for Economic Co-operation and Development," at
　www.oecd.org/home/ (accessed August 5, 2003); "2003 World Population
　Data Sheet," at www.prb.org/pdf/WorldPopulationDS03_Eng.pdf
　(accessed August 5, 2003); "The World Factbook," August 1, 2003, at
　cia.gov/cia/publications/factbook/index.html (accessed October 6, 2003).

Introduction

As recently as 1986, when Spain achieved its long-term ambition of joining the European Community, the idea of the country becoming one of Europe's major players within fifteen years would have been widely dismissed as absurd. Spain had made impressive progress in establishing a democratic polity after the death in late 1975 of dictator General Francisco Franco, yet it remained poorly developed, in both economic and infrastructural terms, compared to most of its European neighbors. Entry to the EC, however, provided the stimulus to a dramatic transformation. By the end of 2002, Spain's standing—at least in economic terms—had advanced to the point where, as one commentator has argued, "[a] solid case can be made for including Spain in the G8's elite club of the wealthiest industrialised nations and renaming it G9."[1] The basis for such a claim lies in the fact that Spain's economy, measured in GDP at purchasing prices, currently ranks eleventh in the world and eighth among the OECD countries. Every year since 1995, Spain's annual GDP growth has comfortably outstripped the average for the EU Fifteen. Moreover, as William Chislett observes, it would be hard to deny that Spain currently enjoys greater political stability and a more secure democratic status than Russia, which was invited in 1998 to join the original G7 club of wealthy industrialized nations. Certainly, under the premiership of José María Aznar, the Spanish government has been keen to portray the country as a major force within the EU—one of the leaders of the "new Europe" identified by the U.S. defense secretary, Donald Rumsfeld, during the buildup to the 2003 war against Saddam Hussein's Iraq.[2] Spain's high-profile involvement in the diplomatic wrangles in the United Nations prior to the conflict was designed at least in part to emphasize the country's growing international stature.

Nonetheless, it seems paradoxical—if not actually bizarre—that Aznar should have sought to align himself so closely with the United States and the UK as part of the "coalition of the willing" against Iraq. Not only has Spain historically been suspicious of, when not outright hostile to, the United States,[3] but Spanish public opinion was also vehemently opposed to any involvement in the conflict. Opinion polls in March 2003 showed that over 90 percent of Spaniards were opposed to military action; 70 percent supported Spanish neutrality; and 60 percent thought the Aznar government was mishandling the Iraq issue. Even after the war was over, 54 percent continued to believe the government had handled the issue badly or very badly.[4] Demonstrations against the war were the largest in Europe, with over two million people taking to the streets in Madrid and Barcelona on February 15—part of a coordinated protest which took place in fifty-seven cities throughout Spain, including all provincial capitals.

Such anti-U.S. sentiments had been compounded in Spain by an embarrassing incident in the Persian Gulf in December 2002, when Spanish naval forces, at the behest of the United States, boarded a vessel bound from North Korea with a cargo of missiles. No sooner had the ship been taken than the United States ordered that it be released, on the grounds that the missiles were legitimately bound for Yemen, one of its allies in the region.

That the government should have taken such a clearly unpopular line seems all the more strange given that voter satisfaction ratings had already fallen to their lowest point since Aznar came to power in 1996. A damaging confrontation with the trade union movement during the summer of 2002 had been followed in November by the government's inept handling of an environmental disaster caused by the sinking of an oil tanker, the *Prestige*, off the Galician coast. Not only had the government initially denied the stricken tanker port access and ordered it to be towed farther out to sea, but it was also very slow to react when the vessel split in two a few days later, causing a massive spillage that devastated the local fishing industry. Worse, the government at first downplayed any suggestion of environmental damage—putting pressure on the broadcast media to support this line—and then took three weeks before it launched a cleanup operation. Aznar's belated apology and promise of economic aid when he visited Galicia in December did little to dampen the hostile reaction he received, with opinion polls putting the ruling *Partido Popular* (PP) behind the Spanish Socialist Workers' Party (PSOE) for the first time since 1996. To compound the sense of a government losing touch with the electorate, the adoption of such a resoundingly unpopular line on the Iraq issue came during the run-up to a major round of regional and municipal elections on May 25, 2003. Yet, in the event—and contrary not just to opinion polls but also to the predictions of a wide range of political commentators—the PP performed far better in the elections than they could have dared imagine.

Part of the purpose of this chapter, therefore, is to unravel the mystery of why the Aznar government aligned itself so closely with a policy rejected by an overwhelming majority of the population, and why, having done so, it was able to avoid paying the expected consequences in the May 2003 elections. The chapter focuses first on the context of the post-Franco transition to democracy, laying emphasis on how the much-heralded consensus that underpinned it belied some important continued tensions, notably in regard to the regional issue. The chapter then turns to the issue of Spain's role within the international community, outlining how membership in the European Community (subsequently the European Union[5]) became a unifying leitmotif for Spain's political elite and provided the basis for defining the country's foreign and security policy. In the third section, the chapter analyzes the reasons for a shift toward a more pro-U.S. foreign policy stance under the PP government of Aznar, and investigates why the electoral consequences were not more damaging. The concluding section highlights some of the challenges posed to the politics of consensus by the recent shifts in Spain's foreign policy emphasis, as well as the continued importance of the regional question.

Democratic Deliverance: Escaping the Dead Hand of Dictatorship

By the time Franco died in 1975, Spain was western Europe's last remaining dictatorship—a political anachronism in a continent won back for democracy through World War II. Although with hindsight the process of transition from dictatorship to democracy looks smooth and rapid, it was neither straightforward nor guaranteed. Parliamentary elections to a constituent assembly were held as early as June 1977, and a new democratic constitution promulgated in December 1978, yet up until the elections of 1982, which brought the Socialist Party (PSOE) to power with a crushing majority (see Figure 12.1), the risk of military intervention remained a looming menace. An attempted coup in February 1981, foiled only through the intervention of King Juan Carlos as commander in chief, was just the most serious of a series of plots against the new democracy.[6] It is thus hardly surprising that the creation of Spain's democratic regime bore the imprint of Franco's legacy. Indeed, the transition was "conditioned" in important ways, with a generalized desire to avoid reopening old wounds leading, on the one hand, to a politics of consensus but, on the other,

Figure 12.1   Spanish Election Results, 1977–2000

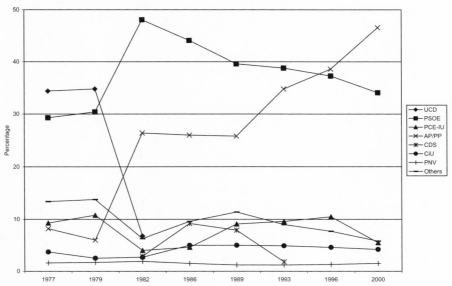

to a politics of avoidance. A number of issues were effectively removed from serious consideration during the constitutional process as forces of the left and the right sought to ensure that compromise and accommodation became the watchwords of the new regime. The monarchy and the military were left broadly untouched, while the need to ensure that regional demands were not ignored and to avoid antagonizing die-hard centralizers at the same time resulted in a rather clumsy compromise over the organizational form of state.

One of the most striking features of the Spanish transition was the so-called *pacto del olvido* (agreement to forget)—an implicit understanding among the key players not to seek to apportion blame and responsibilities for past crimes. While this allowed the transitional process to be driven forward and paved the way for such deals as the 1979 Moncloa Pact, which helped ensure that political reforms would not be derailed by economic crisis, the failure to address directly Franco's legacy would also allow for the construction of a "foundational myth" about the nature of consensus in democratic Spain, which has begun to be contested only recently. In the aftermath of Franco's death, when a range of options seemed open, Spain was faced both with the need to make some form of political adjustment and also to respond to the economic crisis that had followed the 1973 rise in oil prices. This was particularly damaging to a country almost entirely dependent on imported oil to meet its energy needs. Moreover, the growing protagonism of the Basque separatist organization, ETA, which in late 1973 had assassinated Franco's prime minister and chosen successor, Admiral Luis Carrero Blanco, ensured that a profound sense of political uncertainty prevailed.

For many, Spain risked the kind of revolutionary upheaval that Portugal had undergone in the previous year. There was a widespread expectation that the Communist Party (PCE), the most visible opposition to Franco throughout the dictatorship, would seek to emulate its Portuguese counterpart and seize power. Meanwhile, the far right—including much of the military—was determined to ensure that Franco's regime remained intact. In the midst of this potential powder keg stood Spain's new monarch and nominal leader, Juan Carlos, who had assumed power under the terms of Franco's constitution. Juan Carlos's particular skill lay in allowing a middle path to be steered between these extremes, which tapped into the generalized desire among the Spanish population to avoid plunging the country back into civil strife and effected a generational change in its leadership. While the role of Juan Carlos in personally planning and overseeing the transition has probably been exaggerated,[7] he is rightly credited with taking the bold step of dismissing the hapless Carlos Arias Navarro as prime minister in 1976 and replacing him with the young and largely untested Adolfo Suárez. Under Suárez, a series of compromises was engineered between elite actors which enabled the legalization of political parties, freedom of association, and the staging of democratic elections in 1977—won by Suárez's own Democratic Center Union (UCD) party—thus paving the way for the elaboration of a new constitution. Promulgated in December 1978, the constitution marked Spain's formal adoption of democracy within a "state of law" (*estado de derecho*).

While undoubtedly a political triumph, the constitution locked into place a number of features that would have a profound impact on the subsequent functioning of Spanish democracy. Of particular note was Spain's system of asymmetric devolved government: powerful autonomous regions would eventually be able to make significant demands of the central state, especially when national governments were dependent on support from regional parties to remain in power between 1993 and 2000. The issue of self-determination for the Basque country and Catalonia remains one of the most intractable issues on the political agenda. Also of significance was the constitutional power of the central executive, which has led to questions being raised about government accountability and the capacity of parliament and the judiciary to act as effective checks on executive authority—a problem reflected in part through a series of corruption scandals since the early 1990s. Political parties in their turn have struggled to develop solid and secure membership bases and have witnessed significant electoral volatility and partisan dealignment, compounded by low levels of ideological identity and policy consistency.[8]

The relationship between the central state and the regions has been one of the most important political dynamics in Spain's history since the late nineteenth century, with various attempts to establish some form of decentralized structure ending in abject failure. For this reason, the so-called regional question became the single most difficult issue to deal with during the post-Franco transition, linked as it was to the deadly activities of ETA and the responses they elicited from elements in the military. Nearly one-tenth of the 1978 constitution focuses on regional matters. Whereas the left was essentially in favor of a federal state, along the lines of the United States or (West) Germany, the right would not countenance any such perceived threat to the integrity of the nation. In an attempt to satisfy all parties, therefore, the constitution produced a compromise solution that entailed a hybrid formula promising both the "indissoluble unity of the Spanish Nation" and the right to self-government for municipalities, provinces, and autonomous communities.

The process of granting regional autonomy was overshadowed in its early years by political tension. Confusion and perplexity over the nature and structure of the autonomous process fed into a more widespread popular concern over the direction of Spanish democracy at the start of the 1980s and was a factor in the decision of some military conspirators to attempt a coup on February 23, 1981—the most serious of a number of antidemocratic plots. Although the coup attempt failed, it placed the regional issue at the forefront of the political agenda. After warning regions not to make exaggerated demands, the UCD government of Suárez reached an agreement with the Socialist opposition to slow down the autonomy process via the notorious LOAPA (*Ley Orgánica de*

Armonización del Proceso Autonómico), an act passed in September 1981 which required autonomous communities to have their laws endorsed by the central government and ensured that, in the event of conflict, state law would always prevail over regional law. Regional nationalists appealed against the LOAPA to the Constitutional Court, which found in their favor in August 1983. By declaring more than a third of the LOAPA to be unconstitutional, the tribunal's judgment effectively called for the autonomy process to be rethought.

In the meantime, the election in October 1982 of a Socialist (PSOE) government with a commanding majority had restored a sense of stability to the political arena, allowing the regional issue to be confronted in a less tense atmosphere. The new government moved rapidly to complete Spain's autonomous map, and by the end of February 1983 autonomy statutes had been approved for seventeen regions. In May 1983, regional elections were held in thirteen autonomous communities, completing a process which had begun with elections in Catalonia and the Basque country (March 1980), Galicia (October 1981), and Andalusia (May 1982). Undoubtedly, the system of regional devolution has been the most successful and enduring attempt to address the regional question in Spain's modern history. However, its asymmetric structure, designed to recognize the particular claims of the so-called historic regions (Catalonia, the Basque country, and Galicia) has led to an inherent sense of flux, or at least of an ongoing process whose ultimate resolution is unclear. The differentiation between "fast" and "slow" routes to devolution was a transitional measure, and the intention was ultimately to level out powers in the regions. Whereas many see the only logical endpoint of this process being a full-fledged federal structure, the historic regions—most notably Catalonia and the Basque country—have continued to insist on recognition of the *hecho diferencial*, the legacy that sets them apart from the other regions and means that they must always enjoy a qualitatively higher degree of autonomy than Spain's other regions.

Under the PSOE administrations, relations between the regions and the center were initially tense as both sides tested out the limits to their respective competencies and made significant use of the Constitutional Court to resolve disputes. However, over time a more harmonious *modus vivendi* developed as the regional system began to bed down. The relationship between center and the regions became progressively more constructive rather than hostile, although there remained some sharp tensions over the distribution of powers and fiscal responsibility, as well as the use of the vernacular in those regions with their own language. When the PSOE lost its absolute majority in the 1993 general election, it was forced to rely on support from the Catalan nationalist party, *Convergència i Unió* (CiU), and their Basque counterparts in the *Partido Nacionalista Vasco* (PNV) to remain in power. The price was the granting of significant economic concessions to both regions, a move that drew strong criticism from the right-wing opposition Popular Party (PP), led by José María Aznar. In spite of Aznar's own political provenance as a regional leader in Castilla-

León, the PP was opposed to any further concessions to the regions and believed the autonomy process had gone far enough. The PP was particularly
scathing of the CiU leader, Jordi Pujol, whose promotion of the Catalan language was regarded by many as anathema. Yet, when the PP itself fell short of
securing a governing majority in the 1996 elections, it too was forced to rely on
the king-making capacity of the CiU to deliver access to the Moncloa. Aznar
moved quickly to offer an olive branch, even claiming on Catalan television that
he regarded Catalan as "one of the most perfect expressions of language" and
that he liked to speak it himself "among small groups of friends."[9] The price
extracted on this occasion by the CiU leader, Jordi Pujol, was even higher and
obliged the PP to backtrack on its preelection promise to put a stop to the
seemingly inexorable increase in regional power.

In the event, the PP administration soon developed an effective working
relationship with the CiU with little evidence of the kind of tension that many
had predicted. While there was no formal coalition, the mutual dependence of
the PP and CiU made for constructive accommodation and contributed to what
was widely perceived as a period of effective and coherent governance. Aznar
reaped the rewards in the 2000 general elections, this time winning a commanding absolute majority, but the shallow nature of many PP members' support
for the regional process was revealed in their dismissive taunt on election night:
"Pujol, enano, habla castellano" (literally, "Pujol, you dwarf, speak Spanish"—an ironic reference to their leader's tactical claim four years earlier to
speak Catalan). Since the 2000 elections, the PP government has continued to
maintain an effective working relationship with Catalonia, but—as will be discussed further below—relations with the Basque country have plumbed new
depths. It would be an exaggeration to suggest that the tensions between the
government and the Basque region represent any form of immediate threat to
the stability of Spain's system of asymmetric devolution, but they do underline
the continuing significance of the regional question in contemporary Spain.

Spain's "National Project": Europe as Historic Vocation

The question which naturally arises is why—in marked contrast to Spain's historic experience since the late nineteenth century, notably in the 1870s, 1920s,
and 1930s—the regional issue has not led to a breakdown in the post-Franco
democratic political system. The answer is of course complex, and it involves
not just consensus over the need to avoid re-creating the divisions that had led
to civil war in the 1930s, but also the enactment of long-overdue military modernization following the constitutional reforms of the late 1970s. Equally important, however, was the positive commitment, shared across Spain's social

and political spectrum, to a unifying goal, that of securing membership in the European Community. Such was the totemic importance of this ambition that it has been described as Spain's "national project."[10] The desire for membership was driven by both economic and political imperatives. Economic arguments carried considerable weight: although the economy had grown rapidly between 1960 and 1975, the main engines of this growth (migrant remittances, tourism income, foreign investment, and technological imports) were all but exhausted by the late 1970s. Furthermore, the foundations of Spain's industrialization model (protectionism, tariff barriers, state intervention) had by the early 1980s become rigidities that limited further economic development. Spain's political and economic elite thus saw EC membership as an instrument for the elimination of old economic habits that stood in the way of economic rationalization. In addition, Europe would expose the historically protected Spanish economy to the much-needed discipline of the open market.

Despite the importance of these economic issues, they were secondary to the essentially political motivations for accession. EC rejection of the Franco regime had transformed Europe into a symbol of democracy and also contributed to the legitimization of democracy among Spanish elite and public opinion. The aspiration to identify with Europe and the EC became a central element of the political discourse of democratization. Ultimately, therefore, it became one of the elements of political consensus upon which the Spanish transition was built, and Spain's application for membership was unanimously supported by all mainstream political parties. Membership was viewed as an anchor for democracy, a means to end Spain's isolation of the previous two centuries, and a framework for the restoration of human rights and political liberties. According to the PSOE minister who negotiated the final stage of the process, Fernando Morán, accession had a metapolitical value. Indeed, membership even helped reconcile some remaining Francoists to democracy. Alarmed by developments in neighbouring Portugal—where the Communist Party had played a prominent political role following the overthrow of the Salazar/Caetano regime by the Armed Forces Movement—they saw membership of the EC acting as a guarantee of private property and capitalism and also as a bulwark against socialism. Other political reasons that contributed to support for EC membership included the belief that it could help defuse the regional issue and potential demands for independence, that it could legitimize painful measures to bring about economic and social modernization, and that it would provide a framework for defining Spain's international position.

This last point was particularly important, for it set the context within which post-Franco Spain began to formulate a coherent foreign and defense policy. Yet it also represented the issue over which the much-vaunted consensus of the transition would first be seriously challenged. The critical factor at stake was membership of NATO, which became inextricably intertwined with Spain's commitment to the EC. In June 1980, the UCD government announced that Spain would seek to join the Atlantic Alliance, a move which was greeted with strong opposition from all parties of the left. For the left, NATO was inseparable from the United States, which was regarded with cynicism and suspicion. In contrast to other European countries, Spain had not been liberated from fascism by U.S. troops, did not perceive the Soviet Union as a particular threat, and had not enjoyed the benefits of the Marshall Plan. More important, though, Franco had received support from the United States, which had signed a security agreement with him in 1953 and also endorsed Spain's application for UN membership. Nonetheless, following the attempted coup of February 23, 1981, membership of NATO was rushed through with almost indecent haste, a move which proved deeply unpopular with the Spanish electorate. Indeed, capitalizing on the fact that opinion polls showed just 14 percent in favor of NATO membership, Felipe González made the promise of a referendum on the issue a centerpiece of the PSOE's platform for the October 1982 elections. In the event, the PSOE won an overwhelming majority—but to the dismay of many supporters, González soon performed a U-turn on the NATO issue. The promised referendum was long delayed as the new government mounted a propaganda campaign in favor of remaining in NATO: when it finally did take place in March 1986, the issue had been deliberately tied into EC membership by using the argument that a system worth belonging to was a system worth defending.

It is clear that González found himself subjected to considerable pressure to reverse his stance on NATO: not only did West Germany make it clear that progress on EC membership negotiations was contingent on Spain's remaining in NATO, but there was little prospect of any resolution to the Gibraltar issue should Spain withdraw, nor would the United States be keen to reach any agreement to phase out the military bases established in 1953. In turn, though, González was able to use the NATO issue to make progress on EC negotiations, arguing that the Spanish public would accept being in NATO only if it could be presented as a prerequisite to EC entry and only once membership was confirmed. Such confirmation duly came in 1985, with Spain formally joining the EC on January 1, 1986. In order to maximize its voter appeal, the PSOE government's pro-NATO campaign in the run-up to the referendum sought to conflate three issues: a commitment to Europe in regard to security, a certain degree of anti-Americanism, and the defense of national interests in respect of NATO membership, including nonintegration into the military structure. Thus, in an ironic antecedent to the situation his successor Aznar would find himself facing in 2003, González defied public opinion on an issue relating to Spanish foreign policy. However, the unpopularity of NATO was counterbalanced by the very strong support for EC entry, and the government was able to win the referendum on a low turnout.

Once the NATO issue had been resolved, Spain set about seeking to rebuild foreign policy consensus in the domestic arena, as well as demonstrating its commitment to Europe. This meant, in practice, that Spain had to assume the EU's foreign policy concerns alongside its legislative and decision-making mechanisms as set out in the *acquis communautaire*. For instance, the Netherlands insisted that Spain should recognize Israel and establish diplomatic relations, in spite of close ties with the Arab world, while NATO membership required alignment with other EU Atlantic allies on the question of the Soviet Union. In general, though, the relatively calm international context during the period between 1986 and 1989 allowed Spain to assume the community *acquis* without any damage to her special interests in Latin America and the Arab world. However, the fall of the Berlin Wall and subsequent collapse of communism in eastern Europe resulted in a redefinition of Spain's foreign policy concerns within the EU. In particular, there was a shift away from a primarily bilateral, or at best regional, approach to foreign policy toward a more global and multifaceted one. Under the PSOE governments of González, Spain sought to develop its status as a middle power, accepting its responsibilities within the EU but also pressing its own priorities in areas such as the Maghreb. In regard to security and defense, the Socialists pushed for "Europeanization" both within NATO itself through the European Projects Group and also through the West European Union (WEU), which Spain joined as a full member in 1990. The PSOE advocated the progressive integration of the WEU into the EU as the basis of an autonomous European security and defense capacity. The Gulf War of 1991 provided Spain with the opportunity to become actively involved in an overseas security operation, ending over a century of isolationism, and provided concrete expression to the PSOE's argument that the WEU and NATO were "separable but not separate."[11]

The PP government of José María Aznar, which came to power in 1996, adopted the main guidelines of Spain's security and defense policy as established under the PSOE, and maintained the emphasis on building up a European system. In regard to foreign policy, however, the new administration pursued a "neorealist" stance of seeking to link its influence to its main assets: an open economy ranked tenth in the world and the global importance of the Spanish language. For Aznar, international politics was seen as a competition in which the strength of respective players would determine the outcome. There were three areas of foreign policy on which the PP administration diverged from the Socialists: first, it developed much closer ties with the United States and offered full support to such policies as the Strategic Defense Initiative and the Anglo-U.S. bombing raids on Iraq during the late 1990s; second, it moved toward full participation in NATO, including integration into the military structure; third, it took a much more hostile line toward Cuba, with which the PSOE had historically maintained positive relations. Underlining the PP government's policy was a fear of marginalization: hence the 1997 decision to seek full incorporation into NATO; hence also the commitment of troops to various European initiatives, including the EU's Rapid Intervention Force. Aznar sought to secure influence as a mainstream key player within the EU in order to offset the impact of "periphery syndrome" as Europe's attention turned increasingly to the newly democratizing postcommunist regimes. Spain also sought to play a lead role in defining a wide-ranging policy for security issues in the 1997 Treaty of Amsterdam, proposing several initiatives. These included eliminating the right to asylum for EU citizens (aimed at speeding up extradition requests), the granting of operational powers to Europol, and direct cooperation between judges in different member states.

Spain also called for a summit on justice and internal affairs to focus on the fight against terrorism and claimed the lead role in drawing up the agenda for the Tampere meeting of October 1999, which developed guidelines for EU policy on third pillar issues. At the heart of Spanish concerns was the desire to develop a "global approach" to security, which in addition to the usual focus on immigration and asylum issues would also encompass criminal behavior, people-smuggling, and money laundering. The ultimate aim was to create Europe-wide instruments to pursue ETA suspects throughout the EU, and Spain received a significant boost in December 2000 when the EU Council for Home Affairs declared that ETA represented a threat to the whole of Europe. In addition, Spain pursued bilateral agreements with a number of European states beginning in November 2000, when a deal was struck with Italy on mutual recognition of prison sentences for terrorist offenses, organized crime, drug trafficking, child sex abuse, and arms dealing. A similar agreement was signed with the UK a year later. The European Commission also initiated a study of three measures based on Spanish concerns: the development of a common definition of the crime of terrorism; the introduction of a fast-track extradition process (based on the Spanish-Italian agreement); and the sending of suspects for trial in the country where they had allegedly committed their most serious crime, regardless of where they were arrested.

Playing for High Stakes: Spain, Europe, and the Wider World

Although there was no official government document setting out the reasons for Spain's adoption of an "Atlanticist" stance over the Iraq issue, three central factors that follow from the previous discussion can be seen as key: the struggle against terrorism in the Basque country, the strategic projection of Spain within the wider world (most notably in regard to its interests within Europe and Latin America), and the desire to be taken seriously as a major player on the international stage.

First, as reiterated repeatedly by the government, the attack on Iraq was seen as part of the wider "war on global terrorism," in which Spain has a particular involvement on account of the activities of ETA. For Aznar, the struggle against ETA had assumed a very personal dimension following his narrow escape from an assassination attempt in 1995, an experience that reinforced his determination to defeat the organization. Certainly, ETA has represented one of the principal threats to Spanish democracy since the start of the transition process, several times threatening to derail progress in the late 1970s and early 1980s as it became embroiled in a deadly cycle of action and reaction with hard-line elements in the military.[12] Committed to independence for the Basque provinces (including Navarre and those in southwestern France), ETA's use of terrorist tactics has cost over 850 lives since the spectacular assassination of Carrero Blanco. The restoration of democracy made no difference to an organization that remained wedded to the view that Spain represented an occupying force in the Basque country.

After assuming office in 1996, the Aznar government took a firm line on ETA and other organizations associated with its cause. Statements that there would be no negotiation with the separatists while they continued to use violence were seemingly more than rhetorical devices designed for public consumption, and indeed there was an apparent payoff as ETA declared a unilateral cease-fire in September 1998 (influenced, it was widely believed, by the Good Friday Agreement that had successfully been negotiated in Northern Ireland earlier that year). However, little progress was made during talks between the government and ETA representatives, and the cease-fire was abandoned at the end of 1999. Huge demonstrations in protest at a range of seemingly indiscriminate ETA assassinations during 2000 emboldened the government to reassert its hard-line stance, including direct challenges to the PNV administration of the Basque Autonomous Community, accused of offering implicit support for ETA demands. As tension mounted in the Basque country, the Aznar administration adopted an ever more confrontational approach, demanding that the president of the minority nationalist government in the Basque country, Juan José Ibarretxe, resign and call new elections. In the event, the elections did take place early, in May 2001, following a collapse in the governing partnership between the Basque Nationalist Party (PNV) and the more radical Euskal Herritarrok (EH). However, contrary to the PP's expectations, the elections resulted in a significant increase in seats for the PNV, which took over 42 percent of the vote and was able to continue in government. The PP, meanwhile, gained just one extra seat at the expense of the Socialist Party (PSOE).

Amid a growing sense of polarization between the PP and the PNV, which called for the Basque people's right to self-determination, events took a new turn following the 9/11 atrocities in the United States. As the Bush administration developed its strategy of declaring "war on terrorism," so the Aznar government was able to link its anti-ETA activities to the wider issue of global threats to peace. A key part of this approach involved the attempt to ensure that ETA was isolated internationally, which in turn involved collaboration with

U.S. efforts; indeed, there was a growing sense within the Spanish government that the Bush administration had a more realistic perception of the scale and immediacy of the terrorist threat than did neighboring governments in Europe. In this context, the PP developed an approach that focused increasingly on legal proscription, culminating in August 2002 in the outlawing of the radical separatist political party, Batasuna, widely seen as ETA's political wing. Working closely with a Spanish judge, Baltasar Garzón, the PP government secured parliamentary support for an outright ban of Batasuna and the seizure of its assets, under the terms of new legislation directed against all parties that supported terrorism. The subsequent inclusion of Batasuna on the U.S. administration's list of terrorist groups was of great symbolic value to the PP[13]—although, for many, the banning of a political party that could regularly attract some 10 percent of Basque votes (and nearly 20 percent in the local elections of 1999) represented an ominous step in a democratic "state of law" (*estado de derecho*). Moreover, the move was seen as tactically naïve, allowing ETA and Batasuna to claim victimization by the Spanish state and to draw parallels between the PP and the Franco regime.

Undoubtedly, however, the post-9/11 backdrop to the fight against terrorism helped reinforce the realignment of Spain's international focus toward a more pro-U.S. stance. A second reason for adopting an Atlanticist outlook concerns Spain's strategic priorities and projection. Of particular importance in this regard is the Spanish government's conception of the future direction of Europe and her role within an enlarged European Union. Spain's official line on the EU's eastern enlargement has been one of positive support, driven in part by a sense of solidarity with countries that have experienced the transition from dictatorship to democracy. In practice, though, there are real fears about the potential impact of enlargement—not least, that it will lead to a shift in the EU's center of gravity toward the north and east, leaving Spain relegated to a more marginal position. This would leave the Franco-German axis reinforced as the EU's "hard core," with a preponderant weight in shaping Europe's economic and social model. The PP government's concern is that a Franco-German–dominated, enlarged EU would seek to establish a rival pole of power to the United States, based around a federal structure designed to bolster a protectionist conception of "fortress Europe." Although internal barriers will be removed, open markets and labor flexibility would be balanced by a closer link to social protection measures, reinforced by a growing emphasis on interdependencies and coordination.[14] At heart, the issue at stake is the very conception of how the EU should function: in contrast to its Socialist predecessors in government, who were fully aligned with the idea of a "social Europe," the PP's vision is more akin to that of the UK, with a firm commitment to economic deregulation and strong links with the United States as part of the Atlantic Alliance. Spain has therefore sought to develop an alternative pole of influence to the

Franco-German axis within the EU, emphasizing its links not only with the UK but also with Italy, as part of Rumsfeld's "New Europe."

Underlying these broader concerns, however, are more practical issues that explain Spain's desire to have a more prominent say within the EU. Most significant among these is the fear that eastward expansion will cost Spain heavily in terms of access to structural funds. Spain has received the lion's share of EU structural funds, as well as the dedicated "cohesion funds" agreed as part of the Maastricht treaty, but it would find its per capita GDP rising sharply in terms of the EU average once the poorer economies of eastern Europe become members. From a Spanish point of view, this would result in "statistical convergence" of Spain's GDP with the EU average, but those "poor" regions that would no longer qualify for support under the structural funds threshold would be no less poor in reality. While the Laeken summit eased Spanish concerns somewhat by delaying the accession of Romania and Bulgaria—which meant that six regions would continue to qualify for support even after the accession of the ten candidate countries in 2004—negotiations over the issue of convergence pitted Spain against Germany in particular. Although it would be diplomatically damaging to state it openly, Spain wants to ensure that its privileged position in regard to EU support mechanisms—in terms not just of structural and cohesion funds, but also under the European Agricultural Guidance and Guarantee Fund (EAGGF)—is protected within an enlarged Europe. Short of real convergence (a particular challenge given significant differences in human capital, technological development, and employment levels), the best means to achieve such an end is to ensure that Spain is able to play an influential role at EU negotiating tables. The calculation made by the PP government has been that Spain's interests lie in cultivating a stronger relationship with the UK, especially given the apparent personal chemistry between José María Aznar and Tony Blair, rather than in seeking to maintain its traditionally close relations with Germany and France. In practice, of course, the UK's intention to stake its claim to be at the heart of Europe foundered on internal division over economic and monetary union, thereby reducing the potential influence of an Aznar–Blair axis.

A further dimension contributing to the PP's alliance strategy concerns the EU's international focus, where Spain again has looked more toward the UK and its Atlantic links than to its traditional partners in Europe, whose vision is seen as being focused in a more easterly direction. Latin America is relatively low on the list of the EU's international priorities, yet for Spain it is an area of increasingly significant commercial interest, reinforcing long-standing cultural ties. Indeed, Spain has invested more in Latin America since the start of the 1990s than any other country in the world, with the exception of the United States; between 1992 and 2001 it contributed just over 50 percent (80.4 billion) of the EU's total foreign direct investment in the region.[15] The surge of investment, which took off after entry to the EU, has led to Spain becoming a net direct investor—a noteworthy change in the country's economic profile—and has transformed several Spanish companies such as Telefónica, Repsol YPF, and Endesa into some of the largest corporations in Latin America. The downside is that Spain is now far more exposed than in the past to the vicissitudes of the Latin American economy, and the financial crises of 2002 (especially in Argentina) have hurt Spanish companies. Nonetheless, the strength of the links between Latin America and the United States and the potential development of a Free Trade Area of the Americas (FTAA)—proposed by George Bush senior—means that Spain has an increasing interest in relations with North America. From a U.S. point of view, too, Spain's membership of the Eurozone (and the likely continued delay in UK entry) provides a potentially useful point of access—although this factor should not be exaggerated. It is notable that Mexico's economy has tracked the United States' much more closely since it joined the North American Free Trade Association (NAFTA) in 1994, and its attractiveness for Spanish companies has increased as a result. From a Latin American point of view, the growth of Spanish direct investment means that Madrid now stands alongside Miami as a major finance capital. The Madrid Stock Exchange has established Latibex, a market in euros for blue-chip Latin American shares and fixed-income securities.[16]

Cultural ties with Latin America further reinforce Spain's Atlantic focus, not just because of historic bonds, but also because of the growing importance of the Hispanic community in the United States. With some 35 million Hispanics in the United States, according to data released by the Census Bureau in April 2003, the vast majority of whom are of Mexican origin, commentators have spoken of a "Latinization" of the country. Hispanics now account for some 42 percent of New Mexico's population and 32 percent of California's, and they are above the national average in Arizona, Colorado, Florida, Nevada, New Jersey, New York, and Texas. Some cities, such as East Los Angeles and Laredo, Texas, have populations that are more than 90 percent Hispanic.[17] The spending power of the Hispanic community in the United States is virtually equivalent to Spain's GDP, and with numbers expected to reach 60 million by 2015, its political influence will continue to increase. While Mexico, Puerto Rico, and Cuba will remain a more immediate point of reference than Spain for U.S. Hispanics, the developing importance of Spanish as a language means that the cultural activities of the *Instituto Cervantes*—a flagship public body established by the Spanish government in 1991 to promote the Spanish language and Spanish-American culture—will assume ever more relevance in North America. Seen in this context, the PP's desire to build stronger links with the U.S. administration appears logical, in spite of the historic distance between the two countries.

A more immediate concern to Spain that has also inclined the PP administration to look to strengthen ties to the United States is the potential threat to stability posed by developments in the Maghreb. Per capita income differentials between Spain and the Maghreb are as high as those between any two border regions in the world, contributing to real fears of regional destabilization. Key issues at stake from a Spanish perspective concern not just the level of illegal immigration from North Africa (given dramatic focus by the regularity with which the bodies of immigrants have washed up on Spanish beaches) but also drug trafficking routed via southern Spain. In addition, the possible spread of Islamic fundamentalism may lead to greater tension both within the region and with the democratic west, with Spain very much on the front line. Morocco is the Maghrebi country that has historically had the closest as well as the most tense relations with Spain, particularly given its claims to the Spanish enclaves in Ceuta and Melilla. Despite the Euro-Mediterranean Partnership (EMP), also known as the "Barcelona process," which aimed at developing an ongoing dialogue between cultures and civilizations and in which Spain and Morocco played key roles, these tensions came to a head in July 2002. That month a small group of Moroccan soldiers occupied the tiny and uninhabited rocky islet of Perejil, over which Spain exercised historic though legally questionable control. The Moroccan action, seen by many commentators as largely symbolic, precipitated a major diplomatic confrontation between the two countries, with Morocco refusing to give up its claim even after Spain had used special air services troops based in Alicante to retake the contested islet within a week. While for many the confrontation appeared little short of farcical, the potential ramifications of a complete breakdown in relations between Spain and Morocco were of huge significance—a point appreciated by U.S. secretary of state Colin Powell, who intervened to help negotiate a settlement to the dispute. His efforts were seen by some as standing in marked contrast to those of the EU, which proved unable to broker a resolution to the problem. Positive relations between the United States and Morocco provide yet more reasons for the PP administration to seek to bolster its own pro-U.S. stance.

The third factor contributing to the Spanish government's strong support of the U.S. position over Iraq relates to Aznar's desire to seize a "historic opportunity" to bolster Spain's standing in the world. The picture of Spain presented by Aznar in the wake of the war suggested a country with a privileged position in transatlantic dialogues, which could stake a claim to being among the leading world democracies and which was an international power with a voice that would command respect and be taken seriously. For critics, Aznar's desire to be seen to stand alongside Bush and Blair amounted to little more than posturing, dismissed as wishing to "appear in the photograph" but with little genuine credibility of influence. Such views were given credence by the minimal mention made of Aznar by President Bush and Prime Minister Blair during the critical buildup to the war, even though Spain was a cosponsor of the infamous and ultimately abortive second resolution at the United Nations in March 2003. The Spanish premier's claim to international standing was hardly helped by George Bush having called him "Mr. Ansar," or by the president's brother Jeb

Bush referring to Spain as a republic in an address to business leaders in Madrid in February 2003. Certainly, from a U.S. point of view, UK support for its stance on Iraq was welcome, though probably not essential, but Spain's support was of decidedly less significance. It contributed instead to Aznar's wider strategy of seeking to present Spain as possessing credibility as an international power, on a par with its leading European partners.

The PP's pro-U.S. transatlantic vocation did not seem to strike a chord with the Spanish electorate. An opinion poll organized by the Real Instituto Elcano[18] in November 2002 showed that 62 percent of respondents thought that the EU should develop greater independence from the United States, a figure that compared with 60 percent in France, 59 percent in Italy, 51 percent in Germany, and 47 percent in the UK. Just 28 percent of Spaniards felt the EU-U.S. relationship should continue to be as close as it had been historically. In contrast, some 62 percent of respondents placed Europe at the top of their list of geopolitical regions with which Spain should be most strategically concerned, compared with just 20 percent who mentioned the United States at all. More remarkable was the finding in a January 1997 survey by the Centro de Investigaciones Sociológicas (CIS, an autonomous polling organization attached to the Ministry of the Presidency) that just 53 percent of Spaniards saw the United States as unambiguously democratic, while 58 percent described the country as right-wing—some three years before the Republican George W. Bush became president. A follow-up survey by the Real Instituto Elcano in February 2003 found that, when asked to rank democracy, culture, the economy, and science in a range of countries, just 31 percent of Spanish citizens positively approved U.S. democracy. A final point worth noting is that, when asked to place Spain on a scale from 0 (no global influence) to 10 (major world power), the mean location among Spanish respondents was 4.3, compared to 8.8 for the United States, 6.6 for Germany, 6.5 for the UK, 6.2 for France, 6.1 for China, and 5.9 for Russia. Respondents ranked Spain's global influence as being on a par with Italy, greater than Poland and Brazil, but less than Canada. More important, a significant majority—over 60 percent—felt that no further resources or investment should be committed to increasing Spain's influence. Thus, despite Aznar's claims, most Spaniards do not appear to accept the idea that their country can make a credible claim to "major player" status—and do not wish to move in that direction.

Yet, when the regional and municipal elections took place on May 25, 2003, the PP did far better than even its own party leaders had dared to expect. Although it received fewer votes overall than the PSOE, the PP was able to echo the words of the former Socialist premier, Felipe González, who had described his own unexpectedly narrow loss in the 1996 general election as a "sweet defeat" for the PSOE and a "bitter victory" for the PP. Rather than the widely anticipated "punishment vote" for its stance over the Iraq war, the PP saw its support hold up well, highlighting the PSOE's failure to capitalize on its attempts to associate itself directly with the antiwar protests. There are three key reasons that go some way toward providing an explanation for the PP's sweet defeat. First, as opinion polls indicated, the war with Iraq did not have high salience as a *voting* issue, as opposed to being an issue of moral principle: when asked whether opposition to the PP's stance would affect their vote, just 17 percent said it would.[19] Whether that calculation would have been different had the elections taken place while the war was ongoing, as opposed to shortly after the overthrow of the Saddam regime (and before the growing concerns over the seeming absence of weapons of mass destruction), is impossible to answer with any certainty. Second, Spain did not commit any troops to the war, as opposed to providing logistical support; as a result, there were no dramatic images of Spanish casualties, nor grieving relatives (though a number of Spanish reporters lost their lives during the conflict and, indirectly related, sixty-two Spanish peacekeepers were killed in May 2003 when their plane crashed on its return from Afghanistan). To that extent, even though there was strong opposition to Spanish support for the U.S.-led invasion, the actual fighting war remained somewhat remote from people's day-to-day lives. Third, the PSOE under José Rodríguez Zapatero was unable to provide a sufficiently persuasive potential alternative and was seen by many as seeking to jump on the antiwar bandwagon rather than providing credible leadership to the movement. Ultimately, in spite of the unpopularity of his government's stance on the Iraq war, it seems likely that domestic political and economic issues will continue to inform voters' choices.

Conclusion: The End of Consensus and Future Challenges

In the aftermath of the Franco regime, Spain took major strides forward in becoming established as a middle-ranking power within Europe. Much of the credit for that progress must lie with Spain's elite actors, who agreed to set aside key differences in pursuit of the common objective of democratic stability. So much was this the case that "consensus" became a virtual watchword of the transitional process and came to characterize representations of Spanish politics in the post-Franco era. In reality, of course, such consensus was always more apparent than real, as it served to hide some areas of potential tension that would emerge more clearly as Spain's democratic regime became securely established. This chapter has not sought to provide a comprehensive account of the development of Spain's post-Franco democracy but instead has highlighted the continuing significance of the regional issue, the importance of Spain's European vocation, and how foreign and security policy have evolved in recent decades. The central argument is that the consensus over Europe that underpinned Spain's attempt to establish itself as a middle-ranking power in the 1980s and early 1990s has given way to a more contested approach under the PP government of José María Aznar, whose ambition has been to project Spain as a major player within the EU and beyond. Not only is such an approach challenged by political opponents, but it also appears to be deeply unpopular with the Spanish electorate—although it is not in itself an issue likely to determine the outcome of future elections.

Nonetheless, the pro-Atlantic stance of the PP may have sown the seeds of important future tensions. In particular, the antiterrorist focus of both U.S. and Spanish security policy operates within a dynamic that pits the democratic west against "rogue states," principally in the Middle East and Asia. Yet, Spain's more immediate security concerns may follow a very different, north-south dynamic in which developments in Africa assume ever more importance. Already, for the first time in its modern history, Spain is seeing the emergence of significant North African communities in its major cities. Having long prided itself on a generalized lack of racism and the absence of right-wing populist political parties, Spain may have to face up to the uncomfortable fact that such attitudes have been the result more of cultural homogeneity than of racial tolerance. With that homogeneity becoming increasingly diluted, race-based violence has started to emerge in Spanish towns and cities. Race riots against immigrant workers in early 2000 in El Ejido, Almería, attracted international attention, but more routine incidents of racism have become increasingly evident in Spain's urban centers. A report by Amnesty International in April 2002 documented a marked increase in cases of torture and ill-treatment of minorities between 1995 and 2002.[20] The scale of the problem should not be exaggerated, and it is true that Spain does not have any significant extreme right-wing populist movements, but there are no grounds for complacency on an issue that is likely to assume ever more salience in years to come.

Spain's commitment to Europe is essential in regard to border protection and dealing with drug trafficking and related crime. However, the shifting alliance strategy adopted under Aznar, away from Germany and France and toward the UK and Italy, carries risks: while Italy shares some of Spain's concerns, the UK remains committed to an Atlantic rather than a European outlook. For all that the Blair administration declares its desire to be at the heart of Europe, failure to join the euro inevitably reduces the UK's influence and makes it a less powerful ally for Spain. Spain's other main ally in Rumsfeld's conception of the "new Europe" is Italy, but there are serious question marks over the benefits of close association with the highly controversial and mercurial Silvio Berlusconi. In terms of Spain's policy toward Europe, then, the more overtly pro-U.S. line of the Aznar administration may well place Spain at the heart of a vision of the EU other than that supported by the Franco-German axis—but whether this will help Spain assume the "major player" status sought by Aznar remains open to question.

Notes

1. William Chislett, *The Internationalization of the Spanish Economy* (Madrid: Real Instituto Elcano de Estudios Internacionales y Estratégicos, 2002), 19.

2. Although Rumsfeld's comments in early 2003 were explicitly focused on differentiating France and Germany as the "old Europe" from the postcommunist countries of central and eastern Europe, he later clarified that his distinction referred to a matter of "attitude" toward the transatlantic relationship. Radio Free Europe, June 11, 2003.

3. A sentiment that dates back to the humiliating loss of its remaining colonies to the United States in 1898, and which was compounded by U.S. support for the Franco regime at crucial moments during the Cold War, as well as a strong opposition to U.S. policy in Latin and Central America.

4. Figures from surveys by the Centro de Investigaciones Sociológicas (CIS), March and June 2003.

5. This chapter refers to either EC or EU, depending on the appropriate context: EC pre-1992 and EU thereafter.

6. See Paul Preston, *The Politics of Revenge* (London: Routledge, 1995), 175–202.

7. See, for examples, Charles T. Powell, *Juan Carlos. Self-Made Monarch* (London: Macmillan, 1996) and José Luis de Vilallonga, *The King: The Life of King Juan Carlos of Spain* (London: Weidenfeld & Nicolson, 1994). The most recent and comprehensive account of the role of Juan Carlos is Paul Preston's *Juan Carlos: El Rey de un Pueblo* (Barcelona: Plaza Janés, 2003).

8. For further detail on all these issues, see Paul Heywood, ed., *Politics and Policy in Democratic Spain* (London: Frank Cass, 1999).

9. "Shakiness in Catalonia Makes Aznar Wobble," *International Herald Tribune*, December 11, 1996.

10. Carlos Closa and Paul M. Heywood, *Spain and the European Union* (London: Palgrave, in press).

11. Andrés Ortega, "Spain in the Post–Cold War," in *Democratic Spain: Reshaping External Relations in a Changing World*, ed. R. Gillespie, F. Rodrigo, and J. Story (London: Routledge, 1995), 189.

12. Francisco Letamendía Belzunce (Ortzi), *Historia del Nacionalismo Vasco y de E.T.A. 2: E.T.A en la transición (1976–1982)* (San Sebastián: R & B Ediciones, n.d., but 1994).

13. "Designation of Batasuna, Euskal Herritarrok and Herri Batasuna under Executive Order 13224," press statement by Richard Boucher, May 7, 2003.

14. Martin Rhodes, "Globalization, EMU and Welfare State Futures," in *Developments in West European Politics*, ed. Paul Heywood, Erik Jones, and Martin Rhodes (London: Palgrave, 2002), 37–55.

15. William Chislett, *Spanish Direct Investment in Latin America: Challenges and Opportunities* (Madrid: Real Instituto Elcano de Estudios Internacionales y Estratégicos, 2003), 18.

16. Chislett, *Spanish Direct Investment*, 24.

17. *Hispanic News*, April 20, 2003. Online at www.Hispanic.bz.

18. Javier Noya, "La España post-Sadam y su opinion pública," April 29, 2003. On-

line at www.realinstitutoelcano.org/analisis/277.asp?tipo = 1&num = 277&zona = 1& versi on = 1&publicado = Verdadero.

19. Javier Noya, "La España post-Sadam y su opinion pública."

20. Amnesty International, *Spain: The Deadly Consequences of Racism: Torture and Ill-Treatment* (London: Amnesty International, 2002).

Suggestions for Further Reading

Borzel, Tanja A. *States and Regions in the European Union.* Cambridge: Cambridge University Press, 2002.

Closa, Carlos, and Paul M. Heywood. *Spain and the European Union.* London: Palgrave, 2004.

Gil, Federico G., and Joseph S. Tulchin, eds. *Spain's Entry into NATO: Conflicting Political and Strategic Perspectives.* Boulder, Colo.: Lynne Rienner Publishers, 1988.

Gillespie, Richard, and Richard Youngs, eds. *Spain: The European and International Challenges.* London: Frank Cass, 2001.

Heywood, Paul. *The Government and Politics of Spain.* London: Macmillan, 1995.

Heywood, Paul, ed. *Politics and Policy in Democratic Spain.* London: Frank Cass, 1999.

Hooper, John. *The New Spaniards.* London: Penguin, 1995.

Jones, Rachel. *Beyond the Spanish State. Central Government, Domestic Actors and the EU.* London: Palgrave, 2000.

Maravall, José María. *The Transition to Democracy in Spain.* New York: St. Martin's Press, 1982.

Maxwell, Kenneth, and Steven Spiegel. *The New Spain: From Isolation to Influence.* New York: Council on Foreign Relations Press, 1994.

Newton, Michael T. (with Peter J. Donaghy). *Institutions of Modern Spain: A Political and Economic Guide.* Cambridge: Cambridge University Press, 1997.

Pérez-Díaz, Víctor. *The Return of Civil Society.* Cambridge: Harvard University Press, 1993.

Preston, Paul. *The Triumph of Democracy in Spain.* London: Methuen, 1986.

CHAPTER 13

Scandinavia
Still the Middle Way?

Eric S. Einhorn and John Logue

Denmark

Population: 5.4 million
Area in Square Miles: 16,638
Population Density per Square Mile: 325
GDP (in billion dollars, PPP, 2002 est): 155.5
GDP per capita (PPP in dollars, 2002): $29,000
Joined EC/EU: January 1, 1973
Joined NATO: 1949
Key Political Parties:

Social Democratic Party (*Socialdemokratiet*)
Liberal [agrarian] Party (*Venstre*)
Radical Liberal Party (*Det Radikale Venstre*)
Conservative People's Party (*Det Konservative Folkeparti*)
Danish People's Party (*Det Danske Folkeparti*)
Socialist People's Party (*Socialistisk Folkeparti*)

Finland

Population: 5.1 million
Area in Square Miles: 130,100
Population Density per Square Mile: 40
GDP (in billion dollars, PPP, 2002): $136.2
GDP per capita (PPP in dollars, 2002): $26,200
Joined EC/EU: January 1, 1995
Key Political Parties:
Social Democratic Party
  (*Sosialdemokraattinen Puolue*)

Center [agrarian] Party (*Keskustapuolue*)
Conservative Party (*Kansallinen Kokoomus*)
Left Alliance (*Vasemmistoliitto*)
Swedish People's Party (*Svenska Folkpartiet*)
Green League (*Vihrealiitto*)
Finnish Christian Union (*Suomen Kristillinen Liitto*)
True Finnish Party (*Perussuomlaiset*)

Norway

Population: 4.5 million
Area in Square Miles: 125,057
Population Density per Square Mile: 36
GDP (in billion dollars, PPP, 2002): $143.0
GDP per capita (PPP in dollars, 2002): $31,800
Joined NATO: 1949
Joined European Economic Area 1992
Key Political Parties:

Labor Party (*Det Norske Arbeiderpartiet*)
Conservative Party (*Høyre*)
Liberal Party (*Venstre*)
Center [agrarian] Party (*Senterpartiet*)
Progress Party (*Fremskrittspartiet*)
Socialist Left Party (*Socialistisk Venstreparti*)
Christian People's Party (*Kristelig Folkeparti*)

Sweden

Population: 8.9 million
Area in Square Miles: 170,250
Population Density per Square Mile: 52
GDP (in billion dollars, PPP, 2002): $227.4
GDP per capita (PPP in dollars, 2002): $25,400
Joined EC/EU: January 1, 1995
Key Political Parties:
Social Democratic Labor Party (*Sveriges Socialdemokratiska Arbetareparti*)

Moderate Party (*Moderata Samlingspartiet*)
Left Party (*Vänsterpartiet*)
Christian Democratic Party
  (*Kristdemokraterna*)
Center [agrarian] Party (*Centerpartiet*)
Green Party (*Miljöpartiet de Gröna*)
Liberal Party (*Folkpartiet liberalerna*)

Source (all countries): U.S. Central Intelligence Agency, *The World Factbook 2002*, at www.ocdi.gov/ publications/factbook/geos/sw.htm#top (accessed June 2003).
Note: Population statistics are early 2003 estimates.

410

The Rise and Fall of the Scandinavian "Middle Way"

The Scandinavian "middle way" first attracted international attention in the 1930s at the depths of the Great Depression, coinciding with an era when the fragile foundations of democracy were crumbling across Europe. Industrial capitalism based on "free markets," as well as the still-shallow roots of political democracy, was threatened by a rising fascist tide on the right and a brutal but, for many on the left, attractive communist model in the Soviet Union. President Franklin D. Roosevelt's 1933 perception of "a third of the nation, ill-clothed, ill-fed, and ill-housed" described most of the industrial world. Out of this chaos came a unique welfare-state model in Denmark, Norway, and Sweden, offering a "middle way" between these extremes. It developed over time and out of an accumulation of experience. But if you have to pick a "birthday," January 30, 1933, is our choice.

Copenhagen was cold and foggy in its mid-winter gloom. The political and economic situation was as bleak as the weather. Fully 40 percent of Danish wage earners—two out of five—were out of work in this grey third winter of the Great Depression.

The Danish Employers' Federation had announced that it would lock out all union members still working on February 1 to enforce its demand on the unions for a 20 percent wage reduction. Farm mortgage foreclosures, following a general collapse of agricultural prices, cast a long shadow in the countryside. The Danish Social Democrat prime minister, Thorvald Stauning—a former cigar worker who had led the government briefly in the 1920s and formed another government with the center-left Radical Liberals in 1929 on the eve of the Depression—called an extraordinary Sunday-morning parliamentary session. The agenda was legislation to extend the national labor contract under which the unions worked, thus to stave off economic disaster. Behind closed doors, the government negotiated with the Agrarians and Liberals to provide the necessary votes on the bill's third reading the following day. When an acceptable compromise could not be reached, Prime Minister Stauning invited the negotiators home for what turned out to be a historic bargaining session.

The agreement that emerged in the predawn hours of January 30 in Stauning's modest apartment in a city-owned housing block on Kanslergade called for four major actions:

1. an extension of the existing labor agreements without wage reductions;
2. a massive public works program to put the unemployed back to work and to provide winter relief for their families;
3. a devaluation of the currency to stimulate farm exports and agricultural price supports to stabilize farm incomes; and

4. a fundamental restructuring of the Danish patchwork of social insurance and poverty relief measures into a comprehensive program.

The exhausted cabinet members and Agrarian Liberal Party leadership announced the agreement to parliament and struggled through Monday evening to finish putting the deal together. Without realizing it, these Danish politicians were founding what would become known as the Scandinavian middle way.

This was, however, not the only portentous political event of January 30. South of the Danish border that same Monday, the German president, Paul von Hindenburg, facing the Weimar Republic's collapse into economic depression and political extremism, summoned a controversial, untried party leader to form a new government. The recipient of von Hindenburg's confidence was Adolf Hitler.

The Meaning of the Middle Way

Hitler's Third Reich engulfed Europe in flames during the next decade, but it collapsed finally under its own aggressive and self-destructive impulses. The hard-won Danish "Kanslergade Compromise," by contrast, set the pattern for the modern Scandinavian welfare states that have far outlasted Nazism.

The Kanslergade Compromise called for wide-ranging state intervention to manage the market economy. The government became involved in setting wages and agricultural prices, establishing credit and exchange policy, and putting the unemployed back to work. It created a comprehensive economic security net for the unemployed and for all those out of the labor market. And, as a compromise between Social Democrats, Liberals, and Agrarians, it broadened and cemented the center of the political spectrum.

In a way, events in Germany that day changed the very complexion of democratic politics in Scandinavia. Before Hitler's assumption of power, the Scandinavian Social Democrats—by far the largest party in Denmark, Norway, and Sweden—could reasonably strive to win a majority on their own to enact a socialist program, with the political polarization that would ensue. In Finland the Social Democrats had emerged from a civil war in a tie with the Agrarians for the largest percentage of the vote. But with Hitler's rise to power in the Weimar Republic, the handwriting was on the wall: Compromise among democratic parties was vital.

As Hitler consolidated his power by crushing the German Social Democrats, the Communist Party, and the independent trade unions, in Sweden a new Social Democratic government quickly followed the Danish example by agreeing with center parties on minimum farm prices and a public works program to create jobs for the unemployed. Norwegian Labor struck a similar deal with its Agrarian Party in 1935.

A compromise across the dividing line between socialist and "bourgeois" parties was a kind of defeat for the Scandinavian socialist and social democratic parties because it postponed indefinitely the achievement of true socialism. But cooperation did solidify democratic politics in a situation that threatened the very existence of social democracy.

Thereafter, Scandinavian compromise became much more than a tactic; it grew to be seen as virtuous in itself because it solidified a broad national consensus around democracy. The social-democratic welfare state, interventionist and protective of the people, became a surrogate for socialism. Its principle was to achieve redistribution and broadly shared prosperity through compromises acceptable to the nonsocialist center parties. Moreover, compromise worked. State intervention in the collapsing market economy began to stabilize farm income, put the unemployed back to work, reduce conflict in the labor market, and offer hope to the Scandinavian peoples in despair over the Depression and the threat of German aggression.

Right and left faced off despite the Nazi threat, in countries such as France. But in Scandinavia, a "national democratic compromise" started building what the Swedish Social Democratic prime minister, Per Albin Hansson, called "the people's home": a society that took care of all its citizens.

This Scandinavian model—an interventionist state managing the market economy toward a combination of growth, full employment, and large-scale welfare programs supported by agreement between employers and unions— was widely followed subsequently in western Europe. In fact, it was the precursor of the western European "postwar Keynesian consensus" after World War II. In the 1930s the American journalist Marquis Childs dubbed the Scandinavian accord "the middle way"—meaning a middle or third way between "savage" capitalism—i.e., the failed capitalism of the Depression era in the West— and Stalinist communism, the totalitarian regime then reigning in Russia.

After the war, the Scandinavian democracies continued to constitute a middle way in the Cold War ideological and geopolitical conflict, both in domestic and foreign-policy terms. For many in the West (including the United States) the Scandinavian middle way was extremely attractive. It promised "capitalism with a human face"; private production would support full employment and an expanding social welfare network, and it would reduce social and economic inequalities.

In domestic policy, Denmark, Norway, and Sweden built advanced capitalist market economies in which the state played both a regulatory and a redistributive role. Under predominantly Social Democratic governments, the state's role for a generation was far greater than in almost all of the other western capitalist democracies, although policy innovations in Scandinavia often set the pattern for policies elsewhere on the Continent ten or twenty years later.

During the Cold War, the Scandinavians sought a middle way in foreign policy as well. Efforts to fashion a Scandinavian defense union that would provide a viable military foundation for neutrality broke down in 1949, and on Scandinavia's western fringes, Denmark, Norway, and Iceland joined NATO, although they often seemed reluctant members. Finland, which had fought World War II on the German side, signed a separate peace agreement with the Soviet Union in 1944; its neutrality was guaranteed by treaty. Sweden continued to pursue a neutrality policy that had kept it out of war since 1815. Defense strategists wrote of a "Nordic balance," in which Swedish neutrality between NATO in the west and the Warsaw Pact in the east guaranteed Finnish neutrality and independence vis-à-vis the Soviet Union and permitted Denmark and Norway to pursue a strategy of lowering tensions on the northern flank of NATO by refusing to allow foreign troops or nuclear weapons on their territory.

In international economic affairs, there was balance as well. Denmark joined the European Community (now the European Union) when Britain did in 1973, albeit reluctantly; the Norwegians, even more reluctant, voted narrowly against joining Europe. Sweden and Finland held that joining the European Community would compromise their neutrality. All four distinguished themselves by supporting international cooperation that reached across the dividing lines between east and west and between north and south.

Finland developed differently between World War I and World War II—primarily because of the bitter civil war between the "Whites" and the "Reds" in 1917–1918 that the conservative Whites won. Yet in the post–World War II period, Finland came increasingly to resemble the rest of the Scandinavian area in the realm of domestic politics, as it caught up in terms of industrialization, welfare, and living standards. Even its peculiar international position gradually assumed a more Scandinavian "balance."

All this changed at the end of the 1980s. With the end of Soviet dominance of eastern Europe and the collapse of the USSR itself in 1991, the Scandinavian countries found their middle way questioned anew. What was it a middle way between?

The middle way that had served the Scandinavian countries so well domestically and internationally from the 1930s into the 1980s became confused amid economic globalization and political discord at home. Sweden and Finland opted for EU membership and closer ties to Europe in 1995. The middle way's extensive public services, high taxes, and state regulation of the market economy were challenged as well by international economic integration and the growing predominance of free-market thinking. New interest groups and social changes, including new roles for women, an aging population, and significant non-European immigration, challenged the consensus.

The rest of this chapter analyzes the rise and fall of the Scandinavian model in domestic politics, in European integration policy, and in foreign policy generally.

A Social Laboratory

The Nordic countries are idiosyncratic in many ways. They are small in terms of population (see the data on the chapter opening page). With the exception of Iceland (with a quarter of a million inhabitants), they are roughly comparable to medium-sized U.S. states. When compared to other members of the European Union, Sweden is about the size of Greece or Portugal; only Ireland and Luxembourg are smaller than Denmark and Finland.

Denmark, Iceland, Norway, and Sweden share common roots ethnically, linguistically, and culturally; and Finland—despite its distinct ethnic and linguistic origins—shares a common Nordic history and religion with them. Further, Denmark, Norway, and Sweden were distinguished by remarkable internal ethnic, racial, religious, and linguistic homogeneity. This aspect of Scandinavian societies, more than any other, made the development of the solidaristic Scandinavian model possible.

Until they began to receive a substantial flow of immigrants in the 1960s, 97 to 99 percent of the population of each country shared the same cultural, linguistic, and racial roots. About 95 percent of the populations were Lutheran and belonged to the state church. As a consequence, politics and policy in all three countries focused for decades to a unique degree on economic issues rather than the religious, linguistic, and ethnic conflicts that often dominate other societies. However, a generation of immigration, much of it from non-European countries, has literally changed the face of Denmark, Norway, and Sweden. Today, more than one in ten Swedish residents were born abroad. For the first time in more than a century, "ethnic" and immigration issues have become a source of political conflict.

Historically, Finland has been substantially more divided domestically than its Scandinavian neighbors. The legacy of Swedish settlement and rule until 1809 and of Russian rule from 1809 to 1917 left a significant Swedish-speaking population on the southwest coast of Finland and a considerable Russian Orthodox religious minority. Moreover, Finland was torn by a bitter civil war in 1917–1918 between Reds and Whites. The former were radical socialists who sought to emulate Lenin's Bolshevik revolution; the latter were a coalition of primarily antiradical nationalists. The Finnish Whites, backed by German troops, won the war and interned their opponents in concentration camps for a number of years. Half a century later, how Finns voted in national elections still was closely tied to which side of the civil war their grandfathers had fought on. Unlike Denmark, Norway, and Sweden—where the communists played a major role only immediately after World War I and World War II—the Finnish labor movement was split down the middle between communists and social democrats, by the civil war and its aftermath. This division prevented the social democratic dominance in Finland that Denmark, Norway, and Sweden witnessed in the 1930s.

Box 13.1 Why Do the Scandinavian Welfare States Survive?

One mystery to Americans is how political support for the Scandinavian welfare states survives when ordinary working people have to pay 50 percent to 60 percent of their earnings in income and other taxes. When their taxes come due, why don't they rise up in anger and overthrow the government? After all, American taxpayers have rebelled at far lower rates.

The answer is, first, that the Scandinavian welfare states rest on the principle of *solidarity*. By contrast, welfare programs in the United States rest on the principle of social insurance (Social Security, Medicare, workers' compensation, unemployment insurance) or altruism (charity to the poor). The limit of social insurance is that we agree to insure ourselves against only those risks that we cannot afford, and altruism is even more circumscribed, limited to keeping the bodies and souls of the poor together. But solidarity—defined as "reciprocal responsibility or mutual obligation"—has permitted the Scandinavians to build far more elaborate structures of mutual support on a consensual basis.

Second, Scandinavian welfare measures are generally *universal* in scope, rather than means-tested. Thus both transfer payments (such as pensions, sick pay, maternity pay, family allowances) and social services (such as medical and dental care, home assistance for the elderly, free education through college, and daycare and after-school care for children) are available to everyone in the category, whether they are poor, working class, or middle class. Transfer payments are usually taxed, so the post-tax benefit to the best off is much less than the benefit to the worst off. Fees for some social services, such as daycare, also rise with income. But generally speaking everyone is in the same system and receives the same benefits. Every year, almost every family receives some benefits. As a witty phrase describes the situation, "the richest 90 percent help support the poorest 90 percent."

Such universal programs are costly. Scandinavian spending on social security transfer payments is 20 percent to 40 percent higher than elsewhere in Europe.[1] Rising take-up rates for social services such as daycare and after-school care have continued to push up social welfare spending despite the financial constraints on public sector spending. More disturbing, the self-restraint of the older generation about utilizing the welfare net is giving way to a culture of "entitlement" among the younger generation. Thus in Denmark, for example, statistics indicate that the young are sicker than the old, even taking into account legitimate reasons, such as taking care of ill children. Many universal cash benefits in Scandinavia are taxable, so that the wealthier recipients keep a smaller share than the truly needy.

Still, universal public provision of social services generally provides a higher standard and is cheaper than provision through employer-funded, private insurance schemes. The classic case is medical care, which is both far more costly (by about 70 percent) in the United States as a proportion of gross domestic product and less adequately distributed than in Scandinavia. Consequently, the Scandinavian countries' health statistics (infant mortality, lifespan, etc.) beat the United States by a wide margin. Likewise the "top 1 percent" in Scandinavia earn three or four times the median income, and not ten or more times as in the United States. Typical middle-class incomes are very similar to the American level, while low income groups in Scandinavia have a substantially higher living standard than in the United States: after-tax, after-benefit poverty rates in Scandinavia are only about a quarter of the American rate.

Everyone pays, but everyone also benefits.

1. Accounting differences make exact comparison difficult. Social expenditures in Germany, Belgium, and the Netherlands are roughly comparable to Scandinavia, with France not far behind. See William Adema, "Net Social Expenditure," 2nd ed., *Labour Market and Social Policy Occasional Papers*, no. 52 (OECD, 2001).

Geopolitical proximity to "big brother" Russia had to shape the Finns' national political agenda. Finland by itself fought a brave but doomed war against Russia in the winter of 1939–1940. Then, after Germany invaded the Soviet Union in June 1941, Finland reentered the war on the German side, exiting with a separate peace treaty in 1944. Russia held a major naval base on Finnish soil covering the approaches to Helsinki until 1956.

In the postwar period, the decline in the Swedish minority through assimilation and emigration to Sweden has diminished traditional ethnic and linguistic divisions, and memories of the Finnish civil war have gradually faded. Migration into Finland has been much less than that seen in most western European countries. And, of course, Finland's dangerous situation vis-à-vis Russia changed dramatically with the Soviet Union's collapse. In the last twenty-five years, Finnish politics has converged increasingly with the general Scandinavian social democratic model.[1]

Domestic Politics: How Different Is Scandinavia?

Its location on the geographical fringe of Europe has meant that the Scandinavian countries have escaped some European developments entirely, while lagging behind on others.

Throughout most of the nineteenth century, the Scandinavians trailed western Europe in both industrial and political development. Industrialization came late, beginning only about 1855 in Denmark, 1890 in Sweden, and 1905 in Norway—a full century after England, Germany, Belgium, and France. Viewing nineteenth-century European political development in terms of three central themes—constitutionalism, nationalism, and democracy—the Scandinavians lagged behind in all but the first, with Sweden's strong state and well-established constitutional traditions and Norway's 1814 constitution remaining the oldest written European constitution still in force. Nationalism first became a major impulse in Denmark following its confrontations with German nation-alism along its southern boundary after 1848 and the loss of Denmark's Ger-man duchies in 1864.² Norway enjoyed a national cultural revival in the 1880s, and its confrontation with Sweden over full independence in 1905 sharpened national feelings in both countries. Political democracy (parliamentary suprem-acy) came even more slowly: 1884 in Norway, 1901 in Denmark, and 1917 in Sweden.

Late development in these spheres meant that the economic basis for liber-alism developed late. The agrarian and labor movements, which began in Scan-dinavia as elsewhere in Europe in the latter half of the nineteenth century, swept through the countryside and the new industrial towns like a prairie fire. Organ-izing in a virtual vacuum, the "popular movements" of family farmers and in-dustrial workers built their own economic and political organizations, which claimed the high ground of an egalitarian response to industrialization and po-litical democracy. Thanks to the high literacy levels encouraged by Lutheran-ism and by state educational policies in the eighteenth and early nineteenth cen-turies, the democratic popular movements were led from below, and the tie between the leaders and the led remains close even today.³

Even as the Scandinavians lagged behind Europe in many areas in the eigh-teenth and nineteenth centuries, they led in one: the strong state. The Swedes developed in the sixteenth and seventeenth centuries what was probably the most modern state in Europe in terms of its capacity to govern, and Swedish military prowess from the Thirty Years War through Charles XII's misadven-tures in Russia reflected both the state's strength and the success of state-sponsored development of military industries. By the time of the establishment of modern political organizations and democratic institutions in the last part of the nineteenth century, the Scandinavians had a well-established tradition of a strong state and a professional civil service. The right saw the strong state as good in itself; the left, as a tool for reform.

These three factors—relative isolation, powerful popular movements, and a strong state—created the conditions for the Scandinavian middle way in the twentieth century.

SOCIAL DEMOCRACY AND EUROPEAN DEVELOPMENT: SUCCESS, THEN CRISIS

More than any other single factor, what sets Scandinavian politics and policy apart is the predominant role played by the "popular movements"—farmers and labor—that represent the economically disenfranchised. Organizing from below in a virtual political vacuum in the latter half of the nineteenth century, farm and labor organizations swept the countryside, towns, and cities in an evangelical wave. In addition to the creation of the agrarian and labor parties, which came to be the great bearers of the democratic tradition, they created an immense economic and cultural infrastructure.

For the agrarian movement, the economic infrastructure was in the form of purchasing, processing, and marketing cooperatives that created the economies of scale that enabled family farmers to compete with the great estates. The cultural side was provided by the "folk colleges" that educated generation after generation of farm youth between the harvest in the fall and planting in the spring, the community centers in the countryside that offered everything from weekly dances to study circles and political debates, and the agrarian newspapers that preached egalitarianism in a class-bound society.

For labor, it was the trade unions in the crafts and industries; consumer cooperatives for everything from food to clothing to housing to funerals; every kind of cultural group from chess clubs and marching bands to scouts, kindergartens, and adult education; and social democratic newspapers, which were the first Scandinavian mass-circulation papers.

Both agrarian and labor movements shared certain central values. These included egalitarianism, a belief in democracy, and a strong commitment to building their own institutions. Allied in the struggle for political democracy, farmers and workers had much that united them even when ideology—private property versus socialization of the means of production—divided them. It is not inconsequential that the Danish social democrats adopted land reform and support for small farmers as their agrarian policy in the 1890s, much to the chagrin of the more orthodox German social democrats who were otherwise the Danes' mentors.

This massive political organization preceded the establishment of parliamentary democracy everywhere except Norway, where it coincided with the democratic breakthrough. Because numbers had not counted previously in politics, the conservatives had never taken the trouble to organize. Consequently, they found themselves playing catch-up after the agrarian radicals' and labor movement's ideas had already won adherents from their tenants in the countryside and servants in the cities.

Scandinavian popular movements were most remarkable in the degree to which they drew their leadership from the ranks of the movement itself, rather than from the educated elite. The liberal agrarian parties were led predominantly by farmers and the labor parties by workers—not lawyers, teachers, civil servants, or priests. This kept them honest. Government for the people works best when it is by the people and of the people.

The combination of democracy from below—of leaders sprung from and tied to the organizations of those they lead—with relative ethnic and religious homogeneity, overarching agreement of basic values, and relatively small communities offers powerful drivers for a cohesive, solidaristic welfare state based, as one turn-of-the-century trade union tract put it, on the principle of "reciprocal obligation or mutual responsibility."

Despite such advantages, nineteenth-century Scandinavia was a poor, class-ridden, and static region, as reflected in the waves of immigration to North America that also contributed to rapid social changes. Millions of Swedes and Norwegians as well as many Danes and Finns simply left for new opportunities. At first this removed considerable political and economic pressure, but later it stimulated interest in social, economic, and political reforms even among national conservatives. Knowledge of better economic opportunities abroad and the success of democratic government in North America and later Britain encouraged domestic reformers in both the labor and agrarian movements. Nationalists recoiled at the loss of youthful and energetic citizens.

Out of these conflicts emerged a civil society of the strongest sort. Citizens in the popular movements connected in myriad voluntary associations that mediated between them and the state and also provided direct economic, cultural, and social benefits. Organizing successfully around these associations, popular movements ultimately also captured state power. The state was transformed, beginning in the 1930s, to offer many of the benefits that the voluntary organizations had themselves previously provided. In the last thirty years, the welfare, educational, and regulatory functions of the popular-movement organizations were transferred to public administration, and many of the social and cultural functions previously provided by the popular-movement organizations were taken over by local and national government and provided by public employees instead of movement members. This generalized those social services to all the people, but it removed them from control from below. This also left the popular movements—especially the social democratic labor movement—dependent on control of the state to achieve its objectives.

For a half century, this approach was remarkably successful. The existence of a strong state and the tradition of an honest and professional civil service offered the mechanism for building a more egalitarian society. Principles of Keynesian economics advocating job-creating public programs were independently developed by Scandinavian economists during the Depression. Cautiously applied, they offered a route to use the state to improve the performance of capitalist market economies. The combination of the two provided the means to solve the classic problem of industrial capitalism—great and pervasive poverty amid great wealth—without revolution, by a lasting commitment to spread growth more equally than the existing distribution of wealth and income. That commitment lay at the core of the Kanslergade Compromise and the subsequent, similar national compromises in Norway and Sweden. It was driven forward politically by the Social Democrats with what proved to be a virtually unparalleled grasp on power in democratic elections.

Within the lifetime of a single generation, this commitment transformed Scandinavia from a region of great poverty—characterized by the immigrants' "flight to America"—into societies of widely shared affluence. The image of "the fortified poorhouse," as the title of Zeth Höglund's book characterized the Sweden of 1913, gave way to Per Albin Hansson's view of Sweden as "the people's home" in the 1930s as class struggle gave way to national construction under social democratic government. By the 1960s, Sweden and Norway, which had been among the poorest European countries some fifty years earlier, were among the most affluent. The slums and poverty were gone.

The Scandinavian success relied on the use of the state to achieve broad economic goals, and that rested on the assumption that the nation-state was the relevant unit for economic policy. That certainly was true following the collapse of the international trading system in the 1930s, which was anomalous given Scandinavia's long global trading history. It was equally true in the reconstruction after World War II. But by the 1960s and 1970s, as growing national affluence transformed the lives of the working class, the Scandinavian countries once again become fully enmeshed in an interdependent global trading system. This development accelerated prosperity but brought vulnerability to the oil crises of the 1970s and the ever-more-invasive global business cycle.[4]

Political Democracy Scandinavian Style

Denmark, Norway, and Sweden share a great deal in terms of political structures and political actors. Finland is different historically, but it has converged on the other three countries in the postwar period. Much of what they have in common stems from their similarities in terms of cohesion, as discussed earlier.[5] Some of it stems from their close ties in the Nordic Council and various European organizations, which facilitated diffusion of political ideas. The Scandinavian labor movements and the Social Democratic parties have interacted especially closely over the years.

POLITICAL INSTITUTIONS

All four countries are parliamentary democracies. All are clearly democratic in the sense that regular elections determine who holds political office and what policies are made. All are parliamentary systems in the sense that parliament—the legislative body—is the most important branch of government.

Denmark and Sweden are pure parliamentary systems. The legislative majority selects the executive (the prime minister and the cabinet) and can force the executive out by a vote of no confidence. In both cases, parliament is the ultimate arbiter of the constitutionality of its own legislation, although a variety of checks are imposed on parliamentary abuses of power, as we will discuss. In neither country do courts review the constitutionality of parliamentary legislation, as the U.S. Supreme Court does.

Norway also is a parliamentary democracy, but it has a modest tradition of judicial review, and the Norwegian constitution, dating back to 1814, prevents calling early elections, which is otherwise a standard characteristic of parliamentary government.

Finland has a mixed presidential-parliamentary form of government, which has considerable similarity to that of France in the Fifth Republic. The president, who heads the executive branch, is directly elected by a popular vote (prior to 1994, Finnish law provided for indirect election) for a six-year term and directs foreign policy, commands the armed forces, and can dissolve parliament. A new constitution entered into force in 2000, and it clarified and strengthened the primacy of the prime minister and the cabinet, which are selected by the parliament. Together the executive cabinet, led by the prime minister, and parliament share primary responsibility for domestic and EU affairs. Parliament can force the cabinet from office by a vote of no confidence. In practice this division has made the prime minister the most important part of the executive branch in terms of policy making, but there certainly were times during the Cold War when the president's role overshadowed that of his prime minister. There is no judicial review of the constitutionality of legislation.

Despite the multiparty system—today seven to ten or more parties are represented in the national parliaments—and the rarity of single-party majorities, the Scandinavians have had stable and effective government because they practice what Dankwart Rustow called "the politics of compromise." Scandinavian government is coalition government, sometimes through multiparty governments and at other times through bargains worked out in parliament between a minority government and other parties whose agreement has been attained on an issue-by-issue basis.

Although Denmark and Sweden maintained an upper house of parliament until 1953 and 1970, respectively, all four now elect a **unicameral**—single house—**parliament**. The Norwegian parliament (*Stortinget*), divides into two bodies to consider certain types of legislation, although most proceedings take place in the plenary parliament. In all parliaments, much of the detailed legislative and oversight work and most of the necessary multiparty compromises are worked out in standing committees. There are usually parliamentary committees for each governmental ministry, plus some with special competency (constitutional affairs or relations with the European Union). Parties are represented on committees in proportion to their overall strength, but coalitions are usually required for any significant actions. Most proceedings are in secret, precisely to encourage interparty compromises, but occasional hearings are held publicly, and there are increasing demands to "open up" the parliamentary processes to greater media scrutiny.

In all four countries, a proportional representation system is used in electing parliament. Thus, all parties of significant size are represented in parliament with approximately the same proportion of seats as they have support among voters. Although proportional representation was introduced in an existing multiparty system and stabilized it for a number of decades, as new lines of division—including those over the European Union, the environment, and immigration—have come to the fore in recent years, this election system has permitted growing fragmentation in parliament.

The basic principle of parliamentary democracy—that the prime minister and the executive branch are responsible to the majority in the house of parliament with the broadest suffrage—was established in 1884 in Norway, while the country was still under Swedish rule; in 1901 in Denmark; and in 1917 in Sweden. Finland established the same principle in 1917 with independence from Russia, but the losing side in the civil war was pretty much excluded from politics during the 1920s.

Denmark, Norway, and Sweden remain **constitutional monarchies**. Scandinavian monarchs took office within constitutional limits (Karl John in Sweden in 1809 and Norway in 1815; Haakon VII in Norway in 1905) or accepted them with relative grace (Frederik VII in Denmark in 1849). They proved more resistant to yielding the power to choose the prime minister to the elected parliamentary majority (1884 in Norway, 1901 in Denmark, and 1917 in Sweden), but here, too, they bowed to the winds of change. Although the governmental power of the Scandinavian monarchs is virtually nil today, they remain important symbols of national unity, above the lines of party or division by interest. In times of crisis, this symbolic role has had real political significance.

In Finland, the president has the symbolic role played by the monarchs as well as a more practical role in foreign policy. Although elected with a partisan affiliation, the Finnish president stands above party lines while in office. For more than fifty years (1939–1991) the presidents assumed a special role in managing relations with the USSR. This also enhanced presidential internal political powers.

All four countries have **unitary**, rather than federal, **governments** in the sense that all sovereignty resides in the national government, and the powers of the provinces and other subunits of government are derived from the national government. However, Finland provides far-reaching local autonomy for the Swedish-speaking Åland Islands, and Denmark provides even greater autonomy for Greenland and the Faeroe Islands, which have been granted the status of near independence. The Faeroes never joined the European Community, and Greenland, which acquired autonomy in 1979, quickly used its independence to withdraw from the European Community—the only territory to date to do so. In the past decade both have grown increasingly impatient with their ties to Denmark, but with no substitute in sight for the large budgetary subsidies that are sent from Copenhagen, the status quo will continue for a while longer.

Although power is clearly concentrated in the hands of the national government, many governmental services have been delegated to municipal and county government. Thus, most social services, including those for children, families, and the elderly, are provided by municipalities. Indeed, a higher proportion of governmental spending occurs at the local level in Scandinavia than at the state and local levels in the United States. Thus, within unitary states, the Scandinavians have thoroughly decentralized the provision of governmental services.

In order to make this decentralization effective, Denmark, Norway, and Sweden undertook similar consolidations of local government in the end of the 1960s and early 1970s. The consequence was to cut the number of local governments by half in Norway, three-fourths in Sweden, and four-fifths in Denmark. (In Finland, a similar consolidation was blocked, and the number of local administrations was reduced only by about a sixth in this period.) This dramatically reduced the number of elected municipal council members, but it did yield economies of scale and opportunities to build local governmental capacity to satisfy the demands of decentralized service provision. Local and regional governments still enjoy substantial taxing powers, but their dependence on budgetary transfers from the central government and the standardization of social, educational, and other local services has constrained their autonomy. Generally speaking these reforms were successful in establishing the capacity to expand social services in smaller towns and rural areas, but they undercut the relationship between citizens and their government in rural districts. Although the density of elected officials remains high in Scandinavia by comparison to most other democracies, it is much diminished in comparison to the past.

One striking aspect of Scandinavian politics is the degree to which government and the civil service are seen as national resources. This is a result of a convergence of causes. Scandinavian conservatives have traditionally supported a strong state as an instrument of national development. Popular movements, including especially the social democratic labor movement, have seen the government as a mechanism to generalize their egalitarian goals to the entire society. General antigovernment or antistate movements have always been weak. The distrust of government that we see across the political spectrum in the United States has generally been absent in Scandinavia. Furthermore, Scandinavian public administration generally has been deserving of citizen respect: its bureaucrats have been self-effacing, efficient, and honest.

However, that popular belief in the benevolence of public administration does not extend to the transnational public policy dimension. The European Union's multitudinous rules and regulations frequently strike most Scandinavians as downright arcane. For example, the European Union promulgated measures regulating the size of strawberries and curvature of cucumbers shortly before the 1992 Danish referendum on the Maastricht treaty; an effort to harmonize the dimensions of condoms, however, foundered on Italian opposition. One acerbic Danish placard during this referendum put it succinctly: "If you think there are already enough idiots running your life, vote no!" As EU regulations become targets for public ridicule and additional policy responsibilities shift from national capitals to distant EU institutions, the problem of the "democratic deficit" will become more acute.

POLITICAL ACTORS

Scandinavian democracy historically has been based on strong, disciplined mass-membership parties, which organize hundreds of thousands of voters as dues-paying party members. Parties have structured political competition at the local as well as the national level. They provided channels for recruiting political leaders; the career pattern was to start by running for the local municipal council. Municipal office or parliament followed for those who prove themselves. Regular local party meetings ensured close contacts between the elected officials and their party constituency. Because the parties offered different policy choices in the election campaigns, they allowed citizens a means to control not just the people in government but also the policies of government. Problematic for democratic participation has been an accelerating decline in party memberships. Social Democratic parties, which no longer automatically enroll union members, account for much of this decline, but all traditional parties have been hit.

The parties have been complemented by equally strong interest groups that organize workers, farmers, and employers. These groups, which we will look at, have typically been closely linked to individual parties. The unions have traditionally been Social Democratic (except in Finland, where they were hotly contested by the Communists), the farmer organizations have been the mainstays of the agrarian parties, and the employers have typically had a looser association with the Conservatives. Unlike many western countries, Scandinavian labor unions have maintained their remarkably high memberships (often over 80 percent of blue- and white-collar employees). While most are rather passive members, organized labor remains a strong political actor.

Parties and Party Systems

From the origins of parliamentary democracy at the turn of the century to the 1970s, the predominant pattern in all four countries was the five- or six-party system. On the right was the Conservative Party, which had been late to organize a mass base because it had wielded the levers of power on behalf of the elites and propertied classes before the democratic breakthrough. In the center were the nineteenth-century proponents of democracy: the Liberals and the Agrarians. To the left of center were the Social Democrats, their junior allies in the nineteenth-century push for democracy. The Social Democrats outgrew the coalition by the mid-1920s and typically polled about 40 to 45 percent of the vote from the 1930s through the 1970s. On the extreme left were the Radical socialists—Communists from the 1920s through the late 1950s—and the Socialist People's parties, which displaced the Communists in the late 1950s and early 1960s in Denmark and Norway. The remaining Communists in Sweden and Finland became increasingly independent of the Soviet Union after 1960 and evolved into "radical socialist" parties by the 1980s.

There were also some variants on this general theme, especially in the center of the political spectrum. The accommodating proportional representation system allowed small parties to gain parliamentary seats on issues such as prohibition, land taxation, and cultural distinctions. The Finns had a Swedish People's Party to represent the Swedish-speaking minority. The Norwegians supported a strong Christian People's Party, which was culturally and religiously conservative but centrist in economic terms. It gradually grew into a major force in Norwegian politics. Over the past thirty years similar parties have appeared in the other Nordic countries.

From the 1920s through the 1970s, the voters were roughly split between the parties of the right and center (the "bourgeois parties") on the one hand and the left (the "labor" or "socialist" parties") on the other. Although those with bourgeois leanings divided their votes among three or four parties of approximately equal size, the Social Democrats typically captured the lion's share of the labor vote—40 to 45 percent of the total—with the Communists/Socialist People's Party getting 5 to 10 percent. Numerically this gave the Social Democrats an obvious edge. Furthermore, because of the deep historical division during the struggle for parliamentary democracy between the Conservatives on the one hand and the Agrarians and Liberals on the other through the 1930s, the Social Democrats were able to form coalitions with the parties of the center once they put socialization of the means of production on the back burner after 1933.

Thus, the Social Democrats achieved a degree of hegemony in Denmark, Norway, and Sweden that was unparalleled in democratic elections. Social Democrats led the government of Denmark from 1929 to 1968 with only two breaks totaling four years (and two more during the German occupation); of Norway from 1935 to 1965 with a break of two weeks in 1963 and of five years during the German occupation; and of Sweden from 1932 to 1976 with a break only of a couple of months in the summer of 1936. They were able to use these extraordinary periods in government to reshape society through building an exceptionally strong public sector, as we will explore.

Finland constituted something of an exception. The Finnish labor vote (and trade unions as well) was roughly evenly split between the Communist Party and the Social Democrats, and they were direct political competitors. Consequently the fulcrum of Finnish party politics was in the center, especially with the well-led agrarian Center Party. After 1960 the Communist-led electoral alliance vote declined, and it has taken a course similar to that of the radical socialists in the other countries and has been integrated into the parliamentary give-and-take.

The culmination of this period of Social Democratic construction of the Scandinavian welfare state was the reforms of the late 1960s and early 1970s, which expanded social services into rural areas and raised income replacement rates for the unemployed, sick, injured, and disabled from 40 to 50 percent of their market income to 70 to 90 percent. These reforms came on line just about the time the oil price shock of 1973–1974 set off a period of economic adjustment and economic globalization throughout the West. Social democratic ideas and their carefully constructed tools of public economic management, as we will discuss, offered fewer answers in a global economy.

This relatively stable party system changed dramatically in the 1970s and 1980s. New protest parties arose on the right in protest against high taxes, growing immigrant populations, and the fact that the bourgeois parties that finally took governmental power in the late 1960s and 1970s administered the social-democratic system rather than abolishing it; these were the so-called Progress Parties in Denmark and Norway and the New Democracy Party in Sweden. Finland had the somewhat similar but weaker protest parties, including the Rural Party (now known as the "True Finns"). There was further subdivision in the center. Denmark saw the development of a Christian People's Party and a Center Democrat split from the right wing of the Social Democrats. In Sweden, the Christian Democrats also broke into parliament. Environmentalist parties won seats in both Sweden and Finland, and the Danes and Norwegians both sent a few members to parliament from groups to the left of the Socialist People's parties.

The consequence was that the relatively stable five- or six-party model for 1920–1970 gave way to a seven- or eight-party model in which the Christian Democrats in the center and a protest party on the right seemed to be a permanent part of the parliamentary constellation. The Scandinavian Christian Democrats have more of a "Sermon on the Mount" orientation than the rightist orientation of the U.S. Christian Coalition; although socially conservative (especially on the issues of abortion, drugs, pornography, and alcohol), they are strong supporters of the welfare state, foreign aid, and restrained materialism. They show a remarkable streak of religious tolerance as well: although Christian Democratic voters are overwhelmingly devout, evangelical Lutherans, the Danish party was led for some years by a Catholic, and the Swedish party included a prominent immigrant Jewish physician among its leaders and members of parliament. Consequently, they have accommodated themselves easily to the give-and-take of parliamentary compromise.

The protest parties of the right have not, however, and they were initially kept outside the patterns of parliamentary coalitions. Driven originally by opposition to taxes and bureaucracy, they have in recent years become increasingly strident in their opposition to immigrants, particularly those racially or culturally distinguishable, such as Africans, Asians, and Muslims. For a long time they were "heard" but not "listened to." This began to change in the late 1990s as their electoral advances made them too large to be ignored. Nonsocialist governments in Norway and most recently in Denmark have counted on parliamentary votes from the "New Right." In local government the pattern is similar; once radical parties draw 10 to 20 percent of the vote, their political influence grows.

Although the division of the voters between the blocs long remained relatively even, there has been an increasing tilt to the right, especially when the rightist protest parties have won some working-class votes. Further, the Social Democrats were weakened by a seepage of voters to their left, especially over the issue of European Community membership in the 1970s in Denmark and Norway and European Union membership in 1994 in Sweden. For the current division of parliamentary seats among the parties, see Table 13.1.

The cumulative loss of Social Democratic votes in the 1980s and 1990s has been 5 to 15 percentage points (compared to the 1940s–1970s); with proportional representation, this is a significant shift. The forty years of Social Democratic hegemony that began during the Depression came to an end. However, despite the increased party fragmentation, loss of part of their voting base, and a certain poverty of ideas, the Social Democrats remained the largest party in parliament in Denmark (until 2001), Norway, and Sweden. Although they had ceased to be the normal party of government, it was hard to govern against them, and they were perfectly capable of savaging governments of the right that tried to cut the welfare state.

One of the major consequences of the fragmented party system and declining Social Democratic hegemony has been the growing prevalence of minority cabinets. If we split the post–World War II period at the 1972 mark—the Danish and Norwegian European Community referenda—the Danes managed majority governments for 25 percent of the period prior to 1972 and 3 percent of the period since. The Norwegians had majority governments for 80 percent of the pre-1972 period and 6 percent of the period since. The Swedes mustered majority governments for 40 percent of the first period and only 13 percent of the most recent period. Finland remains committed to broad majority coalitions, which have accounted for nearly all its governments over the past thirty years. While one might think that this would produce political paralysis, the governments seem to function about as effectively as in the past.

There are three reasons for this. The first is the value, already discussed, placed on compromise, which makes minority government much less frustrating than it otherwise would be. The second is that various "radical" and "protest" parties on the political left and, more tentatively, on the right have become substantially less radical and more interested in participating in shaping legislation through compromise; Social Democratic minority governments can turn to their left as well as to the center for votes, while nonsocialists look to their

Table 13.1   Party Parliament Strength in November 2003

Country/Party	Seats
Denmark	179
Social Democrats	52
Liberals*	56
Danish People's (rightist)	22
Conservatives*	16
Socialist People's	12
Radical Liberals	9
Christian People's	4
Leftists	4
Greenland and Faeroe Islands	4
Finland	200
Social Democrats*	53
Center [agrarian]*	55
Conservatives	40
Leftists	19
Swedish People's*	9
Greens	14
Christian Democrats	7
True Finns	3
Norway	165
Labor (Social Democrats)	43
Conservatives*	38
Progress (rightist)	26
Leftists	23
Christian People's*	22
Center [agrarian]	10
Liberals*	2
Others	1
Sweden	349
Social Democrats*	144
Moderates (conservatives)	55
Liberals	48
Christian Democrats	33
Leftists	30
Center [agrarian]	22
Greens	17

* In government as of November 2003.

right. The third is that, by and large, Scandinavian governments of the last twenty years have not sought to undertake major domestic reforms. Minority governments have an easier task administering the existing society than seeking to change it.

Interest Groups

The Scandinavian countries are the most thoroughly organized in the world. Practically everybody belongs to his or her economic interest organization. Manufacturers, shopkeepers, renters, farmers, workers, and students are all organized. Even groups that we would think impossible to organize are almost universally members of their union or association. For example, 96 percent of Danish bank employees are reported to be union members. Overall, 75 to 85 percent of all wage and salaried workers are union members, and farmer and employer organizational percentages are equally impressive. School children, university students, priests, and military personnel each have their usually well-ordered group.

Still, as this list suggests, Scandinavian interest organizations are divided primarily along economic lines. This mirrors the lines of political division in these societies. Moreover, the larger of the interest organizations, including both the trade union federation and the employers' organization, are sufficiently inclusive that they have to take broader societal interests into consideration. Furthermore, until recently they were highly centralized: labor agreements were negotiated nationally between the national employers' organization and the national trade union organization. Recently collective bargaining has been decentralized by the economic sector (e.g., metal industry, public sector employees, etc.). In practice, unions and employers keep a close eye across the labor market, and contract provisions tend to move across it in similar directions. Thus, areas of conflict and cooperation spread across the economy and have immediate societal consequences.

As a result, the Scandinavian countries remain models of a peculiar kind of social democratic **corporatism**, in which interest organizations as a matter of course are integrated in making and implementing public policy. Some prefer to call the process "the negotiated economy." Interest organizations have highly professional staffs and constantly are encompassed in governmental commissions in designing policy, including the Swedish "remiss" system of formal consultation on major initiatives with all relevant interest organizations. It is a process of interest representation very different from Washington lobbying.

Not only are Scandinavian interest organizations involved in drafting policy, they implement it. Consider the national labor agreement, for example, in the years that a single overarching national contract for the private sector is negotiated: the unions and the employers, with the government as a third party, hammer out the contract, since the contract essentially determines wage formation for the period. The primary aim of the government, in terms of management of the economy, is to ensure that wage increases are noninflationary.

The practice of corporatism is eased by the small scale of the national political class in the Scandinavian countries. One faces the same people across the table. Working together becomes second nature. Globalization and more particularly European integration may erode this cozy structure.

Restraining the Governors

The concentration of power in unicameral parliaments and the presence of strong, disciplined parties not only permit effective and responsive policy making, it raises the specter of majority tyranny. What prevents a unified parliamentary majority from running roughshod over all opposition? What prevents systematic abuses of citizen rights? In the United States, the system of government has been carefully designed to avert majority tyranny by the division of powers between the three branches of government—legislative, executive, and judicial—and between the federal and state governments. The court system is engaged in a continual review of governmental acts. The Scandinavians do not have those mechanical checks and balances built into their government institutions. They have developed a different set of checks on abuse of power and majority tyranny.

First, the ombudsman—a Scandinavian concept that has entered the English language and U.S. practice—serves as a standing, independent check on abuses of executive power. This position was created in the Swedish constitution of 1809 as a parliamentary restraint on abuse of royal executive power; today it serves as a more general check on abuses throughout the executive branch. The Swedish ombudsman is elected by parliament for a four-year term and is empowered both to respond to formal citizen complaints and to initiate investigations on, for example, the basis of press reports. In recent years, the Swedish ombudsman has handled about three thousand cases a year; about 90 percent are citizen initiated.

The Finns added an ombudsman in 1919 at the birth of the republic on the Swedish model. The Danes added a parliamentary ombudsman in the constitution of 1953, and the Norwegians established a similar office in 1962. The formal powers of ombudsmen are amplified by a strong tradition of parliamentary inquiry (both questions to the government and committee hearings) and investigative journalism.

Second, increasingly voter referenda have checked parliamentary majorities. This is most formalized in Denmark, which has held nineteen referenda since 1915; Denmark is second only to Switzerland in direct citizen votes on key legislation. All constitutional changes go to a citizen vote (after having been approved by two sessions of parliament with an intervening election), any legislation except finance and tax measures can be sent to a vote by one-third of parliament, and any surrender of national sovereignty can be sent to a vote by one-sixth of parliament. Such provisions strengthen the hands of the minority vis-à-vis the majority. While Finland and Norway lack constitutional sanction for binding referenda (and Sweden limits it to constitutional changes), governments have always abided by voter decision except in the case of the Swedish referendum concerning which side of the road they should drive on (in 1955, despite the government's recommendation and common sense, Swedes voted to continue driving on the left; in 1967 the government shifted without a referendum). Increasingly, highly divisive issues such as nuclear power (Sweden, 1980) and European Community/European Union membership (Denmark 1972, Norway 1972 and 1994, Sweden and Finland, 1994) and further integration (Denmark 1986, 1992, 1993, 1998, and 2000; Sweden 2003) have been decided by the people directly.

Third, two aspects of Scandinavian political culture tend to check parliamentary majorities. One is that facts count in Scandinavian politics. The policy debate, both in the media and the parliament, is couched in empirical terms. Demagoguery discredits the user. The other is that a value is placed on broader compromise. Part of the reason for this is purely practical: Parties involved in the compromise will not reverse the policy when they are in government. But part is the concept that legislation passed by narrow majorities is less legitimate than that passed by broad majorities. Thus there is a tendency to seek broader majorities than are necessary simply to pass legislation.

Finally, Scandinavian corporatism provides an open door in policy making. Major legislative initiatives generally are preceded by governmental commissions that involve not only the political parties but all the relevant interest groups. Trade unions, employers, and farmers' organizations are involved in practically all of these, and more specialized interest organizations take part in commissions in their spheres of interest. Such political transparency is reinforced by an active and diverse media and supplemented nowadays by the Internet. Thus major legislation on, for example, changing higher education involves teacher unions and student organizations as well as primary economic interest groups.

THE WELFARE STATE AND ECONOMIC STABILITY

The Scandinavian responses to the economic crises of the 1930s marked a sea change in the role of the state. The old "night watchman state" provided national defense, justice, police protection, roads, and elementary education. The new "welfare state" was to regulate the market economy to ensure full employment and growth and to provide social and economic security for those out of the labor market because of old age, sickness, unemployment, and disability and for families whose market income was small and number of children large.[6] This is what political scientists have come to call the "postwar consensus," but in Scandinavia it started before World War II, driven primarily by the predominant popular movements with more of an egalitarian perspective.

Scandinavian welfare states, like those in Europe generally, are not for the poor alone. They are a method of providing universal social services and economic security for the middle class as well as the working class and the marginalized poor. Practically all social welfare expenses are in the public sector. This includes family allowances, daycare and after-school care, unemployment, health care, maternity and sick pay, pensions, disability, housing subsidies, and social assistance. In the United States, by contrast, a number of these, including medical and dental care, maternity and sick pay, and the bulk of our pensions, are handled privately through employers. Unlike the U.S. provision of these services, which varies tremendously between occupational groups and employers, Scandinavians universally receive about the same benefits.

In the postwar period, Scandinavian governments worked to achieve broadly shared affluence by two mechanisms. First, they sought to manage the economy to limit cyclical unemployment and to bring up the standards of the worst off in the labor market by channeling capital investment and labor from the least efficient firms to the most efficient firms. The trade unions' "solidaristic wage policy" was the most effective mechanism for this purpose. Over time, it raised the wages of the unskilled relative to the skilled and of women relative to men at the same time as it increased the overall efficiency of the economy.

Second, they sought to spread the dividends of economic growth more equally than the existing system distributed income and wealth. Those outside the labor market or in low income groups gained, but no one lost absolutely. As a result, the policy enjoyed widespread political support, and social expenditures expanded rapidly.

Between 1960 and 1974, social spending as a share of GDP nearly doubled in the Scandinavian countries. The growth really was a product of substantial improvements in the social security net that included raising income-replacement ratios for the unemployed and the disabled, raising pension levels, and expanding some services from urban areas to include rural areas. With unemployment at a minimal 2 percent level, it cost little to raise the income replacement ratio to 80 or 90 percent of market wages. All this occurred during a period of prolonged economic growth and, generally speaking, shared the affluence of those in the labor market with those outside and those with low-income families in the labor market with numerous children. (See Table 13.2.)

By contrast, the 1974 to 1984 period was characterized by the two oil crises and the unpredicted combination of economic stagnation and inflation ("stagflation") in most western economies. In Denmark, new social expenditures from the end of the good years finished coming on line, and there was also a rapid expansion of countercyclical social expenditures because of the bad times

Table 13.2   Public Social Security Transfers as a Percentage of GDP, 1960–2000 (Annual Average)

	1960–73	1974–79	1980–89	1990–2000
Denmark	9.5	14.0	17.1	18.9
Finland	6.6	11.2	13.9	20.0
Norway	10.3	12.9	12.7	15.7
Sweden	10.0	15.9	18.3	20.7
EU (15) average	11.4	12.3	16.5	16.8
United States	6.4	10.2	11.0	12.6*

*Average 1990–97.

Source: OECD, Historic Statistics, 1960–97, and Historic Statistics, 1970–2000 (Paris: OECD, 1999 and 2001).

that saw unemployment rise from the frictional level of about 2 percent to 8 percent. Sweden continued to grow the national economy and hold down unemployment by expanding the public sector; this kept unemployment at 3 percent and restrained social spending for countercyclical programs but pushed some economic problems forward. Norway, blessed with North Sea oil, escaped the hard times. Finland's economy benefited from continuing modernization and substantial trade with Soviet Russia and other eastern European states.

Rising social expenditures in a low-growth economy began to squeeze the tax base, private consumption, and capital investment. Increasingly since the 1970s, the Scandinavian countries have struggled with maintaining economic balance. Generous unemployment benefits protected living standards when the economy turned bad, but how long can you sustain using 4 to 5 percent of GDP for that purpose? The answer in Denmark has been "for at least two decades" (1975–1995), but that is very costly. The consequence has been that all the Scandinavians except the oil-rich Norwegians have repeatedly sought to trim welfare programs at the margins. But despite their best efforts to hold down costs, the secular trends pushing costs up combined with growth in unemployment (particularly long-term unemployment) have continued to push spending and taxes up. Governmental expenditures rose roughly 15 percent of GDP between 1974 and 1996 in all Nordic countries except Norway (unchanged thanks to petroleum-fueled prosperity). In the long run, this creates structural problems for competition in a global economy and even in the European Union, where social benefits are significantly better than in the United States but still lower than in Scandinavia.

While the welfare state was being constructed—from the 1930s through the early 1970s—increased expenditures were closely correlated with real gains in living standards. Unemployment compensation was enhanced, maternity and paternity leaves were introduced, pensions went up, housing was improved, daycare centers built, etc. In recent years, however, expenditures have continued to rise without such clear improvements in welfare.

Today, the cost of social programs is being pushed up in Scandinavia by three other forces: demography, technology, and rising take-up rates. Aging populations—and Scandinavians top the list internationally in terms of life expectancy—require more services. Improved (and expensive) medical technology continues to drive the costs of the health-care system higher; despite the comprehensive and efficient national health systems in the four countries, a health-care cost crisis looms. And take-up rates for social programs have continued to rise among the young, who shape their behavior to conform to the mold of the social-benefit system. The result is that increasing expenditures do not necessarily increase welfare. Medical technology certainly extends life, but much of the costs of that new technology are incurred in the last few months of life, when the quality of life is low.

Moreover, the costs of social programs are being driven up by the fact that the small, open Scandinavian economies are very much part of the global economy. Global capital mobility means that investment in high-wage areas, like the Nordic countries, lags unless productivity (and applied research), or currency devaluations, maintain competitiveness. Thus, Danish unemployment rates rose to European Community levels in the 1970s and 1980s, and Swedish rates hit European rates when capital controls were dismantled in the end of the 1980s and public sector employment growth stopped in the 1990s. Finnish unemployment shot through the roof after 1991, but that was primarily due to the collapse of Finland's eastern markets. Good unemployment compensation is inexpensive only when unemployment remains low.[7]

Another issue is the rapid increase in a noticeable immigrant population. About 6 percent of the population of Sweden and 4 percent of that of Denmark and Norway carry foreign passports, and the percentage of foreign-born is higher, especially in Sweden, where more than 10 percent were born somewhere else. To a considerable extent, support for the solidaristic social welfare system rested on the fact that those who benefited and those who paid were very similar. They spoke the same language, worshiped in the same church (at least at Christmas), shared the same culture, and looked very much alike. Under these circumstances, solidarity was easy. It is far from clear that the same solidarity will pertain as immigrant populations grow. Successful integration of non–western European immigrants has so far eluded the Nordic countries. The result has been higher social costs and the rise of explicitly anti-immigrant parties in Denmark and Norway.

In the long run, Scandinavian prosperity in the global economy depends on pursuing the high road of high wages and high performance. That requires action in Brussels, where full employment has not been part of the prevailing ideology of the European Union. And it requires anchoring capital locally. And so the debate over local ownership and control is beginning in Sweden, which in the past has prospered with perhaps the most concentrated ownership of any capitalist country under social democratic economic management.

The past twenty-five years have been a watershed. The great social democratic project—the comprehensive welfare state supported by state economic intervention to manage the market economy—was completed with the able assistance of the center parties. There was no new, equivalent central thrust for reform. Minority governments of the center-right and center-left could administer this system, but it came under increasing pressure. Accelerating demographic changes—an aging and increasingly "multicultural" population—as well as relentless changes in the European Union and in the global economy ensure that the pressure will continue to build.

And so the question becomes whether and how the Scandinavian model can be reshaped to meet the challenges of economic globalization while retaining its comprehensive, solidaristic, and humane structure. That is the challenge for the first decades of the new millennium.

The Roads to Europe

Europe, including Scandinavia, faced four vital questions in the wake of World War II. A century of continental conflict had nearly extinguished European civilization. Armed struggle for control of Europe could not be allowed to occur again. At issue was, first, whether cooperation should be regional or global. A closely related second question was whether states should seek to build intensive integrated communities with like-minded states or whether cooperation should be restrained so as to include the largest number of participating countries (so-called "depth" versus "breadth," or "deepening" versus "widening" arguments). Third, should collaboration focus narrowly on specific economic or other policy problems (i.e., functional issues) or should it seek broad federal arrangements in which states would yield sovereignty over a range of policy matters? Finally, should this new international regime reinforce intergovernmental cooperation or should it carefully construct new international organizations with supranational responsibilities?

The Scandinavian states responded cautiously to these questions. Domestic issues were primary, but defensive isolation had failed between 1939 and 1945. The collapse of world trade in the 1930s had hurt their economies. Sweden had narrowly preserved its traditional neutrality during World War II, but only by accommodating the dominant belligerents. Denmark, Norway, and Finland had been invaded and found traditional nonalignment and neutrality largely discredited at the end of war. All had supported the League of Nations after World War I, only to see ruthless power politics and fanatical nationalism return. After 1945 they hoped that the emerging United Nations organization would allow them to preserve their independence while participating in the global community and a revitalized collective security system. Finland's position as a defeated power made its position especially precarious. Hard-liners in the Soviet Union believed that Finland had been a willing ally of Nazi Germany; instead, Finland's "continuation war" against the Soviet Union had been retaliation for Stalin's attack on Finland in 1939 (which had been encouraged by the Nazi–Soviet pact of August 1939 that established spheres of domination over eastern Europe).

Scandinavia sought security and prosperity through broad European cooperation. All wished to avoid new divisions despite the obvious differences between the western democracies and Stalin's Soviet Union. The term applied to this policy of reconciliation and constructive diplomacy was "bridge building." Bridges are built over chasms; the Scandinavian states recognized the fundamental conflicts that threatened the postwar order.

A useful way to view Scandinavian foreign policies of the past half century is from five perspectives: Nordic, west European, Atlantic, east European, and global. Such geopolitical shorthand is, admittedly, not precise, especially with the transition of many central and east European and Baltic states following the end of the Cold War.

The Nordic perspective reflects history and culture, but it also implies deliberate choices. We have mentioned the common roots of the Scandinavian states, which are traceable to a loose dynastic entity known as the Kalmar Union (1397–1523).[8] The next four hundred years saw frequent and often bitter rivalry in the Nordic region until the current five independent states emerged in the twentieth century. Sweden and Denmark competed for hegemony throughout the Baltic: first against the Hanseatic League and later against the emerging Slavic powers of Poland-Lithuania and finally Russia. The dominance of Russia from the eighteenth century onward and later the growth of German power forced the Scandinavians into an increasingly defensive position. Not until the collapse of the Soviet Union and its sphere of influence after 1990 would the Nordic states take a proactive role (now based on cooperation) in the Baltic.

Yet even as nationalism was shaping five distinct sovereign countries, there were calls for regional cooperation. They followed two lines: a romantic "pan-Scandinavianism" that argued for a federation of the increasingly democratic societies of the north, and pragmatic functional proposals covering a range of public policies common to the industrializing economies of the five states. Although "Scandinavianism" ended historic rivalries, it did not prevent the further division of the region into the five modern nations. The practical policy approach proved most fruitful, starting with a monetary union at the end of the nineteenth century (which collapsed following World War I), an "interparliamentary union" in 1907, and regular meetings between political leaders.

After World War II, the more ambitious goals of advocates for Nordic integration repeatedly ran into two obstacles. First, the interests of the Scandinavian countries were often different and not infrequently competitive. This strengthened historical and nationalist desires in Norway, Finland, and Iceland to maintain full independence from the older Scandinavian states. Second, outside political and economic ties outweighed Scandinavian alternatives. This would be seen most dramatically in security policy after 1948, when Denmark, Norway, and Iceland chose the Atlantic Alliance led by the United States; Finland accommodated its foreign relations within the narrow limits demanded by the Soviet Union; and Sweden reaffirmed its historical and successful nonalignment.

Later economic cooperation followed a similar path with broader European opportunities outweighing the potential of narrower Nordic proposals. Although intra-Scandinavian trade expanded significantly after 1950, access to European and global markets remained the higher priority. Despite these setbacks, in 1952 the Nordic countries established the Nordic Council— essentially an extension of the inter-parliamentary union that would coordinate legislation and encourage Nordic initiatives whenever consensus could be reached. Underlying the development of Nordic policy cooperation was the primacy of Social Democratic and Labor parties during much of the 1945 to 1975 period. Even in Iceland and Finland, where this was not the case, centrist governments adopted much of the Social Democratic agenda on labor, social, and economic issues. This paved the way for regional cooperation.

Nordic cooperation continues on three levels: parliamentary, ministerial, and nongovernmental. The annual meetings of parliamentary delegations from the five countries (plus the three autonomous regions: Åland, Greenland, and the Faeroes) encourage pragmatic cooperation and deepen mutual understanding. Committee work fosters personal contacts across the region as well as a comparative perspective on policy issues. Ministerial contacts are more intense and continuous. Ministries develop expertise on Nordic affairs and also establish contacts among policy experts. Hence, solutions to technical problems may be expedited by a direct phone call to a Nordic bureaucratic neighbor. In addition, there are regular ministerial "summits," since 1971 routinized through the Nordic Council of Ministers, which bring together the top political and administrative people for detailed discussions and planning. A common Nordic political culture that emphasizes consensus, fact-finding, pragmatism, and responsibility helps this process. Finally, there are the various nongovernmental organizations in the educational, cultural, and scientific area that bring Scandinavians together on specific projects and interests. Again, this invigorates Nordic cooperation at the grass roots but also mobilizes important interests in support of these activities.

"Western Europe" was at first a Cold War concept, but it increasingly gained real political and economic significance. The Nordic countries chose not to be part of the evolving European community that started with the Brussels Pact of 1948, the Schuman Plan of 1950 for a coal and steel community, and especially the Treaty of Rome in 1957, which sparked the development of a European common market. Yet all but Finland participated in the European Recovery Program (the Marshall Plan) and became part of looser institutional structures that were also favored by Great Britain. Likewise, Denmark and Norway found that NATO membership brought them closer to the west European democracies and expedited reconciliation with the Federal Republic of Germany. By the 1960s relationships with expanding western European institutions (notably the Common Market) became a permanent issue on the Scandinavian political agenda.

The Atlantic dimension overlaps considerably with the western European, but it has three distinctive facets. After 1940 the Scandinavian states developed sustained and intensive relations with the United States (and to a lesser extent, Canada), with which they had previously had important ethnic ties but no intensive diplomatic history. Further, the Atlantic dimension brought particularly the three Scandinavian NATO members into a much wider community in Europe (especially with the Mediterranean NATO members). Finally it evolved into a broader western community exemplified by the **Organization for Economic Cooperation and Development (OECD)**, which emerged in 1960 out of the narrower Marshall Plan structure. Even after the end of the Cold War, the Scandinavian states have sought to keep the United States immersed in European affairs and have encouraged NATO's enlargement eastward. Interestingly neither Sweden nor Finland considered NATO membership but were satisfied with the Partnership for Peace.

Relations with eastern Europe and the former Soviet Union represent the legacy of the Cold War, which also dominated Scandinavia for more than forty years. For the past two centuries, Scandinavia's relations with eastern Europe have been distant, and Russia was most often seen as a threat. After a period of "bridge building" between 1944 and 1948, the Scandinavian countries chose different options to cope with the east-west struggle. Common to each was a desire to maintain relatively low tensions in the Nordic region and to develop autonomous Nordic relations. Since 1990, Scandinavia's "eastern question" has become far more complex. At present three developments have emerged from the former Eastern Bloc. First is the renewed independence of the Baltic states of Estonia, Latvia, and Lithuania. The Scandinavian countries have greeted this unexpected development with unusual activism. Second, Russia's weakness and tentative steps toward democracy represent an unprecedented challenge for the Nordic states. The norm had been an authoritarian, powerful, but often conservative Russia. Finally, as the expanding EU encompasses central and eastern Europe, the Nordic countries must adjust to changing institutional and political arrangements while maintaining their influence and independence.

Finally, there remains a global perspective that includes Scandinavia's historic commitment to the United Nations and other forms of international cooperation. The Nordic countries have global economic interests and collectively represent a substantial global economic power. They are among the most generous and steadfast contributors to international economic assistance efforts and often champion the less-developed countries in international organizations. Yet they are far from major actors whose decisions can affect global affairs. Here, too, a strategy of bridge building can be constructive, as illustrated by the role of Norway and its late foreign minister, Johann Jørgen Holst, in facilitating the 1993 Israeli-Palestinian Oslo Accords. More recently Norwegian diplomats have brokered peace talks in Sri Lanka.

POSTWAR SECURITY OPTIONS

Initially the Nordic countries placed their trust mainly in the new United Nations and its promise of "collective security" and broad global cooperation. The disappointments of the 1930s were balanced by the lessons of appeasement and the leadership promised by the United States, along with hopes for Soviet cooperation in the postwar order. As a defeated power, Finland was initially denied membership in the UN, but the other four Nordic nations were in from the start. Scandinavians could see that their best foreign policy option was continuing great-power cooperation in the UN. The appointment of Norwegian statesman Trygve Lie as the first secretary general of the UN augured well for Scandinavian engagement.

Denmark and Norway were accepted as victorious powers while Sweden's wartime neutrality was discreetly ignored. Small Danish and Norwegian contingents were part of the Allied occupation forces in Germany. Likewise, temptations to exact retribution against defeated Germany were resisted. Reconciliation would be the goal.

There were similarities with the post–World War I period. Germany was temporarily down, and France and especially Britain enjoyed prestige but clearly were weakened by the war and their protracted efforts to wind down overseas empires. After 1945, there were two major differences: the dominant position of the Soviet Union in eastern Europe and the Baltic and the global stature of the United States. Soviet forces occupied Finland, but their behavior there had been tolerable. Soviet forces had liberated northern Norway and assisted the desperate civilian population as much as they could. They withdrew shortly after the war, and despite some Soviet security claims in the Arctic territories of Svalbard, Soviet-Norwegian relations were cordial. Likewise, Soviet forces occupied the Danish Baltic island of Bornholm in May 1945 but withdrew a year later without incident.

With the apparent breakdown of east-west cooperation in 1946–1947, the Scandinavian states sought to play a mediating role. The term "bridge building" was applied to diplomatic efforts to reconcile the two blocs. Had the focus been northern Europe, such pains might have borne results, but Scandinavia was distant from the conflict's center in central and eastern Europe. The "iron curtain" identified by Winston Churchill in 1946 did not run through Scandinavia, although Finland was vulnerable. Precise fulfillment of the terms of the onerous peace treaty and delicate negotiations by veteran diplomat and later president Juho Paasikivi preserved Finnish sovereignty. Sweden provided the Soviet Union with generous postwar economic credits to atone for its wartime neutrality and to stimulate its postwar economy. All of the Scandinavian countries were handicapped by the weakness of their two main trading partners: Germany and Britain. Hence the Nordic countries were enthusiastic when U.S. Secretary of State George Marshall announced a European Recovery Program in June 1947.

Tensions continued to rise over the next eighteen months. Danish and Norwegian communist parties enjoyed an initial surge of support because of their role in the anti-Nazi resistance, but their strength quickly dissipated. Only in Finland did communists remain a factor as a result of the Soviet support. When the Soviet government rejected participation in the Marshall Plan, the door also slammed for Finland (although the United States found other channels to assist Finland). The February 1948 coup that ousted the democratic Masaryk government in Czechoslovakia was a severe psychological shock. Like Scandinavia, postwar democratic Czechoslovakia had sought to be a bridge-builder between east and west. Yet its regard for Soviet interests had not prevented Stalin from overthrowing a democratic coalition government, installing a ruthless communist regime, and isolating Czechoslovakia from its western European neighbors.

At about the same time Moscow sent a threatening letter to the Finnish government that demanded reassessment of Soviet-Finnish ties. Given the strength of the Finnish communists, the peace terms already imposed a year earlier, and the proximity of Soviet troops to Helsinki, many feared a repetition of the Prague coup. Finnish leaders kept their nerve. Discreetly, Finnish communists were removed from sensitive governmental positions, while Finnish leaders assured Moscow of their understanding of Soviet security needs. A treaty of "friendship, cooperation, and mutual assistance" was negotiated and became the basis of the next forty years of Finnish-Soviet relations. It required Finland to obtain Moscow's approval for political and economic ties with the west and basically gave Moscow a so-called *droit de regard* (veto right) to scrutinize Finnish foreign policy and in practice, for more than twenty years, Soviet veto power over certain Finnish politicians. Crucially, however, it did not end Finland's recovering parliamentary democracy and capitalist economy.

Soviet-Nordic relations eventually stabilized, especially following the marked improvement during the post-Stalin "thaw" when the Russians unilaterally withdrew from their Finnish base in Porkkala in 1955, but in 1948 pessimism prevailed. In the Scandinavian capitals, fear of Soviet intentions and recognition of the limits to the UN as a basis for future security inspired a reappraisal of their security situation. In 1948 the five signatories of the new

Brussels Pact (Britain, France, Belgium, the Netherlands, and Luxembourg) began negotiations with the United States for a broader Atlantic defense alliance.

Neither the United States nor Great Britain had focused on Scandinavia after 1945. The United States had northern strategic concerns, but these were mainly the air bases in Iceland and, to a lesser extent, Greenland. Both were essential for U.S. military operations in Europe, and their strategic importance would grow significantly during the Cold War. There was sympathy for the Finns and their resistance to Soviet pressure; Finnish repayment of earlier U.S. loans had a remarkable impact even on isolationists. While Finnish options were sharply limited, the other Scandinavian states agreed to reassess their collective security in 1948–1949. Isolated neutrality was discredited in Denmark and Norway, and even the Swedes seemed willing to consider a regional security arrangement.

The effort to create a nonaligned Scandinavian Defense Union failed basically because Norway sought closer ties with the emerging western defense alliance that evolved into NATO. As one Norwegian politician put it, "We want to be defended, not liberated." Western (in practice, U.S.) military assistance would be directed at the broader alliance and not at peripheral blocs, and without such assistance Scandinavian military potential would remain at a level characterized by one contemporary observer as a "$0+0+0 = 0$" equation. After Norway's choice, Sweden was uninterested in a bilateral arrangement, and Denmark followed Norway into the North Atlantic Treaty Organization in April 1949. Sweden would preserve its nonalignment in peace and hope for neutrality in war.

For the next forty years, this arrangement prevailed with only marginal adjustments. Norway became initially the most enthusiastic Scandinavian NATO member, although the Norwegians adopted a policy of nonprovocation toward the Soviet Union, with which they shared a border in the far north. Denmark also refused to allow permanent foreign bases on its territory in times of peace, although NATO staff and periodic military exercises were accommodated. Denmark also accepted U.S. bases in Greenland without inquiring too closely about their military activities. Norway made a substantial effort to build up its armed forces; in Denmark defense expenditures were controversial. Nevertheless, both countries developed and maintained military forces and alliance ties that were without historical precedent.

Sweden's nonalignment stimulated initially a considerable defense effort. Swedes believed that their successful neutrality during World War II came from achieving enough military strength to make invasion too costly. That became their defense policy in the Cold War, although we now know that Sweden cooperated secretly with NATO in the 1950s and 1960s in coordinating a defense against the Soviet Union.

THE NORDIC BALANCE

By the 1960s, Nordic foreign policies had established patterns that, with occasional variations, were maintained until the end of the Cold War in 1990. Each Nordic country had, of course, its own interests and priorities. Despite the lack of a formal common Nordic foreign policy, each country has assessed the impact its foreign policy might have on an overall "Nordic balance." In addition, as the Norwegian analyst Arne O. Brundtland and others noted, each Nordic country generally has assumed that the success of one Nordic country's foreign policy would benefit the entire region and minimize regional tensions. Nordic regional cooperation avoided defense and security policy although a *de facto* Nordic bloc emerged in the 1960s in the United Nations and other international organizations. Nordic political leaders continued their tradition of regular informal consultation on issues of common interest.

Traditional small-state discretion gradually gave way to activism; indeed Finland's expansive president, Urho Kekkonen, pursued "active nonalignment" for twenty-five years in order to maximize his country's options and assure the Soviet Union of Finland's friendly intentions. His preemptive anticipation of Soviet requests elicited domestic and foreign criticism, including the notorious concept of "Finlandization." Coined by West German politicians but broadly used by Western conservatives and critics of détente, it implied a passive regard for Soviet interests in lieu of Western cooperation.

Swedish leader Olof Palme also rejected the discretion of his predecessors and tried to shape a Swedish profile of active nonalignment in international affairs. A prominent global figure, Palme increasingly challenged the superpowers and promoted the development agenda for the "Third World" until his assassination in 1986. He pushed a distinctive Swedish policy that gave the country international visibility that it had not had before and has not had since. He became the symbol of a strident criticism of American foreign policy in the wake of the Vietnam War. Both Finland and Sweden put pressure on Denmark and Norway to minimize their engagement in NATO and to reconsider a more active Nordic security commitment. There were many in these countries who were tempted to follow such a line, but the choice of 1949—to rely primarily on broader Western defense cooperation—prevailed.

Nordic balance remained deliberately vague and flexible through the Cold War. NATO and particularly the U.S. guarantee to western Europe formed the foundation of national security policy in Denmark, Iceland, and Norway, and both Finland and Sweden counted on that ultimate source of assistance should things go wrong. All sought to reinforce the reality that northern Europe was not the main axis of east-west tensions. Norwegian restraint along the border with the USSR in the far north and the Danish regard for Soviet concerns in the eastern Baltic, including the Danish island of Bornholm, succeeded in keeping regional tensions under control. Recurring Soviet pressures and interference, highlighted by the provocative submarine violations of Swedish territorial waters, reminded most Scandinavians of the need for a credible security policy.

Despite the different Nordic responses to the Cold War, each country sought to combine credible national security, conflict avoidance with the Soviet Union, and cautious steps toward relaxation of tensions between east and west. From the outset, few Scandinavians believed that the Soviet Union had a timetable for war with the West. War was more likely to occur because of miscalculation or the escalation of conflicts outside of Europe. Hence a policy of "reassurance" and conflict resolution won broad support, although there were genuine arguments about how to carry it out. This was not a policy of "appeasement"; Nordic criticism of Soviet human rights violations and imperialism in eastern Europe became louder through the 1970s and 1980s. As noted earlier, both the Nordic and global dimensions of foreign policy allowed considerable diplomatic opportunities. Not all were successful, but such negotiations would at least communicate to the superpowers (especially the USSR) that the Nordic countries believed in "peaceful coexistence" combined with full respect for national independence.

While successfully restraining most Cold War tensions in their region, the Nordic countries never succeeded in creating a region truly distinct from the larger European context. In the security sphere they had insufficient power; in economic matters their ties to Europe remained supreme. By 1961, however, the dynamic Common Market was a serious issue in Scandinavia. West Germany had become again a vital market for the Scandinavian states, soon surpassing Britain. As security issues waned, economic questions demanded difficult choices: first between competing blocs and models (the **European Economic Community [EEC]** versus the looser **European Free Trade Association [EFTA]**), and then over the extent of integration and its political consequences.

AN END AND A BEGINNING FOR NORDIC BALANCE

Nearly fifteen years after the sudden collapse of communism in Europe and the end of the Cold War, it is hard to recall the passions and tensions of its final phase. First, the failure of east-west détente at the end of the 1970s—despite the Helsinki Accords of 1975, which recognized the geopolitical status quo of the Cold War as well as the legitimacy of human rights issues in Europe—was a severe disappointment to all of the Scandinavian countries. The renewed strategic arms race, especially the frightening "Euromissile" (intermediate-range nuclear missiles stationed in and targeted on Europe) confrontation of the 1980s, was a setback. In addition to the general global atmosphere of political confrontation, the renewed military rivalry threatened the Nordic region. First, the development of new Soviet intermediate-range missiles and their deployment increased the threat of nuclear war in Europe. The Western response, the so-called dual track strategy of deploying U.S. intermediate-range ballistic and cruise missiles in Europe while preparing for an arms-control agreement in Europe, sharpened the confrontation. Antinuclear movements, which had appeared in the early 1960s and waned with détente in the 1970s, quickly sprang up again across western Europe, not least in Scandinavia.[9]

Second, the steady buildup of the Soviet northern fleet (based mainly on the Kola Peninsula close to northern Scandinavia) brought about a Western naval rearmament. Although Scandinavia had been peripheral to the central European arms race, the naval and missile competition intruded into the entire region. This was compounded by a global militarization that saw regional struggles in Central America, Africa, the Middle East, and Asia. Europe seemed to be free of direct military adventures, but it was easy to imagine "horizontal escalation" (the geographic spreading of armed conflict) into the Continent. NATO's call for increased military spending was accepted by Norway but not Denmark.

Third, the collapse of reformist movements in several communist countries, most notably Poland in 1981, gave little hope of evolution toward democracy and human rights. The ideological war between east and west returned to a depth of bitterness not seen for twenty years. There seemed to be little that small states could do to bridge the chasm.

Then, and almost without warning, the political winds shifted. The accession of Mikhail Gorbachev to leadership in the Soviet Union in 1985 was the key element, but both U.S. president Reagan and especially Britain's Margaret Thatcher were quick to sense an opening with the new regime in the Kremlin. The spontaneous summit meeting in Reykjavik, Iceland, between Reagan and Gorbachev in November 1986 failed to produce a conclusive Euromissile agreement, but unlike previous diplomatic disappointments, this meeting seemed to intensify negotiations and the spirit of compromise. The Soviet regime proclaimed "new thinking" in both domestic and foreign policy. Washington, London, and Bonn were prepared to give the Gorbachev proposals a full hearing.

Along with most of the world, the Scandinavians watched these events with growing anticipation. The Finns and Norwegians noticed new flexibility with their Soviet neighbors. Iceland was proud of its emerging status as an international diplomatic venue, and its leading politicians began to visit major capitals to talk about matters more weighty than fish. But the Swedes were still stunned by the assassination of Prime Minister Olof Palme in 1986, which lowered noticeably the country's international profile, and the Danes were distracted by the renewal of sharp partisan struggles over Danish policies with both European Community and NATO partners.

In 1989–1990 Scandinavians, along with Europeans and Americans, watched with amazement as forty years of east-west competition ended and a dozen Marxist-Leninist regimes collapsed. More proactively, the Nordic states gave diplomatic and economic support to the emerging independence movements in the Baltic states (Estonia, Latvia, and Lithuania), which had been forcibly annexed by the Soviet Union fifty years earlier. As in 1918–1920 and 1945–1949, Nordic leaders had to rethink their international position and foreign policy priorities. The challenge would be to balance traditional interests and perspectives with the new opportunities and threats of a changed world.

Scandinavia and the European Union

Scandinavia, as noted earlier, remained on the periphery of the European integration project for nearly twenty-five years after World War II. Three factors have repeatedly deterred the Scandinavian states from aggressively pursuing European integration and unity. First was the alternative attraction of Nordic economic cooperation. Although initial attempts to form a Nordic customs union in the 1950s failed, the project was resurrected in new versions until 1970, when Denmark and Norway declared definitively for the European alternative. However, only Denmark joined the EEC in 1973, while Norwegian voters rejected membership and Sweden and Finland never applied. Denmark would preserve its Nordic links and would even promote regional interests in Brussels, but the limits of Nordic cooperation seemed clear. Second, the ultimate goal of a united Europe enjoyed only modest support among the political leadership and the public in these small states, historically unaligned and mistrustful of larger neighbors. Third, with broader free-trade ambitions, the Nordic countries have resisted having to choose sides in economic communities. Until 1973 Britain and Germany belonged to different European trading blocs, while the attractions of global trade (especially with North America and Japan) and even the socialist countries (Soviet Russia, China, and Eastern Europe) deterred commitment to the European project.

The Scandinavian states favored European cooperation over unity. Cooperation aimed at removing barriers to free trade and investment as well as policy collaboration in areas of common concerns (e.g., environment, refugees, human rights, defense) have come to be regarded as "Europe à la carte." States can pick and choose the collection of projects in which they will participate. The alternative they rejected was more grandiose: a United States of Europe with genuinely federal institutions that would move significant portions of public policy into a European entity. National governments would still have residual powers through the principle of "subsidiarity," but like other federal systems, the whole would be more than the sum of its parts. Ancient cultures and states would be unlikely to disappear or become mere provinces, but the four-hundred-year tradition of state sovereignty largely would be ended in principle as well as practice. This second vision has little support in Scandinavia and has met much vigorous resistance.

ECONOMIC COOPERATION

As trading states, the Scandinavian countries have long been wary of economic isolationism. All suffered from the economic nationalism and mercantilism of the interwar period. In response, domestic protectionism gained a foothold in the agricultural and other primary economic sectors.

The Scandinavian countries did not participate significantly in any of the meetings between 1955 and 1957 that led to the Rome treaty establishing the EEC. Likewise they had not been involved in the precursors of the Schuman Plan and the **European Coal and Steel Community** of 1952. The broader trade bloc did raise concerns, especially in Denmark and Sweden, which had important economic ties to the rapidly growing West German economy. British refusal to consider participation and its establishment of an alternative European Free Trade Association (EFTA) in 1959 confirmed the division of Europe into "sixes and sevens." Generally the Scandinavians favored free trade for industrial goods and international services (e.g., shipping), but only Denmark accepted similar liberalization for the agricultural sector. None of them believed that integration of all economic sectors, as had begun with the European Coal and Steel Community, was relevant for their economic situation. This distinction between free trade versus harmonization would continue.

By 1961 it was clear that the EEC would progress and that EFTA would be less significant. The ambiguous British decision to apply for EEC membership forced the Scandinavian countries to reconsider their position. French President Charles de Gaulle delayed British entry for a decade, but when in 1969 the issue again became germane, it was clear that the EEC was an economic and political success and that there would be no other significant European alternative. As the European option again appeared promising, the Nordic countries (now including Finland) commenced negotiations on a wider Nordic economic community that would possibly lead to a common Nordic entry into the EEC. This possibility threatened especially Finland's special regard for Soviet sensibilities, but Sweden too was concerned about its "nonaligned" status (a point already raised in 1963). In short, whenever a wider European option became promising, the Nordic countries found they each had different perspectives.

The result would be four Scandinavian roads to Europe, with Denmark's entry in 1973, Sweden and Finland in 1995, and Norway's twice (1972 and 1994) failed entry attempts. Just to complicate matters, the two Danish autonomous North Atlantic territories of Greenland and the Faeroe Islands remained outside of the EEC, with Greenland actually withdrawing in 1982.

It is notable that joining Europe has been a divisive issue in domestic politics everywhere, even including Finland, where the European Union seemed to offer guarantees against renewed Russian pressure in the future. The referenda results in Table 13.3 suggest just how disputed this key decision in fact was. Ironically, the strength of domestic opposition has not slowed Danish integration into European structures in those areas approved by the voters; Denmark has typically ranked among the top countries in the European Union in actually adapting national legislation and regulation to fit European requirements. As late entrants, Sweden and Finland had to accept the developing European Union in 1995, including its extensive rules and regulation (the so-called *acquis communautaire*). The ongoing EU debates and, in the case of Denmark, repeated referenda on Europe disrupted the normal patterns of partisan allegiance in domestic politics.

RELUCTANT EUROPEANS

As the European integration project pursues union in the wake of the Maastricht treaty of 1991 (as amended in Edinburgh in 1992 and further in Amsterdam in 1997), the Nordic countries remain reluctant participants. Norway is linked through the agreement on a European Economic Area (EEA), which was negotiated in 1990, took effect in 1993, and essentially gives these countries access to the "Single European Market" in all areas excepting agriculture, natural resources, and other issues of vital national interest. This is the "outer ring" of the European orbit, and although EEA countries (there are only three: Iceland, Norway, and Liechtenstein) have essentially full access to the European market, they have no direct influence on development of the European Union.

Denmark, along with Britain, circles the EU more closely. Both are signa-

Table 13.3 European Community/European Union Referenda

	Denmark						Norway		Sweden		Finland
	1972	1986	1992	1993	1998	2000	1972	1994	1994	2003	1994
Yes	63.3	56.2	49.3	56.7	55.1	46.8	46.5	47.8	52.3	41.8	57.0
No	36.7	43.8	50.7	43.5	44.9	53.2	53.5	52.2	46.8	56.1	43.0
Turnout	90.1	75.4	83.1	86.5	74.8	86.7	79.2	88.8	82.4	81.2	70.8

Sources: Danish Folketinget Website: www.ft.dk; Nordic Council, *Norden i Tal, 2002*; Swedish Riksdag website: www.riksdagen.se.

Note: The referenda were as follows: Denmark 1972: Joining the EC; 1986: EC Single market; 1992: Maastricht; 1993: Edinburgh agreement modifying Maastricht; 1998: Amsterdam treaty; 2000: adopting the Euro; Norway 1972 and 1994, Sweden 1994, Finland 1994: Joining the EC/EU; Sweden 2003: common European currency.

Box 13.2   Why Norway Says No to Europe

For more than thirty years, Norwegians have debated their relationship to the European Community (now the EU). Divisive referenda have put the question to voters, who have twice rejected the European option despite solid parliamentary and governmental support for full membership. The EU debate in Norway shares many elements with the other Scandinavian countries, which (Iceland and Greenland excepted) have now become members of the EU. Norway has always been in favor of international cooperation and has been a stalwart of most international and western organizations. But as a fully independent country only since 1905 and with a history of detachment from European politics, it has tenaciously guarded its sovereignty.

Norway has repeatedly rejected regional economic integration, favoring instead broader economic cooperation and free trade of industrial goods such as raw materials (timber, paper, metals, and, since the 1970s, petroleum and extraction technology), sophisticated specialized chemicals, high technology products, and shipping services.

After 1970, access to the European Economic Community opened, but a coalition of opponents narrowly defeated the issue in a September 1972 referendum. That coalition was strongest in the rural counties (mostly northern and western) where farmers and fishermen and other local interests feared loss of their protected status. They were joined by public sector employees, radical socialists, and even cultural conservatives who resisted the appeal of a greater Europe. In a campaign that generated more heat than light, various European "threats" (Germany, capitalism, agribusiness, Catholicism, etc.) convinced voters to reject the recommendations of most of the country's political and economic elite. Less hysteria but the same coalition produced an identical result in 1994.

The cost of these "noes" has been minimal. The development of enormous offshore oil and then gas resources has pumped billions into the already prosperous Norwegian economy. As one Danish newspaper ironically (in light of Norway's past of poverty and Puritanism) reflected at the start of the "oil age," the country would find prosperity "unavoidable." Despite dependency on world petroleum prices and some initially poor management of the "petrodollar" tidal wave, Norway has been able to avoid most of the austerity, unemployment, and pessimism that has repeatedly swept over much of Europe in the past quarter century. Norway still spends huge sums subsidizing its noncompetitive farmers and small peripheral towns. More ominous is the erosion of traditional manufacturing enterprises by high costs.

Currently a member of the European Economic Area as well as the Schengen passport control area, Norway has full access to the EU but cannot participate readily in EU policy making. With a soaring national Petroleum Fund worth nearly $90 billion (early 2003) that invests oil and gas earnings in sensible economic policies, Norway can well afford to remain aloof. For the other Scandinavian countries the price would have been much higher.

tories to the Maastricht treaty but have significant, though different, reservations. Denmark has rejected monetary union, although its economy is among the strongest in the EU and its currency has been closely tied to the German mark and now the euro since 1982. It has been cautious about harmonization of police and judicial affairs and participation in key elements of the common foreign and security policy. Every significant change in European policy has sparked a bitter fight in Denmark and resulting national referenda. The 1997 Amsterdam revision of the union treaty was approved by the Danish voters, but in September 2001 they rejected the euro as their national currency. The Danish government accepted the Nice treaty of 2000, which prepares the EU for a significant expansion to include eastern and southern European states. Although domestic opponents of the EU have railed against opening the union to hordes of poor eastern Europeans, others see the expansion as postponing "federalism" for an indefinite period. Anti-EU parties (on the extreme right and left) are well represented in parliament, and a quarter of the delegates elected by the Danes to the European parliament are anti-EU activists.

Sweden and Finland became EU members in 1995 after vigorous national debates and referenda. As new members they were forced to swallow the whole EU system, but not without protest and regret. Their EU parliamentary delegations have strong anti-EU contingents, and opinion at home is no less skeptical of the EU project than that of the doubting Danes. Neither is firmly committed to a common European security policy or to federalism. Like the Danes, they have encouraged eastward expansion, especially to the Baltic states and Poland. During their EU presidencies they have pushed the social and labor agenda as well as budgetary and administrative reforms of EU institutions. Only Finland has fully joined the Economic and Monetary Union (EMU), with the euro replacing the Finnish markka as the national currency in 2002, while Sweden rejected the common currency in 2003.

At the start of the new century, the Scandinavian countries still see the EU mainly in pragmatic economic terms. They have been especially cautious about expanded cooperation on foreign and security policy matters despite the turmoil in the Balkans after 1990, the war on terrorism after September 2001, and a host of continuing crises in Africa, the Middle East, and elsewhere that suggest that world politics is not only the global economy. All of the Nordic countries supported—often with military units—the U.S. response to the terrorist attack of 9/11. The reluctant "multilateralism" of the Bush administration and its willingness to work within the UN and NATO seemed a hopeful sign to those suspicious of the raw unilateralism of the new American administration. Unfortunately the confrontation with Iraq in 2002–2003 deepened Nordic concerns and divisions. The Danish government gave wholehearted support to military action against the Saddam regime, while the Swedes, Finns, and Norwegians were critical of the American and British response. It was yet another reminder of the different national perspectives across Scandinavia. Ironically, the differences were mainly "official"; public opinion in Scandinavia is very much in line with the general European public distaste for the Bush administration's unilateralist nationalism.

For the Scandinavian Social Democrats in particular, the European Union and economic globalization more generally pose some ironic dilemmas. Although they have always been rhetorically internationalist—and have lived up to the rhetoric in development aid and in direct support for foreign trade unions and labor parties in the Third World and eastern Europe—their success at home has been premised on the relevance of the nation-state as the unit for making economic policy. The generous and humane provisions of the Social Democratic welfare states in Scandinavia yielded a truly decent society for all, but they were dependent on strong, carefully managed economies and full employment. It is far from clear that those are at the top of the European Union's economic agenda. If the welfare state was the surrogate for socialism for the Scandinavian Social Democrats from the 1930s through the 1980s, what is to be the surrogate for the welfare state?

The habits of nonalignment and independence of all Nordic states, along with their still vigorous sense of nationhood and self-confidence, color their view of Europe. They are also a factor in the continuing debate about non-European immigration and the challenge of multiculturalism. Once again a Nordic "middle way" has emerged toward the regional and global challenges of the new century. Scandinavians are pragmatic skeptics, seeking "just enough Europeanization" to respond to economic, social, and political challenges. As successful states and just societies they see no need to bury themselves in a federal Europe. But they are not isolationists; the past century taught them that their fates are intimately tied to their continent and to global developments. The Nordic bloc of three is likely to support a "social Europe" in which the principles of "subsidiarity" and pragmatism will make the Scandinavians more comfortable in the European home.

Notes

1. For an excellent survey of Scandinavian history, see T. K. Derry, *A History of Scandinavia: Norway, Sweden, Denmark, Finland, and Iceland* (Minneapolis: University of Minnesota Press, 1979). More concise and up-to-date is Byron J. Nordstrom, *Scandinavia since 1500* (Minneapolis: University of Minnesota Press, 2000).

2. Until the war of 1864, the German-speaking duchies of Schleswig, Holstein, and Lauenburg were part of the Danish realm under an exceedingly complex constitutional arrangement. Schleswig had a substantial Danish population that was denied rights under German rule between 1864 and 1918. Following the German defeat in 1918, the Allies supervised a careful referendum that returned the northern third of Schleswig

(Slesvig) to Denmark. Since 1920, the Danish-German border has been fixed, and since the 1950s, the two nationalities have seen greatly improved local relations.

3. Denmark and Norway were under the same monarch from 1380 to 1814. Starting in 1737 in rural Norway, the country was the first in the world to institute universal, compulsory education, culminating in the Danish education act of 1814. Sweden followed with a similar law in 1842. By the second half of the nineteenth century, literacy was nearly universal in Scandinavia, and secondary and adult education was advanced by the "folk colleges" and workers' education movements.

4. There are many excellent studies of the interdependent global economy. See especially Robert O. Keohane and Joseph S. Nye, *Power and Interdependence,* 3rd ed. (Boston: Addison-Wesley, 2000), and for the smaller European states, Peter J. Katzenstein, *Small States in World Markets: Industrial Policy in Europe* (Ithaca, N.Y.: Cornell University Press, 1985).

5. There is a rich literature on Scandinavian political institutions and political actors. For good surveys with copious bibliographies, see the volumes by Olof Petersson and by Eric S. Einhorn and John Logue in Suggestions for Further Reading.

6. For a more comprehensive discussion of the Scandinavian welfare programs and their impact, see Einhorn and Logue, chapters 6–10.

7. Economic policy issues in the Nordic countries are discussed in detail in the economic surveys published every year or two by the Organization for Economic Cooperation and Development as *Economic Surveys: Denmark,* etc. Sweden's economic problems and especially its welfare have received much international attention in the 1990s. The harshest critique may be found in the writings of Assar Lindbeck, most recently in "The Swedish Experiment," *Journal of Economic Literature* 35 (September 1997), 1273–1319. A more technical and less pessimistic survey is Richard B. Freeman et al. (see Suggestions for Further Reading). Both the *Financial Times* and *The Economist* regularly survey the Nordic economies, the latter most recently in June 2003.

8. At the end of the fourteenth century, all three Scandinavian crowns passed to Danish Queen Margrethe I. In 1397, this union was formalized by a treaty drafted in Kalmar, Sweden. Although the Kalmar Union survived until 1523, it was constantly challenged. Norway remained united with Denmark until 1814 and then with Sweden until 1905. Iceland was part of the Danish realm until 1944. The Swedish province of Finland became a Russian Grand Duchy in 1809 and declared its independence in 1917.

9. A concise summary of the Nordic region during the Cold War may be found in "The Nordic Region: Changing Perspectives in International Relations," *The Annals of the American Academy of Political and Social Science* (Martin O. Heisler, special ed.), vol. 512 (November 1990), and in the books by Stephen J. Blank and by Don Snidal and Arne Brundtland (see Suggestions for Further Reading).

Suggestions for Further Reading

Blank, Stephen J. *Finnish Security and European Security Policy.* Carlisle Barracks, Pa.: U.S. Army War College, 1996.
Childs, Marquis. *Sweden: The Middle Way.* New Haven: Yale University Press, 1936.
———. *Sweden: The Middle Way on Trial.* New Haven: Yale University Press, 1980.

Derry, T. K. *A History of Scandinavia: Norway, Sweden, Denmark, Finland, and Iceland*. Minneapolis: University of Minnesota Press, 1979.

Due-Nielsen, Carsten, and Nikolaj Petersen, eds. *Adaptation and Activism: The Foreign Policy of Denmark 1967–1993*. Copenhagen: Dansk Udenrigspolitisk Institut, 1995.

Einhorn, Eric S. "Just Enough (*'Lagom'*) Europeanization: The Nordic States and Europe." *Scandinavian Studies* 74, no. 3 (Fall 2002): 265–86.

Einhorn, Eric S., and John Logue. *Modern Welfare States: Scandinavian Politics and Policy in the Global Age*. New York: Praeger, 2003.

Freeman, Richard B., Robert Topel, and Birgitta Swedenborg. *The Welfare State in Transition: Reforming the Swedish Model*. Chicago: University of Chicago Press, 1997.

Heidar, Knut. *Norway: Elites on Trial*. Boulder, Colo.: Westview, 2001.

Ingebritsen, Christine. *The Nordic States and European Union: From Economic Interdependence to Political Integration*. Ithaca, N.Y.: Cornell University Press, 1998.

Ingebritsen, Christine, ed. "The Scandinavian Way to Europe," special issue of *Scandinavian Studies* 74, no. 3 (Fall 2002).

Jussila, Osmo, Seppo Hentilä, and Jukka Nevakivi. *From Grand Duchy to a Modern State: A Political History of Finland since 1809*. London: Hurst, 1999.

Nordstrom, Byron J. *Dictionary of Scandinavian History*. Westport, Conn.: Greenwood, 1986.

———. *Scandinavia since 1500*. Minneapolis: University of Minnesota Press, 2000.

Organization for Economic Cooperation and Development. *Economic Outlook* (semiannually) (June and December). Paris: OECD.

———. *Historical Statistics, 1970–1999*. Paris: OECD, 2000.

Petersson, Olof. *The Government and Politics of the Nordic Countries*. Stockholm: Fritzes, 1994.

Rustow, Dankwart A. *The Politics of Compromise: A Study of Parties and Cabinet Government in Sweden*. Princeton, N.J.: Princeton University Press, 1955.

Schwartz, Herman. "Small States in Big Trouble." *World Politics* (July 1994): 527–55.

Snidal, Don N., and Arne O. Brundtland. *Nordic-Baltic Security*. Washington, D.C.: Center for Strategic and International Studies, 1993.

CHAPTER 14

Poland

Breaking Multiple Barriers

Ray Taras

Poland

Population: 38.6 million
Area in Square Miles: 124,807
Population Density per Square Mile: 310
GDP (in billion dollars, 2001): $383.9
GDP per capita (purchasing power parity in dollars, 2001): $9,934
Joined EC/EU: will join in 2004
Joined NATO: January 1, 1999
Political Parties:
Solidarity Election Action
Democratic Left Alliance
The Freedom Union
Polish Peasant Party
Movement for the Reconstruction of Poland
The German minority

Sources: "Organisation for Economic Co-operation and Development," at
www.oecd.org/home/ (accessed August 5, 2003); "2003 World Population
Data Sheet," at www.prb.org/pdf/WorldPopulationDS03_Eng.pdf
(accessed August 5, 2003); "Political Resources on the Net," October 6,
2003, at www.politicalresources.net/europe.htm (accessed October 1,
2003).

Introduction

On December 13, 1981, General Wojciech Jaruzelski, acting in the name of a secretly organized Military Council of National Salvation, declared martial law in Poland. The independent trade union Solidarity, which had recruited close to ten million members in the preceding sixteen months and had shaken the Polish Communist Party's monopoly on power, was declared illegal, its leaders throughout the country were arrested in late-night security sweeps, and army tanks and troops appeared in the streets of Poland's towns. The country's bid for a more pluralistic political system that would embrace Western liberal democratic values had been quashed. Sovietization methods—Communist Party rule, a command economy, dependence on the USSR—were reintroduced. Poland had been forcibly reincorporated into the Soviet bloc.

Twenty-one years later to the day, on December 13, 2002, the European Union summit in Copenhagen agreed to enlarge by May 1, 2004. It approved ten new members, most of them from the former Soviet bloc. The largest of the new member states, its citizens constituting close to one-half the population to be added to the EU, was Poland. The democratically elected president of Poland, Aleksander Kwasniewski, who, when martial law was proclaimed, was serving as editor in chief of the weekly Communist student newspaper, described the long road his country had traveled to EU membership. "All governments from 1989 on worked toward Poland's integration into the European Union, if with different degrees of intensity," he observed. "But credit is also due to those who first opened the doors to these changes. This would have to start with General Wojciech Jaruzelski. On that other December 13 he chose the lesser evil. Today, on December 13, we are choosing the greater good." The president then added: "Also making contributions were Solidarity, who opened the door to Europe some time ago, and president Lech Walesa," the union leader whom Kwasniewski ousted as president in 1995.[1]

One other Pole, not mentioned by President Kwasniewski, had played a crucial role in Poland's accession into the EU. John Paul II had helped inspire the Solidarity movement after being chosen Pope in 1978. Twenty-five years later, shortly before the referendum on EU admission, he came to the rescue of pro-Europe forces by declaring, "The entry to the EU on equal terms with other countries is for our nation an expression of historic justice and could enrich Europe." His exhortation for Poles to support EU entry was read from pulpits across the country on the Sunday before the vote. When ballots had been counted the next weekend 59 percent of eligible Poles had voted—50 percent was needed to make the result valid—and 77 percent of the voters had said yes to EU entry. John Paul's intervention had pulled the rug from under the influential Catholic nationalist anti-EU camp that had encouraged Poles to reject EU membership.

To be sure, Poland had been breaking down barriers in communist-run Europe for decades, even before John Paul became pope. The very choice of joining the EU or not was the product in large measure of Poland's unwillingness to accept a geopolitical fate placing it in the shadow of the Kremlin. Repeated popular uprisings against Communist Party rule in the period from 1956 to 1976 culminated in the establishment in 1980 of Solidarity, an independent trade union that effectively evolved into a national movement. Despite the martial law regime's delegalization of trade unions, renewed widespread industrial unrest in the summer of 1988 convinced the Communist leadership to try to co-opt Solidarity and give it a stake in the political system. Accordingly roundtable talks between the Communist government and the Solidarity opposition were convened in the spring of 1989—a historic event that could only occur with Soviet leader Mikhail Gorbachev's acquiescence. The talks produced a political breakthrough: the Communist Party agreed to hold semi-free elections in June of that year.

Though with hindsight it seems unimaginable that any other result was possible, the election produced what at the time seemed an improbable Solidarity landslide in all constituencies where it was allowed to put up candidates. The Soviet bloc's first non-Communist prime minister and government were appointed in August and September 1989. The country's national symbols—name, flag, anthem, constitution—were decommunized quickly after that. By the end of 1989 a blueprint for an accelerated transition to a market economy (called the Balcerowicz Plan after its architect, the finance minister) had been introduced, and by mid-1990 the Polish parliament had approved a sweeping privatization law. It is safe to say, then, that in central Europe the dismantling of the institutions of communism was pioneered by Poland, thereby making it possible for other countries in the region—several of which subsequently leapfrogged Poland in terms of breadth and speed of political and economic transformation—to become plausible candidates for EU enlargement a decade later.

In order to understand how European Union enlargement came about, we need to know something about Poland's domestic politics, in particular the process that led from a standoff between the ruling Communists and the Solidarity movement to a seeming symbiosis of the two around democratic values. In this chapter we also examine the construction of European security architecture that laid the foundation for integration in other areas.

National Politics after 1989

Poland's extrication from communist rule that had been imposed on it by Soviet dictator Joseph Stalin after World War II had arguably as much to do with its wish to redefine its geopolitical position as it had to do with a quest for political liberty. With the exception of a few Communist hard-liners and a small group of right-wing opposition nationalists, the Polish political elite in 1989 had agreed that a "return to Europe" and, more broadly, to the Western world, was "natural." If for forty-five years the Soviet bloc had given Poland authoritarian rule, supplying guns but little butter, the West offered real prospects for democracy and development. Because the United States had done most to roll back communism, in the early years of the transition Poles looked to the United States more than to western Europe to spearhead the political and economic transformation of their country. Even in the 1990s, however, the Polish elite and public became conscious of the fact that the path to Europe was distinct from pro-American policies and attitudes. Membership in NATO would not dramatize this difference—after all, the United States dominated the military pact—as much as would membership in the European Union, an exclusive club for European states. It was the start of the U.S. war in Iraq in March 2003 that finally revealed that the Polish elite's and public's priority—when one had to be identified—was support for the United States over support for western Europe. The emergence of a political cleavage in domestic politics based on attitudes toward Europe was accelerated by U.S. actions in Iraq. It has the potential to become a defining feature of national politics.

NATIONAL CONSENSUS AND CLEAVAGES

Up to 2003 only two often overlapping political cleavages had shaped politics since the 1989 democratic breakthrough. One was based on contrasting attitudes to the communist past; the other was centered on differing relationships with the Catholic Church. The first cleavage separated parties and politicians whose origins lay in the communist past from those who abhorred that tradition. The other cleavage separated devout Catholics who believed that the church should play an important role in Polish society from those who were convinced that a democratic state should be secular and be based on the separation of church and state.[2] Until recently, conflicting views over the desirability of Poland's integration into European structures have *not* represented a salient political cleavage shaping the structure of the party system.

In the early 1990s national politics was dominated by offshoots of the Solidarity movement, which had brought the Communist regime down. Solidarity leader Walesa was elected president in 1991 but quickly became overbearing and polarizing and contributed to the fragmentation of the movement he had helped to found. He flaunted his anticommunist, Catholic credentials and sought to promote apprentices who embodied the same values. Anticommunist but secular-oriented forces—which included much of the intellectual elite—found it hard to work with Walesa. The door was open for former Communists to take advantage of divisions within the Solidarity camp and prepare for a political comeback.

In the first years of transition, prime ministers, cabinets, and political parties came and went but Walesa stood as the reference point for them all—even more so than their common arch-nemesis, the ex-Communists. This latter group scrambled to assume a new political identity in the democratizing system and in 1991 formed the Alliance of the Democratic Left (SLD). This coalition and subsequent political party declared its commitment to the democratic game and to a pro-Western foreign policy. But its candidates still did badly in the 1990 presidential and 1991 parliamentary elections; voters were not ready to believe in the ex-Communists' retooled image.

Not coincidentally, the Solidarity camp began to disintegrate. Walesa's authoritarian manner was one factor, but another was the belief that anticommunist solidarity was no longer important since the former Communists would never be influential in the new system. At this juncture the SLD took the bold step of deciding to champion integration into Europe more doggedly than any other party in the country.[3] The result has been that since 1993 the SLD has controlled either the presidency or the government and, since 2001, both of them.

With hindsight it is easy to trace the failure of the Solidarity camp, and it begins with Walesa. Having honed his political skills struggling against the communist system, he never became an ideas man. His priorities were to consolidate power and build a presidential system—not to join Europe. In addition, the unpopularity of neoliberal economic policies ("shock therapy" that caused widespread unemployment and a precipitous decline in many people's living standards) was reflected at the polls in 1993 when the SLD unexpectedly emerged as the largest party in the Sejm (or parliament). In 1997 the Solidarity bloc regrouped and defeated the SLD, but it was no longer united by a consensus on the virtues of neoliberalism and European integration. Thus, only a year after taking power, the right-leaning coalition government began to unravel when protectionist groups opposed the neoliberals who had been invoking EU directives to insist on less state economic intervention.[4] Divisions within the Solidarity bloc grew, led to its electoral unpopularity, and allowed the SLD to sweep the presidency and parliament in 2000 and 2001.

The string of SLD electoral successes was attributable also to the rise in popularity of President Kwasniewski, one of the founding leaders of the SLD. He had first won the presidency in 1995, narrowly defeating Walesa, and in 2000 he was reelected with an outright majority in the first round over eleven other candidates. Although Kwasniewski officially withdrew from the party after winning the presidency, he made no effort to dissociate himself from it in the electorate's mind. His leadership style that seemed modeled on a media-conscious American president, and his attention-grabbing participation in public events—such as commemorations of the World War II massacres of Jews by Poles in Jedwabne and of Poles by Ukrainians in Wolyn—proved very effective politically. As Kwasniewski went, so did the SLD: in successive parliamentary elections the party increased its share of the vote from 20 percent in 1993 to 27 percent in 1997 to 41 percent in 2001. Serious disagreements in 2003 between Kwasniewski and SLD leaders, especially Prime Minister Miller, provided further evidence that the party had been riding his coattails as successfully as it had been playing the European card: the party's support in public opinion polls dropped dramatically even as it was ushering the country into the EU.

It can be argued that SLD successes owed much to the fact that it appeared to be the most effectual pro-European party in Poland. Its unity over the issue certainly was crucial: rightist parties were, by contrast, badly divided over European integration. A few tapped Euroskeptic constituencies composed of unionized workers, devout Catholics, and Polish nationalists. Others remained committed to joining Europe. It was ironic, then, that the core assumption of the rightist camp of the early 1990s had proven correct: the Europe option would pay major political dividends. Unfortunately for it, it was the SLD that reaped the pro-Europe dividends.

We have suggested that if the communist past and Catholicism formed the most important political cleavages of the 1990s, the EU may become the divisive axis in the first decade of the new century. The electoral breakthrough of two Euroskeptic parties in 2001 has offered support for this proposition.

The first party, Self-Defense, appeared on the political scene in 1991 as a populist and rural movement. It was headed by Andrzej Lepper, a onetime member of the Communist Party and small-scale farmer who organized a hunger strike in 1991 to protest farmers' inability to pay off loans. The following year he became head of the Self-Defense agrarian trade union, which staged radical protests, including occupation of town halls, a march on parliament in 1993, a national demonstration in Warsaw in 1998, and the blockade of a border crossing that same year. These protests were often aimed at government policies that promoted trade with the EU while disadvantaging Polish farmers (for example, imports of agricultural products).

The electoral efforts of Self-Defense met with no success until the parliamentary elections of 2001. Admittedly Lepper had stood as presidential candidate in 1995 and 2000 and increased his share of the vote from 1.3 to 3.1 percent. But by winning 10.2 percent of the 2001 parliamentary vote, Self-Defense sent fifty-three parliamentary deputies to the 460-member Sejm—third most of any party—and even edged out the establishment Polish Peasant Party (PSL). Self-Defense's 2001 success was attributable to its skill in presenting itself as both populist and responsible. In addition, Lepper's criticism of the EU and his support for a pro–Eastern Europe foreign policy spoke to a constituency that had gone unrepresented and had become disaffected by the multiparty consensus favoring EU entry.

The second anti-EU party is the Catholic and rightist League of Polish Families (LPR), which contested its first election in 2001 and surprised everyone by winning nearly 8 percent of the vote and thirty-eight Sejm seats. Arguably even more anti-European than Self-Defense, the LPR capitalized on the fear of practicing Catholics that Polish family values would be eroded after entry into an agnostic western Europe. One LPR spokesman even claimed that the EU was a communist plot: "The way to Moscow is through Brussels."[5] Nationalist parties in Poland had no successes to speak of in the 1990s, but the rise of the LPR was an indication that a narrow ethno-religious understanding of the Polish nation—in contrast to the transnational identity promoted by the EU— was resurfacing, and that it was grounded in xenophobic and ideological paranoia.

The rise of right-wing radicalism made it important for the Catholic Church, historically a pivotal actor in Polish politics, to condemn xenophobia and to express its commitment to the values the EU promoted: tolerance, inclusiveness, and respect for minorities. If Pope John Paul II regarded EU entry as "historic justice," Polish Catholic primate Jozef Glemp was more laconic, calling the country's integration into Europe inevitable—"a historical necessity."[6] The majority of the regular clergy voiced support for the EU, though it should be noted that if 84 percent of clergy favored EU entry in 1998, the figure was down to 59 percent in late 2002.[7] The decline in support was connected with the opinion of 75 percent of priests that the accession negotiations had been poorly managed. Sixty-one percent said that Poland would be a second-class member, while just under half believed that Poland would bear the economic costs of integration.

Conservative Catholics were aware of other dangers posed by EU accession. The religiosity of Poles would be under threat when the country joined a Europe that was primarily secular and materialist, embraced liberal views on many core issues of Catholic doctrine (abortion, euthanasia, homosexuality), separated church and state so categorically, and was dominated by Protestant countries (see Table 14.1). Ultimately the historic pragmatism of Poland's Catholic Church made itself known. The ecclesiastical hierarchy accepted the inevitable—EU accession—but not before extracting benefits for itself from the SLD government. In return for endorsing EU membership in the 2003 referendum campaign, the church convinced the SLD government to appoint senior clergy to key EU-related committees.

EUROPE DEBATED

We have noted how with the 2001 election Euroskeptics finally obtained parliamentary representation. Some Poles who for many years had enthusiastically backed integration into Europe had by 2001 become jaundiced by the slow pace of negotiations. Others had been embarrassed by how far short Poland fell on many EU criteria for membership. Foreign minister Wlodzimierz Cimoszewicz recognized that negotiations with the EU had exposed the country's weak

Table 14.1   Perceptions of the Effects of Polish Integration into the EU in Certain Spheres, 1994–2002 (percentage)

Sphere	Is Likely to Increase					Is Likely to Decrease				
	June '94	May '96	May '99	May '00	Feb '02	June '94	May '96	May '99	May '00	Feb '02
Religiosity	4	5	4	3	2	28	29	33	28	24
Tolerance	31	32	24	24	28	13	15	23	16	15
Liberal mores	51	43	51	46	44	7	10	8	7	8
Efficiency thriftiness	66	66	50	42	45	3	5	9	8	8
Initiative	68	74	61	53	58	3	2	6	8	7
Crime	42	43	57	55	40	16	22	10	15	19

Source: Centrum Badania Opinii Spolecznej (CBOS), "Opinie o integracji polski z Unia Europejska," Warsaw: March 2002, table 11.

credentials in some areas and declared that entry would occur "on favorable terms, taking into account historical and social realities."[8] He envisaged a role for Poland as link between Brussels and Poland's non-EU eastern neighbors. How strong this link would be after Poland, following EU directives, introduced visa requirements for Ukrainians and Russians was unclear.

Euroskeptic parties in the Sejm led the attack on accession negotiations. Lepper accused the SLD government of blindly following a twelve-year foreign policy intended "to transform Poland into an outlet for the West's surplus production," and he advocated closer relations with the east. An LPR deputy framed Poland's relationship with the EU this way: "They're spitting in our face and you [the government] say it's raining."[9]

Economic arguments informed political discourse too. Critics of integration argued that, after over a decade of democratic politics, Poland's economic growth, while impressive, had not lifted up all citizens' boats. The political rhetoric asserting that democracy promotes development came under fire and, with it, the claim that entry into the affluent EU club would promote prosperity. Surveys of Poles revealed their skepticism about who really stood to gain from membership (Table 14.2). Like the long-running debate in Britain over the EU and the euro, contrasting views of what Poland will gain from accession have now become central to politics.

How the Polish left outmaneuvered the right in playing the Europe card is a remarkable story. Assaulting the SLD's political dominance requires the challenger to choose whether or not to attack the SLD's Euro-enthusiasm. For many SLD opponents, attacking it would contradict their own long-standing policy positions. But not attacking it may leave them with little of consequence to differentiate themselves from the SLD in voters' eyes. On the other hand, as we have observed, anti-Europe rightist forces have recently made electoral in-

Table 14.2   Beliefs about Which Countries Will Gain More Benefits from Poland's Entry into the EU, 1993–2002 (percentage)

	July '93	Mar '94	May '95	May '96	Aug '97	Aug '98	May '99	Nov '99	May '00	Sep '00	Mar '01	Feb '02
EU States	41	38	31	19	28	39	39	47	44	50	54	59
Poland	5	8	11	11	11	7	8	8	8	6	6	5
EU & Poland	27	26	33	46	35	30	30	27	29	26	25	19
Hard to say	27	27	26	24	27	24	23	17	19	18	15	17

Source: Centrum Badania Opinii Spolecznej (CBOS), "Opinie o integracji polski z Unia Europejska," Warsaw: March 2002, table 5.

roads. They can be viewed as part of a broader pan-European trend that since 2000 has encompassed Italy, Denmark, Portugal, France, and Holland, in which populist far-right parties have exploited voters' concerns about loss of national identity, immigration, and economic recession to make gains at the expense of establishment parties.[10] EU membership does not end the debate on the wisdom of integration, therefore, and Euroskeptic parties are likely to remain vocal long after Poland's May 2004 entry date.

Poland's Security: Neighbors, NATO, and the United States

In May 2002 British foreign secretary Jack Straw announced "the funeral" of the Cold War following an agreement on cooperation on international security issues between NATO and Russia. Signed by government heads of the nineteen NATO member states and President Vladimir Putin, the agreement was one of the most concrete examples of the impact of the September 11 terrorist attacks on collective security thinking. It also exposed the double-edged sword of the war against terrorism: countries like Poland, which were desperate for the security guarantees that NATO membership provided, could inadvertently be drawn into an alliance with Russia, their most serious historical security threat.

It is not surprising, then, that when the United States attacked Iraq in 2003 and scrambled to build a "coalition of the willing" to support it, Poland signed on, in this way distancing itself from the antiwar position of both Russia and key NATO members in western Europe. Poland's foreign policy options can be framed in the following way: (1) to choose the American side as the rift within NATO deepened; (2) to support NATO as represented by France and Germany, also in this way more accurately reflecting antiwar opinion across all of Europe; and (3) to be on the side that Russia was not—a consideration that should not be taken lightly, given Polish history. In the end the question for Poland is the same as it is for the United States: Is the country more secure following the war in Iraq or is it not? We return to this issue after contextualizing Poland's security dilemma.

NATO VERSUS EASTERN NEIGHBORS

Poland's geopolitical position has always been precarious. It is situated in the central lowlands of Europe with no natural borders in the east or west and with Russia and Germany as neighbors. During a visit to Warsaw in June 1995, U.S. Defense Secretary William Perry called Poland "the key to European security." For Poland, in turn, the key to European security was membership in NATO. In the political conditions of the early 1990s, questioning the wisdom of joining Western alliance systems was virtually untenable.[11]

A normative argument used to justify Poland's membership in the alliance was that NATO enlargement would signify the disappearance of the division of Europe decided upon by the Big Three at the Yalta conference in 1945. By integrating into European-wide security architecture, former Soviet bloc countries would shed their "eastern" status. Successive Polish governments have been sensitive to the charge that a new division of Europe, running along the Bug river (its eastern border), would follow from limited NATO expansion, and they have pursued two foreign policy courses seeking to prevent that from occurring. First, from the early 1990s on, Poland signed bilateral treaties with all of its neighbors, including Belarus and Ukraine. These treaties provided a framework for cooperation that went beyond NATO membership. Second, Poland has given a high priority to promoting the security interests of its eastern neighbors, in particular Lithuania and Ukraine, with which it has historic ties. It championed the cause of the Baltic states and, since their accession, that of Ukraine in gaining admission to NATO. At the May 2002 Iceland summit that cemented NATO cooperation with Russia, the Polish foreign minister was the only advocate of short-listing Ukraine as a NATO membership candidate.

For centuries Russia has been Poland's "Other." Not all Poles are persuaded that Russia is European, and some consider it to be at best Eurasian and at worst Asiatic. So Poland's commitment after 1989 to bridge building between west and east was put to the test when Russia was welcomed as a strategic partner of NATO in May 2002. Polish foreign minister Cimoszewicz poured faint praise on the agreement and instead highlighted its inevitable character. "Keeping Russia at a distance from NATO makes no sense from either the perspective of current security threats or the security of current NATO members. The world is changing and one would have to be blind and stupid not to realize that the decision [to conclude a NATO-Russia security agreement] is a sign of the new geopolitical realities." Cimoszewicz, a former Fulbright scholar in the United States, denied that Poland had opposed granting Russia this new status: "Would Poland feel more secure if there was an increase in tensions with Russia? No."[12] It was clear, however, that the foreign minister's comments belied the lack of enthusiasm that Poland, seeking to escape from Russia's shadow, had for closer secure cooperation with Moscow.

It is ironic to recall that President Boris Yeltsin had urged Poland to return to its interwar foreign policy of maintaining equidistance between Russia and the West. Russia's weakness was never more clearly demonstrated than when NATO pressed ahead with enlargement and in 1997 invited Poland, together with the Czech Republic and Hungary, to become members.

Twelve days after Poland formally joined NATO in 1999, NATO began bombing Serbia in the wake of Yugoslav president Slobodan Milosevic's intransigence on guaranteeing minority rights for Kosovo Albanians. What had Poland gotten into, many asked, in joining the Western military alliance? Of the three new members, Polish public opinion lent the strongest support to the air attacks: 60 percent backed the NATO action. Polish leaders were more circumspect. Then foreign minister Bronislaw Geremek, while acknowledging that NATO's actions might not conform to international law, stressed that the alliance had to do whatever was necessary to halt genocide. In a television address, President Kwasniewski told the nation, just as the air campaign began, "This is a very sad evening." The defense minister, in turn, sought to allay fears about Poland's share of NATO's costs by revealing that it was very low and took into consideration the timing of Poland's entry to NATO. In many respects, Polish leaders expressed more qualms about the war on Serbia (a fellow Slav nation) than it did about the one on Iraq four years later.

NATO actions against Serbia had an impact on Poland's relations with Russia. The two countries were squarely on opposite sides, but other factors complicated the relationship. In January 2000, Warsaw expelled nine Russian diplomats for spying. In March of that year pro-Chechen demonstrators vandalized the Russian consulate in Poznan, infuriating the Kremlin and leading to the temporary recall of Russia's ambassador. In April, in a report that was supposed to be secret, Poland's security service warned that Russian intelligence was stepping up activity in the country. A survey published that month found that only 2 percent of Poles considered relations with Russia to be good, while 40 percent claimed they were bad.[13]

To be sure, a major breakthrough in improving bilateral relations came in January 2002 when President Putin visited Poland. One purpose of his visit was to commemorate the anniversary of the Soviet "liberation" of Warsaw from the Nazis in 1944—a dubious cause for celebration for most Poles. But Putin demonstrated goodwill and political acumen by visiting monuments commemorating the suffering of Poles at the hands of Russian repression—such as the Katyn monument honoring the memory of Polish officers killed by Stalin's forces during World War II.

Given past conflicts, the NATO-Russia agreement of May 2002 could have been bittersweet for Poland. Russia became an equal partner with NATO member states in such matters as nonproliferation, military cooperation, and civil defense. Control over alliance membership, core military decisions, and use of allied troops to defend member states were, however, to remain in the hands of the United States and current NATO countries. As if to assuage Polish unease about Russia's new role, an informal summit of NATO defense ministers and Russia's defense minister Igor Ivanov was held in Warsaw in September 2002. It reported on the already "remarkable" record of the NATO-Russia Council in the defense field, especially concerning theater missile defense and joint conduct of peacekeeping operations. The Warsaw meeting also focused on joint efforts to fight terrorism. The Polish government was thrust into the position of playing host to a bridge-building exercise it might be skeptical about, but it accounted itself well. But within months bridge building suffered a serious setback as Poland unconditionally chose to back the Bush administration in its war on Iraq.

WAR ON IRAQ: A MOMENTOUS CHOICE FOR POLAND

NATO membership brought Poland immeasurable benefits, but it is ironic that just when Poland seemed to have resolved its long-standing security dilemma, international developments conspired to dampen enthusiasm for the alliance. Bombing Serbia, having to cooperate with Russia on terms dictated by NATO, increased military spending, and, to cap it off, deciding to back Bush on Iraq have taken the shine off NATO membership.

The increased threat of international terrorism that followed the September 11 attacks had as one of its most tangible consequences an immediate effort by NATO members to increase their military capability. The alliance's argument—that it now faced unpredictable threats from far away—meant, a NATO communiqué made clear, that it had to be "able to field forces that can move quickly to wherever they are needed." U.S. secretary of state Colin Powell elaborated: "NATO has to have the ability to move to other places. We all need to have highly mobile, sustainable forces with modern combat capabilities, forces that can get to the fight wherever it is and carry out a mission with efficiency and precision."[14] As a result, in 2002 the United States committed to spending 3.7 percent of its gross domestic product on defense. By contrast, one-half of NATO's European members, including Poland, had defense expenditures below 2 percent.

As a step toward assuming a greater security burden, in late 2002 the Polish government awarded Lockheed a contract for forty-eight advanced multi-role F-16 aircraft. The U.S. government had lobbied hard to win this contract and promised Poland $3.8 billion—the cost of the purchase—in low-interest loans. Poland thus spurned a rival European-made fighter jet that had been chosen by several other new NATO members.

The significance of this contract needs to be highlighted, given subsequent developments in the Polish-U.S. relationship. A former Polish defense minister succinctly described the long-term consequences of the choice of the F-16. It was a political and military choice—not just a commercial and technical one—that would affect several generations to come. Poland had chosen a strategic partner in global security, not merely out of sentiment but because of an incisive understanding of politics. With the United States being the only global power, the only country able to carry out global politics, Poland was pursuing a realist foreign policy. "The aircraft's choice was the beginning of a process that is to put Poland in a bilateral alliance with the U.S."[15]

At this time U.S. pressure on Iraq was increasing, as was its efforts to build a multinational coalition. But Europe's major powers seemed to be proving reluctant allies. In January 2003 an impatient U.S. defense secretary Donald Rumsfeld made the much-discussed remark that Europe had moved eastward, and that France and Germany now represented the "old Europe." In turn, French president Chirac began to champion the international antiwar movement while highlighting the large Islamic presence in his country. German chancellor Schröder had won reelection by playing the anti-American card, and he, too, steadfastly refused to support Bush. In response, Pentagon officials began to hint that some American bases in Germany might be moved to Poland, bringing lucrative revenue to neighboring localities. Most Poles welcomed the idea of stationing American troops on their soil. While no final decisions on the issue were taken, for the first time the Bush administration began to use Poland's pro-Americanism to blackmail uncooperative EU states. By July 2003, there were even rumors that the United States was considering moving NATO headquarters from Brussels to somewhere in Poland.

Defense-burden sharing also involves the deployment of Polish troops to far-off regions as part of the war on terrorism. Several units were dispatched to Afghanistan in 2001 after the United States had driven the Taliban from power, but there was no hint yet that Poland was about to assume a security role unprecedented in the country's modern history—occupation and administration of part of a country far removed from central Europe.[16]

In early 2003 it became clear that the Bush administration intended to go to war against Iraq. The Polish government's justification for supporting U.S. action was based on arguments that were subsequently discredited—even by Defense Secretary Donald Rumsfeld—such as the existence of weapons of mass destruction in Iraq, their availability to terrorist groups, and Saddam's supposed purchase of enriched uranium. Not just the substance but the process of Poland coming out with support for Bush's war seemed flawed. In February 2003 it signed "The Letter of Eight"—eight NATO member states in Europe, led by Britain and Spain, that backed Bush's foreign policy in the name of Euro-Atlantic cooperation. Yet the Polish government had not consulted with Paris and Berlin before signing, leading to a political backlash from those countries.

In March 2003 foreign minister Cimoszewicz, the Communist-supported candidate for president in 1990, asserted that he was more frightened by "an arrogant Saddam who for years has humiliated the international community" than by a vision of the United States as global policeman, a superpower imposing its will on the entire international community.[17] Poland's participation was high profile, Cimoszewicz averred, but "it was absolutely necessary from the strategic perspective of its national security." The connection between U.S. war on Iraq and Poland's security was not made clear. Nor was the foreign minister's assertion that Poland was offering support to the logic presented by the United States and the UK in the name of strengthening the Euro-Atlantic Alliance very persuasive. Claiming that his country's special relationship with America was an EU asset also seemed a sophistic argument. Finally, Cimoszewicz seemed to demonstrate inconsistency in rejecting unilateral leadership of the EU even as he was accepting unilateral American leadership.

As the war progressed the U.S. central command singled out Poland's GROM special operations unit fighting in Iraq for praise. However, political observers in Europe, and especially France and Germany, dubbed Poland America's "Trojan horse" and even "Trojan ass." Some EU states, including Germany, were puzzled that a country recently approved for membership was reaching out for billions of euros of EU aid while at the same time sending thousands of troops to Iraq.

Modern diplomacy avoids playing zero-sum games where one side's win is entirely at the cost of the other. But there seemed limits to how Poland could square EU accession with what was perceived as its uncritical pro-Americanism. A testing ground for Poland's priorities is the Weimar Triangle, composed of leaders from Paris, Berlin, and Warsaw. President Chirac, Chancellor Schröder, and President Kwasniewski met in Wroclaw in May 2003 and, on the surface, patched over differences. Even though he was host, the Polish leader took a backseat to Chirac and Schröder. At the same time he adopted a new role as conciliator between the United States and the antiwar coalition formed by France, Germany, and Russia. Kwasniewski stressed that the Poles wanted "understanding and cooperation between Europe and America to be a strong pillar of global security and stability." It seemed doubtful, however, that the fault line had disappeared.

After the fall of the Saddam Hussein regime in Iraq, the Bush administration decided to award command of one of the four Iraqi stabilization zones to Poland. Moreover, alongside the United States and Britain, Poland would, on its own, control an entire zone, the central-southern area. Apart from its un-swerving support for the United States, other factors identified as shaping this decision were Poland's experience in peacekeeping operations, its investments in Iraq dating to the communist period, and the humanitarian consideration of helping with postwar reconstruction. The Polish government was flattered by Washington's choice and accepted the offer immediately, without waiting to see whether the UN might be given a role in the postwar Iraqi administration. The larger EU states seemed shocked by this decision; indeed, the usually well-concealed snobbery that many western European politicians harbor for eastern Europe was unmasked by this unexpected U.S. choice of partner. Poland was criticized for its "immaturity" in assuming a role outstripping its capabilities.

The SLD government found itself in an awkward position (and this setting aside serious financial scandals in which it was implicated at home). It subse-quently behaved awkwardly as well. The foreign minister clumsily hastened to call for joint Polish-German-Danish command of the stabilization force. When some German leaders asserted that the first they had heard of the proposal was from the newspapers, Cimoszewicz claimed it was only an idea anyway. The invitation—such as it was—was haughtily dismissed by the two countries, and Poland instead turned to Lithuania, Thailand, Mongolia, Fiji, and some twenty-five other countries to "internationalize" the sector under its control. The United States pledged financial support for the five-thousand-strong Polish force, while NATO provided additional military equipment. While about two-thirds of Polish respondents in public opinion surveys had at one time ex-pressed support for the war on Iraq, by June 2003 support for a Polish stabiliza-tion force for Iraq had dropped to 40 percent, while more than one-half op-posed Polish troops being sent there.

Many U.S. opponents of Bush's attack on Iraq believed that the war was about control of oil revenues. In Poland some politicians calculated that the greater Poland's commitment to the United States in Iraq, the greater would be its future benefits. Indeed that seemed to be the case when foreign minister Cimoszewicz acknowledged that access to the oilfields had always been "our ultimate objective."[18]

Is there a "Yankee-skeptic" constituency in Poland that parallels the Eu-roskeptic groupings described earlier? Opponents of the "special relationship" with the United States include Euro-enthusiasts, nationalists, and some ex-communists who, for their own reasons, do not want Poland to become depen-dent on a country alien to the region. Interestingly, some Yankee-skeptics invoke not just moral or cultural but also realist reasons. One writer asserts: "Poland is a country in Europe, not on the Yucatan peninsula, and the EU has the right to expect some loyalty from it. So far, Poland has been failing to show that loyalty in virtually all cases where the United States and the EU differed in opinion."[19]

What are we to make, therefore, of Poland's foreign policy conundrum?

Two of its top journalists, Maciej Lukasiewicz and Adam Michnik, have underscored the exceptionalism of Poland's security needs:

> Independence is never given once and for all—no one knows that better than Poles, who have lost it twice. It has to be constantly promoted, constantly strengthened through a network of international treaties and alliances in such a way that it is as closely tied as possible to the democratic commonwealth [the EU], which is more powerful than we are. The Atlantic Alliance is not a sufficient guarantee for a country situated in such a place in Europe.[20]

For reasons of security, then, as well as for economic and democratic development, joining the EU was a top priority for Poland after its democratic breakthrough.

The Road to EU Membership

The jewel in the crown of integration into Europe was always full union membership. In the run-up to the 2001 parliamentary election, SLD leader Leszek Miller boasted that his party would be presiding over the most momentous event in the country's history since Mieszko converted to Christianity in 966: Poland's accession to the European Union. In terms of myth making, Poland was ready for EU entry. European Commission president Romano Prodi regularly invoked historical legends, such as the purported unifying project undertaken by Charlemagne (742–814), king of the Franks, which justified the call for European "reunification."[21]

On December 13, 2002, Prime Minister Miller and EU representatives completed the final round of negotiations on Poland's accession into the EU. A weary Miller announced, "We have removed the heavy burden of the Yalta agreement and the postwar division of Europe. From Polish Solidarity, which won freedom and democracy for Central and Eastern Europe, we are arriving at the genuine solidarity of Europe and of Europeans."[22] From the Polish perspective, joining the EU seemed as decisive as breaking away from the Soviet bloc.[23] Finally, after hearing for more than a decade the rhetorical flourish favored by western European leaders, about how central European nations formed an integral part of Europe but that they had much hard work to do to integrate into Europe, the dissonance was ended.

OPENING MOVES: GETTING TO APPLICANT STATUS

When Poland's communist system collapsed in 1989, optimists predicted that the country would become a member of the EU within five years. They were convinced that, however complicated the process of accession might be, political imperatives in western Europe would ensure that former Soviet-bloc countries would be given fast-track admission. In 1995 the EU duly enlarged, not into central Europe but instead into affluent Austria, Finland, and Sweden.

There was some institutional logic to the EU enlargement strategy. Poland and other central European states were expected to integrate into European structures step by step before full accession became a possibility. Poland had been a member of the Organization for Security and Cooperation in Europe (OSCE), which promotes east-west relations and peaceful resolution of conflicts, since its founding in 1973. It had been an original signatory of the Helsinki Act on Human Rights in 1975. Poland was invited to join the Council of Europe in November 1991 and signed the European Convention on Human Rights and Fundamental Freedoms that came into effect in January 1993.

Integration was also pursued at the regional level. In February 1991 President Walesa attended a summit with his Czechoslovak and Hungarian counterparts in Visegrad, Hungary, to promote trade on the basis of their countries' free-market economies. The summit "was hailed at the time as a major breakthrough in Central European cooperation," but the Visegrad group, as it became known, soon became little more than "a vehicle for coordinating Central Europe's 'road to Europe' while development of closer ties within the region languished on the back burner."[24] But even in this regard, Poland, the Czech Republic, Slovakia, and Hungary became caught up in the prisoner's dilemma and found cooperation difficult. By 2000, when Poland had fallen behind in accession talks, Czech and Hungarian leaders threatened that they would not wait for laggards when seeking EU membership. The Visegrad process proved underwhelming, but at least the EU could see that it was a qualified success in comparison to the wars and ethnic cleansing that were ravaging the Balkans.

In 1993 Poland received associate membership status in the EU and formally applied for full membership in April 1994. In March 1998 the EU officially opened accession negotiations with Poland and four other central European candidates. The Nice Treaty in December 2000 affirmed a commitment to enlargement, thereby setting the stage for a final agreement in Copenhagen two years later.

THE MIDDLE GAME: EU AS MOVING TARGET?

An earlier meeting in Copenhagen, of the European Council in 1993, specified three conditions that had to be met by an applicant state for EU accession:

1. a functioning market economy with the capacity to cope with competitive pressures and market forces within the EU;

2. stable political institutions guaranteeing democracy, the rule of law, and respect for human rights and minority rights; and
3. ability to take on the obligations of EU membership, including the *acquis communautaire*, the EU's legislative corpus.

An additional condition (which was not a focus of discussions with applicant states) specified that the EU had to be able to absorb new members and maintain the momentum of integration.[25] This appeared to be a potentially significant caveat, giving the EU the right to slam the door shut on applicants should problems within the community arise. But it was not invoked, even after September 11 when sealing existing EU borders might have been justified in security terms.

Beginning in 1997 the European Commission began to issue regular progress reports on applicant countries. Commission President Prodi's report of October 1999 deflated hopes of early EU accession for Poland and its Visegrad partners. Central European candidates had recorded little improvement, he asserted, since the Commission had issued an initial "Opinion" in 1997 (which had positively rated Poland's progress). Prodi emphasized that henceforth two procedural considerations were being given greater importance. First, the accession timetable would be based exclusively on merit rather than politics; democratization was not in itself a reason to accelerate the accession timetable if economic and social conditions were unsatisfactory. Second, the Commission would now monitor applicants' claims about progress itself rather than trusting in their self-reporting.

Prodi's 1999 finding was that candidates had "not progressed significantly" in adapting laws and structures to EU criteria. Poland had shown "a notable lack of progress" in implementing reforms in such areas as slashing government aid for ailing industries, restructuring of steel, and modernizing the agricultural sector, fisheries, and infrastructure (especially highways). In short, while the country had fulfilled the first two conditions for membership—a market economy and political stability—it had work to do in harmonizing national laws to the *acquis*.

Another stipulation that could have been used to delay enlargement was the reference under the third Copenhagen condition to minority rights. The 2001 Commission report explicitly recognized the stability of political institutions and the existence of a functioning free market in central Europe. But protection of minorities had become an issue, particularly in the Czech Republic (with its Roma population), Slovakia (with its Hungarian minority), and Hungary (with a rising nationalist movement supporting the idea of a greater Hungary). In the case of Poland, minorities represent a small percentage of the population and seem well integrated, so the EU critique centered instead on a technical matter: "The concept of non-discrimination is enshrined in the Constitution, but to date the transposition of this principle into legislation, including the anti-discrimination *acquis*, has been limited."[26] This criticism was typical of others made in the twenty-nine chapters of the *acquis* as they were being operationalized in Poland.

The 162-page 2002 report offered a more positive assessment. It noted that twenty-seven of the chapters of the accession negotiations with Poland had been closed, with only agriculture, fisheries, and the environment still unresolved. The report observed that "corruption remains a cause for serious concern" but added that the country's administrative capacity had increased. Most importantly, "Overall, Poland has achieved a high degree of alignment with the *acquis* in many areas." The forecast was that Poland would be ready for entry before the 2004 European Parliament elections.[27] A final, intense round of bargaining remained for accession to become a reality.

ENDGAME: THE TERMS OF ACCESSION

The December 2002 summit in Copenhagen came down to a last round of tough negotiations between EU leaders and Polish government ministers who, in contrast to their counterparts from the nine other applicant states, were determined to fight for as many concessions as possible in the terms of accession. The most important compromise reached was an advance payment in 2005–2006 of €1 billion from the EU structural fund for any pressing expenditures faced by the Polish government; originally Poland was to have received this sum after 2007 and then only to finance infrastructural projects. The importance of the advance was that it would allow the country's public finances to absorb additional public expenditures related to EU entry. The concession cost the EU nothing, since it did not allocate any new funds to Poland. Another concession won by Miller was an additional €108 million for securing Poland's eastern borders, above and beyond the €172 million earmarked for this purpose earlier.

Agricultural policy proved the most serious stumbling block in Copenhagen. Polish farmers were offered a better deal than originally proposed. They would be eligible to receive topping-up amounts ranging from 50 to 60 percent of the farm subsidies given to their counterparts in the current EU member states. To be sure, some of this money would come out of the Polish government's budget, and from 2007 any top-ups would be financed entirely out of national funds. Other minor concessions included raising the quota on Polish milk production, maintaining a 7 percent rate of value added tax (VAT) on construction and house building services, and EC recognition of Polish nurses' qualifications.

The rural development package of €5 billion for 2004–2006 was specifically adapted for the ten accession countries. The EU will cofinance many rural development measures at up to 80 percent, including pensions for farmers, support for less favored areas, agroenvironmental programs, and forestation of agricultural land. Franz Fischler, EU Commissioner for Agriculture, Rural Development and Fisheries, concluded, therefore, that the final terms were a "fair and tailor-made package which benefits farmers in accession countries. . . . The leaders of the candidate countries can return home with their heads held high. They have achieved a farm package which is perfectly saleable to their farm community."[28]

Polish negotiators did not come away from Copenhagen empty-handed, even though concessions made were not really substantial. Without doubt Miller had stressed to EU negotiators that nationalist forces were on the rise in Poland. Kwasniewski acknowledged that the hard line taken in negotiations, especially in protecting the agricultural sector, was partly the effect of the right: "The right played its role—one that it is assigned in a democratic state. Every government that is not controlled becomes stupid."[29]

Most of the fundamental institutional questions concerning enlargement had been worked out prior to the Copenhagen summit. By the Nice agreement Poland was to have fifty seats—the same number as Spain—in the expanded European Parliament of 736 members. Only Germany, with ninety-nine MEPs, and Britain, France, and Italy with seventy-two each, had more. As a large country, Poland on admission was entitled to two commissioners on the European Commission. But until an EU constitution finalizes the issue, Poland will have one commissioner.

Poland had earlier committed itself to participating in and contributing to all community programs forming part of the EU general budget and its other financial institutions (the European Development Fund, the European Investment Bank, and the European Central Bank). Poland's fixed contribution to the general budget would be reduced by 90 percent for 2003, but this reduction would be 20 percent less in each succeeding year, reaching 10 percent in 2007. In this way over a five-year transition period Poland would be able to strike a financial balance between contributions paid in to the EU general budget and absorption of budgetary funds benefiting Poland.

Probably the most emotional issue about joining the EU for average Poles has been the sale of land to foreigners. The specter of Germans, in particular, buying land in their ancestral homes in Silesia and Pomerania (provinces that reverted to Polish rule after World War II) was worrying.[30] As one analysis concluded, because of repeated invasions and border changes, "To Polish patriots, land is not so much a good as a heritage never to be betrayed."[31] Land has, of course, more than symbolic value: two-thirds of Poles still live in the countryside and one-quarter of them still make a living from agriculture.

A major negotiating coup, therefore, was the Miller government's agreement with the EU in 2002 for a twelve-year transition period—five years longer than any other candidate country had negotiated—for land sales to EU nationals. For so-called recreation plots the transition period was seven years. Critics of Miller still spoke of betrayal, but elsewhere governments looked enviously at such a gradually phased-in agreement.

THE FUTURE: CONSTITUTIONAL ENACTMENT AND STANDARD SETTING

No sooner had Poland obtained accession into the EU than questions were raised about the drafting of an EU constitution that would precede Poland's formal entry into the Club. The Charter of Fundamental Rights of the European Union adopted at Nice in 2000 referred for the first time to the EU as a constitutionally based entity with a legal personality. A convention to draft a constitution was established under former French president Giscard d'Estaing. The EU's most prosperous and powerful members—Germany, France, and Britain—though attached to their own institutions, would back a European constitution that preserves—and perhaps even enhances—their position within a twenty-five-member EU. If this happens, Poland does not step onto an even playing field in May 2004.

In June 2003 an EU summit—without the ten accession states—was held in Porto Carras, Greece, and approved certain constitutional provisions.[32] Article 10 states that "the constitution and law adopted by the Union's institutions shall have primacy over the law of the Member States." This is no surprise to Poland, which has battled with harmonization of its laws to EU standards for a decade. The EU will have a foreign minister. However, for Poland, with its pro-American dilettantism, the good news is that heads of national governments will retain vetoes over the making of EU foreign policy and control of their own armed forces. More worrying is that the EU's legal personality will allow it to sign treaties in its own right that bind all members. At some point the EU might even have a seat on the UN Security Council in place of Britain and France. If that were the case, Poland's influence would diminish considerably.

The Porto Carras summit agreed to create a presidency of the European Council to complement the presidency of the European Commission. The possibility remains that eventually the two presidencies would be merged into a single president of Europe. Smaller EU states are concerned that the Franco-German axis within the EU will ensure that such a president does its bidding. But for a populous state like Poland, a positive initiative was the expansion of the European Parliament's power to enact legislation by majority vote. In October 2003, an Intergovernmental Conference convened in Rome to finalize the Constitutional Treaty. With it the EU took another step toward federalism even though two basic governmental functions—to raise taxes and to go to war—still eluded it. The timing of the Rome summit was significant: six months later ten new members were joining the EU.

We should remember that the constitutional question involves not just power but also EU standard setting. What has been the record of EU standard setting to date? Has it been consistent? For example, have standards been set for applicants that existing EU members are hard-pressed to meet? More generally, are the issues that were supposed to be standardized in the run-up to accession fully clear yet?

The issue of respect for minority rights is illustrative. The very definition of minorities was contested by some EU states—above all, France. The rise of anti-immigrant parties in the new century throughout Europe has shown the polarization that exists in these societies. As three Norwegian specialists (presumably observing the EU at a critical distance) inferred from this, "There is a risk that on the day of enlargement the applicant states will have a 'higher' standard of rights than the existing EU."[33]

Just as evocative an example of possible EU double-standard setting was on the practical question of ceilings on government budget deficits. It was incongruous that in January 2003, just weeks after agreeing to enlarge to twenty-five members, the European Commission had to warn Germany to reduce its deficit, which had reached 3.9 percent of GDP (the limit was 3 percent; the euro area average was 2.2 percent). Under the Stability and Growth Pact, the Commission had established a set of rules (ironically, at Germany's behest) intended to hold in check the budget deficits of the poorer Eurozone member states such as Greece and Portugal. But in practice, the larger EU economies—Germany, France, and Italy—were more often guilty of profligate spending. Inevitably a number of politicians in the Community criticized the pact as inflexible and unsuited to current economic conditions. Commission president Prodi even called the pact "stupid," and there was talk of doing away with it.

But very few leaders in the existing EU states thought it stupid to apply the criteria to the prospective ten members. Not surprisingly, one Polish finance minister proposed an ingenious, if self-serving, solution to the deficit problem: the government budgets of a bloc of countries—for example, within central Europe—should be pooled so that one country's excessive deficit would be balanced out by others' smaller or nonexistent deficits.[34] The formula was modeled on the Kyoto environmental treaty's concept of transferable pollution rights. While Poland, with a deficit in 2003 slightly higher than Germany's, would stand to gain from such a proposal, other central European states' budgetary discipline would have proved pointless. At least in this regard, Poland as an accession state shared concerns similar to the larger current members—objecting to seemingly arbitrary and unrealistic EU criteria.

PUBLIC OPINION ON INTEGRATION

Even before three-quarters of Polish voters approved EU entry in the June 2003 referendum, it had been clear for some time that public opinion decidedly favored membership.[35] Indeed, the strong endorsement in the referendum more closely reflected the record high level of support found in 1996, when it was 80 percent, than in the first years of the new century, when it hovered around 60 percent.

Popular perceptions of what EU membership would bring Poland were decidedly mixed. Surveys showed that a majority of respondents thought Poland would be admitted as a second-class member: in one national poll 55 percent claimed the country would have an inferior status in the EU, while only 29 percent believed it would rank equally with the existing fifteen.[36]

What were the reasons for skepticism about EU membership? Some believed that the Polish economy was still too weak to compete against EU countries, a consideration that outweighed the prospect of a stronger economy following entry.[37] On the question of whether Poland was ready to become a full EU member, opinions in 2001 differed little from June 1994: in each case 45 to 47 percent thought that Poland was only halfway there.[38]

The frustrating and at times even humiliating process of negotiating accession described above dampened Poles' enthusiasm for membership. As much was acknowledged by EU Enlargement Commissioner Guenter Verheugen in April 2002 when he contended that the drop in public support for the EU in Poland and other candidate states was caused largely by "oversensitivity to reports emanating from Brussels" interpreted as setting new conditions on applicant states.[39]

Undoubtedly Verheugen was right. The view that the EU Club was out to maximize advantages for itself became more common. Thus, in response to a survey question first asked in 1993, the percentage of Polish respondents who believed that Polish entry into the EU would above all benefit current EU members reached an all-time high (59 percent) in 2002—just months before enlargement was approved. Conversely, the percentages claiming it would benefit Poland and EU states equally, or Poland foremost, reached their low points (see Table 14.2).

The most highly critical sector of society has been farmers: 79 percent claimed in 2002 that Poland's entry into the EU would benefit the fifteen EU members most. This conclusion stemmed from the widespread impression that Polish farmers would lose more from EU entry than any other social group (see Table 14.3). Educated people alongside businessmen (especially foreign ones) and political elites were seen as likely to gain most from EU enlargement. Respondents under the age of twenty-four were most positive about mutual benefits of integration.

The profile of those Poles most closely identifying themselves with Europe differs from that of the likely beneficiaries of EU membership. The profile encompasses "men, inhabitants of large towns, those with less sense of national pride, having faith in the EU and UN, activists in voluntary organizations,

Table 14.3   Opinions on Advantages for Particular Social Groups from Poland's Integration into the European Union (May 1998 percentages)

	Will Gain	Will Lose	No Change	Hard to Say
Foreign businessmen	72	5	9	14
Educated people	67	6	13	14
Polish businessmen	64	14	9	13
Political elites	61	9	14	16
Workers	23	40	18	19
Conmen and swindlers	41	22	16	21
Ex-communist nomenclatura	23	22	25	30
Unemployed	33	27	21	19
Clergy	18	18	38	26
Farmers	16	54	12	18

Source: Maria Gerszewska, Jacek Kucharczyk, "Oczekiwania polakow wobec negocjacji z Unia Europejska," in *Polska Eurodebata*, ed. Lena Kolarska-Bobinska (Warsaw: Instytut Spraw Publicznych, 1999), p. 36, Table 7.

those inclined to unconventional political action (participation in protests), and those expressing confidence in democracy."[40]

What was thought to be the impact of EU membership on such values as tolerance, efficiency, initiative, and liberal mores? Respondents in 2002 foresaw less of an impact than those in 1994 (see Table 14.1). The fear of a rise in crime following EU entry was down in 2002, too, though pessimists (40 percent) still outnumbered optimists (19 percent). The apprehension that Poland would be less religious also was waning, though again a significant proportion (one-quarter in 2002) felt that EU membership would produce a decline in religiosity. In general, the perception that radical changes would follow EU entry, characteristic of public opinion in the mid-1990s, was fading.

An intriguing question attenuated by Polish participation in the war on Iraq is whether Poles' desire to be part of Europe is diluted by their ardent pro-Americanism. Sociological surveys have repeatedly shown more support in Poland for the United States as a country and Americans as a nation than in other former Soviet bloc states. But to what degree are Poles more pro-American than people living in current EU states? In a sweeping 2002 study of world public opinion about America, Poles were indeed among the most enthusiastic about American popular culture, 70 percent expressing a liking for it and just 22 percent saying they disliked it; in Europe only Britain, predictably, was even more enthusiastic. Poles liked American ideas on democracy by a margin of 51 to 30 percent—about average for respondents in central and eastern Europe but significantly more positive than in EU states like Britain (43 to 42 percent positive) or France (53 percent negative, 42 percent positive). On the question whether the spread of American ideas and customs was good or bad,

Poles were decidedly negative—31 percent saying good and 55 percent saying bad—again about average for the region, less critical than the British (39 and 50 percent respectively), but not as negative as respondents in Germany (28 and 67 percent) or especially France (25 and 71 percent).[41]

In May 2003 a Polish survey asked respondents whether Poland's recent political and military backing for the United States in Iraq was consistent with its desire to be part of the EU. Thirty-five percent claimed that it was indeed consistent, while only 25 percent (many of them supporters of the nationalist LPR) said it was contradictory. When asked if the EU should promote close cooperation with the United States or should construct its own alternative position in the world, 37 percent contended that the two objectives did not contradict each other. While 23 percent preferred that the EU stake its own international position, 18 percent believed in close cooperation with the United States even if it weakened the EU's international position.[42]

In sum, a substantial number of Poles do not see a conflict between pro-American and pro-EU orientations. That in itself may make Poles different from their counterparts in western Europe. Polish attitudes toward American culture have differed somewhat—but not markedly—from their cohorts in the west. On balance it does not appear that Polish pro-American attitudes—such as they are—have the potential to develop into a serious cleavage with the rest of the EU. On the other hand, failing to recognize when American and EU policy conflict does not make Poles into very discriminating observers.

NOT QUITE THERE? LABOR MIGRATION AND THE SCHENGEN ZONE

One of western Europe's greatest fears is of large-scale immigration. Accordingly the 2003 Porto Carras summit approved the idea of the EU developing a common immigration policy. Westward migration from central and eastern Europe has not evoked the same xenophobic backlash as the flow of immigrants from Africa and Asia, but it is seen as a threat nevertheless. It has been converted into an electoral hot potato in many EU states, ranging from Austria to France to Holland to Scandinavia.

The architects of EU enlargement have had to address the question of job hunters from Poland and its neighbors, where the unemployment rate is high, "flooding" into western Europe as soon as these states join the EU. In 1992 Portuguese workers, who had roughly one-half the income of their German counterparts at that time, migrated in great numbers to the richer EU states when their country became a member. In 2000 Poles' incomes were only one-sixth of those in Germany. If, as one German think tank contended, a direct relationship exists between income gaps and migration, a forecast of 500,000 central Europeans moving to western Europe per year if borders were fully opened could not be ruled out. Especially in Germany, which was wrestling with new citizenship and immigration laws intended to normalize the status of its nine million foreign nationals, a backlash against further labor migrants was probable.

In turn the dilemma for successive Polish governments has been to decide what EU restrictions on migration of people are acceptable. The labor migration formula for Poland's EU accession involves a maximum seven-year transitional period broken down into $2 + 3 + 2$. That is, Polish citizens' right to work in EU countries is to be restricted for the first two years even though, during this period, they will enjoy priority over citizens from so-called third (non-EU) countries. If current EU members decide that their labor markets have been destabilized by immigration from the accession states, they can vote to extend the transition phase by three years. After five years these members can decide to extend restrictions for a final two-year period.[43]

An issue closely related to labor migration is when Poland will be incorporated into the so-called Schengen zone after joining the EU. There is nothing automatic about the dismantling of border controls within the Union upon EU accession: Greece, for example, which joined the EU in 1981, was admitted into the Schengen zone in 1999. Poland's accession into the EU but not quick integration into the Schengen area might complicate Poland's foreign policy toward both west and east.

What is the Schengen zone? It is an agreement signed in 1985 in a Luxembourg village bordering France and Germany; it establishes an open border regime among signatory countries. It grants people the freedom to move around the EU on presentation of a valid passport or identity card. As part of this agreement, the signatory countries undertake to cooperate closely in dealing with security issues and asylum seekers. The first group of signatories included France, Germany, Spain, Portugal, Belgium, Holland, and Luxembourg. Not long after, Italy, Austria, Liechtenstein, Greece, and the five Scandinavian countries (including Norway and Iceland, which are not EU members) signed the agreement. Britain and Ireland have remained outside the zone.

From May 2004, Polish citizens can travel freely within the EU. But "internal border" controls between Poland and existing EU members like Germany and Sweden continue to exist. These controls will be removed when the EU Council of Ministers decides to do so. That decision will depend on the accession states' ability to demonstrate the same level of public safety for European citizens as older EU member states have achieved.

The new "external borders" of the EU brought on by enlargement will require the same degree of monitoring by the accession states as current Schengen members' borders have with their non-Schengen neighbors. As applied to Poland, this means that its "external borders" with non-Schengen states—Belarus, Russia, and Ukraine—will need to be more strictly controlled than hitherto. Such added security will have political costs and may create rifts between Poland and its less stable eastern neighbors.

The need to ensure uniformly high standards of public security within the union was brought home by the 2001 terrorist attacks in the United States—planned in Hamburg and other parts of the EU. Balancing the interests of freedom of movement *within the EU* against secure EU borders *with non-Schengen states* will play out most significantly on Poland's border with former Soviet republics that had nuclear weapons on their territory.

Conclusion

A Polish writer has opined that, no matter how well Poles speak French or English, they never seem to be able to make themselves understood in France or Britain.[44] The long road leading to European integration seemed to confirm the accuracy of this observation. Even after achieving remarkable results within a decade—stable democratic institutions and a functioning market economy—a new set of accession challenges now has to be overcome: disparities in wealth levels, lower environmental standards, the movement of labor, border security, development of backward regions, even a consensus on foreign policy objectives.

How European is Poland? Does it just represent "new Europe," with the implication that its distinguishing feature is, paradoxically, a special relationship with a non-European country, the United States? Or is Poland a nation whose history begins at the birth of European civilization, regardless whether the United States or, for that matter, the EU confer on it a European status in the twenty-first century? Poles have been learning about the histories of EU member states, and about that of America, for many decades. EU accession will hopefully encourage Europeans—and Americans—to learn more about Poland's past.

Notes

1. Quoted in *Gazeta Wyborcza,* December 14, 2002.

2. See "Poland's Transition to a Democratic Republic: The Taming of the Sacred?" in *The Secular and the Sacred: Nation, Religion, and Politics,* ed. William Safran (London: Frank Cass, 2003), 137–54.

3. This point was emphasized by Marjorie Castle in her book with the author, *Democracy in Poland* (Boulder, Colo.: Westview Press, 2002), 123.

4. George Blazyca and Marek Kolkiewicz, "Poland and the EU: Internal Disputes, Domestic Politics and Accession," *Journal of Communist Studies and Transition Politics* 15, no. 4 (December 1999): 131–43.

5. Antoni Macierewicz, LPR spokesman and Polish Interior Minister, 1991–1992, quoted in "Poles and the Catholic Church: Preaching for the European Union," *The Economist*, March 16–22, 2002, 54.

6. Macierewicz, "Poles and the Catholic Church," 54.

7. *Duchowienstwo polskie a integracja europejska*. Warsaw: Instytut Spraw Publicznych, October 2002.

8. Quoted in *Gazeta Wyborcza*, March 14, 2002.

9. Quoted in *Gazeta Wyborcza*, March 14, 2002.

10. See "Europe's Far Right: Toxic but Containable," *Economist,* April 27–May 3, 2002, 47–48.

11. Only a small Catholic parliamentary group, "Our Circle" (*Nasze kolo*), opposed NATO membership in the 1990s.

12. Reported in *Gazeta Wyborcza*, May 15, 2002.

13. Centrum Badania Opinii Publicznej (CBOS), "Poles on the Relations between Poland and Russia and the Political Situation in Russia." Warsaw: April 2000. Online at www.cbos.com.pl.

14. Quoted in *The New York Times*, May 15, 2002.

15. Jan Parys, quoted in *Rzeczpospolita*, February 4, 2003.

16. Poland was involved in six border conflicts between 1918 and 1921, immediately after its independence. In the cases of Czechoslovakia, Lithuania, and Ukraine it seized and went on to govern non-Polish lands. From the perspective of its neighbors, Poland has acted as an imperial power in its recent history.

17. Quoted in *Gazeta Wyborcza*, March 29, 2003.

18. Cimoszewicz's remarks were made to a group of Polish firms that signed a deal with a subsidiary of Vice President Dick Cheney's former company, Halliburton, Kellogg, Brown and Root, which had already won contracts for postwar reconstruction in Iraq. See "Poland Seeks Iraqi Oil Stake," BBC News World Service, July 3, 2003. At news.bbc.co.uk.

19. Lukasz Warzecha, quoted in *Rzeczpospolita*, February 4, 2003.

20. Maciej Lukasiewicz and Adam Michnik, "Polska nie jest przeciez samotna wyspa," *Rzeczpospolita* and *Gazeta Wyborcza*, May 8, 2002. The authors are editors in chief of these two leading dailies, and their article was published in each on the anniversary of the end of World War II in Europe.

21. Romano Prodi, *Europe As I See It*. Cambridge: Polity Press, 2000. For a deconstruction of his vision, see Anders Hellstrom and Bo Petersson, "Temporality in the Construction of EU Identity," Lund, Sweden: Centre for European Studies, CFE Working Paper Series no. 19, 2002.

22. Quoted in *Gazeta Wyborcza*, December 14, 2002.

23. For an informative collection of essays on this, see Karl Cordell, ed., *Poland and the European Union* (London: Routledge, 2000).

24. Sarah Meiklejohn Terry, "Prospects for Regional Cooperation," in *Transition to Democracy in Poland*, 2nd ed., ed. Richard F. Staar (New York: St. Martin's Press), 215–16.

25. "Conclusions of the Presidency," European Council, Copenhagen, June 21–23, 1993, SN/180/93, 13.

26. Commission of the European Communities, "2001 Regular Report on Poland's

Progress Towards Accession," Brussels, November 13, 2001, p. 22. At europa.eu.int/comm/enlargement.

27. Commission of the European Communities, "2002 Regular Report on Poland's Progress Towards Accession," Brussels, October 9, 2002, p. 135. At europa.eu.int/comm/enlargement.

28. At europa.eu.int/comm/enlargement.

29. Quoted in *Gazeta Wyborcza,* December 14, 2002.

30. Poles and central Europeans generally were not the only ones fearing a wave of German second-home hunters. Denmark had earlier negotiated a deal with the EU making it difficult for other EU nationals—in particular Germans—to purchase summer homes along the Danish coast.

31. "Polish Land: A Most Emotional Issue," *Economist*, March 23–29, 2002, 48.

32. "Your Darkest Fears Addressed, Your Hardest Questions Answered—Europe's Constitution," *Economist*, June 21, 2003.

33. Erik Oddvar Eriksen, John Erik Fossum, and Helene Sjursen, "Widening or Reconstituting the EU? Enlargement and Democratic Governance in Europe." Paper prepared for the 43rd Annual International Studies Association Convention, New Orleans, Louisiana, 24–27 March 2002, p. 20.

34. The finance minister was Grzegorz Kolodko, who served in the SLD government until 2003.

35. Krzysztof Jasiewicz, "Reluctantly European?" *Transitions Online*, March 1, 2002. At www.tol.cz/.

36. Lena Kolarska-Bobinska and Jacek Kucharczyk, "Negocjacje z Unia Europejska—opinie Polakow," in *Polska Eurodebata*, ed. Kolarska-Bobinska (Warsaw: Instytut Spraw Publicznych, 1999), 16, Table 1.

37. Beata Roguska, "Opinie o integracji Polski z Unia Europejska," Warsaw: CBOS, March 2002. At www.cbos.com.pl.

38. CBOS, "Opinie o integracji Polski z Unia Europejska," March 2001. At www.cbos.com.pl.

39. Quoted in *Gazeta Wyborcza*, April 5, 2002.

40. Aleksandra Jasinska-Kania and Miroslawa Marody, "Integracja europejska a tozsamosc narodowa polakow," in Jasinska-Kania and Marody, eds., *Polacy wsrod Europejczykow* (Warsaw: Scholar Press, 2002), 286.

41. These results are taken from the Pew Global Attitudes Project, "What the World Thinks in 2002." Washington, D.C.: Pew Research Center, 2002, pp. 63–66.

42. Krzysztof Panowski, "Unia Europejska a wspolpraca transatlantycka—polacy o dylematach polityki zagranicznej," Warsaw: CBOS, May 2003.

43. Sekretariat Europejski, "Bilans negocjacji o czlonkostwo Polski w Unii Europejskiej," Warsaw, December 13, 2002. Published in *Gazeta Wyborcza*.

44. This comment was made by Janusz Tazbir, "Serce z zachodniej strony," *Gazeta Wyborcza*, January 22–23, 1994.

Suggestions for Further Reading

Brzezinski, Matthew. *The Struggle for Constitutionalism in Poland*. London: Macmillan, 2000.

Castle, Marjorie, and Ray Taras. *Democracy in Poland*. 2nd ed. Boulder, Colo.: Westview Press, 2002.

Cordell, Karl, ed. *Poland and the European Union*. London: Routledge, 2000.

European Commission. *Enlargement: Regular Reports on Progress towards Accession*. Brussels: European Commission, 2002.

Kolodko, Grzegorz. *From Shock to Therapy: The Political Economy of Postsocialist Transformation*. New York: Oxford University Press, 2000.

Michta, Andrew A., ed. *America's New Allies: Poland, Hungary, and the Czech Republic in NATO*. Seattle: University of Washington Press, 1999.

Millard, Frances. *Polish Politics and Society*. London: Routledge, 1999.

Pond, Elizabeth. *The Rebirth of Europe*. Washington, D.C.: Brookings Institution Press, 2002.

Prizel, Ilya. *National Identity and Foreign Policy: Nationalism and Leadership in Poland, Russia and Ukraine*. New York: Cambridge University Press, 1998.

Prizel, Ilya, and Andrew A. Michta, eds. *Polish Foreign Policy Reconsidered: The Dilemmas of Independence*. New York: St. Martin's Press, 1995.

Sachs, Jeffrey. *Poland's Jump to the Market Economy*. Cambridge, Mass.: MIT Press, 1994.

Sanford, George. *Democratic Government in Poland*. London: Palgrave, 2002.

Staar, Richard F., ed. *Transition to Democracy in Poland*. 2nd edition. New York: St. Martin's Press, 1998.

Van Brabant, Jozef, ed. *Remaking Europe: The European Union and the Transition Economies*. Lanham, Md.: Rowman & Littlefield, 1999.

Zielonka, Jan, and Alex Pravda, eds. *Democratic Consolidation in Eastern Europe: International and Transnational Factors*. New York: Oxford University Press, 2001.

Glossary

Acquis communautaire: A French term that cannot be precisely translated but that denotes the sum total of EU treaties, regulations, and laws developed since the 1950s; must be accepted by new member states as it exists at the time of accession.

Bretton Woods system: The international monetary system created at the end of World War II in Bretton Woods, New Hampshire. It was designed to establish international management of the global economy and to provide for the cross-convertibility of national currencies through a fixed exchange rate with gold or with currencies backed by gold (such as the U.S. dollar). Its key foundations were the General Agreement on Tariffs and Trade, the International Monetary Fund, and the World Bank.

Common Agricultural Policy (CAP): A controversial, very expensive subsidy system established under the Treaty of Rome to increase agricultural productivity and sustain farm incomes in the European Community. It benefits mainly wealthy European farmers and damages developing world agriculture exports.

Common Assembly: The parliamentary arm of the European Coal and Steel Community; precursor to the European Parliament.

Common Foreign and Security Policy (CFSP): The "second pillar" of the European Union, created under the Maastricht Treaty to replace European Political Cooperation. It establishes the broad foreign policy objectives of the EU and requires member states and the EU institutions to cooperate in promoting these objectives.

Conference on Security and Cooperation in Europe (CSCE): A process designed to promote European cooperation on trade and human rights. Its members include the United States, Canada, Russia, the former Soviet republics, and all of Europe. It was renamed the Organization for Security and Cooperation in Europe (OSCE) in 1994.

constitutional monarchies: The form of monarchy in which the monarch accepts the increasingly stringent limits on his or her power imposed by a constitution.

consumer price inflation: The rate of increase of the prices for goods and services weighted according to their share in a standard consumption bundle.

corporatism: Democratic corporatism provides for the representation of organized interest groups in the policy-making process. Most often such interests are economic, including business, labor, agriculture, etc. In practice such representation may be formal, such as on the EU Economic and Social Council and on national commissions (health, environmental protection, etc.), but most often it is informal through access to governmental policymakers and legislative committees.

Council of Europe: Organization established in 1949 to promote European integration after World War II. Has played an important role in promoting human rights and operates the European Court of Human Rights. Located in Strasbourg.

487

Council of Ministers: The decision-making institution of the EU comprising ministerial-level representatives from each of the member states. In cooperation with the European Parliament, it has the power to adopt or reject EU legislation. Subordinate to the European Council's overall authority.

Council for Mutual Economic Assistance (CMEA): Economic organization established by the Soviet Union in 1949 to coordinate trade among the communist countries of central and eastern Europe. Disbanded in 1991 after the fall of communism.

debt-to-GDP ratio: The ratio of gross public debt to gross domestic product across all levels of government.

euro: The single European currency.

EUROCORPS: The multinational military corps comprising France, Germany, Spain, Belgium, and Italy.

Eurogroup: The ECOFIN representatives of the Eurozone member states.

European Atomic Energy Agency (Euratom): One of the three European communities set up in the 1950s, established simultaneously with the EEC in 1958 to promote the peaceful use of atomic energy. Since 1967 has shared common institutions with the EEC and the ECSC.

European Bank for Reconstruction and Development: A London-based international development bank established in 1991 to promote economic development and political reform in central and eastern Europe. Main shareholders are the EU member states and EU institutions, along with the United States and Japan.

European Central Bank: The European Central Bank is located in Frankfurt, Germany, and is responsible for setting interstate policy for the whole of Europe's economic and monetary union. Oversees the euro.

European Coal and Steel Community (ECSC): The first of the three European communities, created under the 1951 Treaty of Paris. Established a common pool for coal and steel products and strong institutions to regulate the coal and steel industries on a supranational basis.

European Commission: The executive body of the European Union. Initiates legislation, executes EU policies, negotiates on behalf of the EU in international trade forums, and monitors compliance with EU law and treaties by member states.

European Community: Term used informally before 1993 for what the Maastricht Treaty named the European Union.

European Convention: A group comprising representatives from the EU and from member and future-member state governments charged with developing proposals for a first-ever European Constitution. Chaired by Valéry Giscard d'Estaing, the Convention completed a draft constitutional treaty on July 10, 2003, for consideration by the member states and an intergovernmental conference (IGC). In December 2003, the IGC failed to reach agreement on the final text of the constitution, primarily over the key issue of voting weights within the Council of Ministers.

European Council: The EU institution comprising the heads of state or government of the member states and the president of the European Commission. It meets at least twice each year and sets broad guidelines and directions for the development of the EU, as worked out in the Council of Ministers. (See above.)

European Court of Justice (ECJ): The judicial arm of the European Union, which may decide cases brought by EU member states, EU institutions, companies, and, in some cases, individuals. It ensures uniform interpretation of EU law by decisions that are binding upon the member states.

European Currency Unit (ECU): Artificial unit of account established to operate the exchange rate mechanism of the EMS; consists of a basket of member country currencies. Replaced by the euro on January 1, 1999.

European Economic Area: Members of the European Economic Area have full access to the European Union's single market in most areas of trade (agriculture and fisheries are exceptions) but do not have influence on the policy decisions of the European Union. The European Economic Area comprises the EU countries and Iceland, Norway, and Liechtenstein.

European Economic Community (EEC): The most important of the original European communities, set up under the 1957 Treaty of Rome to promote an "ever closer union" among the peoples of Europe through the development of a common market, common external tariff, and common policies in agriculture, transport, and other fields. Renamed the European Community in the Maastricht treaty and made the major part of the first pillar of the European Union.

European Free Trade Association (EFTA): Organization formed in 1960 under British leadership to promote economic cooperation among European states not wishing to become members of the EC. Unlike the EC, did not have strong supranational institutions or a mandate to promote political union. Lost importance as most of its members decided to join the EC.

European Monetary System (EMS): Exchange rate regime, established in 1979, to limit currency fluctuations within the European Community. Operates an exchange rate mechanism (ERM) under which member states are required to maintain the value of their currencies relative to those of other member states. Laid the groundwork for monetary union and the single currency (euro), established in January 1999.

European Political Cooperation (EPC): Foreign policy cooperation among the member states of the EC, established in 1970, conducted on an intergovernmental basis by foreign ministries. Given treaty status in the Single European Act (1987) and replaced by CFSP in the Maastricht Treaty.

Eurozone: The group of countries having adopted the euro.

exchange rate mechanism (ERM): A multilateral framework for the joint management of exchange-rate movements between participating countries to within set tolerance margins.

General Agreement on Tariffs and Trade (GATT): Multilateral trade treaty signed in 1947 establishing rules for international trade. Forum for eight rounds of tariff reductions culminating in the 1994 Uruguay Round agreements and the establishment of the World Trade Organization as successor to the GATT.

GDP (gross domestic product): Annual value of goods and services produced in a country.

High Authority: The executive body of the ECSC. Ceased to exist in July 1967 with the entering into effect of the merger treaty establishing a single commission for the ECSC, Euratom, and the EEC.

intergovernmentalism: Approach to integration in which national governments retain their sovereign powers and cooperate with each other by interstate bargaining and agreement. Opposed to federalism and supranationalism.

Maastricht Treaty: The Treaty on European Union (TEU), known as the Maastricht Treaty, was signed at Maastricht, the Netherlands, on February 7, 1992, the culmination of more than a year of negotiation and debate. By far the most sweeping revision of Community treaties ever attempted, the TEU amended the Treaty of Rome, which established the European Economic Community (EEC) in 1957. The TEU brought into being a new entity called the European Union (EU), a complicated structure of three pillars that has profoundly redefined European economic and political governance.

Marshall Plan: Officially known as the European Recovery Program, plan proposed in 1947 by U.S. Secretary of State George C. Marshall to foster postwar European economic revival through extensive U.S. aid.

nominal long-term interest rate: The rate of return on benchmark government bonds of a set maturity (usually equal to or greater than ten years).

North Atlantic Cooperation Council (NACC): Created by NATO at the Rome summit in November 1991. A U.S. initiative, the NACC was a new institutional relationship of consultation and cooperation on political and security issues open to all of the former, newly independent members of the Warsaw Pact. In July 1997, it was replaced by the Euro-Atlantic Partnership Council (EAPC).

North Atlantic Council: NATO's highest body; the decision-making arm of the organization.

North Atlantic Treaty Organization (NATO): A political-military institution founded in 1949 for the collective defense of its member states, which include the United States, Canada, and fourteen European countries.

Organization for Economic Cooperation and Development (OECD): An international organization established in 1961 comprising mainly industrialized market economy countries of North America, Western Europe, Japan, Australia, and New Zealand. Successor to the OEEC.

Organization for European Economic Cooperation (OEEC): Organization of European Marshall Plan aid recipients, organized at the United States' behest, to administer the aid and serve as a forum to negotiate reductions in intra-European barriers to trade.

parliamentary democracy: The form of democracy in which the composition of the executive branch is determined by the legislative majority, which may also dismiss the executive. The legislative branch of government is elected by the people.

Partnership for Peace (PFP): Framework agreements for non-NATO states to have a military relationship with the alliance.

PPP (purchasing power parity): Adjusts foreign currencies for dollar equivalents in purchasing power.

Rapid Deployment Force: The EU's military arm, still being made.

Schengen Agreement: The EU agreement abolishing border controls, creating free movement of people within its confines. Not all EU member states have joined in.

Single European Act (SEA): First major revision of the founding treaties of the European Community; went into effect in 1987. Increased the powers of the European Parliament, broadened the policy responsibilities of the EC, and, above all, scheduled the completion of a single economic market by December 31, 1992, as a member-state treaty commitment.

Stability and Growth Pact: Establishes several goals for monetary conditions (e.g., no greater than a 3 percent government budget deficit) beyond which EU member states are "admonished" or can even, in theory, be fined by the Commission.

Stability Pact for South Eastern Europe: The Stability Pact was created by the EU on June 10, 1999, to provide a comprehensive, long-term conflict prevention and peace-building strategy for the Balkans. The Stability Pact is not an organization itself; rather it offers a political commitment and a framework agreement to develop a shared international approach to enhance stability and growth in the region.

supranationalism: Approach to integration in which participating states transfer sovereign powers and policymaking responsibilities to transnational institutions whose decisions are binding on those states. An important feature of the first pillar of the EU, and one that distinguishes the EU from international institutions such as NATO or the OECD.

Treaty of Nice: A treaty approved in December 2000 at the European Council that amended the Treaty on European Union to prepare the EU institutions for enlargement. The treaty established the number of seats in the European Parliament, weighted votes in the Council of Ministers, and representatives on the Committee of the Regions and the Economic and Social Committee that the current and future members of the Union would receive. Nice was widely regarded as an awkward set of compromises, and dissatisfaction with the treaty led to the European Convention of 2002–2003.

The Treaty on European Union: See Maastricht Treaty.

unicameral parliament: A legislative body consisting of a single house.

unitary government: The form of government in which the national government is the only repository of sovereign power and in which the powers of subordinate levels of government are determined by the national government.

Warsaw Pact: A military alliance founded by the Soviet Union in 1955 in response to West Germany's entry into NATO. Its membership included the USSR and the countries of eastern Europe.

Western European Union (WEU): An exclusively western European mutual defense organization that grew out of the 1948 Treaty of Brussels. Moribund through much of the Cold War, revived in 1984 as a vehicle to develop European defense cooperation, designated the defense arm of the EU in the Maastricht treaty.

Index

Note: In subheadings, "EU" refers to the European Union and to its predecessors, the European Economic Community (EEC) and the European Community (EC).

257; and Iraq war debate, 15–17, 140,
256, 264–68, 468; and Jospin, 273–74,
287; and Kosovo, 261; on multipolar
world, 256, 295; and nuclear weapons,
261; and Poland, 469; politics of, 286;
and privatization, 280; and Schröder,
238; and taxes, 282–83; and 2002 elec-
tion, 288
Chislett, William, 387
Christian Coalition, U.S., 427
Christian Democratic Union (Germany,
CDU), 217–21, 223
Christian Democrats (Italy, DC), 347,
348, 351, 353, 357, 358–61, 369, 370, 375
Christian Democrats (Scandinavia), 427
Christian Democrats (Sweden), 427
Christian People's Party (Denmark), 427
Christian People's Party (Norway), 426
Christian Social Union (Germany, CSU),
247n6. See also Christian Democratic
Union (Germany, CDU)
Christie's, 280–81
Churchill, Winston: and national identity,
306, 312, 313; and "three overlapping
circles," 308, 335; wartime ties with
Roosevelt of, 254, 269, 307
Ciampi, Carlo Azeglio, 370, 379
Cimoszewicz, Wlodzimierz, 462–63, 465–
66, 469, 470
citizenship: EU, 44; and international law,
182–84, 186, 188, 202–3
CiU. See Convergence and Union (Spain,
CiU)
Clarke, Ken, 330
Clean Hands scandal, 347, 363, 369–70
climate change, global, 8, 57
Clinton, Bill: and Blair, 307, 323, 327; foreign policies of, 57; and Kosovo, 105; on
NATO enlargement, 92, 95; and Northern Ireland, 325
clothing. See textile industry
co-decision, 44
coal industry, 280. See also European Coal
and Steel Community
Cockfield, Lord, 36
cohesion funds, 129, 132, 135, 400
Colbert, Jean-Baptiste, 279
Cold War: and British politics, 300, 307,
335; and Italian politics, 353, 358;
NATO and, 89–90, 94; Scandinavia and,
413–14, 439, 443–45

Collodi, Carlo, 348
Cologne process, 74
colonialism: British, 307; French, 258–59
Comit, 370
Committee of the Regions, 44
Common Agricultural Policy (CAP): establishment of, 28–29; French-German
relations and, 238–39, 272–73, 275; Italy
and, 365; purpose of, 128; reform of,
128
Common Assembly, 25, 27
Common Foreign and Security Policy
(CFSP): British influence on, 316; as EU
second pillar, 43–44; strengthening of,
47, 51
"Common Man" Party (Italy), 356
Common Market. See European Eco-
nomic Community
Commonwealth, 307
communism: Catholic Church and, 351,
352–53, 358, 363; collapse of, 41, 119; in
Finland, 415; in France, 13; in Germany,
225, 230; Middle Way versus, 411, 413;
Polish defeat of, 457–58; U.S. versus,
358
Communist Party (Denmark), 441
Communist Party (Finland), 426–27, 441
Communist Party (France), 285, 352, 353,
361
Communist Party (Germany), 218
Communist Party (Italy). See Italian
Communist Party (PCI)
Communist Party (Norway), 441
Communist Party (Poland). See Polish
Communist Party
Communist Party (Scandinavia), 426
Communist Party (Spain, PCE), 390
Communist Refoundation (Italy), 369,
371, 374, 377
Comprehensive Test Ban Treaty (1998),
261
Confederation of British Industry (CBI),
329
Congress, U.S., anti-French sentiments in,
15
Conservative Party (Britain), 299–301,
309, 312, 330; and EU, 314–18; and
Thatcher revolution, 304–7
Conservative Party (Scandinavia), 425
constitution, EU, 5–6, 52–57, 476

EU, 4, 29–30, 46, 49, 255, 269–72,
274–75; and EU law, 178, 189–90, 198,
199, 200; fiscal policy in, 282; food in,
262–63; Gaullism in, 254–56, 288; German relations with, 23–24, 33, 41, 93,
238–39, 243–44, 255, 266, 269–77,
294–95; German unification effect on,
272–73; GMOs opposed by, 262–63;
grandeur in, 253; immigration to, 259;
and Indochina, 258, 269; and Iraq war
debate, 6–7, 15–17, 18, 109, 140, 256,
264–68; Italian relations with, 364; language in, 255, 262, 290–91, 295; left-
wing politics in, 285, 289; military in,
258–59; military policy of, 254–55,
261–62, 273, 276; Mitterrand government in, 34–35; national identity of,
238, 253–54, 262–63, 295; and NATO,
22, 254, 260; and nuclear weapons, 254,
260–61, 277–78; politics in, 253, 257,
284–89; population of, 256, 293; presidency in, 257, 294; privatization in,
280–82; public opinion in, 267; public
sector in, 292–93; refusal of economic
sanctions by, 72; regions in, 291–92; Resistance movement in, 254; right-wing
politics in, 258, 285, 288–89; security
policy of, 260–61; and Suez Canal, 269;
taxes in, 282–83; Treaty of Dunkirk, 21;
and UN, 265–68; urban planning in,
253; U.S. relation to, 13–15, 254, 256,
260–69, 295; voter behavior in, 285, 288;
and WEU, 21
France Telecom, 280, 281–82
Franco, Francisco, 387, 389–90, 394, 395
François Mitterand Library, 253
Francovich (1991), 186
Frederik VII, King of Denmark, 423
Free Democratic Party (Germany, FDP),
219–21
Free-Trade Area of the Americas (FTAA),
401
freedom fries, 15
Freedom Party (Austria), 171
Freedom Pole, 371, 374
French Institute of International Rela-
tions, 15
Fukuyama, Francis, 9
functionalism, 27

G8, 387
Gaitskell, Hugh Todd Naylor, 332

Galicia, 388, 392
Garton Ash, Timothy, 12, 17–18
Garzón, Baltasar, 399
Gattopardo, Il (Lampedusa), 350, 367
Gaullism, 14, 254–56, 288
Gava family, 359
Gaz de France, 280
General Agreement on Tariffs and Trade,
27
genetically modified organisms (GMOs),
8, 262
genocide. *See* ethnic cleansing
George, Eddie, 333
Georgia, 100
Geremek, Bronislaw, 466
German Democratic Republic, 216
German Trade Union Federation, 232
Germany: Americanization of politics in,
223–24; antiwar sentiments in, 13, 15;
coalition governments in, 219–22; communism in, 225, 230; constitution of,
216, 217, 224, 229, 235, 242; and Czech
Republic, 239–40; democracy in, 215–
18, 233; division of, 216; and Eastern
and Central Europe, 239–40; and ECJ,
190; economy of, 72–74, 225–28, 232;
and ECSC, 4, 23–24; electoral system
in, 218–19; and EU, 4, 41–43, 46, 235–
40, 269–72; and EU law, 200, 203; financial scandals in politics of, 217–18;
foreign policy of, 234–46; French relations with, 23–24, 33, 41, 93, 238–39,
243–44, 255, 266, 269–77, 294–95; immigration to, 228–30, 480–81; and Iraq
war debate, 6, 109, 239, 241; Italian relations with, 380; *Länder* politics in (*see*
regional politics in); language of, 236;
military policy of, 242–43, 245, 276; national interests of, 8; nationalism in, 215;
and NATO, 91, 234; pacifism in, 215,
241, 244; Polish relations with, 96, 240,
470; political party roles in, 217–19; political process in, 217–26; population of,
228; post–World War I, 213; post–World
War II, 213–17, 234; public opinion in,
237–38, 241; red-green coalition in, 220,
241, 244, 246; regional politics in, 218,
221, 223, 224–26, 237; religion in, 224,
233; right-wing politics in, 218, 236;
Russian relations with, 240; significance

Norway: constitution of, 417, 422; and defense, 442; democracy in, 418; economy of, 421, 434; and EFTA, 30; energy resources in, 434, 449; and EU, 4, 414, 428, 432, 447–49; government in, 421–24; immigration to, 435; and Iraq war debate, 450; Middle Way in, 412; monarchs in, 423; and NATO, 414, 442, 443, 445; and peacemaking, 440; right-wing politics in, 428; Soviet relation to, 440; and UN, 440. *See also* Scandinavia

OAS (France, terrorist group), 258
Occhetto, Achille, 369
OEEC. *See* Organization for European Economic Cooperation
oil crisis (1973–1974), 32
"old Europe," 6, 109, 140, 267, 339, 468
Olive Tree, 347, 373–74, 377
ombudsman, in Scandinavia, 431
Operation Deliberate Force, 101
Operation Enduring Freedom, 109, 111
"opt-outs," 43, 45, 46, 316
Organization for Economic Cooperation and Development (OECD), 439
Organization for European Economic Cooperation (OEEC), 22, 357
Organization for Security and Cooperation in Europe (OSCE), 91, 472
Oslo Accords (1993), 440
Oxfam, 147

P2 (Masonic lodge), 367
Paasikivi, Juho, 441
Palestine, 7
Palestine Liberation Organization (PLO), 367
Palme, Olof, 443, 445
Pantelleria, 145
Paribas, 281
parliament, 25. *See also* European Parliament
Partido Nacionalista Vasco. See Basque Nationalist Party (Spain, PNV)
Partito democratico di sinistra (Italy, PDS), 369, 371, 372, 373, 377
Partito Popolare Italiano (PPI), 371, 373
Partito Radicale (Italy, PR), 362
Partnership and Cooperation Agreements, 125

Partnership for Peace (PFP), 92–93, 96, 102, 109, 116, 439
Party of Democratic Socialism (Germany, PDS), 219, 221, 225–26
Party of European Socialists, 320
Pasolini, Pier Paolo, 350
Patten, Chris, 330
Paul VI, Pope, 359
PCI. *See* Italian Communist Party (PCI)
peace: Europeans and international, 10–12; and German pacifism, 215, 241, 244
peacekeeping: in former Yugoslavia, 101–2, 106; German role in, 243; Italy and, 381; U.S. role in, 243
pension benefits: in France, 293; immigrant labor and, 160; threats to, 9
People's Party (Denmark), 171
Perry, William, 95, 465
Persian Gulf War, 46, 242, 261, 336, 337, 381, 396
PFP. *See* Partnership for Peace
PHARE (*Pologne Hongrie: Actions pour la Reconversion Economique*), 120, 121
Philippines, migration encouraged by, 155
Pierson, Paul, 79
pillars, of EU, 43–44, 55
Pinault, François, 280
Pius XII, Pope, 349, 351, 361
Place de Général de Gaulle, Paris, France, 253
Place de la Concorde, Paris, France, 253
Poland: and Afghanistan, 468; agriculture in, 461, 474–75; and Belarus, 464, 481; communist defeat in, 457–58; and Czechoslovakia, 472; and defense, 467–68; democracy in, 463; and Denmark, 470; economy of, 460, 463; and EU, 458–62, 469, 476–77; and Europe agreements, 122; geopolitical situation of, 458, 465; German relations with, 96, 240, 470; and Hungary, 472; integration into EU of, 48, 130–31, 141, 457, 462–64, 471–80; and Iraq war debate, 16, 140, 266–67, 459, 468–70; and labor migration, 480–81; land sales in, 475–76; military in, 97; national identity of, 462; and NATO, 93, 96–97, 464–67; politics in, 459–62; public opinion in, 461, 466, 470, 477–80; reform in, 119–20; religion

About the Contributors

Karen J. Alter is associate professor of political science at Northwestern University, where she specializes in the international politics of international organizations and international law. Alter is author of *Establishing the Supremacy of European Law: The Making of an International Rule of Law in Europe* (2001) and numerous articles and book chapters on the European Union's legal system. Her most recent publications include "Resolving or Exacerbating Disputes? The WTO's New Dispute Resolution System" (*International Affairs*, 2003) and "Do International Courts Enhance Compliance with International Law?" (*Review of Asian and Pacific Studies*, 2003).

Eric S. Einhorn is professor and former chairman in the Department of Political Science, University of Massachusetts Amherst. He has recently published *Modern Welfare States: Scandinavian Politics and Policy in the Global Age* (2003), coauthored with John Logue.

Mark Gilbert is associate professor of contemporary international history at the University of Trento. His books include *The Italian Revolution: The End of Politics, Italian Style?* (1995) and, with Anna Cento Bull, *The Lega Nord and the Northern Question in Italian Politics* (2001). In 2003, he published *Surpassing Realism: The Politics of European Integration since 1945*.

Robert Graham has been the *Financial Times* bureau chief in Paris since 1997. He is the paper's longest serving foreign correspondent, covering many of the major world events over the past thirty-five years in Europe, Latin America, the Middle East, and the Indian subcontinent. He has also been based in Rome, Madrid, and Tehran. He is the author of *Iran: The Illusion of Power* (1979) and *Spain: Change of a Nation* (1984).

Paul M. Heywood is Sir Francis Hill Professor of European Politics and dean of the Graduate School at the University of Nottingham. He is the author of *The Government and Politics of Spain* (1995), editor of *Politics and Policy in Democratic Spain* (1999), and coauthor, with Carlos Closa, of *Spain and the European Union* (2004).

Erik Jones is resident associate professor of European studies at the Johns Hopkins University Bologna Center. He is author of *The Politics of Economic and Monetary Union: Integration and Idiosyncrasy* (2002).

Sean Kay is associate professor of politics and government, and chair of International Studies, at Ohio Wesleyan University. He is also a nonresident fellow in foreign policy at the Eisenhower Institute in Washington, D.C. He is author of *NATO and the Future of European Security* (1998).

John Logue is director of the Ohio Employee Ownership Center and professor of political science, Kent State University. His most recent book, coauthored with Eric Einhorn, is *Modern Welfare States: Scandinavian Politics and Policy in the Global Age* (2003).

Jochen Lorentzen is associate professor of international business at Copenhagen Business School and honorary fellow at the School of Development Studies, University of KwaZulu-Natal, Durban, South Africa. He is the author of *Opening Up Hungary to the World Market* (1995) and coeditor of *Markets and Authorities: Global Finance and Human Choice* (2002).

Michael Mannin is principal lecturer in European studies and Jean Monnet Chair in European Integration, John Moores University, Liverpool. He is editor of *Pushing Back the Boundaries: The EU and Central and Eastern Europe* (1998).

Patrick McCarthy is professor of European studies at the Johns Hopkins University Bologna Center. He is the author of *The Crisis of the Italian State: From the Origins of the Cold War to the Fall of Berlusconi and Beyond* (1995).

Emanuela Poli is director of communication at the Department for Development Policies of the Italian Ministry for Economy. She is the author of *Forza Italia: Organizzazione, leadership e redicamento territoriale* (2001).

Jeffrey Simon is a senior fellow at the Institute for National Strategic Studies, National Defense University. He is the author of *Hungary and NATO: Problems in Civil-Military Relations* (2003), *NATO and the Czech and Slovak Republics: A Comparative Study in Civil-Military Relations* (2004), and *Poland and NATO: A Study in Civil-Military Relations* (2004).

Ray Taras is professor of political science at Tulane University in New Orleans. He is author of *Liberal and Illiberal Nationalisms* (2002).

Ronald Tiersky is Eastman Professor of Politics at Amherst College. He is the author of *France in the New Europe: Changing but Steadfast* (1994) and *François Mitterrand: A Very French President* (2002).

John Van Oudenaren is chief of the European Division, Library of Congress, and adjunct professor at the Elliott School, George Washington University. He is the author of *Uniting Europe: European Integration and the Post–Cold War World* (2000).

Helga A. Welsh is associate professor of political science, Wake Forest University. She has published widely on German history and politics and democratization processes in Central and Eastern Europe, including "The Elite Conundrum in the GDR: Lessons from the District Level" (*German Studies Review*, 2001), "Parliamentary Elites in Times of Political Transition: The Case of Eastern Germany (*West European Politics*, 1996), and "Political Transition Processes in Central and Eastern Europe" (*Comparative Politics*, 1994).